S0-BAN-292

Word Power
Made Easy

**The most effective vocabulary
builder in the English language**

**Including
LATEST WORD-LIST**

**Millenium edition
revised & expanded
Now over 685 pages**

When you want to know How to
say it, spell it, master it, remember it
These are the books that have the answers you need !!

Maxwell Nurnberg and Morris Rosenblum
All About Words
How to Build a Better Vocabulary
Questions you always wanted to ask about English

Norman Lewis

Word Power Made Easy — *Revised and Enlarged*

How to Read Better & Faster

Correct Spelling Made Easy

Better English

Instant Word Power

Instant Spelling Power

Dictionary of Correct Spelling

Rapid Vocabulary Builder

Roget's Thesaurus in Dictionary form

Reading, Spelling, Vocabulary, Pronunciation Book 1, 2 & 3

Norman Lewis and Wilfred Funk

30 Days to a more Powerful Vocabulary

Wilfred Funk

Six Weeks to Words of Power

Word Origins *and their Romantic Stories*

Jerome Agel

Test Your Word Power

Levine, Levine & Levine

The Joy of Vocabulary

Hutchinson Pocket Series *(U.K.)*

Dictionary of Confusible Words

Dictionary of Spelling

Dictionary of Quotations

Word Power Made Easy

The most effective vocabulary builder in the English language

Including LATEST WORD-LIST

NORMAN LEWIS

BLOOMSBURY
G O Y L S $\overline{a\,a}$ b

This Indian Reprint 2005

First Indian edition: 1979
Reprinted 1981, 1983, 1984, 1985, 1986
Second Indian edition: 1987
Reprinted 1988, 1990, 1991, 1992
This completely revised and enlarged edition: 1993
Reprinted 1994, 1995, 1996, 1997, 1998, 1999
Reprinted 2000, 2001, 2002, 2003, 2004, 2005

This special low priced Indian reprint is published by arrangement with **Bloomsbury Publishing Plc.** U.K., for sale in Indian
subcontinent only. This is the only authorised, complete and
unabridged reprint of the latest original edition.

Published by Ashwani Goyal for GOYL SaaB, an imprint of
W.R. GOYAL, Publishers & Distributors
86, U.B. Jawahar Nagar, Delhi - 110007 (India)
Tel. : 011 - 23852986, 23858362, Fax : 23850961
E-mail : goyal@vsnl.com

Printed at Taj Press, New Delhi.

CONTENTS

PART ONE

GETTING OFF TO A GOOD START

and of yourself; why it is necessary to recapture the
'powerful urge to learn'; why your age makes little difference; how this book is designed to build an extensive
vocabulary in two to three months.

(*Sessions 1–3*)

Words that describe all kinds and sorts of people, including terms for self-interest, reactions to the world, attitudes to others, skill and awkwardness, marital states,
hatred of man, of woman, and of marriage. How one session of pleasant work can add more words to your
vocabulary than the average adult learns in an entire
year; why it is necessary to develop a comfortable time
schedule and then *stick to it.*

(*Sessions 4–6*)

Words that relate to medical specialists and specialities.
Terms for experts in disorders of the female organs;
childhood diseases; skin ailments; skeletal deformities;
heart ailments; disorders of the nerves, mind, and personality. How self-discipline and persistence will ultimately lead to complete mastery over words.

(*Sessions 7–10*)

Words that describe a variety of professions, including
those dealing with the human mind, teeth, vision, feet,

Verbs that accurately describe important human activities. Excursions into expressive terms for good and evil, doing, saying, wishing, and pleasing. Further proof that you can learn, in a few weeks or less, more new words than the average adult learns in an entire year.

(*Sessions 24–27*)

Words that explore in depth all degrees and kinds of talk and silence.

(*Sessions 28–31*)

Terms for describing a disciplinarian, toady, dabbler, provocative woman, flagwaver, possessor of a one-track mind, free-thinker, sufferer from imaginary ailments, etc. Excursions into words relating to father and mother, murder of all sorts, sexual desires, and various manias and phobias.

(*Sessions 32–37*)

Terms for describing friendliness, energy, honesty, mental keenness, bravery, charm, sophistication, etc. Excursions into expressive words that refer to ways of eating and drinking, believing and disbelieving, looking and seeing, facing the present, past and future, and living in the city and country. How the new words you are learning have begun to influence your thinking.

A 120-item test of your achievement in *Part II*.

PART THREE

FINISHING WITH A FEELING OF COMPLETE SUCCESS

Words for poverty and wealth, direct and indirect emotions, not calling a spade a spade, banter and other light talk, animal-like contentment, homesickness, meat-eating, and different kinds of secrecy. Excursions into terms expressive of goodness, of hackneyed phraseology, of human similarity to various animals, of kinds of sound, etc. How to react to the new words you meet in your reading.

Verbs that show exhaustion, criticism, self-sacrifice, repetition, mental stagnation, pretence, hinting, soothing, symphathizing, indecision, etc. How you can increase your vocabulary by picking your friends' brains.

Brief intermissions

To:

My family and friends, who accepted, without apparent resentment and with barely audible complaint, my complete self-isolation during the many months in which I totally and shamefully neglected them while working on the revision of this book.

Especially: Mary Margie Baldinger and the kids; Debbie and Allen Hubbert; Milton Lewis; Karen and Bob Kopfstein; Leonard Vogel, one of America's great painters, and Shirley; gourmet cooks David and Janice Potts; Seymour and Nan Prog; Ruth and Leo; Dave and Jan Hopkins; Carol and Marvin Colter; Bob Finnerty, my chess opponent, who says that winning is all that counts; Doris Garcia; Eleanor and Robert Poitou; Mary El and Dick Gayman—

Walter Garcia, Len Grandy, Don Jenkins; Sally Landsburg; Ted and Margaret Synder; Jean Bryan; Rhoda and Ralph Duenewald; George and Phyllis Juric; Bob and Monica Myers, Tony and Kathy Garcia, Jean Kachaturian; Margie Lopez and Jo Watson—

Myrtle and Ace, Dony and Estelle, Helen and Ben, Judy and Bob, Doris and Muriel, Danny and Mary; in memoriam, Max and Frances—

Larry Scher, Chuck Nichamin, Sue Sullivan, Rosemary and Debbie Greenman, Alice Hessing, Dave and Lynn Bisset, Danny Hernandez, John Arcadi and Peggy Arcadi, Norm Ashley, Aaron Breitbart—

Lorin and Gloria Warner, Marty and Ros Chodos, Mahlon and Gwen Woirhaye, Leon and Kay East, Marijane and Paul Paulsen, Helen and Russ Hurford, Elior and Sally Kinarthy—

Carolyn Russell, Rod Sciborski, Vera Laushkin, John Hahn, Liz Johnson, Leonora Davila, Jim Hawley, Jerry Lenington, Jay Loughran, Susan Obler, Marilyn Houseman, Rita Scott, Chris Hamilton, Joan Nay, Mary Lewis, Virginia Sandoval, Hazel Haas—

The staff and all my students at Rio Hondo College—

My editor at Doubleday, Jean Anne Vincent, who so patiently and cheerfully goaded, prodded, pushed, wheedled, and cajoled me into finishing on time.

Also: I wish to thank Karen Kopfstein and Peggy Chulack for their promptness and care in typing the manuscript.

Whittier, California

How to use this book for maximum benefit

1.   This is not a reading book ...

Don't read this book!

Instead, *work* with it. *Write* in it, *talk aloud* to it, *talk back* to it – use your pen or pencil, your voice, not just your eyes and mind.

Learning, *real learning*, goes on only through *active participation*.

When a new word occurs in a chapter, *say it aloud!* (The phonetic respelling will help you pronounce it correctly.)*

When you do the matching exercise, use a pen or pencil. *Write your responses!* (Check the key that immediately follows each exercise after you have filled in all the answers.)

When you do the 'Yes-No,' 'True-False,' or 'Same-Opposite' exercises, use your *pen or pencil to indicate the appropriate response*, then check with the key when you have completed the whole exercise.

When you are asked to fill in words that fit definitions, *write your answers;* then check the key both to see if you have responded with the right word and also to make sure your spelling is correct.

When you do the *Review of Etymology* exercises, make sure to fill in the English word containing the prefix, root, or suffix required – use a word from the chapter, or any other word that comes to mind. (Coin new words if you like!)

Pay special attention to the *Chapter Reviews.* Are the words still fresh in your mind? Do you remember the meaning of each root

---

* The system of pronunciation symbols will be thoroughly explained in Section 2 of this chapter.

studied in the previous sessions? In these *Reviews*, you are not only testing your learning but also tightening up any areas in which you discover lacks, weaknesses, or lapses of memory.

2.   Master the pronunciation system!

Saying words *aloud,* and saying them *right,* is half the battle in feeling comfortable and assured with all the new words you are going to learn. Every word taught is respelt to show its pronunciation, so pay close attention to how the phonetic symbols work.

(a) First, master the 'schwa'!

Almost every English word of two or more syllables contains one or several syllables in which the vowel sound is said *very* quickly. For example:

'*Linda* spoke to her *mother about a different idea* she had.'

Read the *previous sentence* aloud at *normal conversational* speed.

Read it again. Listen to how the *-a* of *Linda;* the *-er* of *mother;* the *a-* of *about;* the *-ent* of *different;* and the *-a* of *idea* sound.

Very quick – very short! Right?

Phonetically respelt, these words are represented as:

1. *Linda*	LIN'-də
2. *mother*	MUTH'-ə
3. *about*	ə-BOWT'
4. *different*	DIF'-rənt
5. *idea*	ī-DI'-ə

The symbol 'ə', called a *schwa,* represents the quick, short vowel sound in the five words above.

Now look back at the sentence preceded by an arrow.

The italicized words are rewritten as:

1. previous	PREE'-vi-əs
2. sentence	SEN'-təns
3. aloud	ə-LOWD'
4. normal	NAW'-məl
5. conversational	kon'-vər-SAY'-shən-əl

You will find ə in almost all words that are phonetically respelt throughout this book. Say the five italicized words aloud and make sure you understand how the *schwa* (ə) sounds.

(b) Next, understand accent.

Look at word (5) above: *conversational:* kon'-vər-SAY'-shən-əl.
Note that there are *two* accent marks, one on *kon'*, another on
SAY'. Note also that *kon'* is in lower-case letters, *SAY'* in capitals.
Both syllables are stressed, but the one in capitals (*SAY'*) sounds
stronger (or louder) than the one in lower case (*kon'*). Say *conversa-
tional* aloud, noting the difference.

Say these three words *aloud*, noticing the variation in stress
between the lower-case and the capitalized syllables:

1.	egotistical	ee'-gō-TIS'-ti-kəl
2.	altercation	awl'-tə-KAY'-shən
3.	anthropological	an'-thrə-pə-LOJ'-i-kəl

(c) Be careful of the letter 'S' (or 's') in phonetic respellings. S (or *s*) is
always *hissed*, as in *see, some, such*. After an *-n*, you will be tempted
to *buzz* (or 'voice') the *-s*, because final *-ns* is usually pronounced
-nz, as in *wins, tons, owns*, etc. (Say these three words aloud – hear
the z at the end?) *Resist the temptation!* S (or *s*) is *always hissed* in
phonetic respellings!

Say these words aloud:

1.	ambivalence†	am-BIV'-ə-ləns
2.	affluence	AF'-loo-əns
3.	opulence	OP'-yoo-ləns
4.	sentence	SEN'-təns

(d) The symbol ī or Ī is pronounced eye, to rhyme with high, sigh, my,
etc., *no matter where you find it.* For example:

1.	fights	FĪTS
2.	spy	SPĪ
3.	malign	mə-LĪN'
4.	civilize	SIV'-i-līz'

[*I* or *i* (without the top bar) is pronounced as in *it, sit, pitch.*]

(e) All consonants have their normal sounds.

Except for G (or *g*), which is *always pronounced as in give, girl, get,*
go.

1.	agree	ə-GREE'
2.	pagan	PAY'-gən

---

† All unusual words in this chapter are taught in later chapters of the book.

3. again   ə-GEN'

(f) The vowel sounds are as follows:

	Symbol	Example
1.	A, a	*cat* (KAT)
2.	E, e	*wet* (WET)
3.	I, i	*sit* (SIT); *ear* (I'-ə); *slowly* (SLŌ'-li)
4.	O, o	*knot* (NOT)
5.	U, u	*nut* (NUT)
6.	AH, ah	*car* (KAH)
7.	AW, aw	*for* (FAW); *north* (NAWTH)
8.	AY, ay	*late* (LAYT); *magnate* (MAG'-nayt)
9.	EE, ee	*equal* (EE'-kwəl); *east* (EEST)
10.	ai	*air* (AIR)
11.	əR, ər	*her* (HəR); *earth* (əRTH)
12.	Ō, ō	*toe* (TŌ)
13.	OͦO, oͦo	*book* (BOͦOK); *put* (POͦOT)
14.	O̅O̅, o̅o̅	*doom* (DO̅O̅M); *blue* (BLO̅O̅); *muse* (MYO̅O̅Z)
15.	OͦOə, oͦoə	*pure* (PYOͦOə); *prurient* (PROͦOəR'-i-ənt)
16.	OW, ow	*about* (ə-BOWT')
17.	OY, oy	*soil* (SOYL)
18.	ING, ing	*taking* (TAYK'-ing)

(g) TH or *th* is pronounced as in *thing; T̄H* or *th* is pronounced as in *this.*

(h) ZH or *zh* is pronounced as in *pleasure.*

3.   Why etymology?

Etymology (et'-i-MOL'-ə-ji) deals with the origin or derivation of words.

  When you know the meaning of a root (for example, Latin *ego*, I or self), you can better understand, and more easily remember, *all* the words built on this root.

  Learn one root and you have the key that will unlock the meanings of up to ten or twenty words in which the root appears.

Learn *ego* and you can immediately get a grasp on *egocentric, egomaniac, egoist, egotist,* and *alter ego.*

Learn *anthropos* (Greek, mankind) and you will quickly understand, and never forget, *anthropology, misanthropy, anthropoid, anthropocentric, anthropomorphic, philanthropy, and anthropophobia.* Meet any word with *anthropo-* in it, and you will have at least some idea of its meaning.

In the *etymological* (et'-i-mə-LOJ'-i-kəl) approach to vocabulary building:

- You will learn about *prefixes, roots,* and *suffixes* –
- You will be able to work out unfamiliar words by recognizing their structure, the building blocks from which they are constructed –
- You will be able to construct words correctly by learning to put these building blocks together in the proper way – and
- You will be able to derive verbs from nouns, nouns and verbs from adjectives, adjectives from nouns, etc. – and do all this correctly.

Learn how to deal with etymology and you will feel comfortable with words – you will use new words with self-assurance – you will be able to understand thousands of words you hear or read even if you have never heard or seen these words before.

That's why the best approach to new words is through etymology‡ – as you will discover for yourself as soon as you start to work on Chapter 3!

4.   But what are nouns, verbs, and adjectives?

You probably know.

But if you don't, you can master these parts of speech (and reference will be made to *noun forms, verb forms,* and *adjectival forms* throughout the book) within the next five minutes.

‡ Incidentally, Latin scholars will notice that I present a Latin verb in the first person singular, present tense (*verso,* I turn), but call it an infinitive (*verto,* to turn). I do this for two reasons: 1) *verto* is easier for a non-Latin scholar to pronounce and 2) when I studied Latin fifty years ago, the convention was to refer to a verb by using the first person singular, present tense.
If you are not a Latin scholar, you need not bother to read this footnote – if you've already done so, forget it!

(a) A *noun* is a word that can be preceded by *a, an, the, some, such,* or *my.*

An *egoist* (noun)

Such *asceticism* (noun)

The *misogynist* (noun)

(Nouns, you will discover, often end in conventional suffixes: *-ness, -ity, -ism, -y, -ion,* etc.)

(b) A *verb* is a word that fits into the pattern, 'Let us _____.' A verb has a past tense.

Let us *equivocate* (verb) — past tense: *equivocated.*

Let us *alternate* (verb) — past tense: *alternated.*

Let us *philander* (verb) — past tense: *philandered.*

(Verbs, you will discover, often end in conventional suffixes: *-ate, -ize, -fy,* etc.)

(c) an *adjective* is a word that fits into the pattern, 'You are very _____.'

You are very *egoistic* (adjective).

You are very *introverted* (adjective).

You are very *misogynous* (adjective).

(Adjectives, you will discover, often end in conventional suffixes: *-ic, -ed, -ous, -al, -ive,* etc.)

And *adverbs,* of course, are generally formed by adding *-ly* to an adjective: *misogynous-misogynously; educational-educationally;* etc.

That's all there is to it! (Did it take more than five minutes? Maybe ten at the most?)

5.   How to work for best results

If you intend to work with this book seriously (that is, if your clear intention is to add a thousand or more new words to your present vocabulary — add them permanently, unforgettably — add them so successfully that you will soon find yourself using them in speech and writing), I suggest that you give yourself every advantage by carefully following the laws of learning:

(a) Space your learning.
Beginning with Chapter 3, every chapter will be divided into
'sessions'. Each session may take half an hour to an hour and a
half, depending on the amount of material and on your own
speed of learning.

Do one or two sessions at a time – three if you're going strong
and are very involved – and always decide when you stop *exactly
when* you will return. (I remind you to do this later in the book,
since such a procedure is of crucial importance.)

(b) Do not rush – go at your own comfortable speed.
Everyone learns at a different pace. Fast learners are no better
than slow learners – it's the end result that counts, not the time it
takes you to finish.

(c) Review.
When you start a new session, go back to the last exercise of the
preious session (usually *Can you recall the words?* or *Chapter Review*),
cover your answers, and test your retention – do you have quick
recall after a day or so has elapsed?

(d) Test yourself.
You are not aiming for a grade, or putting your worth on the line,
when you take the three Comprehensive Tests (Chapters 8, 13,
and 17) – rather you are discovering your weaknesses, if any;
deciding where repairs have to be made; and, especially, experiencing a feeling of success at work well done. (In learning, too,
nothing succeeds like success!)

Use these three tests, as well as the abundant chapter exercises,
as aids to learning. No one is perfect, no one learns in exactly the
same way or at the same rate as anyone else. Find the optimum
technique and speed for *your* unique learning patterns – and then
give yourself every opportunity to exploit your actual, latent, and
potential abilities.

*But most important (as I will remind you several times throughout the
book) – develop a routine and stick to it!*

Disclaimer:

Occasionally in these pages, owing to the deficiency of the English language, I have used *he/him/his* meaning *he or she/him or her/his or her* in order to avoid awkwardness of style.

He, him, and *his* are *not* intended as exclusively masculine pronouns — they may refer to either sex or to both sexes.

Part one

Getting off to a good start

1

HOW TO TEST YOUR PRESENT VOCABULARY

Once – as a child – you were an expert, an accomplished virtuoso, at learning new words.

Today, by comparison, you are a rank and bumbling amateur.

Does this statement sound insulting?

It may be – but if you are the average adult, it is a statement that is, unfortunately, only too true.

Educational testing indicates that children of ten who have grown up in families in which English is the native language have recognition vocabularies of over twenty thousand words –

And that these same ten-year-olds have been learning new words at a rate of many hundreds a year since the age of four.

In astonishing contrast, studies show that adults who are no longer attending school increase their vocabularies at a pace *slower than twenty-five to fifty words annually.*

How do you assess your own vocabulary?

Is it quantitatively healthy?

Rich in overall range?

Responsive to any situation in which you may find yourself?

Truly indicative of your intellectual potential?

More important, is it still growing at the same rapid rate as when you were a child?

Or, as with most adults, has your rate of increase dropped drastically since you left school? And if so do you now feel that your vocabulary is somewhat limited, your verbal skills not as sharp as you would like them to be?

Let us find out.

I challenge you to a series of tests that will measure your vocabulary range, as well as your verbal speed and responsiveness.

A test of vocabulary range

Here are sixty brief phrases, each containing one italicized word; it is up to you to find the closest definition of each such word. To keep your score valid, refrain, as far as possible, from wild guessing. The key will be found at the end of the test.

1. *dishevelled* appearance: (a) untidy, (b) fierce, (c) foolish, (d) peculiar, (e) unhappy .
2. a *baffling* problem: (a) difficult, (b) simple, (c) puzzling, (d) long, (e) new
3. *lenient* parent: (a) tall, (b) not strict, (c) wise, (d) foolish, (e) severe
4. *repulsive* personality: (a) disgusting, (b) attractive, (c) normal, (d) confused, (e) conceited
5. *audacious* attempt: (a) useless, (b) bold, (c) foolish, (d) crazy, (e) necessary
6. *parry* a blow: (a) ward off, (b) fear, (c) expect, (d) invite, (e) ignore
7. *prevalent* disease: (a) dangerous, (b) catching, (c) childhood, (d) fatal, (e) widespread
8. *ominous* report: (a) loud, (b) threatening, (c) untrue, (d) serious, (e) unpleasant
9. an *incredible* story: (a) true, (b) interesting, (c) well-known, (d) unbelievable, (e) unknown
10. an *opthalmologist:* (a) eye doctor, (b) skin doctor, (c) foot doctor, (d) heart doctor, (e) cancer specialist
11. will *supersede* the old law: (a) enforce, (b) specify penalties for, (c) take the place of, (d) repeal, (e) continue
12. an *anonymous* donor: (a) generous, (b) stingy, (c) well-known, (d) one whose name is not known, (e) reluctant
13. performed an *autopsy:* (a) examination of living tissue, (b) examination of a corpse to determine the cause of death, (c) process in the manufacture of optical lenses, (d) operation to cure a disease, (e) series of questions to determine the causes of delinquent behaviour
14. an *indefatigable* worker: (a) well-paid, (b) tired, (c) skilful, (d) tireless, (e) pleasant
15. a confirmed *atheist:* (a) bachelor, (b) disbeliever in God, (c) believer in religion, (d) believer in science, (e) priest

16. endless *loquacity:* (a) misery, (b) fantasy, (c) repetitiousness, (d) ill health, (e) talkativeness

17. a *glib* talker: (a) smooth, (b) awkward, (c) loud, (d) friendly, (e) boring

18. an *incorrigible* optimist: (a) happy, (b) beyond correction or reform, (c) foolish, (d) hopeful, (e) unreasonable

19. an *ocular* problem: (a) unexpected, (b) insoluble, (c) visual, (d) continual, (e) imaginary

20. a notorious *demagogue:* (a) rabble-rouser, (b) gambler, (c) perpetrator of financial frauds, (d) liar, (e) spendthrift

21. a *naïve* attitude: (a) unwise, (b) hostile, (c) unsophisticated, (d) friendly, (e) contemptuous

22. living in *affluence:* (a) difficult circumstances, (b) countrified surroundings, (c) fear, (d) wealth, (e) poverty

23. in *retrospect:* (a) view of the past, (b) artistic balance, (c) anticipation, (d) admiration, (e) second thoughts

24. a *gourmet:* (a) seasoned traveller, (b) greedy eater, (c) vegetarian, (d) connoisseur of good food, (e) skilful chef

25. to *simulate* interest: (a) pretend, (b) feel, (c) lose, (d) stir up, (e) ask for

26. a *magnanimous* action: (a) puzzling, (b) generous, (c) foolish, (d) unnecessary, (e) wise

27. a *clandestine* meeting: (a) prearranged, (b) hurried, (c) important, (d) secret, (e) public

28. the *apathetic* citizens: (a) made up of separate ethnic groups, (b) keenly vigilant of their rights, (c) politically conservative, (d) indifferent, uninterested, uninvolved, (e) terrified

29. to *placate* his son: (a) please, (b) help, (c) find a job for, (d) make arrangements for, (e) change a feeling of hostility to one of friendliness

30. to *vacillate* continually: (a) avoid, (b) swing back and forth in indecision, (c) inject, (d) treat, (e) scold

31. a *nostalgic* feeling: (a) nauseated, (b) homesick, (c) sharp, (d) painful, (e) delighted

32. feel *antipathy:* (a) bashfulness, (b) stage fright, (c) friendliness, (d) hostility, (e) suspense

33. be more *circumspect:* (a) restrained, (b) confident, (c) cautious, (d) honest, (e) intelligent

34. an *intrepid* fighter for human rights: (a) fearless, (b) eloquent, (c) popular, (d) experienced, (e) famous

35. *diaphanous* material: (a) strong, (b) sheer and gauzy, (c) colourful, (d) expensive, (e) synthetic

36. a *taciturn* host: (a) stingy, (b) generous, (c) disinclined to conversation, (d) charming, (e) gloomy

37. to *malign* his friend: (a) accuse, (b) help, (c) disbelieve, (d) slander, (e) introduce

38. a *congenital* deformity: (a) hereditary, (b) crippling, (c) slight, (d) incurable, (e) occurring at or during birth

39. a definite *neurosis*: (a) plan, (b) emotional disturbance, (c) physical disease, (d) feeling of fear, (e) allergic reaction

40. made an *unequivocal* statement: (a) hard to understand, (b) lengthy, (c) politically motivated, (d) clear and forthright, (e) supporting

41. *vicarious* enjoyment: (a) complete, (b) unspoiled, (c) occurring from a feeling of identification with another, (d) long-continuing, (e) temporary

42. *psychogenic* ailment: (a) incurable, (b) contagious, (c) originating in the mind, (d) intestinal, imaginary

43. an *anachronous* attitude: (a) unexplainable, (b) unreasonable, (c) belonging to a different time, (d) out of place, (e) unusual

44. her *iconoclastic* phase: (a) artistic, (b) sneering at tradition, (c) troubled, (d) difficult, (e) religious

45. a *tyro*: (a) dominating personality, (b) beginner, (c) accomplished musician, (d) dabbler, (e) serious student

46. a *laconic* reply: (a) immediate, (b) assured, (c) terse and meaningful, (d) unintelligible, (e) angry

47. *semantic* confusion: (a) relating to the meaning of words, (b) pertaining to money, (c) having to do with the emotions, (d) relating to mathematics, (e) caused by inner turmoil

48. *cavalier* treatment: (a) courteous, (b) haughty and high-handed, (c) negligent, (d) affectionate, (e) expensive

49. an *anomalous* situation: (a) dangerous, (b) intriguing, (c) unusual, (d) pleasant, (e) unhappy

50. *posthumous* child: (a) cranky, (b) brilliant, (c) physically weak, (d) illegitimate, (e) born after the death of the father

51. feels *enervated*: (a) full of ambition, (b) full of strength, (c) completely exhausted, (d) troubled, (e) full of renewed energy

52. shows *perspicacity*: (a) sincerity, (b) mental keenness, (c) love, (d) faithfulness, (e) longing

53. an unpopular *martinet:* (a) candidate, (b) supervisor, (c) strict disciplinarian, (d) military leader, (e) discourteous snob
54. *gregarious* person: (a) outwardly calm, (b) very sociable, (c) completely untrustworthy, (d) vicious, (e) self-effacing and timid
55. generally *phlegmatic:* (a) smug, self-satisifed, (b) easily pleased, (c) nervous, high-strung, (d) emotionally unresponsive, (e) lacking in social graces
56. an *inveterate* gambler: (a) impoverished, (b) successful, (c) habitual, (d) occasional, (e) superstitious
57. an *egregious* error: (a) outstandingly bad, (b) slight, (c) irreparable, (d) unnecessary, (e) deliberate
58. *cacophony* of a large city: (a) political administration, (b) crowded living conditions, (c) cultural advantages, (d) unpleasant noises, harsh sounds, (e) busy traffic
59. a *prurient* adolescent: (a) tall and gangling, (b) sexually longing, (c) clumsy, awkward, (d) sexually attractive, (e) soft-spoken
60. *uxorious* husband: (a) henpecked, (b) suspicious, (c) guilty of infidelity, (d) fondly and foolishly doting on his wife, (e) tightfisted, penny-pinching

Key   1--a, 2--c, 3--b, 4--a, 5--b, 6--a, 7--e, 8--b, 9--d, 10--a, 11--c, 12--d, 13--b, 14--d, 15--b, 16--e, 17--a, 18--b, 19--c, 20--a, 21--c, 22--d, 23--a, 24--d, 25--a, 26--b, 27--d, 28--d, 29--e, 30--b, 31--b, 32--d, 33--c, 34--a, 35--b, 36--c, 37--d, 38--e, 39--b, 40--d, 41--c, 42--c, 43--c, 44--b, 45--b, 46--c, 47--a, 48--b, 49--c, 50--e. 51--c, 52--b, 53--c, 54--b, 55--d, 56--c, 57--a, 58--d, 59--b, 60--d

Your score (one point for each correct choice): _____
The Meaning of Your Score:
0-11: below average
12-35: average
36-48: above average
49-54: excellent
55-60: superior

A test of verbal speed

Part 1
This is a timed test.

In no more than three minutes (time yourself, or have someone time you), decide whether the word in column B is the *same* (or *approximately the same*) in meaning as the word in column A; *opposite* (or *approximately opposite*) in meaning; or whether the two words are merely *different.*

Circle **S** for *same,* **O** for *opposite,* and **D** for *different.*

You will not have time to dawdle or think too long, so go as fast as you can.

Column A	Column B			
1. sweet	sour	S	O	D
2. crazy	insane	S	O	D
3. stout	fat	S	O	D
4. big	angry	S	O	D
5. danger	peril	S	O	D
6. help	hinder	S	O	D
7. splendid	magnificent	S	O	D
8. love	hate	S	O	D
9. stand	rise	S	O	D
10. furious	violent	S	O	D
11. tree	apple	S	O	D
12. doubtful	certain	S	O	D
13. handsome	ugly	S	O	D
14. begin	start	S	O	D
15. strange	familiar	S	O	D
16. male	female	S	O	D
17. powerful	weak	S	O	D
18. beyond	under	S	O	D
19. live	die	S	O	D
20. go	get	S	O	D
21. return	replace	S	O	D
22. growl	weep	S	O	D
23. open	close	S	O	D
24. nest	home	S	O	D
25. chair	table	S	O	D
26. want	desire	S	O	D
27. can	container	S	O	D

28. idle	working	S	O	D
29. rich	luxurious	S	O	D
30. building	structure	S	O	D

Part 2
This is also a timed test.

In no more than three minutes (again, time yourself or have someone time you), write down as many *different* words as you can think of that start with the letter *D*.

Do *not* use various forms of a word, such as *do, doing, does, done, doer,* etc.

Space is provided for 125 words. You are not expected to reach that number, but write as fast as you can and see how many blanks you can fill in before your time is up.

1. _____
2. _____
3. _____
4. _____
5. _____
6. _____
7. _____
8. _____
9. _____
10. _____
11. _____
12. _____
13. _____
14. _____
15. _____
16. _____
17. _____
18. _____
19. _____
20. _____
21. _____
22. _____
23. _____
24. _____
25. _____
26. _____

27. _____
28. _____
29. _____
30. _____
31. _____
32. _____
33. _____
34. _____
35. _____
36. _____
37. _____
38. _____
39. _____
40. _____
41. _____
42. _____
43. _____
44. _____
45. _____
46. _____
47. _____
48. _____
49. _____
50. _____
51. _____
52. _____
53. _____
54. _____
55. _____
56. _____
57. _____
58. _____
59. _____
60. _____
61. _____
62. _____
63. _____
64. _____
65. _____
66. _____

67. _____
68. _____
69. _____
70. _____
71. _____
72. _____
73. _____
74. _____
75. _____
76. _____
77. _____
78. _____
79. _____
80. _____
81. _____
82. _____
83. _____
84. _____
85. _____
86. _____
87. _____
88. _____
89. _____
90. _____
91. _____
92. _____
93. _____
94. _____
95. _____
96. _____
97. _____
98. _____
99. _____
100. _____
101. _____
102. _____
103. _____
104. _____
105. _____
106. _____

107. _____
108. _____
109. _____
110. _____
111. _____
112. _____
113. _____
114. _____
115. _____
116. _____
117. _____
118. _____
119. _____
120. _____
121. _____
121. _____
122. _____
123. _____
124. _____
125. _____

Key: Part 1: 1–O, 2–S, 3–S, 4–D, 5–S, 6–O, 7–S, 8–O, 9–S,
10–S, 11–D, 12–O, 13–O, 14–S, '15–O, 16–O,
17–O, 18–D, 19–O, 20–D, 21–S, 22–D, 23–O,
24–S, 25–D, 26–S, 27–S, 28–O, 29–S, 30–S

Part 2: Any English word starting with *D* is correct unless it
is merely another form of a previous word on the
list.

Scoring:

Part 1
If you have up to 10 correct answers, credit your score with 25
points.
If you have 11–20 correct answers, credit your score with 50
points.
21–25 correct answers – 75 points.
26–30 correct answers – 100 points.
        Your Score on Part 1:_____

Part 2

       Up to 30 words: 25 points
       31–50 words: 50 points
       51–70 words: 75 points
       71–125 words: 100 points
       Your Score on Part 2:_____

       Total Score
       On Verbal Speed:_____

The meaning of your verbal speed score:
       50: below average
       75: average
       100: above average
       125–150: excellent
       175–200: superior

A test of verbal responsiveness

Part 1
Write in the blank in column B a word starting with the letter *P*
that is the *same*, or *approximately the same*, in meaning as the word
given in column A.
    Example: look   *peer*
    Warning: Every answer *must* start with the letter *P*.

A	B	A	B
1. bucket	_____	14. location	_____
2. faultless	_____	15. stone	_____
3. maybe	_____	16. inactive	_____
4. forgive	_____	17. fussy	_____
5. separate	_____	18. suffering	_____
6. likely	_____	19. castle	_____
7. annoy	_____	20. gasp	_____
8. good-looking	_____	21. fear	_____
9. picture	_____	22. twosome	_____
10. choose	_____	23. artist	_____
11. ugly	_____	24. sheet	_____
12. go	_____	25. collection	_____
13. dish	_____		

Part 2

Write in the blank in column B a word starting with the letter *G* that is *opposite, approximately opposite,* or *in contrast to* the word given in column A.

Example: stop   *go*

Warning: Every answer *must* start with the letter *G.*

A	B	A	B
1. lose	_____	14. ugly	_____
2. midget	_____	15. stingy	_____
3. special	_____	16. awkward	_____
4. lady	_____	17. little	_____
5. take	_____	18. rough	_____
6. moron	_____	19. bride	_____
7. sad	_____	20. ripe	_____
8. boy	_____	21. generous	_____
9. happy	_____	22. unprotected	_____
10. plain	_____	23. experienced	_____
11. hello	_____	24. scarcity	_____
12. here	_____	25. unappreciative	_____
13. bad	_____		

Key, Part 1: If more than one answer is given, count as correct any word you have written that is the same as any *one* of the answers.

1–pail, 2–perfect, 3–perhaps, possibly, probably, 4–pardon, 5–part. 6–probable, possible, perhaps, 7–pester, 8–pretty, 9–photograph, painting, 10–pick, 11–plain, 12–proceed, 13–plate, platter, 14–place, 15–pebble, 16–passive, 17–particular, 18–pain, 19–palace, 20–pant, puff, 21–panic, 22–pair, 23–painter, 24–page, 25–pack

Part 2: If more than one answer is given, count as correct any word you have written that is the same as any *one* of the answers.

1–gain, get, garner, grab, glean, grasp, grip, 2–giant, gigantic, great, gross, 3–general, 4–gentleman, 5–give, 6–genius, 7–glad, gleeful, gleesome,

8–girl, 9–gloomy, glum, grieving, grumpy,
10–gaudy, grand, grandiose, 11–goodbye,
12–gone, 13–good, 14–good-looking, 15–generous, giving, 16–graceful, 17–great, giant, gigantic,
18–gentle, 19–groom, 20–green, 21–greedy,
grasping, 22–guarded, 23–green, 24–glut,
25–grateful

Scoring:
Score Parts 1 and 2 together. Write in the blank the *total number of
correct responses you gave:* _____
The meaning of your verbal responsiveness score:

> 0–10: below average
> 11–20: average
> 21–30: above average
> 31–40: excellent
> 41–50: superior

Vocabulary and success
Now you know where you stand. If you are in the below average
or average group, you must consider, seriously, whether an inade-
quate vocabulary may be holding you back. (If you scored above
average, excellent, or superior, you have doubtless already discovered the unique and far-reaching value of a rich vocabulary, and
you are eager to add still further to your knowledge of words.)

Educational research has discovered that your I.Q. is intimately
related to your vocabulary. Take a standard vocabulary test and
then an intelligence test – the results in both will be substantially
the same.

You can increase your vocabulary
The more extensive your vocabulary, the better your chances of
success, other things being equal – success in attaining your educational goals, success in moving ahead in your business or professional career, success in achieving your intellectual potential.

And you *can* increase your vocabulary – faster and more easily
than you may realize.

You can, in fact, accomplish a tremendous gain in less than two to three months of concentrated effort, even if you do only one session a day – in less time if you do two or more sessions a day.

Furthermore –

You can start improving your vocabulary immediately – and within a few days you can be cruising along at such a rapid rate that there will be an actual change in your thinking, in your ability to express your thoughts, and in your powers of understanding.

Does this sound as if I am promising you the whole world in a neat package with a pretty pink ribbon tied around it? I am. And I am willing to make such an unqualified promise because I have seen what happens to those of my students who make sincere, methodical efforts to learn more, many more, words.

2

HOW TO START BUILDING YOUR VOCABULARY

When you have finished working with this book, you will no longer be the same person.

You can't be.

If you honestly read every page, if you do every exercise, if you take every test, if you follow every principle, you will go through an intellectual experience that will effect a radical change in you.

For if you systematically increase your vocabulary, you will also sharpen and enrich your thinking; push back your intellectual horizons; build your self-assurance; improve your facility in handling the English language and thereby your ability to express your thoughts effectively; and acquire a deeper understanding of the world in general and of yourself in particular.

Increasing your vocabulary does not mean merely learning the definitions of large numbers of obscure words; it does not mean memorizing scores of unrelated terms. What it means – what it can only mean – is becoming acquainted with the multitudinous and fascinating phenomena of human existence for which words are, obviously, only the verbal descriptions.

Increasing your vocabulary – properly, intelligently, and systematically – means treating yourself to an all-round, liberal education.

And surely you cannot deny that such an experience will change you intellectually –

Will have a discernible effect on your methods of thinking – on your store of information – on your ability to express your ideas – on your understanding of human problems.

How children increase their vocabularies

The typical ten-year-old, you will recall, has a recognition vocabulary of over twenty thousand words – and has been learning many hundreds of new words every year since the age of four.

You were once that typical child.

You were once an accomplished virtuoso of vocabulary building.

What was your secret?

Did you spend hours every day poring over a dictionary?

Did you keep notebooks full of all the new words you ever heard or read?

Did you immediately look up the meaning of any new word that your parents or older members of your family used?

Such procedures would have struck you as absurd then, as absurd as they would be for your today.

You had a much better, much more effective, and considerably less self-conscious method.

Your method was the essence of simplicity: day in and day out you kept learning; you kept squeezing every possible ounce of learning out of every waking moment; you were an eternal question box, for you had a constant and insatiable desire to know and understand.

How adults stop building their vocabularies

Then, eventually, at some point in your adult life (unless you are the rare exception), you gradually lost your compulsive drive to discover, to understand, to know.

Eventually, therefore, you gradually lost your need to increase your vocabulary – your need to learn the words that could verbalize your new discoveries, your new understanding, your new knowledge.

Roland Gelatt, in a review of Caroline Pratt's book *I Learn from Children*, describes this phenomenon as follows:

All normal human beings are born with a powerful urge to learn. Almost all of them lose this urge, even before they have reached maturity. It is only the few . . . who are so constituted that lack of learning becomes a nuisance. This is perhaps the most insidious of human tragedies.

Children are wonders at increasing their vocabularies because of their 'powerful urge to learn'. They do not learn solely by means of words, but as their knowledge increases, so does their vocabulary – for words are the symbols of ideas and understanding.

(If you are a parent, you perhaps remember that crucial and trying period in which your child constantly asked 'Why?'. The 'Why?' is the child's method of finding out. How many adults that you know go about asking and thinking 'Why?'? How often do your yourself do it?)

The adults who 'lose this urge', who no longer feel that 'lack of learning becomes a nuisance', stop building their vocabularies. They stop learning, they stop growing intellectually, they stop changing. When and if such a time comes, then, as Mr. Gelatt so truly says, 'This is perhaps the most insidious of human tragedies'. But fortunately the process is far from irreversible.

If you have lost the 'powerful urge to learn', you can regain it – you can regain your need to discover, to understand, to know.

And thus you can start increasing your vocabulary at the same rate as when you were a child.

I am not spouting airy theory. For over thirty-five years I have worked with thousands of adults in my college courses in vocabulary improvement, and I can state as a fact, and without qualification, that:

If you can recapture that 'powerful urge to learn' with which you were born, you can go on increasing your vocabulary at a prodigious rate –
No matter what your present age.

Why age makes little difference in vocabulary building

I repeat, *no matter what your present age.*

You may be labouring under a delusion common to many older people.

You may think that after you pass your twenties you rapidly and inevitably lose your ability to learn.

That is simply not true.

There is no doubt that the years up to eighteen or twenty are the best period for learning. Your own experience no doubt bears that out. And of course *for most people* more learning goes on faster up to the age of eighteen or twenty than ever after, even if they live to be older than Methuselah. (That is why vocabulary in-

creases so rapidly for the first twenty years of life and comparatively at a snail's pace thereafter.)

But (and follow me closely) —

The fact that most learning is accomplished before the age of
twenty does not mean that very little learning can be achieved
beyond that age.

What *is* done by most people and what *can* be done under
proper guidance and motivation are two very, very different
things — as scientific experiments have conclusively shown.

Furthermore —

The fact that your learning ability may be best up to the age of
twenty does not mean that it is absolutely useless as soon as your
twentieth birthday is passed.

Quite the contrary.

Edward Thorndike, the famous educational psychologist,
found in experiments with people of all ages that although the
learning curve rises spectacularly up to twenty, it remains steady
for at least another five years. After that, ability to learn (according to Professor Thorndike) drops very, very slowly up to the age
of thirty-five, and drops a bit more but *still slowly* beyond that age.

And —

Right up to senility the *total* decrease in learning ability after the
age of twenty is never more than fifteen per cent!

That does not sound, I submit, as if no one can ever learn
anything new after the age of twenty.

Believe me, the old saw that claims you cannot teach an old dog
new tricks is a baseless, if popular, superstition.

So I repeat: no matter what your age, you can go on learning
efficiently, or start learning once again if perhaps you have
stopped.

You can be thirty, or forty, or fifty, or sixty, or seventy — or
older.

No matter what your age, you can once again increase your
vocabulary at a prodigious rate — providing you recapture the
'powerful urge to learn' that is the key to vocabulary improvement.

Not the urge to learn 'words' — words are only symbols of ideas.

But the urge to learn facts, theories, concepts, information,
knowledge, understanding — call it what you will.

Words are the symbols of knowledge, the keys to accurate thinking. Is it any wonder then that the most successful and intelligent people in this country have the biggest vocabularies?

It was not their large vocabularies that made these people successful and intelligent, but their *knowledge*.

Knowledge, however, is gained largely through words.

In the process of increasing their knowledge, these successful people increased their vocabularies.

Just as children increase *their* vocabulary at a tremendous, phenomenal rate during those years when their knowledge is increasing most rapidly.

Knowledge is chiefly in the form of words, and from now on, in this book, you will be thinking *about*, and thinking *with*, new words and new ideas.

What this book can do for you

This book is designed to get you started building your vocabulary – effectively and at jet-propelled speed – by helping you regain the intellectual atmosphere, the keen, insatiable curiosity, the 'powerful urge to learn' of your childhood.

The organization of the book is based on two simple principles: 1) words are the verbal symbols of ideas, and 2) the more ideas you are familiar with, the more words you know.

So, chapter by chapter, we will start with some central idea – personality types, doctors, science, unusual occupations, liars, actions, speech habits, insults, compliments, etc. – and examine ten basic words that express various aspects of the idea. Then, using each word as a springboard, we will explore any others which are related to it in meaning or derivation, so that it is not unlikely that a single chapter may discuss, teach, and test close to one hundred important words.

Always, however, the approach will be from the idea. First there will be a 'teaser preview' in which the ideas are briefly hinted at; then a 'headline', in which each idea is examined somewhat more closely; next a clear, detailed paragraph or more will analyse the idea in all its ramifications; finally the word itself, which you will meet only after you are completely familiar with the idea.

In the *etymology* (derivation of words) section, you will learn what Greek or Latin root gives the word its unique meaning and what other words contain the same, or related, roots. You will thus be continually working in related fields, and there will never be any possibility of confusion from 'too muchness', despite the great number of words taken up and tested in each chapter.

Successful people have superior vocabularies. People who are intellectually alive and successful in the professional or business worlds are accustomed to dealing with ideas, are constantly on the search for new ideas, build their lives and their careers on the ideas they have learned. And it is to readers whose goal is *successful* living (in the broadest meaning of the word *successful*) that this book is addressed.

A note on time schedules

From my experience over many years in teaching, I have become a firm believer in setting a goal for all learning and a schedule for reaching that goal.

You will discover that each chapter is divided into approximately equal sessions, and that each session will take from thirty to forty-five minutes of your time, depending on how rapidly or slowly you enjoy working – and bear in mind that everyone has an optimum rate of learning.

For best results, do one or two sessions at a time – spaced studying, with time between sessions so that you can assimilate what you have learned, is far more efficient, far more productive, than gobbling up great amounts in indigestible chunks.

Come back to the book every day, or as close to every day as the circumstances of your life permit.

Find a schedule that is comfortable for you, and then stick to it.

Avoid interrupting your work until you have completed a full session, and always decide, before you stop, *exactly when* you will plan to pick up the book again.

Working at your own comfortable rate, you will most likely finish the material in two to three months, give or take a few weeks.

However long you take, you will end with a solid feeling of accomplishment, a new understanding of how English words work, and – most important – how to make words work for you.

3

HOW TO TALK ABOUT PERSONALITY TYPES

(Sessions 1–3)

Teaser preview
What word best describes your personality if you:

- *are interested solely in your own welfare?*
- *constantly talk about yourself?*
- *dedicate your life to helping others?*
- *turn your mind inwards?*
- *turn your mind outwards?*
- *hate humanity?*
- *hate women?*
- *hate marriage?*
- *lead a lonely, austere existence?*

Session 1

HOW TO TALK ...

PERSONALITY TYPES

You have ... ... exciting
yourself ... ... own mind
and, how ... ... when ... about

Every human being is, in one way or another, unique.

Everyone's personality is determined by a combination of genetic and environmental factors.

Let us examine ten personality types (one of which might by chance be your very own) that result from the way culture, growth, family background, and environment interact with heredity.

And, of course, we begin not with the words, but with the ideas.

Ideas

1.   Me first

Your attitude to life is simple, direct, and aboveboard — every decision you make is based on the answer to one question: 'What's in it for me?' If your selfishness, greed, and ruthless desire for self-advancement hurt other people, that's too bad. 'This is a tough world, pal, dog eat dog and all that, and I, for one, am not going to be left behind!'

       An *egoist*

2.   The height of conceit

'Now, let's see. Have you heard about all the money I'm making? Did I tell you about my latest amorous conquest? Let me give you my opinion — I know, because I'm an expert at practically everything!' You are boastful to the point of being obnoxious — you have only one string to your conversational bow, namely, *yourself*; and on it you play a number of monotonous variations: what *you* think, what *you* have done, how good *you* are, how *you* would solve the problems of the world, etc. ad nauseam.

    An *egotist*

3.   Let me help you

You have discovered the secret of true happiness – concerning yourself with the welfare of others. Never mind your own interests, how's the next fellow getting along?

    an *altruist*

4.   Leave me alone

Like a biochemist studying a colony of bacteria under the microscope, you minutely examine your every thought, feeling, and action. Probing futile questions like 'what do other people think of me?', 'How do I look?', and 'Maybe I shouldn't have said that?' are your constant nagging companions, for you are unable to realize that other people do not spend as much time and energy analysing you as you think.

You may seem unsocial, yet your greatest desire is to be liked and accepted. You may be shy and quiet, you are often moody and unhappy, and you prefer solitude or at most the company of one person to a crowd. You have an aptitude for creative work and are uncomfortable engaging in activities that require cooperation with other people. You may even be a genius, or eventually turn into one.

    An *introvert*

5.   Let's do it together

You would be great as a teacher, counsellor, administrator, insurance agent. You can always become interested – sincerely, vitally interested – in other people's problems. You're the life of the party, because you never worry about the effect of your actions, never inhibit yourself with doubts about dignity or propriety. You are usually happy, generally full of high spirits; you love to be with people – lots of people. Your thoughts, your interests, your whole personality are turned outwards.

    An *extrovert*

6.   Neither extreme

You have both introverted and extroverted tendencies – at different times and on different occasions. Your interests are turned, in about equal proportions, both inwards and outwards. Indeed, you're quite normal – in the sense that your personality is like that of most people.

An *ambivert*

7.   People are no damn good

Cynical, embittered, suspicious, you hate everyone. (Especially, but never to be admitted, *yourself*?) The perfectibility of the human race? 'Nonsense! No way!' The stupidity, the meanness, and the crookedness of most mortals ('Most? Probably all!') – that is your favourite theme.

A *misanthrope*

8.   Women are no damn good

Sometime in your dim past, you were crossed, scorned, or deeply wounded by a woman (a mother, or mother figure, perhaps?). So now you have a carefully constructed defence against further hurt – you hate *all* women.

A *misogynist*

9.   'Marriage is an institution – and who wants to live in an institution?'

You will not make the ultimate *legal* commitment. Members of the opposite sex are great as lovers, roommates, flat- or house-sharers, but *not* as lawfully wedded spouses. The ties that bind are too binding for you. You may possibly believe, and possibly, for yourself, be right, that a commitment is deeper and more meaningful if freedom is available without judicial proceedings.

A *misogamist*

10.   ' . . . that the flesh is heir to . . .

Self-denial, austerity, lonely contemplation – these are the characteristics of the good life, so you claim. The simplest food and the least amount of it that will keep body and soul together, combined with abstinence from fleshly, earthly pleasures, will eventually lead to spiritual perfection – that is your philosophy.
       An *ascetic*

Using the words

You have been introduced to ten valuable words – but in each case, as you have noticed, you have first considered the ideas that these words represent. Now *say* the words – each one is respelled phonetically so that you will be sure to pronounce it correctly.*

Say each word aloud. This is the first important step to complete mastery. As you hear a word in your own voice, think of its meaning. Are you quite clear about it? If not, reinforce your learning by rereading the explanatory paragraph or paragraphs.

Can you pronounce the words?

1. *egoist*	EE'-gō-ist
2. *egotist*	EE'-gō-tist
3. *altruist*	AL'-trōō-ist
4. *introvert*	IN'-trə-vərt'
5. *extrovert*	EKS'-trə-vərt'
6. *ambivert*	AM'-bi-vərt'
7. *misanthrope*	MIZ'-ən-thrōp'
8. *misogynist*	mi-SOJ'-ə-nist
9. *misogamist*	mi-SOG'-ə-mist
10. *ascetic*	ə-SET'-ik

Can you work with the words?

You have taken two long steps towards mastery of the expressive words in this chapter – you have thought about the ideas behind them, and you have said them aloud.

* See Introduction, Section 2, *Master the pronunciation system.*

For your third step, match each personality with the appropriate characteristic, action, or attitude.

1. egoist	a.	turns thoughts inwards
2. egotist	b.	hates marriage
3. altruist	c.	talks about accomplishments
4. introvert	d.	hates people
5. extrovert	e.	does not pursue pleasures of the flesh
6. ambivert	f.	is interested in the welfare of others
7. misanthrope	g.	believes in self-advancement
8. misogynist	h.	turns thoughts both inwards and outwards
9. misogamist	i.	hates women
10. ascetic	j.	turns thoughts outwards

Key: 1–g, 2–c, 3–f, 4–a, 5–j, 6–h, 7–d, 8–i, 9–b, 10–e

Do you understand the words?

Now that you are becoming more and more involved in these ten words, find out if they can make an immediate appeal to your understanding. Here are ten questions – can you indicate, quickly, and without reference to any previous definitions, whether the correct answer to each of these questions is *yes* or *no*?

	YES	NO
1. Is an *egoist* selfish?	YES	NO
2. Is modesty one of the characteristics of the *egotist*?	YES	NO
3. Is an *altruist* selfish?	YES	NO
4. Does an *introvert* pay much attention to himself?	YES	NO
5. Does an *extrovert* prefer solitude to companionship?	YES	NO
6. Are most normal people *ambiverts*?	YES	NO
7. Does a *misanthrope* like people?	YES	NO
8. Does a *misogynist* enjoy the company of women?	YES	NO
9. Does an *ascetic* lead a life of luxury?	YES	NO

10. Does a *misogamist* try to avoid   YES   NO
    marriage?

Key: 1–yes, 2–no, 3–no, 4–yes, 5–no, 6–yes, 7–no, 8–no,
        9–no, 10–yes

Can you recall the words?

You have thus far reinforced your learning by saying the words
aloud, by matching them to their definitions, and by responding
to meaning when they were used in context.

Can you recall each word, now, without further reference to
previous material? And can you spell it correctly?

1. Who lives a lonely, austere   1. A_____
   life?
2. Whose interests are   2. E_____
   turned outwards?
3. Who is supremely selfish?   3. E_____
4. Who hates people?   4. M_____
5. Whose interests are   5. A_____
   turned both inwards and
   outwards?
6. Who is incredibly   6. E_____
   conceited?
7. Who is more interested in   7. A_____
   the welfare of others than
   in his own?
8. Who hates women?   8. M_____
9. Whose interests are   9. I_____
   turned inwards?
10. Who hates marriage?   10. M_____

Key: 1–ascetic, 2–extrovert, 3–egoist, 4–misanthrope,
        5–ambivert, 6–egotist, 7–altruist, 8–misogynist, 9–in-
        trovert, 10–misogamist

End of Session 1)

Session 2

Origins and related words

Every word in the English language has a history – and these ten are no exception. In this section you will learn a good deal more about the words you have been working with; in addition, you will make excursions into many other words allied either in meaning, form, or history to our basic ten.

1. The ego

Egoist and *egotist* are built on the same Latin root – the pronoun *ego*, meaning *I*. *I* is the greatest concern in the *egoist's* mind, the most overused word in the *egotist's* vocabulary. (Keep the words differentiated in your own mind by thinking of the *t* in *talk*, and the additional *t* in *egotist*). *Ego* itself has been taken over from Latin as an important English word and is commonly used to denote one's concept of oneself, as in, 'What do you think your constant criticisms do to my *ego*?'. *Ego* has also a special meaning in psychology – but for the moment you have enough problems without going into *that*.

If you are an *egocentric* (ee'-gō-SEN'-trik), you consider yourself the *centre* of the universe – you are an extreme form of the *egoist*. And if you are an *egomaniac* (ee'-gō-MAY'-ni-ak), you carry *egoism* to such an extreme that your needs, desires, and interests have become a morbid obsession, a *mania*. The *egoist* or *egotist* is obnoxious, the *egocentric* is intolerable, and the *egomaniac* is dangerous and slightly mad.

Egocentric is both a noun ('What an *egocentric* her new roommate is!') and an adjective ('He is the most *egocentric* person I have ever met!').

To derive the adjective form of *egomaniac*, add *-al*, a common adjective suffix. Say the adjective aloud:

egomaniacal   ee'-gō-mə-NI'-ə-kəl

2.   Others

In Latin, the word for *other* is *alter*, and a number of valuable English words are built on this root.

Altruism (AL'-trōō-iz-əm), the philosophy practiced by *altruists*, comes from one of the variant spellings of Latin *alter*, other. *Altruistic* (al-trōō-IS'-tik) actions look towards the benefit of *others*. If you *alternate* (AWL'-tə-nayt'), you skip one and take the *other*, so to speak, as when you play golf on *alternate* (awl-TƏR'-nət) Saturdays. If you have no *alternative* (awl-TƏR'-nə-tiv), you have no *other* choice.

You see how easy it is to understand the meanings of these words once you realize that they all come from the same source. And keeping in mind that *alter* means *other*, you can quickly understand words like *alter ego, altercation,* and *alteration*.

An *alteration* (awl'-tə-RAY'-shən) is of course a change – a making into something *other*. When you *alter* (AWL'-tə) your plans, you make *other* plans.

An *altercation* (awl'-tə-KAY'-shən) is a verbal dispute. When you have an *altercation* with someone, you have a violent disagreement, a 'fight' with words. And why? Because you have *other* ideas, plans, or opinions than those of the person on the *other* side of the argument. *Altercation*, by the way, is stronger than *quarrel* or *dispute* – the sentiment is more heated, the disagreement is likely to be angry or even hot-tempered, there may be recourse, if the disputants are human, to profanity or obscenity. You have *altercations*, in short, over pretty important issues, and the word implies that you get quite excited.

Alter ego (AWL'-tə EE'-gō), which combines *alter*, other, with *ego*, I, self, generally refers to someone with whom you are so close that you both do the same things, think alike, react similarly, and are, in temperament, almost mirror images of each other. Any such friend is your *other I*, your *other self*, your *alter ego*.

Using the words

Can you pronounce the words?

Digging a little into the derivation of three of our basic words, *egoist, egotist,* and *altruist,* has put us in touch with two important Latin roots, *ego,* I, self, and *alter,* other, and has made it possible for us to explore, with little difficulty, many other words derived from these roots. Pause now, for a moment, to digest these new acquisitions, and to say them *aloud.*

1. *ego*	EE'-gō
2. *egocentric*	ee'-gō-SEN'-trik
3. *egomaniac*	ee'-gō-MAY'ni-ak
4. *egomaniacal*	ee'-gō-mə-NĪ'-ə-kəl
5. *altruism*	AL'-trōō-iz-əm
6. *altruistic*	al-trōō-IS'-tik
7. to *alternate (v.)*	AWL'-tə-nayt'
8. *alternate (adj.)*	awl-TəR'-nət
9. *alternative*	awl-TəR'-nə-tiv
10. *alteration*	awl'-tə-RAY'-shən
11. to *alter*	AWL'-tə
12. *altercation*	awl'-tə-KAY'-shən
13. *alter ego*	AWL'-tə EE'-gō

Can you work with the words? (I)

You have seen how these thirteen words derive from the two Latin roots *ego,* I, self, and *alter,* other, and you have pronounced them aloud and thereby begun to make them part of your active vocabulary.

Are you ready to match definitions to words?

1. ego	a.	one who is excessively fixated on his own desires, needs, etc.
2. egocentric	b.	to change
3. altruism	c.	argument
4. to alternate	d.	one's concept of oneself
5. to alter	e.	to take one, skip one, etc.
6. altercation	f.	philosophy of putting another's welfare above one's own

Key: 1–d, 2--a, 3–f, 4–e, 5–b, 6–c

Can you work with the words? (II)

1. egomaniacal	a.	a change
2. altruistic	b.	other possible
3. alternative	c.	interested in the welfare of others
4. alteration	d.	one's other self
5. alter ego	e.	a choice
6. alternate (*adj.*)	f.	morbidly, obsessively wrapped up in oneself

Key: 1–f, 2–c, 3–e, 4–a, 5–d, 6–b

Do you understand the words?

If you have begun to understand these thirteen words, you will be able to respond to the following questions.

1. Is rejection usually a blow to one's *ego*?	YES	NO
2. Are *egocentric* people easy to get along with?	YES	NO
3. Does an *egomaniac* have a normal personality?	YES	NO
4. Are *egomaniacal* tendencies a sign of maturity?	YES	NO
5. Is *altruism* a characteristic of selfish people?	YES	NO
6. Are *altruistic* tendencies common to egoists?	YES	NO
7. Is an *alternate* plan necessarily inferior?	YES	NO
8. Does an *alternative* allow you some freedom of choice?	YES	NO
9. Does *alteration* imply keeping things the same?	YES	NO

10. Do excitable people often engage in *altercations*?   YES   NO

11. Is your *alter ego* usually quite similar to yourself?   YES   NO

Key: 1—yes, 2—no, 3—no, 4—no, 5—no, 6—no, 7—no, 8—yes, 9—no, 10—yes, 11—yes

Can you recall the words?

Have you learned these words so well that you can summon each one from your mind when a brief definition is offered? Review first if necessary; then, without further reference to previous pages, write the correct word in each blank. Make sure to check your spelling when you refer to the Key.

1. one's other self
2. to change
3. a heated dispute
4. excessively, morbidly obsessed with one's own needs, desires, or ambitions
5. unselfish; more interested in the welfare of others than in one's own
6. utterly involved with oneself; self-centred
7. a choice
8. one who substitutes for another

1. A_____
2. A_____
3. A_____
4. E_____

5. A_____

6. E_____

7. A_____
8. A_____

Key: 1—alter ego, 2—alter, 3—altercation, 4—egomaniacal, 5—altruistic, 6—egocentric, 7—alternative, 8—alternate

(End of Session 2)

Session 3

Origins and related words

1.   Depends how you turn

Introvert, extrovert, and *ambivert* are built on the Latin verb *verto,* to turn. If your thoughts are constantly turned inwards (*intro-*), you are an *introvert*; outwards (*extro-*), an *extrovert*; and in both directions (*ambi-*), an *ambivert*. The prefix *ambi-,* both, is also found in *ambidextrous* (am'-bi-DEKS'-trəs), *able to use both hands with equal skill.* The noun is *ambidexterity* (am'-bi-deks-TER'-ə-ti).

Dexterous (DEKS'-trəs) means *skilful,* the noun *dexterity* (desk-TER'-ə-ti) is *skill.* The ending *-ous* is a common adjective suffix (*famous, dangerous, perilous,* etc.); *-ity* is a common noun suffix (*vanity, quality, simplicity,* etc.).

(Spelling caution: Note that the letter following the *t-* in *ambidextrous* is *-r,* but that in dexterous the next letter is *-e.*)

Dexter is actually the Latin word for *right hand* – in the *ambidextrous* person, both hands are *right hands,* so to speak.

The right hand is traditionally the more skilful one; it is only within recent decades that we have come to accept that left-handers are just as normal as anyone else – and the term *left-handed* is still used as a synonym of *awkward.*

The Latin word for the *left hand* is *sinister.* Sinister (SIN'-i-stə), in English, means *threatening, evil,* or *dangerous,* a further commentary on our early suspiciousness of left-handed persons. There may still be some parents who insist on forcing left-handed children to change (though left-handedness is inherited, and as much an integral part of its possessor as eye colour or nose shape), with various unfortunate results to the child – sometimes stuttering or an inability to read with normal skill.

The French word for the *left hand* is *gauche*, and, as you would suspect, when we took this word over into English we invested it with an uncomplimentary meaning. Call someone *gauche* (GŌSH) and you imply clumsiness, generally social rather than physical. (We're right back to our age-old misconception that left-handed people are less skilful than right-handed ones.) A *gauche* remark is tactless; a *gauche* offer of sympathy is so bumbling as to be embarrassing; *gaucherie* (GŌ'-shə-ri) is an awkward, clumsy, tactless, embarrassing way of saying things or of handling situations. The *gauche* person is totally without finesse.

And the French word for the *right hand* is *droit*, which we have used in building our English word *adroit* (ə-DROYT'). Needless to say, *adroit*, like *dexterous*, means *skilful*, but especially in the exercise of the mental facilities. Like *gauche*, *adroit*, or its noun *adroitness*, usually is used figuratively. The *adroit* person is quick-witted, can get out of difficult spots cleverly, can handle situations ingeniously. *Adroitness* is, then, quite the opposite of *gaucherie*.

2.   Love, hate, and marriage

Misanthrope, misogynist, and *misogamist* are built on the Greek root *misein,* to hate. The *misanthrope* hates mankind (Greek *anthropos,* mankind); the *misogynist* hates women (Greek *gyne,* woman); the *misogamist* hates marriage (Greek *gamos,* marriage).

Anthropos, mankind, is also found in *anthropology* (an'-thrə-POL'-ə-ji), the study of the development of the human race; and in *philanthropist* (fi-LAN'-thrə-pist), one who loves mankind and shows such love by making substantial financial contributions to charitable organizations or by donating time and energy to helping those in need.

The root *gyne,* woman, is also found in *gynaecologist* (gīna-ə-KOL'-ə-jist), the medical specialist who treats female disorders. And the root *gamos,* marriage, occurs also in *monogamy* (mə-NOG -ə-mi), *bigamy* (BIG'-ə-mi), and *polygamy* (pə-LIG'-ə-mi).

(As we will discover later, *monos* means *one,* *bi* means *two, polys* means *many.*)

So *monogamy* is the custom of only *one* marriage (at a time).

Bigamy, by etymology, is *two* marriages – in actuality, the unlawful act of contracting another marriage without divorcing one's current legal spouse.

And *polygamy*, by derivation *many* marriages, and therefore etymologically denoting plural marriage for either males *or* females, in current usage generally refers to the custom practiced in earlier times by the Mormons, and before them by King Solomon, in which the man has as many wives as he can afford financially and/or emotionally. The correct, but rarely used, term for this custom is *polygyny* (pə-LIJ'-ə-ni) – *polys*, many, plus *gyne*, woman.

What if a woman has two or more husbands, a form of marriage practiced in the Himalaya Mountains of Tibet? That custom is called *polyandry* (pol-i-AN'-dri), from *polys* plus Greek *andros*, male.

3.   Making friends with suffixes

English words have various forms, using certain suffixes for nouns referring to persons, other suffixes for practices, attitudes, philosophies, etc., and still others for adjectives.

Consider:

Person	*Practice, etc.*	*Adjective*
1. misanthrope *or* misanthropist	misanthropy	misanthropic
2. misogynist	misogyny	misogynous *or* misogynistic
3. gynaecologist	gynaecology	gynaecological
4. monogamist	monogamy	monogamous
5. bigamist	bigamy	bigamous
6. polygamist	polygamy	polygamous
7. polygynist	polygyny	polygynous
8. polyandrist	polyandry	polyandrous
9. philanthropist	philanthropy	philanthropic
10. anthropologist	anthropology	anthropological

You will note, then, that *-ist* is a common suffix for a person; *-y* for a practice, attitude, etc.; and *-ic* or *-ous* for an adjective.

4.   Living alone and liking it

Ascetic is from the Greek word *asketes*, monk or hermit.

A monk lives a lonely life – not for him the pleasures of the fleshpots, the laughter and merriment of convivial gatherings, the dissipation of high living. Rather, days of contemplation, study, and rough toil, nights on a hard bed in a simple cell, and the kind of self-denial that leads to a purification of the soul.

That person is an *ascetic* who leads an existence, voluntarily of course, that compares in austerity, simplicity, and rigorous hardship with the life of a monk.

The practice is *asceticism* (ə-SET'-i-siz-əm), the adjective *ascetic*.

Review of etymology

Notice how efficiently you can master words by understanding their etymological structure. Stop for a moment to review the roots, prefixes, and suffixes you have studied. Can you recall a word we have discussed in this chapter that is built on the indicated prefix, root, or suffix?

Prefix, Root, Suffix	Meaning	Example
1. *ego*	self, I	_____
2. *alter*	other	_____
3. *intro-*	inside	_____
4. *extro-*	outside	_____
5. *verto*	turn	_____
6. *ambi-*	both	_____
7. *misein*	hate	_____
8. *anthropos*	mankind	_____
9. *gyne*	woman	_____
10. *gamos*	marriage	_____
11. *asketes*	monk	_____
12. *centrum*	centre	_____
13. *mania*	madness	_____
14. *dexter*	right hand	_____
15. *sinister*	left hand	_____
16. *gauche*	left hand	_____
17. *droit*	right hand	_____
18. *monos*	one	_____
19. *bi-*	two	_____
20. *polys*	many	_____
21. *andros*	male	_____
22. *-ist*	person who (*noun suffix*)	_____

23.	-y	Practice, custom, etc. (*noun suffix*)	_____
24.	-ous	adjective suffix	_____
25.	-ity	quality, condition, etc. (*noun suffix*)	_____

Using the words

Can you pronounce the words? (I)

Say each word aloud! Hear it in your own voice! *Say it often enough so that you feel comfortable with it, noting carefully from the phonetic respelling exactly how it should sound.*

Remember that the first crucial step in mastering a word is to be able to say it with ease and assurance.

1.	*ambidextrous*	am-bi-DEKS'-trəs
2.	*ambidexterity*	am'-bi-deks-TER'-ə-ti
3.	*dexterous*	DEKS'-trəs
4.	*dexterity*	deks-TER'-ə-ti
5.	*sinister*	SIN'-i-stə
6.	*gauche*	GŌSH (Say the English word *go*, then quickly add -*sh*.)
7.	*gaucherie*	GŌ'-shə-ri
8.	*adroit*	ə-DROYT'
9.	*adroitness*	ə-DROYT'-nəss)
10.	*anthropology*	an'-thrə-POL'-ə-ji
11.	*anthropologist*	an'-thrə-POL'-ə-jist
12.	*anthropological*	an'-thrə-pə-LOJ'-i-kəl
13.	*philanthropist*	fi-LAN'-thrə-pist
14.	*philanthropy*	fi-LAN'-thrə-pi
15.	*philanthropic*	fil'-ən-THROP'-ik
16.	*gynaecologist*	gīna-ə-KOL'-ə-jist
17.	*gynaecology*	gīna-ə-KOL'-ə-jee
18.	*gynaecological*	gīna-ə-kə-LOJ'-i-kəl
19.	*monogamist*	mə-NOG'-ə-mist
20.	*monogamy*	mə-NOG'-ə-mi
21.	*monogamous*	mə-NOG'-ə-məs

Can you pronounce the words? (II)

1.	*bigamist*	BIG'-ə-mist
2.	*bigamy*	BIG'-ə-mi
3.	*bigamous*	BIG'-ə-məs
4.	*polygamist*	pə-LIG'-ə-mist
5.	*polygamy*	pə-LIG'-ə-mi
6.	*polygamous*	pə-LIG'-ə-məs
7.	*polygynist*	pə-LIJ'-ə-nist
8.	*polygyny*	pə-LIJ'-ə-ni
9.	*polygynous*	pə-LIJ'-ə-nəs
10.	*polyandrist*	pol-i-AN'-drist
11.	*polyandry*	pol-i-AN'-dri
12.	*polyandrous*	pol-i-AN'-drəs
13.	*misnathropist*	miz-AN'-thrə-pist
14.	*misanthropy*	miz-AN'-thrə-pi
15.	*misanthropic*	miz-ən-THROP'-ik
16.	*misogyny*	mə-SOJ'-ə-ni
17.	*misogynous*	mi-SOJ'-ə-nəs
18.	*misogynistic*	mi-soj'-ə-NIS'-tik
19.	*misogamy*	mi-SOG'-ə-mi
20.	*misogamous*	mi-SOG'-ə-məs
21.	*asceticism*	ə-SET'-i-siz-əm

Can you work with the words? (I)

Check on your comprehension! See how successfully you can match words and meanings!

1.	ambidextrous	a.	evil, threatening
2.	dexterous	b.	hating mankind
3.	sinister	c.	skilful
4.	gauche	d.	awkward
5.	misanthropic	e.	capable of using both hands with equal skill

Key: 1–e, 2–c, 3–a, 4–d, 5–b

Can you work with the words? (II)

1.	anthropology	a.	system of only one marriage

2. gynaecology   b. hatred of women
3. monogamy   c. illegal plurality of marriages
4. bigamy   d. study of human development
5. misogyny   e. study of female ailments

Key: 1–d, 2–e, 3–a, 4–c, 5–b

Can you work with the words? (III)

1. polygamy   a. devotion to a lonely and austere life
2. misogamy   b. skill, cleverness
3. asceticism   c. custom in which one man has many wives
4. philanthropy   d. love of mankind
5. adroitness   e. hatred of marriage

Key: 1–c, 2–e, 3–a, 4–d, 5–b

Can you work with the words? (IV)

1. polygynist   a. student of the development of mankind
2. polyandrist   b. one who engages in charitable works
3. anthropologist   c. male with a plurality of wives
4. gynaecologist   d. women's doctor
5. philanthropist   e. female with a plurality of husbands

Key: 1–c, 2–e, 3–a, 4–d, 5–b

Do you understand the words?

1. Can *ambidextrous* people use either the left or right hand equally well?   YES   NO

2. Should a surgeon be manually   YES   NO
   dexterous?

3. Is a *sinister*-looking person   YES   NO
   frightening?

4. Is *gaucherie* a social asset?   YES   NO

5. Is an *adroit* speaker likely to be a   YES   NO
   successful lawyer?

6. Is a student of *anthropology*   YES   NO
   interested in primitive tribes?

7. Does a *gynaecologist* have more male   YES   NO
   than female patients?

8. Is *monogamy* the custom in Western YES   NO
   countries?

9. Is a *misogamist* likely to show   YES   NO
   tendencies towards *polygamy?*

10. Is a *bigamist* breaking the law?   YES   NO

11. Is a *philanthropist* generally altruistic?   YES   NO

12. Does a *misanthropist* enjoy human YES   NO
    relationships?

13. Does a *misogynist* enjoy female   YES   NO
    companionship?

14. Are unmarried people necessarily   YES   NO
    misogamous?

15. Are bachelors necessarily *misogynous?*   YES   NO

16. Is *asceticism* compatible with   YES   NO
    luxurious living and the pursuit of
    pleasure?

17. Does a *polyandrist* have more than YES   NO
    one husband?

Key: 1–yes, 2–yes, 3–yes, 4–no, 5–yes, 6–yes, 7–no, 8–yes,
        9–no, 10–yes, 11–yes, 12–no, 13–no, 14–no. 15–no,
        16–no, 17–yes

Can you recall the words?

1. philosophy of living   1. A_____
   austerely

2. hatred of women   2. M_____

3. hatred of marriage	3. M_____
4. hatred of mankind	4. M_____
5. skilful	5. D_____
6. awkward	6. G_____
7. evil, threatening	7. S_____
8. describing hatred of women (*adj.*)	8. M_____
	or M_____
9. skill	9. A_____
10. pertaining to hatred of marriage (*adj.*)	10. M_____
11. pertaining to hatred of mankind (*adj.*)	11. M_____
12. social custom of plural marriage	12. P_____
	or P_____
	or P_____
13. unlawful state of having more than one spouse	13. B_____
14. doctor specializing in female disorders	14. G_____
15. custom of one marriage at a time	15. M_____
16. one who hates the human race	16. M_____
	or M_____
17. able to use both hands with equal skill	17. A_____
18. study of mankind	18. A_____
19. one who loves mankind	19. P_____
20. skill in the use of both hands	20. A_____

Key: 1–asceticism, 2–misogyny, 3–misogamy, 4–misanthropy, 5–dexterous, 6–gauche, 7–sinister, 8–misogynous or misogynistic, 9–adroitness, 10–misogamous, 11–misanthropic, 12–polygamy, polyandry, *or* polygyny, 13–bigamy, 14–gynaecologist, 15–monogamy, 16–misanthropist *or* misanthrope, 17–ambidextrous, 18–anthropology, 19–philanthropist, 20–ambidexterity

---

Chapter review

A.   Do you recognize the words?

1. Puts selfish desires first: (a) egoist, (b) egotist, (c) altruist
2. Is self-analytical: (a) extrovert, (b) introvert, (c) ambivert
3. Hates women: (a) misogamist, (b) misanthrope, (c) misogynist
4. One's other self: (a) altercation, (b) alter ego, (c) alteration
5. Awkward, clumsy: (a) adroit, (b) dexterous, (c) gauche
6. Plural marriage as a custom: (a) bigamy, (b) polygamy, (c) monogamy
7. Study of human development: (a) asceticism, (b) philanthropy, (c) anthropology
8. Plurality of husbands as a custom: (a) misogyny, (b) polygyny, (c) polyandrv

---

Key: 1–a, 2–b, 3–c, 4–b, 5–c, 6–b, 7–c, 8–c

B.   Can you recognize roots?

Root	Meaning	Example
1. *ego*	_____	egoist
2. *alter*	_____	alternative
3. *verto*	_____	introvert
4. *misein*	_____	misogynist
5. *anthropos*	_____	anthropologist
6. *gyne*	_____	gynaecologist
7. *gamos*	_____	bigamy
8. *centrum*	_____	egocentric
9. *dexter*	_____	dexterous
10. *droit*	_____	adroit
11. *monos*	_____	monogamy
12. *andros*	_____	polyandry

Key: 1–self, 2–other, 3–to turn, 4–to hate, 5–mankind
       6–woman, 7–marriage, 8–centre, 9–right hand,
       10–right hand, 11–one, 12–male

Teaser questions for the amateur etymologist

Suppose you met the following words in your reading. Recognizing the roots on which they are constructed, could you work out
the meanings? Write your answers on the blank lines.

1. *anthropocentric:* _____

2. *andromania:* _____

3. *gynandrous:* _____

4. *monomania:* _____

5. *misandrist:* _____

(*Answers in Chapter 18.*)

Stick to your time schedule!

In three sessions, you have become acquainted with scores of new,
vital, exciting words. You understand the ideas behind these
words, their various forms and spellings, their pronunciation,
their derivation, how they can be used, and exactly what they
mean. I do not wish to press a point unduly, but it is possible that
you have learned more new words in the short time it took you to
cover this chapter than the average adult learns in an entire year.
This realization should make you feel both gratified and excited.

Funny thing about time. Apart from the fact that we all, rich or
poor, sick or well, have the same amount of time, exactly twenty-
four hours every day (that is looking at time from a static point of
view), it is also true that we can always find time for the things we
enjoy doing, almost never for the things we find unpleasant (and
that is looking at time from the dynamic point of view). I am not

merely being philosophical – I am sure you will agree with this concept if you give it a little thought.

If you have enjoyed learning new words, accepting new challenges, gaining new understanding, and discovering the thrill of successful accomplishment, then make sure to stay with the time schedule you have set for yourself.

A crucial factor in successful, continuous learning is routine.

Develop a comfortable time routine, persevere against all distractions, and you will learn anything you sincerely want to learn.

So, to give yourself an edge, write here the day and hour you plan to return to your work:

DAY: _____

DATE: _____

TIME: _____

(End of Session 3)

Test your grammar

How good is your English? Have you ever said *me* and then wondered if it shouldn't have been *I* – or vice versa? Do you sometimes get a little confused about *lay* and *lie* or *who* and *whom*? Perhaps you are often a little less than certain about the distinction between *effect* and *affect, principal* and *principle, childish* and *childlike*?

Here is a series of quick tests that will show you how skilful you are in using the right word in the right place, that will give you a reliable indication of how your language ability compares with the average.

Test 1 – easy

If your English is every bit as good as average, you will have no difficulty making a proper choice in at least eight of the following ten sentences.

1. There is a beautiful moon out tonight and Estelle and I are going for a stroll – would you like to come along with (she and I, her and me)?
2. Your husband doesn't believe that you are older than (I, me).
3. Maybe we're not as rich as (they, them), but I bet we're a lot happier.
4. Does your child still (lay, lie) down for a nap after lunch?
5. When we saw Mary openly flirting with Nellie's husband, we (could, couldn't) hardly believe our eyes.
6. You should (of, have) put more gin into the martini.
7. Does your company (leave, let) you have as long a lunch break as you would like?

8. Harriet feels that her (brothers-in-law, brother-in-laws) are impossible to get along with.
9. 'What (kind of, kind of a) car are you looking for?' asked the salesman.
10. Mrs. White was delighted that the Fennells had invited John and (she, her) to their party.

Is your English up to par? HERE ARE THE CORRECT ANSWERS
1–her and me, 2–I, 3–they, 4–lie, 5–could, 6–have, 7–let, 8–brothers-in-law, 9–kind of, 10–her

Test II – harder

Choose correctly in at least seven of the following problems to consider that your skill is distinctly above average – get all ten right to conclude that you rarely, if ever, make an error in grammar.

1. What (effect, affect) has the new administration had on investor confidence?
2. A feeling of one's worth is one of the (principle, principal) goals of psychological therapy.
3. There's no sense (in, of) carrying on that way.
4. I can't remember (who, whom) it was.
5. The infant (lay, laid) quietly sucking its thumb.
6. No one but (she, her) ever made a perfect score on the test.
7. In the early days of frontier history, horse thieves were (hanged, hung).
8. Neither of your responses (are, is) satisfactory.
9. Either of these two small cars, if properly maintained, (is, are) sure to give over thirty miles per gallon in long-distance driving.
10. Tell (whoever, whomever) is waiting to come in.

Is your English above average? HERE ARE THE CORRECT ANSWERS
1–effect, 2–principal, 3–in, 4–who, 5–lay, 6–her, 7–hanged, 8–is, 9–is, 10–whoever

Test III – hardest

Now you can discover how close you are to being an expert in English. The next ten sentences are not easy – you will be acquitting yourself creditably if you choose the correct word five times out of ten. And you have every right to consider yourself an expert if you get nine or ten right.

1. We have just interviewed an applicant (who, whom) the committee believes is best qualified for the position.
2. She is one of those gifted writers who (turns, turn) out one best seller after another.
3. Don't sound so (incredulous, incredible); what I am saying is absolutely true.
4. We were totally (disinterested, uninterested) in the offer.
5. This recipe calls for two (cupsful, cupfuls) of sugar.
6. Are you trying to (infer, imply) by those words that he is not to be trusted?
7. We thought the actress to be (she, her), but we weren't sure.
8. Was it (she, her) you were talking about?
9. Your criteria (is, are) not valid.
10. 'It is I who (is, am) the only friend you've got,' she told him pointedly.

Are you an expert? HERE ARE THE CORRECT ANSWERS

1–who, 2–turn, 3–incredulous, 4–uninterested,
5–cupfuls, 6–imply, 7–her, 8–she, 9–are, 10–am

4

HOW TO TALK ABOUT DOCTORS

(Sessions 4–6)

Teaser preview

What is the title of the doctor who specialies in:
- *female ailments?*
- *pregnancy and childbirth?*
- *the treatment and care of infants and young children?*
- *skin disorders?*
- *diseases of the eye?*
- *heart problems?*
- *the brain and nervous system?*
- *mental and emotional disturbances?*

Session 4

In this chapter we discuss medical specialists – what they do, how they do it, what they are called.

Ideas

1.   Female troubles?

This specialist treats the female reproductive and sexual organs.
        A *gynaecologist*

2.   Having a baby?

This specialist delivers babies and takes care of the mother during and immediately after the period of her pregnancy.
        An *obstetrician*

3.   Is your baby ill?

You know the common childhood maladies – mumps, whooping cough, chicken pox, measles. This specialist limits his practice to youngsters, taking care of babies directly after birth, supervising their diet and watching over their growth and development, giving them the series of inoculations that has done so much to decrease infant mortality, and soothing their anxious parents.
        A *paediatrician*

4.   Skin clear?

You have heard the classic riddle: 'What is the best use for pig-skin?' answer: 'To keep the pig together.'. Human skin has a similar purpose: it is, if we get down to fundamentals, what keeps us all in one piece. And our outer covering, like so many of our internal organs, is subject to diseases and infections of various kinds, running the gamut from simple acne and eczemas to impetigo, psoriasis, and cancer. There is a specialist who treats all such skin diseases.

A *dermatologist*

5.   Eyes okay?

The physician whose speciality is disorders of vision (myopia, astigamtism, cataracts, glaucoma, etc.) may prescribe glasses, administer drugs, or perform surgery.

An *opthalmologist*

6.   How are your bones?

This specialist deals with the skeletal structure of the body, treating bone fractures, slipped discs, clubfoot, curvature of the spine, dislocations of the hip, etc., and may correct a condition either by surgery or by the use of braces or other appliances.

An *orthopaedist*

7.   Does your heart go pitter-patter?

This specialist treats disorders of the heart and circulatory system.

A *cardiologist*

8.   Is your brain working?

This physician specialises in the treatment of disorders of the brain, spinal cord, and the rest of the nervous system.

A *neurologist*

9. Are you neurotic?

This specialist attempts to alleviate mental and emotional disturbances by means of various techniques, occasionally drugs or electroconvulsive therapy, more often private or group psychotherapy.

A *psychiatrist*

Using the words

Can you pronounce the words?

Words take on a new colour if you hear them in your own voice; they begin to belong to you more personally, more intimately, than if you merely hear or read them. As always, therefore *say the words aloud* to take the first, crucial step towards complete mastery.

1. *gynaecologist*   gīna'-ə-KOL'-ə-jist
2. *obstetrician*   ob-stə-TRISH'-ən
3. *paediatrician*   pee'-di-ə-TRISH'-ən
4. *dermatologist*   dər-mə-TOL'-ə-jist
5. *ophthalmologist*   off-thal-MOL'-ə-jist
6. *orthopaedist*   aw-thə-PEE'-dist
7. *cardiologist*   kah-di-OL'-ə-jist
8. *neurologist*   nyoŏr (or nyoŏər)-OL'-ə-jist
9. *psychiatrist*   sī-KĪ'-ə-trist

Can you work with the words?

Match each doctor to the field.

Fields	Doctors
1. mental or emotional disturbances	a. gynaecologist
2. nervous system	b. obstetrician
3. skin	c. paediatrician
4. infants	d. dermatologist
5. female reproductive organs	e. ophthalmologist
6. eyes	f. orthopaedist
7. heart	g. cardiologist

8. pregnancy,   h. neurologist
   childbirth
9. skeletal system   i. psychiatrist

Key: 1–i, 2–h, 3–d, 4–c, 5–a, 6–e, 7–g, 8–b, 9–f

Do you understand the words?

1.	Is a *gynaecologist* familiar with the female reproductive organs?	YES	NO
2.	Does an *obstetrician* specialize in diseases of childhood?	YES	NO
3.	Does a *paediatrician* deliver babies?	YES	NO
4.	If you had a skin disease, would you visit a *dermatologist*?	YES	NO
5.	If you had trouble with your vision would you vist an *orthopaedist*?	YES	NO
6.	Is an *ophthalmologist* an eye specialist?	YES	NO
7.	Does a *cardiologist* treat bone fractures?	YES	NO
8.	Is a *neurologist* a nerve specialist?	YES	NO
9.	If you were nervous, tense, overly anxious, constantly fearful for no apparent reasons, would a *psychiatrist* be the specialist to see?	YES	NO

Key: 1–yes, 2–no, 3–no, 4–yes, 5–no, 6–yes, 7–no, 8–yes, 9–yes

Can you recall the words?

Write the name of the specialist you might visit or be referred to:
1. for a suspected brain   1. N_____
   disorder
2. if you have a skin disease   2. D_____
3. if you have a heart   3. C_____
   problem

4. if you are tense, fearful, insecure   4. P_____

5. if you are pregnant   5. O_____

6. for some disorder of the female reproductive organs   6. G_____

7. for a checkup for your two-month-old child   7. P_____

8. for faulty vision   8. O_____

9. for curvature of the spin   9. O_____

Key: 1–neurologist, 2–dermatologist, 3–cardiologist, 4–psychiatrist, 5–obstetrician, 6–gynaecologist, 7–paediatrician, 8–ophthalmologist, 9–orthopaedist

---

(End of Session 4).

Session 5

Origins and related words

1. Doctors for women

The word *gynaecologist* is built on Greek *gyne*, woman, plus *logy*, science, which comes from the original Greek *logos*, meaning word; etymologically, *gynaecology* is the science (in actual use, the medical science) of women. Adjective: *gynaecological* (gīn'-ə-kə-LOJ'-i-kəl).

Obstetrician derives from Latin *obstetrix*, midwife, which in turn has its source in a Latin verb meaning *to stand* – midwives stand in front of the woman in labour to aid in the delivery of the infant.

The suffix *-ician*, as in *obstetrician, physician, musician, magician, electrician,* etc., means *expert.*

The medical speciality dealing with childbirth is *obstetrics* (ob-STET'-riks). Adjective: *obstetric* (ob-STET'-rik) or *obstetrical* (ob-STET'-ri-kəl).

2. Children

Paediatrician is a combination of Greek *paidos*, child; *iatreia*, medical healing; and *-ician*, expert.

Paediatrics (pee-di-AT'-riks), then, is by etymology the medical healing of a child. Adjective: *paediatric* (pee-di-AT'-rik).

Pedagogy (PED'-ə-go'-ji), which loses the 'a' but still combines *paidos* with *agogos*, leading, is, etymologically, *the leading of children*. And to what do you lead them? To learning, to development, to growth, to maturity. From the moment of birth, infants are led by adults – they are taught, first by parents and then by teachers, to be self-sufficient, to fit into the culture in which they are born. Hence, *pedagogy*, which by derivation means *the leading of a child*, refers actually to the principles and methods of teaching. Adjective: *pedagogic* (ped'-ə-GOJ'-ik) or *pedagogical* (ped'-ə-GOJ'-i-kəl).

(the *ped-* you see in words like *pedestal*, *pedal*, and *pedestrian* is from the Latin *pedis*, foot, and despite the identical spelling in English has no relationship to Greek *paidos*.)

A *pedagogue* (PED'-ə-gog) is versed in *pedagogy*. But *pedagogue* has an unhappy history. From its original, neutral meaning of *teacher*, it has deteriorated to the point where it refers, today, to a narrow-minded, strait-laced, old-fashioned, dogmatic teacher. It is a word of contempt and should be used with caution.

Like *pedagogue*, *demagogue* (DEM'-ə-gog) has also deteriorated in meaning. By derivation a leader (*agogos*) of the people (*demos*), a *demogague* today is actually one who attempts, in essence, to *mislead* the people, a politician who foments discontent among the masses, rousing them to fever pitch by wild oratory, in an attempt to be voted into office.

Once elected, *demagogues* use political power to further their own personal ambitions or fortunes.

Masny 'leaders' of the past and present in countries around the world, have been accused of *demagoguery* (dem'-ə-GOG'-ə-ri). Adjective: *demagogic* (dem'-ə-GOG'-ik).

3. Skin-deep

The *dermatologist*, whose specialty is *dermatology* (dər'-mə-TOL'-ə-ji), is so named from Greek *derma*, skin. Adjective: *dermatological* (dər'-mə-tə-LOJ'-i-kəl).

See the syllables *derma* in any English word and you will know there is some reference to *skin* – for example, a *hypodermic* (hī-pə-DəR'-mik) needle penetrates *under* (Greek, *hypos*) the *skin*; the *epidermis* (ep-i-DəR'-mis) is the outermost layer of *skin*; a *taxidermist* (TAKS'-i-dər-mist), whose business is *taxidermy* (TAKS'-i-dər-mi), prepares, stuffs, and mounts the *skins* of animals; a *pachyderm* (PAK'-i-dərm) is an animal with an unusually thick *skin*, like an elephant, hippopotamus, or rhinoceros; and *dermatitis* (dər-mə-TĪ'-tis) is the general name for any *skin* inflammation, irritation, or infection.

4.   The eyes have it

Ophthalmologist – note the *ph* preceding *th* – is from Greek *ophthalmos*, eye, plus *logos*, science or study. The speciality is *ophthalmology* (off-thal-MOL'-ə-ji), the adjective *ophthalmological* (off'-thal-mə-LOJ'-i-kəl).

An earlier title for this physician is *oculist* (OK'-yoo-list), from Latin *oculus*, eye, a root on which the following English words are also built:

1. *ocular* (OK'-yoo-lə) – an adjective that refers to the eye
2. *monocle* (MON'-ə-kəl) – a lens for one (*monos*) eye, sported by characters in old films as a symbol of the British so-called upper class
3. *binoculars* (bi-NOK'-yoo-ləz) – field glasses that increase the range of two (*bi-*) eyes
4. And, strangely enough, *inoculate* (in-OK'-yoo-layt'), a word commonly misspelt with two *n*s. When you are *inoculated* against a disease, an 'eye', puncture, or hole is made in your skin, through which serum is injected.

Do not confuse the *ophthalmologist*, a medical specialist, with two other practitioners who deal with the eye – the *optometrist* (op-TOM'-ə-trist) and *optician* (op-TISH'-ən).

Optometrists are not doctors, and do not perform surgery or administer drugs; they measure vision, test for glaucoma, and prescribe and fit glasses.

Opticians fall into two categories. The first type, often called *ophthalmic opticians*, perform the same functions as *optometrists*. The second type make or dispense glasses and contact lenses. They fill an *optometrist's* or *ophthalmologist's* prescription, grinding and fitting lenses according to specifications; they do not examine patients.

Optometrist combines Greek *opsis, optikos*, sight or vision, with *metron*, measurement – the *optometrist*, by etymology, is one who measures vision. The specialty is *optometry* (op-TOM'-ə-tri).

Optician is built on *opsis, optikos*, plus *-ician*, expert. The specialty is *optics* (OP'-tiks).

Adjectives: *optometric* (op-tə-MET'-rik) or *optometrical* (op-tə-MET'-ri-kəl), *optical* (OP'-ti-kəl).

Review of etymology

Prefix, Root, Suffix	Meaning	English word
1. *gyne*	woman	_____
2. *obstetrix*	midwife	_____
3. *paidos*	child	_____
4. *pedis*	foot	_____
5. *agogos*	leading, leader	_____
6. *demos*	people	_____
7. *derma*	skin	_____
8. *hypos*	under	_____
9. *ophthalmos*	eye	_____
10. *oculus*	eye	_____
11. *monos*	one	_____
12. *bi-*	two	_____
13. *-ician*	expert	_____
14. *opsis, optikos*	vision, sight	_____
15. *metron*	measurement	_____

Using the words

Can you pronounce the words? (II)

1. *gynaecology*	gīn-ə-KOL'-ə-ji
2. *gynaecological*	gīn-ə-kə-LOJ'-i-kəl
3. *obstetrics*	ob-STET'-riks
4. *obstetric*	ob-STET'-rik
5. *paediatrics*	pee-di-AT'-riks
6. *paediatric*	pee-di-AT'-rik
7. *pedagogy*	PED'-ə-go-ji
8. *pedagogical*	ped'-ə-GOJ'-i-kəl
9. *pedagogue*	PED'-ə-gog
10. *demagogue*	DEM'-ə-gog
11. *demagoguery*	dem'-ə-GOG'-ə-ri
12. *demagogic*	dem'-ə-GOG'-ik

Can you pronounce the words? (II)

1. *dermatology*   dər-mə-TOL'-ə-ji

2. *dermatological* — dər'-mə-tə-LOJ'-i-kəl
3. *hypodermic* — hī-pə-DəR'-mik
4. *epidermis* — ep-i-DəR'-mis
5. *taxidermist* — TAKS'-i-dər-mist
6. *taxidermy* — TAKS'-i-dər-mi
7. *pachyderm* — PAK'-i-dərm
8. *dermatitis* — dər-mə-TĪ'-tis
9. *ophthalmology* — off-thal-MOL'-ə-ji
10. *ophthalmological* — off'-thal-mə-LOJ'-i-kəl
11. *oculist* — OK'-yoö-list
12. *ocular* — OK'-yoö-lə
13. *monocle* — MON'-ə-kəl
14. *binoculars* — bi-NOK'-yoö-ləz
15. *inoculate* — in-OK'-yoö-layt'
16. *optometrist* — op-TOM'-ə-trist
17. *optometry* — op-TOM'-ə-tri
18. *optometric* — op-tə-MET'-rik
19. *optometrical* — op-tə-MET'-ri-kəl
20. *optician* — op-TISH'-ən
21. *optics* — OP'-tiks
22. *optical* — OP-ti-kəl

Can you work with the words? (II)

1. gynaecology — a. principles of teaching
2. obstetrics — b. stuffing of skins of animals
3. paediatrics — c. speciality dealing with the delivery of newborn infants
4. pedagogy — d. stirring up discontent among the masses
5. demagoguery — e. treatment of skin diseases
6. dermatology — f. speciality dealing with women's diseases
7. taxidermy — g. speciality dealing with the treatment of children

Key: 1–f, 2–c, 3–g, 4–a, 5–d, 6–e, 7–b

Can you work with the words? (III)

1. hypodermic	a. elephant
2. epidermis	b. eye doctor
3. pachyderm	c. under the skin
4. dermatitis	d. one who measures vision
5. ophthalmologist	e. outer layer of skin
6. optometrist	f. inflammation of the skin

Key: 1–c, 2–e, 3–a, 4–f, 5–b, 6–d

Do you understand the words?

1. Does a treatise on *obstetrics* deal with childbirth?	YES	NO
2. Does *gynaecology* deal with the female reproductive organs?	YES	NO
3. Is *paediatrics* concerned with the diseases of old age?	YES	NO
4. Does *pedagogy* refer to teaching?	YES	NO
5. Is a *pedagogue* an expert teacher?	YES	NO
6. Is a *demogogue* interested in the welfare of the people?	YES	NO
7. Is a lion a *pachyderm*?	YES	NO
8. Is the *epidermis* one of the layers of the skin?	YES	NO
9. Is *dermatitis* an inflammation of one of the limbs?	YES	NO
10. Is a *taxidermist* a medical practitioner?	YES	NO
11. Is an *ophthalmologist* a medical doctor?	YES	NO
12. Is an *optometrist* a medical doctor?	YES	NO

Key: 1–yes, 2–yes, 3–no, 4–yes, 5–no, 6–no, 7–no, 8–yes, 9–no, 10–no, 11–yes, 12–no

Can you recall the words?

1.	speciality of child delivery	1. O_____
2.	outer layer of skin	2. E_____
3.	principles of teaching	3. P_____
4.	thick-skinned animal	4. P_____
5.	skin inflammation	5. D_____.
6.	one who foments political discontent	6. D_____
7.	one who sells optical equipment	7. O_____
8.	treatment of childhood diseases	8. P_____
9.	practice of stirring up political dissatisfaction for purely personal gain	9. D_____
10.	one who stuffs the skins of animals	10. T_____
11.	treatment of female ailments	11. G_____
12.	medical speciality relating to diseases of the eye	12. O_____
13.	one-lens eyeglass	13. M_____
14.	pertaining to the eye	14. O_____
15.	one who measures vision	15. O_____

Key: 1–obstetrics, 2–epidermis, 3–pedagogy, 4–pachyderm,
         5–dermatitis, 6–demagogue, 7–optician, 8–paediatrics,
         9–demagoguery,   10–taxidermist,   11–gynaecology,
         12–ophthalmology, 13–monocle, 14–ocular, 15–op-
         tometrist or (ophthalmic) optician

(End of Session 5)

Session 6

Origins and related words

1.   The straighteners

The *orthopaedist* is so called from the Greek roots *orthos*, straight or correct, and *paidos*, child. The *orthopaedist*, by etymology, straightens children. The term was coined in 1741 by the author of a textbook on the prevention of childhood diseases — at that time the correction of spinal curvature in children was a main concern of practitioners of *orthopaedics* (aw-thə-PEE'-diks).

Today the speciality treats deformities, injuries, and diseases of the bones and joints (of adults as well as children, of course), often by surgical procedures.

Adjective: *orthopaedic* (aw-thə-PEE'-dik).

Orthodontics (aw-thə-DON'-tiks), the straightening of teeth, is built on *orthos* plus *odontos*, tooth. The *orthodontist* (aw-thə-DON'-tist) specializes in improving your 'bite', retracting 'buck teeth', and by means of braces and other techniques seeing to it that every molar, incisor, bicuspid, etc. is exactly where it belongs in your mouth.

Adjective: *orthodontic* (aw-thə-DON'-tik).

2.   The heart

Cardiologist combines Greek *kardia*, heart, and *logos*, science.

The speciality is *cardiology* (kah-di-OL'-ə-ji), the adjective *cardiological* (kah'-di-ə-LOJ'-i-kəl).

So a *cardiac* (KAH'-di-ak) condition refers to some malfunctioning of the heart; a *cardiogram* (KAH'-di-ə-gram') is an electrically produced record of the heartbeat. The instrument that produces this record is called a *cardiograph* (KAH'-di-ə-grahf').

3.   The nervous system

Neurologist derives from Greek *neuron*, nerve, plus *logos*, science.
    Speciality: *neurology* (nyŏŏr(or nyŏŏr)-OL'-ə-ji); adjective: *neurological* (nyŏŏr-ə-LOJ'-i-kəl).
    Neuralgia (nyŏŏr-AL'-jə) is acute pain along the nerves and their branches; the word comes from *neuron* plus *algos*, pain.
    Neuritis (nyŏŏr-Ī'-tis), is inflammation of the nerves.
    Neurosis (nyŏŏr-Ō'-sis), combining *neuron* with *-osis*, a suffix meaning *abnormal or diseased condition*, is not, despite its etymology, a disorder of the nerves, but rather, as described by the late Eric Berne, a psychiatrist, '. . . an illness characterized by excessive use of energy for unproductive purposes so that personality development is hindered or stopped. A man who spends most of his time worrying about his health, counting his money, plotting revenge, or washing his hands, can hope for little emotional growth.'.
    Neurotic (nyŏŏr-OT'-ik) is both the adjectival form and the term for a person suffering from *neurosis*.

4.   The mind

A *neurosis* is not a form of mental unbalance. A full-blown mental disorder is called a *psychosis* (sī-KŌ'-sis), a word built on Greek *psyche*, spirit, soul, or mind, plus *-osis*.
    A true *psychotic* (sī-KOT'-ik) has lost contact with reality – at least with reality as most of us perceive it, though no doubt *psychotic* (note that this word, like *neurotic*, is both a noun and an adjective) people have their own form of reality.
    Built on *psyche* plus *iatreia*, medical healing, a *psychiatrist*, by etymology, is a mind-healer. The speciality is *psychiatry* (sī-KĪ'-ə-tri); the adjective is *psychiatric* (sī-ki-AT'-rik).
    Paediatrics, as you know, is also built on *iatreia*, as is *geriatrics* (jer'-i-AT'-riks), the speciality dealing with the particular medical needs of the elderly. (This words combines *iatreia* with Greek *geras*, old age.)

The specialist is a *geriatrician* (jer'-i-ə-TRISH'-ən), the adjective is *geriatric* (jer'-i-AT'-rik).

Review of etymology

Root, Suffix	Meaning	English Word
1. *orthos*	straight, correct	_____
2. *paidos* (*paed-*)	child	_____
3. *odontos*	tooth	_____
4. *kardia*	heart	_____
5. *logos*	science; study	_____
6. *neuron*	nerve	_____
7. *algos*	pain	_____
8. *-osis*	abnormal or diseased condition	_____
9. *-itis*	inflammation	_____
10. *psyche*	spirit, soul, mind	_____
11. *iatreia*	medical healing	_____
12. *geras*	old age	_____

Using the words

Can you pronounce the words (I)

1. *orthopaedics*	aw-thə-PEE'-diks
2. *orthopaedic*	aw-thə-PEE'-dik
3. *orthodontics*	aw-thə-DON'-tiks
4. *orthodontist*	aw-thə-DON'-tist
5. *orthodontic*	aw-thə-DON'-tik
6. *cardiology*	kah-di-OL'-ə-ji
7. *cardiological*	kah-di-ə-LOJ'-i-kəl
8. *cardiac*	KAH'-di-ak
9. *cardiogram*	KAH'-di-ə-gram'
10. *cardiograph*	KAH'-di-ə-grahf'

Can you pronounce the words? (II)

1. *neurology*	nyŏŏr (or nyŏŏbər)-OL'-ə-ji

2.	*neurological*	nyŏŏr-ə-LOJ'-i-kəl
3.	*neuralgia*	nyŏŏr-AL'-jə
4.	*neuritis*	nyŏŏr-Ī'-tis
5.	*neurosis*	nyŏŏr-Ō'-sis
6.	*neurotic*	nyŏŏr-OT'-ik
7.	*psychosis*	sī-KŌ'-sis
8.	*psychotic*	sī-KOT'-ik
9.	*psychiatry*	sī-KĪ'-ə-tri
10.	*psychiatric*	sī-ki-AT'-rik
11.	*geriatrics*	jer'-i-AT'-riks
12.	*geriatrician*	jer'-i-ə-TRISH'-ən
13.	*geriatric*	jer'-i-AT'-rik

Can you work with the words? (I)

1.	orthopaedics	a.	nerve pain
2.	orthodontics	b.	speciality dealing with medical problems of the elderly
3.	neuralgia	c.	straightening of teeth
4.	neuritis	d.	inflammation of the nerves
5.	geriatrics	e.	treatment of skeletal deformities

Key: 1–e, 2–c, 3–a, 4–d, 5–b

Can you work with the words? (II)

1.	cardiogram	a.	record of heart beats
2.	cardiograph	b.	mental unbalance
3.	neurosis	c.	emotional disturbance
4.	psychosis	d.	treatment of personality disorders
5.	psychiatry	e.	instrument for recording heartbeats

Key: 1–a, 2–e, 3–c, 4–b, 5–d

Do you understand the words?

1.	A *gynaecologist's* patients are mostly men.	TRUE	FALSE·
2.	*Ophthalmology* is the study of eye diseases.	TRUE	FALSE
3.	*Orthopaedics* is the speciality dealing with the bones and joints.	TRUE	FALSE
4.	A *cardiac* patient has a heart ailment.	TRUE	FALSE
5.	A person with a bad 'bite' may profit from *orthodontics*.	TRUE	FALSE
6.	*Neuralgia* is a disease of the bones.	TRUE	FALSE
7.	A *neurosis* is the same as a *psychosis*.	TRUE	FALSE
8.	*Neuritis* is inflammation of the nerves.	TRUE	FALSE
9.	*Psychiatry* is a medical speciality that deals with mental, emotional, and personality disturbances.	TRUE	FALSE
10.	A *cardiograph* is a device for recording heartbeats.	TRUE	FALSE
11.	*Psychiatric* treatment is designed to relieve tension, fears, and insecurities.	TRUE	FALSE
12.	A doctor who specializes in *paediatrics* has very old patients.	TRUE	FALSE
13.	A *geriatrician* has very young patients.	TRUE	FALSE

Key: 1–F, 2–T, 3–T, 4–T, 5–T, 6–F, 7–F, 8–T, 9–T, 10–T, 11–T, 12–F, 13–F

Can you recall the words?

1.	specialist who straightens teeth	1.	O_____
2.	nerve pain	2.	N_____
3.	medical speciality dealing with bones and joints	3.	O_____

4. medical speciality dealing with emotional disturbances and mental illness   4. P_____

5. inflammation of the nerves   5. N_____

6. emotional or personality disorder   6. N_____

7. mentally unbalanced   7. P_____

8. pertaining to the heart   8. C_____

9. speciality dealing with medical problems of the elderly   9. G_____

10. instrument that records heart action   10. C_____

11. record produced by such an instrument   11. C_____

Key: 1–orthodontist, 2–neuralgia, 3–orthopaedics, 4–psychiatry, 5–neuritis, 6–neurosis, 7–psychotic, 8–cardiac, 9–geriatrics, 10–cardiograph, 11–cardiogram

Chapter review

A. Do you recognize the words?

1. Specialist in female ailments:
   (a) obstetrician, (b) gynaecologist, (c) dermatologist
2. Specialist in children's diseases:
   (a) orthopaedist, (b) paediatrician, (c) psychiatrist
3. Specialist in eye diseases:
   (a) cardiologist, (b) ophthalmologist, (c) optician
4. Specialist in emotional disorders:
   (a) neurologist, (b) demagogue, (c) psychiatrist
5. Pertaining to medical treatment of the elderly:
   (a) neurological, (b) obstetric, (c) geriatric
6. Straightening of teeth:
   (a) orthodontics, (b) orthopaedic, (c) optometry

7. Personality disorder:
 (a) neuritis, (b) neuralgia, (c) neurosis
8. Mentally unbalanced:
 (a) neurotic, (b) psychotic, (c) cardiac
9. Principles of teaching:
 (a) demagoguery, (b) pedagogy, (c) psychosis

Key: 1–b, 2–b. 3–b, 4–c, 5–c, 6–a, 7–c, 8–b, 9–b

B.   Can you recognize roots?

Root	Meaning	Example
1. *gyne*	_____	gynaecologist
2. *paidos (paed-)*	_____	paediatrician
3. *pedis*	_____	pedestrian
4. *agogos*	_____	pedagogue
5. *demos*	_____	demagogue
6. *derma*	_____	dermatologist
7. *hypos*	_____	hypodermic
8. *ophthalmos*	_____	ophthalmologist
9. *oculus*	_____	monocle
10. *opsis, optikos*	_____	optician
11. *metron*	_____	optometrist
12. *orthos*	_____	orthopaedist
13. *odontos*	_____	orthodontist
14. *kardia*	_____	cardiologist
15. *logos*	_____	anthropologist
16. *neuron*	_____	neurologist
17. *algos*	_____	neuralgia
18. *psyche*	_____	psychiatrist
19. *iatreia*	_____	psychiatry
20. *geras*	_____	geriatrics

Key: 1–woman, 2–child, 3–foot, 4–leading, 5–people,
6–skin, 7–under, 8–eye, 9–eye, 10–view, sight,
11–measurement, 12–straight, correct, 13–tooth,
14–heart, 15–science, study, 16–nerve, 17–pain,
18–mind, 19–medical healing, 20–old age

Teaser questions for the amateur etymologist

1. Thinking of the roots *odontos* and *paidos* (spelled *paed-* in English), work out the meaning of *paedodontics*: _____

2. Recall the roots *kardia* and *algos*. What is the meaning of *cardialgia*? _____

3. Of *odontalgia*? _____

4. *Nostos* is the Greek word for a *return* (home). Can you combine this root with *algos*, pain, to construct the English word meaning *homesickness*? _____

(Answers in Chapter 18)

Two keys to success: self-discipline and persistence

You can achieve a superior vocabulary in a phenomenally short time — given self-discipline and persistence.

The greatest aid in building self-discipline is, as I have said, a matter of devising a practical and comfortable schedule for yourself and then *keeping to that schedule*.

Make sure to complete *at least* one session each time you pick up the book, and always decide exactly when you will continue with your work before you put the book down.

There may be periods of difficulty — then is the time to exert the greatest self-discipline, the most determined persistence.

For every page that you study will help you attain a mastery over words; every day that you work will add to your skill in understanding and using words.

(End of Session 6)

Random notes on modern usage

English grammar is confusing enough as it is — what makes it doubly confounding is that it is slowly but continually changing.

This means that some of the strict rules you memorized so painfully at school may no longer be completely valid.

Following such outmoded principles, you may think you are speaking 'perfect' English, and instead you may sound stuffy and pedantic.

The problem boils down to this: if grammatical usage is gradually becoming more liberal, where does educated, unaffected, informal speech end? And where does illiterate, ungrammatical speech begin?

The following notes on current trends in modern usage are intended to help you come to a decision about certain controversial expressions. As you read each sentence, pay particular attention to the italicized word or words. Does the usage square with your own language patterns? Would you be willing to phrase your thoughts in such terms? Decide whether the sentence is right or wrong, then compare your conclusion with the opinion given in the explanatory paragraphs that follow the test.

Test yourself

1. If you drink too much vodka, you   RIGHT   WRONG
   will *get* drunk.
2. Have you *got* a pound?   RIGHT   WRONG
3. No one loves you except *I*.   RIGHT   WRONG

4. Please *lay* down.	RIGHT	WRONG
5. *Who* do you love?	RIGHT	WRONG
5. Neither of these cars *are* worth the money.	RIGHT	WRONG
7. The judge sentenced the murderer to be *hung*.	RIGHT	WRONG
8. Mother, *can* I go out to play?	RIGHT	WRONG
9. Take two *spoonsful* of this medicine every three hours.	RIGHT	WRONG
10. Your words seem to *infer* that Jack is a liar.	RIGHT	WRONG
11. I *will* be happy to go to the concert with you.	RIGHT	WRONG
12. It is *me*.	RIGHT	WRONG
13. Go *slow*.	RIGHT	WRONG
14. I *would* like to ask you a question.	RIGHT	WRONG

1. If you drink too much vodka, you will *get* drunk.

RIGHT. The puristic objection is that *get* has only one meaning – namely, *obtain*. However, as any modern dictionary will attest, *get* has scores of different meanings, one of the most respectable of which is *become*. You can *get* tired, *get* dizzy, *get* drunk, or *get* sick – and your choice of words will offend no one but a pedant.

2. Have you *got* a pound?

RIGHT. If purists get a little pale at the sound of '*get* sick', they turn chalk white when they hear *have got* as a substitute for *have*. But the fact is that *have got* is an established idiomatic form of expression.

3. No one loves you except *I*.

WRONG. In educated speech, *me* follows the preposition *except*. This problem is troublesome because, to the unsophisticated, the sentence sounds as if it can be completed to read 'No one loves you, except *I* do', but current educated usage adheres to the technical rule that a preposition requires an objective pronoun (*me*).

4. Please *lay* down.

WRONG. Liberal as grammar has become, there is still no sanction for using *lay* with the meaning of *recline*. *Lay* means to place, as in '*Lay* your hand on mine'. *Lie* is the correct choice.

5. *Who* do you love?

RIGHT. The rules for *who* and *whom* are complicated, and few educated speakers have the time, patience, or expertise to bother with them. Use the democratic *who* in your everyday speech whenever it sounds right.

6. Neither of these cars *are* worth the money.

WRONG. The temptation to use *are* in this sentence is, I admit, practically irresistible. However, 'neither of' means neither *one* of and *is*, therefore, is the preferable verb.

7. The judge sentenced the murderer to be *hung*.

WRONG. A distinction is made, in educated speech, between *hung* and *hanged*. A picture is *hung*, but a person is *hanged* – that is, if such action is intended to bring about an untimely demise.

8. Mother, *can* I go out to play?

RIGHT. If you insist that your child say *may*, and nothing but *may*, when asking for permission, you may be considered puristic. *When speaking informally, can* is not discourteous, incorrect, or vulgar.

9. Take two *spoonsful* of this medicine every three hours.

WRONG. There is a strange affection, on the part of some people, for *spoonsful* and *cupsful*, even though *spoonsful* and *cupsful* do not exist as acceptable words. The plurals are *spoonfuls* and *cupfuls*.

I am taking for granted, of course, that you are using one spoon and filling it twice. If, for secret reasons of your own, you prefer to take your medicine in two separate spoons, you may then properly speak of 'two *spoons full* (not *spoonsful*) of medicine'.

10. Your words seem to *infer* that Jack is a liar.

WRONG. *Infer* does not mean *hint* or suggest. *Imply* is the proper word; to *infer* is to draw a conclusion from another's words.

11. I *will* be happy to go to the concert with you.

RIGHT. In informal speech, you need no longer worry about the technical and unrealistic distinctions between *shall* and *will*.

12. It is *me*.

RIGHT. This 'violation' of grammatical 'law' has been completely sanctioned by current usage. When the late Winston Churchill made a nationwide radio address from New Haven, Connecticut, many, many years ago, his opening sentence was: 'This is *me*, Winston Churchill.' I imagine that the purists who were listening fell into a deep state of shock at these words, but of course

Churchill was simply using the kind of down-to-earth English that had long since become standard in informal educated speech.

13. Go *slow*.

RIGHT. 'go *slow*' is not, and never has been, incorrect English – every authority concedes that *slow* is an adverb as well as an adjective.

14. I *would* like to ask you a question.

RIGHT. In current usage, *would* may be used with *I*, though old-fashioned rules demand *I should*.

Indeed, in modern speech, *should* is almost entirely restricted to expressing probability, duty, or responsibility.

As in the case of the charitable-looking dowager who was approached by a seedy character seeking a handout.

'Madam,' he whined, 'I haven't eaten in five days.'

'My good man,' the matron answered with great concern, 'you should force yourself!'

5

HOW TO TALK ABOUT VARIOUS PRACTITIONERS

(Sessions 7–10)

Teaser Preview

What practitioner:

- *is a student of human behaviour?*
- *follows the techniques devised by Sigmund Freud?*
- *straightens teeth?*
- *measures vision?*
- *treats minor ailments of the feet?*
- *analyses handwriting?*
- *deals with the problems of aging?*
- *uses manipulation and massage as curative techniques?*

Session 7

An ancient Greek mused about the meaning of life, and *philosophy* was born. The first Roman decided to build a road instead of cutting a path through the jungle, and *engineering* came into existence. One day in primitive times, a human being lent to another whatever then passed for money and got back his original investment plus a little more – and *banking* had started.

Most people spend part of every working day at some gainful employment, honest or otherwise, and in so doing often contribute their little mite to the progress of the world.

We explore in this chapter the ideas behind people's occupations – and the words that translate these ideas into verbal symbols.

Ideas

1. Behaviour

By educating and training, this practitioner is an expert in the dark mysteries of human behaviour – what makes people act as they do, why they have certain feelings, how their personalities were formed – in short, what makes them tick. Such a professional is often employed by industries and institutions to devise means for keeping workers productive and happy and inmates contented. This person may also do private or group therapy.

A *psychologist*

2.   Worries, fears, conflicts

This practitioner is a physician, psychiatrist, or psychologist who has been specially trained in the techniques devised by Sigmund Freud, encouraging you to delve into that part of your mind called 'the unconscious'. By reviewing the experiences, traumas, feelings, and thoughts of your earlier years, you come to a better understanding of your present worries, fears, conflicts, repressions, insecurities, and nervous tensions – thus taking the first step in coping with them. Treatment, consisting largely of listening to, and helping you to interpret the meaning of, your free-flowing ideas, is usually given in frequent sessions that may well go on for a year or more.

A *psychoanalyst*

3.   Teeth

This practitioner is a dentist who has specialized in the straightening of teeth.

An *orthodontist*

4.   Eyes

This practitioner measures your vision and prescribes the type of glasses that will give you a more accurate view of the world.

An *optometrist* or (*ophthalmic*) *optician*

5.   Glasses

This practitioner makes or supplies lenses according to the specifications prescribed by your optometrist or ophthalmologist.

A (*dispensing*) *optician*

6.   Bones and blood vessels

This practitioner is a member of the profession that originated in 1874, when Andrew T. Still devised a drugless technique of curing diseases by massage and other manipulative procedures, a technique based on the theory that illness may be caused by the undue pressure of displaced bones on nerves and blood vessels.

An *osteopath*

Treatment, consists of manipulating most of the articulations of
the body, especially those connected to the spinal column.

 A *chiropractor*

8. Feet

This practitioner treats minor foot ailments – corns, calluses,
bunions, fallen arches, etc.

 A *chiropodist*

9. Writing

This practitioner analyses handwriting to determine character,
personality, or aptitudes, and is often called upon to verify the
authenticity of signatures, written documents, etc.

 A *graphologist*

10. Getting old

This person deals with the economic, sexual, social, retirement,
and other problems of the elderly.

 A *gerontologist*

Using the words

Can you pronounce the words?

1. *psychologist* — sī-KOL'-ə-jist
2. *psychoanalyst* — sī-kō-AN'-ə-list
3. *orthodontist* — aw-thə-DON'-tist
4. *optometrist* — op-TOM'-ə-trist
5. *optician* — op-TISH'-ən
6. *osteopath* — OS'-ti-ə-path
7. *chiropractor* — KĪ'-rə-prak'-tə
8. *chiropodist* — ki-ROP'-ə-dist

9. *graphologist*   graf-OL'-ə-jist
10. *gerontologist*   jer'-ən-TOL'-ə-jist

Can you work with the words?

Practitioners	Interests
1. psychologist	a. vision
2. psychoanalyst	b. 'the unconscious'
3. orthodontist	c. bones and blood vessels
4. optometrist	d. feet
5. osteopath	e. teeth
6. chiropractor	f. problems of aging
7. chiropodist	g. joints of the spine
8. graphologist	h. handwriting
9. gerontologist	i. behaviour

Key: 1–i, 2–b, 3–e, 4–a, 5–c, 6–g, 7–d, 8–h, 9–f

Do you understand the words?

1. A *psychologist* must also be a doctor.	TRUE	FALSE
2. A *psychoanalyst* follows Freudian techniques.	TRUE	FALSE
3. An *orthodontist* specializes in straightening teeth.	TRUE	FALSE
4. An *optometrist* prescribes and fits glasses.	TRUE	FALSE
5. An *osteopath* may use massage and other manipulative techniques	TRUE	FALSE
6. A *chiropractor* treats corns and bunions.	TRUE	FALSE
7. A *graphologist* analyses character from handwriting.	TRUE	FALSE
8. A *gerontologist* is interested in the problems of adolescence.	TRUE	FALSE

Key: 1–F, 2–T, 3–T, 4–T, 5–T, 6–F, 7–T, 8–F

Can you recall the words?

1. delves into the
   unconscious
   1. P_____

2. uses either massage and
   manipulation or other
   standard medical
   procedures to treat illness
   2. O_____

3. takes care of minor
   ailments of the feet
   3. C_____

4. straightens teeth
   4. O_____

5. analyses handwriting
   5. G_____

6. dispenses glasses and
   contact lenses
   6. O_____

7. deals with the problems
   of aging
   7. G_____

8. manipulates articulations
   connected to the spinal
   column
   8. C_____

9. studies and explains
   human behaviour
   9. P_____

10. measures vision and
    prescribes glasses
    10. O_____

Key: 1–psychoanalyst, 2–osteopath, 3–chiropodist, 4–ortho-
        dontist, 5–graphologist, 6–optician, 7–gerontologist,
        8–chiropractor, 9–psychologist, 10–optometrist or
        ophthalmic optician

(End of Session 7)

Session 8

Origins and related words

1. The mental life

Psychologist is built upon the same Greek root as *psychiatrist* – *psyche*, spirit, soul, or mind. In *psychiatrist*, the combining form is *iatreia*, medical healing. In *psychologist*, the combining form is *logos*, science or study; a *psychologist*, by etymology, is one who studies the mind.

The field is *psychology* (sī-KOL.'-ə-ji), the adjective *psychological* (sī-kə-LOJ'-i-kəl).

Psyche (SĪ-ki) is also an English word in its own right – it designates the mental life, the spiritual or non-physical aspect of one's existence. The adjective *psychic* (SĪ'-kik) refers to phenomena or qualities that cannot be explained in purely physical terms. People may be called *psychic* if they seem to possess a sixth sense, a special gift of mind reading, or any mysterious aptitudes that cannot be accounted for logically. A person's disturbance is *psychic* if it is emotional or mental, rather than physical.

Psyche combines with the Greek *pathos*, suffering or disease, to form *psychopathic* (sī-kə-PATH'-ik), an adjective that describes someone suffering from a severe mental or emotional disorder. The noun is *psychopathy* (sī'-KOP'-ə-thi).*

---

* *Psychopathy* is usually characterized by antisocial and extremely egocentric behaviour. A *psychopath* (SĪ'-kə-path'), sometimes called a *psychopathic personality*, appears to be lacking an inner moral censor, and often commits criminal acts, without anxiety or guilt, in order to obtain immediate gratification of desires. Such a person may be utterly lacking in sexual restraint, or addicted to hard drugs. Some psychologists

The root *psyche* combines with Greek *soma*, body, to form *psych-somatic* (sī'-kō-sə-MAT'-ik), an adjective that delineates the powerful influence that the mind, especially the unconscious, has on bodily diseases. Thus, a person who fears the consequence of being present at a certain meeting will suddenly develop a bad cold or backache, or even be injured in a traffic accident, so that his appearance at this meeting is made impossible. It's a real cold, it's far from an imaginary backache, and of course one cannot in any sense doubt the reality of the vehicle that injured him. Yet, according to the *psychosomatic* theory of medicine, his unconscious made him susceptible to the cold germs, caused the backache, or forced him into the path of the car.

A *psychosomatic* disorder actually exists insofar as symptoms are concerned (headache, excessive urination, pains, paralysis, heart palpitations), yet there is no organic cause within the body. The cause is within the *psyche*, the mind.

Psychoanalysis (sī-kō-ə-NAL'-ə-sis) relies on the technique of deeply, exhaustively probing into the unconscious, a techique developed by Sigmund Freud. In oversimplified terms, the general principle of *psychoanalysis* is to guide the patient to an awareness of the deep-seated, unconscious causes of anxieties, fears, conflicts, and tension. Once found, exposed to the light of day, and thoroughly understood, claim the *psychoanalysts*, these causes may vanish like a light snow that is exposed to strong sunlight.

Consider an example: You have asthma, let us say, and your doctor can find no physical basis for your ailment. So you are referred to a *psychoanalyst* (or *psychiatrist* or clinical *psychologist* who practices *psychoanalytically* oriented therapy).

With your therapist you explore your past life, dig into your unconscious, and discover, let us say for the sake of argument, that your mother or father always used to set for you impossibly high goals. No matter what you accomplished in school, it was not good enough – in your mother's or father's opinion (and such opinions were always made painfully clear to you), you could do better if you were not so lazy. As a child you built up certain resentments and anxieties because you seemed unable to please your parent – and (this will sound far-fetched, but it is perfectly possible) as a result you became asthmatic. How else were you

prefer the label *sociopath* (SŌ'-si-ə-path') for this type of personality to indicate the absence of a social conscience.

going to get the parental love, the approbation, the attention you needed and that you felt you were not receiving?

In your sessions with your therapist, you discover that your asthma is emotionally, rather than organically, based – your ailment is *psychogenic* (sī-kō-JEN'-ik), of *psychic* origin, or (the terms are used more or less interchangeably although they differ somewhat in definition) *psychosomatic*, resulting from the interaction of mind and body. (*Psychogenic* is built on *psyche* plus Greek *genesis*, birth or origin.)

And your treatment? No drugs, no surgery – these may help the body, not the emotions. Instead, you 'work out' (this is the term used in *psychoanalytic* [sī-kō-an'-ə-LIT'-ik] parlance) early trauma in talk, in remembering, in exploring, in interpreting, in reliving childhood experiences. And if your asthma is indeed *psychogenic* (or *psychosomatic*), therapy will very likely help you; your attacks may cease, either gradually or suddenly.

Freudian therapy is less popular today than formerly; many newer therapies – Gestalt, bioenergetics, transactional analysis, to name only a few – claim to produce quicker results.

In any case, *psychotherapy* (sī-kō-THER'-ə-pi) of one sort or another is the indicated treatment for *psychogenic* (or *psychosomatic*) disorders, or for any personality disturbances. The practitioner is a *psychotherapist* (sī-kō-THER'-ə-pist) or *therapist*, for short; the adjective is *psychotherapeutic* (sī-kō-ther'-ə-PYOO'-tik).

Review of etymology

Root, Suffix	Meaning	English Word
1. *psyche*	spirit, soul, mind	_____
2. *iatreia*	medical healing	_____
3. *-ic*	adjective suffix	_____
4. *soma*	body	_____
5. *genesis*	birth, origin	_____
6. *pathos*	suffering, disease	_____

Using the words

Can you pronounce the words?

1.	*psychology*	sī-KOL'-ə-ji
2.	*psychological*	sī-kə-LOJ'-i-kəl
3.	*psyche*	SĪ'-ki
4.	*psychic*	SĪ'-kik
5.	*psychopathic*	sī-kə-PATH'-ik
6.	*psychopathy*	sī-KOP'-ə-thi
7.	*psychopath*	SĪ'-kə-path
8.	*psychosomatic*	sī-kō-sə-MAT'-ik
9.	*psychoanalysis*	sī-kō-ə-NAL'-ə-sis
10.	*psychoanalytic*	sī-kō-an'-ə-LIT'-ik
11.	*psychogenic*	sī-kō-JEN'-ik
12.	*psychotherapy*	sī-kō-THER'-ə-pi
13.	*psychotherapist*	sī-kō-THER'-ə-pist
14.	*psychotherapeutic*	sī-kō-ther'-ə-PYOO'-tik

Can you work with the words?

1.	psychology	a.	mental or emotional disturbance
2.	psyche	b.	psychological treatment based on Freudian techniques
3.	psychic	c.	general term for psychological treatment
4.	psychopathy	d.	originating in the mind or emotions
5.	psychosomatic	e.	one's inner or mental life, or self-image
6.	psychoanalysis	f.	study of the human mind and behaviour
7.	psychogenic	g.	describing the interaction of mind and body
8.	psychotherapy	h.	pertaining to the mind; extrasensory
9.	psychopath	i.	person lacking in social conscience or inner censor

Key: 1–f, 2–e, 3–h, 4–a, 5–g, 6–b, 7–d, 8–c, 9–i

Do you understand the words?

1.	*Psychological* treatment aims at sharpening the intellect.	TRUE	FALSE
2.	*Psychic* phenomena can be explained on rational or physical grounds.	TRUE	FALSE
3.	*Psychopathic* personalities are normal and healthy.	TRUE	FALSE
4.	A *psychosomatic* symptom is caused by organic disease.	TRUE	FALSE
5.	Every therapist uses *psychoanalysis*.	TRUE	FALSE
6.	A *psychogenic* illness originates in the mind or emotions.	TRUE	FALSE
7.	A *psychotherapist* must have a medical degree.	TRUE	FALSE
8.	*Psychoanalytically* oriented therapy uses Freudian techniques.	TRUE	FALSE
9.	A *psychopath* is often a criminal.	TRUE	FALSE

Key: 1–F, 2–F, 3–F, 4–F, 5–F, 6–T, 7–F, 8–T, 9–T

Can you recall the words?

1. one's inner or mental life, or self-image   1. P_____

2. the adjective that denotes the interactions, especially in illness, between mind and body   2. P_____

3. mentally or emotionally disturbed   3. P_____

4. study of behaviour   4. P_____

5. extrasensory   5. P_____

6. treatment by Freudian techniques   6. P_____

7. pertaining to the study of behaviour (*adj.*)   7. P_____

8. of mental or emotional origin   8. P_____

9. general term for
   treatment of emotional
   disorders

                    9. P_____

10. antisocial person   10. P_____

Key: 1–psyche, 2–psychosomatic, 3–psychopathic, 4–psychology, 5–psychic, 6–psychoanalysis, 7–psychological, 8–psychogenic, 9–psychotherapy, 10–psychopath

(End of Session 8)

Session 9

Origins and related words

1. The whole tooth

Orthodontist, as we discovered in Chapter 4, is built on *orthos*, straight, correct, plus *odontos*, tooth.

A *periodontist* (per'-i-ō-DON'-tist) is a gum specialist – the term combines *odontos* with the prefix *peri-*, around, surrounding. (As a quick glance in the mirror will tell you, the gums surround the teeth, more or less.) The speciality: *periodontics* (per'-i-ō-DON'-tiks); the adjective: *periodontic* (per'-i-ō-DON'-tik).

An *endodontist* (en'-dō-DON'-tist) specializes in work on the pulp of the tooth and in root-canal therapy – the prefix in this term is *endo-*, from Greek *endon*, inner, within.

Try your hand again at constructing words. What is the speciality?_____. And the adjective?

_____

The prefix *ex-*, out, combines with *odontos* to form *exodontist* (eks'-ō-DON'-tist). What do you suppose, therefore, is the work in which this practitioner specializes? _____. And the term for the speciality? _____. For the adjective? _____.

2. Measurement

The *optometrist*, by etymology, measures vision – the term is built on *opsis, optikos*, view, vision, plus *metron*, measurement.

Metron is the root in many other words:

1. *thermometer* (thə-MOM'-i-tə) – an instrument to measure heat (Greek *therme*, heat).

2. *barometer* (bə-ROM'-i-tə) – an instrument to measure atmospheric pressure (Greek *baros*, weight); the adjective is *barometric* (bar'-ə-MET'-rik).

3. *sphygmomanometer* (sfig'-mō-mə-NOM'-i-tə) – a device for measuring blood pressure (Greek *sphygmos*, pulse).

4. *metric* system – a decimal system of weights and measures.

3.   Bones, feet, and hands

Osteopath combines Greek *osteon*, bone, with *pathos*, suffering, disease. *Osteopathy* (os'-ti-OP'-ə-thi), you will recall, was originally based on the theory that disease is caused by pressure of the bones on blood vessels and nerves. An *osteopathic* (os'-ti-ə-PATH'-ik) practitioner is *not* a bone specialist, despite the misleading etymology – and should not be confused with the *orthopaedist*, who is.

The *chiropodist* (Greek *cheir*, hand, spelt *chiro-* in English words, plus *pons, podos,* foot) practices chiropody (ki-ROP'-ə-di). The term was coined in the days before labour-saving machinery and push-button devices, when people worked with their hands and developed calluses on their upper extremities as well as on their feet.

Chiropractors heal with their hands – the speciality is *chiropractic* (kī-rō-PRAK'-tik).

Cheir (*chiro-*), hand, is also the root in *chirography* (kī-ROG'-rə-fi). Recalling the *graph-* in *graphologist*, can you work out by etymology what *chirography* is? _____
_____

An expert in writing by hand, or in penmanship (a lost art in these days of electronic word-processing,† would be a *chirographer* (kī-ROG'-rə-fə); the adjective is *chirographic* (kī-rə-GRAF'-ik).

If the suffix *-mancy* comes from a Greek word meaning *foretelling* or *prediction,* can you decide what *chiromancy* (KĪ'-rə-man'-si) must be? _____

The person who practises *chiromancy* is a *chiromancer* (KĪ'-rə-man'-sə); the adjective is *chiromantic* (kī-rə-MAN'-tik).

The root *pous, podos* is found in:

---

† But see *calligrapher* in the next session.

1. *octopus* (OK'-tə-pəs), the eight-armed (or, as the etymology has it, eight-footed) sea creature (Greek *okto*, eight)

2. *platypus* (PLAT'-i-pəs), the strange water mammals with a duck's bill, webbed feet, and a beaver-like tail that reproduces by laying eggs (Greek *platys*, broad, flat – hence, by etymology, a flatfoot!).

3. *podium* (PŌ'-di-əm), a speaker's platform, etymologically a place for the feet. (The suffix *-ium* often signifies 'place where', as in *gymnasium, stadium, auditorium*, etc.)

4. *tripod* (TRĪ'-pod), a three-legged (or 'footed') stand for a camera or other device (*tri-*, three).

5. *podiatrist* (pō-DĪ'-ə-trist), another name for a *chiropodist*. The speciality is *podiatry* (pō-DĪ'-ə-tri).

Review of etymology

Prefix, Root, Suffix	Meaning	English Word
1. *orthos*	straight, correct	_____
2. *odontos*	tooth	_____
3. *paidos (paed-)*	child	_____
4. *-ic*	adjective suffix	_____
5. *peri-*	around, surrounding	_____
6. *endo-*	inner, within	_____
7. *ex-*	out	_____
8. *opsis, optikos*	vision	_____
9. *metron*	measurement	_____
10. *therme*	heat	_____
11. *baros*	weight	_____
12. *sphygmos*	pulse	_____
13. *osteon*	bone	_____
14. *pathos*	suffering, disease	_____
15. *pous, podos*	foot	_____
16. *okto*	eight	_____
17. *platys*	broad, flat	_____
18. *-ium*	place where	_____
19. *tri-*	three	_____
20. *cheir (chiro-)*	hand	_____
21. *mancy*	prediction	_____

22. *iatreia*   medical healing   _____

Using the words

Can you pronounce the words? (I)

1. *periodontist*   per'-i-ō-DON'-tist
2. *periodontics*   per'-i-ō-DON'-tiks
3. *periodontic*   per'-i-ō-DON'-tik
4. *endodontist*   en'-dō-DON'-tist
5. *endodontics*   en'-dō-DON'-tiks
6. *endodontic*   en'-dō-DON'-tik
7. *exodontist*   eks'-ō-DON'-tist
8. *exodontics*   eks'-ō-DON'-tiks
9. *exodontic*   eks'-ō-DON'-tik
10. *thermometer*   thə-MOM'-i-tə
11. *barometer*   bə-ROM'-i-tə
12. *barometric*   bar'-ə-MET'-rik
13. *sphygmomanometer*   sfig'-mō-mə-NOM'-i-tə

Can you pronounce the words? (II)

1. *osteopathy*   os'-ti-OP'-ə-thi
2. *osteopathic*   os'-ti-ə-PATH'-ik
3. *chiropody*   ki-ROP'-ə-di
4. *octopus*   OK'-tə-pəs
5. *platypus*   PLAT'-i-pəs
6. *podium*   PŌ'-di-əm
7. *tripod*   TRĪ'-pod
8. *podiatrist*   pō-DĪ'-ə-trist
9. *podiatry*   pō-DĪ'-ə-tri
10. *chiropractic*   kī-rō-PRAK'-tik
11. *chirography*   kī-ROG'-rə-fi
12. *chirographer*   kī-ROG'-rə-fə
13. *chirographic*   kī-rə-GRAF'-ik
14. *chiromancy*   KĪ'-rə-man'-si
15. *chiromancer*   KĪ'-rə-man'-sə
16. *chiromantic*   kī'-rə-MAN'-tik

Can you work with the words? (I)

1.	orthodontics	a.	dental speciality involving the pulp and root canal
2.	periodontics	b.	instrument that measures atmospheric pressure
3.	endodontics	c.	speciality arising from the theory that pressure of the bones on nerves and blood vessels may cause disease
4.	exodontics	d.	blood-pressure apparatus
5.	barometer	e.	treatment of minor ailments of the foot
6.	sphygmomanometer	f.	instrument to measure heat
7.	osteopathy	g.	speciality of tooth extraction
8.	chiropody	h.	speciality of tooth straightening
9.	thermometer	i.	speciality of the gums

Key: 1–h, 2–i, 3–a, 4–g, 5–b, 6–d, 7–c, 8–e, 9–f

Can you work with the words? (II)

1.	octopus	a.	speaker's platform
2.	platypus	b.	maintenance of integrity of the nervous system by manipulation and massage
3.	podium	c.	palm reading
4.	chiropractic	d.	eight-armed sea creature
5.	chirography	e.	handwriting
6.	chiromancy	f.	egg-laying mammal with webbed feet

Key: 1–d, 2–f, 3–a, 4–b, 5–e, 6–c

Do you understand the words?

1. *Orthodontics* is a branch of dentistry.   TRUE   FALSE
2. Doctors use *sphygmomanometers* to   TRUE   FALSE
   check blood pressure.

3. *Osteopathic* physicians may use standard medical procedures.   TRUE   FALSE
4. *Chiropractic* deals with handwriting.   TRUE   FALSE
5. *Chiropody* and *podiatry* are synonymous terms.   TRUE   FALSE
6. A *podium* is a place from which a lecture might be delivered.   TRUE   FALSE
7. A *periodontist* is a gum specialist.   TRUE   FALSE
8. A *endodontist* does root-canal therapy.   TRUE   FALSE
9. An *exodontist* extracts teeth.   TRUE   FALSE
10. A *barometer* measures heat.   TRUE   FALSE
11. An *octopus* has eight arms.   TRUE   FALSE
12. A *platypus* is a land mammal.   TRUE   FALSE
13. A *tripod* has four legs.   TRUE   FALSE
14. A *chirographer* is an expert at penmanship.   TRUE   FALSE
15. A *chiromancer* reads palms.   TRUE   FALSE

Key: 1–T, 2–T. 3–T, 4–F, 5–T, 6–T, 7–T, 8–T, 9–T, 10–F, 11–T, 12–F, 13–F, 14–T, 15–T .

Do you recall the words? (I)

1. blood-pressure apparatus   1. S_____
2. three-legged stand   2. T_____
3. pertaining to the treatment of diseases by manipulation to relieve pressure of the bones on nerves and blood vessels (*adj.*)   3. O_____
4. pertaining to handwriting (*adj.*)   4. C_____
5. gum specialist   5. P_____
6. treatment of ailments of the foot   6. P_____

    or C_____
7. stand for a speaker   7. P_____

8. dentist specializing in   8. E_____
   treating the pulp of the
   tooth or in doing root-
   canal therapy

Key: 1–sphygmomanometer,   2–tripod,   3–osteopathic,
       4–chirographic, 5–periodontist, 6–chiropody *or* podia-
       try, 7–podium, 8–endodontist

Can you recall the words? (II)

1. pertaining to the speciality   1. E_____
   of tooth extraction (*adj.*)
2. pertaining to the   2. B_____
   measurement of
   atmospheric pressure
   (*adj.*)
3. palm reading (*noun*)   3. C_____
4. handwriting   4. C_____
5. the practice of   5. C_____
   manipulating bodily
   articulations to relieve
   ailments
6. egg-laying mammal   6. P_____
7. eight-armed sea creature   7. O_____
8. instrument to measure   8. T_____
   heat

Key: 1–exodontic, 2–barometric, 3–chiromancy, 4–chirog-
       raphy, 5–chiropractic, 6–platypus, 7–octopus, 8–ther-
       mometer

(End of Session 9)

Session 10

Origins and related words

1. Writing and writers

The Greek verb *graphein*, to write, is the source of a great many English words.

We know that the *graphologist* analyses handwriting, the term combining *graphein* with *logos*, science, study. The speciality is *graphology* (gra-FOL'-ə-ji), the adjective *graphological* (graf'-ə-LOJ'-i-kəl).

Chirographer is built on *graphein* plus *cheir* (*chiro-*), hand. Though *chirography* may be a lost art, *calligraphy* (kə-LIG'-rə-fi) is enjoying a revival. For centuries before the advent of printing, *calligraphy*, or penmanship as an artistic expression, was practiced by monks.

A *calligrapher* (kə-LIG'-rə-fə) is called upon to design and write announcements, place cards, etc., as a touch of elegance. The adjective is *calligraphic* (kal'-i-GRAF'-ik).

Calligraphy combines *graphein* with Greek *kallos*,‡ *beauty, and so, by etymology, means beautiful writing.*

If a word exists for artistic handwriting, there must be one for the opposite – bad, scrawly, or illegible handwriting. And indeed there is – *cacography* (kə-KOG'-rə-fi), combining *graphein* with Greek *kakos*, bad, harsh.

‡ An entrancing word that also derives from *kallos* is *callipygian* (kal'-i-PIJ'-i-ən), an adjective describing a shapely or attractive rear end, or a person so endowed – the combining root is *pyge*, buttocks.

By analogy with the forms of *calligraphy*, can you write the word for:

One who uses bad or illegible handwriting?

_____

Pertaining to, or marked by, bad handwriting (*adjective*)?

_____

Graphein is found in other English words:

1. *cardiograph* (discussed in Chapter 4) – etymologically a 'heart writer' (*kardia*, heart).

2. *photograph* – etymologically, 'written by light' (Greek *photos*, light).

3. *phonograph* – etymologically, a 'sound writer' (Greek *phone*, sound).

4. *telegraph* – etymologically, a 'distance writer' (Greek *tele-*, distance).

5. *biography* – etymologically 'life writing' (Greek, *bios*, life).

Many of these new roots will be discussed in greater detail in later chapters.)

2.   Aging and the old

We know that a *geriatrician* specializes in the medical care of the elderly. The Greek word *geras*, old age, has a derived form, *geron*, old man, the root in *gerontologist*. The speciality is *gerontology* (jer'-ən-TOL'-ə-ji), the adjective is *gerontological* (jer'-ən-tə-LOJ'-i-kəl).

The Latin word for *old* is *senex*, the base on which *senile, senescent, senior*, and *senate* are built.

1. *senile* (SEE'-nīl) – showing signs of the physical and/or mental detioriation that generally marks very old age. The noun is *senility* (si-NIL'-i-ti).

2. *senescent* (si-NES'-ənt) – aging, growing old. (Note the same suffix in this word as in *adolescent*, growing into an adult, *convalescent*, growing healthy again, and *obsolescent*, growing or becoming obsolete.) The noun is *senescence* (si-NES'-əns).

3. *senior* (SEEN'-yə) – older. Noun: *seniority* (seen-i-OR'-i-ti).

4. *senate* (SEN'-ət) – originally a council of older, and presumably wiser, citizens.

Review of etymology

Prefix, Root, Suffix	Meaning	English Word
1. *graphein*	to write	_____
2. *cheir (chiro-)*	hand	_____
3. *kallos*	beauty	_____
4. *-er*	one who	_____
5. *-ic*	adjective suffix	_____
6. *pyge*	buttocks	_____
7. *kakos*	bad, harsh	_____
8. *kardia*	heart	_____
9. *photos*	light	_____
10. *tele-*	distance	_____
11. *bios*	life	_____
12. *geras*	old age	_____
13. *geron*	old man	_____
14. *senex*	old	_____
15. *-escent*	growing, becoming	_____

Using the words

Can you pronounce the words?

1. *graphology*	gra-FOL'-ə-ji
2. *graphological*	graf'-ə-LOJ'-i-kəl
3. *calligraphy*	kə-LIG'-rə-fi
4. *calligrapher*	kə-LIG'-rə-fə
5. *calligraphic*	kal'-i-GRAF'-ik
6. *callipygian*	kal'-i-PIJ'-i-ən
7. *cacography*	kə-KOG'-rə-fi
8. *cacographer*	kə-KOG'-rə-fə
9. *cacographic*	kak'-ə-GRAF'-ik
10. *gerontology*	jer'-ən-TOL'-ə-ji
11. *gerontological*	jer'-ən-tə-LOJ'-i-kəl
12. *senile*	SEE'-nīl
13. *senility*	si-NIL'-i-ti
14. *senescent*	si-NES'-ənt
15. *senescence*	si-NES'-əns

Can you work with the words?

1.	graphology	a.	possessed of beautiful buttocks
2.	calligraphy	b.	science of the social, economic, etc. problems of the aged
3.	callipygian	c.	condition of aging or growing old
4.	cacography	d.	deteriorated old age
5.	gerontology	e.	analysis of handwriting
6.	senility	f.	ugly, bad, illegible handwriting
7.	senescence	g.	beautiful handwriting; handwriting as an artistic expression

Key: 1–e, 2–g, 3–a, 4–f, 5–b, 6–d, 7–c

Do you understand the words?

1. *Graphology* analyses the grammar, spelling, and sentence structure of written material.	TRUE	FALSE
2. A *calligrapher* creates artistic forms out of alphabetical symbols.	TRUE	FALSE
3. Tight trousers are best worn by those of *callipygian* anatomy.	TRUE	FALSE
4. *Cacographic* writing is easy to read.	TRUE	FALSE
5. *Gerontology* aims to help old people live more comfortably.	TRUE	FALSE
6. *Senile* people are old but still vigorous and mentally alert.	TRUE	FALSE
7. In a society dedicated to the worship of youth, *senescence* is not an attractive prospect.	TRUE	FALSE

Key: 1–F, 2–T, 3–T, 4–F, 5–T, 6–F, 7–T

Can you recall the words?

1.	pertaining to the study of the problems of the aged (*adj.*)	1. G_____
2.	growing old (*adj.*)	2. S_____
3.	pertaining to handwriting as an artistic expression (*adj.*)	3. C_____
4.	one who uses ugly, illegible handwriting	4. C_____
5.	mentally and physically deteriorated from old age	5. S_____
6.	pertaining to the analysis of handwriting (*adj.*)	6. G_____
7.	possessed of beautiful or shapely buttocks	7. C_____

Key: 1–gerontological, 2–senescent, 3–calligraphic, 4–cacographer, 5–senile, 6–graphological, 7–callipygian

Chapter review

A. Do you recognize the words?

1. Practitioner trained in Freudian techniques: (a) psychologist, (b) psychoanalyst, (c) psychotherapist
2. Foot doctor: (a) chiropodist, (b) osteopath, (c) chiropractor
3. Handwriting analyst: (a) graphologist, (b) chirographer, (c) cacographer
4. Mentally or emotionally disturbed: (a) psychological, (b) psychopathic, (c) psychic
5. Originating in the emotions: (a) psychic, (b) psychogenic, (c) psychoanalytic
6. Describing bodily ailments tied up with the emotions: (a) psychosomatic, (b) psychopathic, (c) psychiatric
7. Gum specialist: (a) periodontist, (b) orthodontist, (c) endodontist

8. Specialist in tooth extraction: (a) orthodontist, (b) exodontist, (c) endodontist
9. Blood-pressure apparatus: (a) barometer, (b) thermometer, (c) sphygmomanometer
10. Prediction by palm reading: (a) chirography, (b) chiropody, (c) chiromancy
11. Possessed of a shapely posterior: (a) calligraphic, (b) callipygian, (c) adolescent
12. Artistic handwriting: (a) calligraphy, (b) chirography, (c) graphology
13. Growing old: (a) senile, (b) geriatric, (c) senescent
14. Medical speciality dealing with the aged: (a) gerontology, (b) geriatrics, (c) chiropractic
15. Antisocial person who may commit criminal acts: (a) psychopath, (b) sociopath, (c) osteopath

Key: 1–b, 2–a, 3–a, 4–b, 5–b, 6–a, 7–a, 8–b, 9--c, 10–c, 11–b, 12–a, 13–c, 14–b, 15–a *and* b

B.   Can you recognize roots?

Root	Meaning	Example
1. *psyche*	_____	psychiatry
2. *soma*	_____	psychosomatic
3. *pathos*	_____	osteopath
4. *orthos*	_____	orthodontics
5. *odontos*	_____	exodontist
6. *pous, podos*	_____	platypus
7. *cheir (chiro-)*	_____	chiropodist
8. *okto*	_____	octopus
9. *graphein*	_____	graphology
10. *kallos*	_____	calligraphy
11. *pyge*	_____	callipygian
12. *kakos*	_____	cacography
13. *photos*	_____	photography
14. *tele-*	_____	telegraph
15. *bios*	_____	biography
16. *geras*	_____	geriatrics
17. *geron*	_____	gerontology

18. *senex*   _____   senate

Key: 1—mind, 2—body, 3—disease, 4—straight, correct,
         5—tooth, 6—foot, 7—hand, 8—eight, 9—to write,
         10—beauty, 11—buttocks, 12—bad, ugly, 13—light,
         14—distance, 15—life, 16—old age, 17—old man, 18—old

---

Teaser question for the amateur etymologist

1. Latin *octoginta* is a root related to Greek *okto*, eight. How old is
an *octogenarian* (ok'-tə-jə-NAIR'-i-ən)? _____

2. You are familiar with *kakos*, bad, harsh, as in *cacography*, and
with *phone*, sound, as in *phonograph*. Can you construct a word
ending in the letter *y* that means *harsh, unpleasant sound*?
_____(Can you pronounce it?)

3. Using *callipygian* as a model, can you construct a word to
describe an ugly, unshapely rear end? _____.
(Can you pronounce it?)

4. Using the prefix *tele-*, distance, can you think of the word for
a field glass that permits the viewer to see great distances?
_____. How about a word for the instrument
that transmits sound over a distance? _____.
Finally, what is it that makes it possible for you to view happenings
that occur a great distance away? _____.

(Answers in Chapter 18)

Becoming word-conscious

Perhaps, if you have been working as assiduously with this book as
I have repeatedly counselled, you have noticed an interesting
phenomenon.

This phenomenon is as follows: you read a magazine article and
suddenly you see one or more of the words you have recently
learned. Or you open a book and there again are some of the
words you have been working with. In short, all your reading
seems to call to your attention the very words you've been studying.

Why? Have I, with uncanny foresight, picked words which have suddenly and inexplicably become popular among writers? Obviously, that's nonsense.

The change is in you. You have now begun to be alert to words, you have developed what is known in psychology as a 'mind-set' towards certain words. Therefore, whenever these words occur in your reading you take special notice of them.

The same words occurred before – and just as plentifully – but since they presented little communication to you, you reacted to them with an unseeing eye, with an ungrasping mind. You were figuratively, and almost literally, blind to them.

Do you remember when you bought, or contemplated buying, a new car? Let's say it was a Toyota. Suddenly you began to see Toyotas all around you – you had a Toyota 'mind-set'.

It is thus with anything new in your life. Development of a 'mind-set' means that the new experience has become very real, very important, almost vital.

If you have become suddenly alert to the new words you have been learning, you're well along towards your goal of building a superior vocabulary. *You are beginning to live in a new and different intellectual atmosphere – nothing less!*

On the other hand, if the phenomenon I have been describing has not yet occurred, do not despair. It will. I am alerting you to its possibilities – recognize it and welcome it when it happens.

(End of Session 10)

How grammar changes

If you think that grammar is an exact science, get ready for a shock. Grammar is a science, all right – but it is most inexact. There are no inflexible laws, no absolutely hard and fast rules, no unchanging principles. Correctness varies with the times and depends much more on geography, on social class, and on collective human caprice than on the restrictions found in textbooks.

In mathematics, which is an exact science, five and five make ten the world over. There are no two opinions on the matter – we are dealing, so far as we know, with a universal and indisputable fact.

In grammar, however, since the facts are highly susceptible to change, we have to keep an eye peeled for trends. What are educated people saying these days? Which expressions are generally used and accepted on educated levels, which others are more or less restricted to the less educated levels of speech? The answers to these questions indicate the trends of usage, and if such trends come into conflict with academic rules, then the rules are no longer of any great importance.

Grammar follows the speech habits of the majority of educated people – not the other way around. That is the important point to keep in mind.

The following notes on current trends in modern usage are intended to help you come to a decision about certain controversial expressions. As you read each sentence, pay particular attention to the italicized word or words. Does the usage square with your own language patterns? Would you be willing to phrase your thoughts in such terms? Decide whether the sentence is right or wrong, then compare your conclusion with the opinions given following the test.

Test yourself

1. Let's keep this between you and *I*.   RIGHT   WRONG
2. Five and five *is* ten.   RIGHT   WRONG
3. Every one of his sisters *are*   RIGHT   WRONG
   unmarried.
4. Do you *prophecy* another world war?   RIGHT   WRONG
5. *Leave* go of me.   RIGHT   WRONG
6. If you expect to *eventually succeed*,   RIGHT   WRONG
   you must keep trying.

1. Let's keep this between you and *I*.

WRONG. Children are so frequently corrected by parents and teachers when they say *me* that they cannot be blamed if they begin to think that this simple syllable is probably a naughty word. Dialogues such as the following are certainly typical of many households.

'Mother, can me and Johnnie go out and play?'

'No, dear, not until you say it correctly. You mean "May Johnnie and I go out to play?"'

'Who wants an apple?'

'Me!'

'Then use the proper word.'

(The child becomes a little confused at this point – there seem to be so many 'proper' and 'improper' words.)

'Me, *please*!'

'No, dear, not *me*.'

'Oh. *I*, please?'

(This sounds terrible to a child's ear. It completely violates his sense of language, but he does want the apple, so he grudgingly conforms.)

'Who broke my best vase?'

'It wasn't me!'

'Is that good English, Johnnie?'

'Okay, it wasn't *I*. But honest, Mum, it wasn't me – I didn't even touch it!'

And so, if the child is strong enough to survive such constant corrections, he decides that whenever there is room for doubt, it is safest to say *I*.

Some adults, conditioned in childhood by the kind of misguided censorship detailed here, are likely to believe that 'between you and *I*' is the more elegant form of expression, but most educated speakers, obeying the rule that a preposition governs the objective pronoun, say 'between you and *me*'.

3. Five and five *is* ten.

RIGHT. But don't jump to the conclusion that 'five and five *are* ten' is wrong — both verbs are equally acceptable in this or any similar construction. If you prefer to think of 'five-and-five' as a single mathematical concept, say *is*. If you find it more reasonable to consider 'five and five' a plural idea, say *are*. Use whichever verb has the greater appeal to your sense of logic.

5. Every one of his sisters *are* unmarried.

WRONG. *Are* is perhaps the more logical word, since the sentence implies that he has more than one sister and they are all unmarried. In educated speech, however, the tendency is to make the verb agree with the subject, even if logic is violated in the process — and the better choice here would be *is*, agreeing with the singular subject, *every one*.

4. Do you *prophecy* another world war?

WRONG. Use *prophecy* only when you mean *prediction*, a noun. When you mean *predict*, a verb, as in this sentence, use *prophesy*. This distinction is simple and foolproof. Therefore we properly say: 'His *prophecy* (*prediction*) turned out to be true', but 'He really seems able to *prophesy* (*predict*) political trends'. There is a distinction also in the pronunciation of these two words. *Prophecy* is pronounced PROF'-ə-si; *prophesy* is pronounced PROF'-ə-sī'.

5. *Leave* go of me.

WRONG. On the less sophisticated levels of speech, *leave* is a popular substitute for *let*. On educated levels, the following distinction is carefully observed: *let* means *allow*; *leave* means *depart*. (There are a few idiomatic exceptions to this rule, but they present no problem.) '*Let* me go' is preferable to '*Leave* me go' even on the most informal of occasions.

6. If you expect to *eventually succeed*, you must keep trying.

RIGHT (but with reservations). We have here, in case you're puzzled, an example of that notorious bugbear of academic grammar, the 'split infinitive.' (An infinitive is a verb preceded by *to*: *to succeed, to fail, to remember*.)

Splitting an infinitive is not at all difficult – you need only insert a word between the *to* and the verb: *to eventually succeed, to completely fail, to quickly remember.*

Now that you know how to split an infinitive, the important question is, is it legal to do so? Although it is common, even among good writers, it is disliked by many people and so should be avoided if possible. However, there are some instances in which it is clearer, more effective, or less ambiguous to split the infinitive than not. Compare 'He failed to completely understand the problem', meaning he partly understood, with 'He failed to understand the problem completely' meaning he did not begin to understand it.

6

HOW TO TALK ABOUT SCIENCE AND SCIENTISTS

(Sessions 11–13)

Teaser Preview

What scientist:

- *is interested in the development of the human race?*
- *is a student of the heavens?*
- *explores the physical qualities of the earth?*
- *studies all living matter?*
- *is a student of plant life?*
- *is a student of animal life?*
- *is pr fessionally involved in insects?*
- *is a student of language?*
- *is a student of the psychological effects of words?*
- *studies the culture, structure, and customs of different societies?*

Session 11

A true scientist lives up to the etymological meaning of his title 'one who knows'. Anything scientific is based on facts – observable facts that can be recorded, tested, checked, and verified.

Science, then, deals with human knowledge – as far as it has gone. It has gone very far indeed since the last century or two, when we stopped basing our thinking on guesses, wishes, theories that had no foundation in reality, and concepts of how the world *ought* to be; and instead began to explore the world as it *was*, and not only the world but the whole universe. From Galileo, who looked through the first telescope atop a tower in Pisa, Italy, Pasteur, who watched microbes through a microscope, to Einstein, who deciphered riddles of the universe by means of mathematics, we have at last begun to fill in a few areas of ignorance.

Who are some of the more important explorers of knowledge – and by what terms are they known?

Ideas

1.   Whither mankind?

The field is all mankind – how we developed in mind and body from primitive cultures and early forms.

   An *anthropologist*

2.   What's above?

The field is the heavens and all that's in them – planets, galaxies, stars, and other universes.

   An *astronomer*

3.   And what's below?

The field is the comparatively little and insignificant whirling ball on which we live – the earth. How did our planet come into being, what is it made of, how were its mountains, oceans, rivers, plains, and valleys formed, and what's down deep if you start digging?

A *geologist*

4.   What is life?

The field is all living organisms – from the simplest one-celled amoeba to the amazingly complex and mystifying structure we call a human being. Plant or animal, flesh or vegetable, denizen of water, earth, or air – if it lives and grows, this scientist wants to know more about it.

A *biologist*

5.   Flora

Biology classifies life into two great divisions – plant and animal. This scientist's province is the former category – flowers, trees, shrubs, mosses, marine vegetation, blossoms, fruits, seeds, grasses, and all the rest that make up the plant kingdom.

A *botanist*

6.   And Fauna

Animals of every description, kind, and condition, from birds to bees, fish to fowl, reptiles to humans, are the special area of exploration of this scientist.

A *zoologist*

7.   And all the little bugs

There are over 650,000 different species of insects, and millions of individuals of every species – and this scientist is interested in every one of them.

An *entomologist*

8.   Tower of Babel

This linguistic scientist explores the subtle, intangible, elusive uses of that unique tool that distinguishes human beings from all other forms of life – to wit: language. This person is, in short, a student of linguistics, ancient and modern, primitive and cultured, Chinese, Hebrew, Icelandic, Slavic, Teutonic, and every other kind spoken now or in the past by human beings, not excluding that delightful hotchpotch known as 'pidgin English', in which a piano is described as 'big box, you hit 'um in teeth, he cry', and in which Hamlet's famous quandary, 'To be or not to be, that is the question . . . ' is translated into 'Can do, no can do – how fashion?'.
      A *philologist*

9.   What do you really mean?

This linguistic scientist explores the subtle, intangible, elusive relationship between language and thinking, between meaning and words; and is interested in determining the psychological causes and effects of what people say and write.
      A *semanticist*

10.   Who are your friends and neighbours?

This scientist is a student of the ways in which people live together, their family and community structures and customs, their housing, their social relationships, their forms of government, and their layers of caste and class.
      A *sociologist*

Using the words

      Can you pronounce the words?

1.	*anthropologist*	an'-thrə-POL'-ə-jist
2.	*astronomer*	ə-STRON'-ə-mə
3.	*geologist*	jee (*or* ji)-OL'-ə-jist
4.	*biologist*	bī-OL'-ə-jist
5.	*botanist*	BOT'-ə-nist

6. *zoologist*   zŏo-OL'-ə-jist
7. *entomologist*   en'-tə-MOL'-ə-jist
8. *philologist*   fi-LOL'-ə-jist
9. *semanticist*   si-MAN'-ti-sist
10. *sociologist*   sō'-si-OL'-ə-jist

Can you work with the words?

Scientist	Professional Field
1. anthropologist	a. community and family life
2. astronomer	b. meanings and psychological effects of words
3. geologist	c. development of the human race
4. biologist	d. celestial phenomena
5. botanist	e. anguage
6. zoologist	f. insect forms
7. entomologist	g. the earth
8. philologist	h. all forms of living matter
9. semanticist	i. animal life
10. sociologist	j. plant life

Key: 1–c, 2–d, 3–g, 4–h, 5–j, 6–i, 7–f, 8–e, 9–b, 10–a

Can you recall the words?

1. insects	1.	E_____
2. language	2.	P_____
3. social conditions	3.	S_____
4. history of development of mankind	4.	A_____
5. meanings of words	5.	S_____
6. plants	6.	B_____
7. the earth	7.	G_____
8. the heavenly bodies	8.	A_____
9. all living things	9.	B_____
10. animals	10.	Z_____

Key: 1—entomologist, 2—philologist, 3—sociologist, 4—anthropologist, 5—semanticist, 6—botanist, 7—geologist, 8—astronomer, 9—biologist, 10—zoologist

(End of Session 11)

Session 12

Origins and related words

1. People and the stars

Anthropologist is constructed from roots we are familiar with — *anthropos*, mankind, and *logos*, science, study.

The science is *anthropology* (an'-thrə-POL'-ə-ji). Can you write the adjective form of this word? _____. (Can you pronounce it?)

Astronomer is built on Greek *astron*, star, and *nomos*, arrangement, law, or order. The *astronomer* is interested in the arrangement of stars and other celestial bodies. The science is *astronomy* (ə-STRON'-ə-mi), the adjective is *astronomical* (as'-trə-NOM'-i-kəl), a word often used in a non-heavenly sense, as in 'the *astronomical* size of the national debt'. *Astronomy* deals in such enormous distances (the sun, for example, is 149 million kilometres/93 million miles from the earth, and light from stars travels towards the earth at 300,000 kilometres/186,000 miles per *second*) that the adjective *astronomical* is applied to any tremendously large figure.

Astron, star, combines with *logos* to form *astrology* (ə-STROL'-ə-ji), which assesses the influence of planets and stars on human events. The practitioner is an *astrologer* (ə-STROL'-ə-jə). Can you form the adjective? _____. (Can you pronounce it?)

By etymology, an *astronaut* (AS'-trə-nawt') is a sailor among the stars (Greek *nautes*, sailor). This person is termed with somewhat less exaggeration a *cosmonaut* (KOZ'-mə-nawt') by the Russians (Greek, *kosmos*, universe). *Nautical* (NAWT'-i-kəl), relating to sailors, sailing, ships, or navigation, derives also from *nautes*, and *nautes* in turn is from Greek *naus*, ship – a root used in *nausea* (etymologically, ship-sickness or seasickness!).

Aster (AS'-tə) is a star shaped flower. *Asterisk* (AS'-tə-risk), a star-shaped symbol (*), is generallky used in writing or printing to direct the reader to look for a footnote. *Astrophysics* (as'-trō-FIZ'-iks) is that branch of physics dealing with heavenly bodies.

Disaster (di-ZAHS'-tə) and *disastrous* (di-ZAHS'-trəs) also come from *astron*, star. In ancient times it was believed that the stars ruled human destiny; any misfortune or calamity, therefore, happened to someone because the stars were in opposition. (*Dis-*, a prefix of many meanings, in this word signifies *against*.)

Nomos, arrangement, law, or order, is found in two other interesting English words.

For example, if you can make your own laws for yourself, if you needn't answer to anyone else for what you do, in short, if you are independent, then you enjoy *autonomy* (aw-TON'-ə-mi), a word that combines *nomos*, law, with *autos*, self. *Autonomy*, then, is self-law, self-government. A self-governing state is *autonomous* (aw-TON'-ə-məs).

You know the instrument that beginners at the piano use to guide their timing? A pendulum swings back and forth, making an audible click at each swing, and in that way governs or orders the measure (or timing) of the player. Hence it is called a *metronome* (MET'-rə-nōm'), a word that combines *nomos* with *metron*, measurement.

2. The earth and its life

Geologist derives from Greek *ge* (*geo-*), earth. The science is *geology* (jee-(*or* ji)-OL'-ə-ji). Can you write the adjective?
_____. (Can you pronounce it?)

Geometry (jee-(*or* ji)-OM'-ə-tri) – *gee* plus *metron* – by etymology 'measurement of the earth', is that branch of mathematics dealing with the measurement and properties of solid and plane figures, such as angles, triangles, squares, spheres, prisms, etc. (The etymology of the word shows that this ancient science was originally concerned with the measurement of land and space on the earth.)

The mathematician is a *geometrician* (jee'-(or ji')-ə-mə-TRISH'-ən), the adjective is *geometric* (jee'-(or ji')-ə-MET'-rik).

Geography (jee-(or ji')-OG'-rə-fi) is writing about (*graphein*, to write), or mapping, the earth. A practitioner of the science is a *geographer* (jee-(or ji)-OG'-rə-fə), the adjective is *geographic* (jee'-(or ji')-ə-GRAF'-ik).

(The name *George* is also derived from *ge* (*geo-*), earth, plus *ergon*, work — the first George was an earth-worker or farmer.)

Biologist combines *bios*, life with *logos*, science, study. The science is *biology* (bī-OL'-ə-ji). The adjective? _____

Bios, life, is also found in *biography* (bī-OG'-rə-fi), writing about someone's *life*; *autobiography* (aw'-tə-bī-OG'-rə-fi), the story of one's *life* written by *oneself*; and *biopsy* (BĪ'-op-si), a medical examination, or view (*opsis, optikos*, view, vision), generally through a microscope, of living tissue, frequently performed when cancer is suspected. A small part of the tissue is cut from the affected area and under the microscope its cells can be investigated for evidence of malignancy. A *biopsy* is contrasted with an *autopsy* (AW'-top-si), which is a medical examination of a corpse in order to discover the cause of death. The *autos* in *autopsy* means, as you know, *self* — in an *autopsy*, etymologically speaking, the surgeon or pathologist determines, by actual view or sight rather than by theorizing (i.e., 'by viewing or seeing for oneself'), what brought the corpse to its present grievous state.

Botanist is from Greek *botane*, plant. The field is *botany* (BOT'-ə-ni); the adjective is *botanical* (bə-TAN'-i-kəL).

Zoologist is from Greek *zoion*, animal. The science is *zoology*. The adjective? _____. The combination of the two *o*'s tempts many people to pronounce the first three letters of these words in one syllable, thus: *zoo*. However, the two *o*'s should be separated, as in *co-operate*, even though no hyphen is used in the spelling to indicate such separation. Say zōō-OL'-ə-jist, zōō-ə-LOJ'-i-kəl. *Zoo*, a park for animals, is a shortened form of *zoological gardens*, and is, of course, pronounced in one syllable.

The *zodiac* (ZŌ-di-ak) is a diagram used in astrology, of the paths of the sun, moon, and planets; it contains, in part, Latin names for various animals — *scorpio*, scorpion; *leo*, lion; *cancer*, crab; *taurus*, bull; *aries*, ram; and *pisces*, fish. Hence its derivation from *zoion*, animal.

The adjective is *zodiacal* (zō-DĪ'-ə-kəl).

Review of Etymology

Prefix, Root	Meaning	English Word
1. *anthropos*	mankind	_____
2. *logos*	science, study	_____
3. *astron*	star	_____
4. *nautes*	sailor	_____
5. *naus*	ship	_____
6. *dis-*	against	_____
7. *nomos*	arrangement, law, order	_____
8. *autos*	self	_____
9. *metron*	measurement	_____
10. *ge (geo-)*	earth	_____
11. *graphein*	to write	_____
12. *bios*	life	_____
13. *opsis, optikos*	view, vision, sight	_____
14. *botane*	plant	_____
15. *zoion*	animal	_____

Using the words

Can you pronounce the words? (I)

1.	*anthropology*	an'-thrə-POL'-ə-ji
2.	*anthropological*	an'-thrə-pə-LOJ'-i-kəl
3.	*astronomy*	ə-STRON'-ə-mi
4.	*astronomical*	as'-trə-NOM'-i-kəl
5.	*astrology*	ə-STROL'-ə-ji
6.	*astrological*	as'·trə-LOJ'-i-kəl
7.	*astronaut*	AS'-trə-nawt'
8.	*cosmonaut*	KOZ'-mə-nawt'
9.	*nautical*	NAWT'-i-kəl
10.	*aster*	AS'-tə
11.	*asterisk*	AS'-tə-risk
12.	*disaster*	di-ZAHS'-tə
13.	*disastrous*	di-ZAHS'-trəs

Can you pronounce the words? (II)

1. *geology* — jee-(or ji)-OL'-ə-ji
2. *geological* — jee'-(or ji')-ə-LOJ'-i-kəl
3. *geometry* — jee-(or ji)-OM'-ə-tri
4. *geometrician* — jee'-(or ji')-ə-mə-TRISH'-ən
5. *geometric* — jee-(or ji)-ə-MET'-rik
6. *geography* — jee'-(or ji')-OG'-rə-fi
7. *geographer* — jee-(or ji)-OG'-rə-fə
8. *geographical* — jee'-(or ji)'-ə-GRAF'-ə-kəl
9. *biology* — bī-OL'-ə-ji
10. *biological* — bī-ə-LOJ'-i-kəl
11. *biography* — bī-OG'-rə-fi
12. *biographer* — bī-OG'-rə-fə
13. *biographical* — bī-ə-GRAF'-i-kəl

Can you pronounce the words? (III)

1. *autonomy* — aw-TON'-ə-mi
2. *autonomous* — aw-TON'-ə-məs
3. *metronome* — MET'-rə-nōm'
4. *autobiography* — aw'-tə-bī-OG'-rə-fi
5. *autobiographer* — aw'-tə-bī-OG'-rə-fə
6. *autobiographical* — aw-tə-bī'-ə-GRAF'-i-kəl
7. *biopsy* — BĪ'-op-si
8. *autopsy* — AW'-top-si
9. *botany* — BOT'-ə-ni
10. *botanical* — bə-TAN'-i-kəl
11. *zoology* — zōō-OL'-ə-ji
12. *zoological* — zōō-ə-LOJ'-i-kəl
13. *zodiac* — ZŌ'-di-ak
14. *zodiacal* — zō-DĪ'-ə-kəl

Can you work with the words? (I)

1. anthropology — a. theory of the influence of planets and stars on human events
2. astronomy — b. science of earth-mapping
3. astrology — c. science of all living matter
4. geology — d. science of human development

5. biology	e.	science of plants
6. geometry	f.	science of the composition of the earth
7. botany	g.	science of animal life
8. zoology	h.	science of the heavens
9. geography	i.	mathematical science of figures, shapes, etc.

Key: 1–d, 2–h, 3–a, 4–f, 5–c, 6–i, 7–e, 8–g, 9–b

Can you work with the words? (II)

1. autopsy	a.	'sailor among the stars'
2. biopsy	b.	star-shaped flower
3. biography	c.	story of one's own life
4. autobiography	d.	dissection and examination of a corpse to determine the cause of death
5. zodiac	e.	great misfortune
6. astronaut	f.	'sailor of the universe'
7. cosmonaut	g.	story of someone's life
8. aster	h.	diagram of paths of sun, moon, and planets
9. disaster	i.	instrument to measure musical time
10. autonomy	j.	self-rule
11. metronome	k.	examination of living tissue

Key: 1–d, 2–k, 3–g, 4–c, 5–h, 6–a, 7–f, 8–b, 9–e, 10–j, 11–i

Do you understand the words?

1. Are *anthropological* studies concerned with plant life?   YES   NO

2. Are *astronomical* numbers extremely small?   YES   NO

3. Is an *astrologer* interested in the time
   and date of your birth?   YES   NO

4. Are *nautical* manoeuvres carried on
   at sea?   YES   NO

5. Does a *disastrous* earthquake take a
   huge toll of life and property?   YES   NO

6. Do *geological* investigations
   sometimes determine where oil is to
   be found?   YES   NO

7. Does a *geometrician* work with
   mathematics?   YES   NO

8. Do *geographical* shifts in population
   sometimes affect the economy of an
   area?   YES   NO

9. Does a *biographical* novel deal with
   the life of a real person?   YES   NO

10. Is *botany* a biological science?   YES   NO

11. Is the United States politically
    autonomous?   YES   NO

12. Is a *biopsy* performed on a dead
    body?   YES   NO

13. Is a *metronome* used in the study of
    mathematics?   YES   NO

14. Is an *autopsy* performed to correct a
    surgical problem?   YES   NO

15. Does an author write an
    autobiography about someone else's
    life?   YES   NO

Key: 1–no, 2–no, 3–yes, 4–yes, 5–yes, 6–yes, 7–yes, 8–yes,
         9–yes, 10–yes, 11–yes, 12–no, 13–no, 14–no, 15–no

Can you recall the words? (I)

1. pertaining to the science   1. Z_____
   of animals (*adj.*)

2. pertaining to the science   2. B_____
   of plants (*adj.*)

3. dissection of a corpse to determine the cause of death

3. A_____

4. story of one's life, self-written

4. A_____

5. pertaining to the science of all living matter (*adj.*)

5. B_____

6. science of the measurement of figures

6. G_____

7. pertaining to the science of the earth's composition (*adj.*)

7. G_____

8. branch of physics dealing with the composition of celestial bodies

8. A_____

9. star-shaped flower

9. A_____

10. very high in number; pertaining to the science of the heavens (*adj.*)

10. A_____

11. science of heavenly bodies

11. A_____

12. science of the development of mankind

12. A_____

13. person who believes human events are influenced by the paths of the sun, moon, and planets

13. A_____

Key: 1–zoological, 2–botanical, 3–autopsy, 4–autobiography, 5–biological, 6–geometry, 7–geological, 8–astrophysics, 9–aster, 10–astronomical, 11–astronomy, 12–anthropology, 13–astrologer

Can you recall the words? (II)

1. microscopic examination of living tissue

1. B_____

2. self-government

2. A_____

3. time measurer for music

3. M_____

4. voyager among the stars   4. A_____
5. traveller through the   5. C_____
   universe
6. great misfortune   6. D_____
7. mapping of the earth   7. G_____
   (*noun*)
8. self-governing (*adj.*)   8. A_____
9. diagram used in astrology   9. Z_____
10. pertaining to such a   10. Z_____
    diagram (*adj.*)
11. pertaining to ships,   11. N_____
    sailing, etc.
12. star-shaped symbol   12. A_____
13. story of a person's life   13. B_____

Key: 1–biopsy, 2–autonomy, 3–metronome, 4–astronaut,
      5–cosmonaut, 6–disaster, 7–geography, 8–autono-
      mous, 9–zodiac, 10–zodiacal, 11–nautical, 12–asterisk,
      13–biography

(End of Session 12)

Session 13

Origins and related words

1.   Cutting in and out

Flies, bees, beetles, wasps, and other insects are segmented creatures – head, thorax, and abdomen. Where these parts join, there
appears to the imaginative eye a 'cutting in' of the body.

Hence the branch of zoology dealing with insects is aptly named
entomology, from Greek *en-*, in, plus *tome*, a cutting. The adjective is
entomological (en'-tə-mə-LOJ'-i-kəl).

(The word *insect* makes the same point – it is built on Latin *in-*,
in, plus *sectus*, a form of the verb meaning *to cut*.)

The prefix *ec-*, from Greek *ek-*, means *out*. (The Latin prefix,
you will recall, is *ex-*.) Combine *ec-* with *tome* to derive the words for
surgical procedures in which parts are 'cut out', or removed: *tonsil-
lectomy* (the tonsils), *appendectomy* (the appendix), *mastectomy* (the
breast), *hysterectomy* (the uterus), *prostatectomy* (the prostate), etc.

Combine *ec-* with Greek *kentron*, centre (the Latin root, as we
have discovered, is *centrum*), to derive *eccentric* (ik-SEN'-trik) – *out
of the centre*, hence deviating from the normal in behaviour, attitudes, etc., or unconventional odd, strange. The noun is *eccentricity* (ek'-sen-TRIS'-i-ti).

2.   More cuts

The Greek prefix *a-* makes a root negative; the *atom* (A'-təm) was
so named at a time when it was considered the smallest possible
particle of an element, that is, one that could *not* be cut any fur-

ther. (We have long since split the atom, of course, with results, as in most technological advances, both good and evil.) The adjective is *atomic* (ə-TOM'-ik).

The Greek prefix *ana-* has a number of meanings, one of which is *up*, as in *anatomy* (ə-NAT'-ə-mi), originally the *cutting up* of a plant or animal to determine its structure, later the bodily structure itself. The adjective is *anatomical* (an'-ə-TOM'-i-kəl).

Originally any book that was part of a larger work of many volumes was called a *tome* (TOM) – etymologically, a part *cut* from the whole. Today, a *tome* designates, often disparagingly, an exceptionally large book, or one that is heavy and dull in content.

The Greek prefix *dicha-*, in two, combines with *tome* to construct *dichotomy* (dī-KOT'-ə-mi), a splitting in two, a technical word used in astronomy, biology, botany, and the science of logic. It is also employed as a non-technical term, as when we refer to the *dichotomy* in the life of a man who is a bank clerk all day and a night-school teacher after working hours, so that his life is, in a sense, split into two parts. The verb is *dichotomize* (dī-KOT'-ə-mīz'); the adjective is *dichotomous* (dī-KOT'-ə-məs). *Dichotomous* thinking is the sort that divides everything into two parts – good and bad, white and black, Democrats and Republicans, etc. An unknown wit has made this classic statement about *dichotomous* thinking: 'There are two kinds of people: those who divide everything into two parts, and those who do not.'

Imagine a book, a complicated or massive report, or some other elaborate document – now figuratively cut through it so that you can get to its essence, the very heart of the idea contained in it. What you have is an *epitome* (i-PIT'-ə-mi), a condensation of the whole. (From *epi-*, on, upon, plus *tome*.)

An *epitome* may refer to a summary, condensation, or abridgment of language, as in 'Let me have an *epitome* of the book', or 'Give me the *epitome* of his speech'.

More commonly, *epitome* and the verb *epitomize* (i-PIT'-ə-mīz') are used in sentences like 'She is the *epitome* of kindness', or 'That one act *epitomizes* her philosophy of life'. If you cut everything else away to get to the *essential* part, that part is a representative cross-section of the whole. So a woman who is the *epitome* of kindness stands for all people who are kind, and an act that *epitomizes* a philosophy of life represents, by itself, the complete philosophy.

3. Love and words

Logos, we know, means *science* or *study*; it may also mean *word* or *speech*, as it does in *philology* (fi-LOL'-ə-ji) etymologically *the love of words* (from Greek *philein*, to love, plus *logos*), or what is more commonly called *linguistics* (lin-GWIS'-tiks), the science of language, a term derived from Latin *lingua*, tongue.

Can you write, and pronounce, the adjectival form of *philology*?

---

4. More love

Philanthropy (fi-LAN'-thrə-pi) is, by etymology, the love of mankind – one who devotes himself to *philanthropy* is a *philanthropist* (fi-LAN'-thrə-pist), as we learned in Chapter 3; the adjective is *philanthropic* (fil-ən-THROP'-ik).

The verb *philander* (fi-LAN'-də), to 'play around' sexually, be promiscuous, or have extramarital relations, combines *philein* with *andros*, male. (*Philandering*, despite its derivation, is not, of course, exclusively the male province. The word is, in fact, derived from the proper name conventionally given to male lovers in plays and romances of the 1500s and 1600s.) One who engages in the interesting activities catalogued above is a *philanderer* (fi-LAN'-dər-ə).

By etymology, *philosophy* is the love of wisdom (Greek *sophos*, wise); *Philadelphia* is the City of Brotherly Love (Greek *adelphos*, brother); *philharmonic* is the love of music or harmony (Greek *harmonia*, harmony); and a *philtre*, a rarely used word, is a love potion. Today, we call whatever arouses sexual desire an *aphrodisiac* (af'-rə-DIZ'-i-ak'), from Aphrodite, the Greek goddess of love and beauty.

Aphrodisiac is an adjective as well as a noun, but a longer adjectival form, *aphorodisiacal* (af'-rə-də-ZI'-ə-kəl), is also used.

A *bibliophile* (BIB'-li-ə-fil') is one who loves books as collectibles, admiring their binding, typography, illustrations, rarity, etc. – in short, a book collector. The combining root is Greek *biblion*, book.

An *Anglophile* (AN'-glō-fil') admires and is fond of the British people, customs, culture, etc. The combining root is Latin *Anglus*, English.

5.   Words and how they affect people

The *semanticist* is professionally involved in *semantics* (si-MAN'-tiks). The adjective is *semantic* (si-MAN'-tik).

Semantics, like *orthopaedics*, *paediatrics*, and *obstetrics*, is a singular noun despite the -s ending. Semantics *is*, not *are*, an exciting study. However, this rule applies only when we refer to the word as a science or area of study. In the following sentence, *semantics* is used as a plural: 'The *semantics* of your thinking *are* all wrong.'

6.   How people live

The profession of the *sociologist* is *sociology* (sō-si-OL'-ə-ji). Can you write, and pronounce, the adjective? _____

Sociology is built on Latin *socius*, companion,* plus *logos*, science, study. *Socius* is the source of such common words as *associate*, *social*, *socialize*, *society*, *sociable*, and *antisocial*; as well as *asocial* (ay-SŌ'-shəl), which combines the negative prefix *a-* with *socius*.

The *antisocial* person actively dislikes people, and often behaves in ways that are detrimental or destructive to society or the social order (*anti-*, against).

On the other hand, someone who is *asocial* is withdrawn and self-centred, avoids contact with others, and feels completely indifferent to the interests or welfare of society. The *asocial* person doesn't want to 'get involved.'

Review of etymology

Prefix, Root	Meaning	English Word
1. *en-*	in	_____
2. *tome*	a cutting	_____
3. *in-*	in	_____
4. *sectus*	cut	_____
5. *kentron* (*centrum*)	centre	_____
6. *a-*	not, negative	_____
7. *ana-*	up	_____

* *Companion* itself has an interesting etymology – Latin *com-*, with, plus *panis*, bread. If you are social, you enjoy breaking bread with companions. *Pantry* also comes from *panis*, though far more than bread is stored there.

8. *dicha-*	in two	_____
9. *epi-*	on, upon	_____
10. *logos*	word, speech	_____
11. *lingua*	tongue	_____
12. *philein*	to love	_____
13. *sophos*	wise	_____
14. *adelphos*	brother	_____
15. *biblion*	book	_____
16. *Anglus*	English	_____
17. *socius*	companion	_____
18. *anti-*	against	_____

Using the words

Can you pronounce the words? (I)

1.	*entomology*	en'-tə-MOL'-ə-ji
2.	*entomological*	en'-tə-mə-LOJ'-i-kəl
3.	*eccentric*	ik-SEN'-trik
4.	*eccentricity*	ek'-sen-TRIS'-i-ti
4.	*atom*	A'-təm
6.	*atomic*	ə-TOM'-ik
7.	*anatomy*	ə-NAT'-ə-mi
8.	*anatomical*	an'-ə-TOM'-i-kəl
9.	*tome*	TŌM
10.	*dichotomy*	dī-KOT'-ə-mi
11.	*dichotomous*	dī-KOT'-ə-məs
12.	*dichotomize*	dī-KOT'-ə-mīz'

Can you pronounce the words? (II)

1.	*epitome*	i-PIT'-ə-mi
2.	*epitomize*	i-PIT'-ə-mīz'
3.	*philology*	fi-LOL'-ə-ji
4.	*philological*	fil'-ə-LOJ'-i-kəl
5.	*linguistics*	lin-GWIS'-tiks
6.	*philanthropy*	fi-LAN'-thrə-pi
7.	*philanthropist*	fə-LAN'-thrə-pist
8.	*philanthropic*	fil'-ən-THROP'-ik

9. *philander*   fi-LAN'-də
10. *philanderer*   fi-LAN'-dər-ə

Can you pronounce the words? (III)

1. *philtre*   FIL'-tə
2. *aphrodisiac*   af'-rə-DIZ'-i-ak'
3. *aphrodisiacal*   af'-rə-də-ZĪ'-ə-kəl
4. *bibliophile*   BIB'-li-ə-fīl'
5. *Anglophile*   AN'-glō-fīl'
6. *semantics*   si-MAN'-tiks
7. *semantic*   si-MAN'-tik
8. *sociology*   sō'-si-OL'-ə-ji
9. *sociological*   sō-si-ə-LOJ'-i-kəl
10. *asocial*   ay-SŌ'-shəl

Can you work with the words? (I)

1. entomology	a. physical structure
2. eccentricity	b. summary; representation of the whole
3. anatomy	c. science of the meanings and effects of words
4. dichotomy	d. linguistics
5. epitome	e. science dealing with insects
6. philology	f. science of social structures and customs
7. semantics	g. charitable works
8. sociology	h. that which causes sexual arousal
9. aphrodisiac	i. strangeness; oddness; unconventionality
10. philanthropy	j. condition or state of being split into two parts

Key: 1–e, 2–i, 3–a, 4–j, 5–b, 6–d, 7–c, 8–f, 9–h, 10–g

_____

Can you work with the words? (II)

1. dichotomize	a. dull, heavy book

2.	epitomize	b.	love potion; aphrodisiac
3.	philander	c.	pertaining to the study of language
4.	philtre	d.	one fond of English people, customs, etc.
5.	bibliophile	e.	pertaining to the science of group cultures, conventions, etc.
6.	Anglophile	f.	to split in two
7.	asocial	g.	withdrawn from contact with people
8.	tome	h.	book collector
9.	philological	i.	to summarize
10.	sociological	j.	to engage in extramarital sex

Key: 1–f, 2–i, 3–j, 4–b, 5–h, 6–d, 7–g, 8–a, 9–c, 10–e

Do you understand the words?

1.	Is a *philanderer* likely to be faithful to a spouse?	YES	NO
2.	Did Dr. Jekyll-Mr. Hyde lead a *dichotomous* existence?	YES	NO
3.	Is an egoist the *epitome* of selfishness?	YES	NO
4.	Is a *philanthropist* antisocial?	YES	NO
5.	Is an *aphrodisiac* intended to reduce sexual interest?	YES	NO
6.	Is a *bibliophile's* chief aim the enjoyment of literature?	YES	NO
7.	Does a *philologist* understand etymology?	YES	NO
8.	Is a *semanticist* interested in more than the dictionary meanings of words?	YES	NO
9.	Is an *asocial* person interested in improving social conditions?	YES	NO
10.	Is a light novel considered a *tome*?	YES	NO

Key: 1—no, 2—yes, 3—yes, 4—no, 5—no, 6—no, 7—yes, 8—yes, 9—no, 10—no

Can you recall the words?

1.	pertaining to the study of social customs (*adj.*)	1. S_____
2.	pertaining to the psychological effects of words (*adj.*)	2. S_____
		or S_____
3.	lover and collector of books	3. B_____
4.	make love promiscuously	4. P_____
5.	pertaining to the science of linguistics (*adj.*)	5. P_____
6.	pertaining to the study of insects (*adj.*)	6. E_____
7.	one who admires English customs	7. A_____
8.	smallest particle, so-called	8. A_____
9.	pertaining to the structure of a body (*adj.*)	9. A_____
10.	a dull, heavy book	10. T_____
11.	split in two (*adj.*)	11. D_____
12.	to split in two	12. D_____
13.	a condensation, summary, or representation of the whole	13. E_____
14.	to stand for the whole; to summarize	14. E_____
15.	pertaining to charitable activities (*adj.*)	15. P_____
16.	out of the norm; odd	16. E_____
17.	one who 'plays around'	17. P_____
18.	arousing sexual desire (*adj.*)	18. A_____
		or A_____

19. science of the manner in which groups function

19. S_____

20. self-isolated from contact with people

20. A_____

Key: 1–sociological, 2–semantic, 3–bibliophile, 4–philander, 5–philological, 6–entomological, 7–Anglophile, 8–atom, 9–anatomical, 10–tome, 11–dichotomous, 12–dichotomize, 13–epitome, 14–epitomize, 15–philanthropic, 16–eccentric, 17–philanderer, 18–aphrodisiac *or* aphrodisiacal, 19–sociology, 20–asocial

Chapter review

A.   Do you recognize the words?

1. Student of the stars and other heavenly phenomena: (a) geologist, (b) astronomer, (c) anthropologist
2. Student of plant life: (a) botanist, (b) zoologist, (c) biologist
3. Student of insect life: (a) sociologist, (b) entomologist, (c) etymologist
4. Student of the meaning and psychology of words: (a) philologist, (b) semanticist, (c) etymologist
5. Analysis of living tissue: (a) autopsy, (b) biopsy, (c) autonomy
6. That which arouses sexual desire: (a) zodiac, (b) bibliophile, (c) aphrodisiac
7. Self-governing: (a) autobiographical, (b) autonomous, (c) dichotomous
8. Part that represents the whole: (a) epitome, (b) dichotomy, (c) metronome
9. One who physically travels in space: (a) astronomer, (b) astrologer, (c) astronaut
10. One who has extramarital affairs: (a) cosmonaut, (b) philanderer, (c) philanthropist

Key: 1–b, 2–a, 3–b, 4–b, 5–b, 6–c, 7–b, 8–a, 9–c, 10–b

B.   Can you recognize roots?

Root	Meaning	Example
1. *anthropos*	_____	anthropology
2. *logos*	_____	philology
3. *astron*	_____	astronomy
4. *nautes*	_____	astronaut
5. *nomos*	_____	metronome
6. *autos*	_____	autonomy
7. *ge (geo-)*	_____	geology
8. *graphein*	_____	biography
9. *opsis, optikos*	_____	autopsy
10. *zoion*	_____	zodiac
11. *tome*	_____	entomology
12. *sectus*	_____	insect
13. *lingua*	_____	linguistics
14. *philein*	_____	philanthropy
15. *sophos*	_____	philosophy
16. *biblion*	_____	bibliophile
17. *Anglus*	_____	Anglophile
18. *socius*	_____	sociology
19. *logos*	_____	biology
20. *bios*	_____	biopsy

Key: 1—mankind, 2—word, speech, 3—star, 4—sailor, 5—law,
order, arrangement, 6—self, 7—earth, 8—to write,
9—view, vision, sight, 10—animal, 11—a cutting, 12—cut,
13—tongue, 14—to love, 15—wise, 16—book, 17—English,
18—companion, 19—science, study, 20—life

Teaser question for the amateur etymologist

1. Recalling the root *sophos*, wise, what word means *worldly-wise*?
_____.

2. Thinking of *bibliophile*, define *bibliomaniac*: _____
_____
_____.

3. These three words, based on *lingua*, tongue, use prefixes we
have discussed. Can you define each one?
(1)   monolingual   _____

(2)   bilingual   _____
(3)   trilingual   _____

Can you, now, guess at the meaning of *multilingual*? _____
_____
_____.

How about *linguist*? _____
_____.

What do you suppose the Latin root *multus* means? _____
_____. (Think of *multitude*.)

4. With *Anglophile* as your model, can you work out what country and its people, customs, etc. each of the following admires?
(a)   Francophile   _____
(b)   Russophile   _____ _____
(c)   Hispanophile   _____
(d)   Germanophile   _____ _____
(e)   Nipponophile   _____
(f)   Sinophile   _____

5. Using roots you have learned, and with *bibliophile* as your mode, can you construct a word for:
(a)   one who loves males: _____
(b)   one who loves women: _____
(c)   one who loves animals: _____
(d)   one who loves plants: _____

(Answers in Chapter 18)

Where to get new ideas

People with superior vocabularies, I have submitted, are the people with ideas. The words they know are verbal symbols of the ideas they are familiar with – reduce one and you must reduce the other, for ideas cannot exist without verbalization. Freud once had an idea – and had to coin a whole new vocabulary to make his idea clear to the world. Those who are familiar with Freud's theories know all the words that explain them – the *unconscious*, the *ego*, the *id*, the *supergo*, *rationalization*, *Oedipus complex*, and so on. Splitting the atom was once a new idea – anyone familiar with it knew something about *fission*, *isotope*, *radioactive*, *cyclotron*, etc.

Remember this: your vocabulary indicates the alertness and range of your mind. The words you know show the extent of your understanding of what's going on in the world. The size of your vocabulary varies directly with the degree to which you are growing intellectually.

You have covered so far in this book several hundred words. Having learned these words, you have begun to think of an equal number of new ideas. A new word is not just another pattern of syllables with which to clutter up your mind – a new word is a new idea to help you think, to help you understand the thoughts of others, to help you express your own thoughts, to help you live a richer intellectual life.

Realizing these facts, you may become impatient. You will begin to doubt that a book like this can cover all the ideas that an alert and intellectually mature adult wishes to be acquainted with. Your doubt is well-founded.

One of the chief purposes of this book is to get you started, to give you enough of a push so that you will begin to gather momentum, to stimulate you enough so that you will want to start gathering your own ideas.

Where can you gather them? From good books on new topics.

How can you gather them? By reading on a wide range of new subjects.

Reference has repeatedly been made to psychology, psychiatry, and psychoanalysis in these pages. If your curiosity has been aroused by these references, here is a good place to start. In these fields there is a tremendous and exciting literature – and you can read as widely and as deeply as you wish.

(End of Session 13)

How to avoid being a purist

Life, as you no doubt realize, is complicated enough these days. Yet puristic textbooks and English teachers with puristic ideas are striving to make it still more complicated. Their contribution to the complexity of modern living is the repeated claim that many of the natural, carefree, and popular expressions that most of us use every day are 'bad English', 'incorrect grammar', 'vulgar', or 'illiterate'.

In truth, many of the former restrictions and 'thou shalt nots' of academic grammar are now outmoded.

Students in my grammar classes are somewhat nonplussed when they discover that correctness is not determined by textbook rules and cannot be enforced by school-teacher edict. They invariably ask: 'Aren't you going to draw the line somewhere?'

It is neither necessary nor possible for any one person to 'draw the line'. That is done — and quite effectively — by the people themselves, by the millions of educated people throughout the nation.

Of course certain expressions may be considered 'incorrect' or 'illiterate' or 'bad grammar' — not because they violate puristic rules, but only because they are rarely, if ever, used by educated speakers.

Correctness, in short, is determined by current educated usage.

The following notes on current trends in modern usage are intended to help you come to a decision about certain controversial expressions. As you read each sentence, pay particular attention to the italicized word or words. Does the usage square with your own language patterns? Would you be willing to phrase your thoughts in such terms? Decide whether the sentence is 'right' or 'wrong', then compare your conclusions with the opinions given after the test.

Test yourself

1. Let's not walk any *further* right now.   RIGHT   WRONG
2. Some people admit that their   RIGHT   WRONG
   principle goal in life is to become
   wealthy.
3. What a *nice* thing to say!   RIGHT   WRONG
4. He's *pretty* sick today.   RIGHT   WRONG
5. I feel *awfully* sick.   RIGHT   WRONG
6. Are you going to invite Doris and *I*   RIGHT   WRONG
   to your party?

1. Let's not walk any *further* right now.

RIGHT. In the nineteenth century, when professional grammarians attempted to Latinize English grammar, an artificial distinction was drawn between *farther* and *further*, to wit: *farther* refers to space, *further* means *to a greater extent* or *additional*. Today, as a result, many teachers who are still under the forbidding influence of nineteenth-century restrictions insist that it is incorrect to use one word for the other.

To check on current attitudes towards this distinction, I sent the test sentence above to a number of dictionary editors, authors, and professors of English, requesting their opinion of the acceptability of *further* in reference to actual distance. Sixty out of eighty-seven professors, over two-thirds of those responding, accepted the usage without qualification. Of twelve dictionary editors, eleven accepted *further*, and in the case of the authors, thirteen out of twenty-three accepted the word as used. The conclusion to be drawn from this is, as applied to spatial distance, *further* and *farther* are interchangeable.

2. Some people admit that their *principle* goal in life is to become wealthy.

WRONG. In speech, you can get *principal* and *principle* confused as often as you like, and no one will ever know the difference – both words are pronounced identically. In writing, however, your spelling will give you away.

There is a simple memory trick that will help you if you get into trouble with these two words. *Rule* and *principle* both end in *-le-* and a princip*le* is a ru*le*. On the other hand, *principal* contains an *a*, and so does *main* – and princip*al* means m*ain*. Get these points straight and your confusion is over.

Heads of schools are called *principals*, because they are the *main* person in that institution of learning. The money you have invested in the bank is your *principal*, your *main* financial assets. And the stars of a play are *principals* – the *main* actors.

Thus, 'Some people admit that their *principal* (main) goal in life is to become wealthy', but 'Such a *principle* (rule) is not guaranteed to lead to happiness'.

3. What a *nice* thing to say!

RIGHT. Purists object to the popular use of *nice* as a synonym for *pleasant, agreeable*, or *delightful*. They wish to restrict the word to its older and more erudite meaning of *exact* or *subtle*. You will be happy to hear that they aren't getting anywhere.

When I polled a group of well-known authors on the acceptability in everyday speech of the popular meaning of *nice*, their opinions were unanimous; not a single dissenting voice, out of the twenty-three authors who answered, was raised against the usage.

Editors of magazines and newspapers questioned on the same point were just a shade more conservative. Sixty out of sixty-nine accepted the usage. One editor commented: 'I think we do not have to be nice about *nice* any longer. No one can eradicate it from popular speech as a synonym for *pleasant*, or *enjoyable*, or *kind*, or *courteous*. It is a workhorse of the vocabulary, and properly so.'

The only valid objection to the word is that it is *overworked* by some people, but this shows a weakness in vocabulary rather than in grammar.

As in the famous story of the editor who said to her secretary: 'There are two words I wish you would stop using so much. One is "nice" and the other is "lousy".'

'Okay,' said the secretary, who was eager to please. 'What are they?'

4. He's *pretty* sick today.

RIGHT. One of the purist's pet targets of attack is the word *pretty* as used in the sentence under discussion. Yet all modern dictionaries accept such use of *pretty* as established English.

5. I feel *awfully* sick.

RIGHT. Dictionaries accept this usage in informal speech.

The great popularity of *awfully* in educated speech is no doubt due to the strong and unique emphasis that the word gives to an adjective – substitute, *very*, *extremely*, or *severely* and you considerably weaken the force.

On the other hand, it is somewhat less than cultivated to say 'I feel *awful* sick', and the wisdom of using *awfully* to intensify a *pleasant* concept ('What an *awfully* pretty child'; 'That book is *awfully* interesting') is perhaps still debatable, though getting less and less so as the years go on.

6. Are you going to invite Doris and *I* to your party?

WRONG. Some people are almost irresistibly drawn to the pronoun *I* in constructions like this one. However, not only does such use of *I* violate a valid and useful grammatical principle, but, more important, it is rarely heard in educated speech. The meaning of the sentence is equally clear no matter which form of the pronoun is employed, of course, but the use of *I*, the less popular choice, may stigmatize the speaker as uneducated.

Consider it this way: You would normally say, 'Are you going to invite *me* to your party?' It would be wiser, therefore, to say, 'Are you going to invite Doris and *me* to your party?

7

HOW TO TALK ABOUT LIARS AND LYING

(Sessions 14—17)

Teaser preview

What kind of liar are you if you:

- *have developed a reputation for falsehood?*
- *are particularly skilful?*
- *cannot be reformed?*
- *have become habituated to your vice?*
- *started to lie from the moment of your birth?*
- *always lie?*
- *cannot distinguish fact from fancy?*
- *suffer no pangs of conscience?*
- *are suspiciously smooth and fluent in your lying?*
- *tell vicious lies?*

Session 14

It was the famous Greek philosopher and cynic Diogenes who went around the streets of Athens, lantern in hand, looking for an honest person.

This was over two thousand years ago, but I presume that Diogenes would have as little success in his search today. Lying seems to be an integral weakness of mortal character – I doubt that few human beings would be so brash as to claim that they have never in their lives told at least a partial untruth. Indeed, one philologist goes as far as to theorize that language must have been invented for the sole purpose of deception. Perhaps so. It is certainly true that animals seem somewhat more honest than humans, maybe because they are less gifted mentally.

Why do people lie? To increase their sense of importance, to escape punishment, to gain an end that would otherwise be denied them, out of long-standing habit, or sometimes because they actually do not know the difference between fact and fancy. These are the common reasons for falsification. No doubt there are other, more unusual, motives that impel people to distort the truth. And, to come right down to it, can we always be certain what is true and what is false?

If lying is a prevalent and all-too-human phenomenon, there would of course be a number of interesting words to describe different types of liars.

Let us pretend (not to get personal, but only to help you become personally involved in the ideas and words) that you are a liar.

The question is, what kind of liar *are* you?

Ideas

1.   You don't fool even some of the people

Everybody knows your propensity for avoiding facts. You have built so solid and unsavoury a reputation that only a stranger is likely to be misled – and then, not for long.
     A *notorious* liar

2.   To the highest summits of artistry

Your ability is top drawer – rarely does anyone lie as convincingly or as artistically as you do. Your skill has, in short, reached the zenith of perfection. Indeed, your mastery of the art is so great that your lying is almost always crowned with success – and you have no trouble seducing an unwary listener into believing that you are telling gospel truth.
     A *consummate* liar

3.   Beyond redemption or salvation

You are impervious to correction. Often as you may be caught in your fabrications, there is no reforming you – you go right on lying despite the punishment, embarrassment, or unhappiness that your distortions of truth may bring upon you.
     An *incorrigible* liar

4.   Too old to learn new tricks

You are the victim of firmly fixed and deep-rooted habits. Telling untruths is as frequent and customary an activity as brushing your teeth in the morning, or having toast and coffee for breakfast, or lighting up a cigarette after dinner (if you are a smoker). And almost as reflexive.
     An *inveterate* liar

5.   An early start

You have such a long history of persistent falsification that one can only suspect that your vice started when you were reposing in your mother's womb. In other words, and allowing for a great deal of exaggeration for effect, you have been lying from the moment of your birth.

A *congenital* liar

6.   No let-up

You never stop lying. While normal people lie on occasion, and often for special reasons, you lie continually – not occasionally or even frequently, but over and over.

A *chronic* liar

7.   A strange disease

You are not concerned with the difference between truth and falsehood; you do not bother to distinguish fact from fantasy. In fact, your lying is a disease that no antibiotic can cure.

A *pathological* liar

8.   No regrets

You are completely without a conscience. No matter what misery your fabrications may cause your innocent victims, you never feel the slightest twinge of guilt. Totally unscrupulous, you are a dangerous person to get mixed up with.

An *unconscionable* liar

9.   Smooth!

Possessed of a lively imagination and a ready tongue, you can distort facts as smoothly and as effortlessly as you can say your name. But you do not always get away with your lies.

Ironically enough, it is your very smoothness that makes you suspect: your answers are too quick to be true. Even if we can't immediately catch you in your lies, we have learned from unhappy past experience not to suspend our critical faculties when you are talking. We admire your nimble wit, but we listen with a sceptical ear.

A *glib* liar

10.   Outstanding!

Lies, after all, are bad – they are frequently injurious to other people, and may have a particularly dangerous effect on you as a liar. At best, if you are caught you suffer some embarrassment. At worst, if you succeed in your deception your character becomes warped and your sense of values suffers. Almost all lies are harmful; some are no less than vicious.

If you are one type of liar, *all* your lies are vicious – calculatedly, predeterminedly, coldly, and advisedly vicious. In short, your lies are so outstandingly hurtful that people gasp in amazement and disgust at hearing them.

                    An *egregious* liar

In this chapter the ten basic words revolve rather closely around a central core. Each one, however, has a distinct, a unique meaning, a special implication. Note the differences.

Type of Liar	Special Implication
1. *notorious*	*famous* – or *infamous* – for lying; tendency to falsify is *well-known*
2. *consummate*	*great skill*
3. *incorrigible*	too far gone to be *reformed* – *impervious to rehabilitation*
4. *inveterate*	lying has become a *deep-rooted habit*
5. *congenital*	lying had *very early beginnings* – as if *from birth*
6. *chronic*	*over and over*
7. *pathological*	an irresistible *compulsion* to lie – often for no rational reason; lying is a *disease*
8. *unconscionable*	*lack of regret or remorse*
9. *glib*	great *smoothness*
10. *egregious*	*viciousness* of the lies

These ten expressive adjectives, needless to say, are not restricted to lying or liars. Note their general meanings:

1. *notorious*	well-known for some bad quality – a *notorious* philanderer
2. *consummate*	perfect, highly skilled – *consummate* artistry at the keyboard

3. *incorrigible*	beyond reform – an *incorrigible* optimist
4. *inveterate*	long-accustomed, deeply habituated – an *inveterate* smoker (this adjective, like *notorious*, usually has an unfavourable connotation)
5. *congenital*	happening at or during birth – a *congenital* deformity
6. *chronic*	going on for a long time, or occurring again and again – *chronic* appendicitis
7. *pathological*	diseased – a *pathological* condition
8. *unconscionable*	without pangs of conscience – *unconscionable* cruelty to children
9. *glib*	smooth, suspiciously fluent – a *glib* witness
10. *egregious*	outstandingly bad or vicious – *egregious* error

With the exception of *consummate* and *congenital*, all ten adjectives have strongly derogatory implications and are generally used to describe people, characteristics, or conditons we disapprove of.

Using the words

Can you pronounce the words? (I)

1.	*notorious*	nō-TAW'-ri-əs
2.	*consummate*	kən-SUM'-ət *or* KON'-sə-mət
3.	*incorrigible*	in-KOR'-i-jə-bəl
4.	*inveterate*	in-VET'-ə-rət
5.	*congenital*	kən-JEN'-i-təl
6.	*chronic*	KRON'-ik
7.	*pathological*	path'-ə-LOJ'-i-kəl
8.	*unconscionable*	un-KON'-shə-nə-bəl
9.	*glib*	GLIB
10.	*egregious*	i-GREE'-jəs

Can you work with the words?

1.	notorious	a.	beyond reform
2.	consummate	b.	continuing over a long period of time; recurring
3.	incorrigible	c.	diseased
4.	inveterate	d.	from long-standing habit
5.	congenital	e.	suspiciously smooth
6.	chronic	f.	without conscience or scruples
7.	pathological	g.	outstandingly bad or vicious
8.	unconscionable	h.	unfavourably known
9.	glib	i.	from birth
10.	egregious	j.	finished, perfect, artistic

Key: 1–h, 2–j, 3–a, 4–d, 5–i, 6–b, 7–c, 8–f, 9–e, 10–g

Do you understand the words?

1. Do people become *notorious* for good acts?	YES	NO
2. Is Beethoven considered a *consummate* musical genius?	YES	NO
3. If a criminal is truly *incorrigible*, is there any point in attempting rehabilitation?	YES	NO
4. Does an *inveterate* smoker smoke only occasionally?	YES	NO
5. Is a *congenital* deformity one that occurs late in life?	YES	NO
6. Is a *chronic* invalid ill much of the time?	YES	NO
7. Is a *pathological* condition normal and healthy?	YES	NO
8. If a person commits an *unconscionable* act of cruelty, is there any regret, remorse, or guilt?	YES	NO
9. Is a *glib* talker awkward and hesitant in speech?	YES	NO
10. Is an *egregious* error very bad?	YES	NO

Key: 1–no, 2–yes, 3–no, 4–no, 5–no, 6–yes, 7–no, 8–no, 9–no, 10–yes

Can you recall the words?

1. outstandingly vicious; so bad as to be in a class by itself
2. starting at birth
3. happening over and over again; continuing for a long time
4. widely and unfavourably known (as for antisocial acts, character weakness, immoral or unethical behaviour, etc.)
5. beyond correction
6. smooth and persuasive; unusually, almost suspiciously, fluent
7. long addicted to a habit
8. perfect in the practice of an art; extremely skilful
9. unscrupulous; entirely without conscience
10. diseased

1. E_____
2. C_____
3. C_____
4. N_____
5. I_____
6. G_____
7. I_____
8. C_____
9. U_____
10. P_____

Key: 1–egregious, 2–congenital, 3–chronic, 4–notorious, 5–incorrigible, 6–glib, 7–inveterate, 8–consummate, 9–unconscionable, 10–pathological

Can you use the words?

As a result of the tests you are taking, you are becoming more and more familiar with these ten valuable and expressive words. Now, as a further check on your learning, write the word that best fits each blank.

1. This person has gambled, day in and day out, for as long as anyone can remember – gambling has become a deep-rooted habit.
1. An _____ gambler

2. Born with a clubfoot.

2. A _____ deformity

3. Someone known the world over for criminal acts.
3. A _____ criminal

4. An invading army kills, maims, and tortures without mercy, compunction, or regret.
4. _____ acts of cruelty

5. The suspect answers the detective's questions easily, fluently, almost too smoothly.
5. _____ responses

6. A person reaches the acme of perfection as an actress or actor.

6. A _____ performer

7. No one can change someone's absurdly romantic attitude towards life.

7. An _____ romantic

8. A mistake so bad that it defies description.

8. An _____ blunder

9. Drunk almost all the time, again and again and again periods of sobriety are few and very, very far between.

9. A _____ alcoholic

10. Doctors find a persistent, dangerous infection in the bladder.

10. A _____ condition

Key: 1–inveterate, 2–congenital, 3–notorious, 4–uncon-
       scionable, 5–glib, 6–consummate, 7–incorrigible,
       8–egregious, 9–chronic, 10–pathological

(End of Session 14)

Session 15

Origins and related words

1. Well-known

'Widely but unfavourably known' is the common definition for
notorious. Just as a *notorious* liar is well-known for unreliable statements, so a *notorious* gambler, a *notorious* thief, or a *notorious* killer
has achieved a wide reputation for some form of antisocial behaviour. The noun is *notoriety* (nō-tə-EĪ'-ə-ti).

The derivation is from Latin *notus*, known, from which we also
get *noted*. It is an interesting characteristic of some words that a
change of syllables can alter the emotional impact. Thus, an ad-
mirer of certain business executives will speak of them as '*noted*
industrialists'; these same people's enemies will call them '*notorious*
exploiters'. Similarly, if we admire a man's or a woman's unworldliness, we refer to it by the complimentary term *childlike*; but if we
are annoyed by the trait, we describe it, derogatively, as *childish*.
Change '-like' to '-ish' and our emotional tone undergoes a complete reversal.

2. Plenty of room at the top

The top of a mountain is called, as you know, the *summit*, a word
derived from Latin *summus*, highest, which also gives us the
mathematical term *sum*, as in addition. A *consummate* artist has
reached the very highest point of perfection; and to *consummate*
(KON'-sə-mayt') a marriage, a business deal, or a contract is, ety-

mologically, to bring it to the highest point; that is, to put the final touches to it, to bring it to completion.

[Note how differently *consummate* (kən-SUM'-ət *or* KON'-sə-mət), the adjective, can be pronounced, compared with the verb to *cosummate* (KON'-sə-mayt').]

Nouns are formed from adjectives by the addition of the noun suffix *-ness: sweet — sweetness; simple — simpleness; envious — envious-ness;* etc.

Many adjectives, however, have alternate noun forms, and the adjective *consummate* is one of them. To make a noun out of *consummate*, add either *-ness* or *-acy; consummateness* (kən-SUM'-ət-nəs) or *consummacy* (kən-SUM'-ə-si).

Verbs ending in *-ate* invariably tack on the noun suffix *-ion* to form nouns: *create — creation; evaluate — evaluation;* etc.

Can you write the noun form of the verb to *consummate*?

---

3.   No help

Call people *incorrigible* (in-KOR'-i-jə-bəl) if they do anything to excess, and if all efforts to correct or reform them are to no avail. Thus, one can be an *incorrigible* idealist, an *incorrigible* criminal, an *incorrigible* optimist, or an *incorrigible* philanderer. The word derives from Latin *corrigo,* to correct or set straight, plus the negative prefix *in-*. (This prefix, depending on the root it precedes, may be negative, may intensify the root, as in *invaluable,* or may mean *in*.)

The noun is *incorrigibility* (in-kor'-i-jə-BIL'-ə-ti) or, alternatively, *incorrigibleness.*

4.   Veterans

Inveterate, from Latin *vetus,* old,* generally indicates disapproval.

Inveterate gamblers have grown old in the habit, etymologically speaking; *inveterate* drinkers have been imbibing for so long that they, too, have formed old, well-established habits; and *inveterate* liars have been lying for so long, and their habits are by now so deep-rooted, that one can scarcely remember (the word implies) when they ever told the truth.

---

* Latin *senex,* source of *senile* and *senescent,* also, you will recall, means *old.* In *inveterate, in-* means *in*; it is not the negative prefix found in *incorrigible.*

The noun is *inveteracy* (in-VET'-ər-ə-si) or *inveterateness*.

A *veteran* (VET'-ə-rən), as of the Armed Forces, grew older serving the country; otherwise a *veteran* is an old hand at the game (and therefore skilful). The word is both a noun and an adjective: a *veteran* at (or in) swimming, tennis, police work, business, negotiations, diplomacy — or a *veteran* actor, teacher, diplomat, political reformer.

5.   Birth

Greek *genesis*, birth or origin, a root we discovered in discussing *psychogenic* (Chapter 5), is the source of a great many English words.

Genetics (jə-NET'-iks) is the science that deals with the transmission of hereditary characteristics from parents to offspring. The scientist specializing in the field is a *geneticist* (jə-NET'-i-sist), the adjective is *genetic* (jə-NET'-ik). The particle carried on the chromosome of the germ cell containing a hereditary characteristic is a *gene* (JEEN).

Genealogy (jeen'-i-AL'-ə-ji) is the study of family trees or ancestral origins (*logos*, study). The practitioner is a *genealogist* (jeen'-i-AL'-ə-jist). Can you form the adjective? _____
_____. (And can you pronounce it?)

The *genital* (JEN'-i-təl), or sexual, organs are involved in the process of conception and birth. The *genesis* (JEN'-ə-sis) of anything — a plan, idea, thought, career, etc. — is its beginning, birth, or origin, and *Genesis*, the first book of the Old Testament, describes the creation, or birth, of the universe.

Congenital is constructed by combining the prefix *con-*, with or together, and the root *genesis*, birth.

So a *congenital* defect, deformity, etc. occurs during the nine-month birth process (or period of gestation, to become technical). *Hereditary* (hi-RED'-i-ter'-i) characteristics, on the other hand, are acquired at the moment of conception. Thus, eye colour, nose shape, hair texture, and other such qualities are *hereditary*; they are determined by the *genes* in the germ cells of the mother and father. But a thalidomide baby resulted from the use of the drug by a pregnant woman, so the deformities were *congenital*.

Congenital is used both literally and figuratively. Literally, the word generally refers to some medical deformity or abnormality occurring during gestation. Figuratively, it wildly exaggerates, for effect, the very early existence of some quality: *congenital* liar, *congenital* fear of the dark, etc.

Review of etymology

Prefix, Root	Meaning	English Word
1. *notus*	known	_____
2. *summus*	highest	_____
3. *corrigo*	to correct, set straight	_____
4. *vetus*	old	_____
5. *senex*	old	_____
6. *genesis*	birth, origin	_____
7. *logos*	science, study	_____
8. *in-*	negative prefix	_____

Using the Words

Can you pronounce the words? (I)

1. *notoriety*	nō-tə-RĪ'-ə-ti
2. *to consummate* (*v.*)	KON'-sə-mayt'
3. *consummacy*	kən-SUM'-ə-si
4. *consummation*	kon'-sə-MAY'-shən
5. *incorrigibility*	in-kor'-i-jə-BIL'-ə-ti
6. *inveteracy*	in-VET'-ə-rə-si
7. *veteran*	VET'-ə-rən
8. *genetics*	jə-NET'-iks
9. *geneticist*	jə-NET'-i-sist
10. *genetic*	jə-NET'-ik
11. *gene*	JEEN
12. *genealogy*	jee'-ni-AL'-ə-ji
13. *genealogist*	jee'-ni-AL'-ə-jist
14. *genealogical*	jee'-ni-ə-LOJ'-i-kəl
15. *genital*	JEN'-i-təl
16. *genesis*	JEN'-ə-sis
17. *hereditary*	hi-RED'-i-ter'-i

Can you work with the words?

1.	notoriety	a.	state of artistic height
2.	to consummate (*v.*)	b.	state of being long established in a habit
3.	consummacy	c.	beginning, origin
4.	incorrigibility	d.	science of heredity
5.	inveteracy	e.	bring to completion
6.	genetics	f.	study of ancestry
7.	genealogy	g.	referring to characteristics passed on to offspring by parents
8.	genital	h.	referring to reproduction, or to the reproductive or sexual organs
9.	genesis	i.	ill fame
10.	hereditary	j.	particle that transmits hereditary characteristics
11.	gene	k.	state of being beyond reform or correction

Key: 1–i, 2–e, 3–a, 4–k, 5–b, 6–d, 7–f, 8–h, 9–c, 10–g, 11–j

Do you understand the words?

1.	Does *notoriety* usually come to perpetrators of mass murders?	YES	NO
2.	Is the product of a *consummately* skilful counterfeiter likely to be taken as genuine?	YES	NO
3.	Is *incorrigibility* in a criminal a sign that rehabilitation is possible?	YES	NO
4.	Is a *geneticist* interested in your parents' characteristics	YES	NO
5.	Does *inveteracy* suggest that a habit is new?	YES	NO
6.	When you *consummate* a deal, do you back out of it?	YES	NO

7. Is a *veteran* actress long experienced at her art?   YES   NO

8. Do *genes* determine heredity?   YES   NO

9. Is a *genealogist* interested in your family origins?   YES   NO

10. Are the *genital* organs used in reproduction?   YES   NO

11. Is the *genesis* of something the final point?   YES   NO

12. Are *hereditary* characteristics derived from parents?   YES   NO

Key: 1–yes, 2–yes, 3–no, 4–yes, 5–no, 6–no, 7–yes, 8–yes, 9–yes, 10–yes, 11–no, 12–yes

Can you recall the words?

1. sexual; reproductive   1. G_____
2. to complete   2. C_____
3. wide and unfavourable reputation   3. N_____
4. particle carried on the chromosome of a cell that transmits a characteristic from parent to offspring   4. G_____
5. completion   5. C_____
6. inability to be reformed   6. I_____
7. the science that deals with the transmission of characteristics from parents to children   7. G_____
8. referring to a quality or characteristic that is inherited (*adj.*)   8. H_____
9. beginning or origin   9. G_____
10. student of family roots or origins   10. G_____
11. height of skill or artistry   11. C_____
    or C_____

12. transmitted by heredity   12. G_____

13. quality of a habit that has   13. I_____
     been established over
     many years

                          or I_____

14. a person long experienced   14. V_____
     at a profession, art, or
     business

15. pertaining to a study of   15. G_____
     family origins (*adj.*)

Key: 1–genital,   2–consummate,   3–notoriety,   4–gene,
        5–consummation, 6–incorrigibility, 7–genetics, 8–he-
        reditary, 9–genesis, 10–genealogist, 11–consummacy *or*
        consummateness, 12–genetic, 13–inveteracy *or* inveter-
        ateness, 14–veteran, 15–genealogical

(End of Session 15)

Session 16

Origins and related words

1.   Of time and place

A *chronic* liar lies constantly, again and again and again; a *chronic* invalid is ill time after time, frequently, repeatedly. The derivation of the word is Greek *chronos*, time. The noun form is *chronicity* (krə-NIS'-ə-ti).

An *anachronism* (ə-NAK'-rə-niz-əm) is someone or something out of time, out of date, belonging to a different era, either earlier or later. (The prefix *ana-* like *a-*, is negative.) The adjective is *anachronous* (ə-NAK'-rə-nəs) or *anachronistic* (ə-nak'-rə-NIS'-tik).

Read a novel in which a scene is supposedly taking place in the nineteenth century and imagine one of the characters turning on a TV set. An *anachronism!*

Your friend talks, thinks, dresses, and acts as if he were living in the time of Shakespeare. Another *anachronism!*

Science fiction is deliberately *anachronous* − it deals with phenomena, gadgetry, accomplishment far off (possibly) in the future.

An *anachronism* is out of *time*; something out of *place* is *incongruous* (in-KONG'-groo-əs), a word combining the negative prefix *in-*, the prefix *con-*, with or together, and a Latin verb meaning to *agree* or *correspond*.

Thus, it is *incongruous* to wear a sweater and slacks to a formal wedding; it is *anachronous* to wear the wasp waist, conspicuous bustle, or powdered wig of the eighteenth century. The noun form of *incongruous* is *incongruity* (in-kəng-GROO'-ə-ti).

Chronological (kron-əl-LOJ'-i-kəl), in correct time order, comes from *chronos*. To tell a story *chronologically* is to relate the events in the time order of their occurrence. *Chronology* (krə-NOL'-ə-ji) is the science of time order and the accurate dating of events (*logos*, science) – the expert in this field is a *chronologist* (krə-NOL'-ə-jist) – or a list of events in the time order in which they have occurred or will occur.

A *chronometer* (krə-NOM'-i-tə), combining *chronos* with *metron*, measurement, is a highly accurate timepiece, especially one used on ships. *Chronometry* (krə-NOM'-ə-tri) is the measurement of time – the adjective is *chronometric* (kron'-ə-MET'-rik).

Add the prefix *syn-*, together, plus the verb suffix *-ize*, to *chronos*, and you have constructed *synchronize* (SIN'-krə-nīz'), etymologically *to time together*, or to move, happen, or cause to happen, at the same time or rate. If you and your friend *synchronize* your watches, you set them at the same time. If you *synchronize* the activity of your arms and legs, as in swimming, you move them at the same time or rate. The adjective is *synchronous* (SIN'-krə-nəs); the noun form of the verb *synchronize* is *synchronization* (sin'-krə-nī-ZAY'-shən).

2.   Disease, suffering, feeling

Pathological is *diseased* (a *pathological* condition) – this meaning of the word ignores the root *logos*, science, study.

Pathology (pə-THOL'-ə-ji) is the science or study of disease – its nature, cause, cure, etc. However, another meaning of the noun ignores *logos*, and *pathology* may be any morbid, diseased, or abnormal physical condition or conditions; in short, simply *disease*, as in 'This case involves so many kinds of *pathology* that several different specialists are working on it.'

A *pathologist* (pə-THOL'-ə-jist) is an expert who examines tissue, often by autopsy or biopsy, to diagnose disease and interpret the abnormalities in such tissue that may be caused by specific diseases.

Pathos occurs in some English words with the additional meaning of *feeling*. If you feel or suffer with someone, you are *sympathetic* (sim-pə-THET'-ik) – *sym-* is a respelling before the letter *p* of the Greek prefix *syn-*, with or together. The noun is *sympathy* (SIM'-pə-thi), the verb *sympathize* (SIM'-pə-thīz). Husbands, for example, so the story goes, may have *sympathetic* labour pains when their wives are about to deliver.

The prefix *anti-*, you will recall, means *against*. If you experience *antipathy* (an-TIP'-ə-thi) to people or things, you feel *against* them – you feel strong dislike or hostility. The adjective is *antipathetic* (an'-ti-pə-THET'-ik), as in 'an *antipathetic* reaction to an authority figure'.

But you may have *no* feeling at all – just indifference, lack of any interest, emotion, or response, complete listlessness, especially when some reaction is normal or expected. Then you are *apathetic* (ap-ə-THET'-ik); *a-*, as you know, is a negative prefix. The noun is *apathy* (AP'-ə-thi), as in voter *apathy*, student *apathy*, etc.

On the other hand, you may be so sensitive or perceptive that you do not only share the feelings of another, but you also *identify* with those feelings, in fact experience them yourself as if momentarily you were that other person. What you have, then, is *empathy* (EM'-pə-thi); you *empathize* (EM'-pə-thīz), you are *empathetic* (em-pə-THET'-ik), or, to use an alternate adjective, *empathic* (em-PATH'-ik). *Em-* is a respelling before the letter *p* of the Greek prefix *en-*, in.

Someone is *pathetic* (pə-THET'-ik) who is obviously suffering – such a person may arouse sympathy or pity (or perhaps *antipathy*?) in you. A *pathetic* story is about suffering and, again, is likely to arouse sadness, sorrow, or pity.

What makes it possible for two people separated by miles of space to communicate with each other without recourse to messenger, telephone, telegraph, or postal service? It can be done, say the believers in *telepathy* (tə-LEP'-ə-thi), also called *mental telepathy*, though they do not yet admit to knowing how. How can one person read the mind of another? Simple – by being *telepathic* (tel-i-PATH'-ik), but no one can explain the chemistry or biology of it. *Telepathy* is built by combining *pathos*, feeling, with the prefix *tele-*, distance, the same prefix we found in *telephone*, *telegraph*, *telescope*.

Telepathic communication occurs when people can feel each other's thoughts from a distance, when they have ESP.

Review of etymology

Prefix, Root, Suffix	Meaning	English Word
1. *chronos*	time	_____

2. *ana-, a-*	negative prefix	_____
3. *con-*	with, together	_____
4. *in-*	negative prefix	_____
5. *logos*	science, study	_____
6. *metron*	measurement	_____
7. *syn-, sym-*	with, together	_____
8. *-ize*	verb suffix	_____
9. *pathos*	disease, suffering, feeling	_____
10. *anti-*	against	_____
11. *en-, em-*	in	_____
12. *tele-*	distance	_____

Using the words

Can you pronounce the words? (I)

1. *chronicity*	krə-NIS'-ə-ti
2. *anachronism*	ə-NAK'-rə-niz-əm
3. *anachronous*	ə-NAK'-rə-nəs
4. *anachronistic*	ə-nak'-rə-NIS'-tik
5. *incongruous*	in-KONG'-groo-əs
6. *incongruity*	in'-kəng-GROO'-ə-ti
7. *chronological*	kron'-ə-LOJ'-i-kəl
8. *chronology*	krə-NOL'-ə-ji
9. *chronologist*	krə-NOL'-ə-jist
10. *chronometer*	krə-NOM'-i-tə
11. *chronometry*	krə-NOM'-ə-tri
12. *chronometric*	kron'-ə-MET'-rik
13. *synchronize*	SIN'-krə-nīz'
14. *synchronization*	sin'-krə-nī-ZAY'-shən
15. *synchronous*	SIN'-krə-nəs

Can you pronounce the words? (II)

1. *pathology*	pə-THOL'-ə-ji
2. *pathologist*	pə-THOL'-ə-jist
3. *sympathy*	SIM'-pə-thi
4. *sympathetic*	sim-pə-THET'-ik

5. *sympathize*   SIM'-pə-thīz
6. *antipathy*   an-TIP'-ə-thi
7. *antipathetic*   an'-ti-pə-THET'-ik
8. *apathy*   AP'-ə-thi
9. *apathetic*   ap-ə-THET'-ik
10. *empathy*   EM'-pə-thi
11. *empathize*   EM'-pə-thīz'
12. *empathetic*   em-pə-THET'-ik
13. *empathic*   em-PATH'-ik
14. *pathetic*   pə-THET'-ik
15. *telepathy*   tə-LEP'-ə-thi
16. *telepathic*   tel'-i-PATH'-ik

Can you work with the words? (I)

1. chronicity
2. anachronism
3. incongruity
4. chronology
5. chronometer
6. chronometry
7. synchronization
8. pathology
9. sympathy
10. telepathy

a. something, or state of being, out of place
b. timepiece; device that measures time very accurately
c. condition of continual or repeated recurrence
d. act of occurring, or of causing to occur, at the same time
e. calendar of events in order of occurrence
f. something, or someone, out of time
g. measurement of time
h. a sharing or understanding of another's feeling
i. ESP; communication from a distance
j. disease; study of disease

Key: 1–c, 2–f, 3–a, 4–e, 5–b, 6–g, 7–d, 8–j, 9–h, 10–i

Can you work with the words? (II)

1.	pathologist	a.	identification with another's feelings
2.	antipathy	b.	share another's feelings so strongly as to experience those feelings oneself
3.	apathy	c.	out of time
4.	empathy	d.	one who examines tissue to diagnose disease
5.	synchronize	e.	occurring at the same time or rate
6.	empathize	f.	relating to extrasensory perception
7.	anachronous	g.	suffering; arousing sympathy or pity
8.	incongruous	h.	lack of feeling; non-responsiveness
9.	synchronous	i.	out of place
10.	pathetic	j.	happen, or cause to happen, at the same time or rate
11.	telepathic	k.	hostility; strong dislike

Key: 1–d, 2–k, 3–h, 4–a, 5–j, 6–b, 7–c, 8–i, 9–e, 10–g, 11–f

Do you understand the words?

1. Are these dates in *chronological* order? 1492, 1941, 1586   YES   NO
2. Is *pathology* the study of healthy tissue?   YES   NO
3. Is *telepathic* communication carried on by telephone?   YES   NO
4. Does a *sympathetic* response show an understanding of another's feelings?   YES   NO
5. Is one *antipathetic* to things, ideas, or people one finds agreeable?   YES   NO
6. Do *apathetic* people react strongly?   YES   NO

7. Does an *empathic* response show identification with the feelings of another?   YES   NO

8. Is a swimsuit *incongruous* attire at a formal ceremony?   YES   NO

9. Is an *anachronistic* attitude up to date?   YES   NO

10. Are *synchronous* movements out of time with one another?   YES   NO

Key: 1—no, 2—no, 3—no, 4—yes, 5—no, 6—no, 7—yes, 8—yes, 9—no, 10—no

Can you recall the words?

1. in order of time	1. C_____
2. out of place	2. I_____
3, 4. out of time (two forms)	3. A_____
	4. A_____
5. something, or state of being, out of place	5. I_____
6. lack of feeling	6. A_____
7. measurer of time	7. C_____
8. study of disease	8. P_____
9. feeling of hostility or dislike	9. A_____
10. to occur, or cause to occur, at the same time or rate	10. S_____
11. evoking sorrow or pity	11. P_____
12. something out of time	12. A_____
13. state of recurring again and again	13. C_____
14. extrasensory perception	14. T_____
15. one who examines tissue to diagnose disease	15. P_____
16. identification with the feelings of another	16. E_____

17. happening at the same   17. S_____
    time or rate (*adj.*)
18. skilful at thought   18. T_____
    transference without
    sensory communication
19. calendar of events in time 19. C_____
    sequence
20. referring to the   20. C_____
    measurement of time
    (*adj.*)

Key: 1–chronological, 2–incongruous, 3, 4–anachronous,
        anachronistic, 5–incongruity, 6–apathy, 7–chronome-
        ter, 8–pathology, 9–antipathy, 10–synchronize, 11–pa-
        thetic, 12–anachronism, 13–chronicity, 14–telepathy,
        15–pathologist, 16–empathy, 17–synchronous, 18–tel-
        epathic, 19–chronology, 20–chronometric

End of Session 16)

Session 17

Origins and related words

1. Knowing

Psychopaths commit antisocial and *unconscionable* acts – they are not troubled by *conscience*, guilt, remorse, etc. over what they have done.

Unconscionable and *conscience* are related in derivation – the first word from Latin *scio*, to know, the second from Latin *sciens*, knowing, and both using the prefix *con-*, with, together.

Etymologically, then, your *conscience* is your knowledge *with* a moral sense of right and wrong; if you are *unconscionable*, your conscience is not (*un-*) working, or you have no conscience. The noun form is *unconscionableness* or *unconscionability* (un-kon'-shə-nə-BIL'-ə-ti).

conscious, also from *con-* plus *scio*, is knowledge or awareness of one's emotions or sensations, or of what's happening around one.

Science, from *sciens*, is systematized *knowledge* as opposed, for example, to belief, faith, intuition, or guesswork.

Add Latin *omnis*, all, to *sciens*, to construct *omniscient* (om-NIS'-si-ənt), all-knowing, possessed of infinite knowledge. The noun is *omniscience* (om-NIS'-si-əns).

Add the prefix *pre-*, before, to *sciens*, to construct *prescient* (PRES'-si-ənt) – knowing about events *before* they occur, i.e., psychic, or possessed of unusual powers of prediction. The noun is *prescience* (PRES'-si-əns).

And, finally, add the negative prefix *ne-* to *sciens* to produce *nescient* (NES'-si-ənt), not knowing, or ignorant. Can you, by anal-

ogy with the previous two words, write the noun form of *nescient*?
_____ (Can you pronounce it?)

2.   Fool some of the people . . .

Glib is from an old English root that means *slippery*. *Glib* liars or *glib* talkers are smooth and slippery; they have ready answers, fluent tongues, a persuasive air – but, such is the implication of the word, they fool only the most *nescient*, for their smoothness lacks sincerity and conviction.

The noun is *glibness* (GLIB'-nəs).

3.   Herds and flocks

Egregious (remember the proncunciation? i-GREE'-jəs) is from Latin *grex, gregis,* herd or flock. An *egregious* lie, act, crime, mistake, etc. is so exceptionally vicious that it conspicuously stands *out* (*e-*, a shortened form of the prefix *ex-,* out) from the *herd* or *flock* of other bad things.

The noun is *egregiousness* (i-GREE'-jəs-nəs).

A person who enjoys companionship, who, etymologically, likes to be with the herd, who reaches out for friends and is happiest when surrounded by people – such a person is *gregarious* (gri-GAIR'-i-əs).

Extroverts are of course *gregarious* – they prefer human contact, conversation, laughter, interrelationships, to solitude.

The suffix *-ness*, as you know, can be added to an adjective to construct a noun form. Write the noun for *gregarious:*
_____.

Add the prefix *con*, with, together, to *grex, gregis,* to get the verb *congregate* (KONG'-gri-gayt'); add the prefix *se-,* apart, to build the verb *segregate* (SEG'-ri-gayt'); add the prefix *ad-,* to, towards (*ad-* changes to *ag-* before a root starting with *g-*), to construct the verb *aggregate* (AG-ri-gayt').

Let's see what we have. When people gather *together* in a *herd* or *flock,* they (write the verb) _____. The noun is *congregation* (con'-gri-GAY'-shən), one of the meanings of which is a religious 'flock'.

Put people or things apart from the *herd,* and you (write the verb) _____ them. Can you construct the

noun   by   adding   the   suitable   noun   suffix?
_____.

Bring individual items to or towards the *herd* or *flock*, and you (write the verb) _____ them. What is the noun form of this verb? _____.

The verb *aggregate* also means *to come together to or towards the herd*, that is, *to gather into a mass or whole*, or by extension, *to total or amount to*. So *aggregate*, another noun form, pronounced AG'-ri-gət, is a group or mass of individuals considered as a whole, a *herd*, or a *flock*, as in the phrase 'people in the *aggregate* . . .'

Review of etymology

Prefix, Root, Suffix	Meaning	English Word
1. *grex, gregis*	herd, flock	_____
2. *e-, ex-*	out	_____
3. *-ness*	noun suffix	_____
4. *con-*	with, together	_____
5. *ad-, ag-*	to, towards	_____
6. *un-*	negative prefix	_____
7. *scio*	to know	_____
8. *sciens*	knowing	_____
9. *omnis*	all	_____
10. *pre*	before	_____
11. *ne-*	negative prefix	_____
12. *se-*	apart	_____
13. *-ion*	noun suffix added to verbs	_____

Using the words

Can you pronounce the words? (I)

1. *unconscionability*	un-kon'-shə-nə-BIL'-ə-ti
2. *omniscient*	om-NIS'-si-ənt
3. *omniscience*	om-NIS'-si-əns
4. *prescient*	PRES'-si-ənt
5. *prescience*	PRES'-si-əns

6. *nescient*   NES'-si-ənt
7. *nescience*   NES'-si-əns
8. *glibness*   GLIB'-nəs
9. *egregiousness*   i-GREE'-jəs-nəs
10. *gregarious*   gri-GAIR'-i-əs
11. *gregariousness*   gri-GAIR'-i-əs-nəs
12. *congregate*   KONG'-gri-gayt'
13. *congregation*   kong'-gri-GAY'shən
14. *segregate*   SEG'-ri-gayt'
15. *segregation*   seg'-ri-GAY'-shən
16. *aggregate* (*v.*)   AG'-ri-gayt
17. *aggregate* (*n.*)   AG'-ri-gət
18. *aggregation*   ag'-ri-GAY'-shən

Can you work with the words?

1. unconscionability
2. omniscience
3. prescience
4. nescience
5. glibness
6. egregiousness
7. gregariousness
8. congregation
9. segregation
10. aggregate (*n.*)

a. ignorance
b. outstanding badness or viciousness
c. religious group; a massing together
d. total; mass; whole
e. exclusion from the herd; a setting apart
f. infinite knowledge
g. friendliness; enjoyment of mixing with people
h. lack of conscience
i. suspiciously smooth fluency
j. foreknowledge

Key: 1–h, 2–f, 3–j, 4–a, 5–i, 6–b, 7–g, 8–c, 9–e, 10–d

Do you understand the words?

1. Is *unconscionability* one of the signs of the psychopath?   YES   NO
2. Can anyone be truly *omniscient*?   YES   NO

3. Does a *prescient* fear indicate some knowledge of the future?   YES   NO
4. Is *nescience* a result of learning?   YES   NO
5. Does *glibness* make someone sound sincere and trustworthy?   YES   NO
6. Is *egregiousness* an admirable quality?   YES   NO
7. Do *gregarious* people enjoy parties?   YES   NO
8. Do spectators *congregate* at sports events?   YES   NO
9. Do we often *segregate* hardened criminals from the rest of society?   YES   NO
10. Is an *aggregation* of problems a whole mass of problems?   YES   NO

Key: 1–yes, 2–no, 3–yes, 4–no, 5–no, 6–no, 7–yes, 8–yes, 9–yes, 10–yes

Can you recall the words?

1. enjoying groups and companionship   1. G_____
2. ignorant   2. N_____
3. state of *not* being held back from antisocial behaviour by one's conscience   3. U_____
                    or U _____
4. having knowledge of an event before it occurs (*adj.*)   4. P_____
5. a religious 'flock'   5. C_____
6. a total, whole, or mass   6. A_____
                    or A_____
7. to separate from the rest   7. S_____
8. suspiciously smooth fluency   8. G_____
9. all-knowing (*adj.*)   9. O_____
10. to come together into a group or mass   10. C_____

Key: 1–gregarious, 2–nescient, 3–unconscionability *or* un-
        conscionableness, 4–prescient, 5–congregation, 6–ag-
        gregate *or* aggregation, 7–segregate, 8–glibness, 9–om-
        niscient, 10–congregate

Chapter review

A.   Do you recognize the words?

1. Highly skilled:
   (a) consummate, (b) inveterate, (c) notorious
2. Beyond reform:
   (a) inveterate, (b) incorrigible, (c) glib
3. Dating from birth:
   (a) inveterate; (b) congenital, (c) psychopathic
4. Outstandingly bad:
   (a) egregious, (b) unconscionable, (c) chronic
5. Science of heredity:
   (a) pathology, (b) genetics, (c) orthopaedics
6. Out of time:
   (a) incongruous, (b) anachronous, (c) synchronous
7. Study of disease:
   (a) pathology, (b) telepathy, (c) antipathy
8. fond of company, friends, group activities, etc.:
   (a) apathetic, (b) gregarious, (c) chronological
9. Indifferent:
   (a) antipathetic, (b) pathetic, (c) apathetic
10. Long accustomed in habit:
    (a) incorrigible, (b) notorious, (c) inveterate
11. Study of family ancestry:
    (a) genealogy, (b) genetics, (c) genesis
12. To complete, finish, top off:
    (a) synchronize, (b) consummate, (c) empathize
13. Accurate timepiece:
    (a) anachronism, (b) chronology, (c) chronometer
14. Identification with the feelings of another:
    (a) sympathy, (b) apathy, (c) empathy

15. thought transference; extrasensory perception:
    (a) telepathy, (b) empathy, (c) omniscience
16. Ignorance:
    (a) omniscience, (b) prescience, (c) nescience
17. to gather into a group:
    (a) congregate, (b) segregate, (c) synchronize

Key: 1–a, 2–b, 3–b, 4–a, 5–b, 6–b, 7–a, 8–b, 9–c, 10–c,
        11–a, 12–b, 13–c, 14–c, 15–a, 16–c, 17–a

B.   Can you recognize roots?

Root	Meanings	Example
1. *notus*	_____	notorious
2. *summus*	_____	summit
3. *corrigo*	_____	incorrigible
4. *vetus*	_____	veteran
5. *senex*	_____	senile
6. *genesis*	_____	congenital
7. *logos*	_____	genealogy
8. *chronos*	_____	chronic
9. *metron*	_____	chronometer
10. *pathos*	_____	pathology
	_____	empathy
11. *grex, gregis*	_____	gregarious
12. *scio*	_____	unconscionable
13. *sciens*	_____	prescience
14. *omnis*	_____	omniscient

Key: 1–known, 2–highest, 3–to correct, set straight, 4–old,
        5–old, 6–birth, 7–science, study, 8–time, 9–measure-
        ment, 10–disease, suffering, feeling, 11–herd, flock,
        12–to know, 13–knowing, 14–all

Teaser questions for the amateur etymologist

1. 'She was one of many *notables* who attended the convention.'
Recognizing that the italicized word is built on the root *notus*, can
you define the noun *notable* in the context of *known*?
_____
_____

2. *Notify* and *notice* derive from the same root. Can you define
these two words, again in the context of *known*? *Notify*:
_____. *Notice*: _____. What do
you suppose the verb suffix *-fy* of *notify* means? (Think also of
simplify, clarify, liquefy, etc.) _____.

3. You are familiar with the roots *chronos* and *graphein*. Suppose
you came across the word *chronograph* in your reading. Can you
make an educated guess as to the meaning? _____
_____
_____.

4. Recognizing the root *genesis* in the verb *generate*, how would
you define the word? _____
_____
_____.

How about *regenerate*? _____
_____
_____.

What do you suppose the prefix *re-* means? _____
_____.

5. Recognizing the root *omnis* in *omnipotent* and *omnipresent*, can
you define the words?
    Omnipotent: _____.
    Omnipresent: _____.
Recalling how we formed a noun from the adjective *omniscient*,
write the noun forms of:
    Omnipotent: _____.
    Omnipresent: _____.

6. Think of the negative prefix in *anachronism*; think next of the
noun *aphrodisiac*. Can you construct a word for *that which reduces or
eliminates sexual desire*? _____.

(Answers in Chapter 18)

Four lasting benefits

You know by now that it is easy to build your vocabulary if you work diligently and intelligently. Diligence is important — to come to the book occasionally is to learn new words and ideas in an aimless fashion, rather than in the continuous way that characterizes the natural, uninterrupted, intellectual growth of a child. (You will recall that children are experts in increasing their vocabularies.) And an intelligent approach is crucial — new words can be completely understood and permanently remembered only as symbols of vital ideas, never if memorized in long lists of isolated forms.

If you have worked diligently and intelligently, you have done much more than merely learned a few hundred new words. Actually, I needn't tell you what else you've accomplished, since, if you really have accomplished it, you can feel it for yourself; but it may be useful if I clarify the feelings you may have.

In addition to learning the meanings, pronunciation, background, and use of 300–350 valuable words, you have:

1. *Begun to sense a change in your intellectual atmosphere.* (You have begun to do your thinking with many of the words, with many of the ideas behind the words. You have begun to use the words in your speech and writing, and have become alert to their appearance in your reading.)

2. *Begun to develop a new interest in words as expressions of ideas.*

3. *Begun to be aware of the new words you hear and that you see in your reading.*

4. *Begun to gain a new feeling for the relationship between words.* (For you realize that many words are built on roots from other languages and are related to other words which derive from the same roots.)

Now, suppose we pause to see how successful your learning has been.

In the next chapter, I offer you a comprehensive test on the first part of your work.

(End of Session 17)

8

HOW TO CHECK YOUR PROGRESS

Comprehensive Test I

Session 18

If you have worked diligently thus far, you have:
1. Become acquainted, or perhaps reacquainted, with approximately 300–350 expressive words –
2. Learned scores of important Latin and Greek prefixes, roots, and suffixes –
3. Set up valuable habits of self-discipline and self-directed learnings –
4. Explored your attitudes towards grammar and current usage, meanwhile erasing any confusion you may once have felt about specific problems of correctness in your use of words –
5. And, finally, taken good, long steps towards your ultimate goal, namely, the development of a better, richer, more expressive – in short, *superior* – vocabulary.

Here is your chance both to review and to check your learning. (Bear in mind that without careful and periodic review, a significant amount of learning is lost.)

Methods of scoring your achievement on this test, and the meaning of your results, will be explained at the end of the chapter.

I   Etymology

Root	Meaning	Example
1. *ego*	———————	egoism
2. *misein*	———————	misanthrope
3. *gamos*	———————	bigamy
4. *gyne*	———————	gynaecology
5. *derma*	———————	dermatology
6. *orthos*	———————	orthodontics
7. *psyche*	———————	psychotic
8. *neuron*	———————	neurology
9. *logos*	———————	biology
10. *bios*	———————	biopsy
11. *opsis, optikos*	———————	autopsy, optical
12. *algos*	———————	neuralgia
13. *agogos*	———————	demagogue
14. *pedis*	———————	pedestrian
15. *paidos (paed-)*	———————	paediatrician
16. *demos*	———————	democracy
17. *oculus*	———————	ocular
18. *iatreia*	———————	psychiatry
19. *metron*	———————	optometrist
20. *geras*	———————	geriatrics
21. *soma*	———————	psychosomatic
22. *pathos*	———————	osteopath
23. *odontos*	———————	exodontist
24. *pous, podos*	———————	octopus, podium
25. *cheir (chiro-)*	———————	chirography

II   More etymology

Root	Meaning	Example
1. *graphein*	———————	graphology

2.	*kallos*	_____	calligrapher
3.	*pyge*	_____	callipygian
4.	*kakos*	_____	cacophony
5.	*senex*	_____	senescent
6.	*anthropos*	_____	anthropology
7.	*astron*	_____	astronomy
8.	*nautes*	_____	astronaut
9.	*ge (geo-)*	_____	geology
10.	*zoion*	_____	zodiac
11.	*lingua*	_____	bilingual
12.	*philein*	_____	philanthropy
13.	*biblion*	_____	bibliophile
14.	*autos*	_____	autonomous
15.	*socius*	_____	asocial
16.	*notus*	_____	notorious
17.	*summus*	_____	consummate
18.	*vetus*	_____	inveterate
19.	*genesis*	_____	congenital
20.	*chronos*	_____	chronic
21.	*pathos*	_____	empathy
22.	*grex, gregis*	_____	egregious
23.	*sciens*	_____	prescient
24.	*omnis*	_____	omniscient
25.	*nomos*	_____	metronome

III   Same or opposite

1.	egoistic – altruistic	*Same*	*Opposite*
2.	misnathropic – philanthropic	*Same*	*Opposite*
3.	misogamous – polygamous	*Same*	*Opposite*
4.	dexterous – skilful	*Same*	*Opposite*
5.	sinister – threatening	*Same*	*Opposite*
6.	optical – visual	*Same*	*Opposite*
7.	notorious – infamous	*Same*	*Opposite*
8.	consummate (*adj.*) – unskilled	*Same*	*Opposite*
9.	chronic – acute	*Same*	*Opposite*
10.	glib-halting	*Same*	*Opposite*
11.	ophthalmologist – oculist	*Same*	*Opposite*
12.	geriatric – paediatric	*Same*	*Opposite*
13.	endodontist – exodontist	*Same*	*Opposite*

14.	calligraphy – cacography	*Same*	*Opposite*
15.	astronaut – cosmonaut	*Same*	*Opposite*
16.	biopsy – autopsy	*Same*	*Opposite*
17.	dichotomous – cut in two	*Same*	*Opposite*
18.	congenital – hereditary	*Same*	*Opposite*
19.	veteran – 'old hand'	*Same*	*Opposite*
20.	anachronous – timely	*Same*	*Opposite*

IV   Matching

I		II	
1.	dislikes women	a.	entomologist
2.	is pathologically self-interested	b.	taxidermist
3.	studies the development of the human race	c.	egomaniac
4.	is an expert on insects	d.	bibliophile
5.	collects books	e.	ophthalmologist
6.	mounts and stuffs animal skins	f.	psychopath
7.	is an eye doctor	g.	philologist
8.	is a student of linguistics	h.	anthropologist
9.	has 'split off' from reality	i.	psychotic
10.	commits antisocial acts without guilt or pangs of conscience	j.	misogynist

V   More matching

I		II	
1.	delivers babies	a.	paediatrician
2.	treats female ailments	b.	cardiologist
3.	treats infants	c.	psychiatrist
4.	treats skin diseases	d.	chiropodist
5.	treats skeletal deformities	e.	dermatologist
6.	is a heart specialist	f.	periodontist
7.	treats mental or emotional disturbances	g.	obstetrician
8.	treats disorders of the nervous system	h.	neurologist

9. treats minor ailments of the feet   i.   orthopaedist

10. treats ailments of the gums   j.   gynaecologist

VI   Recall a word

1. ruthless; without conscience   1. U_____

2. suspiciously fluent or smooth   2. G_____

3. outstandingly bad; vicious   3. E_____

4. out of place   4. I_____

5. study of the family tree; speciality of tracing ancestry   5. G_____

6. science of heredity   6. G_____

7. in correct order of time   7. C_____

8. socially awkward   8. G_____

9. record of heart action   9. C_____

10. equally skilful with both the right and left hand   10. A_____

11. doctor who deals with the problems of aging   11. G_____

12. extrasensory perception   12. T_____

13. branch of dentistry specializing in the pulp and root canal   13. E_____

14. blood-pressure apparatus   14. S_____

15. growing old (*adj.*)   15. S_____

16. palm reader   16. C_____

17. that which arouses sexual desire   17. A_____

18. representation of the whole   18. E_____

19. diseased; pertaining to the study of disease (*adj.*)   19. P_____

20. measurement of time   20. C_____

21. hostility; strong dislike; aversion   21. A_____

22. to occur, or cause to occur, at the same time or rate

22. S_____

23. ignorant

23. N_____

24. knowledge of an occurrence beforehand

24. P_____

25. enjoying being with the herd; liking companionship

25. G_____

26. to identify strongly with the feelings of another

26. E_____

27. instrument to measure atmospheric pressure

27. B_____

28. to separate from the herd

28. S_____

29. possessed of shapely buttocks

29. C_____

30. ugly, illegible handwriting

30. C_____

Key: A correct answer counts as one point. Count up your points for each part of the test, then add them together for a total.

I

1—I, self, 2—to hate, 3—marriage, 4—woman, 5—skin, 6—straight, correct, 7—mind, soul, spirit, 8—nerve, 9—science, study, 10—life, 11—view, sight, vision, 12—pain, 13—leading, 14—foot, 15—child, 16—people, 17—eye, 18—medical healing, 19—measurement, 20—old age, 21—body, 22—disease, 23—tooth, 24—foot, 25—hand

    Your score: _____

II

1—to write, 2—beauty, 3—buttock, 4—harsh, ugly, bad, 5—old, 6—mankind, 7—star, 8—sailor, 9—earth, 10—animal, 11—tongue, 12—to love, 13—book. 14—self, 15—companion, 16—known, 17—highest, 18—old, 19—birth (beginning, origin), 20—time, 21—feeling, 22—herd, flock, 23—knowing, 24—all, 25—law, order, arrangement

    Your score: _____

III

1—O, 2—O, 3—O, 4—S, 5—S, 6—S, 7—S, 8—O, 9—O, 10—O, 11—S, 12—O, 13—O, 14—O, 15—S, 16—O, 17—S, 18—O, 19—S, 20—O

Your score: _____

IV

1-j, 2-c, 3-h, 4-a, 5-d, 6-b, 7-e, 8-g, 9-i, 10-f

Your score: _____

V

1-g, 2-j, 3-a, 4-e, 5-i, 6-b, 7-c, 8-h, 9-d, 10-f

Your score: _____

VI

1-unconscionable, 2-glib, 3-egregious, 4-incongruous, 5-gen-ealogy, 6-genetics, 7-chronological, 8-gauche, 9-cardiogram, 10-ambidextrous, 11-geriatrician, 12-telepathy, 13-endodon-tist, 14-sphygmomanometer, 15-senescent, 16-chiromancer, 17-aphrodisiac, 18-epitome, 19-pathological, 20-chronome-try, 21-antipathy, 22-synchronize, 23-nescient, 24-prescience, 25-gregarious, 26-empathize, 27-barometer, 28-segregate, 29-callipygian, 30-cacography

Your score: _____

Your total score: _____

Significance of your total score:

100-120: Masterly work; you are ready to move on.

80- 90: Good work; this review was useful to you.

65- 79: Average work, you're getting a good deal out of your study, but perhaps you should revise thoroughly after each session.

50- 64: Barely acceptable; work harder.

35- 49: Poor; further revision is suggested before you go on.

0- 34: You can do much better if you really try; continue with firmer resolve and more determination.

Part Two

Gaining Increased Momentum

9

HOW TO TALK ABOUT ACTIONS

(Sessions 19–23)

Teaser preview

What verb means to:

- *belittle?*
- *be purposely confusing?*
- *tickle someone's fancy?*
- *flatter fulsomely?*
- *prohibit some food or activity?*
- *make unnecessary?*
- *work against?*
- *spread slander?*
- *give implicit forgiveness for a misdeed?*
- *change hostility to friendliness?*

Session 19

Verbs are incalculably useful to you.

Every sentence you think, say, read, or write contains an implied or expressed verb, for it is the verb that carries the action, the movement, the force of your ideas.

As a young child, you used verbs fairly early.

Your first words, of course, were probably *nouns*, as you identified the things or people around you.

Mama, Dada, doll, baby, bottle, etc. perhaps were the first standard syllables you uttered, for naming concrete things or real persons is the initial step in the development of language.

Soon there came the ability to express *intangible* ideas, and then you began to use simple verbs – *go, stop, stay, want, eat, sleep*, etc.

As you gained maturity, your verbs expressed ideas of greater and greater complexity; as an adult you can describe the most involved actions in a few simple syllables – if you have a good store of useful verbs at your command.

The richer and more extensive your vocabulary of verbs, the more accurately and expressively you can communicate your understanding of actions, reactions, attitudes, and emotions.

Let's be specific.

Ideas

1.   Playing it down

Ready to go back thirty or more years? Consider some post-World War II American political history:

Harry Truman couldn't win the 1948 election. The pollsters said so, the Republicans heartily agreed, even the Democrats, some in high places, believed it. Mr. Truman himself was perhaps the only voter in the country who was not entirely convinced.

His election was no mean accomplishment, thought many people. Pure accident, said others. If one out of twelve voters in a few key states had changed his vote, Harry could have gone back to selling ties, one Republican apologist pointed out. It wasn't anything Truman did, said another; it was what his Republican opponent, Thomas Dewey, didn't do. No credit to Truman, said a third; it was the farmers – or manual workers –or the Republicans who hadn't bothered to vote – or the ingenious miscounting of ballots. No credit to Truman, insisted a fourth; it was the Democrats – it was Republican overconfidence – it was sunspots – it was the Communists – it was the civil service workers who didn't want to lose their cushy jobs.

Anyway Harry didn't accomplish a thing – he was just a victim of good fortune.

What were the apolgoists for Dewey's failure doing?

They were *disparaging* Truman's achivement.

2.   Playing it safe

Of course, Dewey did campaign, in his own way, for the presidency. As the Republican aspirant, he had to take a stand on the controversial Taft-Hartley Act which limited the power and activities of trade unions.

Was he for it? He was for that part of it which was *good*. Naturally, he was against any of the provisions which were *bad*. Was he for it? The answer was *yes* – and also *no*. Take whichever answer you wanted most to hear.

What was Dewey doing?

He was *equivocating*.

3.   Enjoying the little things

Have you every gone through a book that was so good you kept hugging yourself mentally as you read? Have you ever seen a play or film that was so charming that you felt sheer delight as you watched? Or perhaps you have had a portion of lemon meringue pie, light and airy and mildly flavoured, and with a flaky, delicious crust, that was the last word in gustatory enjoyment?

Now notice the examples I have used. I have not spoken of books that grip you emotionally, of plays and films that keep you on the edge of your seat in suspense, or of food that satisfies a ravenous hunger. These would offer quite a different, perhaps more lasting and memorable, type of enjoyment. I have detailed, rather, mental or physical stimuli that excite enjoyably but not too sharply – a delightful novel, a charming play, a delicious dessert.

How do such things affect you?

They *titillate* you.

4.   Hero worship

You know how the teenagers of an earlier generation adored, idolized, and overwhelmed Frank Sinatra, Elvis Presley, the Beatles?

And of course you know how certain people fall all over visiting celebrities – best-selling authors, much publicized artists, or famous entertainers. They show them ingratiating, almost servile attention, worship and flatter them fulsomely.*

How do we say it in a single word?

They *adulate* such celebrities.

5.   Accentuating the negative

What does the doctor say to you if you have low blood sugar? 'No sweets, no pastries, no chocolate cake, no ice cream!', your morale dropping lower and lower as each favourite goody is placed on the forbidden list.

What, in one word, is the doctor doing?

The doctor is *proscribing* harmful items in your diet.

6.   Accentuating the affirmative

You are warm, friendly, enthusiastic, outgoing, easy to please; you are quick to show appreciation, yet accept, without judgment or criticism, the human weaknesses of others.

---

* *Fulsome* (FOOL'-səm) does not mean, despite its apperance, *fully* or *completely*, but rather, *offensive because of excessiveness or insincerity*, often in reference to compliments, praise, admiration, or flattery.

You are a fascinating talker, an even better listener.

You believe in, and practise, honest self-disclosure; you feel comfortable with yourself and therefore with everyone else; and you have a passionate interest in experiencing, in living, in relating to people.

Need you have any fears about making friends? Obviously not.

Your characteristics and temperament *obviate* such fears.

7. Playing it wrong

Theodor Reik, in his penetrating book on psychoanalysis *Listening with the Third Ear*, talks about neurotic people who unconsciously wish to fail. In business interviews they say exactly the wrong words, they do exactly the wrong things, they seem intent (as, *unconsciously*, they actually are) on insuring failure in every possible way, though consciously they are doing their best to court success.

What effect does such a neurotic tendency have?

It *militates* against success.

8. Playing it dirty

'Harry? *He's a closet alcoholic.* Maud? *She's sleeping around* – and her stupid husband doesn't suspect a thing. Bill? *He's embezzling from his own company.* Paul? *He's a child molester.* Tom? You don't know that *he's a notorious wife beater?*'

What is this character doing?

He's maligning everyone.

9. Giving the benefit of any doubt

Do you think it's all right to cheat on your income tax? At least just a little? It's wrong, of course, but doesn't everybody do it?

How do you feel about marital infidelity? Are you inclined to overlook the occasional philandering of the male partner, since, after all, to invent a cliché, men are essentially polygamous by nature?

If your answers are in the affirmative, how are you reacting to such legal or ethical transgressions?

You *condone* them.

10. Changing hostility

Unwittingly you have done something that has aroused anger and resentment in your best friend. You had no desire to hurt him, yet he makes it obvious that he feels pretty bitter about the whole situation. (Perhaps you failed to invite him to a gathering he wanted to come to; or you neglected to consult him before making a decision on a matter in which he felt he should have some say.) His friendship is valuable to you and you wish to restore yourself in his good graces. What do you do?

You try to *placate* him.

Using the words

Can you pronounce the words?

1.	*disparage*	dis-PAR'-ij
2.	*equivocate*	i-KWIV'-ə-kayt'
3.	*titillate*	TIT'-i-layt'
4.	*adulate*	AD'-yoo-layt'
5.	*proscribe*	prō-SKRĪB'
6.	*obviate*	OB'-vi-ayt'
7.	*militate*	MIL'-i-tayt
8.	*malign*	mə-LĪN'
9.	*condone*	kən-DŌN'
10.	*placate*	plə-KAYT'

Can you work with the words?

1.	disparage	a.	flatter lavishly
2.	equivocate	b.	work against
3.	titillate	c.	prohibit
4.	adulate	d.	forgive
5.	proscribe	e.	change hostility to friendliness
6.	obviate	f.	purposely talk in such a way as to be vague and misleading
7.	militate	g.	slander
8.	malign	h.	play down
9.	condone	i.	make unnecessary
10.	placate	j.	tickle; stimulate pleasurably

Key: 1–h, 2–f, 3–j, 4–a, 5–c, 6–i, 7–b, 8–g, 9–d, 10–e

Do you understand the words?

1. Do you normally *disparage* something you admire?	YES	NO
2. Do you *equivocate* if you think it unwise to take a definite stand?	YES	NO
3. Do pleasant things *titillate* you?	YES	NO
4. Do emotionally mature people need constant *adulation?*	YES	NO
5. Is sugar *proscribed* for most diabetics?	YES	NO
6. Does a substantial fortune *obviate* financial fears?	YES	NO
7. Does a worker's inefficiency often *militate* against his keeping his job?	YES	NO
8. Do people enjoy being *maligned?*	YES	NO
9. Do we generally *condone* the faults of those we love?	YES	NO
10. Can you sometimes *placate* a person by apologizing?	YES	NO

Key: 1–no, 2–yes, 3–yes, 4–no, 5–yes, 6–yes, 7–yes, 8–no, 9–yes, 10–yes

Can you use the words?

In this exercise you gain the value of actually writing a new word as an accurate solution to a problem. To think about a word, to say it, to write it, to use it – that is the road to word mastery. Write the verb that best fits each situation.

1. You've been asked to take a stand on a certain issue, but you don't have the courage to be either definitely for or against. You _____.

2. You spread an unpleasant story that you know will blacken someone's reputation.

    You _____ that person.

3. Your friend is justifiably angry – you asked him to go to a party with you, ignored him all evening, and then finally left with someone else. What must you do if you wish to restore the relationship?

    You must try to _____ him.

4. You virtually worship your driving instructor. You express your admiration in lavish flattery; you priase her in such excessive terms that she appears devoid of all human frailty.

    You _____ her.

5. Your weight is soaring, so your doctor warns against high calorie meals, rich desserts, second helpings, etc.

    The doctor _____ these foods.

6. Your child Johnnie has hit the neighbour's child entirely without provocation, you are forced to admit. But after all, you think, tomorrow the other kid will, with equal lack of provocation, probably hit Johnnie.

    You _____ Johnnie's behaviour.

7. When your son, understandly expects praise, mentions the three B's and two A's he earned in his school courses, you respond, callously, 'Is that the best you can do? What stopped you from getting *all* A's?'

    You _____ his accomplishment.

8. You have run out of cash and plan to go to the bank to make a withdrawal; then unexpectedly you discover a twenty-pound note you secreted in your desk drawer months ago.

    Your find _____ a trip to the bank.

9. You are the soul of honesty, but unfortunately, you have a sneaky, thievish, sinister look – and no one ever trusts you.

    Your appearance _____ against you.

10. The centrefold of *Playboy* or *Playgirl* provides a mild and agreeable stimulation.

The centrefold _____ you.

Key: 1–equivocate, 2–malign, 3–placate, 4–adulate, 5–proscribes, 6–condone, 7–disparage, 8–obviates, 9–militates, 10–titillates

Can you recall the words?

1.	change hostility into friendliness	1.	P_____
2.	make unnecessary	2.	O_____
3.	belittle	3.	D_____
4.	overlook or forgive a transgression	4.	C_____
5.	tickle; delight; stimulate pleasurably	5.	T_____
6.	spread malicious rumours about	6.	M_____
7.	purposely use language susceptible of opposite interpretations	7.	E_____
8.	act to disadvantage of	8.	M_____
9.	forbid	9.	P_____
10.	worship; flatter fulsomely	10.	A_____

Key: 1–placate, 2–obviate, 3–disparage, 4–condone, 5–titillate, 6–malign, 7–equivocate, 8–militate (against), 9–proscribe, 10–adulate

(End of Session 19)

Session 20

Origins and related words

1. Equality

If you play golf, you know that each course or hole has a certain *par*, the number of strokes allowed according to the results achieved by expert players. Your own accomplishment on the course will be at *par*, above *par*, or below *par*.

Similarly, some days you may feel up to *par*, other days below *par*.

Par is from a Latin word meaning *equal*. You may try, when you play golf, to *equal* the expert score; and some days you may, or may not, feel *equal* to your usual self.

When we speak of *parity* payments, we refer to payments that show an *equality* to earnings for some agreed-upon year.

So when you *disparage*, you lower someone's *par* , or feeling of *equality*, (*dis-* as you know, may be a negative prefix). The noun is *disparagement* (dis-PAR'-ij-mənt), the adjective *disparaging* (dis-PAR'-ij-ing), as in 'Why do you always make *disparaging* remarks about me?'

Parity (PAR'-it-ti) as a noun means *equality*; *disparity* (dis-PAR'-ə-tee) means a lack of *equality*, or a difference. We may speak, for example, of the *disparity* between someone's promise and performance; or of the *disparity* between the rate of vocabulary growth of a child and of an adult. The adjective *disparate* (DIS'-pə-rət) indicates *essential* or *complete* difference or inequality, as in 'Our philosophies are so *disparate* that we can never come to any agreement on action'.

The word *compare* and all its forms (*comparable*, *comparative*, etc.) derive from *par*, equal. Two things are *compared* when they have certain *equal* or similar qualities (*con-*, *com-*, together, with).

Pair and *peer* are also from *par*. Things (shoes, socks, gloves, etc.) in *pairs* are *equal* or similar; your *peers* are those *equal* to you, as in age, position, rank, or ability. Hence the expression 'to be judged by a jury of one's peers'.

(British *peers*, however, such is the contradiction of language, are *nobles*.)

2.   How to say yes and no

Equivocate is built on another Latin word meaning *equal* – *aequus* (the spelling in English is always *equ-*) – plus *vox*, *vocis*, voice.

When you *equivocate* (i-KWIV'-ə-kayt'), you seem to be saying both *yes* and *no* with *equal voice*. An *equivocal* (i-KWIV'-ə-kəl) answer, therefore, is by design vague, indefinite, and susceptible of contradictory interpretations, quite the opposite of an *unequivocal* (un'-i-KWIV'-ə-kəl) response, which says *Yes!* or *No!*, and no kidding. Professional politicians are masters of *equivocation* (i-kwiv'-ə-KAY'-shən) – on most vital issues they sit on the fence. You will often hear candidates for office say, publicly, that they *unequivocally* promise, if elected, to ... ; and then they start *equivocating* for all they are worth, like people who say, 'Let me be perfectly *frank* with you' – and then promptly and glibly lie through their teeth.

3.   Statements of various kinds

Do not confuse *equivocal* with *ambiguous* (am'-BIG'yoŏ-əs). An *equivocal* statement is purposely, deliberately (and with malice aforethought) couched in language that will be deceptive; an *ambiguous* statement is *accidentally* couched in such language. *Equivocal* is, in short, purposely *ambiguous*.

You will recall that *ambi-*, which we last met in *ambivert* and *ambidextrous*, is a root meaning *both*; anything *ambiguous* may have *both* one meaning and another meaning. If you say, 'That sentence is the height of *ambiguity*', you mean that you find it vague because it admits of both affirmative and negative interpretations, or because it may mean two different things. *Ambiguity* is pronounced am'-bi-GYŌŌ-i-ti.

Another type of statement or word contains the possibility of two interpretations – one of them suggestive, risqué, or sexy. Such a statement or word is a *double entendre*. This is from the French and translates literally as *double meaning*. Give the word as close a French pronunciation as you can – DŌŌB'-lahn-TAHN'-drə. (The *n*'s are nasalized, the *r* somewhat throaty, and the final syllable is barely audible.)

Review of etymology

Prefix, Root, Suffix	Meaning	English Word
1. *par*	equal	_____
2. *-ment*	noun suffix attached to verbs	_____
3. *-ity*	noun suffix attached to adjectives	_____
4. *dis-*	negative prefix	_____
5. *con-, com-*	with, together	_____
6. *aequus (equ-)*	equal	_____
7. *vox, vocis*	voice	_____
8. *-ate*	verb suffix	_____
9. *-ion*	noun suffix attached to verbs ending in *-ate*	_____
10. *-ous*	adjective suffix	_____
11. *ambi-*	both	_____

Using the words

Can you pronounce the words?

1. *parity*   PAR'-i-ti
2. *disparity*   dis-PAR'-i-ti
3. *disparate*   DIS'-pə-rət
4. *disparagement*   dis-PAR'-ij-mənt

5. *disparaging*   dis-PAR'-ij-ing
6. *peer*   PI-ə
7. *equivocate*   i-KWIV'-ə-kayt'
8. *equivocation*   i-kwiv'-ə-KAY'-shən
9. *equivocal*   i-KWIV'-ə-kəl
10. *unequivocal*   un'-i-KWIV'-ə-kəl
11. *ambiguous*   am-BIG'-yŏŏ-əs
12. *ambiguity*   am'-bi-GYOO'-i-ti
13. *double entendre*   DOOB'-lahn-TAHN'-drə

Can you work with the words?

1. parity   a. belittlement
2. disparity   b. act of being deliberately vague or indirectly deceptive; statement that is deceptive or purposely open to contrary interpretations
3. disparagement   c. quality of being open to misinterpretation; statement with this quality
4. peer   d. statement or word with two meanings, one of them risqué, indelicate, or of possible sexual connotation
5. equivocation   e. inequality
6. ambiguity   f. equality
7. double entendre   g. one's equal

Key: 1–f, 2–e, 3–a, 4–g, 5–b, 6–c, 7–d

Do you understand the words?

1. Is there a *disparity* in age between a grandfather and his granddaughter?   YES   NO
2. Is an *equivocal* statement clear and direct?   YES   NO
3. Is an *unequivocal* answer vague and misleading?   YES   NO

4. Are politicians often masters of
    equivocation?   YES   NO

5. Are *ambiguous* sentences somewhat   YES   NO
    confusing?

6. Are people with *disparate*   YES   NO
    perceptions of life likely to
    experience reality in the same way?

7. Is a *disparaging* look one of   YES   NO
    admiration?

8. When people *equivocate*, are they   YES   NO
    evading the issue?

9. Is the deliberate use of *double*   YES   NO
    entendres likely to shock puritanical
    people?

10. Are supervisors and their   YES   NO
    subordinates *peers?*

Key: 1–yes, 2–no, 3–no, 4–yes, 5–yes, 6–no, 7–no, 8–yes,
        9–yes, 10–no

Can you recall the words?

1. accidentally vague   1. A_____
2. purposely vague   2. E_____
3. equality   3. P_____
4. word or statement one   4. D_____
    meaning of which may be
    interpreted as risqué
5. lack of equality   5. D_____
6. belittlement   6. D_____
7. clear; direct; capable of   7. U_____
    only one interpretation
8. essentially or widely   8. D_____
    unequal or different
9. one's equal in age, rank,   9. P_____
    etc.

10. to use words in a   10. E_____
    calculated effort to
    mislead or to be
    ambiguous

Key: 1–ambiguous, 2–equivocal, 3–parity, 4–double enten-
        dre, 5–disparity, 6–disparagement, 7–unequivocal,
        8–disparate, 9–peer, 10–equivocate

(End of Session 20)

Session 21

Origins and related words

1.   More on equality

The root *aequus*, spelled *equ-* in English words, is a building block of:

1. *equity* (EK'-wi-ti) – justice, fairness; i.e., equal treatment. By extension, stocks in the financial markets are *equities*, and the value of your home or other property over and above the amount of the mortgage you owe is your *equity* in it.) The adjective is *equitable* (EK'-wi-tə-bəl).

2. *inequity* (in-EK'-wi-ti) – injustice, unfairness (*equity* plus the negative prefix *in-*). Adjective: *inequitable* (in-EK'-wi-tə-bəl).

3. *iniquity* (in-IK'-wi-ti) – by one of those delightful surprises and caprices characteristic of language, the change of a single letter (*e* to *i*), extends the meaning of a word far beyond its derivation and original denotation. Injustice and unfairness are sinful and wicked, especially if you naively believe that life is fair. So a 'den of *iniquity*' is a place where vice flourishes; an *iniquity* is a sin or vice, or an egregiously immoral act; and *iniquity* is wickedness, sinfulness. Adjective: *iniquitous* (in-IK'-wi-təs).

4. *equinox* (EE'-kwi-noks' *or* EK'-wi-noks') – etymologically, 'equal night', a combination of *aequus* and *nox, noctis,* night. The *equinox*, when day and night are of equal length, occurs twice a year: about March 21 and again about September 21 or 22. (The adjective is *equinoctial* – ee'kwi-NOK'-shəl *or* ek'-wi-NOK'-shəl.) *Nocturnal* (nok-TURN'-əl), derived from *nox, noctis*, describes people, animals, or plants that are active or flourish at night rather

than during daylight hours. Cats and owls are *nocturnal*, as in the moonflower, whose blossoms open at night; not to mention 'night people', whose biorhythms are such that they function better after the sun goes down, and who like to stay up late and sleep well into midmorning. A *nocturne* (NOK'-turn) is a musical composition of dreamy character (i.e., night music), or a painting of a night scene.

5. *equanimity* (ee'kwə-NIM'-i-ti *or* ek'-wə-NIM'-i-ti) – etymologically *aequus* plus *animus*, mind, hence 'equal mind'. Maintain your *equanimity*, your evenness of temper, your composure, your coolness or calmness, when everyone around you is getting excited or hysterical, and you will probably be considered an admirable person, though one might wonder what price you pay for such emotional control. (Other words built on *animus*, mind, will be discussed in Chapter 12.)

6. *equability* (ek'-wə-BIL'-i-ti) – a close synonym of *equanimity*. A person of *equable* (EK'-wə-bəl) temperament is characteristically calm, serene, unflappable, even-tempered.

7. *equilibrium* (ee'-kwi-LIB'-ri-əm *or* ek'-wi-LIB'-ri-əm) – by derivation *aequus* plus *libra*, balance, weight, pound, hence 'equal balance'. *Libra* (LĪ'-brə) is the seventh sign of the zodiac, represented by a pair of scales. Now you know, in case the question has been bothering you, why the abbreviation for the word *pound* is *lb.* and why the symbol for *pound*, the monetary unit, is £. *Equilibrium* is a state of *physical* balance, especially between opposing forces. When you are very drunk you may have difficulty keeping your *equilibrium* – the force of gravity is stronger than your ability to stay upright. An *equilibrist* (i-KWIL'-i-brist), as you might guess, is a professional tightrope walker – a performer successfully defying the law of gravity (when sober) by *balancing* on a thin overhead wire.

The *equator* divides the earth into *equal* halves, and words like *equation*, *equivalent*, *equidistant*, *equiangular*, and *equilateral* (from Latin *latus, lateris*, side) are self-explanatory.

2.   Not to be confused with horses

Equestrian (i-KWES'-tri-ən) is someone on a horse (as *pedestrian* is someone on foot); an *equestrienne* (i-kwes'-tri-əN') is a woman on a horse (if you *must* make the distinction); and *equine* (E'-kwīn) is like a horse, as in appearance or characteristics, or descriptive of horses.

Equestrian is also an adjective referring to horseback riding, as an *equestrian* statue; and *equine* is also a noun, i.e., a horse.

So the *equ-* in these words, from Latin *equus*, horse, is not to be confused with the *equ-* in the words of the previous section – that *equ-* is from *aequus*, equal.

3.   Hear voices?

Equivocal, you will recall, combines *aequus* with *vox, vocis*, voice; and *vox, vocis* combines with *fero*, to bear or carry, to form *vociferous* (vō-SIF'-ər-əs), etymologically 'carrying (much) voice', hence loud, noisy, clamorous, as *vociferous* demands (not at all quiet or subtle), or the *vociferous* play of young children ('Please! Try to be quiet so Dad can get his work done!'), though unfortunately TV addiction has abnormally eliminated child noises. (*Vociferous* will be discussed at greater length in Chapter 10.)

If you are *vocal* (VŌ'-kəl), you express yourself readily and freely by voice; *vocal* sounds are voiced; *vocal* music is sung; and you know what your *vocal* cords are for.

To *vocalize* (VŌ'-kə-līz') is to give voice to ('*vocalize* your anger, dont" hold it in!'), or to sing the *vocals* (or voice parts) of music. (Can you write the noun form of the verb *vocalize*? ――――――――――――――――) A *vocalist* (VŌ'-kə-list) is a singer.

Review of etymology

Prefix, Root, Suffix	Meaning	English Word
1. *aequus (equ-)*	equal	＿＿＿＿＿＿
2. *in-*	negative prefix	＿＿＿＿＿＿
3. *nox, noctis*	night	＿＿＿＿＿＿
4. *animus*	mind	＿＿＿＿＿＿
5. *-ity*	noun suffix	＿＿＿＿＿＿
6. *libra*	balance, weight, pound	＿＿＿＿＿＿
7. *-ist*	person who	＿＿＿＿＿＿
8. *latus, lateris*	side	＿＿＿＿＿＿
9. *equus*	horse	＿＿＿＿＿＿

10.	*-ine*	like, descriptive of	_____
11.	*vox, vocis*	voice	_____
12.	*fero*	to bear, carry	_____

Using the words

Can you pronounce the words? (I)

1.	*equity*	EK'-wi-ti
2.	*equitable*	EK'-wi-tə-bəl
3.	*inequity*	in-EK'-wi-ti
4.	*inequitable*	in-EK'-wi-tə-bəl
5.	*iniquity*	in-IK'-wi-ti
6.	*iniquitous*	in-IK'-wi-təs
7.	*equinox*	EE'-kwi(*or* EK'-wi)-noks'
8.	*equinoctial*	ee'-kwi(*or* ek'-wi)-NOK'-shəl
9.	*nocturnal*	nok-TURN'-əl
10.	*nocturne*	NOK'-turn

Can you pronounce the words? (II)

1.	*equanimity*	ee'-kwə(*or* ek'-wə)-NIM'-i-ti
2.	*equability*	ek'-wə-BIL'-i-ti
3.	*equable*	EK'-wə-bəl
4.	*equilibrium*	ee'-kwi(*or* ek'-wi)-LIB'-ri-əm
5.	*equilibrist*	i-KWIL'-i-brist
6.	*equilateral*	ee'-kwi(*or* ek'-wi)-LAT'-ər-əl
7.	*equestrian*	i-KWES'-tri-ən
8.	*equine*	E'-kwīn
9.	*vociferous*	vō-SIF'-ər-əs
10.	*vocal*	VŌ'-kəl
11.	*vocalize*	VŌ'-kə-līz'
12.	*vocalization*	vō-kə-lī-ZAY'-shən
13.	*vocalist*	VŌ'-kə-list

Can you work with the words? (I)

| 1. equity | a. time when night and day are of equal length. |

2. inequity   b. balance of mind; composure; calmness under trying circumstances

3. iniquity   c. horseback rider

4. equinox   d. a horse

5. nocturne   e. sinfulness; wickedness; immoral act; sin

6. equanimity   f. unfairness, injustice

7. equilibrium   g. tightrope walker

8. equestrian   h. singer

9. equilibrist   i. fairness, justice

10. equine   j. balance, especially between opposing forces

11. vocalist   k. night music

Key: 1–i, 2–f, 3–e, 4–a, 5–k, 6–b, 7–j, 8–c, 9–g, 10–d, 11–h

Can you work with the words? (II)

1. equitable   a. descriptive of time when night and day are of equal length

2. inequitable   b. give voice to; sing

3. iniquitous   c. having equal sides

4. equinoctial   d. using, or referring to, the voice; freely expressing by voice

5. nocturnal   e. noisy, loud, clamorous

6. equable   f. calm, unruffled, even-tempered

7. equilateral   g. fair, just

8. vociferous   h. referring or pertaining to, or active at, night

9. vocal   i. sinful, wicked, immoral

10. vocalize   j. unfair, unjust

Key: 1–g, 2–j, 3–i, 4–a, 5–h, 6–f, 7–c, 8–e, 9–d, 10–b

Do you understand the words?

1.	Is life always *equitable*?	YES	NO
2.	Does the cynic expect more *inequity* than *equity* in life?	YES	NO
3.	Do ethical people practice *iniquity*?	YES	NO
4.	Does the *equinox* occur once a month?	YES	NO
5.	Are *nocturnal* animals active at night?	YES	NO
6.	If you generally preserve your *equanimity*, do you often get very excited?	YES	NO
7.	Is it easy to maintain your *equilibrium* on icy ground?	YES	NO
8.	Is *equability* the mark of a calm, even-tempered person?	YES	NO
9.	Does an *equilateral* triangle have equal sides?	YES	NO
10.	Is an *equine* a dog?	YES	NO
11.	If you demand something *vociferously*, do you make a lot of noise?	YES	NO
12.	If you are *vocal*, do you have difficulty expressing yourself?	YES	NO
13.	Is a *vocalist* the same as an instrumentalist?	YES	NO

Key: 1–no, 2–yes, 3–no, 4–no, 5–yes, 6–no, 7–no, 8–yes, 9–yes, 10–no, 11–yes, 12–no, 13–no

Can you recall the words? (I)

1. to give voice to; to   1. V_____
express aloud; to sing

2. tightrope walker   2. E_____
3. active or flourishing at   3. N_____
   night
4. descriptive or   4. E_____
   characteristic of, or like, a
   horse
5. referring to the voice·   5. V_____
   skilful or fluent in
   expressing by voice
6. calm and unflappable in   6. E_____
   temperament
7. wicked, sinful   7. I_____
8. night music   8. N_____
9. fairness, justice   9. E_____

Key: 1–vocalize, 2–equilibrist, 3–nocturnal, 4–equine,
        5–vocal, 6–equable, 7–iniquitous, 8–nocturne, 9–equi-
        ty

Can you recall the words? (II)

1. loud, noisy, clamorous   1. V_____
2. person on horseback   2. E_____
                                      or E_____
3. calmness or evenness of   3. E_____
   temper
                                      or E_____
4. unfair, unjust   4. I_____
5. sin; wickedness; grossly   5. I_____
   immoral behaviour
6. time when day and night   6. E_____
   are of equal length
7. fair, just, evenhanded   7. E_____
8. physical balance, balance   8. E_____
   between opposing forces
9. having equal sides   9. E_____
10. singer   10. V_____

Key: 1–vociferous, 2–equestrian *or* equestrienne, 3–equanimity *or* equability, 4–inequitable, 5–iniquity, 6–equinox, 7–equitable, 8–equilibrium, 9–equilateral, 10–vocalist

(End of Session 21)

Session 22

Origins and related words

1.   How to tickle

Titillate comes from a Latin verb meaning *to tickle*, and may be used both literally and figuratively. That is (literally), you can *titillate* by gentle touches in strategic places; you are then causing an actual (and always very pleasant) physical sensation. Or you can (figuratively) *titillate* people, or their minds, fancies, palates (and this is the more common use of the word), by charm, brilliance, wit, promises, or in any other way your imagination can conceive.

Titillation (tit'-i-LAY'-shən) has the added meaning of light sexual stimulation. (Note that both noun and verb are spelled with a double *l*, *not* a double *t*.)

2.   How to flatter

A *compliment* is a pleasant and courteous expression of praise; *flattery* is stronger than a compliment and often considered insincere. *Adulation* (ad'-yŏŏ-LAY'-shən) is flattery and worship carried to an excessive, ridiculous degree. There are often public figures (entertainers, musicians, government officials, etc.) who receive widespread *adulation*, but those not in the public eye can also be *adulated*, as a teacher by students, a wife by husband (and vice versa), a doctor by patients, and so on. (The derivation is from a Latin verb meaning to *fawn upon*.)

The adjective *adulatory* (ad'-yŏŏ-LAY'-tə-ri) ends in *-ory*, a suffix we are meeting for the first time in these pages. (Other adjectives suffixes; *-al, -ic, -ical, -ous*.)

3. Ways of writing

Proscribe, to forbid, is commonly used for medical, religious, or legal prohibitions.

A doctor *proscribes* a food, drug, or activity that might prove harmful to the patient. The church *proscribes*, or announces a *proscription* (prō-SKRIP'-shən) against, such activities as may harm its parishioners. The law *proscribes* behaviour detrimental to the public welfare.

The derivation is the prefix *pro-*, before, plus *scribo, scriptus*, to write. In ancient Roman times, a man's name was written on a public bulletin board if he had committed some crime for which his property or life was to be forfeited; Roman citizens in good standing would thereby know to avoid him. In a similar sense, the doctor writes down those foods or activities that are likely to commit crimes against the patient's health – in that way the patient knows to avoid them.

Scribo, scriptus is the building block of scores of common English words: *scribe, scribble, prescribe, describe, subscribe, script, the Scriptures, manuscript, typescript*, etc. *Describe* uses the prefix *de-*, down – to *describe* is, etymologically, 'to write down' about. *Manuscript*, combining *manus*, hand (as in *manual* labour), with *scriptus*, is something handwritten – the word was coined before the invention of the typewriter. *The Scriptures* are holy writings. To *subscribe* (as to a magazine) is to write one's name *under* an order or contract (*sub*, under, as in *subway, subsurface*, etc.); to *subscribe* to a philosophy or a principle is figuratively to write one's name *under* the statement of such philosophy or principle.

To *inscribe* is to write *in* or *into* (a book, for example, or metal or stone). A *postscript* is something written after (Latin *post*, after) the main part is finished.

Note how *-scribe* verbs change to nouns and adjectives:

VERB	NOUN	ADJECTIVE
prescribe	prescription	prescriptive
subscribe	subscription	subscriptive

Can you follow the pattern?

describe	_____	_____
inscribe	_____	_____
proscribe	_____	_____

4.   It's obvious

You are familiar with the word *via*, by way of, which is from the Latin word for *road*. (The *Via Appia* was one of the famous highways of ancient Roman times.) When something is *obvious*, etymologically it is right there in the middle of the road where no one can fail to see it — hence, easily seen, not hidden, conspicuous. And if you meet an obstacle in the road and dispose of it forthwith, you are doing what *obviate* says. Thus, if you review your work daily in some college subject, frenzied 'cramming' at the end of the term will be *obviated*. A large and steady income *obviates* fears of financial insecurity; leaving for work early will *obviate* worry about being late. *To obviate*, then, is to make unnecessary, to do away with, to prevent by taking effective measures or steps against (an occurrence, a feeling, a requirement, etc.). The noun is *obviation* (ob'-vi-AY'-shən).

Surprisingly, *via*, road, is the root in the English word *trivial* (tri-, three). Where three roads intersect, you are likely to find busy traffic, lots of people, in short a fairly public place, so you are not going to talk of important or confidential matters, lest you be overheard. You will, instead, talk of *trivial* (TRIV'-i-əl) things — whatever is unimportant, without great significance; you will confine your conversation to *trivialities* (triv'-i-AL'-i-tiz) or to *trivia* (also a plural noun, pronounced TRIV'-i-ə), insignificant trifles.

5.   War

Militate derives from *militis*, one of the forms of the Latin noun meaning *soldier* or *fighting man*. If something *militates* against you, it fights against you, i.e., works to your disadvantage. Thus, your timidity may *militate* against your keeping your friends. (*Militate* is always followed by the preposition *against* and, like *obviate*, never takes a personal subject — *you* don't *militate* against anyone, but some habit, action, tendency, etc. *militates* against someone or something.)

The adjective *militant* (MIL.'-i-tənt) comes from the same root. A *militant* reformer is one who fights for reforms; a *militant* campaign is one waged aggressively and with determination. The noun is *militancy* (MIL'-i-tən-si), and *militant* is also a noun for the person – 'Sally is a *militant* in the Women's Liberation movement.'

Military and *militia* also have their origin in *militis*.

6.   First the bad news

Built on Latin *malus*, bad, evil, to *malign* is to speak evil about, to defame, to slander. *Malign* is also an adjective meaning *bad, harmful, evil, hateful*, as in 'the *malign* influence of his unconscious will to fail'. Another adjective form is *malignant* (mə-LIG'-nənt), as in 'a *malignant* glance', i.e., one showing deep hatred, or 'a *malignant* growth', i.e., one that is cancerous (bad).

The noun of *malignant* is *malignancy* (mə-LIG'-nən-si), which medically, is a cancerous growth, or, generally, the condition, state, or attitude of harmfulness, hatefulness, evil intent, etc. The noun form of the adjective *malign* is *malignity* (mə-LIG'-nə-ti).

Observe how we can construct English words by combining *malus* with other Latin roots.

Add the root *dico, dictus*, to say or tell, to form *malediction* (mal'-ə-DIK'-shən), a curse, i.e., an evil saying. Adjective: *maledictory* (mal'-ə-DIK'-tə-ri).

Add the root *volo*, to wish, to will, or to be willing, and we can construct the adjective *malevolent* (mə-LEV'-ə-lent), wishing evil or harm – a *malevolent* glance, attitude, feeling, etc. The noun is *malevolence* (mə-LEV'-ə-ləns).

Add the root *facio, factus*, to do or make (also spelled, in English words, *fec-*, *fic-*, *factus*, or, as a verb ending, *-fy*), to form the adjective *maleficent* (mə-LEF'-i-sənt), doing harm or evil, or causing hurt – *maleficent* acts, deeds, behaviour.

Can you figure out, and pronounce, the noun form of *maleficent*? _____.

A *malefactor* (MAL'-i-fak'-tə) is a wrongdoer, an evildoer, a criminal – a *malefactor* commits a *malefaction* (mal'-i-FAK'-shən), a crime, an evil deed.

French is a 'Romance' language, that is, a language based on Roman or Latin (as are, also, Spanish, Portuguese, Italian, and Romanian), and so Latin *malus* became French *mal*, bad, the source of *maladroit* (mal'-ə-DROYT'), clumsy, bungling, awkward, unskilful, etymologically, having a 'bad right hand'. (See *adroit*, Chapter 3.) The noun is *maladroitness*. Also from French *mal*: *malaise* (ma-LAYZ'), an indefinite feeling of bodily discomfort, as in a mild illness, or as a symptom preceding an illness; etymologically, 'bad ease', just as *disease* (dis-ease) is 'lack of ease'.

Other common words that you are familiar with also spring from Latin *malus*: *malicious*, *malice*, *malady*; and the same *malus* functions as a prefix in words like *maladjusted*, *malcontent*, *malpractice*, *malnutrition*, etc., all with the connotation of *badness*.

And what's the *good* news? See Session 23.

Review of etymology

Prefix, Root, Suffix	Meaning	English Word
1. *-ory*	adjective suffix	_____
2. *scribo, scriptus*	to write	_____
3. *de-*	down	_____
4. *manus*	hand	_____
5. *sub-*	under	_____
6. *in-*	in, into	_____
7. *post*	after	_____
8. *via*	road	_____
9. *tri-*	three	_____
10. *militis*	soldier	_____
11. *malus*	bad, evil	_____
12. *disco, dictus*	to say, tell	_____
13. *volo*	to wish	_____
14. *facio (fec-, fic-, -fy)*	to do, make	_____
15. *-ence, -ancy*	noun suffix	_____

Working with the words

Can you pronounce the words? (I)

1. *titillation*   tit'-i-LAY'-shən

2. *adulation* — ad'-yŏŏ-LAY'-shən
3. *adulatory* — ad'-yŏŏ-LAY'-tə-ri
4. *proscription* — prō-SKRIP'-shən
5. *proscriptive* — prō-SKRIP'-tiv
6. *obviation* — ob'-vi-AY'-shən
7. *trivial* — TRIV'-i-əl
8. *trivialities* — triv'-i-AL'-i-tiz
9. *trivia* — TRIV'-i-ə
10. *militant* — MIL'-i-tənt
11. *militancy* — MIL'-i-tən-si
12. *malign (adj.)* — mə-LĪN'
13. *malignity* — mə-LIG'-nə-ti
14. *malignant* — mə-LIG'-nənt
15. *malignancy* — mə-LIG'-nən-si

Can you pronounce the words? (II)

1. *malediction* — mal'-ə-DIK'-shən
2. *maledictory* — mal'-ə-DIK'-tə-ri
3. *malevolent* — mə-LEV'-ə-lənt
4. *malevolence* — mə-LEV'-ə-ləns
5. *maleficent* — mə-LEF'-i-sənt
6. *maleficence* — mə-LEF'-i-səns
7. *malefactor* — MAL'-i-fak'-tə
8. *malefaction* — mal'-i-FAK'-shən
9. *maladroit* — mal'-ə-DROYT'
10. *maladroitness* — mal'-ə-DROYT'-nəs
11. *malaise* — ma-LAYZ'

Can you work with the words? (I)

1. titillation   a. prohibition
2. adulation   b. hatefulness; harmfulness
3. proscription   c. clumsiness
4. militancy   d. quality of wishing evil; ill-will
5. malignity   e. prevention; fact or act of making unnecessary or of doing away with

6. malediction   f. worship; excessive flattery

7. maladroitness   g. vague feeling of bodily discomfort

8. obviation   h. pleasurable stimulation; tickling

9. malevolence   i. a curse

10. malaise   j. aggressiveness

Key: 1–h, 2–f, 3–a, 4–j, 5–b, 6–i, 7–c, 8–e, 9–d, 10–g

Can you work with the words? (II)

1. adulatory   a. aggressive; 'fighting'

2. proscriptive   b. of no great consequence

3. militant   c. bearing ill-will; wishing harm

4. malign   d. of the nature of curses

5. trivial   e. clumsy, awkward

6. maledictory   f. worshipful, adoring

7. malevolent   g. bad, harmful, hurtful

8. maladroit   h. relating or pertaining to prohibitions

Key: 1–f, 2–h, 3–a, 4–g, 5–b, 6–d, 7–c, 8–e

Do you understand the words?

1. Does a *malignant* look indicate kindly feelings?   YES   NO

2. Is a cancer sometimes called a *malignancy*?   YES   NO

3. Are *trivialities* important?   YES   NO

4. If your house is cluttered with *trivia*, are these objects of great value?   YES   NO

5. Do people enjoy having *maledictions* hurled at them?   YES   NO

6. Is a *maleficent* act likely to cause harm or hurt?   YES   NO

7. Does *maladroitness* show skill?   YES   NO

8. Is a *malefactor* a wrongdoer?   YES   NO

9. Does an *adulatory* attitude show exaggerated admiration?   YES   NO

10. Is *militancy* the same as passiveness?   YES   NO

Key: 1–no, 2–yes, 3–no, 4–no, 5–no, 6–yes, 7–no, 8–yes, 9–yes, 10–no

Can you recall the words? (I)

1. clusmy, awkward — 1. M_____
2. bearing ill-ill; wishing harm — 2. M_____
3. pleasurable stimulation — 3. T_____
4. a person aggressively fighting for a cause — 4. M_____
5. prohibition against something injurious — 5. P_____ __
6. excessive flattery; exaggerated admiration — 6. A_____
7. vague feeling of general physical discomfort — 7. M_____
8. a criminal; a wrongdoer — 8. M_____
9. a curse — 9. M_____
10. a crime; bad or evil act or behaviour — 10. M_____

Key: 1–maladroit, 2–malevolent, 3–titillation, 4–militant, 5–proscription, 6–adulation, 7–malaise, 8–malefactor, 9–malediction, 10–malefaction

Can you recall the words? (II)

1. fact or act or making unnecessary or of taking effective steps towards prevention — 1. O_____
2. aggressive attitude — 2. M_____

3. harmful, hurtful, bad

3. M_____
   or M_____
   or M_____

4. unimportant, insignificant

4. T_____

5. unimportant, insignificant things; trifles

5. T_____

   or T_____

6. cursing; of the nature of, or relating to, curses (*adj.*)

6. M_____

7. worshipful

7. A_____

Key: 1–obviation, 2–militancy, 3–malign, malignant, *or* maleficent, 4–trivial, 5–trivialities *or* trivia, 6–maledictory, 7–adulatory

---

(End of Session 22)

Session 23

Origins and related words

1.   So now what's the good news?

Malus is *bad*; *bonus* is *good*. The adverb from the Latin adjective *bonus* is *bene*, and *bene* is the root found in words that contrast with the *mal-* terms we studied in the previous session.

So *benign* (bi-NĪN') and *benignant* (bi-NIG'-nənt) are kindly, good-natured, not harmful, as in *benign* neglect, a *benign* judge, a *benign* tumour (not cancerous), a *benignant* attitude to malefactors and scoundrels. The corresponding nouns are *benignity* (bi-NIG'-ni-ti) and *benignancy* (bi-NIG'-nən-si).

A *malediction* is a curse; a *benediction* (ben'-i-DIK'-shən) is a blessing, a 'saying good'. The adjective is *benedictory* (ben'-i-DIK'-tə-ri).

In contrast to *maleficent* is *beneficent* (bi-NEF'-i-sənt), doing good. The noun? _____.

In contrast to *malefactor* is *benefactor* (BEN'-i-fak'-tə), one who does good things for another, as by giving help, providing financial gifts or aid, or coming to the rescue when someone is in need. If you insist on making sexual distinctions, a woman who so operates is a *benefactress* (BEN'-i-fak'-tris). And, of course, the person receiving the *benefaction* (ben-i-FAK'-shən), the recipient of money, help, etc., is a *beneficiary* (ben'-i-FISH'-ər-i). *Benefit* and *beneficial* are other common words built on the combination of *bene* and a form of *facio*, to do or make.

So let others be *malevolent* towards you – confuse them by being *benevolent* (bi-NEV'-ə-lənt) – wish them well. (Turn the other cheek? Why not?) The noun? _____.

The adjective *bonus*, good, is found in English *bonus*, extra pay ment, theoretically – but not necessarily – for some good act; in *bonbon*, a sweet (a 'good-good', using the French version of the Latin adjective); and in *bona fide* (BŌ-nə-FĪ-di), etymologically, 'in good faith', hence valid, without pretence, deception, or fraudu- lent intent – as a *bona fide* offer, a *bone fide* effort to negotiate differences, etc. *Fides* is Latin for *faith* or *trust*, as in *fidelity* (fi- DEL'-i-ti), faithfulness; *Fido*, a stereotypical name for a dog, one's faithful friend; *infidel* (IN'-fi-dəl), one who does *not* have the right faith or religion (depending on who is using the term), or one who has *no* religion (Latin *in-*, not); and *infidelity* (in'-fi-DEL'-i-ti), un- faithfulness, especially to the marriage vows.

2.   Say, do, and wish

Benediction and *malediction* derive from *dico, dictus*, to say, tell. *Dictate, dictator, dictation, dictatorial* (dik'-tə-TAWR'-i-əl) – words that signify telling others what to do ('Do as I say!') – are built on *dico*, as is *predict*, to tell beforehand, i.e., to say that something will occur before it actually does (*pre-*, before, as in *prescient*).

The brand name *Dictaphone* combines *dico* with *phone*, sound; *contradict*, to say against, or to make an opposite statement ('Don't *contradict* me!'; 'That *contradicts* what I know') combines *dico* with *contra-*, against, opposite; and *addiction*, etymologically 'a saying to or towards', or the compulsion to say 'yes' to a habit, combines *dico* with *ad-*, to, towards.

Facio, factus, to do or make (as in *malefactor, benefactor*), has, as noted, variant spellings in English words: *fec-, fic-*, or, as a verb ending, *-fy*.

Thus *factory* is a place where things are *made* (*-ory*, place where); a *fact* is something *done* (i.e., something that occurs, or exists, or is; therefore, true); *fiction*, something *made* up or invented; *manufac- ture*, to *make* by hand (*manus*, hand, as in *manuscript, manual*), a word coined before the invention of machinery; *artificial, made* by human art rather than occurring in nature, as *artificial* flowers, etc.; and *clarify, simplify, liquefy* (to *make* clear, simple, liquid), and *magnify* (*magnus*, large) among hundreds of other *-fy* verbs.

Volo, to wish, to will, to be willing (as in *malevolent, benevolent*), occurs in *voluntary, involuntary, volunteer*, words too familiar to need definition, and each quite obviously expressing *wish* or *will-*

ingness. Less common, and from the same root, is *volition* (vǝ-LISH'-ǝn), the act or power of willing or wishing, as in 'of her own *volition*', i.e., *voluntarily*, or 'against her *volition*'.

3.   If you please!

Placate is built on the root *plac-* which derives from two related Latin verbs meaning, 1) *to please*, and 2) *to appease, soothe*, or *pacify*.

If you succeed in *placating* an angry colleague, you turn that person's hostile attitude into one that is friendly or favourable. The noun is *placation* (plǝ-KAY'-shǝn), the adjective either *placative* (plǝ-KAY'-tiv *or* PLAK'-ǝ-tiv) or *placatory* (plǝ-KAY'-tǝ-ri *or* PLAK'-ǝ-tǝ-ri). A more *placatory* attitude to those you have offended may help you regain their friendship; when husband and wife, or lovers, quarrel, one of them finally makes a *placative* gesture if the war no longer fulfills his or her neurotic needs – one of them eventually will wake up some bright morning in a *placatory* mood.

But then, such is life, the other one may at that point be *implacable* (im-PLAK'-ǝ-bǝl) – *im-* is a respelling of *in-*, not, before the letter *p*. One who can be soothed, whose hostility *can* be changed to friendliness, is *placable* (PLAK'-ǝ-bǝl).

Implacable has taken on the added meaning of *unyielding to entreaty or pity*; hence, *harsh, relentless*, as 'The governor was *implacable* in his refusal to grant clemency'.

The noun form of *implacable* is *implacability* (im-plak'-ǝ-BIL'-i-ti). Can you write (and pronounce) the noun derived from *placable*? _____.

If you are *placid* (PLAS'-id), you are calm, easygoing, serene, undisturbed – etymologically, you are pleased with things as they are. Waters of a lake or sea, or the emotional atmosphere of a place, can also be *placid*. The noun is *placidity* (plǝ-SID'-i-ti).

If you are *complacent* (kǝm-PLAY'-sǝnt), you are pleased with yourself (*com-*, from *con-*, with, together); you may, in fact, such is one common connotation of the word, be smug, *too* pleased with your position or narrow accomplishments, too easily self-satisfied, and the hour of reckoning may be closer than you realize. (Humans, as you know, are delighted to be critical of the contentment of others.)

The noun is *complacence* (kəm-PLAY'-səns) or *complacency* (kəm-PLAY'-sən-si).

4.   How to give – and forgive

To *condone* is to forgive, overlook, pardon, or be uncritical of (an offence, or of an antisocial or illegal act). You yourself might or might not indulge in such behaviour or commit such an offence, but you feel no urge to protest, or to demand censure or punishment for someone else who does. You may *condone* cheating on one's income tax, shoplifting from a big, impersonal supermarket, or exceeding the speed limit, though you personally observe the law with scrupulousness. (Not everyone, however, is so charitable or forgiving.) The noun is *condonation* (kon'-dō-NAY'-shən).

condone is built on Latin *dono*, to give, the root found in *donor*, one who gives; *donate*, to give; and *donation*, a gift.

Review of etymology

Prefix, Root, Suffix	Meaning	English Word
1. *bonus, bene*	good, well	_____
2. *fides*	faith	_____
3. *dico, dictus*	to say, tell	_____
4. *pre-*	before, beforehand	_____
5. *phone*	sound	_____
6. *contra-*	against, opposite	_____
7. *ad-*	to, towards	_____
8. *facio, factus, fec-, fic-, -fy*	to make or do	_____
9. *-ory*	place where	_____
10. *manus*	hand	_____
11. *volo*	to wish, to will, to be willing	_____
12. *plac-*	to please, appease, soothe, pacify	_____
13. *-ive*	adjective suffix	_____
14. *-ory*	adjective suffix	_____
15. *im- (in-)*	not; negative prefix	_____
16. *com- (con-)*	with, together	_____

17. *dono*   to give   _____

Using the Words

Can you pronounce the words?

1.	*benign*	bi-NĪN'
2.	*benignity*	bi-NIG'-ni-ti
3.	*benignant*	bi-NIG'-nənt
4.	*benignancy*	bi-NIG'-nən-si
5.	*benediction*	ben'-i-DIK'-shən
6.	*benedictory*	ben'-i-DIK'-tə-ri
7.	*beneficent*	bi-NEF'-i-sənt
8.	*beneficence*	bi-NEF'-i-səns
9.	*benefactor*	BEN'-i-fak'-tə
10.	*benefaction*	ben'-i-FAK'-shən
11.	*beneficiary*	ben'-i-FISH'-ər-i
12.	*benevolent*	bi-NEV'-ə-lənt
13.	*benevolence*	bi-NEV'-ə-ləns
14.	*bona fide*	BŌ'-nə- FĪ-di
15.	*fidelity*	fi-DEL'-i-ti
16.	*infidelity*	in'-fi-DEL'-i-ti
17.	*infidel*	IN'-fi-dəl

Can you pronounce the words? (II)

1.	*dictatorial*	dik'-tə-TAWR'-i-əl
2.	*volition*	və-LISH'-ən
3.	*placation*	plə-KAY'-shən
4.	*placative*	plə-KAY'-tiv *or* PLAK'-ə-tiv
5.	*placatory*	plə-KAY'-tə-ri *or* PLAK'-ə-tə-ri
6.	*placable*	PLAK'-ə-bəl
7.	*implacable*	im-PLAK'-ə-bəl
8.	*placability*	plak'-ə-BIL'-i-ti
9.	*implacability*	im-plak'-ə-BIL'-i-ti
10.	*placid*	PLAS'-id
11.	*placidity*	plə-SID'-i-ti
12.	*complacent*	kəm-PLAY'-sənt
13.	*complacence*	kəm-PLAY'-səns

14. *complacency*   kəm-PLAY'-sən-si
15. *condonation*   kon'-dō-NAY'-shən

Can you work with the words? (I)

1. benign   a. wishing good things (for another); well disposed
2. benedictory   b. domineering; giving orders in a manner permitting no refusal
3. benevolent   c. not to be soothed or pacified; unyielding to pity or entreaty
4. bona fide   d. tending, or intended, to pacify, to soothe, or to change hostility to friendliness
5. dictatorial   e. kindly, good-natured, not cancerous
6. placatory   f. calm, unruffled, undisturbed
7. implacable   g. self-satisifed; smug
8. placid   h. of the nature of, or relating to, blessings
9. complacent   i. in good faith; sincere; valid

Key: 1—e, 2—h, 3—a, 4—i, 5—b, 6—d, 7—c, 8—f, 9—g

Can you work with the words? (II)

1. benevolence   a. recipient of money, kindness, etc.
2. benefaction   b. free will
3. beneficiary   c. act of overlooking, or of forgiving, an offence or transgression
4. infidelity   d. faithfulness
5. volition   e. self-satisfaction; smugness
6. placation   f. calmness
7. fidelity   g. act of pacifying, or of turning hostility or anger into friendly feelings

8. condonation	h.	attitude of wishing good things for another
9. placidity	i.	faithlessness
10. complacency	j.	good deed; act of charity or kindness

Key: 1–h, 2–j, 3–a, 4–i, 5–b, 6–g, 7–d, 8–c, 9–f, 10–e

Do you understand the words? (I)

1. Are *benedictions* given in houses of worship?	YES	NO
2. Is it pleasant to be the recipient of a *beneficent* act?	YES	NO
3. Are kind people *benevolent*?	YES	NO
4. Do *placatory* gestures often heal wounds and soothe disgruntled friends?	YES	NO
5. Are some unambitious people *complacent*?	YES	NO
6. Does *benignity* show malice?	YES	NO
7. Is a *benefaction* an act of philanthropy?	YES	NO
8. Is an *implacable* foe of corruption likely to *condone* corrupt acts?	YES	NO
9. Is a *bona fide* offer made insincerely?	YES	NO
10. Does a *benignant* attitude indicate hostility?	YES	NO

Key: 1–yes, 2–yes, 3–yes, 4–yes, 5–yes, 6–no, 7–yes, 8–no, 9–no, 10–no

Do you understand the words? (II)

1. benign – hateful	SAME	OPPOSITE
2. benignant – kindly	SAME	OPPOSITE
3. benediction – malediction	SAME	OPPOSITE
4. benefactor – evildoer	SAME	OPPOSITE

5. beneficiary – giver   SAME   OPPOSITE
6. benevolent – well disposed   SAME   OPPOSITE
7. bona fide – valid   SAME   OPPOSITE
8. fidelity – unfaithfulness   SAME   OPPOSITE
9. infidel – true believer   SAME   OPPOSITE
10. dictatorial – submissive   SAME   OPPOSITE
11. placative – pacifying   SAME   OPPOSITE
12. implacable – unyielding   SAME   OPPOSITE
13. placid – calm   SAME   OPPOSITE
14. complacent – discontented   SAME   OPPOSITE
15. condonation – forgiveness   SAME   OPPOSITE

Key: 1–O, 2–S, 3–O, 4–O, 5–O, 6–S, 7–S, 8–O, 9–O,
        10–O, 11–S, 12–S, 13–S, 14–O, 15–S

Can you recall the words?

1. tending to give orders	1. D_____
2. act of overlooking (an offence, etc.)	2. C_____
3. unyieldingly hostile; beyond soothing; relentless; pitiless	3. I_____
4. intended to soothe or pacify (*adj.*)	4. P_____ *or* P_____
5. one's desire, wishes, or unforced will	5. V_____
6. calmness	6. P_____
7. self-satisfaction; smugness	7. C_____ *or* C_____
8. non-believer in the 'true' religion	8. I_____
9. kindly; well-disposed	9. B_____ *or* B_____ *or* B_____
10. unfaithfulness	10. I_____
11. involving a blessing (*aaj.*)	11. B_____
12. doing something good or kind (*adj.*)	12. B_____

13. faithfulness   13. F_____
14. sincere; valid; in good faith   14. B_____
15. one who does something good, kind, or charitable (for another)   15. B_____
16. a kind or charitable deed   16. B_____
17. recipient of kindness, gift, etc.   17. B_____
18. able to be soothed or pacified   18. P_____

Key: 1–dictatorial, 2–condonation, 3–implacable, 4–placatory *or* placative, 5–volition, 6–placidity, 7–complacence *or* complacency, 8–infidel, 9–benign, benignant, *or* benevolent, 10–infidelity, 11–benedictory, 12–beneficent, 13–fidelity, 14–bona fide, 15–benefactor, 16–benefaction, 17–beneficiary, 18–placable

Chapter review

A.   Do you recognize the words?

1. To belittle:
 (a) titillate, (b) disparage, (c) adulate
2. To be purposely confusing:
 (a) equivocate, (b) obviate, (c) proscribe
3. To work to the disadvantage of:
 (a) malign, (b) militate, (c) placate
4. To slander:
 (a) malign, (b) condone, (c) placate
5. Lack of equality:
 (a) parity, (b) disparity, (c) ambiguity
6. Phrase that may have two interpretations, one of them indelicate or risqué:
 (a) equivocation, (b) ambiguity, (c) double entendre
7. Hateful:
 (a) malignant, (b) benignant, (c) malaise

8. Ill-will:
   (a) malaise, (b) malevolence, (c) maleficence
9. Kindly:
   (a) benevolent, (b) placid, (c) complacent
10. Inflexibly hostile:
   (a) implacable, (b) placatory, (c) militant
11. Giving orders imperiously:
   (a) benedictory, (b) dictatorial, (c) adulatory
12. Self-satisfaction:
   (a) complacency, (b) placation, (c) placidity

Key: 1–b, 2–a, 3–b, 4–a, 5–b, 6–c, 7–a, 8–b, 9–a, 10–a, 11–b, 12–a

B.   **Can you recognize roots?**

Root	Meaning	Example
1. *par*	_____	parity
2. *aequus (equ-)*	_____	equivocal
3. *vox, vocis*	_____	vocal
4. *nox, noctis*	_____	nocturnal
5. *libra*	_____	equilibrist
6. *latus, lateris*	_____	equilateral
7. *equus*	_____	equine
8. *fero*	_____	vociferous
9. *magnus*	_____	magnify
10. *scribo, scriptus*	_____	proscribe
11. *manus*	_____	manuscript
12. *post*	_____	postscript
13. *via*	_____	trivial
14. *militis*	_____	militate
15. *malus*	_____	malefactor
16. *dico, dictus*	_____	dictatorial
17. *volo*	_____	volition
18. *facio (fec-, fic-, -fy)*	_____	benefactor
	_____	fiction
	_____	simplify
19. *bonus*	_____	bona fide
20. *fides*	_____	fidelity

21. *phone*   ————————   Dictaphone
22. *plac-*   ————————   placate
23. *dono*   ————————   donation

Key: 1–equal,   2–equal,   3–voice,   4–night,   5–balance, 6–side, 7–horse, 8–carry, bear, 9–large, 10–write, 11–hand, 12–after, 13–road, 14–soldier, 15–bad, 16–say, tell, 17–wish, 18–do, make, 19–good, 20–faith, 21–sound, 22–please, soothe, pacify, 23–give

Teaser questions for the amateur etymologist

1. Keeping in mind the roots *animus* in *equanimity* and *magnus* in *magnify*, can you combine these two roots to form a noun meaning, etymologically, *largeness of mind*? ———————————————. Can you work out the adjectival form, ending in *-ous*, of the noun you have constructed? ——————————.

2. If *equilateral* means *equal-sided*, can you construct an adjective meaning *two-sided*? ——————————.

3. *Trans-* is a prefix meaning *across*. Build a verb meaning *to write across* (from one form or language to another): ———————— ————————————. What is the noun derived from this verb? ——————————.

4. What disease was so named on the erroneous assumption that it was caused by 'bad air'? ——————————.

5. *Facio* may appear in English words as *fec-*. Using the prefix *con-*, together, can you form a noun sometimes used as a synonym for a sweet, cake, or ice cream (etymologically, 'something made together')? ——————————.

(Answers in Chapter 18)

The thrill of recognition

You have been adding, over the past twenty-three sessions, hundreds of words to your vocabulary; you have been learning hundreds of prefixes, roots, and suffixes that make it possible for you to work out the meaning of many unfamiliar words you may come across in your reading.

As time goes on and you notice more and more of the words you have studied whenever you read, or whenever you listen to lectures, the radio, or TV, the thrill of recognition plus the immediate comprehension of complex ideas will provide a dividend of incalculable value.

You will hear these words in conversation, and you will begin to use them yourself, unselfconsciously, whenever something you want to say is best expressed by one of the words that exactly verbalizes your thinking. Another priceless dividend!

So keep on! You are involved in a dividend-paying activity that will eventually make you intellectually rich.

(End of Session 23)

How to speak naturally

Consider this statement by Louis Bromfield, a noted American author: 'If I, as a novelist, wrote dialogue for my characters which was meticulously grammatical, the result would be the creation of a speech which rendered the characters pompous and unreal'.

And this one by Jacques Barzun, former literary critic for *Harper's*: 'Speech, after all, is in some measure an expression of character, and flexibility in its use is a good way to tell your friends from the robots'.

These are typical reactions of professional people to the old restrictions of formal English grammar. Do the actual teachers of English feel the same way?

'Grammar is only an analysis after the facts, a post-mortem on usage,' said the Canadian economist and humorist Stephen Leacock in *How to Write*. 'Usage comes first and usage must rule.'

One way to discover current trends in usage is to poll a cross section of people who use the language professionally, inquiring as to their opinion of the acceptability, in everyday speech, of certain specific and controversial expressions. A questionnaire I prepared recently was answered by eighty-two such people – thirty-one authors, seven book reviewers, thirty-three editors, and eleven professors of English. The results, some of which will be detailed below, may possibly prove startling to you if you have been conditioned to believe, as most of us have, that correct English is rigid, unchangeable, and exclusively dependent on grammatical rules.

Test yourself

1. Californians boast of the *healthy* climate of their state.	RIGHT	WRONG
2. Her new novel is not *as* good as her first one.	RIGHT	WRONG
3. We *can't* hardly believe it.	RIGHT	WRONG
4. This is *her*.	RIGHT	WRONG
5. *Who* are you waiting for?	RIGHT	WRONG
6. Please take care of *whomever* is waiting.	RIGHT	WRONG
7. *Whom* would you like to be if you weren't yourself?	RIGHT	WRONG
8. My wife has been *robbed*.	RIGHT	WRONG
9. Is this *desert* fattening?	RIGHT	WRONG

1. Californians boast of the *healthy* climate of their state.

RIGHT. There is a distinction, says formal grammar, between *healthy* and *healthful*. A person can be *healthy* – I am still quoting the rule – if he possesses good health. But climate must be *healthful*, since it is *conducive* to health. This distinction is sometimes observed in writing but rarely in everyday speech, as you have probably noticed. Even the dictionaries have stopped splitting hairs – they permit you to say *healthy* no matter which of the two meanings you intend.

'*Healthy* climate' was accepted as current educated usage by twenty-six of the thirty-three editors who answered the questionnaire, six of the seven book reviewers, nine of the eleven professors of English, and twenty of the thirty-one authors. The earlier distinction, in short, is rapidly becoming obsolete.

2. Her new novel is not *as* good as her first one.

RIGHT. If you have studied formal grammar, you will recall that after a negative verb the 'proper' word is *so*, not *as*. Is this rule observed by educated speakers? Hardly ever.

The tally on this use of *as* showed seventy-four for, only eight against.

3. We *can't* hardly believe it.

WRONG. Of the eighty-two professional people who answered my questionnaire, seventy-six rejected this sentence; it is evident that *can't hardly* is far from acceptable in educated speech. Preferred usage: We *can* hardly believe it.

4. This is *her*.

WRONG. This substitution of *her* where the rule requires *she* was rejected by fifty-seven of my eighty-two respondents. Paradoxically enough, although 'It's *me*' and 'This is *me*' are fully established in educated speech, 'This is *her*' still seems to be condemned by the majority of cultivated speakers. Nevertheless, the average person, I imagine, may feel a bit uncomfortable saying 'This is *she*' — it sounds almost too sophisticated.

This is more than an academic problem. If the voice at the other end of a telephone conversation makes the opening move with 'I'd like to speak to Jane Doe [your name, for argument's sake]', you are, unfortunately, on the horns of a very real dilemma. 'This is *she*' may sound prissy — 'This is *her*' may give the impression that you're uneducated. Other choices are equally doubtful. 'Speaking!' is suspiciously businesslike if the call comes to your home, and 'I am Jane Doe!' may make you feel like the opening line of a school play. The need for a decision arises several times in a busy day — and, I am sorry to report, the English language is just deficient enough not to be of much help. I wonder how it would be if you just grunted affably?

5. *Who* are you waiting for?

RIGHT. *Formal grammar* not only requires *whom* but demands that the word order be changed to 'For whom are you waiting?' (Just try talking with such formality on everyday occasions and see how long you'll keep your friends.)

Who is the normal, popular form as the first word of a sentence, no matter what the grammatical construction. The score for acceptance of the sentence as it stands (with *who*) was sixty-six out of eighty-two. If, like most unpedantic speakers, you prefer *who* to *whom* for informal occasions, you will be happy to hear that modern trends in English are all on your side.

6. Please take care of *whomever* is waiting.

WRONG. *Whomever* is awkward and a little silly in this sentence. It is also contrary to grammatical rule. People who are willing to be sufficiently insufferable to use *whomever* in this construction have been tempted into error by the adjacent word *of*. They believe that since they are following a preposition with an objective pronoun they are speaking impeccable grammar. In actuality, however, *whomever* is not the object of the preposition *of* but the subject of the verb *is waiting*. Preferable form: Please take care of *whoever* is waiting.

7. *Whom* would you like to be if you weren't yourself.

WRONG. Here is another and typical example of the damage which an excessive reverence for *whom* can do to an innocent person's speech. Judged by grammatical rule, *whom* is incorrect in this sentence (the verb *to be* requires *who*); judged by normal speech patterns, it is absurd. This use of *whom* probably comes from an abortive attempt to sound elegant.

8. My wife has been *robbed*

RIGHT — If something your wife owns was taken by means of theft. However, if your wife herself was kidnapped, or in some way talked into leaving you, she was *stolen*, not *robbed*. To *rob* is to abscond with the contents of something — to *steal* is to walk off with the thing itself. Needless to say, both forms of activity are highly antisocial and equally illegal.

9. Is this *desert* fattening?

WRONG. The *dessert* that is fattening is spelt with double *s*. With one *s*, it's a desert, like the Sahara. Remember the double *s* in dessert by thinking how much you'd like *two* portions, if only your waistline permitted.

10

HOW TO TALK ABOUT VARIOUS SPEECH HABITS

(Sessions 24–27)

Teaser Preview

What adjective describes people who:

- *are disinclined to conversation?*
- *are brief and to the point in their speech?*
- *are blocked or incoherent in their speech?*
- *show by their speech that they are trite and unimaginative?*
- *use more words than necessary?*
- *are forcefully compelling and logical in their speech?*
- *talk rapidly and fluently?*
- *are noisy and clamorous?*
- *are talkative?*

Session 24

Perhaps some of your richest and most satisfying experiences have been with people to whom you can just talk, talk, talk. As you speak, previously untapped springs of ideas and emotions begin to flow; you hear yourself saying things you never thought you knew.

What kinds of people might you find yourself in conversation with? In this chapter we start by examining ten types, discovering the adjective that aptly describes each one.

Ideas

1. Saying little

There are some people who just don't like to talk. It's not that they prefer to listen. Good listeners hold up their end of the conversation delightfully – with appropriate facial expressions; with empathetic smiles, giggles, squeals, and sighs at just the right time; and with encouraging nods or phrases like 'go on!', 'Fantastic!', 'And then what happened?'.

These people like neither to talk nor to listen – they act as if conversation is a bore, even a painful waste of time. Try to engage them, and the best you may expect for your efforts is a vacant stare, a noncommittal grunt, or an impatient silence. Finally, in frustration, you give up, thinking 'Are they self-conscious? Do they hate people? Do they hate *me*?'.

The adjective: *taciturn*

2.   Saying little – meaning much

There is an anecdote about Calvin Coolidge, who, when he was president of the USA, was often called (though probably not to his face) 'silent Cal':

A young newspaperwoman was sitting next to him at a banquet, so the story goes, and turned to him mischievously.

'Mr. Coolidge,' she said, 'I have a bet with my editor that I can get you to say more than two words to me this evening.'

'*You lose*', Coolidge rejoined simply.

The adjective: *laconic*

3.   When the words won't come

Under the pressure of some strong emotion – fear, rage, anger, for example – people may find it difficult, or even impossible, to utter words, to get their feelings unjumbled and untangled enough to form understandable sentences. They undoubtedly have a lot they want to say, but the best they can do is splutter!

The adjective: *inarticulate*

4.   Much talk, little sense

Miss Bates, a character in the novel *Emma*, by Jane Austen:

'So obliging of you! No, we should not have heard, if it had not been for this particular circumstance, of her being able to come here so soon. My mother is so delighted. For she is to be three months with us at least. Three months, she says so, positively, as I am going to have the pleasure of reading to you. The case is, you see, that the Campbells are going to Ireland. Mrs. Dixon has persuaded her father and mother to come over and see her directly. I was going to say, but, however, different countries, and so she wrote a very urgent letter to her mother, or her father, I declare I do not know which it was, but we shall see presently in Jane's letter . . .'

The adjective: *garrulous*

5.   Unoriginal

Some people are completely lacking in originality and imagination – and their talk shows it. Everything they say is trite, hackneyed, commonplace, humourless — their speech patterns are full of clichés and stereotypes, their phraseology is without sparkle.

The adjective: *banal*

6.   Words, words, words!

They talk and talk and talk — it's not so much the quantity you object to as the repetitiousness. They phrase, rephrase, and re-rephrase their thoughts — using far more words than necessary, overwhelming you with words, drowning you with them, until your only thought is how to escape, or maybe how to die.

The adjective: *verbose*

7.   Words in quick succession

They are rapid, fluent talkers, the words seeming to roll off their tongues with such ease and lack of effort, and sometimes with such copiousness, that you listen with amazement.

The adjective: *voluble*

8.   Words that convince

They express their ideas persuasively, forcefully, brilliantly, and in a way that calls for wholehearted assent and agreement from an intelligent listener.

The adjective: *cogent*

9.   The sound and the fury

Their talk is loud, noisy, clamorous, vehement. What may be lacking in content is compensated for in force and loudness.

The adjective: *vociferous*

10.   Quantity

They talk a great deal — a very great deal. They may be voluble, vociferous, garrulous, verbose, but never inarticulate, taciturn, or laconic. No matter. It's the quantity and continuity that are most conspicuous.

The adjective: *loquacious*

These ten words revolve around the idea of varying kinds and ways of talking and not talking. Many of the adjectives are close in meaning, but each contains its unique difference.

Quality	Adjective
1. silence, unresponsiveness	taciturn
2. economy, brevity, meaningfulness	laconic
3. awkwardness, spluttering, incoherence	inarticulate
4. rambling chatter	garrulous
5. hackneyed, unoriginal phraseology	banal
6. wordiness, repetitiousness	verbose
7. fluency, rapidity	voluble
8. logic, clarity, persuasiveness	cogent
9. noise, vehemence	vociferous
10. talkativeness	loquacious

Using the words

Can you pronounce the words?

1.	*taciturn*	TAS'-i-tərn
2.	*laconic*	lə-KON'-ik
3.	*inarticulate*	in'-ah-TIK'-yŏo-lət
4.	*garrulous*	GAR'-ŏo-ləs
5.	*banal*	bə-NAHL'
6.	*verbose*	vər-BŌS'
7.	*voluble*	VOL'-yŏo-bəl
8.	*cogent*	KŌ'-jənt
9.	*vociferous*	vō-SIF'-ər-əs
10.	*loquacious*	lə-KWAY'-shəs

Can you work with the words?

1. taciturn	a.	chattering meaninglessly
2. laconic	b.	wordy
3. inarticulate	c.	trite, hackneyed, unoriginal

4. garrulous   d. fluent and rapid
5. banal   e. noisy, loud
6. verbose   f. spluttering unintelligbly
7. voluble   g. talkative
8. cogent   h. brilliantly compelling, persuasive
9. vociferous   i. unwilling to engage in
                         conversation
10. loquacious   j. using few words packed with
                         meaning

Key: 1–i, 2–j, 3–f, 4–a, 5–c, 6–b, 7–d, 8–h, 9–e, 10–g

Do you understand the words?

1. Do *taciturn* people usually make others feel comfortable and welcome?	YES	NO
2. Does a *laconic* speaker use more words than necessary?	YES	NO
3. Does rage make some people *inarticulate*?	YES	NO
4. Is it interesting to listen to *garrulous* old men?	YES	NO
5. Do *banal* speakers show a great deal of originality?	YES	NO
6. Is *verbose* a complimentary term?	YES	NO
7. Is it easy to be *voluble* when you don't know the subject you are talking about?	YES	NO
8. Do unintelligent people usually make *cogent* statements?	YES	NO
9. Is a *vociferous* demand ordinarily made by a shy, quiet person?	YES	NO
10. Do *loquacious* people spend more time talking than listening?	YES	NO

Key: 1–no, 2–no, 3–yes, 4–no, 5–no, 6–no, 7–no, 8–no,
        9–no, 10–yes

Can you recall the words?

Do you know that new nerve patterns are formed by repeated actions? As a very young child, you tied your shoelaces and buttoned your clothing with great concentration – the activity was directed, controlled, purposeful, exciting. As you grew older and more skilful, you tied and buttoned with scarcely a thought of what you were doing. Your fingers flew about their task almost automatically – for the habit had formed a nerve pattern and the action needed little if any conscious attention.

That's simple enough to understand. If you do not remember your own experiences, you can observe the phenomenon of struggling with a skill, mastering it, and finally making it a self-starting habit by watching any young child. Or you can simply take my word for it.

You need not take my word for the way a mastery of new words is acquired. You can see in yourself, as you work with this book, how adding words to your vocabulary is exactly analogous to a child's mastery of tying shoelaces. First you struggle with the concepts; then you eventually master them; finally, by frequent work with the new words (now you see the reason for the great number of exercises, the repetitious writing, saying, thinking) you build up new nerve patterns and you begin to use the new words with scarcely any consciousness of what you are doing.

Watch this common but important phenomenon closely as you do the next exercise. Your total absorption of the material so far has given you complete mastery of our ten basic words. Prove that you are beginning to form new nerve patterns in relation to these words by writing the one that fits each brief definition. The more quickly you think of the word that applies, the surer you can be that using these words will soon be as automatic and unself-conscious as putting on your shoes or buttoning up your clothes in the morning.

1. talkative   1. L_____
2. noisy, vehement, clamorous   2. V_____
3. incoherent; spluttering   3. I_____
4. talking ceaselessly and with little meaning   4. G_____
5. disinclined to conversation   5. T_____

6. talking in hackneyed phraseology	6. B	_____
7. showing a fine economy in the use of words	7. L	_____
8. forceful and convincing	8. C	_____
9. talking rapidly and fluently	9. V	_____
10. using more words than necessary	10. V	_____

Key: 1—loquacious, 2—vociferous, 3—inarticulate, 4—garru-
        lous, 5—taciturn, 6—banal, 7—laconic, 8—cogent,
        9—voluble, 10—verbose

(End of Session 24)

Session 25

Origins and related words

1. About keeping one's mouth shut

If you let your mind play over some of the *taciturn* people you know, you will realize that their abnormal disinclination to conversation makes them seem morose, sullen, and unfriendly. Calvin Coolidge's *taciturnity* (tas-i-TƏRN'-i-ti) was world-famous, and no one, I am sure, ever conceived of him as cheerful, overfriendly, or particularly sociable. There are doubtless many possible causes of such verbal rejection of the world: perhaps lack of self-assurance, feelings of inadequacy or hostility; excessive seriousness or introspection, or just plain having nothing to say. Who knows, the cause may be geographical and climatic, rather than psychological.

Taciturn is from a Latin verb *taceo*, to be silent, and is one of those words whose full meaning cannot be expressed by any other combination of syllables. It has many synonyms, among them *silent, uncommunicative, reticent, reserved, secretive, tight-lipped,* and *close-mouthed;* but no other word indicates the *permanent, habitual,* and *temperamental* disinclination to talk implied by *taciturn.*

2. Better left unsaid

Tacit (TAS'-it) derives also from *taceo.*

Here is a man dying of cancer. He suspects what his disease is, and everyone else, of course, knows. Yet he never mentions the dread word, and no one who visits him ever breathes a syllable of it in his hearing. It is *tacitly* understood by all concerned that the word will remain forever unspoken.

(Such a situation today, however, may or may not be typical – there appears to be a growing tendency among doctors and families to be open and honest with people who are dying.)

Consider another situation:

An executive is engaging in extracurricular activities with his secretary. Yet during office time they are as formal and distant as any two human beings can well be. Neither of them ever said to the other, 'Now, look here, we may be lovers after five o'clock, but between nine and five we must preserve the utmost decorum, okay?' Such speech, such a verbal arrangement, is considered unnecessary – so we may say that the two have a *tacit* agreement (i.e. nothing was ever actually *said*) to maintain a complete employer-employee relationship during office hours.

Anything *tacit*, then, is unspoken, unsaid, not verbalized. We speak of a *tacit* agreement, arrangement, acceptance, rejection, assent, refusal, etc. A person is never called *tacit*.

The noun is *tacitness* (TAS'-it-nəs). (Bear in mind that you can transform any adjective into a noun by adding *-ness*, though in many cases there may be a more sophisticated, or more common, noun form.)

Changing the *a* of the root *taceo* to *i*, and adding the prefix *re-*, again, and the adjective suffix *-ent*, we can construct the English word *reticent* (RET'-i-sənt).

Someone is *reticent* who prefers to keep silent, whether out of shyness, embarrassment, or fear of revealing what should not be revealed. (The idea of 'againness' in the prefix has been lost in the current meaning of the word.)

We have frequently made nouns out of *-ent* adjectives. The noun form of *reticent* is *reticence* (RET'-i-səns).

3.   Talk, talk, talk!

Loquacious people love to talk. This adjective is not necessarily a put-down, but the implication, when you so characterize such people, is that you wish they would pause for breath once in a while so that *you* can have your turn. The noun is *loquacity* (lə-KWAS'-i-ti), or, of course, *loquaciousness*.

The word derives from Latin *loquor*, to speak, a root found also in:

1. *soliloquy* (sə-LIL'-ə-kwi) – a speech to oneself (*loquor* plus *solus*, alone), or, etymologically, a speech when alone.

We often talk to ourselves, but usually silently, the words going through our minds but not actually passing our lips. The term *soliloquy* is commonly applied to utterances made in a play by characters who are speaking their thoughts aloud so the audience won't have to guess. The *soliloquist* (sə-LIL'-ə-kwist) may be alone; or other members of the cast may be present on stage, but of course they don't hear what's being said, because they're not supposed to know. Eugene O'Neill made novel uses of *soliloquies* in *Mourning Becomes Electra* – the characters made honest disclosures of their feelings and thoughts to the audience, but kept the other players in the dark.

The verb is to *soliloquize* (sə-LIL'-ə-kwīz').

2. A *ventriloquist* (ven-TRIL'-ə-kwist) is one who can throw his voice. A listener thinks the sound is coming from some source other than the person speaking. The combining root is Latin *venter, ventris*, belly; etymologically, *ventriloquism* (ven-TRIL'-ə-kwiz-əm) is the art of 'speaking from the belly'. The adjective is *ventriloquistic* (ven-tril'-ə-KWIS'-tik) or *ventriloquial* (ven'-tri-LŌ'-kwi-əl). Can you work out how the verb will end? Write the verb:

_____

3. *Colloquial* (kə-LŌ-kwi-əl) combines *loquor*, to speak, with the prefix *con-*. (*Con-* is spelled *col-* before a root starting with *l*; *cor-* before a root starting with *r*; *com-*before a root starting with *m, p,* or *b*.) When people speak together they are engaging in conversation – and their language is usually more informal and less rigidly grammatical than what you might expect in writing or in public addresses. *Colloquial* patterns are perfectly correct – they are simply informal, and suitable to everyday conversation.

A *colloquialism* (kə-LŌ'-kwi-ə-liz-əm), therefore, is a *conversational-style* expression, like 'He hasn't got any' or 'Who are you going with?' as contrasted to the formal or literary 'He has none' or 'With whom are you going?' *Colloquial* English is the English you and I talk on everyday occasions – it is not slangy, vulgar, or illiterate.

4. A *circumlocution* (sər-kəm-lə-KYŌŌ'-shən), is, etymologically, a 'talking around' (*circum-*, around). Any way of expressing an

idea that is roundabout or indirect is *circumlocutory* (sər-kəm-LOK'-yə-tər'-i) – you are now familiar with the common adjective suffix *-ory*.

Review of etymology

Prefix, Root, Suffix	Meaning	English Word
1. *taceo*	to be silent	_____
2. *-ity*	noun suffix	_____
3. *-ness*	noun suffix	_____
4. *-ent*	adjective suffix	_____
5. *-ence, -ency*	noun suffix	_____
6. *re-*	again	_____
7. *loquor*	to speak	_____
8. *solus*	alone	_____
9. *-ist*	one who	_____
10. *-ize*	verb suffix	_____
11. *venter, ventris*	belly	_____
12. *-ic*	adjective suffix	_____
13. *-ous*	adjective suffix	_____
14. *con-, col-, com-, cor-*	with, together	_____
15. *-al*	adjective suffix	_____
16. *-ism*	noun suffix	_____

Working with the words

Can you pronounce the words?

1. *taciturnity*	tas-i-TəRN'-i-ti
2. *tacit*	TAS'-it
3. *tacitness*	TAS'-it-nəs
4. *reticent*	RET'-i-sənt
5. *reticence*	RET'-i-səns
6. *loquaciousness*	lə-KWAY'-shəs-nəs
7. *loquacity*	lə-KWAS'-i-ti
8. *soliloquy*	sə-LIL'-ə-kwi
9. *soliloquist*	sə-LIL'-ə-kwist

10. *soliloquize*   sə-LIL'-ə-kwīz'
11. *ventriloquist*   ven'-TRIL'-ə-kwist
12. *ventriloquism*   ven-TRIL'-ə-kwiz-əm
13. *ventriloquistic*   ven-tril'-ə-KWIS'-tik
14. *ventriloquial*   ven-tri-LŌ'-kwi-əl
15. *ventriloquize*   ven-TRIL'-ə-kwīz'
16. *colloquial*   kə-LŌ'-kwi-əl
17. *colloquialism*   kə-LŌ'-kwi-ə-liz-əm
18. *circumlocution* sər-kəm-lə-KYŌŌ'-shən
19. *circumlocutory* sər'-kəm-LOK'-yə-tər'-i

Can you work with the words?

1. tacituniry   a. unwillingness to talk, out of fear, shyness, reserve, etc.

2. tacitness   b. talking, or a speech, 'to oneself'
3. reticence   c. art of throwing one's voice
4. loquacity   d. unwillingness to engage in conversation

5. soliloquy   e. informal expression used in everyday conversation

6. ventriloquism   f. state of being understood though not actually expressed

7. colloquialism   g. a talking around; method of talking indirectly or in a roundabout way

8. circumlocution   h. talkativeness

Key: 1–d, 2–f, 3–a, 4–h, 5–b, 6–c, 7–e, 8–g

Do you understand the words?

1. A *tacit* understanding is put into words.   TRUE   FALSE

2. Inhibited people are seldom *reticent* about expressing anger.   TRUE   FALSE

3. A *soliloquist* expresses his thoughts aloud.   TRUE   FALSE

4. A *ventriloquial* performance on stage involves a dummy who appears to be talking.   TRUE   FALSE

5. A *colloquial* style of writing is ungrammatical.   TRUE   FALSE

6. *Circumlocutory* speech is direct and forthright.   TRUE   FALSE

7. *Inarticulate* people are generally given to *loquaciousness*.   TRUE   FALSE

8. A *soliloquy* is a dialogue.   TRUE   FALSE

Key: 1–F, 2–F, 3–T, 4–T, 5–F, 6–F, 7–F, 8–F

Can you recall the words?

1. to speak to oneself   1. S_____
2. to throw one's voice   2. V_____
3. unwillingness to engage in conversation   3. T_____
4. unspoken   4. T_____
5. referring to an indirect, roundabout style of expression (*adj.*)   5. C_____
6. suitable for informal conversation   6. C_____
7. talkativeness   7. L_____
    or   L_____
8. reluctance to express one's feelings or thoughts   8. R_____
    or   R_____
9. a speech to oneself, especially in a play   9. S_____
10. an indirect, roundabout expression   10. C_____

Key: 1--soliloquize, 2--ventriloquize, 3--taciturnity, 4--tacit, 5--circumlocutory, 6--colloquial, 7--loquaciousness *or* loquacity, 8--reticence, 9--soliloquy, 10--circumlocution

(End of Session 25)

Session 26

Origins and related words

1.   A Spartan virtue

In ancient Sparta, originally known as *Laconia*, the citizens were long-suffering, hard-bitten, stoical, military-minded, and noted for their economy of speech. Legend has it that when Philip of Macedonia was storming the gates of Sparta (or Laconia), he sent a message to the besieged king saying, 'If we capture your city we will burn it to the ground.' A one-word answer came back: 'If.' It was now probably Philip's turn to be speechless, though history does not record his reaction.

It is from the name *Laconia* that we derive our word *laconic* – pithy, concise, economical in the use of words almost to the point of curtness; precisely the opposite of *verbose*.

Like the man who was waiting at a snack bar for a ham sandwich. When it was ready, the assistant inquired politely, 'Will you eat it here, or take it with you?'

'Both' was the *laconic* reply.

Or like the woman who was watching a drunk imbibing dry martinis at a cocktail bar. The drunk downed the contents of each cocktail glass at one gulp, daintily nibbled and swallowed the bowl, then finally turned the glass over and ate the base. The stem he threw into a corner. This amazing gustatory feat went on for half an hour, until a dozen stems were lying shattered in the corner, and the drunk had chewed and swallowed enough bowls and bases to start a glass factory. He suddenly turned to the lady and asked belligerently, 'I suppose you think I'm crazy, don't you?' 'Sure – the stem is the best part' was the *laconic* answer.

We have learned that -*ness*, -*ity*, and -*ism* are suffixes that transform adjectives into nouns – and all three can be used with *laconic*:

. . . with characteristic *laconicness* (lə-KON'-ik-nəs)

. . . her usual *laconicity* (lak'-ə-NIS'-ə-ti)

. . . his habitual *laconism* (LAK'-ə-niz-əm)

. . . with, for him, unusual *laconicism* (lə-KON'-i-siz-əm)

A *laconism* or *laconicism* is also the expression that is pithy and concise, as the famous report from a naval commander in World War II: 'Saw sub, sank same'.

2.   Brilliant

Cogent is a term of admiration. A *cogent* argument is well put, convincing, hardly short of brilliant. *Cogency* (KŌ'-jən-si) shows a keen mind, an ability to think clearly and logically. The word derives from the Latin verb *cogo*, to drive together, compel, force. A *cogent* argument *compels* acceptance because of its logic, its persuasiveness, its appeal to one's sense of reason.

3.   Back to talk

You will recall that *loquor*, to speak, is the source of *loquacity*, *soliloquy*, *ventriloquism*, *colloquialism*, *circumlocution*. This root is also the base on which *eloquent* (EL'-ə-kwənt), *magniloquent* (mag-NIL'-ə-kwənt), and *grandiloquent* (gran-DIL'-ə-kwənt) are built.

The *eloquent* person speaks *out* (*e*-, from *ex*-, out), is vividly expressive, fluent, forceful, or persuasive in language ('the prosecutor's *eloquent* plea to the jury'). The word is partially synonymous with *cogent*, but *cogent* implies irresistible logical reasoning and intellectual keenness, while *eloquent* suggests artistic expression, strong emotional appeal, the skilful use of language to move and arouse a listener.

Magniloquent (*magnus*, large) and *grandiloquent* (*grandis*, grand) are virtually identical in meaning. *Magniloquence* or *grandiloquence* is the use of high-flown, grandiose, even pompous language; of large and impressive words; of lofty, flowery, or overelegant phraseology. Home is *a place of residence;* wife is *helpmate, helpmeet,* or *better half;* women are *the fair sex;* children are *offspring* or *progeny;* a doctor is a *member of the medical fraternity;* people are the *species Homo sapiens,* etc., etc.

Loquacious, verbose, voluble, and *garrulous* people are all talkative; but each type, you will recall, has a special quality.

If you are *verbose,* you smother your ideas with excess words, with such an overabundance of words that your listener either drops into a state of helpless confusion or falls asleep.

If you are *voluble,* you speak rapidly, fluently, glibly, without hesitation, stutter, or stammer; you are vocal, verbal, and highly articulate.

If you are *garrulous,* you talk constantly, and usually aimlessly and meaninglessly, about trifles. We often hear the word used in 'a *garrulous* old man' or 'a *garrulous* old woman', since in very advanced age the mind may wander and lose the ability to discriminate between the important and the unimportant, between the interesting and the dull.

Verbose is from Latin *verbum,* word – the *verbose* person is wordy.

Voluble comes from Latin *volvo, volutus,* to roll – words effortlessly roll off the *voluble* speaker's tongue.

And *garrulous* derives from Latin *garrio,* to chatter – a *garrulous* talker chatters away like a monkey.

The suffix *-ness* can be added to all these adjectives to form nouns. Alternate noun forms end in *-ity:*

verbosity	(vər-BOS'-i-ti)
volubility	(vol'-yoo-BIL'-i-ti)
garrulity	(ga-ROO'-li-ti)

4.   At large

We discovered *magnus,* large, big, great, in Chapter 9, and find it again in *magniloquent* (etymologically, 'talking big'). The root occurs in a number of other words:

1. *Magnanimous* (mag-NAN'-i-məs) – big-hearted, generous, forgiving (etymologically, 'great-minded'). (*Magnus* plus *animus,* mind.) We'll discuss this word in depth in Chapter 12.

2. *Magnate* (MAG'-nayt) – a person of great power or influence, a big wheel, as a business *magnate.*

3. *Magnify* – to make larger, or make seem larger (*magnus* plus *-fy* from *facio,* to make), as in '*magnify* your problems'.

4. *Magnificent* – *magnus* plus *fic-*, from *facio*.

5. *Magnitude* – *magnus* plus the common noun suffix *-tude*, as in *fortitude*, *multitude*, *gratitude*, etc.

6. *Magnum* (as of champagne or wine) – a large bottle, generally twice the size of a standard bottle.

7. *Magnum opus* (MAG'-nəm Ō'-pes) – etymologically, a 'big work'; actually, the greatest work, or masterpiece, of an artist, writer, or composer. *Opus* is the Latin word for *work;* the plural of *opus* is used in the English word *opera*, etymologically, 'a number of works', actually a musical drama containing overture, singing, and other forms of music, i.e. many musical works. The verb form *opero*, to work, occurs in *operate*, *co-operate*, *operator*, etc.

5. Words, words, words!

Latin *verbum* is *word*. A *verb* is the important word in a sentence; *verbatim* (vər-BAY'-tim) is word-for-word (a *verbatim* report).

Verbal (vər-bəl), ending in the adjectival suffix *-al*, may refer either to a *verb*, or to words in general (a *verbal* fight); or it may mean, loosely, *oral* or *spoken*, rather than written (*verbal* agreement or contract); or, describing people ('she is quite *verbal*'), it may refer to a ready ability to put feelings or thoughts into words.

Working from *verbal*, can you add a common verb suffix to form a word meaning *to put into words*?

_____

Verbiage (VƏR'-bi-ij) has two meanings: an excess of words ('Such *verbiage!*'); or a style or manner of using words (medical *verbiage*, military *verbiage*).

6. Roll on, and on!

Volvo, volutus, to roll, the source of *voluble*, is the root on which many important English words are based.

Revolve (ri-VOLV') – roll again (and again), or keeping turning round. Wheels *revolve*, the earth *revolves* around the sun, the cylinder of a revolver *revolves*. (The prefix is *re-*, back or again.)

The noun is *revolution* (rev-ə-LOO'-shən), which can be one such complete rolling, or, by logical extension, a radical change of any sort (TV was responsible for a *revolution* in the entertainment industry), especially political (the American, or French, *Revolu-*

tion). The adjective *revolutionary* (rev'-ə-LŌO'-shən-ə-ri) introduces us to a new adjective suffix, *-ary*, as in *contrary, disciplinary, stationary, imaginary*, etc. (But *-ary* is sometimes also a noun suffix, as in *dictionary, commentary*, etc.)

Add different prefixes to *volvo* to construct two more English words:

1. *involve* – etymologically, 'roll in' ('I didn't want to get *involved!*'). Noun: *involvement*.

2. *evolve* (i-VOLV') – etymolgoically, 'roll out' (*e-*, out); hence to unfold, or gradually develop ('The final plan *evolved* from some informal discussions'; 'The political party *evolved* from a group of interested citizens who met frequently to protest against government actions').

By analogy with the forms derived from *revolve*, can you construct the noun and adjective of *evolve*?

Noun: _____.

Adjective: _____.

Review of etymology

Prefix, Root, Suffix	Meaning	English Word
1. *Laconia*	Sparta	_____
2. *-ness*	noun suffix	_____
3. *-ism*	noun suffix	_____
4. *-ity*	noun suffix	_____
5. *e- (ex-)*	out	_____
6. *-ent*	adjective suffix	_____
7. *-ence*	noun suffix	_____
8. *magnus*	big	_____
9. *grandis*	grand	_____
10. *verbum*	word	_____
11. *volvo, volutus*	to roll	_____
12. *garrio*	to chatter	_____
13. *animus*	mind	_____
14. *-fy*	to make	_____
15. *-tude*	noun suffix	_____
16. *opus*	work	_____
17. *opero*	to work	_____
18. *-al*	adjective suffix	_____

19. *-ize*	verb suffix	_____
20. *re-*	again, back	_____
21. *-ary*	adjective suffix	_____
22. *in-*	in	_____

Using the words

Can you pronounce the words? (I)

1. *laconicity*	lak'-ə-NIS'-ə-ti
2. *laconism*	LAK'-ə-niz-əm
3. *laconicism*	lə-KON'-i-siz-əm
4. *eloquent*	EL'-ə-kwənt
5. *eloquence*	EL'-ə-kwəns
6. *magniloquent*	mag-NIL'-ə-kwənt
7. *magniloquence*	mag-NIL'-ə-kwəns
8. *grandiloquent*	gran-DIL'-ə-kwənt
9. *grandiloquence*	gran-DIL'-ə-kwəns
10. *verbosity*	vər-BOS'-i-ti
11. *volubility*	vol'-yo͝o-BIL'-i-ti
12. *garrulity*	ga-RO͞O'-li-ti
13. *cogency*	KŌ'-jən-si

Can you pronounce the words? (II)

1. *magnanimous*	mag-NAN'-i-məs
2. *magnate*	MAG'-nayt
3. *magnum opus*	MAG'-nəm Ō'-pəs
4. *verbatim*	vər-BAY'-tim
5. *verbal*	VəR'-bəl
6. *verbalize*	VəR'-bə-līz'
7. *verbiage*	VəR'-bi-ij
8. *revolve*	ri-VOLV'
9. *revolution*	rev'-ə-LO͞O'-shən
10. *revolutionary*	rev'-ə-LO͞O-shən-ə-ri
11. *evolve*	i-VOLV'
12. *evolution*	eev'(or ev')-ə-LO͞O'-shən
13. *evolutionary*	eev'(or ev')-ə-LO͞O'-shən-ə-ri

.

.

.

Can you work with the words? (I)

1. laconicity
2. eloquence
3. magniloquence
4. verbosity
5. volubility
6. garrulity
7. magnum opus
8. magnate
9. revolution
10. evolution
11. cogency

a. floweriness, pompousness, or elegance in speech
b. incessant chatter with little meaning
c. big wheel; important or influential person
d. great artistic work; masterpiece
e. a gradual unfolding or development; 'a rolling out'
f. 'a rolling round'; radical change; political upheaval
g. great economy in speech
h. fluency, ease, and/or rapidity of speech
i. great, artistic, or emotional expressiveness
j. wordiness
k. persuasiveness through logic; keen-mindedness in reasoning

Key: 1–g, 2–i, 3–a, 4–j, 5–h, 6–b, 7–d, 8–c, 9–f, 10–e, 11–k

Can you work with the words? (II)

1. laconism
2. verbiage
3. verbalize
4. verbal
5. verbatim
6. revolutionary
7. evolutionary

a. word for word
b. to put into words
c. causing, or resulting from, radical change; new and totally different
d. resulting or developing gradually from (something)
e. expressive; emotionally moving
f. pithiness or economy of expression; word or phrase packed with meaning
g. big-hearted; generous, forgiving

8. grandiloquent h. referring or pertaining to, or involving, words; oral, rather than written

9. eloquent i. using flowery, elegant, or impressive phraseology

10. magnanimous j. wordiness; style or manner of using words; type of words

Key: 1–f, 2–j, 3–b, 4–h, 5–a, 6–c, 7–d, 8–i, 9–e, 10–g

Do you understand the words?

1.	Is *laconicism* characteristic of a verbose speaker?	YES	NO
2.	Does a *magniloquent* speaker use short, simple words?	YES	NO
3.	Does a frog *evolve* from a tadpole?	YES	NO
4.	Is an *eloquent* speaker interesting to listen to?	YES	NO
5.	Do verbose people use a lot of *verbiage*?	YES	NO
6.	Is *volubility* characteristic of an inarticulate person?	YES	NO
7.	Does *verbosity* show a careful and economical use of words?	YES	NO
8.	Is a *verbal* person usually inarticulate?	YES	NO
9.	Is a *magnum opus* one of the lesser works of a writer, artist, or composer?	YES	NO
10.	Is a *magnanimous* person selfish and petty-minded?	YES	NO

Key: 1–no, 2–no, 3–yes, 4–yes, 5–yes, 6–no, 7–no, 8–no, 9–no, 10–no

Can you recall the words?

1. gradually unfolding, resulting, or developing (*adj.*)	1. E_____
2. causing, or resulting from, radical change (*adj.*)	2. R_____
3. quality of conciseness and economy in the use of words	3. L_____ or L_____ or L_____ or L_____
4. expressiveness in the use of words	4. E_____
5. turn round and round	5. R_____
6. important person, as in the commercial world	6. M_____
7. unselfish; generous; noble in motive; big-hearted; forgiving	7. M_____
8. using words easily; vocal; articulate; referring to, or involving, words; oral, rather than written	8. V_____
9. style of word usage; type of words; overabundance of words	9. V_____
10. wordiness; quality of using excess words	10. V_____
11. elegance in word usage	11. M_____ or G_____
12. quality of chattering on and on about trivia, or with little meaning	12. G_____
13. fluency and ease in speech	13. V_____
14. word for word	14. V_____
15. masterpiece; great artistic work	15. M_____O_____

16. persuasiveness and
forcefulness in speech or
writing through closely
reasoned logic

16. C_____

Key: 1–evolutionary, 2–revolutionary, 3–laconism, laconicism, laconicity, *or* laconicness, 4–eloquence, 5–revolve, 6–magnate, 7–magnanimous, 8–verbal, 9–verbiage, 10–verbosity, 11–magniloquence *or* grandiloquence, 12–garrulity, 13–volubility, 14–verbatim, 15–magnum opus, 16–cogency

---

(End of Session 26)

Session 27

Origins and related words

1. Front and back – and uncles

The *ventriloquist* appears to talk from the belly (*venter, ventris* plus *loquor*) rather than through the lips (or such was the strange perception of the person who first used the word).

Venter, ventris, belly, is the root on which *ventral* (VEN'-trəl) and *ventricle* are built.

The *ventral* side of an animal, for example, is the front or anterior side – the belly side.

A *ventricle* (VEN'-tri-kəl) is a hollow organ or cavity, or, logically enough, belly, as one of the two chambers of the heart, or one of the four chambers of the brain. The *ventricles* of the heart are the lower chambers, and receive blood from the upper chambers, known as the *atria* or *auricles*. The *auricle* (AW'-ri-kəl), so named because it is somewhat ear-shaped (Latin *auris*, ear), receives blood from the veins; the *auricles* send the blood into the *ventricles*, which in turn pump the blood into the arteries. (It's all very complicated, but fortunately it works.)

The adjective form of *ventricle* is *ventricular* (ven-TRIK'-yoo-lə), which may refer to a *ventricle*, or may mean *having a bellylike bulge*.

Now that you see how *ventricular* is formed from *ventricle*, can you work out the adjective of *auricle*? _____.

How about the adjective of *vehicle*? _____

Or *circle*? _____

No doubt you wrote *auricular* (aw-RIK'-yŏŏ-lə), *vehicular*, and *circular*, and have discovered that nouns ending in *-cle* form adjectives ending in *-cular*.

So now work out the adjective derived from:

clavicle: _____

cuticle: _____

vesicle: _____

testicle: _____

uncle: _____

The answers of course are *clavicular, cuticular, vesicular, testicular* – and for *uncle* you have every right to shout 'Not fair!' (But where is it written that life is fair?)

The Latin word for *uncle* (actually, uncle on the mother's side) is *avunculus*, from which we get *avuncular* (ə-VUNG'-kyŏŏ-lə), referring to an uncle.

Now what about an uncle? Well, traditional or stereotypical uncles are generally kindly, permissive, indulgent, protective – and often give helpful advice. So anyone who exhibits one or more of such traits to another (usually younger) person is *avuncular* or acts in an *avuncular* capacity.

So, at long last, to get back to *ventral*. If there's a front or belly side, anatomically, there must be a reverse – a back side. This is the *dorsal* (DAW'-səl) side, from Latin *dorsum*, the root on which the verb *endorse* (in-DAWS') is built.

If you *endorse* a cheque, you sign it on the back side; if you *endorse* a plan, an idea, etc., you *back* it, you express your approval or support. The noun is *endorsement* (in-DAWS'-mənt).

2.   The noise and the fury

Vociferous derives from Latin *vox, vocis*, voice (a root you met in Chapter 9), plus *fero*, to bear or carry. A *vociferous* rejoinder carries a lot of voice – i.e., it is vehement, loud, noisy, clamorous, shouting. The noun is *vociferousness* (vō-SIF'-ə-rəs-ııəs); the verb is to *vociferate* (vō-SIF'-ə-rayt'). Can you form the noun derived from the verb? _____

3.   To sleep or not to sleep — that is the question

The root *fero* is found also in *somniferous* (som-NIF'-ə-rəs), carrying, hearing, or bringing sleep. So a *somniferous* lecture is so dull and boring that it is sleep-inducing.

Fero is combined with *somnus*, sleep, in *somniferous*. (The suffix -*ous* indicates what part of speech? _____.)

Tack on the negative prefix *in-* to *somnus* to construct *insomnia* (in-SOM'-ni-ə), the abnormal inability to fall asleep when sleep is required or desired. The unfortunate victim of this disability is an *insomniac* (in-SOM'-ni-ak), the adjective is *insomniac* or *insomnious* (in-SOM'-ni-əs). (So -*ous*, in case you could not answer the question in the preceding paragraph, is an *adjective* suffix.)

Add a different adjective suffix to *somnus* to derive *somnolent* (SOM'-nə-lənt), sleepy, drowsy. Can you construct the noun form of *somnolent*? _____ *or* _____.

Combine *somnus* with *ambulo*, to walk, and you have *somnambulism* (som-NAM'-byoŏ-liz-əm), walking in one's sleep. With your increasing skill in using etymology to form words, write the term for the person who is a sleepwalker. _____.
Now add to the word you wrote a two-letter adjective suffix we have learned, to form the adjective: _____.

4.   A walkaway

A *ambulatory* (AM'-byoŏ-lət-ə-ri) patient, as in a hospital or convalescent home, is finally well enough to get out of bed and walk around. A *perambulator* (pə-RAM'-byoŏ-lay'-tə), often shortened to *pram*, is a baby carriage, a vehicle for walking an infant through the streets (*per-*, through). To *perambulate* (pə-RAM'-byoŏ-layt') is, etymologically, 'to walk through'; hence, to stroll around. Can you write the noun form of this verb? _____.

To *amble* (AM'-bəl) is to walk aimlessly; an *ambulance* is so called because originally it was composed of two stretcher-bearers who *walked* off the battlefield with a wounded soldier; and a *preamble* (PREE'-am-bəl) is, by etymology, something that 'walks before' (*pre-*, before, beforehand), hence an introduction or introductory statement, a *preamble* to the speech, etc; or any event that is introductory or preliminary to another, as in 'An increase in inflationary factors in the economy is often a *preamble* to a drop in the stock market.'

5.   Back to sleep

Somnus is one Latin word for sleep – *sopar* is another. A *soporific* (sop'-ə-RIF'-ik) lecture, speaker, style of delivery, etc. will put the audience to sleep (*fic-* from *facio,* to make), and a *soporific* is a sleeping pill.

6.   Noun suffixes

You know that *-ness* can be added to any adjective to construct the noun form. Write the noun derived from *inarticulate:* _____. *Inarticulate* is a combination of the negative prefix *in-* and Latin *articulus,* a joint. The *inarticulate* person has trouble joining words together coherently. If you are quite *articulate* (ah-TIK'-yoo-lət), on the other hand, you join your words together easily, you are verbal, vocal, possibly even voluble. The verb to *articulate* (ah-TIK'-yoo-layt') is to join (words), i.e., to express your vocal sounds – as in 'Please *articulate* more clearly.' Can you write the noun derived from the verb *articulate?* _____.

Another, and very common, noun suffix attached to adjectives is, as you have discovered, *-ity.* So the noun form of *banal* is either *banalness,* or, more commonly, *banality* (bə-NAL'-i-ti).

Bear in mind, then, that *-ness* and *-ity* are common noun suffixes attached to adjectives, and *-ion* (or *-ation*) is a noun suffix frequently affixed to verbs (to *articulate* – *articulation;* to *vocalize* – *vocalization;* to *perambulate* – *perambulation*).

Review of etymology

Prefix, Root, Suffix	Meaning	English Word
1. *venter, ventris*	belly	_____
2. *loquor*	to speak	_____
3. *auris*	ear	_____
4. *avunculus*	uncle	_____
5. *dorsum*	back	_____
6. *vox, vocis*	voice	_____
7. *fero*	to carry, bear	_____
8. *somnus*	sleep	_____
9. *-ous*	adjective suffix	_____

10. *in-*	negative suffix	_____
11. *ambulo*	to walk	_____
12. *-ory*	adjective suffix	_____
13. *per-*	through	_____
14. *pre-*	before, beforehand	_____
15. *sopor*	sleep	_____
16. *fic- (facio)*	to make or do	_____
17. *-ness*	noun suffix	_____
18. *-ity*	noun suffix	_____
19. *-ion (-ation)*	noun suffix attached to verbs	_____
20. *-ent*	adjective suffix	_____
21. *-ence, -ency*	noun suffix	_____

Using the words

Can you pronounce the words? (I)

1. *ventral*	VEN'-trəl
2. *ventricle*	VEN'-tri-kəl
3. *auricle*	AW'-ri-kəl
4. *ventricular*	ven-TRIK'-yoŏ-lə
5. *auricular*	aw-RIK'-yoŏ-lə
6. *avuncular*	ə-VUNG'-kyoŏ-lə
7. *dorsal*	DAW'-səl
8. *endorse*	in-DAWS'
9. *endorsement*	in-DAWS'-mənt
10. *vociferousness*	vō-SIF'-ə-rəs-nəs
11. *vociferate*	vō-SIF'-ə-rayt'
12. *vociferation*	vō-sif'-ə-RAY'-shən

Can you pronounce the words? (II)

1. *somniferous*	som-NIF'-ər-əs
2. *insomnia*	in-SOM'-ni-ə
3. *insomniac*	in-SOM'-ni-ak'
4. *insomnious*	in-SOM'-ni-əs
5. *somnolent*	SOM'-nə-lənt
6. *somnolence*	SOM'-nə-ləns
7. *somnolency*	SOM'-nə-lən-si

8.	*somnambulism*	som-NAM'-byo͝o-liz-əm
9.	*somnambulist*	som-NAM'-byo͝o-list
10.	*somnambulistic*	som-nʌm'-byo͝o-LIST'-ik

Can you pronounce the words? (III)

1.	*ambulatory*	AM'-byo͝o-lət-ə-ri
2.	*perambulator*	pə-RAM'-byo͝o-lay'-tə
3.	*perambulate*	pə-RAM'-byo͝o-layt'
4.	*perambulation*	pə-ram'-byo͝o-LAY'-shən
5.	*amble*	AM'-bəl
6.	*preamble*	PREE'-am-bəl
7.	*soporific*	sop-ə-RIF'-ik
8.	*inarticulateness*	in'-ah-TIK'-yo͝o-lət-nəs
9.	*articulate (adj.)*	ah-TIK'-yo͝o-lət
10.	*banality*	bə-NAL'-i-ti

Can you work with the words? (I)

1. ventral	a. unable to fall asleep
2. dorsal	b. pertaining to sleepwalking
3. somniferous	c. drowsy
4. insomnious	d. able to walk, after being bedridden
5. somnolent	e. verbal, vocal
6. somnambulistic	f. like an uncle; kindly; protective
7. ambulatory	g. pertaining to one of the chambers of the heart
8. articulate	h. referring to the front or belly side
9. ventricular, auricular	i. sleep-inducing
10. avuncular	j. referring to the back side

Key: 1–h, 2–j, 3–i, 4–a, 5–c, 6–b, 7–d, 8–e, 9–g, 10–f

Can you work with the words? (II)

1.	ventricle, auricle	a.	inability to fall asleep
2.	endorsement	b.	sleepwalking
3.	vociferousness	c.	introduction; preliminary or introductory occurrence
4.	insomnia	d.	incoherence; spluttering; inability to get words out
5.	somnolence	e.	chamber of the heart
6.	somnambulism	f.	sleeping pill
7.	perambulator	g.	support; approval
8.	preamble	h.	lack of originality; lack of imagination
9.	soporific	i.	drowsiness
10.	inarticulateness	j.	baby carriage
11.	banality	k.	loudness; clamorousness

Key: 1–e, 2–g, 3–k, 4–a, 5–i, 6–b, 7–j, 8–c, 9–f, 10–d, 11–h

Can you work with the words? (III)

1.	endorse	a.	one who cannot fall asleep
2.	vociferate	b.	sleepwalker
3.	insomniac	c.	walk aimlessly
4.	somnolency	d.	stroll through; walk around
5.	somnambulist	e.	to sign on the back; support; approve of
6.	perambulate	f.	drowsiness
7.	amble	g.	say loudly and with great vehemence
8.	soporific	h.	causing sleep
9.	insomnious	i.	wakeful; unable to fall asleep

Key: 1–e, 2–g, 3–a, 4–f, 5–b, 6–d, 7–c, 8–h, 9–i

Do you understand the words?

1.	Does an *insomniac* often need a *soporific*?	YES	NO
2.	Does a *somnambulist* always stay in bed when asleep?	YES	NO
3.	Are *ambulatory* patients bedridden?	YES	NO
4.	Does a *preamble* come after another event?	YES	NO
5.	Are *articulate* people verbal?	YES	NO
6.	Does *banality* show creativeness?	YES	NO
7.	Does an *avuncular* attitude indicate affection and protectiveness?	YES	NO
8.	Is *vociferation* habitual with quiet, shy people?	YES	NO
9.	Is a *somnolent* person wide awake?	YES	NO
10.	Is a *somniferous* speaker stimulating and exciting?	YES	NO

Key: 1–yes, 2–no, 3–no, 4–no, 5–yes, 6–no, 7–yes, 8–no, 9–no, 10–no

Can you recall the words?

1.	lack of imagination or originality in speech, actions, or style of life; hackneyed or trite phraseology	1. B_____
2.	sleep-inducing	2. S_____ *or* S_____
3.	unable to fall asleep (*adj.*)	3. I_____ *or* I_____
4.	verbal, vocal, speaking fluently	4. A_____
5.	acting like an uncle	5. A_____
6.	referring to the front; anterior	6. V_____
7.	referring to the back; posterior	7. D_____

8. approve of; support; sign   8. E_____
   on the back of
9. shout vehemently   9. V_____
10. one who cannot fall   10. I_____
    asleep
11. drowsy; sleepy   11. S_____
12. sleepwalker   12. S_____
13. now able to walk; though   13. A_____
    previously bedridden
14. walk aimlessly   14. A_____
15. introduction; introductory 15. P_____
    event
16. incoherence   16. I_____

Key: 1−banality, 2−somniferous *or* soporific, 3−insomniac *or*
        insomnious, 4−articulate, 5−avuncular, 6−ventral,
        7−dorsal, 8−endorse, 9−vociferate, 10−insomniac,
        11−somnolent, 12−somnambulist, 13−ambulatory,
        14−amble, 15−preamble, 16−inarticulateness

Chapter review

A.   Do you recognize the words?

1. Disinclined to conversation:
   (a) loquacious, (b) laconic, (c) taciturn
2. Trite:
   (a) inarticulate, (b) banal, (c) verbose
3. Rapid and fluent:
   (a) voluble, (b) verbose, (c) garrulous
4. Forceful and compelling:
   (a) vociferous, (b) cogent, (c) laconic
5. Unspoken:
   (a) verbatim, (b) eloquent, (c) tacit
6. Using elegant and impressive words:
   (a) verbose, (b) grandiloquent, (c) colloquial
7. Back:
   (a) dorsal, (b) ventral, (c) somniferous

8. Sleep-inducing:
   (a) soporific, (b) somnolent, (c) ventral
9. Inability to fall asleep:
   (a) somnambulism, (b) ambulatory, (c) insomnia
10. Talkativeness:
    (a) reticence, (b) ventriloquism, (c) loquacity
11. Expressing indirectly or in a roundabout way:
    (a) circumlocutory, (b) colloquial, (c) laconic
12. Elegance in expression:
    (a) magniloquence, (b) grandiloquence, (c) verbiage
13. Wordiness:
    (a) laconism, (b) cogency, (c) verbosity
14. Big-hearted, generous, unselfish:
    (a) grandiloquent, (b) magnanimous, (c) garrulous
15. Causing radical changes:
    (a) evolutionary, (b) revolutionary, (c) ventricular
16. To shout vehemently:
    (a) endorse, (b) perambulate, (c) vociferate
17. Like an uncle:
    (a) ventricular, (b) auricular, (c) avuncular
18. Drowsy:
    (a) somniferous, (b) somnolent, (c) soporific
19. Sleepwalking:
    (a) insomnia, (b) somnolency, (c) somnambulism
20. Introduction:
    (a) preamble, (b) perambulator, (c) evolution

Key: 1–c, 2–b, 3–a, 4–b, 5–c, 6–b, 7–a, 8–a, 9–c, 10–c,
        11–a, 12–a *and* b, 13–c, 14–b, 15–b, 16–c, 17–c, 18–b,
        19–c, 20–a

B.   Can you recognize roots?

Root	Meaning	Example
1. *taceo*	_____	taciturn
2. *loquor*	_____	loquacity
3. *solus*	_____	soliloquize
4. *venter, ventris*	_____	ventral
5. *magnus*	_____	magniloquent

6. *grandis*	_____	grandiloquent
7. *verbum*	_____	verbatim
8. *volvo, volutus*	_____	revolution
9. *garrio*	_____	garrulous
10. *animus*	_____	magnanimous
11. *opus*	_____	magnum opus
12. *opero*	_____	operator
13. *auris*	_____	auricle
14. *avunculus*	_____	avuncular
15. *dorsum*	_____	dorsal
16. *vox, vocis*	_____	vociferate
17. *fero*	_____	somniferous
18. *ambulo*	_____	preamble
19. *sopor*	_____	soporific
20. *somnus*	_____	somnolency

Key: 1–to be silent, 2–to speak, 3–alone, 4–belly, 5–big, large, great, 6–grand, 7–word, 8–to roll, 9–to chatter, 10–mind, 11–work, 12–to work, 13–ear, 14–uncle, 15–back, 16–voice, 17–to carry or bear, 18–to walk, 19–sleep, 20–sleep

Teaser questions for the amateur etymologist

1. The present participle (or *-ing* form) of the Latin verb *opero*, to work, is *operans*, working. The form *operandi* means *of working*. Can you work out the literal meaning of the phrase *modus operandi*, sometimes used to signify the characteristic methods or procedures used by certain criminals? _____

_____ .

2. *Circum-*, we have learned, is a prefix meaning *around*, as in *circumlocution, circumference, circumcision, circumnavigation*, etc. Thinking of the root *scribo, scriptus*, to write, can you work out the word meaning *writing*, or *written material*, *around* (the edge of something)? _____

_____ .

3. You know the roots *somnus* and *loquor*. Can you combine these two roots to form an adjective meaning *talking in one's sleep?*

_____. Can you write the
noun form of this adjective? _____
_____.

4. We have discovered *auris*, ear, as in *auricle*. Can you work out
the speciality of the doctor called an *aurist?*
_____

5. *Verbal*, from *verbum*, refers to words; *oral*, from *os, oris*, the
mouth, refers to spoken words or sounds. Can you analyse *aural*
and decide on its meaning? _____
_____.

6. A *somnambulist* walks in his sleep. What does a *noctambulist* do?
_____

7. *Soporific*, combining *sopor*, sleep, with *fic-* (from *facio*), to
make, means *inducing or causing sleep*. Use *somnus*, another root for
sleep, to construct a word that has the same form and meaning as
soporific: _____
8. *Perambulate* is *to walk through*. Use another Latin prefix to
construct a verb meaning *to walk around*. _____
_____.

(Answers in Chapter 18)

Do you always use the proper word?

The fact is that grammar is getting more liberal every day. Common usage has put a stamp of approval on many expressions which your grandmother would not have dared utter in her most intimate conversation – not if she believed she was in the habit of using good English. *It is me; have you got a cold?; it's a nice day; can I have another piece of cake?; she is a most aggravating child; will everybody please remove their hats* – all these today represent perfectly correct grammar for everyday conversation. Modern grammar research reports that these expressions have become universal in educated speech.

However, such a liberal policy does not mean that all bars are down. Only a person whose speech borders on the illiterate would make such statements as: *can you learn me to swim?; he don't live here no more; we ain't working so good; me and my husband are glad to see you.* There are still certain minimum essentials of good English that the cultivated speaker carefully observes.

Is your grammar as good as the next person's? Here's a quick test by which you can measure your ability.

Tick the preferable choice in each sentence, then compare your results with the key at the end. Allowing 4 per cent for each correct answer, consider 92–100 excellent, 76–88 good, 68–72 average.

1. What (a–effect, b–affect) does Margaret Thatcher have on you?
2. What's the sense (a–in, b–of) looking for a needle in a haystack?
3. She won't (a–leave, b–let) us meet her new boyfriend.

0

4. What (a–kind of, b–kind of a) dress do you want?
5. Her (a–principle, b–principal) objection to neurotics is that they are difficult to live with.
6. The murderer was (a–hanged, b–hung) two hours before the governor's pardon arrived.
7. Many men feel great affection for their (a–mother-in-laws, b–mothers-in-law).
8. For a light cake, use two (a–spoonfuls, b–spoonsful) of baking powder.
9. Everyone likes you but (a–she, b–her).
10. Sally sent a gift for (a–him and me, b–he and I).
11. The criteria you are using (a–is, b–are) not valid.
12. The cost of new houses (a–is, b–are) finally stabilizing.
13. Irene as well as her husband (a–has, b–have) come to see you.
14. (a–Is, b–Are) either of your sisters working?
15. As soon as the editor or her secretary (a–comes, b–come) in, let me know.
16. One or two of her features (a–is, b–are) very attractive.
17. Can you visit Mary and (a–I, b–me) tonight?
18. He is totally (a–uninterested, b–disinterested) in your personal affairs.
19. She (a–laid, b–lay) on the beach while her son splashed at the water's edge.
20. (a–Who, b–Whom) would you rather be if you weren't yourself?
21. You should not (a–have, b–of) spoken so harshly.
22. She is one of those women who (a–believes, b–believe) that husbands should share in doing housework and taking care of the children.
23. Was it you who (a–was, b–were) here yesterday?
24. What we need in this country (a–is, b–are) honest politicians.
25. I'm smarter than Gladys, but she's richer than (a–I, b–me).

Key: 1–a, 2–a, 3–b, 4–a, 5–b, 6–a, 7–b, 8–a, 9–b, 10–a, 11–b, 12–a, 13–a, 14–a, 15–a, 16–b, 17–b, 18–a, 19–b, 20–a, 21–a, 22–b, 23–b, 24–a, 25–a

11

HOW TO INSULT YOUR ENEMIES

(Sessions 28–31)

Teaser preview

What do you call a person who:

- *insists on complete and blind obedience?*
- *toadies to the rich or influential?*
- *dabbles in the fine arts?*
- *is a loud-mouthed, quarrelsome woman?*
- *has a one-track mind?*
- *sneers at other people's cherished traditions?*
- *does not believe in God?*
- *has imaginary ailments?*

Session 28

There are few of us who do not need warm and nourishing relationships to lead a fulfilled life.

Psychology makes clear that loving and being loved are important elements in emotional health, but also points out the necessity for expressing, rather than repressing, our hostilities. (You know how good you feel once you blow off steam? And how much closer you can become attached to someone once you directly and honestly vent your anger, resentment, or irritation instead of bottling it up and seething in fury?)

It is a mark of your own emotional maturity if you can *accept* hostility as well as dish it out. So let us pretend, in order to encourage you to become personally involved in the introductory ten words of this chapter, that each paragraph in the next few pages accurately describes *you*. What label exactly fits your personality?

Ideas

1.   Slave driver

You make everyone toe the line – right down to the last centimetre. You exact blind, unquestioning obedience; demand the strictest conformity to rules, however arbitrary or tyrannical; and will not tolerate the slightest deviation from your orders. You are, in short, the very epitome of the army drill sergeant.

   You are a *martinet*.

2.   Bootlicker

You toady to rich or influential people, catering to their vanity, flattering their ego. On top of this, you're a complete hypocrite. All your servile attention and unceasing adulation spring from your own selfish desires to get ahead, not out of any sincere admiration. You cultivate people of power or property so that you can curry favour at the opportune moment.

You are a *sycophant*.

3.   Dabbler

Often, though not necessarily, a person of independent income, you engage superficially in the pursuit of one of the fine arts – painting, writing, sculpturing, composing, etc. You do this largely for your own amusement and not to achieve any professional competence; nor are you at all interested in monetary rewards. Your artistic efforts are simply a means of passing time pleasantly.

You are a *dilettante*.

4.   Battle-axe

You are a loud-mouthed, shrewish, turbulent woman; you're quarrelsome and aggressive, possessing none of those gentle and tender qualities stereotypically associated with femininity. You're strong-minded, unyielding, sharp-tongued, and dangerous. You can curse like a stevedore and yell like a fishwife – and often do.

You are a *virago*.

5.   Superpatriot

Anything you own or belong to is better – simply because you own it or belong to it, although you will be quick to find more justifiable explanations. Your religion, whatever it may be, is far superior to any other; your political party is the only honest one; your neighbourhood puts all others in the city in the shade; members of your own sex are more intelligent, more worthy, more emotionally secure, and in every way far better than people of the opposite sex; your car is faster, more fun to drive, and gets better fuel mileage than any other, no matter in what price range; and of course your country and its customs leave nothing to be desired, and inhabitants of other nations are in comparison barely civilized. In short, you are exaggeratedly, aggressively, absurdly, and excessively devoted to your own affiliations – and you make no bones about advertising such prejudice.

You are a *chauvinist*.

6.   Fanatic

You have a one-track mind – and when you're riding a particular hobbyhorse, you ride it hard. You have such an excessive, all-inclusive zeal for one thing (and it may be your business, your profession, your husband or wife, your children, your stomach, your money, or whatever) that your obsession is almost absurd. You talk, eat, sleep that one thing – to the point where you bore everyone to distraction.

You are a *monomaniac*.

7.   Attacker

You are violently against established beliefs, revered traditions, cherished customs – such, you say, stand in the way of reform and progress and are always based on superstition and irrationality. Religion, family, marriage, ethics – you weren't there when these were started and you're not going to conform simply because most unthinking people do.

You are an *iconoclast*.

8.   Sceptic

There is no God – that's your position and you're not going to budge from it.

You are an *atheist*.

9.   Self-indulger

You are, as a male, lascivious, libidinous, lustful, lewd, wanton, immoral – but more important, you promiscuously attempt to satisfy (and are often successful in so doing) your sexual desires with any woman within your arm's reach.

You are a *lecher*.

10.   Worrier

You are always sick, though no doctor can find an organic cause for your ailments. You know you have ulcers, though medical tests show a healthy stomach. You have heart palpitations, but a cardiogram fails to show any abnormality. Your headaches are caused (you're sure of it) by a rapidly growing brain tumour – yet X-rays show nothing wrong. These maladies are not imaginary, however; to you they are most real, non-existent as they may be in fact. And as you travel from doctor to doctor futilely seeking confirmation of your imminent death, you become more and more convinced that you're too weak to go on much longer. Organically, of course, there's nothing the matter with you. Perhaps tensions, insecurities, or a need for attention is taking the form of simulated bodily ills.

You are a *hypochondriac*.

Using the words

Can you pronounce the words?

1.	*martinet*	mah-ti-NET'
2.	*sycophant*	SIK'-ə-fant
3.	*dilettante*	dil'-i-TAN'-ti
4.	*virago*	vi-RAH'-gō
5.	*chauvinist*	SHŌ'-və-nist
6.	*monomaniac*	mon'-ō-MAY'-ni-ak
7.	*iconoclast*	ī-KON'-ə-klast'
8.	*atheist*	AY'-thi-ist
9.	*lecher*	LECH'-ə
10.	*hypochondriac*	hī-pə-KON'-dri-ak

Can you work with the words?

Words	Key Ideas
1. martinet	a. superficiality
2. sycophant	b. patriotism
3. dilettante	c. godlessness
4. virago	d. single-mindedness
5. chauvinist	e. antitradition

6. monomaniac	f. sex
7. iconoclast	g. illness
8. atheist	h. discipline
9. lecher	i. turbulence
10. hypochondriac	j. flattery

Key: 1–h, 2–j, 3–a, 4–i, 5–b, 6–d, 7–e, 8–c, 9–f, 10–g

Do you understand the words?

1.	Does a *martinet* condone carelessness and neglect of duty?	YES	NO
2.	Is a *sycophant* a sincere person	YES	NO
3.	Is a *dilettante* a hard worker?	YES	NO
4.	Is a *virago* sweet and gentle?	YES	NO
5.	Is a *chauvinist* modest and self-effacing?	YES	NO
6.	Does a *monomaniac* have a one-track mind?	YES	NO
7.	Does an *iconoclast* scoff at tradition?	YES	NO
8.	Does an *atheist* believe in God?	YES	NO
9.	Is a *lecher* misogynous?	YES	NO
10.	Does a *hypochondriac* have a lively imagination?	YES	NO

Key: a–no, 2–no, 3–no, 4–no, 5–no, 6–yes, 7–yes, 8–no, 9–no, 10–yes

Can you recall the words?

1.	a person whose emotional disorder is reflected in non-organic or imaginary bodily ailments	1. H_____ __
2.	a strict disciplinarian	2. M_____
3.	a lewd and sexually aggressive male	3. I_____

4. a toady to people of wealth or power   4. S_____

5. a disbeliever in God   5. A_____

6. a dabbler in the arts   6. D_____

7. a shrewish, loud-mouthed female   7. V_____

8. a scoffer at tradition   8. I_____

9. person with a one-track mind   9. M_____

10. a blatant superpatriot   10. C_____

Key: 1–hypochondriac, 2–martinet, 3–lecher, 4–sycophant, 5–atheist, 6–dilettante, 7–virago, 8–iconoclast, 9–monomaniac, 10–chauvinist

Can you use the words?

1. She scoffs at beliefs you have always held dear.   1. _____

2. You know he's hale and hearty – but he constantly complains of his illness.   2. _____

3. She insists her political affiliations are superior to yours.   3. _____

4. She insists on her subordinates toeing the line.   4. _____

5. He makes sexual advances to everyone else's wife – and is too often successful.   5. _____

6. He cultivates friends that can do him good – financially.   6. _____

7. She dabbles with water colours.   7. _____

8. She insists there is no Deity.

    8. _____

9. She's a shrew, a harridan, a scold, and a nag.

    9. _____

10. His only interest in life is his fish collection – and he is fanatically, almost psychotically, devoted to it.

    10. _____

Key: 1–iconoclast, 2–hypochondriac, 3–chauvinist, 4–martinet, 5–lecher, 6–sycophant, 7–dilettante, 8–atheist, 9–virago, 10–monomaniac

(End of Session 28)

Session 29

Origins and related words

1. The French drillmaster

Jean Martinet was the Inspector-General of Infantry during the reign of King Louis XIV – and a stricter, more fanatic drillmaster France had never seen. It was from this time that the French Army's reputation for discipline dated, and it is from the name of this Frenchman that we derive our English word *martinet*. The word is always used in a derogatory sense and generally shows resentment and anger on the part of the user. The secretary who calls his boss a *martinet*, the wife who applies the epithet to her husband, the worker who thus refers to the foreman – these speakers all show their contempt for the excessive, inhuman discipline to which they are asked to submit.

Since *martinet* comes from a man's name (in the Brief Intermission which follows we shall discover that a number of picturesque English words are similarly derived), there are no related forms built on the same root. There is an adjective *martinetish* (mah-ti-NET'-ish) and another noun form, *martinetism*, but these are used only rarely.

2. A Greek 'fig-shower'

Sycophant comes to us from the Greeks. According to Shipley's *Dictionary of Word Origins*:

The Greeks had a name for it: *fig-shower*. Sycophant is from Gr. *sykon*, fig, [and] *phanein*, to show. This was the fellow that informed the officers in charge when (1) the figs in the sacred groves were being taken, or (2) when the Smyrna fig-dealers were dodging the tariff.

Thus, a *sycophant* may appear to be a sort of 'grass', since the latter curries the favour of police officials by informing on his fellow criminals. *Sycophants* may use this means of ingratiating themselves with influential citizens of the community; or they may use flattery, servile attentions, or any other form of insinuating themselves into someone's good graces. A *sycophant* practices *sycophancy* (SIK'-ə-fan-si), and has a *sycophantic* (sik-ə-FAN'-tik) attitude. All three forms of the word are highly uncomplimentary – use them with care.

Material may be so delicate or fine in texture that anything behind it will show through. The Greek prefix *dia-* means *through*; and *phanein*, as you now know, means *to show* – hence such material is called *diaphanous* (dī-AF'-ə-nəs). Do not use the adjective in reference to all material that is transparent (for example, you would not call glass *diaphanous*, even though you can see right through it), but only material that is silky, gauzy, filmy, and, in addition, transparent or practically transparent. The word is often applied to female garments – nightgowns, negligees, etc.

3.   Just for one's own amusement

Dilettante is from the Italian verb *dilettare*, to delight. The *dilettante* paints, writes, composes, plays a musical instrument, or engages in scientific experiments purely for amusement – not to make money, become famous, or satisfy a deep creative urge (the latter, I presume, being the justifications for the time that professional artists, writers, composers, musicians, poets, and scientists spend at their chosen work). A *dilettantish* (dil-i-TAN'-tish) attitude is superficial, unprofessional; *dilettantism* (dil-i-TAN'-tiz-əm) is superficial, part-time dabbling in the type of activity that usually engages the full time and energy of the professional artist or scientist.

Do not confuse the *dilettante*, who has a certain amount of native talent or ability, with the *tyro* (TĪ'-rō), who is the inexperienced beginner in some art, but who may be full of ambition, drive, and energy. To call a person a *tyro* is to imply that he is just starting in some artistic, scientific, or professional field — he's not much good yet because he has not had time to develop his skill, if any. The *dilettante* usually has some skill but isn't doing much with it. On the other hand, anyone who has developed consummate skill in an artistic field, generally allied to music, is called a *virtuoso* (vər'-tyōō-ō'-sō *or* vər'-tyōō-ō'-zō) — like Yehudi Menuhin on the violin or Arthur Rubinstein on the piano. Pluralize *virtuoso* in the normal way — *virtuosos;* or if you wish to sound more sophisticated, give it the continental form — *virtuosi* (vər'-tyōō-ō'-si). Similarly, the plural of *dilettante* is either *dilettantes* or *dilettanti* (dil-i-TAN'-ti).

The *i* ending for a plural is the Italian form and is common in musical circles. For example, *libretto,* the story (or book) of an opera, may be pluralized to *libretti; concerto,* a form of musical composition, is pluralized *concerti.* However, the Anglicized *librettos* and *concertos* are perfectly correct also. *Libretto* is pronounced li-BRET'-ō; *libretti* is li-BRET'-i; *concerto* is kən-CHəR'-tō; and *concerti* is kən-CHəR'-ti. Suit your plural form, I would suggest, to the sophistication of your audience.

4.   'Masculine' women

Virago comes, oddly enough, from the Latin word for man, *vir.* Perhaps the derivation is not so odd after all; a *virago,* far from being stereotypically feminine (i.e. timid, delicate, low-spoken, etc.), is stereotypically masculine in personality — coarse, aggressive, loud-mouthed. *Termagant* (TəR'-mə-gənt) and *harridan* (HAR'-i-dən) are words with essentially the same uncomplimentary meaning as *virago.* To call a brawling woman a *virago,* a *termagant,* and a *harridan* is admittedly repetitious, but is successful in relieving one's feelings.

5.   The old man

Nicolas Chauvin, soldier of the French Empire, so vociferously and unceasingly aired his veneration of Napoleon Bonaparte that he became the laughing-stock of all Europe. Thereafter, an exaggerated and blatant patriot was known as a *chauvinist* — and still is today. *Chauvinism* (SHŌ'-və-niz-əm), by natural extension, applies to blatant veneration of, or boastfulness about, any other affiliation besides one's country.

To be *patriotic* is to be normally proud of, and devoted to, one's country – to be *chauvinistic* (shō-və-NIS'-tik) is to exaggerate such pride and devotion to an obnoxious degree.

We might digress here to investigate an etymological side road down which the word *patriotic* beckons. *Patriotic* is built on the Latin word *pater, patris,* father – one's country is, in a sense, one's fatherland.

Let us see what other interesting words are build on this same root.

1. *patrimony* (PAT'-ri-mō-ni) – an inheritance from one's father. The *-mony* comes from the same root that gives us *money*, namely *Juno Moneta*, the Roman goddess who guarded the temples of finance. The adjective is *patrimonial* (pat'-ri-MŌ'-ni-əl).

2. *patronymic* (pat'-rə-NIM'-ik) – a name formed on the father's name, like *Johnson* (son of John), *Martinson, Aaronson,* etc. The word combines *pater, patris* with Greek *onyma*, name. *Onyma* plus the Greek prefix *syn-*, with or together, forms *synonym* (SIN'-ə-nim), a word of the same name (or meaning), etymologically 'a together name'. *Onyma* plus the prefix *anti-* against, forms *antonym* (AN'-tə-nim), a word of opposite meaning, etymologically 'an against name'. *Onyma* plus Greek *homos*, the same, forms *homonym* (HOM'-ə-nim), a word that sounds like another but has a different meaning and spelling, like *bare – bear, way – weigh, to – too – two,* etc., etymologically 'a same name'. A *homonym* is more accurately called a *homophone* (HOM'-ə-fōn'), a combination of *homos*, the same, and *phone*, sound. The adjective form of *synonym* is *synonymous* (si-NON'-i-məs). Can you write, and pronounce, the adjective derived from:

antonym? _____

homonym? _____

homophone? _____

3. *paternity* (pə-TəR'-ni-ti) – fatherhood, as to question someone's *paternity*, to file a *paternity* suit in order to collect child support from the assumed, accused, or self-acknowledged father. The adjective is *paternal* (pə-TəR'-nəl), fatherly. *Paternalism* (pə-TəR'-nə-liz-əm) is the philosophy or system of governing a country, or of managing a business or institution, so that the citizens, employees, or staff are treated in a manner suggesting a father-

children relationship. (Such a system sounds, and often is, benign and protective, but plays havoc with the initiative, independence, and creativity of those in subordinate roles.) The adjective is *paternalistic* (pə-tər'-nə-LIS'-tik).

4. *patriarch* (PAY'-tri-ahk') – a venerable, fatherlike old man; an old man in a ruling, fatherlike position. Here *pater, patris* is combined with the Greek root *archein*, to rule. The adjective is *patriarchal* (pay'-tri-AHR'-kəl), the system is a *patriarchy* (PAY'-tri-ah'-ki).

5. *patricide* (PAT'-ri-sīd') – the killing of one's father. *Pater, patris* combines with *-cide*, a suffix derived from the Latin verb *caedo*, to kill. The adjective is *patricidal* (pat-ri-SĪ'-dəl).

This list does not exhaust the number of words built on *pater*, father, but is sufficient to give you an idea of how closely related many English words are. In your reading you will come across other words containing the latters *pater* or *patr* – you will be able to work them out once you realize that the base is the word *father*. You might, if you feel ambitious, puzzle out the relationship to the 'father idea' in the following words, checking with a dictionary to see how good your linguistic intuition is:

1. patrician
2. patron
3. patronize
4. patronizing (*adj.*)
5 paterfamilias
6. padre

6.   The old lady

Pater, patris is *father. Mater, matris* is *mother.*
For example:

1. *matriarch* (MAY'-tri-ahk') – the mother-ruler; the 'mother person' that controls a large household, tribe, or country. This word, like *patriarch*, is built on the root *archein*, to rule. During the reign of Queen Victoria, England was a *matriarchy* (MAY'-tri-ah'-ki). Can you work out the adjective form? _____
_____.

2. *maternity* (mə-TəR'-ni-ti) – motherhood.
3. *maternal* (mə-TəR'-nəl) – motherly.
4. *matron* (MAY'-trən) – an older woman, one sufficiently mature to be a mother. The adjective *matronly* (MAY'-trən-li) con-

jures up for many people a picture of a woman no longer in the glow of youth and possibly with a bit of added weight in the wrong places, so this word should be used with caution; it may be hazardous to your health if the lady you are so describing is of a tempestuous nature, or is a *virago*.

5. *alma mater* (AL'-mə-MAH'-tə *or* AL'-mə-MAY'-tə) – etymologically, 'soul mother'; actually, the school or college which one attended, and which in a sense is one's intellectual mother.

6. *matrimony* (MAT'-ri-mə-ni) – marriage. Though this word is similar to *patrimony* in spelling, it does not refer to *money*, as *patrimony* does; unless, that is, you are cynical enough to believe that people marry for money. As the language was growing, marriage and children went hand in hand – it is therefore not surprising that the word for *marriage* should be built on the Latin root for *mother*. Of course, times have changed, but the sexist nature of the English language has not. The noun suffix -*mony* indicates state, condition, or result, as in *sanctimony*, *parsimony*, etc. The adjective is *matrimonial* (mat'-ri-MŌ'-ni-əl).

7. *matricide* (MAT'-ri-sīd' *or* MAY'-tri-sīd') – the killing of one's mother. The adjective? _____.

7.   Murder most foul . . .

Murder unfortunately is an integral part of human life, so there is a word for almost every kind of killing you can think of. Let's look at some of them.

1. *suicide* (SOO'-i-sīd') – killing oneself (intentionally); -*cide* plus *sui*, of oneself. This is both the act and the person who has been completely successful in performing the act (*partially* doesn't count). The adjective? _____.

2. *fratricide* (FRAT'-ri-sīd') – the killing of one's brother; -*cide* plus *frater, fratris*, brother. The adjective? _____
_____.

3. *sororicide* (sə-ROR'-i-sīd') – the killing of one's sister; -*cide* plus *soror*, sister. The adjective? _____.

4. *homicide* (HOM'-i-sīd') – the killing of a human being; -*cide* plus *homo*, person. In law, *homicide* is the general term for any slaying. If intent and premeditation can be proved, the act is *murder* and punishable as such. If no such intent is present, the act is called *manslaughter* and receives a lighter punishment. Thus, if

your mate/lover/spouse makes your life unbearable and you slip some arsenic into his/her coffee one bright morning, you are committing murder — that is, if he/she succumbs. On the other hand, if you run your victim down — quite accidentally — with your car, bicycle, or wheelchair, with no intent to kill, you will be accused of *manslaughter* — that is, if death results and if you can prove you didn't really mean it. It's all rather delicate, however, and you might do best to put thoughts of justifiable *homicide* out of your mind. The adjective? _____.

5. *regicide* (REJ'-i-sīd') — the killing of a king. Adjective? _____. Derivation: Latin *rex, regis*, king, plus *-cide*.

6. *uxoricide* (uk-SAW'-ri-sīd') — the killing of one's wife. Adjective? _____. Derivation: Latin *uxor*, wife, plus *-cide*.

7. *mariticide* (mə-RIT'-i-sīd') — the killing of one's husband. Adjective? _____. Derivation: Latin *maritius*, husband, plus *-cide*.

8. *infanticide* (in-FAN'-ti-sīd') — the killing of a newborn child. Adjective? _____. Derivation: Latin *infans, infantis*, baby, plus *-cide*.

9. *genocide* (JEN'-ō-sīd') — the killing of a whole race or nation. This is a comparatively new word, coined in 1944 by a UN official named Raphael Lemkin, to refer to the mass murder of the Jews, Poles, etc. ordered by Hitler. Adjective? _____ _____. Derivation: Greek *genos*, race, kind, plus *-cide*.

10. *parricide* (PAR'-i-sīd') — the killing of either or both parents. Adjective? _____.

Review of Etymology

Prefix, Root, Suffix	Meaning	English Word
1. *sykon*	fig	_____
2. *phanein*	to show	_____
3. *dia-*	through	_____
4. *vir*	man (male)	_____
5. *pater, patrix*	father	_____
6. *syn-*	with, together	_____

7. *onyma*	name	_____
8. *anti*	against	_____
9. *homos*	the same	_____
10. *phone*	sound	_____
11. *-ity*	noun suffix	_____
12. *-ism*	noun suffix	_____
13. *-al*	adjective suffix	_____
14. *-ic*	adjective suffix	_____
15. *archein*	to rule	_____
16. *-cide*	killing	_____
17. *mater, matrix*	mother	_____
18. *alma*	soul	_____
19. *-mony*	noun suffix	_____
20. *sui*	of oneself	_____
21. *frater, fratis*	brother	_____
22. *soror*	sister	_____
23. *homo*	person, human	_____
24. *rex, regis*	king	_____
25. *uxor*	wife	_____
26. *maritus*	husband	_____
27. *infans, infantis*	baby	_____
28. *genos*	race, kind	_____

Using the words

Can you pronounce the words? (I)

1. *martinetish*	mah-ti-NET'-ish
2. *sycophancy*	SIK'-ə-fan-si
3. *sycophantic*	sik'-ə-FAN'-tik
4. *diaphanous*	dī-AF'-ə-nəs
5. *dilettanti*	dil'-i-TAN'-ti
6. *dilettantism*	dil-i-TAN'-tiz-əm
7. *dilettantish*	dil-i-TAN'-tish
8. *tyro*	TĪ-rō
9. *virtuoso*	vər'-tyo͞o-Ō'-sō (*or* -zō)
10. *virtuosi*	vər'-tyo͞o-Ō-si
11. *termagant*	TəR'-mə-gənt
12. *harridan*	HAR'-i-dən

Can you pronounce the words? (II)

1. *chauvinism*	SHŌ'-və-niz-əm
2. *chauvinistic*	shō-və-NIS'-tik
3. *patrimony*	PAT'-ri-mō-ni
4. *patronymic*	pat'-rə-NIM'-ik
5. *synonym*	SIN'-ə-nim
6. *synonymous*	si-NON'-i-məs
7. *antonym*	AN'-tə-nim
8. *antonymous*	an-TON'-i-məs
9. *homonym*	HOM'-ə-nim
10. *homonymous*	ho-MON'-i-məs
11. *homophone*	HOM'-ə-fōn
12. *homophonous*	ho-MOF'-ə-nəs

Can you pronounce the words? (III)

1. *paternity*	pə-TəR'-ni-ti
2. *paternal*	pə-TəR'-nəl
3. *paternalism*	pə-TəR'-nə-liz-əm
4. *paternalistic*	pə-tər'-nə-LIS'-tik
5. *patriarch*	PAY'-tri-ahk'
6. *patriarchal*	pay'-tri-AH'-kəl
7. *patriarchy*	PAY'-tri-ah'-ki
8. *patricide*	PAT'-ri-sīd'
9. *patricidal*	pat'-ri-SĪ'-dəl

Can you pronounce the words? (IV)

1. *matriarch*	MAY'-tri-ahk'
2. *matriarchy*	MAY'-tri-ah'-ki
3. *matriarchal*	may'-tri-AH'-kəl
4. *maternity*	mə-TəR'-ni-ti
5. *maternal*	mə-TəR'-nəl
6. *matron*	MAY'-trən
7. *matronly*	MAY'-trən-li
8. *alma mater*	AL'-mə MAH'-tə or AL'-mə MAY'-tə
9. *matrimony*	MAT'-ri-mə-ni
10. *matrimonial*	mat-ri-MŌ'-ni-əl
11. *matricide*	MAT'-ri-sīd' *or* MAY'-tri-sīd'

12. *matricidal*   mat-ri-SĪ'-dəl *or* may-tri-SĪ-dəl

Can you pronounce the words? (V)

1. *suicide*   SOO'-i-sīd'
2. *suicidal*   soo-i-SĪ'-dəl
3. *fratricide*   FRAT'-ri-sīd'
4. *fratricidal*   frat-ri-SĪ'-dəl
5. *sororicide*   sə-ROR'-i-sīd'
6. *sororicidal*   sə-ror'-i-SĪ'-dəl
7. *homicide*   HOM'-i-sīd'
8. *homicidal*   hom'-i-SĪ'-dəl
9. *regicide*   REJ'-i-sīd'
10. *regicidal*   rej'-i-SĪ'-dəl

Can you pronounce the words? (VI)

1. *uxoricide*   uk-SAW'-ri-sīd'
2. *uxoricidal*   uk-SAW'-ri-SĪ'-dəl
3. *mariticide*   mə-RIT'-i-sīd'
4. *mariticidal*   mə-rit'-i-SĪ'-dəl
5. *infanticide*   in-FAN'-ti-sīd'
6. *infanticidal*   in-fan'-ti-SĪ'-dəl
7. *genocide*   JEN'-ō-sīd'
8. *genocidal*   jen'-ō-SĪ'-dəl
9. *parricide*   PAR'-i-sīd'
10. *parricidal*   PAR'-i-SĪ'-dəl

Can you work with the words? (I)

1. sycophancy   a. murder of one's father
2. dilettantism   b. excessive patriotism
3. chauvinism   c. murder of one's king
4. patrimony   d. inheritance from one's father
5. patricide   e. murder of one's sister
6. matricide   f. murder of one's brother
7. fratricide   g. murder of a person
8. sororicide   h. toadying
9. homicide   i. murder of one's mother
10. regicide   j. dabbling

Key: 1–h, 2–j, 3–b, 4–d, 5–a, 6–i, 7–f, 8–e, 9–g, 10–c

Can you work with the words? (II)

1.	uxoricide	a.	marriage
2.	infanticide	b.	killing of one's child
3.	genocide	c.	fatherhood
4.	matrimony	d.	mother-ruler
5.	matriarch	e.	killing of one's wife
6.	maternity	f.	older woman
7.	matron	g.	one's school or college
8.	alma mater	h.	motherhood
9.	paternity	i.	old man in governing position
10.	patriarch	j.	killing of whole groups of people

Key: 1–e, 2–b, 3–j, 4–a, 5–d, 6–h, 7–f, 8–g, 9–c, 10–i

Can you work with the words? (III)

1.	parricide	a.	catering to people of power or position
2.	patronymic	b.	name from father
3.	chauvinistic	c.	dabblers.
4.	sycophantic	d.	an accomplished musician
5.	diaphanous	e.	filmy, gauzy
6.	dilettanti	f.	blatantly overpatriotic
7.	tyro	g.	loud-mouthed woman
8.	virtuoso	h.	a beginner
9.	termagant	i.	killing of either or both parents

Key: 1–i, 2–b, 3–f, 4–a, 5–e, 6–c, 7–h, 8–d, 9–g

Can you work with the words? (IV)

1.	synonyms	a.	system in which those in power have a father-child relationship with subordinates
2.	antonyms	b.	like a strict disciplinarian
3.	homonyms	c.	self-killing
4.	paternalism	d.	fatherly
5.	suicide	e.	referring to, or like, those who 'play at' an art
6.	mariticide	f.	words that sound alike but are spelt differently and have unrelated meanings
7.	martinetish	g.	words of similar meaning
8.	dilettantish	h.	referring to, or like, an older woman
9.	paternal	i.	husband-killing
10.	matronly	j.	words of opposite meaning

Key: 1–g, 2–j, 3–f, 4–a, 5–c, 6–i, 7–b, 8–e, 9–d, 10–h

Can you work with the words? (V)

1.	harridan	a.	motherly
2.	homophones	b.	similar in meaning
3.	maternal	c.	referring to a system in which older men are in power
4.	matrimonial	d.	the same in sound but not in spelling or meaning
5.	synonymous	e.	likely to kill; referring to the killing of a person
6.	antonymous	f.	referring to a system in which older women are in power
7.	homonymous	g.	virago
8.	patriarchal	h.	opposite in meaning
9.	matriarchal	i.	referring to marriage
10.	homicidal	j.	words that sound the same

Key: 1–g, 2–j, 3–a, 4–i, 5–b, 6–h, 7–d, 8–c, 9–f, 10–e

Do you understand the words?

1.	Does a *sycophantic* attitude show sincere admiration?	YES	NO
2.	Is a *diaphanous* gown revealing?	YES	NO
3.	Does *dilettantism* show firmness and tenacity?	YES	NO
4.	Is a *tyro* particularly skilful?	YES	NO
5.	Is a violin *virtuoso* an accomplished musician?	YES	NO
6.	Is a *termagant* a pleasant person?	YES	NO
7.	Does *chauvinism* show modesty?	YES	NO
8.	Does a substantial *patrimony* obviate financial insecurity?	YES	NO
9.	If you know a person's *patronymic* can you deduce his father's name?	YES	NO
10.	Is a *patriarch* a male?	YES	NO
11.	Does a *matriarch* have a good deal of power?	YES	NO
12.	Does *fratricide* mean murder of one's sister?	YES	NO
13.	Do dictators and tyrants sometimes commit *genocide*?	YES	NO
14.	Are an *uxoricidal* husband and his *mariticidal* wife likely to have a peaceful and affectionate marriage?	YES	NO

Key: 1–no, 2–yes, 3–no, 4–no, 5–yes, 6–no, 7–no, 8–yes, 9–yes, 10–yes, 11–yes, 12–no, 13–yes, 14–no

Can you recall the words? (I)

1.	father-killing (*noun*)	1.	P_____
2.	wife-killing (*noun*)	2.	U_____
3.	mature woman	3.	M_____
4.	toadying to people of influence (*adj.*)	4.	S_____
5.	skilled musician	5.	V_____
6.	exaggerated patriotism	6.	C_____

7. turbulent female (three words)

7. T_____

or H_____

or V_____

8. named derived from father's name

8. P_____

9. powerful father figure in a ruling position

9. P_____

10. powerful mother figure in a ruling position

10. M_____

11. motherly

11. M_____

12. motherhood

12. M_____

13. marriage

13. M_____

14. one's school or college

14. A_____

15. attitude of catering to wealth or prestige (*noun*)

15. S_____

16. killing of a race or nation

16. G_____

17. dabbling in the fine arts (*noun*)

17. D_____

18. a beginner in a field

18. T_____

19. plural of *virtuoso* (Italian form)

19. V_____

20. having an attitude of excessive patriotism (*adj.*)

20. C_____

21. inheritance from father

21. P_____

22. sheer, transparent

22. D_____

23. mother-killing (*noun*)

23. M_____

24. brother-killing (*noun*)

24. F_____

25. sister-killing (*noun*)

25. S_____

26. killing of a human being

26. H_____

27. killing of one's king

27. R_____

28. killing of a baby

28. I_____

29. killing of one's husband

29. M_____

30. killing of either parent or of both parents

30. P_____

Key: 1—patricide, 2—uxoricide, 3—matron, 4—sycophantic, 5—virtuoso, 6—chauvinism, 7—termagant, harridan, virago, 8—patronymic, 9—patriarch, 10—matriarch, 11—maternal, 12—maternity, 13—matrimony, 14—alma mater, 15—sycophancy, 16—genocide, 17—dilettantism,

8–tyro, 19–virtuosi, 20–chauvinistic, 21–patrimony, 22–diaphanous, 23–matricide, 24–fratricide, 25–sororicide, 26–homicide, 27–regicide, 28–infanticide, 29–mariticide, 30–parricide

---

Can you recall the words? (II)

1. words of similar meaning	1. S_____s
2. words of opposite meaning	2. A_____s
3. words of the same sound	3. H_____s
	or H_____s
4. fatherly	4. P_____
5. protective and fatherly toward one's subordinates (*adj.*)	5. P_____
6. older woman	6. M_____
7. self-destructive	7. S_____
8. meaning the same (*adj.*)	8. S_____
9. having opposite meanings (*adj.*)	9. A_____
10. sounding the same but spelt differently (*adj.*)	10. H_____
	or H_____

Key: 1–synonyms, 2–antonyms, 3–homonyms *or* homophones, 4–paternal, 5–paternalistic, 6–matron, 7–suicidal, 8–synonymous, 9–antonymous, 10–homonymous *or* homophonous

---

(End of Session 29)

Session 30

Origins and related words

1.   Brothers and sisters, wives and husbands

Frater, brother; *soror*, sister; *uxor*, wife; and *maritus*, husband –
these roots are the source of a number of additional English
words:

1. to *fraternize* (FRAT'-ə-nīz') – etymologically, to have a brotherly relationship (with). This verb may be used to indicate social
intercourse between people, irrespective of sex, as in, 'Members of
the faculty often *fraternized* after school hours.'

Additionally, and perhaps more commonly, there may be the
implication of having a social relationship with one's subordinates
in an organization, or even with one's so-called inferiors, as in,
'The head of the college was reluctant to *fraternize* with faculty
members, preferring to keep all her contacts with them on an
exclusively professional basis'; or as in, 'The artist enjoyed *frater-
nizing* with thieves, drug addicts, prostitutes, and pimps, partly
out of social perversity, partly to find interesting faces to put in his
paintings.'

The verb also gained a new meaning during and after World
War II, when soldiers of occupying armies had sexual relations
with the women of conquered countries, as in, 'Military personnel
were strictly forbidden to *fraternize* with the enemy.' (How euphemistic can you get?)

Can   you   write   the   noun   form   of   *fraternize?*

2. *fraternal* (frə-TəR'-nəl) – brotherly. The word also designates *non-identical* (twins).

3. *fraternity* (frə-TəR'-ni-ti) – a brotherhood or guild; an American men's organization in school or college; or any group of people of similar interests or profession (the medical *fraternity*, the financial *fraternity*).

4. *sorority* (sə-ROR'-i-ti) – a women's organization, especially one in an American school or college; or any women's social club.

5. *uxorious* (uk-SAW'-ri-əs) – an adjective describing a man who excessively, even absurdly, caters to, dotes on, worships, and submits to the most outlandish or outrageous demands of his wife. This word is *not* synonymous with *henpecked*, as the henpecked husband is dominated by his wife, perhaps because of his own fear or weakness, while the *uxorious* husband is dominated only by his neurosis, and quite likely the wife finds his *uxoriousness* (uk-SAW'-ri-əs-nəs) comical or a pain in the neck. (There can, indeed, be too much of a good thing!)

6. *uxorial* – pertaining to, characteristic of, or befitting, a wife, as *uxorial* duties, privileges, attitudes, etc.

7. *marital* (MAR'-i-təl) – etymologically, pertaining or referring to, or characteristic of, a husband; but the meaning has changed to include the marriage relationship of both husband *and* wife (don't ever let anyone tell you that our language is not sexist!), as *marital* duties, obligations, privileges, arguments, etc. Hence *extramarital* is literally *outside the marriage*, as in *extramarital* affairs (hanky-panky with someone other than one's spouse). And *premarital* (Latin prefix *pre-*, before) describes events that occur before a planned marriage, as *premarital* sex, a *premarital* agreement as to the division of property, etc.

2.   Of cabbages and kings (without the cabbage)

Rex, regis is Latin for *king. Tyrannosaurus rex* was the king (i.e. the largest) of the dinosaurs (etymologically, 'king of the tyrant lizards'). Dogs are often named *Rex* to fool them into thinking they are kings rather than slaves. And *regal* (REE'-gəl) is royal, or fit for a king, hence magnificent, stately, imperious, splendid, etc., as in *regal* bearing or manner, a *regal* mansion, a *regal* reception, etc. The noun is *regality* (ree-GAL'-i-ti).

Regalia (ri-GAYL'-iə), a plural noun, designated the emblems or insignia or dress of a king, and now refers to any impressively formal clothes; or, more commonly, to the decorations, insignia, or uniform of a rank, position, office, social club, etc. 'The five-star general appeared in full *regalia*,', etc.

3.   'Madness' of all sorts

The *monomaniac* develops an abnormal obsession in respect to *one* particular thing (Greek *monos,* one), but is otherwise normal. The obsession itself, or the obsessiveness, is *monomania* (mon'-ō-MAY'-ni-ə), the adjective is *monomaniacal* (mon'-ō-mə-NĪ'-ə-kəl). *Monomaniacal,* like the adjective forms of various other manias, is tricky to pronounce – practise carefully to make sure you can say it correctly without stuttering.

Psychology recognizes other abnormal states, all designating obsessions, and built on Greek *mania,* madness.

1. *dipsomania* (dip'-sō-MAY'-ni-ə) – morbid compulsion to keep on absorbing alcoholic beverages (Greek *dipsa,* thirst). The *dipsomaniac* has been defined as the person for whom one drink is too many, a thousand not enough. Recent investigations suggest that *dipsomania,* or alcoholism, may not necessarily be caused by anxieties or frustrations, but possibly by a metabolic or physiological disorder.

Adjective: *dipsomaniacal* (dip'·sō-mə-NĪ'-ə-kəl).

2. *kleptomania* (klep'-tō-MAY'-ni-ə) – morbid compulsion to steal, not from any economic motive, but simply because the urge to take another's possessions is irresistible. The *kleptomaniac* (Greek *klepte,* thief) may be wealthy, and yet be an obsessive shoplifter. The *kleptomaniac,* for reasons that psychologists are still arguing about, is more often a female than a male, and may pinch her best friend's valueless trinket, or a cheap ashtray or salt shaker from a restaurant, not because she wants, let alone needs, the article, but because she apparently can't help herself; she gets carried away. (When she arrives home, she may toss it in a drawer with other loot, and never look at it again.)

Can you write (and *correctly* pronounce) the adjective?

---

3. *pyromania* (pī'-rō-MAY'-ni-ə) – morbid compulsion to start fires. *Pyromania* should not be confused with *incendiarism* (in-

SEN'-di-ə-riz-əm), which is the malicious and deliberate burning of another's property, and is *not* a compulsive need to see the flames and enjoy the thrill of the heat and the smoke. Some *pyromaniacs* join volunteer fire companies, often heroically putting out the very blaze they themselves have started. An *incendiary* (in-SEN'-di-ə-ri) is antisocial, and usually starts fires for revenge. Either of these two dangerous characters is called, colloquially, a 'firebug'.

In law, setting fire to another's, or to one's own, property for an improper purpose, such as economic gain (e.g., the collection of the proceeds of an insurance policy) is called *arson* (AH'-sən) and is a criminal act. The *pyromaniac* sets fire to property for the thrill; the *incendiary* for revenge; the *arsonist* (AH'-sə-nist) for money.

Pyromania is built on Greek *pyros*, fire; *incendiarism* on Latin *incendo, incensus*, to set fire; *arson* on Latin *ardo, arsus*, to burn.

Can you write, and pronounce, the adjectival form of *pyromaniac*? _____.

4. *megalomania* (meg'-ə-lō-MAY'-ni-ə) – morbid delusions of grandeur, power, importance, godliness, etc. Jokes accusing the heads of governments of *megalomania* are common. Here's an old chestnut from the forties:

Churchill, Roosevelt, and Stalin were talking about their dreams.
Churchill: I dreamed last night that God had made me *Prime Minister* of the whole world.
Roosevelt: I dreamed that God had made me *President of* the whole world.
Stalin: How could you gentlemen have such dreams? *I* didn't dream of offering you those positions!

Hitler, Napoleon, and Alexander the Great have been called *megalomaniacs* – all three certainly had delusions about their invincibility.

Can you write (and pronounce correctly!) the adjective derived from *megalomaniac*? _____

Megalomania is built on Greek *megas*, great, big, large, plus *mania*.

Can you think of the word for an instrument that someone speaks through to make the *sound* (*phone*) of his voice *greater?*

_____

5. *nymphomania* (nim'-fə-MAY'-ni-ə) – morbid, incessant, uncontrollable, and intense desire, on the part of a female, for sexual intercourse (from Greek *nymphe*, bride, plus *mania*).

The person? _____.

The adjective? _____.

6. *satyromania* (sə-tir'-ə-MAY'-ni-ə) – the same morbid, incessant, etc. desire on the part of a male (from Greek *satyros*, satyr, plus *mania*).

A *satyr* (SAT'-ə) was a mythological Greek god, notorious for lechery. He had horns, pointed ears, and the legs of a goat; the rest of him was in human form. *Satyromania* is more commonly called *satyriasis* (sat'-ə-RĪ'-ə-sis).

4.   And now phobias

So much for *maniacs*. There is another side to the coin. Just as personality disorders can cause morbid *attraction* towards certain things or acts (stealing, fire, power, sex, etc.), so also other emotional ills can cause violent or morbid *repulsions* to certain conditions, things, or situations. There are people who have irrational and deep-seated dread of cats, dogs, fire, the number thirteen, snakes, thunder or lightning, various colours, and so on almost without end:* Such morbid dread or fear is called, in the language of psychology, a *phobia*, and we might pause to investigate the three most common ones. These are:

1. *claustrophobia* (klaw'-strə-FŌ'-bi-ə *or* klo'-strə-FŌ'-bi-ə) – morbid dread of being physically hemmed in, of enclosed spaces, of crowds, etc. From Latin *claustrum*, enclosed place, plus Greek *phobia*, morbid fear. The person: *claustrophobe* (KLAW'-strə-fōb' *or* KLO'-strə-fōb'). Adjective: *claustrophobic* (klaw-strə-FŌ'-bik *or* klo'-strə-FŌ'-bik).

2. *agoraphobia* (ag'-ə-rə-FŌ'-bi-ə) – morbid dread of open space, the reverse of *claustrophobia*. People suffering from *agoraphobia* prefer to stay shut up in their homes as much as possible, and become panic-stricken in such places as open fields, large public

_____

* For some of these esoteric phobias, see Appendix

buildings, airport terminals, etc. From Greek *agora*, market place, plus *phobia*.

The person? _____

The adjective? _____

3. *acrophobia* (ak'-rə-FŌ'-bi-ə) – morbid dread of high places. The victims of this fear will not climb ladders or trees, or stand on top of furniture. They refuse to go onto the roof of a building or look out the window of one of the higher floors. From Greek *akros*, highest, plus *phobia*.

The person? _____

The adjective? _____

Review of etymology

Prefix, Root, Suffix	Meaning	English Word
1. *frater, fratris*	brother	_____
2. *soror*	sister	_____
3. *uxor*	wife	_____
4. *maritus*	husband	_____
5. *rex, regis*	king	_____
6. *mania*	madness	_____
7. *monos*	one	_____
8. *-ac*	noun suffix 'one who'	_____
9. *-al*	adjective suffix	_____
10. *dipsa*	thirst	_____
11. *klepte*	thief	_____
12. *pyros*	fire	_____
13. *incendo, incensus*	to set fire	_____
14. *ardo, arsus*	to burn	_____
15. *mega*	great, large, big	_____
16. *phone*	sound	_____
17. *satyros*	satyr	_____
18. *nymphe*	bride	_____
19. *claustrum*	enclosed place	_____
20. *agora*	market place	_____
21. *akros*	highest	_____
22. *-ic*	adjective suffix	_____
23. *phobia*	morbid dread	_____

24. *pre-*	before	_____
25. *extra-*	outside	_____

Using the words

Can you pronounce the words? (I)

1.	*fraternize*	FRAT'-ə-nīz'
2.	*fraternization*	frat'-ə-ni-ZAY'-shən
3.	*fraternal*	frə-TəR'-nəl
4.	*fraternity*	frə-TəR'-ni-ti
5.	*sorority*	sə-ROR'-i-ti
6.	*uxorious*	uk-SAW'-ri-əs
7.	*uxorial*	uk-SAW'-ri-əl
8.	*marital*	MAR'-i-təl
9.	*extramarital*	ek'-strə-MAR'-i-təl
10.	*premarital*	pree-MAR'-i-təl
11.	*regal*	REE'-gəl
12.	*regality*	ree-GAL'-i-ti
13.	*regalia*	ri-GAYL'-iə

Can you work with the words? (I)

1. fraternize	a.	pertaining to, characteristic of, or befitting, a wife
2. fraternal	b.	outside the marriage
3. sorority	c.	kingly, royal; splendid, stately, magnificent, etc.
4. uxorious	d.	referring to marriage
5. uxorial	e.	before marriage
6. marital	f.	socialize
7. extramarital	g.	excessively indulgent to, or doting on, one's wife
8. premarital	h.	brotherly
9. regal	i.	badges, insignia, dress, etc. of rank or office
10. regalia	j.	sisterhood

Key: 1–f, 2–h, 3–j, 4–g, 5–a, 6–d, 7–b, 8–e, 9–c, 10–i

Can you pronounce the words? (II)

1. *monomania*	mon'-ō-MAY'-ni-ə
2. *monomaniac*	mon'-ō-MAY'-ni-ak
3. *monomaniacal*	mon'-ō-mə-NĪ'-ə-kəl
4. *dipsomania*	dip'-sō-MAY'-ni-ə
5. *dipsomaniac*	dip'-sō-MAY'-ni-ak
6. *dipsomaniacal*	dip'-sō-mə-NĪ'-ə-kəl
7. *kleptomania*	klep'-tō-MAY'-ni-ə
8. *kleptomaniac*	klep'-tō-MAY'-ni-ak
9. *kleptomaniacal*	klep'-tō-mə-NĪ'-ə-kəl
10. *pyromania*	pī'-rō-MAY'-ni-ə
11. *pyromaniac*	pī'-rō-MAY'-ni-ak
12. *pyromaniacal*	pī'-rō-mə-NĪ'-ə-kəl

Can you work with the words? (II)

1. monomania		a.	obsession for alcohol
2. dipsomania		b.	obsession for starting fires
3. kleptomania		c.	obsession in one area
4. pyromnia		d.	obsession for theft

Key: 1–c, 2–a, 3–d, 4–b

Can you pronounce the words? (III)

1. *incendiarism*	in-SEN'-di-ə-riz-əm
2. *incendiary*	in-SEN'-di-ə-ri
3. *arson*	AH'-sən
4. *arsonist*	AH'-sə-nist
5. *megalomania*	meg'-ə-lō-MAY'-ni-ə
6. *megalomaniac*	meg'-ə-lō-MAY'-ni-ak
7. *megalomaniacal*	meg'-ə-lō-mə-NĪ'-ə-kəl
8. *nymphomania*	nim'-fə-MAY'-ni-ə
9. *nymphomaniac*	nim'-fə-MAY'-ni-ak
10. *nymphomaniacal*	nim'-fə-mə-NĪ'-ə-kəl
11. *satyromania*	sə-tir-ə-MAY'-ni-ə
12. *satyriasis*	sat'-ə-RĪ'-ə-sis

Can you pronounce the words? (IV)

1. *claustrophobia*   klaw(*or* klo')-strə-FŌ'-bi-ə
2. *claustrophobe*   KLAW'(*or* KLO')-strə-fōb'
3. *claustrophobic*   klaw'(*or* klo')-strə-FŌ'-bik
4. *agoraphobia*   ag'-ə-rə-FŌ'-bi-ə
5. *agoraphobe*   AG'-ə-rə-fōb'
6. *agoraphobic*   ag'-ə-rə-FŌ'-bik
7. *acrophobia*   ak'-rə-FŌ'-bi-ə
8. *acrophobe*   AK'-rə-fōb'
9. *acrophobic*   ak'-rə-FŌ'-bik

Can you work with the words? (III)

1. incendiarism
2. megalomania
3. nymphomania
4. satyromania
5. claustrophobia
6. agoraphobia
7. acrophobia

a. delusions of grandeur
b. compulsive sexual needs on the part of a male
c. morbid dread of open spaces
d. morbid dread of enclosed places
e. malicious setting of fires, as for revenge, etc.
f. morbid dread of heights
g. compulsive sexual needs on the part of a female

Key: 1–e, 2–a, 3–g, 4–b, 5–d, 6–c, 7–f

Can you work with the words? (IV)

1. arsonist
2. megalomaniac
3. nymphomaniac
4. satyriasis
5. claustrophobe
6. agoraphobe

a. one who has delusions of greatness or power
b. male compulsion for sexual intercourse
c. one who fears shut-in or crowded places
d. one who fears heights
e. one who fears large or open spaces
f. one who maliciously starts fires, as for economic and illegal profit

7. acrophobe   g. woman with compulsive, incessant sexual desire

Key: 1–f, 2–a, 3–g, 4–b, 5–c, 6--e, 7–d

Do you understand the words?

1.	Is a *sorority* a men's organization?	YES	NO
2.	Is an *uxorious* husband likely to be psychologically dependent on his wife?	YES	NO
3.	Are *extramarital* affairs adulterous?	YES	NO
4.	Do VIPs often receive *regal* treatment?	YES	NO
5.	Is an admiral of the fleet in *regalia* informally dressed?	YES	NO
6.	Do *monomaniacal* people have varied interests?	YES	NO
7.	Can a *dipsomaniac* safely indulge in social drinking?	YES	NO
8.	Do people of *pyromaniacal* tendencies fear fire?	YES	NO
9.	Is *incendiarism* an uncontrollable impulse?	YES	NO
10.	Is it necessary to seduce a *nymphomaniac*?	YES	NO
11.	Do *megalomaniacs* have low opinions of themselves?	YES	NO
12.	Is a *satyromaniac* lecherous?	YES	NO
13.	Are *satyriasis* and *asceticism* compatible conditions?	YES	NO
14.	Does a *claustrophobe* enjoy cramped quarters?	YES	NO
15.	Would an *agoraphobe* be comfortable in a small cell-like room?	YES	NO
16.	Does an *acrophobe* enjoy mountain-climbing?	YES	NO

Key: 1–no, 2–yes, 3–yes, 4–yes, 5–no, 6–no, 7–no, 8–no,
      9–no, 10–no, 11–no, 12–yes, 13–no, 14–no, 15–yes,
      16–no

Can you recall the words?

1. to socialize	1. F_____
2. excessively indulgent to, and doting on, one's wife	2. U_____
3. full dress, with ribbons, insignia, badges of office, etc.	3. R_____
4. obsessed in one area or with one overriding interest (*adj.*)	4. M_____
5. having a compulsion to start fires (*adj.*)	5. P_____
6. having a psychological compulsion to steal (*adj.*)	6. K_____
7. person who sets fires for revenge	7. I_____
8. criminal act of setting fire to property, e.g., for economic profit	8. A_____
9. obsessive need for sexual gratification by a male	9. S_____ *or* S_____
10. morbidly dreading enclosed or cramped places (*adj.*)	10. C_____
11. morbidly dreading heights (*adj.*)	11. A_____
12. morbidly dreading wide-open spaces (*adj.*)	12. A_____
13. having delusions of grandeur or power (*adj.*)	13. M_____
14. referring to a female who obsessively needs sexual gratification (*adj.*)	14. N_____

15. alcoholism	15. D_____
16. stealing for thrills or out of psychological compulsion (*adj.*)	16. K_____
17. brotherly	17. F_____
18. characteristic of, or befitting, a wife	18. U_____
19. referring to, characteristic of, or involved in, the matrimonial relationship	19. M_____
20. kingly; royal; splendid; etc.	20. R_____
21. outside the marriage (*adj.*)	21. E_____
22. before marriage (*adj.*)	22. P_____

Key: 1–fraternize, 2–uxorious, 3–regalia, 4–monomaniacal, 5–pyromaniacal, 6–kleptomaniacal, 7–incendiary, 8–arson, 9–satyromania *or* satyriasis, 10–claustrophobic, 11–acrophobic, 12–agoraphobic, 13–megalomaniacal, 14–nymphomaniacal, 15–dipsomania, 16–kleptomaniacal, 17–fraternal, 18–uxorial, 19–marital, 20–regal, 21–extramarital, 22–premarital

(End of Session 30)

Session 31

Origins and related words

1. No reverence

The *iconoclast* sneers at convention and tradition, attempts to expose our cherished beliefs, our revered traditions, or our stereotypical thinking as shams and myths.

Adolescence is that confused and rebellious time of life in which *iconoclasm* (ī-KON'-ə-klaz'-əm) is quite normal – indeed the adolescent who is not *iconoclastic* (ī-kon'-ə-KLAST'-ik) to some degree might be considered either immature or maladjusted. The words are from the Greek *eikon*, a religious image, plus *klaein*, to break. *Iconoclasm* is not of course restricted to religion.

2. Is there a God?

Atheist combines the Greek negative prefix *a-* with *theos*, God. Do not confuse *atheism* (AY'-thi-iz-əm) with *agnosticism* (ag-NOS'-ti-siz-əm), the philosophy that claims that God is unknowable, that He may or may not exist, and that human beings can never come to a final conclusion about Him. The *agnostic* (ag-NOS'-tik) does not deny the existence of a deity, as does the *atheist*, but simply holds that no proof can be adduced one way or the other.

3. How to know

Agnostic (which is also an adjective) is built on the Greek root *gnostos*, known, and the negative prefix *a-*. An *agnostic* claims that all but material phenomena is unknown, and, indeed, unknowable.

A *diagnosis* (dī-əg-NŌ'-sis), constructed on the allied Greek root *gnosis*, knowledge, plus *dia-*, through, is a knowing through examination or testing. A *prognosis* (prog-NŌ'-sis), on the other hand, is, etymologically, a knowing beforehand, hence a prediction, generally, but not solely, as to the course of a disease. (The Greek prefix *pro-*, before, plus *gnosis*.)

Thus, you may say to a doctor: 'What's the *diagnosis*, Doctor?'
'Diabetes.'

Then you say, 'And what's the *prognosis*?'

'If you take insulin and watch your diet, you'll soon be as good as new.'

The doctor's *prognosis*, then, is a forecast of the development or trend of a disease. The doctor knows beforehand, from previous similar cases, what to expect.

The verb form of *diagnosis* is *diagnose* (DĪ'-əg-nōz' *or* dī'-əg-NŌZ'); the verb form of *prognosis* is *prognosticate* (prog-NOS'-ti-kayt'). To use the verb *prognosticate* correctly, be sure that your meaning involves the forecasting of developments from a consideration of symptoms or conditions – whether the problem is physical, mental, political, economic, psychological, or what have you.

In school, you may have taken *diagnostic* (dī'-əg-NOS'-tik) tests; these measured not what you were supposed to have learned during the term, but your general knowledge in a field, so that your teachers would know what steps to take, just as doctors rely on their *diagnosis* to decide what drugs or treatment to prescribe.

In a reading centre, various *diagnostic* machines and tests are used – these tell the clinician what is wrong with a student's reading and what measures will probably increase such a student's reading efficiency.

The medical specialist in *diagnosis* is a *diagnostician* (dī'-əg-nos-TISH'-ən).

The noun form of the verb *prognosticate* is *prognostication* (prog-nos'-ti-KAY'-shən).

4.   Getting back to God

Theos, God, is also found in:

1. *Monotheism* (MON'-ō-thee'-iz-əm) – belief in *one* God. (*Monos,* one, plus *theos,* God.)

Using *atheism, atheist,* and *atheistic* as a model, write the word for the person who believes in one God: _____.
The adjective? _____.

2. *Polytheism* (POL'-i-thee-iz-əm) – belief in *many* gods, as in ancient Greece or Rome, (*Polys,* many, plus *theos.*)

The person with such a belief? _____. The adjective? _____.

3. *Pantheism* (PAN'-thi-iz-əm) – belief that God is not in man's image, but is a combination of all forces of the universe. (*Pan,* all, plus *theos.*) The person? _____. The adjective? _____.

4. *Theology* (thi-OL'-ə-jee) – the study of God and religion. (*Theos* plus *logos,* science or study.)

The student is a *theologian* (thee'-ə-LŌ-jən), the adjective is *theological* (thee'-ə-LOJ'-i-kəl).

5.   Of sex and the tongue

A *lecher* practices lechery (LECH'-ər-i). The derivation is Old French *lechier,* to lick. The adjective *lecherous* (LECH'-ə-rəs) has many close or not-so-close synonyms, most of them also, and significantly, starting with the letter *l,* a sound formed with the tongue, supposedly the seat of sensation.

1. *libidinous* (li-BID'-i-nəs) – from Latin *libido,* pleasure.

2. *lascivious* (lə-SIV'-i-əs) – from *lascivia,* wantonness.

3. *lubricious* (loo-BRISH'-əs) – from *lubricus,* slippery, the same root found in *lubricate.* The noun is *lubricity* (loo-BRIS'-i-ti).

4. *licentious* (lī-SEN'-shəs) – from Latin *licere,* to be permitted, the root from which we get *license,* etymologically, 'permission', and *illicit,* etymologically, 'not permitted'.

5. *lewd* – the previous four words derive from Latin, but this one is from Anglo-Saxon *lewed,* vile.

6. *lustful* – from an Anglo-Saxon word meaning *pleasure, desire.* Noun: *lust.*

Libidinous, lascivious, lubricious, licentious, lewd, lecherous, lustful are seven adjectives that indicate sexual desire and/or activity. The implication of all seven words is more or less derogatory.

Each adjective becomes a noun with the addition of the noun suffix *-ness; lubricity* and *lust* are alternative noun forms of two of the adjectives.

6.   Of sex and the itch

Prurient (PRO'OǝR'-i-ǝnd), from Latin *prurio,* to itch, to long for, describes someone who is filled with great sexual curiosity, desire, longing, etc. Can you form the noun? _____

Pruritis (proŏr-Ī'-tǝs *or* proŏǝr-Ī'-tǝs), from the same root, is a medical condition in which the skin is very itchy, but without a rash or eruptions. (Scratch enough, of course, as you will be irresistibly tempted to do, and something like a rash will soon appear.) The adjective is *pruritic* (proŏr-IT'-ik *or* proŏǝr-IT'-ik).

7.   Under and over

Hypochondria (hī-pǝ-KON'-dri-ǝ) is built on two Greek roots: *hypos,* under, and *chondros,* the cartilage of the breastbone. This may sound farfetched until you realize that under the breastbone is the abdomen; the ancient Greeks believed that morbid anxiety about one's health arose in the abdomen – and no one is more morbidly, unceasingly, and unhappily anxious about health than the *hypochondriac.*

Hypochondriac is also an adjective – an alternative adjectival form is *hypochondrical* (hī-pǝ-kon-DRĪ'-ǝ-kǝl).

Hypos, under, is a useful root to know. The *hypodermic* needle penetrates *under* the skin; a *hypothyroid* person has an *under-work-ing* thyroid gland; *hypotension* is abnormally low blood pressure.

On the other hand, *hyper* is the Greek root meaning *over.* The *hypercritical* person is excessively fault-finding; *hyperthyroidism* is an overworking of the thyroid gland; *hypertension* is high blood pressure; and you can easily work out the meanings of *hyperacidity, hyperactive, hypersensitive,* etc.

The adjectival forms of *hypotension* and *hypertension* are *hypotensive* and *hypertensive.*

Review of Etymology

Prefix, Root, Suffix	Meaning	English Word
1. *eikon*	religious image	_____
2. *klaein*	to break	_____
3. *a-*	negative prefix	_____
4. *theos*	God	_____
5. *gnostos*	known	_____
6. *-ism*	noun suffix	_____
7. *-ic*	adjective suffix	_____
8. *gnosis*	knowledge	_____
9. *dia-*	through	_____
10. *pro-*	before	_____
11. *-ate*	verb suffix	_____
12. *-ion*	noun suffix for verbs ending in *-ate*	_____
13. *-ician*	one who; expert	_____
14. *monos*	one	_____
15. *polys*	many	_____
16. *pan*	all	_____
17. *logos*	science, study	_____
18. *-al*	adjective suffix	_____
19. *prurio*	to itch, to long for	_____
20. *hypos*	under	_____
21. *hyper*	over	_____
22. *-ive*	adjective suffix	_____

Using the words

Can you pronounce the words? (I)

1. *iconoclasm* ī-KON'-ə-klaz-əm
2. *iconoclastic* ī-kon'-ə-KLAS'-tik
3. *atheism* AY'-thi-iz-əm
4. *atheistic* ay'-thi-IS'-tik
5. *agnostic* ag-NOS'-tik
6. *agnosticism* ag-NOS'-ti-siz-əm
7. *diagnosis* dī-əg-NŌ-sis
8. *diagnose* DĪ-əg-nōz' or dī-əg-NŌZ'

9. *diagnostic*   dī-əg-NOS'-tik
10. *diagnostician*   dī-əg-nos-TISH'-ən
11. *prognosis*   prog-NŌ'-sis
12. *prognostic*   prog-NOS'-tik
13. *prognosticate*   prog-NOS'-ti-kayt'
14. *prognostication*   prog-nos'-ti-KAY'-shən

Can you pronounce the words? (II)

1. *monotheism*   MON'-ō-thee'-iz-əm
2. *monotheist*   MON'-ō-thee'-ist
3. *monotheistic*   mon'-ō-thee-IS'-tik
4. *polytheism*   POL'-i-thee-iz-əm
5. *polytheist*   POL'-i-thee'-ist
6. *polytheistic*   pol'-i-thee-IS'-tik
7. *pantheism*   PAN'-thi-iz-əm
8. *pantheist*   PAN'-thi-ist
9. *pantheistic*   pan'-thi-IS'-tik
10. *theology*   thi-OL'-ə-ji
11. *theologian*   thi'-ə-LŌ'-jən
12. *theological*   thee'-ə-LOJ'-i-kəl

Can you pronounce the words? (III)

1. *lechery*   LECH'-ər-i
2. *lecherous*   LECH'-ər-əs
3. *libidinous*   li-BID'-i-nəs
4. *lascivious*   lə-SIV'-i-əs
5. *lubricious*   loo-BRISH'-əs
6. *lubricity*   loo-BRIS'-i-ti
7. *licentious*   li-SEN'-shəs
8. *lewd*   LOOD *or* LYOOD
9. *lustful*   LUST'-fəl
10. *lust*   LUST

Can you pronounce the words? (IV)

1. *prurient*   PROO'Oər-i-ənt
2. *prurience*   PROO'Oər'-i-əns
3. *pruritis*   proŏr(*or* proŏər)-Ī'-təs

4. *pruritic*   proŏr(or proŏər)-IT'-ik
5. *hypochondria*   hī-pə-KON'-dri-ə
6. *hypochondriacal*   hī-pə-kon-DRI'-ə-kəl
7. *hypotension*   hī'-pō-TEN'-shən
8. *hypertension*   hī'-pə-TEN'-shən
9. *hypotensive*   hī'-pō-TEN'-siv
10. *hypertensive*   hī-pə-TEN'-siv

This has been a long chapter, and we have discussed, more or less in detail, over one hundred words. Just to keep everything straight in your mind now, see how successfully you can work out the following matching exercises, which will concern any of the words discussed in this chapter.

Can you work with the words? (I)

1. martinet   a. lack of seriousness in an art or profession
2. sycophancy   b. harridan, shrew
3. dilettantism   c. excessive patriotism
4. tyro   d. name from father
5. virtuoso   e. venerable and influential old man
6. termagant   f. beginner
7. chauvinism   g. brilliant performer
8. patrimony   h. bootlicking
9. patronymic   i. inheritance from father
10. patriarch   j. strict disciplinarian

Key: 1–j, 2–h, 3–a, 4–f, 5–g, 6–b, 7–c, 8–i, 9–d, 10–e

Can you work with the words? (II)

1. patricide   a. mother-killing
2. alma mater   b. tending to fixate obsessively on one thing
3. matricide   c. wife-killing
4. fratricide   d. father-killing
5. uxoricide   e. tending to start fires

6. uxorious   f. alcoholic
7. monomaniacal   g. wife-doting
8. pyromaniacal   h. one's school or college
9. megalomaniacal   i. tending to delusions of grandeur
10. dipsomaniacal   j. brother-killing

Key: 1–d, 2–h, 3–a, 4–j, 5–c, 6–g, 7–b, 8–e, 9–i, 10–f

Can you work with the words? (III)

1. kleptomania   a. disbelief in God
2. libidinous   b. belief in many gods
3. atheism   c. lewd
4. agnosticism   d. belief that God is in nature
5. polytheism   e. morbid anxiety about health
6. monotheism   f. belief in one God
7. theology   g. study of religion
8. pantheism   h. obsessive theft
9. satyriasis   i. abnormal male sexual needs
10. hypochondria   j. scepticism about God

Key: 1–h, 2–c, 3–a, 4–j, 5–b, 6–f, 7–g, 8–d, 9–i, 10–e

Can you work with the words? (IV)

1. hypotension   a. high blood pressure
2. lascivious   b. criminal setting fire to property
3. hypertension   c. abnormally low blood pressure
4. agnostic   d. to forecast (probably
                        developments)
5. arson   e. a determination through
                        examination or testing of the
                        nature, type, causes, etc. of a
                        condition
6. iconoclasm   f. one who claims that ultimate
                        reality is unknowable
7. prognosticate   g. sexually immoral

8. diagnosis   h. a foretelling of probable developments

9. prognosis   i. a scoffing at tradition

Key: 1–c, 2–g, 3–a, 4–f, 5–b, 6–i, 7–d, 8–e, 9–h

Can you work with the words? (V)

1. prurience   a. abnormal need for sexual intercourse by a male
2. satyriasis   b. fear of enclosed places
3. agoraphobia   c. student of religion
4. claustrophobia   d. sexual longing or curiosity
5. acrophobia   e. fear of heights
6. theologian   f. fear of open spaces
7. lubricious   g. having, or referring to, abnormally low blood pressure
8. hypochondriacal   h. itching
9. hypotensive   i. having, or referring to, high blood pressure
10. hypertensive   j. sexually immoral; lewd
11. pruritis   k. beset by anxieties about one's health

Key: 1–d, 2–a, 3–f, 4–b, 5–e, 6–c, 7–j, 8–k, 9–g, 10–i, 11–h

Can you recall the words? (I)

1.   Manias and phobias
   1. single fixed obsession   1. M_____
   2. irresistible compulsion to start fires   2 P_____

3. unceasing desire, on the part of a woman, for sexual intercourse	3. N_____
4. obsessive desire to steal	4. K_____
5. delusions of grandeur	5. M_____
6. alcoholism	6. D_____
7. compulsion for sexual intercourse by a male	7. S_____ *or* S_____
8. dread of heights	8. A_____
9. dread of open spaces	9. A_____
10. dread of cramped quarters	10. C_____

Key: 1–monomania,   2–pyromania,   3–nymphomania,
4–kleptomania, 5–megalomania, 6–dipsomania, 7–satyriasis *or* satyromania, 8–acrophobia, 9–agoraphobia,
10–claustrophobia

Can you recall the words? (II)

II.   Sex

Write seven adjectives; all starting with *L*, more or less meaning
'sexually immoral, desirous, etc.'; write the adjective starting with
P meaning 'sexually curious or longing'.

1. L_____   5. L_____
2. L_____   6. L_____
3. L_____   7. L_____
4. L_____   8. P_____

Key: (*1–7 in any order*) 1–lecherous, 2–libidinous, 3–lascivious, 4–lubricious, 5–licentious, 6–lewd, 7–lustful, 8–prurient

Can you recall the words? (III)

III. God

1. study of religion	1. T_____
2. belief that God is the sum total of natural forces	2. P_____
3. belief that there is no God	3. A_____
4. belief that God's existence is unknowable	4. A_____
5. belief in one God	5. M_____
6. belief in many gods	6. P_____

Key: 1–theology, 2–pantheism, 3–atheism, 4–agnosticism, 5–monotheism, 6–polytheism

Can you recall the words? (IV)

1. morbid anxiety about one's health	1. H_____
2. high blood pressure	2. H_____
3. malicious fire-starting	3. I_____
4. the criminal act of maliciously starting fires	4. A_____
5. sneering contempt for convention or tradition	5. I_____
6. a forecast of development (of a disease, etc.)	6. P_____
7. designed to discover causes or conditions (*adj.*)	7. D_____
8. abnormally low blood pressure	8. H_____

9. to forecast (probably future developments) by examining present conditions

9. P_____

10. to determine the nature of a disease, condition, or state by examination

10. D_____

11. the act of forecasting (probably future developments) by examining present conditions

11. P_____

12. doctor who is an expert at recognizing the nature of disease or condition

12. D_____

13. possessed of, or referring to, high blood pressure

13. H_____

14. possessed of, or referring to, abnormally low blood pressure

14. H_____

15. one who studies religion

15. T_____

Key: 1–hypochondria,   2–hypertension,   3–incendiarism, 4–arson, 5–iconoclasm, 6–prognosis, 7–diagnostic, 8–hypotension,   9–prognosticate,   10–diagnose, 11–prognostication, 12–diagnostician, 13–hyperten- sive, 14–hypotensive, 15–theologian

---

Chapter review

A.   Do you recognize the words?

1. Disciplinarian:
 (a) martinet, (b) virago, (c) dilettante
2. Bootlicker:
 (a) chauvinist, (b) sycophant, (c) lecher
3. Scoffer at tradition:
 (a) monomaniac, (b) hypochondriac, (c) iconoclast

4. Disbeliever in God:
  (a) agnostic, (b) atheist, (c) chauvinist
5. Accomplished musician:
  (a) tyro, (b) dilettante, (c) virtuoso
6. Sheer, flimsy:
  (a) diaphanous, (b) uxorious, (c) paternal
7. Abusive woman:
  (a) termagant, (b) virtuoso, (c) matriarch
8. Murder of one's wife:
  (a) genocide, (b) uxoricide, (c) sororicide
9. Old man in ruling position:
  (a) matriarch, (b) patricide, (c) patriarch
10. Morbid compulsion to steal:
  (a) dipsomania, (b) nymphomania, (c) kleptomania
11. Delusions of grandeur:
  (a) megalomania, (b) egomania, (c) pyromania
12. Lewd, lustful:
  (a) prurient, (b) agnostic, (c) hypochondriac
13. Belief in many gods:
  (a) polytheism, (b) monotheism, (c) agnosticism
14. Starting fires for thrills:
  (a) pyromania, (b) incendiarism, (c) arson
15. Morbid fear of heights:
  (a) agoraphobia, (b) acrophobia, (c) claustrophobia
16. High blood pressure:
  (a) hypotension, (b) hypertension, (c) hypochondria
17. Abnormal need for sexual intercourse by a male:
  (a) lechery, (b) lubricity, (c) satyriasis

Key: 1–a, 2–b, 3–c, 4–b, 5–c, 6–a, 7–a, 8–b, 9–c, 10–c, 11–a, 12–a, 13–a, 14–a, 15–b, 16–b, 17–c

B.   Can you recognize roots?

Root	Meaning	Example
1. *sykon*	_____	sycophant
2. *phanein*	_____	diaphanous
3. *vir*	_____	virago
4. *pater, patris*	_____	paternal

5. *onyma*	_____	synonym
6. *homos*	_____	homonym
7. *phone*	_____	homophone
8. *archein*	_____	matriarchy
9. *mater, matris*	_____	maternity
10. *alma*	_____	alma mater
11. *sui*	_____	suicide
12. *caedo (-cide)*	_____	parricide
13. *frater, fratris*	_____	fraternity
14. *soror*	_____	sorority
15. *homo*	_____	homicide
16. *rex, regis*	_____	regal
17. *uxor*	_____	uxorious
18. *maritus*	_____	mariticide
19. *infans, infantis*	_____	infanticide
20. *genos*	_____	genocide
21. *mania*	_____	egomania
22. *monos*	_____	monomania
23. *dipsa*	_____	dipsomania
24. *klepte*	_____	kleptomania
25. *pyros*	_____	pyromania
26. *incendo, incensus*	_____	incendiarism
27. *ardo, arsus*	_____	arson
28. *mega*	_____	megalomaniac
29. *satyros*	_____	satyriasis
30. *nymphe*	_____	nymphomaniac
31. *claustrum*	_____	claustrophobia
32. *agora*	_____	agoraphobia
33. *akros*	_____	acrophobia
34. *phobia*	_____	zoophobia
35. *eikon*	_____	iconoclastic
36. *klaein*	_____	iconoclasm
37. *theos*	_____	monotheism
38. *gnostos*	_____	agnostic
39. *gnosis*	_____	prognosis
40. *polys*	_____	polytheism
41. *pan*	_____	pantheism
42. *logos*	_____	theology
43. *prurio*	_____	pruritis
45. *hypos*	_____	hypotension

45. *hyper* _____ hypertension

Key: 1–fig, 2–to show, 3–man (male), 4–father, 5–name,
6–the same, 7–sound, 8–to rule, 9–mother, 10–soul,
11–of oneself, 12–to kill, killing, 13–brother, 14–sister,
15–person, 16–king, 17–wife, 18–husband, 19–baby,
20–race, kind, 21–madness, 22–one, 23–thirst,
24–thief, 25–fire, 26–to set fire, 27–to burn, 28–great,
large, 29–satyr, 30–bride, 31–enclosed place, 32–market
place, 33–highest, 34–morbid dread, 35–religious
image, 36–to break, 37–God, 38–known, 39–knowledge,
40–many, 41–all, 42–science, study, 43–to itch,
44–under, 45–over

Teaser questions for the amateur etymologist

1. If a *patronymic* is a name derived from the name of one's
father, can you work out the word for a name derived from one's
mother's name? _____.

2. *Incendo, incensus*, to set on fire, is the origin of the adjective
incendiary, the noun *incense*, and the verb to *incense*.

    (a) What is an *incendiary* statement or speech? _____

    (b) Why do people use *incense*, and why is it called *incense?*

(c) If someone *incenses* you, or if you feel *incensed*, how does the
meaning of the verb derive from the root? _____

3. *Ardo, arsus*, to burn, is the source of *ardent* and *ardour*. Explain
these two words in terms of the root.

    (a) ardent: _____
    (b) ardour: _____

4. What is used to make sound greater (use of the roots for *great*
and *sound*)? _____

5. A *metropolis*, by etymology, is the mother city (Greek *meter*,
mother, plus *polis*, city, state). Construct a word for a *great city*
(think of *megalomania*, delusions of greatness):
_____.

6. *Polis,* city, state, is the origin of the word for the uniformed group guarding the city or state. The English word? _____. Can you think of the word from the same root for the art of governing the city or state? _____

7. What is a *bibliokleptomaniac?* _____

Coin a word for one who has an irresistible compulsion to steal *women:* _____. To steal *children* (use the Greek, not the Latin, root for *child*): _____. To steal *males* (use the Greek root): _____. To steal *people* (use the Greek root): _____.

8. What word can you coin for someone who has an obsession to reach the highest places? _____. To be in the market place, or in wide-open spaces? _____. To be in confined places? _____

9. Coin a word for one who has a morbid dread of thieves: _____; of fire: _____; of women: _____; of males: _____; of people: _____.

10. Guess at the meaning, thinking of the roots you have learned, of *gnosiology:* _____

11. Wolfgang Amadeus Theophilus Gottlieb Mozart was a famous eighteenth-century Austrian composer. You can recognize the roots in *Theophilus.* How are his other two middle names similar to *Theophilus?* _____

12. Thinking of the root *phanein,* define *cellophane:* _____

13. Recognizing the root *hypos,* can you define *hypoglycaemia?* _____

Construct a word that is the opposite of *hypoglycaemia:* _____

14. *Pan,* all, occurs in *Pantheon, pandemonium,* and *panorama.* Can you work out the meanings?
                    (a) Pantheon: _____

(b) pandemonium: _____

_____

(c) panorama: _____

_____

15. Recognizing the **roots** in *monarchy*, define the word: _____

_____

(Answers in Chapter 18)

Magazines will help you

When a pregnant woman takes calcium pills, she must make sure also that her diet is rich in vitamin D, since this vitamin makes the absorption of the calcium possible. In building your vocabulary by learning great quantities of new words, you too must take a certain vitamin, metaphorically speaking, to help you absorb, understand, and remember these words. This vitamin is reading – for it is in books and magazines that you will find the words that we have been discussing in these pages. To learn new words without seeing them applied in the context of your reading is to do only half the job and to run the risk of gradually forgetting the additions to your vocabulary. To combine your vocabulary-building with increased reading is to make assurance doubly sure.

You are now so alert to the words and roots we have discussed that you will find that most of your reading will be full of the new words you have learned – and every time you do see one of the words used in context in a book or magazine, you will understand it more fully and will be taking long steps towards using it yourself.

(End of Session 31)

Some interesting derivations

People who made our language

Bloomers

Mrs. Elizabeth Smith Miller invented them in 1849, and showed a working model to a famous women's rights advocate, *Amelia J. Bloomer*. Amelia was fascinated by the idea of garments that were both modest (they then reached right down to the ankles) and convenient – and promptly sponsored them . . . .

Boycott

Charles C. Boycott was an English land agent whose difficult duty it was to collect high rents from Irish farmers. In protest, the farmers ostracized him, not even allowing him to make purchases in town or hire workers to harvest his crops.

Marcel

Marcel was an ingenious Parisian hairdresser who felt he could improve on the button curls popular in 1875. He did, and made a fortune.

Silhouette

Finance Minister of France just before the Revolution, *Etienne de Silhouette* advocated the *simple* life, so that excess money could go into the treasury instead of into luxurious living. And the profile is the *simplest* form of portraiture, if you get the connection.

Derrick

A seventeenth-century English hangman, *Derrick* by name, hoisted to their death some of the most notorious criminals of the day.

Sadist

Because the *Marquis de Sade*, an eighteenth-century Frenchman, found his greatest delight in torturing friends and mistresses, the term *sadist* was derived from his name. His works shocked his nation and the world by the alarming frankness with which he described his morbid and bloodthirsty cruelty.

Galvanism

Luigi Galvani, the Italian physiologist, found by accident that an electrically charged scalpel could send a frog's corpse into muscular convulsions. Experimenting further, he eventually discovered the principles of chemically produced electricity. His name is responsible not only for the technical expressions *galvanism*, *galvanized iron*, and *galvanometer*, but also for that highly graphic phrase, '*galvanized* into action'.

Guppies

In 1868, *R. J. Lechmere Guppy*, president of the Scientific Association of Trinidad, sent some specimens of a tiny tropical fish to the British Museum. Ever since, fish of this species have been called *guppies*.

Nicotine

Four hundred years ago, *Jean Nicot*, a French ambassador, bought some tobacco seeds from a Flemish trader. Nicot's successful efforts to popularize the plant in Europe brought him linguistic immortality.

Places that made our language

Bayonne, France

Where first was manufactured the daggerlike weapon that fits over the muzzle end of a rifle – the *bayonet*.

Cantalupo, Italy

The first place in Europe to grow those luscious melons we now call *cantaloupes*.

Calicut, India

The city from which a kind of cotton cloth now known as *calico* was first imported.

Tuxedo Park, New York

In the country club of this exclusive and wealthy community, the short (no tails) dinner coat for men, or *tuxedo*, was popularized.

Egypt

It was once supposed that the colourful, fortune-telling travellers, or *Gypsies*, hailed from this ancient land.

Damascus, Syria

Where an elaborately patterned silk, *damask*. was first made.

Tzu-t'ing, China

Once a great seaport in Fukien Province. Marco Polo called it *Zaitun,* and in time a silk fabric made there was called *satin*.

Frankfurt, Germany

Where the burghers once greatly enjoyed their smoked beef and pork sausages, which we now ask for in delicatessen stores and supermarkets by the name of *frankfurters* or *hot dogs*.

12

HOW TO FLATTER YOUR FRIENDS

(Sessions 32–37)

Teaser preview

What adjective aptly describes people who are:

- *friendly and easy to get along with?*
- *tireless?*
- *simple, frank, aboveboard?*
- *keen-minded?*
- *generous, noble, and forgiving?*
- *able to do many things skilfully?*
- *unflinching in the face of pain or disaster?*
- *brave, fearless?*
- *charming and witty?*
- *smooth, polished, cultured?*

Session 32

Words are the symbols of emotions, as well as ideas. You can show your feeling by the tone you use ('You're silly' can be an insult, an accusation, or an endearment, depending on how you say it) or by the words you choose (you can label a quality either 'childish' or 'childlike', depending on whether you admire it or condemn it – it's the same quality, no matter what you call it).

In Chapter 11 we discussed ten basic words that you might use to show your disapproval. In this chapter we discuss ten adjectives that indicate wholehearted approval.

Consider the interesting types of people described in the following paragraphs, then note how accurately the adjective applies to each type.

Ideas

1.   Put the kettle on, Polly

They are friendly, happy, extroverted, and gregarious – the sort of people who will invite you out for a drink, who like to transact business around the lunch table, who offer coffee as soon as company drops in. They're sociable, genial, cordial, affable – and they like parties and all the eating and drinking that goes with them.

The adjective is: *convivial*

2.   You can't tire them

Arnold Bennett once pointed out that we all have the same amount of time – twenty-four hours a day. Strictly speaking, that's as inconclusive an observation as Bennett ever made. It's not time that counts, but energy – and of that wonderful quality we all have very different amounts, from the people who wake up tired, no matter how much sleep they've had, to lucky, well-adjusted mortals who hardly ever need to sleep.

Energy comes from a healthy body, of course; it also comes from a psychological balance, a lack of conflicts and insecurities.

Some people apparently have boundless, illimitable energy – they're on the go from morning to night, and often far into the night, working hard, playing hard, never tiring, never worn out or exhausted – and getting twice as much done as any three other human beings.

The adjective is: *indefatigable*

3.   No tricks, no secrets

They are pleasingly frank, utterly lacking in pretence or artificiality, in fact quite unable to hide their feelings or thoughts – and so honest and aboveboard that they can scarcely conceive of trickery, chicanery, or dissimulation in anyone. There is, then, about them the simple naturalness and unsophistication of a child.

The adjective is: *ingenuous*

4.   Sharp as a razor

They have minds like steel traps; their insight into problems that would confuse or mystify people of less keenness or discernment is just short of amazing.

The adjective is: *perspicacious*

5.   No placating necessary

They are most generous about forgiving a slight, an insult, an injury. Never do they harbour resentment, store up petty grudges, or waste energy or thought on means of revenge or retaliation. How could they? They're much too big-hearted.

The adjective is: *magnanimous*

6.   One-person orchestras

The range of their aptitudes is truly formidable. If they are writers, they have professional facility in poetry, fiction, biography, criticism, essays — you just mention it and they've done it, and very competently. If they are musicians, they can play the oboe, the bassoon, the French horn, the cello, the piano, the celesta, the xylophone, even the clavichord if you can dig one up. If they are artists, they use oils, water colours, gouache, charcoal, pen and ink — they can do anything! Or maybe the range of their abilities cuts across all fields, as in the case of Michelangelo, who was an expert sculptor, painter, poet, architect, and inventor. In case you're thinking 'Jack of all trades . . . ', you're wrong — they're *masters* of all trades.

The adjective is: *versatile*

7.   No grumbling

They bear their troubles bravely, never ask for sympathy, never yield to sorrow, never wince at pain. It sounds almost superhuman, but it's true.

The adjective is: *stoical*

8.   No fear

There is not, as the hackneyed phrase has it, a cowardly bone in their bodies. They are strangers to fear, they're audacious, dauntless, contemptuous of danger and hardship.

The adjective is: *intrepid*

9.   No dullness

They are witty, clever, delightful; and naturally, also, they are brilliant and entertaining conversationalists.

The adjective is: *scintillating*

10.   City slickers

They are cultivated, poised, tactful, socially so experienced, sophisticated, and courteous that they're at home in any group, at ease under all circumstances of social intercourse. You cannot help admiring (perhaps envying) their smoothness and self-assurance, their tact and congeniality.

The adjective is: *urbane*

Using the words

Can you pronounce the words?

1. *convivial*   kən-VIV'-i-əl
2. *indefatigable*   in'-di-FAT'-i-gə-bəl
3. *ingenuous*   in-JEN'-yoŏ-əs
4. *perspicacious*   pər'-spi-KAY'-shəs
5. *magnanimous*   mag-NAN'-i-məs
6. *versatile*   VəR'-sə-tīl
7. *stoical*   STÖ-i-kəl
8. *intrepid*   in-TREP'-id
9. *scintillating*   SIN'-ti-layt'-ing
10. *urbane*   ər-BAYN'

Can you work with the words?

1. convivial	a.	frank
2. indefatigable	b.	unflinching
3. ingenuous	c.	noble
4. perspicacious	d.	capable in many directions
5. magnanimous	e.	tireless
6. versatile	f.	fearless
7. stoical	g.	keen-minded
8. intrepid	h.	witty
9. scintillating	i.	friendly
10. urbane	j.	polished, sophisticated

Key: 1–i, 2–e, 3–a, 4–g, 5–c, 6–d, 7–b, 8–f, 9–h, 10–j

Do you understand the words? (I)

1. *Convivial* people are unfriendly.   TRUE   FALSE

2. Anyone who is *indefatigable* tires easily.   TRUE   FALSE

3. An *ingenuous* person is artful and untrustworthy.   TRUE   FALSE

4. A *perspicacious* person is hard to fool.   TRUE   FALSE

5. A *magnanimous* person is easily insulted.   TRUE   FALSE

6. A *versatile* person may do many things well.   TRUE   FALSE

7. A *stoical* person always complains of his hard lot.   TRUE   FALSE

8. An *intrepid* explorer is not easily frightened.   TRUE   FALSE

9. A *scintillating* speaker is interesting to listen to.   TRUE   FALSE

10. Someone who is *urbane* is always making enemies.   TRUE   FALSE

Key: 1–F, 2–F, 3–F, 4–T, 5–F, 6–T, 7–F, 8–T, 9–T, 10–F

Do you understand the words?

1. convivial – hostile   SAME   OPPOSITE
2. indefatigable – enervated   SAME   OPPOSITE
3. ingenuous – worldly   SAME   OPPOSITE
4. perspicacious – obtuse   SAME   OPPOSITE
5. magnanimous – petty   SAME   OPPOSITE
6. versatile – well-founded   SAME   OPPOSITE
7. stoical – unemotional   SAME   OPPOSITE
8. intrepid – timid   SAME   OPPOSITE
9. scintillating – banal   SAME   OPPOSITE
10. urbane – rude   SAME   OPPOSITE

Key: 1–O, 2–O, 3–O, 4–O, 5–O, 6–S, 7–S, 8–O, 9–O, 10–O

Can you recall the words?

1.	witty	1. S_____
2.	noble, forgiving	2. M_____
3.	capable in many fields	3. V_____
4.	keen-minded	4. P_____
5.	uncomplaining	5. S_____ _____
6.	friendly	6. C_____
7.	poised; polished	7. U_____
8.	courageous	8. I_____
9.	tireless	9. I_____
10.	simple and honest; frank	10. I_____

Key: 1—scintillating, 2—magnanimous, 3—versatile, 4—perspicacious, 5—stoical, 6—convivial, 7—urbane, 8—intrepid,
9—indefatigable, 10—ingenuous

(End of Session 32)

Session 33

Origins and related words

1.   Eat, drink, and be merry

The Latin verb *vivo*, to live, and the noun *vita*, life, are the source of a number of important English words.

Convivo is the Latin verb *to live together;* from this, in Latin, was formed the noun *convivium* (don't get impatient; we'll be back to English directly), which meant a *feast* or *banquet;* and from *convivium* we get our English word *convivial*, an adjective that describes the kind of person who likes to attend feasts and banquets, enjoying (and supplying) the jovial good fellowship characteristic of such gatherings.

Using the suffix *-ity* can you write the noun form of the adjective *convivial*? _____. (Can you pronounce it?)

2.   Living it up

Among many others, the following English words derive from Latin *vivo*, to live:

1. *vivacious* (vi-VAY'-shəs) – full of the joy of living; animated; peppy – a *vivacious* personality. Noun: *vivacity* (vi-VAS'-i-ti). You can, as you know, also add *-ness* to any adjective to form a noun. Write the alternate noun form of *vivacious:* _____

2. *vivid* – possessing the freshness of life; strong; sharp – a *vivid* imagination; a *vivid* colour. Add *-ness* to form the noun:

_____

3. *revive* (ri-VĪV') – bring back to life. In the 1960s, men's fashions of the twenties were *revived*. Noun: *revival* (ri-VĪ'-vəl).

4. *vivisection* (viv'-i-SEK'-shən) – operating on a live animal. *Sect-* is from a Latin verb meaning *to cut. Vivisection* is the process of experimenting on live animals to discover causes and cures of disease. *Antivivisectionists* object to the procedure, though many of our most important medical discoveries were made through *vivisection*.

5. *viviparous* (vi-VIP'-ər-əs or vī-VIP'-ər-əs) – producing live babies. Human beings and most other mammals are *viviparous*. *Viviparous* is contrasted with *oviparous* (ō-VIP'-ər-əs), producing young from eggs. Most fish, fowl, and other lower forms of life are *oviparous*.

The combining root in both these adjectives is Latin *pareto,* to give birth (*parent* comes from the same root). In *oviparous,* the first two syllables derive from Latin *ovum,* egg.

Ovum, egg, is the source of *oval* and *ovoid,* egg-shaped; *ovulate* (O'-vyoŏ-layt') to release an egg from the *ovary: ovum* (Ō'-vəm), the female germ cell which, when fertilized by a sperm, develops into an embryo, then into a *foetus* (FEE'-təs), and finally, in about 280 days in the case of humans, is born as an infant.

The adjectival form of *ovary* is *ovarian* (ō-VAIR'-i-ən); of *foetus, foetal* (FEE'-təl). Can you write the noun form of the verb *ovulate?*

_____

Love, you may or may not be surprised to hear, also comes from *ovum.*

No, not the kind of love you're thinking of. Latin *ovum* became *oeuf* in French, or with 'the' preceding the noun (*the egg*), *l'oeuf,* pronounced something like LəRF. *Zero* (picture it for a moment) is shaped like an egg (O), so if your score in tennis is '*fifteen,* and your opponent's is *zero,* you shout triumphantly, fifteen love!'

3.   More about life

Latin *vita,* life, is the origin of:

1. *vital* (VĪ'-təl) – essential to life; of crucial importance – a *vital* matter; also full of life, strength, vigour, etc. Add the suffix *-ity* to

form the noun: _____. Add a verb suffix to
construct the verb: _____ (meaning: *to give
life to*). Finally, write the noun derived from the verb you have
constructed: _____.

   2. *Revitalize* (ree-VĪ'-tə-līz') is constructed from the prefix *re-*,
again, back, the root *vita*, and the verb suffix. Meaning?
_____. Can you write the noun formed from
this verb? _____.

   3. The prefix *de-* has a number of meanings, one of which is
essentially negative, as in *defrost, decompose, declassify*, etc. Using
this prefix, can you write a verb meaning *to rob of life, to take life
from?* _____. Now write the noun form of
this verb: _____.

   4. *vitamin* – one of the many nutritional elements on which life
is dependent. Good eyesight requires vitamin A (found, for example, in carrots); strong bones need vitamin D (in sunlight and cod-
liver oil); etc.

   Vitalize, revitalize, and *devitalize* are used figuratively – for example, a programme or plan is *vitalized, revitalized,* or *devitalized*,
according to how it's handled.

4.   French life

Sometimes, instead of getting our English words directly from
Latin, we work through one of the Latin-derived or Romance
languages. (As you will recall, the Romance languages – French,
Spanish, Italian, Portuguese, and Romanian – are so called because they were originally dialects of the old Roman tongue. English, by the way, is not a Romance language, but a Teutonic one.
Our tongue is a development of a German dialect imposed on our
ancestors by the Angles, Saxons, and Jutes. Though we have taken
over into English more than 50 per cent of the Latin vocabulary
and almost 30 per cent of the classical Greek vocabulary as roots
and prefixes, our basic language is nevertheless German).

   The French, using the same Latin root *vivo*, to live, formed two
expressive phrases much used in English. French pronunciation
is, of course, tricky, and if you are not at least superficially acquainted with that language, your pronunciation may sound a bit
awkward to the sophisticated ear – but try it anyway. These
phrases are:

1. *joie de vivre* – pronounced something like zhwah'-də-VEEV' (*zh* is identical in sound to the *s* of *pleasure*).

Literally *joy of living*, this phrase describes an immense delight in being alive, an effervescent keenness for all the daily activities that humam beings can indulge in. People who possess *joie de vivre* are never moody, depressed, bored, or apathetic – on the contrary, they are full of sparkle, eager to engage in all group activities, and, most important, always seem to be having a good time, no matter what they are doing. *Joie de vivre* is precisely the opposite of *ennui* (this is also a word of French origin, but is easy to pronounce: on-WEE'), which is a feeling of boredom, discontent, or weariness resulting sometimes from having a jaded, oversophisticated appetite, sometimes from just finding all of life tedious and unappetizing, and sometimes implying in addition physical lassitude and general inactivity. Young children and simple people rarely experience *ennui* – to them life is always exciting, always new.

2. *bon vivant*, pronounced something like BON'-vee-VONH' – the -NH a muted nasal sound.

A *bon vivant* is a person who lives luxuriously, especially in respect to rich food, good drink, expensive theatre parties, operas, and other accoutrements of upper-class life. *Bon vivant* means, literally, a *good liver;* actually, a *high liver*, one who lives a luxurious life. When you think of a *bon vivant* (usually, language being sexist, a male), you get the picture of someone attired in top hat and dinner jacket, raising his cane to call a taxi while a beautiful, evening-gowned and sophisticated-looking woman, sparkling in diamonds and furs, waits at his side. They're going to a champagne and partridge supper at an outrageously expensive restaurant, etc. – fill in your own details of the high life.

The *bon vivant* is of course a *convivial* person – and also likely to be a *gourmet* (goobər-MAY'), another word from French.

5.   Food and how to enjoy it

The *gourmand* (GOOOəR'-mənd) enjoys food with a sensual pleasure. To *gourmands* the high spots of the day are the times for breakfast, lunch, dinner, and midnight supper; in short, they like to eat, but the eating must be good. The verb form, *gormandize* (GAW'-mən-dīz'), however, has suffered a degeneration in meaning – it signifies *to stuff oneself like a pig*.

A *gourmand* is significantly different from a *gourmet*, who has also a keen interest in food and drink, but is much more fastidious, is more of a connoisseur, has a most discerning palate for delicate tastes, flavours, and differences; goes in for rare delicacies (like hummingbirds' tongues and other such absurdities); and approaches the whole business from a scientific, as well as a sensual, viewpoint. *Gourmet* is always a complimentary term, *gourmand* somewhat less so.

The person who eats voraciously, with no discernment whatever, but merely for the purpose of stuffing himself ('I know I haven't had enough to eat till I feel sick'), is called a *glutton* (GLUT'-ən) – obviously a highly derogatory term. The verb *gluttonize* is stronger than *gormandize;* the adjective *gluttonous* (GLUT'-ə-nəs) is about the strongest epithet you can apply to someone whose voracious eating habits you find repulsive. Someone who has a voracious, insatiable appetite for money, sex, punishment, etc. is also called a *glutton*.

Review of etymology

Prefix, Root, Suffix	Meaning	English Words
1. *vivo*	to live	_____
2. *-ous*	adjective suffix	_____
3. *re-*	again, back	_____
4. *sectus*	cut	_____
5. *anti-*	against	_____
6. *pareo*	to give birth, produce	_____
7. *ovum*	egg	_____
8. *vita*	life	_____
9. *-ize*	verb suffix	_____
10. *-ation*	noun suffix added to verbs ending in *-ize*	_____
11. *de-*	negative prefix	_____
12. *bon*	good	_____
13. *-ate*	verb suffix	_____

Using the words

Can you pronounce the words? (I)

1. *conviviality* — kən-viv'-i-AL'-i-ti
2. *vivacious* — vi-VAY'-shəs
3. *vivacity* — vi-VAS'-i-ti
4. *vivid* — VIV'-id
5. *vividness* — VIV'-id-nəs
6. *revive* — ri-VĪV'
7. *revival* — ri-VĪV'-əl
8. *vivisection* — viv'-i-SEK'-shən
9. *antivivisectionist* — an'-ti-viv'-i-SEK'-shən-ist
10. *viviparous* — vi(or vī)-VIP'-ər-əs
11. *oviparous* — ō-VIP'-əR-əs
12. *oval* — Ō'-vəl
13. *ovoid* — Ō'-voyd'
14. *ovary* — Ō-və-ri
15. *ovarian* — ō-VAIR'-i-ən
16. *ovulate* — O'-vyŏŏ-layt'
17. *ovulation* — o-vyŏŏ-LAY'-shən

Can you pronounce the words? (II)

1. *vital* — VĪ-təl
2. *vitality* — vī-TAL'-ə-ti
3. *vitalize* — VĪ'-tə-līz'
4. *vitalization* — vī'-tə-lī-ZAY'-shən
5. *revitalize* — ree-VĪ'-tə-līz'
6. *revitalization* — ree-vī'-tə-lī-ZAY'-shən
7. *devitalize* — dee-VĪ'-tə-līz'
8. *devitalization* — dee-vī-tə-lī-ZAY'-shən
9. *joie de vivre* — zhwah'-də-VEEV'
10. *ennui* — on-WEE'
11. *bon vivant* — BON'-vee-VONH'
12. *gourmand* — GŎŎəR'-mənd
13. *gourmet* — gŏŏər-MAY'
14. *gourmandize* — GAW'-mən-dīz'
15. *glutton* — GLUT'-ən
16. *gluttonous* — GLUT'-ə-nəs

17. *gluttonize*   GLUT'-ə-nīz'
18. *vitamin*   VI'(*or* VĪ')-tə-min

Can you work with the words? (I)

1. oval, ovoid   a. peppy
2. revitalize   b. bearing live young
3. gluttonous   c. strong, sharp
4. vivacious   d. piggish; greedy
5. vivid   e. egg-shaped
6. viviparous   f. bearing young in eggs
7. oviparous   g. give new life to

Key: 1–e, 2–g, 3–d, 4–a, 5–c, 6–b, 7–f

Can you work with the words? (II)

1. conviviality   a. release of the egg
2. vivisection   b. a 'high liver'
3. antivivisectionist   c. experimentation on live animals
4. ovulation   d. one who is a connoisseur of
                            good food
5. vitality   e. effervescence; joy of living
6. *joie de vivre*   f. one who enjoys food
7. ennui   g. one who eats greedily; one who
                            is greedy (as for punishment,
                            etc.)
8. *bon vivant*   h. boredom
9. gourmand   i. congeniality
10. gourmet   j. strength, vigour
11. glutton   k. one who is against
                            experimentation on live animals

Key: 1–i, 2–c, 3–k, 4–a, 5–j, 6–e, 7–h, 8–b, 9–f, 10–d,
        11–g

Can you work with the words? (III)

1. revive		a.	rob of life or strength
2. vital		b.	nutritional element necessary for life
3. vitalize		c.	important, crucial
4. devitalize		d.	stuff oneself like a pig
5. gluttonize		e.	breathe life into
6. vitamin		f.	bring back to life

Key: 1–f, 2–c, 3–e, 4–a, 5–d, 6–b

Do you understand the words? (I)

1. conviviality – asceticism	SAME	OPPOSITE
2. vivacious – apathetic	SAME	OPPOSITE
3. vivid – dull	SAME	OPPOSITE
4. revive – kill	SAME	OPPOSITE
5. revitalize – rejuvenate	SAME	OPPOSITE
6. ennui – boredom	SAME	OPPOSITE
7. *bon vivant* – 'man about town'	SAME	OPPOSITE
8. gourmandize – starve	SAME	OPPOSITE
9. glutton – ascetic	SAME	OPPOSITE
10. *joie de vivre* – boredom	SAME	OPPOSITE

Key: 1–O, 2–O, 3–O, 4–O, 5–S, 6–S, 7–S, 8–O, 9–O, 10–O

Do you understand the words? (II)

1. vivacity – liveliness	SAME	OPPOSITE
2. revival – renewal	SAME	OPPOSITE
3. vivisection – experimentation on corpses	SAME	OPPOSITE
4. ovulation – egg-releasing	SAME	OPPOSITE
5. devitalize – reinvigorate	SAME	OPPOSITE
6. vitality – fatigue	SAME	OPPOSITE
7. gluttonous – greedy	SAME	OPPOSITE
8. gourmand – ascetic	SAME	OPPOSITE

9. ovoid – egg-shaped	SAME	OPPOSITE

Key: 1–S, 2–S, 3–O, 4–S, 5–O, 6–O, 7–S, 8–O, 9–S

Do you understand the words? (III)

1. Humans are *viviparous*.	TRUE	FALSE
2. Cows are *oviparous*.	TRUE	FALSE
3. *Ovulation* takes place in females only when they are married.	TRUE	FALSE
4. An *antivivisectionist* believes in experimenting on live animals.	TRUE	FALSE
5. *Vitamins* are essential to good health.	TRUE	FALSE
6. A *bon vivant* lives like a hermit.	TRUE	FALSE
7. A *gourmet* stuffs himself with food.	TRUE	FALSE
8. It is normal for young children to be overwhelmed with *ennui*.	TRUE	FALSE
9. People who are keenly alive possess *joie de vivre*.	TRUE	FALSE

Key: 1–T, 2–F, 3–F, 4–F, 5–T, 6–F, 7–F, 8–F, 9–T

Can you recall the words?

1. bearing young by eggs (*adj.*)	1. O_____
2. bearing live young (*adj.*)	2. V_____ _____
3. good-fellowship	3. C_____
4. operating on live animals	4. V_____
5. one who is opposed to such an activity	5. A_____
6. the process of releasing an egg from the ovary	6. O_____
7. to remove life or vigour from	7. D_____
8. joy of living	8. J_____
9. one who eats like a pig	9. G_____ _____
10. a 'high liver'	10. B_____

11. one who is a connoisseur of good food

11. G_____

12. one who gets a sensual enjoyment from good food

12. G_____

13. to stuff oneself like a pig; to eat greedily

13. G_____

               or G_____

14. boredom; discontent; tedium

14. E_____

15. liveliness, pep

15. V_____

               or V_____

               or V_____

16. egg-shaped

16. O_____

               or O_____

17. to bring renewed life or vigour to

17. R_____

               or R_____

18. referring to the ovary (*adj.*)

18. O_____

19. essential to life; crucial; of utmost importance

19. V_____

Key: 1–oviparous, 2–viviparous, 3–conviviality, 4–vivisection, 5–antivivisectionist, 6–ovulation, 7–devitalize, 8–*joie de vivre,* 9–glutton, 10–*bon vivant,* 11–gourmet, 12–gourmand, 13–gluttonize *or* gormandize, 14–ennui, 15–vivacity, vivaciousness, *or* vitality, 16–oval *or* ovoid, 17–revitalize *or* revive, 18–ovarian, 19–vital

---

(End of Session 33)

Session 34

Origins and related words

1. No fatigue

Indefatigable is a derived form of *fatigue* — *in-* is a negative prefix, the suffix *-able* means *able to be;* hence, literally, *indefatigable* means *unable to be fatigued.* The noun is *indefatigability* (in'-di-fat'-i-gə-BIL'-i-ti).

2. How simple can one be?

Ingenuous is a complimentary term, though its synonyms *naïve, gullible,* and *credulous* are faintly derogatory.

To call people *ingenuous* implies that they are frank, open, artless — in other words, not likely to try to put anything over on you, nor apt to hide feelings or thoughts that more sophisticated persons would consider it wise, tactful, or expedient to conceal.

Ingenuous should not be confused with *ingenious* (in-JEEN'-i-əs) — note the slight difference in spelling — which on the contrary means *shrewd, clever, inventive.*

The noun form of *ingenuous* is *ingenuousness;* of *ingenious, ingenuity* (in'-ji-NYOO'-i-ti) or *ingeniousness.*

To call people *naïve* (nah-EEV' *or* nī-EEV') is to imply that they have not learned the ways of the world, and are therefore idealistic and trusting beyond the point of safety; such idealism and trust have probably come from ignorance or inexperience. The noun is *naïveté* (nah-EEV'-tay *or* nī-EEV'-tay) or *naïvety* (nah-EEV'-ti *or* nī-EEV'-ti).

Credulous (KRED'-yŏo-ləs) implies a willingness to believe almost anything, no matter how fantastic. *Credulity* (kri-DYOO'-li-ti), like *naïveté*, usually results, again, from ignorance or inexperience, or perhaps from an inability to believe that human beings are capable of lying.

Gullible (GUL'-ə-bəl) means *easily tricked, easily fooled, easily imposed on.* It is a stronger word than *credulous* and is more derogatory. *Gullibility* (gul'-ə-BIL.'-i-ti) results more from stupidity than from ignorance or inexperience.

These four synonyms, *ingenuous, naïve, credulous,* and *gullible,* are fairly close, but they contain areas of distinction worth remembering. Let's review them:

1. *ingenuous* – frank, not given to concealment
2. *naïve* – inexperienced, unsophisticated, trusting
3. *credulous* – willing to believe; not suspicious or sceptical
4. *gullible* – easily tricked

3.   Belief and disbelief

Credulous comes from Latin *credo,* to believe, the same root found in *credit* (if people *believe* in your honesty, they will extend *credit* to you; they will *credit* what you say). *-Ous* is an adjective suffix that usually signifies *full of.* So, strictly, *credulous* means *full of believing-ness.*

Do not confuse *credulous* with *credible* (KRED'-i-bəl). In the latter word we see combined the root *credo,* believe, with *-ible,* a suffix meaning *can be.* Something *credible* can be believed.

Let's note some differences:

Credulous listeners – those who fully believe what they hear

A *credible* story – one that can be believed

An *incredulous* (in-KRED'-yŏo-ləs) attitude – an attitude of scepticism, of non-belief

An *incredible* (in-KRED'-i-bəl) story – one that cannot be believed

Incredible characters – persons who are so unusual that you can scarcely believe they exist.

Nouns are formed as follows:

credulous – credulity (krə-JOO'-lə-tee *or* kri-DYOO-li-ti)
incredulous – incredulity (in-krə-JOO-lə-tee *or* in-kri-DYOO-li-ti)
credible – credibility (kred'-i-BIL'-i-ti)
incredible – incredibility (in-kred'-i-BIL'-i-ti)

To check your understanding of these distinctions, try the next test.

Can you use these words correctly?

Use *credulous, credible,* or corresponding negative or noun forms in the following sentences:

1. She listened _____ly to her husband's confession of his frequenty infidelity, for she had always considered him a paragon of moral uprightness.
2. He told his audience an _____ and fantastic story of his narrow escapes.
3. He'll believe you – he's very _____
4. Make your characters more _____ if you want your readers to believe in them.
5. We listened dumb-struck, full of _____, to the shocking details of corruption and vice.
6. He has the most _____ good luck.
7. The _____ of it! How can such things happen?
8. Naïve people accept with complete _____, whatever anyone tells them.
9. 'Do you believe me?' 'Sure – your story is _____ ____ enough.'
10. I'm not objecting to the total _____ of your story, but only to your thinking that I'm _____ enough to believe it!

Key: 1–incredulously, 2–incredible, 3–credulous, 4–credible, 5–incredulity, 6–incredible, 7–incredibility, 8–credulity, 9–credible, 10–incredibility, credulous

4.   What people believe in

Credo, to believe, is the origin of four other useful English words.

1. *Credo* (KREE'-dō *or* KRAY'-dō) – personal belief, code of ethics; the principles by which people guide their actions.

2. *Creed* – a close synonym of *credo;* in addition, a religious belief, such as Catholicism, Judaism, Protestantism, Hinduism, etc.

3. *Credence* (KREE¸-dəns) – belief, as in, 'I place no *credence* in his stories', or 'Why should I give any *credence* to what you say?'

4. *Credentials* (kri-DEN'-shəls) – a document or documents proving a person's right to a title or privilege (i.e. a right to be believed), as in, 'The new ambassador presented his *credentials* to the State Department.'

5.   Heads and tails

We can hardly close our book on the words suggested by *ingenuous* without looking at the other side of the coin. If *ingenuous* means *frank, open,* then *disingenuous* (dis-in-JEN'-yo͝o-əs) should mean *not frank or open*. But *disingenuous* people are far more than simply *not ingenuous*. They are crafty, cunning, dishonest, artful, insincere, untrustworthy – and they are all of these while making a pretence of being simple, frank, and aboveboard. You are thinking of a wolf in sheep's clothing? It's a good analogy.

Similarly, a remark may be *disingenuous*, as may also a statement, an attitude, a confession, etc.

Add *-ness* to form the noun derived from *disingenuous*:

_____.

Review of etymology

Prefix, Root, Suffix	Meaning	English Word
1. *in-*	negative prefix	_____
2. *-ness*	noun suffix	_____
3. *credo*	to believe	_____
4. *-ous*	adjective suffix	_____
5. *-ible*	can be; able to be	_____
6. *-ity*	noun suffix	_____
7. *-ence*	noun suffix	_____

8. *dis-* negative prefix _____

Using the words

Can you pronounce the words?

1. *indefatigability* — in'-di-fat'-i-gə-BIL'-i-ti
2. *ingenuousness* — in-JEN'-yŏo-əs-nəs
3. *ingenious* — in-JEEN'-i-əs
4. *ingenuity* — in'-ji-NYŌŌ'-i-ti
5. *naïve* — nah(*or* nī)-EEV'
6. *naïveté* — nah(*or* nī)-EEV'-tay
7. *credulous* — KRED'-yŏo-ləs
8. *incredulous* — in-KRED'-yŏo-ləs
9. *gullible* — GUL'-ə-bəl
10. *gullibility* — gul'-ə-BIL'-i-ti
11. *credible* — KRED'-i-bəl
12. *incredible* — in-KRED'-i-bəl
13. *credulity* — kri-DYŌŌ'-li-ti
14. *incredulity* — in-kri-DYŌŌ-li-ti
15. *credibility* — kred'-ə-BIL'-i-ti
16. *incredibility* — in-kred'-ə-BIL'-i-ti
17. *credo* — KREE'-dō *or* KRAY'-dō
18. *creed* — KREED'
19. *credence* — KREE'-dəns
20. *credentials* — kri-DEN'-shəlz
21. *disingenuous* — dis'-in-JEN'-yŏo-əs
22. *disingenuousness* — dis'-in-JEN'-yŏo-əs-nəs

Can you work with the words? (I)

1. indefatigability
2. ingenuousness
3. disingenuousness
4. naïveté
5. credibility
6. incredulity
7. credence
8. credo

a. cunning
b. scepticism
c. personal code of ethics
d. frankness
e. belief, trust
f. tirelessness
g. believability
h. inexperience; unworldliness

Key: 1–f, 2–d, 3–a, 4–h, 5–g, 6–b, 7–e, 8–c

Can you work with the words? (II)

1. ingenious		a.	easily tricked
2. credulous		b.	religious belief
3. gullible		c.	inexperienced; unworldly
4. incredible		d.	document proving privileges, identity, etc.
5. creed		e.	unbelievable
6. credentials		f.	shrewdness; cleverness
7. ingenuity		g.	clever; inventive; shrewd
8. naïve		h.	willing to believe

Key: 1–g, 2–h, 3–a, 4–e, 5–b, 6–d, 7–f, 8–c

Do you understand the words?

1. Is *indefatigability* a sign of physical and emotional health?	YES	NO
2. Is *ingenuousness* a normal quality of young childhood?	YES	NO
3. Is *ingenuity* a characteristic of inventors?	YES	NO
4. Are some adolescents naïve?	YES	NO
5. Are unintelligent people often *gullible*?	YES	NO
6. Is *incredulity* the mark of the agnostic?	YES	NO
7. Does an *incredible* story invite belief?	YES	NO
8. Do people generally live by a *credo*?	YES	NO
9. Are *ingenious* people sometimes *disingenuous*?	YES	NO
10. Do we generally give *credence* to *incredible* statements?	YES	NO

Key: 1–yes, 2–yes, 3–yes, 4–yes, 5–yes, 5–yes, 6–yes, 7–no, 8–yes, 9–yes, 10–no

Can you recall the words?

1.	inexperience; unsophistication	1.	N_____
2.	believing (*adj.*)	2.	C_____
3.	religious belief	3.	C_____
4.	believable	4.	C_____
5.	great reservoir of energy	5.	I_____
6.	frankness	6.	I_____
7.	crafty; dishonest	7.	D_____
8.	inventive; clever	8.	I_____
9.	easily tricked	9.	G_____
10.	sceptical	10.	I_____
11.	unbelievable	11.	I_____
12.	personal code	12.	C_____

Key: 1–naïve, 2–credulous, 3–creed, 4–credible, 5–indefatigability, 6–ingenuousness, 7–disingenuous, 8–ingenious, 9–gullible, 10–incredulous, 11–incredible, 12–credo

(End of Session 34)

Session 35

Origins and related words

1.   How to look

The Latin root *specto*, to look, is the source of a host of common English words: *spectacle*, *spectator*, *inspect*, *retrospect* (a looking back), *prospect* (a looking ahead), etc. In a variant spelling, *spic-*, the root is found in *conspicuous* (easily seen or looked at), *perspicacious*, and *perspicuous*.

A *perspicacious* (pər'-spi-KAY'-shəs) person is keen-minded, mentally sharp, astute. *Per-* is a prefix meaning *through;* so the word etymologically means *looking through* (matters, etc.) keenly, intelligently. The noun: *perspicacity* (pər -spi-KAS'-i-ti). Write an alternative noun ending in *-ness:* _____.

Perspicacity is a synonym of *acumen* (AK'-yŏŏ-mən), mental keenness, sharpness, quickness; keen insight. The root is Latin *acuo*, to sharpen.

2.   Sharpness

From *acuo*, to sharpen, come such words as *acute*, sharp, sudden, as *acute pain*, an *acute* attack of appendicitis, *acute* reasoning, etc; and *acupuncture* (AK'-yŏŏ-pungk'-chə), the insertion of a (sharp) needle into the body for medical purposes. The noun form of *acute*, referring to the mind or thinking, is *acuteness* or *acuity* (ə-KYŎŎ'-i-ti); in other contexts, *acuteness* only.

Acupuncture combines *acuo*, to sharpen, with *punctus*, point. When you *punctuate* a sentence, you put various *points* (full stops, commas, etc.) where needed; when lightning *punctuates* the storm, or when the silence is *punctuated* by the wailing of police sirens, again *points*, etymologically speaking, interrupt the atmosphere, the quiet, etc.

If you are *punctual*, you're right on the point of time (noun: *punctuality*); if you're *punctilious* (pungk-TIL'-i-əs), you are exact, scrupulous, very careful to observe the proper *points* of behaviour, procedure, etc. (noun: *punctiliousness*). And to *puncture* something, of course, is to make a hole in it with a sharp *point* – as to *puncture* someone's tyre, or figuratively, illusions, fantasies, or ego. *Pungent* (PUN'-jənt) comes from another form of the root *punctus* (*pungo*, to pierce sharply), so a *pungent* smell or taste is sharp, spicy, prick-ing the nose or taste buds, so to speak; and a *pungent* wit sharply pierces one's sense of humour. Can you write the noun forms of this adjective? _____ or _____.

3.   Some more looking

Perspicacious should not be confused with *perspicuous* (pə-SPIK'-yŏŏ-əs). Here is the important distinction:

Perspecacious means *smart, sharp, able to look through and under-stand quickly*. This adjective applies to persons, their reasoning, minds, etc.

Perspicuous is the obverse side of the coin – it means *easily understood from one look*, and applies to writing, style, books, and like things that have to be understood. Hence it is a synonym of *clear, simple, lucid*. If you write with *perspicuous* style, your language is clear, easy to understand. If you are *perspicacious*, you understand quickly, easily.

The noun form of *perspicuous* is *perspicuity* (pər'-spi-KYŌŌ'-i-ti), or, of course, *perspicuousness*.

A *spectacle* is something to *look at*; *spectacles* (glasses) are the means by which you get a comfortable and accurate *look* at the world. Anything *spectacular* is, etymologically, worth *looking* at.

A *spectator* is one who *looks* at what's happening.

To *inspect* is to *look into* something.

Retrospect (RET'-rō-spekt') is a backward *look* – generally the word is preceded by the preposition *in*, for instance, 'His life *in retrospect* seemed dreary and dull', or 'Most experiences seem more enjoyable *in retrospect* than in actuality' (*retro*-backward).

Prospect (PROS'-pekt') is a forward *look; prospective* (prə-SPEK'-tiv) is the adjective. What's the *prospect* for inflation, for world peace, for the domestic energy supply? Your *prospective* mother-in-law is the one you can look forward to if you marry a certain person; similarly, your *prospective* bride, groom, child, job, holiday, etc. is the person, thing, or activity in the future that you look forward to. (The prefix is *pro-*, forward, ahead, before.)

If you enjoy looking at yourself, figuratively speaking, then you like to examine your mental processes and emotional reactions, in the intense way characteristic of the *introvert* (see Chapter 3). Your mind's eye turns inwards, and you spend a good deal of time analysing yourself, your character, your personality, your actions. Hence, since you look *inwards,* you are *introspective* (in'-trə-SPEK'-tiv) – the prefix is *intro-*, inside, within. If you *introspect* (in'-trə-SPEKT'), you look inwards and examine your inner reactions. Too much *introspection* (in'-trə-SPEK'-shən) or *introspectiveness* may lead to unhappiness or to depressing thoughts or feelings of anxiety – few people have the courage to see themselves as they really are.

There are times when you have to look *around* most carefully; you must then be *circumspect* (SəR'-kəm-spekt') – watchful, cautious, alert (*circum-*, around).

The noun is *circumspection* (sər'-kəm-SPEK'-shən) or *circumspectness.*

If something looks good or sensible, but actually is not, we call it *specious* (SPEE'-shəs). A *specious* argument sounds plausible, but in reality is based on an error, a fallacy, or an untruth. The noun is *speciousness.*

Review of etymology

Prefix, Root, Suffix	Meaning	English Word
1. *specto*	to look	_____
2. *per-*	through	_____
3. *acuo*	to sharpen	_____
4. *punctus*	point	_____
5. *-ate*	verb suffix	_____
6. *-al*	adjective suffix	_____

7. *pungo*	to pierce sharply	_____
8. *-ent*	adjective suffix	_____
9. *-ence, -ency*	noun suffixes	_____
10. *-ness*	noun suffix	_____
11. *-ity*	noun suffix	_____
12. *retro-*	backward	_____
13. *pro-*	forward, ahead, before	_____
14. *intro-*	inside, within	_____
15. *-ion*	noun suffix	_____
16. *-ive*	adjective suffix	_____
17. *circum-*	around	_____

Using the words

Can you pronounce the words? (I)

1. *perspicacious*	pər'-spi-KAY'-shəs
2. *perspicacity*	pər'-spi-KAS'-i-ti
3. *acumen*	AK'-yŏŏ-mən
4. *acute*	ə-KYŌŌT'
5. *acuity*	ə-KYŌŌ'-i-ti
6. *acupuncture*	AK'-yŏŏ-pungk-chə
7. *punctuate*	PUNGK'-chŏŏ-ayt'
8. *punctilious*	pungk-TIL'-i-əs
9. *puncture*	PUNGK'-chə
10. *pungent*	PUN'-jənt
11. *pungence*	PUN'-jəns
12. *pungency*	PUN'-jən-si

Can you pronounce the words? (II)

1. *perspicuous*	pə-SPIK'-yŏŏ-əs
2. *perspicuity*	pər'-spi-KYŌŌ'-i-ti
3. *retrospect*	RET'-rō-spekt'
4. *prospect*	PROS'-pekt'
5. *prospective*	prə-SPEK'-tiv
6. *introspective*	in'-trə-SPEK'-tiv
7. *introspect*	in'-trə-SPEKT'

8. *introspection*   in'-trə-SPEK'-shən
9. *circumspect*   SəR'-kəm-spekt'
10. *circumspection*   sər'-kəm-SPEK'-shən
11. *specious*   SPEE'-shəs

Can you work with the words? (I)

1. perspicacious
2. acumen
3. acupuncture
4. punctilious
5. pungent
6. perspicuous
7. retrospect
8. prospect
9. introspective
10. circumspect

a. extremely careful, exact, or proper in procedure
b. clear; easy to understand
c. a forward look
d. looking inside, or examining or analysing, oneself
e. keen-minded
f. sharp; spicy; piercing
g. careful, watchful, wary, cautious; 'looking around'
h. sharpness of mind or thinking
i. a backward look
j. medical insertion of needles

Key: 1–e, 2–h, 3–j, 4–a, 5–f, 6–b, 7–i, 8–c, 9–d, 10–g

Can you work with the words? (II)

1. acute
2. acuity
3. punctuate
4. puncture
5. pungence, pungency
6. perspicuity

a. pierce; make a hole in; (noun) a small hole
b. clarity; lucidity; ability to be understood quickly and easily
c. sounding plausible, or looking right, but actually false or untrue
d. in the future; describing that which, or one who, can be looked forward to
e. care; watchfulness; caution
f. sharp; sudden; keen-minded

7. prospective	g.	tending to examine and to think about one's motives, feelings, etc.
8. introspective	h.	interrupt sharply or suddenly
9. circumspection	i.	sharpness or spiciness of taste, smell, wit, etc.
10. specious	j.	keenness of mind, thinking, or intellect

Key: 1–f, 2–j, 3–h, 4–a, 5–i, 6–b, 7–d, 8–g, 9–e, 10–c

Do you understand the words?

1. perspicacious – dull witted	SAME	OPPOSITE
2. acumen – stupidity	SAME	OPPOSITE
3. acute – sharp	SAME	OPPOSITE
4. acuity – perspicacity	SAME	OPPOSITE
5. punctilious – casual	SAME	OPPOSITE
6. pungent – flat, dull	SAME	OPPOSITE
7. perspicuous – clear	SAME	OPPOSITE
8. retrospect – backward look	SAME	OPPOSITE
9. prospect – expectation	SAME	OPPOSITE
10. introspective – extroverted	SAME	OPPOSITE
11. prospective – in the past	SAME	OPPOSITE
12. circumspect – careless	SAME	OPPOSITE
13. specious – true	SAME	OPPOSITE

Key: 1–O, 2–O, 3–S, 4–S, 5–O, 6–O, 7–S, 8–S, 9–S, 10–O, 11–O, 12–O, 13–O

Can you recall the words? (I)

1. plausible, but false or incorrect   1. S_____
2. spiciness, sharpness; piercing quality   2. P_____

    or P_____
3. clear; easily understood   3. P_____

4. sharpness of mind or of intelligence

4. A_____
   or A_____
   or A_____

5. care and caution; wariness

5. C_____
   or C_____

6. piercing of the skin with needles for medical purposes

6. A_____

7. tending to examine one's motives, etc.; looking inwards (*adj.*)

7. I_____

8. exact in the observance of proper procedure

8. P_____

9. to pierce and make a small hole in

9. P_____

10. a backward look or view

10. R_____

Key: 1—specious, 2—pungence *or* pungency, 3—perspicuous, 4—acumen *or* acuteness *or* acuity, 5—circumspection *or* circumspectness, 6—acupuncture, 7—introspective, 8—punctilious, 9—puncture, 10—retrospect

Can you recall the words? (II)

1. keenness of mind

1. P_____
   or P_____

2. sharp; sudden; keen-minded

2. A_____

3. to interrupt suddenly

3. P_____

4. spicy; piercing in taste, smell, wit, etc.

4. P_____

5. clarity; clearness of style or language

5. P_____
   or P_____

6. keen-minded; perceptive

6. P_____

7. a look forward

7. P_____

8. act or process of looking inwards

8. I_____

9. carefully looking around; cautious; wary

9. C_____

10. anticipated; 'to be'; looked   10. P_____
forward to (*adj.*)

Key: 1–perspicacity *or* perspicaciousness, 2–acute, 3–punctuate, 4–pungent, 5–perspicuity *or* perspicuousness, 6–perspicacious, 7–prospect, 8–introspection, 9–circumspect, 10–prospective

---

(End of Session 35)

Session 36

Origins and related words

1.   The great and the small

You are familiar with Latin *animus*, mind. *Animus* and a related root, *anima*, life principle, soul, spirit (in a sense, these meanings are all very similar), are the source of such words as *animal, animate* and *inanimate, animated,* and *animation;* knowing the meaning of the roots, you have a better understanding of any word built on them.

Magnanimous contains, in addition to *animus*, mind, the root *magnus*, large, great, which you recall from *magniloquent. Magnanimous* people have such great, noble minds or souls that they are beyond seeking petty revenge.

The noun is *magnanimity* (mag'-nə-NIM'-i-ti).

On the other hand, people who have tiny, tiny minds or souls are *pusillanimous* (pyoo'-si-LAN'-i-məs) – Latin *pusillus*, tiny. Hence, they are contemptibly petty and mean. The noun is *pusilla-nimity* (pyoo'-si-lə-NIM'-i-ti).

Other words built on *animus*, mind:

1. *unanimous* (yoo-NAN'-i-məs) – of one *mind*. If the judges of a competition are *unanimous*, they are all of *one* mind (Latin *unus*, one). The noun is *unanimity* (yoo-nə-NIM'-i-ti).

2. *equanimity* (ee'-kwə-NIM'-i-ti *or* ek'-wə-NIM'-i-ti) – etymolog-ically, 'equal (or balanced) mind'. Hence, evenness or calmness of mind; composure. If you preserve your *equanimity* under trying circumstances, you keep your temper, you do not get confused, you remain calm (Latin *aequus*, equal).

3. *animus* (AN'-i-məs) – hostility, ill will, malevolence. Etymologically, *animus* is simply *mind*, but has degenerated, as words often do, to mean *unfriendly mind*. The word is most often used in a statement such as 'I bear you no *animus*, even though you have tried to destroy me'. (Such a statement shows real *magnanimity!*)

4. *animosity* (an'-i-MOS'-ə-ti) – ill will, hostility. An exact synonym of *animus,* and a more common word. It is used in patterns like, 'You feel a good deal of *animosity*, don't you?', 'There is real *animosity* between Bill and Ernie', 'If you bear me no *animosity*, why do you treat me so badly?'.

2. Turning

Versatile comes from *verto, versus,* to turn – *versatile* people can turn their hand to many things successfully. The noun is *versatility* (vər'-sə-TIL'-i-ti).

3. Zeno and the front porch

Centuries ago, in ancient Greece, the philosopher Zeno lectured on a topic that still piques the human mind, to wit: 'How to Live a Happy Life'. Zeno would stand on a porch (the Greek word for which is *stoa*) and hold forth somewhat as follows: people should free themselves from intense emotion, be unmoved by both joy and sorrow, and submit without complaint to unavoidable necessity.

Today, psychologists suggest pretty much the exact opposite – let your emotions flow freely, express your love or animosity, don't bottle up your feelings. But in the fourth century B.C., when Zeno was expounding his credo, his philosophy of control of the passions fell on receptive ears. His followers were called *Stoics,* after the *stoa,* or porch, from which the master lectured.

If we call people *stoical,* we mean that they bear their pain or sorrow without complaint, they meet adversity with unflinching fortitude. This sounds very noble, you will admit – actually, according to modern psychological belief, it is healthier not to be so *stoical. Stoicism* (STŌ'-i-siz-əm) may be an admirable virtue (mainly because we do not then have to listen to the *stoic's* troubles), but it can be overdone.

4.   Fear and trembling

Intrepid is from Latin *trepido*, to tremble. *Intrepid* people exhibit courage and fearlessness (and not a single tremble!) when confronted by dangers from which you and I would run like the cowards we are. (You recognize the negative prefix *in-*.)

The noun: *intrepidity* (in'-trǝ-PID'-i-ti), or, of course, *intrepidness*.

Trepido is the source also of *trepidation* (trep'-i-DAY'-shǝn) – great fear, trembling, or alarm.

5.   Quick flash

Scintilla, in Latin, is a quick, bright spark; in English the word *scintilla* (sin-TIL'-ǝ) may also mean *a spark*, but more commonly refers to a very small particle (which, in a sense, a spark is), as in, 'There was not a *scintilla* of evidence against him'.

In the verb *scintillate* (SIN'-ti-layt'), the idea of the spark remains; someone who *scintillates* sparkles with charm and wit, flashes brightly with humour. The noun is *scintillation* (sin'-ti-LAY'-shǝn).

6.   City and country

People who live in the big city go to theatres, attend the opera, visit museums and art galleries, browse in book shops, and shop at large department stores.

These activities fill them with culture and sophistication.

Also, they crowd into jammed tube trains or buses, squeeze into packed lifts, cross the street in competition with high-powered motorcars, and patiently stand in line outside cinemas.

Also, they have the privilege of spending two hours a day going to and coming from work.

As a result, city-dwellers are refined, polished, courteous – or so the etymology of *urbane* (from Latin *urbs*, city) tells us. (And you must be absurdly credulous, if not downright gullible, to believe it.) The noun is *urbanity* (ǝr-BAN'-i-ti).

So *urbane* people are gracious, affable, cultivated, suave, tactful – add any similar adjectives you can think of.

Urban (əR'-bən) as an adjective simply refers to cities – *urban* affairs, *urban* areas, *urban* populations, *urban* life, *urban* development, etc.

Consider some prefixes: *sub-*, near; *inter*, between; *intra-*, inside, within; *ex-*, out.

Add each prefix to the root *urbs*, using the adjectival suffix *-an:*

        sub_____: near the city

    (*Sub-* has a number of
meanings: *under, near, close to,*
etc.)

        inter_____: between cities

        intra_____: within a city

        ex_____: out of the city

The *suburbs* are residential sections, or small communities, close to a large city.

Suburbia (sə-BəR'-bi-ə) may designate *suburbs* as a group; *suburban* residents, or *suburbanites* (sə-BəR'-bə-nīts'), as a group; or the typical manners, modes of living, customs, etc. of suburban residents.

An *interurban* bus travels *between* cities, an *intraurban* bus *within* a single city.

An *exurb* (EKS'-ərb) lies well beyond, way outside, a large city, and generally refers to a region inhabited by well-to-do families. *Exurb* has derived forms corresponding to those of *suburb*. Can you construct them?

        Plural noun: _____

        Adjective: _____

        Resident: _____

As a group; manners, customs, _____
etc.:

Urbs is the city; Latin *rus, ruris* is the country, i.e. farmland, fields, etc. So *rural* (ROÖəR'-əl) refers to country or farm regions, agriculture, etc. – a wealthy *rural* area.

Rustic (RUS'-tik) as an adjective may describe furniture or dwellings made of rough-hewn wood, or furnishings suitable to a farmhouse; or, when applied to a person, is an antonym of *urbane* – unsophisticated, boorish, lacking in social graces, uncultured. Noun: *rusticity* (rus-TIS'-i-ti). *Rustic* is also a noun designating a person with such characteristics, as in, 'He was considered a *rustic* by his classmates, all of whom came from cultured and wealthy backgrounds.'

Urbane and *rustic*, when applied to people, are emotionally charged words. *Urbane* is complimentary, *rustic* derogatory.*

To *rusticate* (RUS'-ti-kayt') is to spend time in the country, away from the turmoil and tensions of big-city life. Can you construct the noun? _____.

Review of Etymology

Prefix, Root, Suffix	Meaning	English Word
1. *animus*	mind	_____
2. *anima*	soul, spirit, life principle	_____
3. *magnus*	large, great	_____
4. *pusillus*	tiny	_____
5. *unus*	one	_____
6. *aequus (equ-)*	equal	_____
7. *verto, versus*	to turn	_____
8. *stoa*	porch	_____
9. *in-*	negative prefix	_____
10. *trepido*	to tremble	_____
11. *scintilla*	a spark	_____
12. *urbs*	city	_____
13. *sub-*	near, close to, under	_____
14. *inter-*	between	_____
15. *intra-*	within, inside	_____
16. *ex-*	out	_____
17. *rus, ruris*	country, farmlands	_____
18. *-ate*	verb suffix	_____
19. *-ion*	noun suffix added to *-ate* verbs	_____

* Incidentally, a word used with a derogatory connotation (*bitch, piggish, glutton, idiot,* etc.) is called a *pejorative* (pe-JO'-rə-tiv). *Pejorative* is also an adjective, as in, 'She spoke in *pejorative* terms about her ex-husband.' The derivation is Latin *pejor*, worse.

Using the words

Can you pronounce the words? (I)

1. *magnanimity*   mag'-nə-NIM'-i-ti
2. *pusillanimous*   pyōo'-si-LAN'-i-məs
3. *pusillanimity*   pyōo'-si-lə-NIM'-i-ti
4. *unanimous*   yōo-NAN'-i-məs
5. *unanimity*   yōo-nə-NIM'-i-ti
6. *equanimity*   eek'(*or* ek')-wə-NIM'-i-ti
7. *animus*   AN'-i-məs
8. *animosity*   an'-i-MOS'-i-ti
9. *versatility*   vər'-sə-TIL'-ə-tee
10. *stoic*   STŌ'-ik
11. *stoicism*   STŌ'-i-siz-əm

Can you pronounce the words? (II)

1. *intrepidity*   in'-trə-PID'-i-ti
2. *trepidation*   trep'-i-DAY'-shən
3. *scintilla*   sin-TIL'-ə
4. *scintillate*   SIN'-ti-layt'
5. *scintillation*   sin'-ti-LAY'-shən
6. *urbanity*   ər-BAN'-i-ti
7. *suburbia*   sə-BəR'-bi-ə
8. *interurban*   in'-tə-əR'-bən
9. *intraurban*   in'-trə-əR'-bən
10. *exurbs*   EKS'-ərbz
11. *exurban*   eks-əR'-bən
12. *exurbanite*   eks-əR'-bən-īt'
13. *exurbia*   eks-əR'-bi-ə

Can you pronounce the words? (III)

1. *rural*   ROO'əR'-əl
2. *rustic*   RUS'-tik
3. *rusticity*   rus-TIS'-i-ti
4. *rusticate*   RUS'-ti-kayt'
5. *rustication*   'rus'-ti-KAY'-shən
6. *pejorative*   pə-JO'-rə-tiv

Can you work with the words? (I)

1.	magnanimity	a.	calmness, composure
2.	pusillanimity	b.	ability either to do many different things well, or to function successfully in many areas
3.	unanimity	c.	fearlessness; great courage
4.	equanimity	d.	unemotionality; bearing of pain, etc. without complaint
5.	animosity	e.	big-heartedness; generosity; quality of forgiving easily
6.	versatility	f.	a sparkling with wit ,r cleverness
7.	stoicism	g.	fear and trembling; alarm
8.	intrepidity	h.	complete agreement, all being of one mind
9.	trepidation	i.	petty-mindedness
10.	scintillation	j.	anger, hostility, resentment, hatred

Key: 1—e, 2—i, 3—h, 4—a, 5—j, 6—b, 7—d, 8—c, 9—g, 10—f

Can you work with the words? (II)

1.	urbanity	a.	referring to the countryside
2.	suburbia	b.	word with negative or derogatory connotation; describing such a word or words
3.	exurbia	c.	to spend time in the country
4.	animus	d.	residential areas near big cities; customs, etc. of the inhabitants of such areas
5.	interurban	e.	residential areas far from big cities; customs, etc. of the inhabitants of such areas
6.	intraurban	f.	between cities
7.	rural	g.	rough-hewn, farmlike; unsophisticated, uncultured
8.	rustic	h.	sophistication, courtesy, polish, etc.

9. rusticate   i. anger, hatred, hostility
10. pejorative   j. within one city

Key: 1–h, 2–d, 3–e, 4–i, 5–f, 6–j, 7–a, 8–g, 9–c, 10–b

(End of Session 36)

Session 37

Ready for revision?

Review, review, review! This is the secret of remembering, assimilating, digesting, and keeping as permanent acquisitions all the new words you have learned.

So pitch in with enthusiasm to the rest of this chapter, made up of a series of valuable tests on all the chapter words. Ready?

Can you work with the words? (I)

1. retrospect	a.	complete agreement
2. acumen	b.	pettiness
3. magnanimity	c.	malevolence
4. pusillanimity	d.	backward look
5. unanimity	e.	calmness
6. equanimity	f.	ability in many fields
7. animosity	g.	mental keenness
8. versatility	h.	generosity

Key: 1–d, 2–g, 3–h, 4–b, 5–a, 6–e, 7–c, 8–f

Can you work with the words? (II)

1. stoicism	a.	fearlessness
2. intrepidity	b.	sparkle
3. trepidation	c.	inward look
4. scintillation	d.	uncomplaining attitude to pain or trouble

5. urbanity   e. falsity
6. introspection   f. polish, cultivation
7. circumspection   g. care, cautiousness
8. speciousness   h. fear

Key: 1–d, 2–a, 3–h, 4–b, 5–f, 6–c, 7–g, 8–e

Can you work with the words? (III)

1. exurbs   a. of one mind
2. pusillanimous   b. ill will
3. unanimous   c. pertaining to the city
4. animus   d. petty
5. rustic   e. self-analytical
6. urban   f. regions far from the city
7. introspective   g. cautious
8. circumspect   h. false, though plausible
9. specious   i. countrified

Key: 1–f, 2–d, 3–a, 4–b, 5–i, 6–c, 7–e, 8–g, 9–h

Can you work with the words? (IV)

1. perspicacity   a. clearness
2. perspicuity   b. to be witty
3. stoic   c. spend time in the country
4. scintilla   d. one who controls his emotions
5. scintillate   e. to look inwards
6. rural   f. a very small amount
7. rusticate   g. keen intelligence
8. introspect   h. clear, understandable
9. perspicuous   i. keen-minded
10. perspicacious j. pertaining to the country

Key: 1–g, 2–a, 3–d, 4–f, 5–b, 6–j, 7–c, 8–e, 9–h, 10–i

Do you understand the words? (I)

1.	Does life often seem pleasanter in *retrospect*?	YES	NO
2.	Are people of *acuity* gullible?	YES	NO
3.	Is *perspicacity* a common characteristic?	YES	NO
4.	Is a person of *acumen* likely to be naïve?	YES	NO
5.	Is a *perspicuous* style of writing easy to read?	YES	NO
6.	Should all writers aim at *perspicuity*?	YES	NO
7.	Is *magnanimity* a characteristic of small-minded people?	YES	NO
8.	Does a person of *pusillanimous* mind often think of petty revenge?	YES	NO
9.	Is a *unanimous* opinion one in which all concur?	YES	NO

Key: 1–yes, 2–no, 3–no, 4–no, 5–yes, 6–yes, 7–no, 8–yes, 9–yes

Do you understand the words? (II)

1.	Is it easy to preserve one's *equanimity* under trying circumstances?	YES	NO
2.	Do we bear *animus* towards our enemies?	YES	NO
3.	Do we usually feel great *animosity* towards our friends?	YES	NO
4.	Do we admire *versatility*?	YES	NO
5.	Does a *stoic* usually complain?	YES	NO
6.	Is *stoicism* a mark of an uninhibited personality?	YES	NO
7.	Do cowards show *intrepidity* in the face of danger?	YES	NO
8.	Do cowards often feel a certain amount of *trepidation*?	YES	NO
9.	Is a *scintilla* of evidence a great amount?	YES	NO

10. Do dull people *scintillate?*   YES   NO
11. Is *urbanity* a characteristic of boorish   YES   NO
    people?

Key: 1—no, 2—yes, 3—no, 4—yes, 5—no, 6—no, 7—no, 8—yes, 9—no, 10—no, 11—no

Do you understand the words? (III)

1. Is New York City a *rural*   YES   NO
    community?
2. Is a village an *urban* community?   YES   NO
3. Do you *rusticate* in the city?   YES   NO
4. Are extroverts very *introspective?*   YES   NO
5. Does an introvert spend a good deal   YES   NO
    of time in *introspection?*
6. In dangerous circumstances, is it   YES   NO
    wise to be *circumspect?*
7. Do *specious* arguments often sound   YES   NO
    convincing?

Key: 1—no, 2—no, 3—no, 4—no, 5—yes, 6—yes, 7—yes

Do you understand the words? (IV)

1. retrospect – prospect   SAME   OPPOSITE
2. acute – perspicacious   SAME   OPPOSITE
3. acumen – stupidity   SAME   OPPOSITE
4. perspicuous – confused   SAME   OPPOSITE
5. magnanimous – noble   SAME   OPPOSITE
6. pusillanimous – petty   SAME   OPPOSITE
7. unanimous – divided   SAME   OPPOSITE
8. equanimity – nervousness   SAME   OPPOSITE
9. animosity – hostility   SAME   OPPOSITE
10. animus – friendliness   SAME   OPPOSITE
11. versatility – monomania   SAME   OPPOSITE
12. stoicism – cowardice   SAME   OPPOSITE
13. intrepidity – fear   SAME   OPPOSITE

14. trepidation – courage	SAME	OPPOSITE
15. scintilla – slight amount	SAME	OPPOSITE
16. urbanity – refinement	SAME	OPPOSITE
17. rustic – crude	SAME	OPPOSITE
18. rural – urban	SAME	OPPOSITE
19. introspective – self-analytic	SAME	OPPOSITE
20. circumspect – careless	SAME	OPPOSITE
21. specious – true	SAME	OPPOSITE

Key: 1–O, 2–S, 3–O, 4–O, 5–S, 6–S, 7–O, 8–O, 9–S,
         10–O, 11–O, 12–O, 13–O, 14–O, 15–S, 16–S, 17–S,
         18–O, 19–S, 20–O, 21–O

Can you recall the words? (I)

1. ability in many fields?   1. V_____
2. pertaining to the city   2. U_____
   (*adj.*)
3. to spend time in the   3. R_____
   country
4. merest spark; small   4. S_____
   amount
5. courage   5. I_____

Key: 1–versatility, 2–urban, 3–rusticate, 4–scintilla, 5–in-
         trepidity

Can you recall the words? (II)

1. unflinching fortitude   1. S_____
2. countrified; unpolished   2. R_____
3. pertaining to the   3. R_____
   countryside (*adj.*)
4. a looking back to the past   4. R_____
5. nobleness of mind or   5. M_____
   spirit

Key: 1–stoicism, 2–rustic, 3–rural, 4–retrospect, 5–magnanimity

Can you recall the words? (III)

1. keen-mindedness
2. clear, lucid
3. petty, mean
4. all of one mind or opinion
5. ill will

1. A_____
2. P_____
3. P_____
4. U_____
5. A_____
   or A_____

Key: 1–acuity, 2–perspicuous, 3–pusillanimous, 4–unanimous, 5–animus *or* animosity

Can you recall the words? (IV)

1–4. keenness of mind

1. P_____
   or P_____
2. A_____
3. A_____
4. A_____

5. clearness of style or language
6. one who keeps his emotions, during times of trouble, hidden
7. sophistication, courtesy, refinement

5. P_____
6. S_____
7. U_____

Key: 1–perspicacity *or* perspicaciousness, 2–acumen, 3–acuity, 4–acuteness (2–4 in any order), 5–perspicuity, 6–stoic, 7–urbanity

Can you recall the words? (V)

1. pettiness of character	1. P_____
2. noun form of *unanimous*	2. U_____
3. mental calmness, balance	3. E_____
4. fear and trembling	4. T_____
5. to sparkle with wit and humour	5. S_____

Key: 1—pusillanimity, 2—unanimity, 3—equanimity, 4—trepidation, 5—scintillate

Can you recall the words? (VI)

1. a looking inwards; an examining of one's mental processes or emotional reactions	1. I_____
2. cautious	2. C_____
3. seemingly true, actually false	3. S_____
4. to think of one's mental processes	4. I_____
5. care, watchfulness	5. C_____

Key: 1—introspective, 2—circumspect, 3—specious, 4—introspect, 5—circumspection

Three further tests

1.   Matching

Word	Meaning
1. convivial	a. frank
2. indefatigable	b. noble, forgiving
3. ingenuous	c. unflinching; unemotional
4. perspicacious	d. courteous; polished; suave
5. magnanimous	e. companionable, gregarious

6. versatile   f. witty
7. stoical   g. capable in many directions
8. intrepid   h. brave
9. scintillating   i. keen-minded
10. urbane   j. tireless

Key: 1–e, 2–j, 3–a, 4–i, 5–b, 6–g, 7–c, 8–h, 9–f, 10–d

II.   Same or opposite?

1. vivacious – sluggish	SAME	OPPOSITE
2. vital – crucial	SAME	OPPOSITE
3. ennui – boredom	SAME	OPPOSITE
4. *bon vivant* – gourmand	SAME	OPPOSITE
5. gourmet – ascetic	SAME	OPPOSITE
6. ingenuous – crafty	SAME	OPPOSITE
7. naïve – sophisticated	SAME	OPPOSITE
8. credulous – sceptical	SAME	OPPOSITE
9. disingenuous – insincere	SAME	OPPOSITE
10. credo – belief	SAME	OPPOSITE

Key: 1–O, 2–S, 3–S, 4–S, 5–O, 6–O, 7–O, 8–O, 9–S, 10–S

III.   Changing parts of speech

Change these adjectives to nouns *not* ending in *-ness*.

1. indefatigable   1. _____
2. perspicacious   2. _____
3. stoical   3. _____
4. urbane   4. _____
5. naïve   5. _____
6. incredulous   6. _____
7. incredible   7. _____
8. perspicuous   8. _____
9. magnanimous   9. _____
10. pusillanimous   10. _____

Key: 1—indefatigability, 2—perspicacity, 3—stoicism, 4—urbanity, 5—naïveté *or* naïvety, 6—incredulity, 7—incredibility, 8—perspicuity, 9—magnanimity, 10—pusillanimity

Chapter review

A.   Do you recognize the words?

1. Tireless:
   (a) convivial, (b) indefatigable, (c) versatile
2. Frank, unsophisticated:
   (a) ingenuous, (b) ingenious, (c) intrepid
3. Unflinching, uncomplaining:
   (a) perspicacious, (b) urbane, (c) stoical
4. Noble, forgiving, generous:
   (a) pusillanimous, (b) unanimous, (c) magnanimous
5. Between cities:
   (a) interurban, (b) intraurban, (c) exurban
6. Giving birth to live young:
   (a) oviparous, (b) ovulation, (c) viviparous
7. Tedium, boredom:
   (a) ennui, (b) *joie de vivre*, (c) vitality
8. Connoisseur of choice food:
   (a) gourmet, (b) gourmand, (c) glutton
9. Inexperienced in the ways of the world:
   (a) credulous, (b) naïve, (c) credible
10. Easily tricked:
    (a) gullible, (b) incredulous, (c) ingenious
11. Backward look:
    (a) prospect, (b) retrospect, (c) introspection
12. Clearness:
    (a) perspicacity, (b) perspicuity, (c) intrepidity
13. Resentment:
    (a) animosity, (b) stoicism, (c) urbanity
14. Countrified:
    (a) rustic, (b) specious, (c) circumspect

Key: 1–b, 2–a, 3–c, 4–c, 5–a, 6–c, 7–a, 8–a, 9–b, 10–a, 11–b, 12–b, 13–a, 14–a

---

B. Can you recognize roots?

Root	Example	Meaning
1. *vivo*	_____	vivacious
2. *sectus*	_____	vivisection
3. *pareo*	_____	viviparous
4. *ovum*	_____	oviparous
5. *vita*	_____	vital
6. *bon*	_____	*bon vivant*
7. *credo*	_____	credible
8. *specto*	_____	spectator
9. *acuo*	_____	acupuncture
10. *punctus*	_____	punctuate
11. *pungo*	_____	pungent
12. *animus*	_____	animosity
13. *pusillus*	_____	pusillanimous
14. *magnus*	_____	magnanimous
15. *unus*	_____	unanimous
16. *aequus (equ-)*	_____	equanimity
17. *verto, versus*	_____	versatile
18. *stoa*	_____	stoical
19. *trepido*	_____	trepidation
20. *scintilla*	_____	scintillate
21. *urbs*	_____	urban
22. *rus, ruris*	_____	rural, rustic

Key: 1–to live, 2–cut, 3–to give birth, produce, 4–egg, 5–life, 6–good, 7–to believe, 8–to look, 9–to sharpen, 10–point, 11–to pierce sharply, 12–mind, 13–tiny, 14–big, great, large, 15–one, 16–equal, 17–to turn, 18–porch, 19–to tremble, 20–spark, 21–city, 22–country, countryside

Teaser questions for the amateur etymologist

1. Recalling the root *vivo*, to live, can you think of the verb that means *to live on?* _____.

Can you write the noun form? _____.

2. How would you explain a *vivarium?* _____
_____.

3. *Unus* is Latin for *one*. Can you use this root to construct words meaning:

(a) animal with *one* horn: _____

(b) of *one* form: _____

(c) to make *one:*   _____

(d) *one*ness: _____

(e) *one*-wheeled vehicle: _____

4. *Annus* is Latin for *year; verto, versus,* as you know, means *to turn.* Can you, then, explain the word *anniversary* in terms of its roots? _____
_____.

5. How about *universe* and *university* in terms of their roots (*unus,* one; *verto, versus* to turn)?

(a) universe: _____

(b) university: _____

6. Use *inter-*, between, to form words of the following meanings:

(a) *between* states (*adj.*)   _____

(b) *between* nations (*adj.*):   _____

(c) in the middle *between*   _____
elementary and advanced
(*adj.*):

(d) to break in (*between* people _____
conversing):

(e) *between persons* (*adj.*):   _____

7. Use *intra-*, within, to form words with the following meaning (all *adjectives*):

(a) *within* one state: _____

(b) *within* one nation: _____

(c) *within* one's own person or   _____
mind:

(d) *within* the muscles: _____

(*Answers in Chapter 18*)

Words influence your thinking

By now, you have thoroughly explored hundreds upon hundreds of valuable words and scores upon scores of important Greek and Latin roots.

As you went along you stopped at frequent intervals to say aloud, think about, work with, and recall the words you were adding to your vocabulary.

By now, therefore, the words you have been learning are probably old friends of yours; they have started to influence your thinking, have perhaps begun to appear in your conversation, and have certainly become conspicuous in your reading. In short, they have been effective in making changes in your intellectual climate.

Let us pause now for another check-up of the success of your study. In the next chapter, you will find a second Comprehensive Test. Take the test cold if you feel that all the material is at your fingertips; or spend a little time reviewing Chapters 9, 10, 11, and 12 if you believe such review is necessary.

(End of Session 37)

13

HOW TO CHECK YOUR PROGRESS

Comprehensive Test II

Session 38

I—Etymology

Root	Meaning	Example
1. *scribo, scriptus*	_____	proscribe
2. *aequus (equ-)*	_____	equivocal
3. *malus*	_____	malign
4. *dico, dictus*	_____	malediction
5. *volo*	_____	malevolent
6. *facio*	_____	malefactor
7. *bonus, bene*	_____	benevolent
8. *fides*	_____	infidelity
9. *dono*	_____	condone
10. *nox, noctis*	_____	equinox

12. *libra*	_____	equilibrium
13. *taceo*	_____	taciturn
14. *loquor*	_____	loquacious
15. *solus*	_____	soliloquy
16. *venter, ventris*	_____	ventral
17. *magnus*	_____	magniloquence
18. *verbum*	_____	verbatim
19. *volvo, volutus*	_____	voluble
20. *animus*	_____	pusillanimous
21. *dorsum*	_____	endorse
22. *vox, vocis*	_____	vocal
23. *fero*	_____	vociferous
24. *ambulo*	_____	somnambulist
25. *somnus*	_____	somnolent

II—More etymology

Root	Meaning	Example
1. *phanein*	_____	sycophant
2. *vir*	_____	virago
3. *pater, patris*	_____	patricide
4. *onyma*	_____	synonym
5. *homos*	_____	homonym
6. *phone*	_____	homophone
7. *archein*	_____	matriarch
8. *mater, matris*	_____	matron
9. *caedo (-cide)*	_____	suicide
10. *homo*	_____	homicide
11. *uxor*	_____	uxorious
12. *maritus*	_____	matricide
13. *pyros*	_____	pyromania
14. *theos*	_____	atheist
15. *vivo*	_____	viviparous
16. *credo*	_____	credulous
17. *pungo*	_____	pungency
18. *unus*	_____	unanimous
19. *trepido*	_____	intrepid
20. *scintilla*	_____	scintillate
21. *urbs*	_____	urbanity
22. *rus, ruris*	_____	rural, rustic

23. *gnosis*   _____   prognosis
24. *pan*   _____   pantheism
25. *omnis*   _____   omniscient

III—Same or opposite?

1. disparage – praise		S	O
2. proscribe – prohibit		S	O
3. placate – irritate		S	O
4. taciturn – talkative		S	O
5. cogent – brilliant		S	O
6. atheistic – religious		S	O
7. convivial – unfriendly		S	O
8. ingenuous – naïve		S	O
9. perspicacious – keen-minded		S	O
10. intrepid – fearful		S	O
11. malign – praise		S	O
12. inarticulate – verbal		S	O
13. verbose – laconic		S	O
14. tyro – virtuoso		S	O
15. megalomania – modesty		S	O
16. satyriasis – nymphomania		S	O
17. claustrophobia – agoraphobia		S	O
18. indefatigability – tirelessness		S	O
19. credulous – sceptical		S	O
20. animosity – hostility		S	O

IV—Matching

1. is lewd and lustful   a. chauvinist
2. caters to the rich   b. sycophant
3. is an accomplished   c. dilettante
   musician
4. sneers at traditions   d. iconoclast
5. is the mother-ruler of a   e. lecher
   family, tribe, or nation
6. has an irresistible urge to   f. tyro
   steal
7. is excessively patriotic   g. virtuoso
8. is a loud-mouthed woman   h. termagant

9. is a beginner
10. is a dabbler

i. matriarch
j. kleptomaniac

V—More matching

1. does not know whether or not God exists
2. is a criminal
3. is a connoisseur of good food
4. sets fire to property for revenge
5. meets adversity or pain without flinching
6. walks in his sleep
7. is obsessively addicted to drink
8. has imaginary ailments
9. compulsively starts fires
10. is a woman who is sexually insatiable

a. dipsomaniac
b. pyromaniac
c. agnostic
d. hypochondriac
e. gourmet
f. stoic
g. malefactor
h. somnambulist
i. nymphomaniac
j. incendiary

VI—Recall a word

1. to make unnecessary
2. to flatter fulsomely
3. to spread slander about
4. economical in speech
5. trite and hackneyed
6. word for word
7. killing of masses of people
8. inheritance from one's father
9. belief in many gods
10. a person aggressively fighting for a cause
11. sincere; valid; in good faith

1. O_____
2. A_____
3. M_____
4. L_____
5. B_____
6. V_____
7. G_____
8. P_____
9. P_____
10. M_____
11. B_____
F_____

12. babbling ceaselessly about trivia (*adj.*)

12. G_____

13. to speak to oneself, as in a play

13. S_____

14. masterpiece

14. M_____
O_____

15. unselfish; not revengeful

15. M_____

16. able to walk after being bedridden

16. A_____

17. inability to fall asleep

17. I_____

18. morbid fear of heights

18. A_____

19. the killing of one's brother

19. F_____

20. opposite in meaning (*adj.*)

20. A_____

21. 'joy of life'

21. J_____D_____
V_____

22. to rob of life or vigour

22. D_____

23. inexperience, unsophistication

23. N_____

24. scrupulously careful in the observance of proper procedure

24. P_____

25. clear, understandable (of style or language)

25. P_____

26. wary, cautious, watchful

26. C_____

27. a backward look

27. R_____

28. all of one mind (*adj.*)

28. U_____

29. uncomplaining in face of pain, misfortune, or emotional difficulties (*adj.*)

29. S_____

30. between cities (*adj.*)

30. I_____

Key: A correct answer counts as one point. Count up your points for each part of the test, then add together for a total.

I

1–to write, 2–equal, 3–bad, evil, 4–to say or tell, 5–to wish, 6–to do or make, 7–good, well, 8–faith, 9–to give, 10–night, 11–horse, 12–balance, pound, 13–to be silent, 14–to speak,

15–alone, 16–belly, 17–big, large, great, 18–word, 19–to roll, 20–mind, 21–back, 22–voice, 23–to bear or carry, 24–to walk, 25–sleep

Your score: _____

II

1–to show, 2–man, male, 3–father, 4–name, 5–the same, 6–sound, 7–to rule, 8–mother, 9–to kill, killing, 10–person, 11–wife, 12–husband, 13–fire, 14–God, 15–to live, 16–to believe, 17–to pierce sharply, 18–one, 19–to tremble, 20–spark, 21–city, 22–country (countryside), 23–knowledge, 24–all, 25–all

Your score: _____

III

1–O, 2–S, 3–O, 4–O, 5–S, 6–O, 7–O, 8–S, 9–S, 10–O, 11–O, 12–O, 13–O, 14–O, 15–O, 16–O, 17–O, 18–S, 19–O, 20–S

Your Score: _____

IV

1–e, 2–b, 3–g, 4–d, 5–i, 6–j, 7–a, 8–h, 9–f, 10–c

Your score: _____

V

1–c, 2–g, 3–e, 4–j, 5–f, 6–h, 7–a, 8–d, 9–b, 10–i

Your score: _____

VI

1–obviate, 2–adulate, 3–malign, 4–laconic, 5–banal, 6–verbatim, 7–genocide, 8–patrimony, 9–polytheism, 10–militant, 11–bona fide, 12–garrulous, 13–soliloquize, 14–magnum opus, 15–magnanimous, 16–ambulatory, 17–insomnia, 18–acrophobia; 19–fratricide, 20–antonymous, 21–*joie de vivre*, 22–devitalize, 23–naïveté *or* naïvety, 24–punctilious, 25–perspicuous.

26–circumspect, 27–retrospect, 28–unanimous, 29–stoical, 30–interurban

Your score: _____

Your total score: _____

Significance of Your Total Score:

100–120: Masterly work; you are ready to move on.

80–99: Good work; this review was useful to you.

65–79: Average work: you're getting a good deal out of your study, but perhaps you should revise thoroughly after each session.

50–64: Barely acceptable; work harder.

35–49: Poor; further revision is suggested before you go on.

0–34: You can do much better if you really try.

You might turn back for a moment to Chapter 8, in which you recorded your score on the first Comprehensive Test. Did you do better this time? Let's make a record of both scores at this point for the sake of comparison and to give you a mark to aim for in the Comprehensive Test you will take in Chapter 17.

SCORES

Test I (Chapter 8):   _____ **out of 120**
Test II (Chapter 13):   _____ **out of 120**

(End of Session 38)

Part Three

Finishing with a Feeling of Complete Success

14

HOW TO TALK ABOUT COMMON PHENOMENA AND OCCURRENCES

(*Sessions 39–41*)

Teaser preview

What word aptly describes:

- *dire poverty?*
- *emotion experienced without direct participation?*
- *something which lasts a very short time?*
- *an inoffensive word for an unpleasant idea?*
- *light and easy banter?*
- *someone who is cowlike in his stolidity?*
- *homesickness?*
- *harsh sound?*
- *a meat-eating animal?*
- *something kept secret?*

Session 39

This world, Robert Louis Stevenson once claimed – with, I think, questionable logic – is so full of a number of things that we should all be as happy as kings.

I doubt very strongly that happiness comes from the outside, or that kings are necessarily happy. But I will go this far (and no further) with Stevenson: the world is certainly full of a number of things. For instance, poverty and misery, hospitals and insane asylums, slums and racial restrictions, cut-down forests and once fertile lands becoming progressively more arid, war and death and taxes and bumbling diplomats. I know that Stevenson had a different sort of thing in mind, for romantic poets tend to view the world through rose-tinted spectacles, but it is often necessary to counter one extreme with another – and I simply wish to set the record straight.

In this chapter we are going to discuss a number of things to be found in the word and in the minds of its inhabitants – poverty and wealth; secondhand emotions; the relativity of time; praise of various sorts; small talk and how to indulge in it; animals; longings for the past; sounds; eating habits; and many kinds and conditions of secrecy.

As you see, when you start exploring ideas, as we constantly do in these chapters, you never know what will turn up.

Ideas

1.   For want of funds

There are those people who are forced (often through no fault of their own) to pursue an existence not only devoid of such luxuries as radios, television sets, sunken bathtubs, electric orange-juice squeezers, cars, Jacuzzis, private swimming pools, etc., but lacking also in many of the pure necessities of living – sufficient food, heated homes, hot water, vermin- and rodent-free surroundings, decent clothing, etc.

Such people live:

in *penury*

2.   At least watch it

All normal people want and need love and at least a modicum of excitement in their lives – so say the psychologists. If no one loves them, and if they can find no one on whom to lavish their own love, they may often satisfy their emotional longings and needs by getting their feelings secondhand – through reading love stories, attending films, watching soap operas, etc.

These are:

vicarious feelings

3.   Time is fleeting

During the late winter and early spring of 1948–49 in the USA, great numbers of people went practically berserk joining and forming 'pyramid clubs'. If you have not heard of this amazing phenomenon, I won't attempt to describe it in any of its multifarious ramifications, but the main point was that you paid two dollars, treated some people to coffee and doughnuts, and shortly thereafter (if you were gullible enough to fall for this get-rich-quick scheme) supposedly received a return of some fantastic amount like $2,064 for your investment.

For a short time, pyramid clubs were a rage – soon they had vanished from the American scene.

Anything that lasts for but a short time and leaves no trace is:

ephemeral

4.   How not to call a spade . . .

Words are only *symbols* of things – they are not the things themselves. (This, by the way, is one of the basic tenets of semantics.) But many people identify the word and the thing so closely that they fear to use certain words that symbolize things that are unpleasant to them.

I know that this is confusing, so let me illustrate.

Words having to do with death, sex, certain portions of the anatomy, excretion, etc. are avoided by certain people.

These people prefer circumlocutions – words that 'talk around' an idea or that mean or imply something but don't come right out and say so directly.

For example:

Word	Circumlocution
die	expire; depart this life; pass away; leave this vale of tears
sexual intercourse	(intimate) relations; 'intimacy'; 'shacking up'
prostitute	lady of the night; *fille de joie;* painted woman; lady of easy virtue; *fille de nuit;* streetwalker
house of prostitution	house of ill-fame; bawdyhouse; house of ill-repute; bagnio; bordello; 'house'; 'massage parlour'
buttocks	derrière; rear end; behind; backside; posterior
breasts	bosom; bust
toilet	powder room; little girl's room; facilities; washroom

The left-hand column is the direct, non-pussyfooting word. The right-hand column is made up of:

euphemisms

5.   Small talk

'Whenever I'm down in the sumps, I get a new suit.'
'Oh, so that's where you get them!'
'The doctor says I have snoo in my blood!'
'Snoo? What's snoo?'

'Not a thing! What's new with you?'
'What are twins?'
'Okay, what are twins?'"
'Womb mates!'
'I took a twip yesterday.'
'A twip?'
'Yes, I took a twip on a twain!'

These are examples of:

badinage

6.   Everything but give milk

You've seen a cow contentedly munching the cud. Nothing seems capable of disturbing this animal — and the animal seems to want nothing more out of life than to lead a simple, vegetable existence.

Some people are like a cow — calm, patient, placid, phlegmatic, vegetable-like. They are:

*bovine**

7.   Good old days

Do you sometimes experience a keen, almost physical, longing for associations or places of the past?

When you pass the neighbourhood in which you were born and where you spent your early years, do you have a sharp, strange reaction, almost akin to mild nausea?

When you are away from home and friends and family, do pleasant remembrances crowd in on your mind to the point where your present loneliness becomes almost unbearable, and you actually feel a little sick?

This common feeling is called:

nostalgia

---

* Remember Ogden Nash's delightful definition? The cow is of the bovine ilk, One end moo, the other end milk

8.   Sounds that grate

Some sounds are so harsh, grating, and discordant that they offend the ear. They lack all sweetness, harmony, pleasantness. Traffic noises of a big city, chalk squeaking on a blackboard . . .

Such blaring, ear-splitting, or spine-tingling sounds are called:

cacophonous

9.   Eating habits

Lions, tigers, wolves, and some other mammals subsist entirely on flesh. No spinach, salads, whole-wheat cereals, sugar, or spices — just red meat.

These mammals are:

carnivorous

10.   Private and public

There are certain things most of us do in private, like taking a bath. Some people like to engage in other activities in complete privacy — eating, reading, watching TV, sleeping, for example.

The point is that, while these activities may be conducted in privacy, there is never a reason for keeping them secret.

But there are other activities that are kept not only private, but well-shrouded in secrecy and concealed from public knowledge. These activities are unethical, illegal, or unsafe — like having an affair with someone whose spouse is your best friend, betraying military secrets to the enemy, trading in narcotic drugs, bribing public officials, etc.

Arrangements, activities, or meetings that fall under this category are called:

clandestine

Using the words

Can you pronounce the words?

1. *penury*   PEN'-yŏo-ri
2. *vicarious*   vī-KAIR'-i-əs
3. *ephemeral*   i-FEM'-ə-rəl

4. *euphemism*   YOO'-fə-mizəm
5. *badinage*   BAD'-i-nahzh
6. *bovine*   BŌ'-vīn'
7. *nostalgia*   no-STAL'-jə
8. *cacophony*   kə-KOF'-ə-ni
9. *carnivorous*   kah-NIV'-ə-rəs
10. *clandestine*   klan-DES'-tin

Can you work with the words?

1. penury	a. impermanent
2. vicarious	b. banter
3. ephemeral	c. homesickness
4. euphemism	d. meat-eating
5. badinage	e. circumlocution
6. bovine	f. harsh noise
7. nostalgia	g. poverty
8. cacophony	h. secret
9. carnivorous	i. placid; stolid; cowlike
10. clandestine	j. secondhand

Key: 1–g, 2–j, 3–a, 4–e, 5–b, 6–i, 7–c, 8–f, 9–d, 10–h

Do you understand the words? (I)

1. Do wealthy people normally live in *penury*?   YES   NO
2. Is a *vicarious* thrill one that comes from direct participation?   YES   NO
3. Do *ephemeral* things last a very short time?   YES   NO
4. Is a *euphemism* the substitution of an inoffensive term for another of the same meaning that may sound offensive, vulgar, or indelicate?   YES   NO
5. Does *badinage* show lighthearted frivolity?   YES   NO
6. Are *bovine* people highly-strung and nervous?   YES   NO

7. Does one get a feeling of *nostalgia*   YES   NO
   for past occurrences and
   relationships?
8. Is *cacophony* pleasant and musical?   YES   NO
9. Do *carnivorous* animals eat meat?   YES   NO
10. Is a *clandestine* meeting conducted in   YES   NO
    secrecy?

Key: 1–no, 2–no, 3–yes, 4–yes, 5–yes, 6–no, 7–yes, 8–no,
        9–yes, 10–yes

Do you understand the words? (II)

1. penury – affluence	SAME	OPPOSITE
2. vicarious – actual	SAME	OPPOSITE
3. ephemeral – eternal	SAME	OPPOSITE
4. euphemism – less offensive word	SAME	OPPOSITE
5. badinage – light, teasing talk	SAME	OPPOSITE
6. bovine – highly-strung	SAME	OPPOSITE
7. nostalgia – longing for the past	SAME	OPPOSITE
8. cacophony – euphony	SAME	OPPOSITE
9. carnivorous – herbivorous	SAME	OPPOSITE
10. clandestine – hidden	SAME	OPPOSITE

Key: 1–O, 2–O, 3–O, 4–S, 5–S, 6–O, 7–O, 8–O, 9–O,
        10–S

(The new words used in this test will be discussed in later sections of this chapter.)

Can you recall the words?

1. harsh sound   1. C_____
2. having a short life   2. E_____
3. dire poverty   3. P_____

4. substitution of an indirect or pleasant word or phrase for a possibly offensive one of the same meaning

4. E_____

5. experienced as a spectator, rather than as a participant

5. V_____

6. acute feeling of homesickness

6. N_____

7. light, half-teasing banter

7. B_____

8. subsisting solely on meat

8. C_____

9. cowlike; stolid

9. B_____

10. secret; concealed

10. C_____

Key: 1–cacophony, 2–ephemeral, 3–penury, 4–euphemism, 5–vicarious, 6–nostalgia, 7–badinage, 8–carnivorous, 9–bovine, 10–clandestine

(*End of Session 39*)

Session 40

Origins and related words

1. Money, and what it will buy

The modern world operates largely by means of a price structure – wealth and poverty are therefore words that indicate the possession, on the one hand, or the lack, on the other, of money. *Penury*, from Latin *penuria*, need, neediness, is dire, abject poverty, complete lack of financial resources. It is one of the two strongest English words there are to denote absence of money. The adjectival form, *penurious* (pi-NYOO'OƏR'-i-əs), strangely enough, may mean *poverty-stricken*, but more commonly signifies *stingy, close-fisted, niggardly;* so sparing in the use of money as to give the appearance of *penury*.

Penurious is a synonym of *parsimonious* (pah'-si-mō-ni-əs), but is much stronger in implication. A *parsimonious* person is stingy; a *penurious* person is twice as stingy. *Penury*, then, is poverty; *penuriousness* is stinginess, excessive frugality. The noun form of *parsimonious* is *parsimony* (PAH'-si-mə-ni).

A somewhat milder word than *penury* for poverty (if you can imagine a mild degree of poverty) is *indigence* (IN'-di-jəns). *Indigent* (IN'-di-jənt) people are not absolutely penniless – they are simply living in reduced circumstances, forgoing many creature comforts, forced to undergo the type of hardships that may accompany a lack of sufficient funds.

On the other hand, a close synonym of *penury*, and one of equal strength, is *destitution* (des-ti-TYOO-shən). *Destitute* (DES'-ti-tyoot) people do not even have the means for mere subsistence – as such, they are perhaps on the verge of starvation. *Penury* and *destitution* are not merely straitened circumstances – they are downright desperate circumstances.

To turn now to the brighter side of the picture, the possession of money, especially in increasing amounts, is expressed by *affluence* (AF'-loo-əns). *Affluent* (AF'-loo-ənt) people, people of *affluence*, or those living in *affluent* circumstances, are more than comfortable; in addition, there is the implication that their wealth is increasing. People who live in *affluence* probably own large and costly homes, run big, new cars, belong to expensive golf or country clubs, etc.

A much stronger term is *opulence* (OP'-yoo-ləns), which not only implies much greater wealth than *affluence*, but in addition suggests lavish expenditures and ostentatiously luxurious surroundings. People of *opulence* own estates; drive only outrageously expensive and specially equipped cars (Rolls-Royces, Mercedes-Benzes, Porsches, etc.); have a corps of servants, including a butler; belong to golf and yacht and country clubs, etc., etc. Embroider the fantasy as much as you wish. *Opulent* (OP'-yoo-lənt) may describe people, surroundings, styles of life, or the like.

Affluent is a combination of the prefix *ad-*, to, towards (changing to *af-* before a root beginning with *f*), plus the Latin verb *fluo*, to flow – *affluence* is that delightful condition in which money keeps flowing to us, and no one ever turns off the tap. Other words from the same root, *fluo*, to flow, are *fluid*, *influence*, *confluence* (a 'flowing together'), *fluent* (the words flow smoothly), etc.

Opulent is from Latin *opulentus*, wealthy. No other English words derive from this root.

2. Doing and feeling

If you watch a furious athletic event, and *you* get tired, though the athletes expend all the energy – that's *vicarious* fatigue.

➤ If your friend goes on a bender, and as you watch him absorb one drink after another, *you* begin to feel giddy and stimulated, that's *vicarious* intoxication.

If you watch a mother in a film or play suffer horribly at the death of her child, and *you* go through the same agony, that's *vicarious* torment.

You can experience an emotion, then, in two ways: firsthand, through actual participation; or *vicariously*, by becoming empathetically involved in another person's feelings.

Some people, for example, lead essentially dull and colourless lives. Through their children, through reading or attending the theatre, however, they can experience all the emotions felt by others whose lives move along at a swift, exciting pace. These people live at second hand; they live *vicariously*.

3.   Time is relative

Elephants and turtles live almost forever; human beings in Western Europe and the United States have a life expectancy in general of sixty-eight to seventy-six years (though the gradual conquest of disease is constantly lengthening our span); dogs live from seven to ten years; and some insects exist for only a few hours or days.

One such short-lived creature is the mayfly, which in Greek was called *ephemera*. Hence anything so short-lived, so unenduring that it scarcely seems to outlast the day, may be called *ephemeral*. The noun is *ephemerality* (i-fem'-ər-Al'-i-ti).

A synonym of *ephemeral* is *evanescent* (ev-ə-NES'-ənt), fleeting, staying for a remarkably short time, vanishing. Something intangible, like a feeling, may be called *evanescent*; it's here, and before you can quite comprehend it, it's gone – vanished.

The noun is *evanescence* (ev'-ə-NES'-əns); the verb is to *evanesce* (ev-ə-NES').

Evanescent is built on the prefix *e-* (*ex-*), out, the root *vanesco*, to vanish, and the adjective suffix *-ent*.

The suffix *-esce* often, but not always, means *begin to*. *-Escent* may mean *becoming* or *beginning to*. Thus:

adolescent – beginning to grow up; beginning to become an adult evanesce – begin to vanish convalesce – begin to get well after illness putrescent – beginning to rot; beginning to become putrid obsolescent – becoming obsolete

4.   An exploration of various good things

A *euphemism* is a word or expression that has been substituted for another that is likely to offend – it is built on the Greek prefix *eu-*, good, the root *pheme*, voice, and the noun suffix *-ism*. (Etymologically, 'something said in a good voice!') Adjective: *euphemistic* (yōō'-fə-MIS'-tik)

Other English words constructed from the prefix *eu-*:

1. *euphony* (YŌŌ'-fə-ni) – good sound; pleasant lilt or rhythm (*phone, sound*)

Adjective: *euphonic* (yōō-FON'-ik) or *euphonious* (yōō-FŌ'-ni-əs)

2. *eulogy* (YŌŌ'-lə-ji) – etymologically, 'good speech'; a formal speech of praise, usually delivered as a funeral oration. *Logos* in this term means *word* or *speech*, as it did in *philology* (Chapter 6). *Logos* more commonly means *science* or *study*, but has the alternative meaning in *eulogy, philology, monologue, dialogue, epilogue* (words upon the other words, or 'after-words'), and *prologue* (words before the main part, 'before-words', or introduction).

Adjective: *eulogistic* (yōō-lə-JIS'-tik); verb: *eulogize* (YŌŌ-lə-jīz'); person who delivers a *eulogy: eulogist* (YŌŌ-lə-jist)

3. *euphoria* (yōō-FAW'-ri-ə) – good feeling, a sense of mental buoyancy and physical well-being

Adjective: *euphoric* (yōō-FOR'-ik)

4. *euthanasia* (yōō'-thə-NAY'-zi-ə) – etymologically, 'good death'; method of painless death inflicted on people suffering from incurable diseases – not legal at the present time, but advocated by many people. The words derives from *eu-* plus Greek *thanatos*, death.

5.   Exploration of modes of expression

Badinage is a half-teasing, non-malicious, frivolous banter, intended to amuse rather than wound. *Badinage* has a close synonym, *persiflage* (PƏR'-sə-flahzh'), which is a little more derisive, a trifle more indicative of contempt or mockery – but still totally unmalicious.

In line with *badinage* and *persiflage*, there are four other forms of expression you should be familiar with: *cliché* (KLEE'-shay), *bromide* (BRŌ'-mīd), *platitude* (PLAT'-i-tyōōd), and *anodyne* (AN'-ə-dīn').

A *cliché* is a pattern of words which was once new and fresh, but which now is so old, worn, and threadbare that only banal, unimaginative speakers and writers ever use it. Examples are: *fast and furious; unsung heroes; by leaps and bounds; conspicuous by its absence; green with envy;* etc. The most devastating criticism you can make of a piece of writing is to say, 'It is full of *clichés*'; the most pointed insult to a person's way of talking is, 'You speak in *clichés*.'

A *bromide* is any trite, dull, and probably fallacious remark that shows little evidence of original thinking, and that therefore convinces a listener of the total absence of perspicacity on the part of the speaker.

For instance, some cautious, dull-minded individual might warn you not to take a chance in these words: 'Remember it's better to be safe than sorry!'

Your sneering response might be: 'Oh, that old *bromide!*'

A *platitude* is similar to a *cliché* or *bromide*, in that it is a dull, trite, hackneyed, unimaginative pattern of words – but, to add insult to injury (*cliché*), the speaker uses it with an air of novelty – as if he just made it up, and isn't he the brilliant fellow!

An *anodyne*, in the medical sense, is a drug that allays pain without curing an illness, like aspirin or morphine. Figuratively, an *anodyne* is a statement made to allay someone's fears or anxieties, not believed by the speaker, but intended to be believed by the listener. 'Prosperity is just around the corner' was a popular *anodyne* of the 1930s.

A *bromide* is also a drug, formerly used as a sedative. Sedatives dull the senses – the statement labelled a *bromide* comes from a speaker of dull wit and has a sedative effect on the listener. The adjective is *bromidic* (brō-MID'-ik), as in 'his *bromidic* way of expressing himself'.

Platitude derives from Greek *platys*, broad or flat, plus the noun suffix *-tude*. Words like *plateau* (flat land), *plate* and *platter* (flat dishes), and *platypus* (flat foot) all derive from the same root as *platitude*, a flat statement, i.e., one that falls flat, despite the speaker's high hopes for it. The adjective is *platitudinous* (plat'-i-TYOO-di-nəs), as in, 'What a *platitudinous* remark.'

Anodyne is a combination of the negative prefix *an-* with Greek *odyne*, pain. *Anodynes*, as drugs, lessen pain; as statements, they are intended to reduce or eliminate emotional pain or anxiety.

Review of etymology

Prefix, Root, Suffix	Meaning	English Word
1. *penuria*	need, neediness	_____
2. *ad- (af-)*	to, towards	_____
3. *fluo*	to flow	_____
4. *opulentus*	wealthy	_____
5. *ephemera*	mayfly	_____
6. *e-, ex-*	out	_____
7. *vanesco*	to vanish	_____
8. *-esce*	begin to	_____
9. *-ent*	adjective suffix	_____
10. *-ence*	noun suffix	_____
11. *eu-*	good	_____
12. *pheme*	voice .	_____
13. *-ism*	noun suffix	_____
14. *phone*	sound	_____
15. *-ic*	adjective suffix	_____
16. *-ous*	adjective suffix	_____
17. *logos*	word, speech	_____
18. *-ize*	verb suffix	_____
19. *thanatos*	death	_____
20. *platys*	broad or flat	_____
21. *an-*	negative prefix	_____
22. *odyne*	pain	_____

Using the words

Can you pronounce the words? (I)

1. *penurious*	pi-NYOOəR'-i-əs
2. *penuriousness*	pi-NYOOəR'-i-əs-nəs
3. *parsimonious*	pah'-si-MŌ'-ni-əs
4. *parsimony*	PAH'-si-mə-ni
5. *indigence*	IN'-di-jəns
6. *indigent*	IN'-di-jənt
7. *destitutin*	des-ti-TYOO'-shən
8. *destitute*	DES'-ti-tyoॕot
9. *affluence*	AF'-loŏ-əns

10. *affluent*	AF'-lŏo-ənt
11. *opulence*	OP'-yŏo-ləns
12. *opulent*	OP'-yŏo-lənt

Can you pronounce the words? (II)

1. *evanescent*	ev'-ə-NES'-ənt
2. *evanescence*	ev'-ə-NES'-əns
3. *evanesce*	ev'-ə-NES'
4. *euphemistic*	yŏo-fə-MIS'-tik
5. *euphony*	YŌO'-fə-ni
6. *euphonic*	yŏo-FON'-ik
7. *euphonious*	yŏo-FÔ-ni-əs
8. *eulogy*	YOO'-lə-ji
9. *eulogistic*	yŏo'-lə-JIS'-tik
10. *eulogize*	YŌO'-lə-jīz'

Can you pronounce the words? (III)

1. *euphoria*	yŏo-FAW'-ri-ə
2. *euphoric*	yŏo-FOR'-ik
3. *euthanasia*	yŏo'-thə-NAY'-zi-ə
4. *persiflage*	PəR'-si-flahzh'
5. *cliché*	KLEE'-shay
6. *bromide*	BRÔ'-mīd'
7. *bromidic*	brō-MID'-ik
8. *platitude*	PLAT'-i-tyŏod
9. *platitudinous*	plat'-i-tyŏo-di-nəs
10. *anodyne*	AN'-ə-dīn'

Can you work with the words? (I)

1. penurious	a. poor; of limited means
2. indigent	b. inoffensive
3. affluent	c. flat, trite
4. evanescent	d. feeling tip-top
5. euphemistic	e. wealthy
6. euphonious	f. pleasant in sound
7. euphoric	g. stingy; tight-fisted
8. platitudinous	h. fleeting

Key: 1–g, 2–a, 3–e, 4–h, 5–b, 6–f, 7–d, 8–c

Can you work with the words? (II)

1.	parsimony	a.	lavish luxury
2.	destitution	b.	painless death
3.	opulence	c.	pleasant sound
4.	evanescence	d.	trite remark
5.	euphony	e.	impermanence
6.	euphoria	f.	feeling of well-being
7.	euthanasia	g.	stinginess
8.	platitude	h.	poverty

Key: 1–g, 2–h, 3–a, 4–e, 5–c, 6–f, 7–b, 8–d

Can you work with the words? (III)

1.	anodyne	a.	light, teasing banter
2.	bromide	b.	tightfistedness
3.	persiflage	c.	statement intended to allay anxiety
4.	eulogy	d.	poverty, want
5.	penuriousness	e.	high, formal praise
6.	indigence	f.	wealth
7.	affluence	g.	trite statement

Key: 1–c, 2–g, 3–a, 4–e, 5–b, 6–d, 7–f

Can you work with the words? (IV)

1.	parsimonious	a.	begin to vanish
2.	destitute	b.	stingy, frugal
3.	opulent	c.	highly praising
4.	vicarious	d.	hackneyed phrase
5.	euphonic	e.	ostentatiously wealthy
6.	eulogistic	f.	stilted in expression

7. evanesce		g.	pleasant-sounding
8. eulogize		h.	in want
9. bromidic		i.	secondhand
10. cliché		j.	praise

Key: 1–b, 2–h, 3–e, 4–i, 5–g, 6–c, 7–a, 8–j, 9–f, 10–d

Do you understand the words? (I)

1. Do *penurious* people satisfy their extravagant desires.   YES   NO
2. Is *penuriousness* the characteristic of a miser?   YES   NO
3. If you are *parsimonious* with praise, do you lavish it on others?   YES   NO
4. Are people with extremely low incomes forced to live a life of *parsimony?*   YES   NO
5. Is *indigence* a sign of wealth?   YES   NO
6. Are *indigent* people often aided by state welfare?   YES   NO
7. If you live in a state of *destitution*, do you have all the money you need?   YES   NO
8. Is a completely *destitute* person likely to have to live in want?   YES   NO
9. Does a person of *affluence* generally have petty money worries?   YES   NO
10. Are *opulent* surroundings indicative of great wealth?   YES   NO

Key: 1–no, 2–yes, 3–no, 4–yes, 5–no, 6–yes, 7–no, 8–yes, 9–no, 10–yes

Do you understand the words? (II)

1. Can you engage in *vicarious* exploits by reading spy novels?   YES   NO

2. Does an *evanescent* feeling remain   YES   NO
   for a considerable time?
3. Do parents generally indulge in   YES   NO
   euphemisms in front of young
   children?
4. Is poetry generally *euphonious*?   YES   NO
5. Does a sincere *eulogy* indicate one's   YES   NO
   feeling of admiration?
6. Is *euphoria* a feeling of malaise?   YES   NO
7. Is *euthanasia* practised on animals?   NO
   YES
8. Is *persiflage* an indication of   YES   NO
   seriousness?
9. Does a liberal use of *clichés* show   YES   NO
   original thinking?
10. Is an *anodyne* intended to relieve   YES   NO
    fears?

Key: 1–yes, 2–no, 3–yes, 4–yes, 5–yes, 6–no, 7–yes, 8–no,
      9–no, 10–yes

Do you understand the words? (III)

1. Is a *platitude* flat and dull?   YES   NO
2. If a person uses *bromides*, is he likely   YES   NO
   to be an interesting
   conversationalist?
3. If you indulge in *persiflage*, are you   YES   NO
   being facetious?
4. Are the works of Beethoven   YES   NO
   considered *euphonious*?
5. Can parents receive a *vicarious* thrill   YES   NO
   from their children's triumphs?

Key: 1–yes, 2–no, 3–yes, 4–yes, 5–yes

Can you recall the words?

1. a statement, usually untrue, meant to alleviate fear
1. A_____

2. light banter
2. P_____

3. a hackneyed phrase
3. C_____

4. fleeting – lasting a very short time (*adj.*)
4. E_____
or E_____

5. laudatory – delivered in tones of formal praise (*adj.*)
5. E_____

6. process of painlessly putting to death a victim of an ncurable disease
6. E_____

7. stingy (*adj.*)
7. P_____
or P_____

8. in want (*adj.*)
8. D_____

9. wealth
9. A_____

10. immense wealth
10. O_____

11. adverb describing the manner of responding empathetically to another's acts
11. V_____

12. stinginess (*noun*)
12. P_____
or P_____

13–14. poverty
13. I_____
14. D_____

15. impermanence
15. E_____
or E_____

16. pleasing sound
16. E_____

17. substituting inoffensive words (*adj.*)
17. E_____

18. sense of well-being
18. E_____

19. trite remark
19. B_____

20. banal remark
20. P_____

21. begin to vanish (*v.*)
21. E_____

22. poverty-stricken (*adj.*)
22. I_____

23–24. wealthy (two *adjs.*)
23. A_____
24. O_____

25. feeling tip-top (*adj.*)
25. F_____

26. pleasant in sound (*adj.*) 26. E_____
   or E_____
27. formal praise 27. E_____
28. trite (*adj.*) 28. B_____
29. flat, dull (*adj.*) 29. P_____
30. to praise 30. E_____

Key: 1–anodyne, 2–persiflage, 3–cliché, 4–evanescent *or* ephemeral, 5–eulogistic, 6–euthanasia, 7–parsimonious *or* penurious, 8–destitute, 9–affluence, 10–opulence, 11–vicariously, 12–parsimony *or* penuriousness, 13–indigence, 14–destitution, 15–evanescence *or* ephemerality, 16–euphony, 17–euphemsitic, 18–euphoria, 19–bromide, 20–platitude, 21–evanesce, 22–indigent, 23–affluent, 24–opulent, 25–euphoric, 26–euphonic *or* euphonious, 27–eulogy, 28–bromidic, 29–platitudinous, 30–eulogize

(End of Session 40)

Session 41

Origins and Related words

1.   People are the craziest animals

Bovine, placid like a cow, stolid, patient, unexcitable, is built on the Latin word for *ox* or *cow, bovis,* plus the suffix *-ine,* like, similar to, or characteristic of. To call someone *bovine* is of course far from complimentary, for this adjective is considerably stronger than *phlegmatic,* and implies a certain mild contempt on the part of the speaker. A *bovine* person is somewhat like a vegetable: eats and grows and lives, but apparently is lacking in any strong feelings.

Humans are sometimes compared to animals, as in the following adjectives:

1. *leonine* (LEE'-ə-nīn') – like a lion in appearance or temperament.
2. *canine* (KAY'-nīn') – like a dog. As a noun, the word refers to the species to which dogs belong. Our *canine* teeth are similar to those of a dog.
3. *feline* (FEE'-līn') – catlike. We may speak of *feline* grace; or (insultingly) of *feline* temperament when we mean that a person is 'catty'.
4. *porcine* (PAW'-sīn') – piglike
5. *vulpine* (VUL'-pīn') – foxlike in appearance or temperament. When applied to people, this adjective usually indicates the shrewdness of a fox.
6. *ursine* (əR'-sīn') – bearlike.
7. *lupine* (LOO'-pīn) – wolflike.
8. *equine* (E'-kwīn') – horselike; 'horsy'.

9. *piscine* (PIS'-īn') -- fishlike.

All these adjectives come from the corresponding Latin words for the animals; and, of course, each adjective also describes, or refers to, the specific animal as well as to the person likened to the animal.

1. *leo*	lion
2. *canis*	dog
3. *felis*	cat
4. *porcus*	pig
5. *vulpus*	fox
6. *ursus*	bear
7. *lupus*	wolf
8. *equus*	horse
9. *piscis*	fish

The word for meat from a pig -- *pork* -- derives obviously, from *porcus*. *Ursa Major* and *Ursa Minor*, the *Great Bear* and the *Little Bear*, the two conspicuous groups of stars in the northern sky (conspicuous, of course, only on a clear night), are so labelled because in formation they resemble the outlines of bears. The feminine name *Ursula* is, by etymology, 'a little bear', which, perhaps, is a strange name to burden a child with. The skin disease *lupus* was so named because it eats into the flesh, as a wolf might.

2.   You can't go home again

Nostalgia, built on two Greek roots, *nostos*, a return, and *algos*, pain (as in *neuralgia*, *cardialgia*, etc.) is a feeling you can't ever understand until you've experienced it -- and you have probably experienced it whenever some external stimulus has crowded your mind with scenes from an earlier day.

You know how life often seems much pleasanter in retrospect? Your conscious memory tends to store up the pleasant experiences of the past (the trauma and unpleasant experiences may get buried in the unconscious), and when you are lonely or unhappy you may begin to relive these pleasant occurrences. It is then that you feel the emotional pain and longing that we call *nostalgia*.

The adjective is *nostalgic* (nos-TAL'-jik), as in films that are *nostalgic* of the fifties', or as in 'he feels *nostalgic* whenever he passes Vaughan Gardens and sees the house in which he grew up'.

3. Soundings

Cacophony is itself a harsh-sounding word – and is the only one that exactly describes the unmusical, grating, ear-offending noises you are likely to hear in man-made surroundings: the underground trains thundering through their tunnels (they are also eye-offending, for which we might coin the term *cacopsis*, noun, and *cacoptic*, adjective), the traffic bedlam of rush hours in a big city, a steel mill, a car factory, a blast furnace, etc. Adjective: *cacophonous* (kə-KOF'-ə-nəs).

These words are built on the Greek roots *kakos*, bad, harsh, or ugly, and *phone*, sound.

Phone, sound, is found also in:

1. *telephone* – etymologically, 'sound from afar'
2. *euphony* – pleasant sound
3. *phonograph* – etymologically, 'writer of sound'
4. *saxophone* – a musical instrument (hence *sound*) invented by Adolphe Sax
5. *xylophone* – a musical instrument; etymologically, 'sounds through wood' (Greek *xylon*, wood)
6. *phonetics* (fə-NET'-iks) – the science of the sounds of language; the adjective is *phonetic* (fə-NET'-ik), the expert a *phonetician* (fō'-nə-TISH'-ən)
7. *phonics* – the science of sound; also the method of teaching reading by practising the sounds of letters and syllables

4. The flesh and all

Carnivorous combines *carnis*, flesh, and *voro*, to devour. A *carnivorous* animal, or *carnivore* (KAH'-ni-vaw'), is one whose main diet is meat.

Voro, to devour, is the origin of other words referring to eating habits:

1. *herbivorous* (hər-BIV'-ər-əs) – subsisting on grains, grasses, and other vegetation, as do cows, deer, horses, etc. The animal is a *herbivore* (HƏR'-bi-vaw). Derivation: Latin *herba*, herb, plus *voro*, to devour.

2. *omnivorous* (om-NIV'-ər-əs) – eating everything: meat, grains, grasses, fish, insects, and anything else digestible. The only species so indiscriminate in their diet are humans and rats, plus, of course, some cats and dogs that live with people (in contrast to *felines* and *canines* – lions, tigers, bobcats, wolves, etc. – that are not domesticated). *Omnivorous* (combining Latin *omnis*, all, with *voro*, plus the adjective suffix *-ous*) refers not only to food. An *omnivorous* reader reads everything in great quantities (that is, devours *all* kinds of reading matter).

3. *voracious* (və-RAY'-shəs) – *devouring;* hence, greedy or gluttonous; may refer either to food or to any other habits. One may be a *voracious* eater, *voracious* reader, *voracious* in one's pursuit of money, pleasure, etc. Think of the two noun forms of *loquacious*. Can you write two nouns derived from *voracious?*

(1)_____ (2)_____.

5.   'Allness'

Latin *omnis*, all, is the origin of:

1. *omnipotent* (om-NIP'-ə-tənt) – all-powerful, an adjective usually applied to God; also, to any ruler whose governing powers are unlimited, which allows for some exaggeration, as King Canute proved to his sycophantic courtiers when he ordered the tide to come so far up the beach and no further. He got soaking wet! (*Omnis* plus Latin *potens*, *potentis*, powerful, as in *potentate*, a powerful ruler; *impotent* (IM'-pə-tənt), powerless; *potent*, powerful; and *potential*, possessing power or ability not yet exercised). Can you write the noun form of *omnipotent?*

_____

2. *omniscient* (om-NIS'-i-ənt) all-knowing: hence, infinitely wise. (*Omnis* plus *sciens*, knowing.) We have discussed this adjective in a previous chapter, so you will have no problem writing the noun:_____.

3. *omnipresent* (om'-ni-PREZ'-ənt) – present in all places at once. Fear was *omnipresent* in Europe during 1939 just before World War II. A synonym of *omnipresent* is *ubiquitous* (yōō-BIK'-wi-təs), from Latin *ubique*, everywhere. The *ubiquitous* ice cream vendor seems to be *everywhere* at the same time, tinkling those little bells, once spring arrives. The *ubiquitous* little wagon travels around *everywhere* in airports to refuel departing planes. '*Ubiquitous* laughter greeted the press secretary's remark', i.e., laughter was heard *everywhere* in the room. The noun forms are *ubiquity* (yōō-BIK'-wi-ti) or _____ (Can you think of the alternative form?)

4. *omnibus* (OM'-ni-bəs) – etymologically, 'for all, including all'. In the shortened form *bus* we have a public vehicle for *all* who can pay; in a John Galsworthy *omnibus* we have a book containing *all* of Galsworthy's works; in an *omnibus* legislative bill we have a bill containing *all* the miscellaneous provisions and appropriations left out of other bills.

6.   More flesh

Note how *carnis*, flesh, is the building block of:

1. *carnelian* (kah-NEEL'-yən) – a reddish gemstone, the colour of red *flesh*.

2. *carnival* (KAH'-ni-vəl) – originally the season of merrymaking just before Lent, when people took a last fling before saying '*Carne vale!*' 'Oh *flesh*, farewell!' (Latin *vale*, farewell, goodbye). Today a *carnival* is any exuberant or riotous merrymaking or festivities.

3. *carnal* (KAH'-nəl) – most often found in phrases like '*carnal* pleasures' or '*carnal* appetites', and signifying pleasures or appetites of the *flesh* rather than of the spirit – hence, sensual, lecherous, lascivious, lubricious, etc. The noun is *carnality* (kah-NAL'-i-ti).

4. *carnage* (KAH'-nij) – great destruction of life (that is, of human *flesh*), as in war or mass murders.

5. *reincarnation* (ree'-in-kah-NAY'-shən) – a rebirth or re-appearance. Believers in *reincarnation* maintain that one's soul persists after it has fled the *flesh*, and eventually reappears in the body of a newborn infant or animal, or in another form. Some of us, according to this interesting philosophy, were once Napoleon, Alexander the Great, Cleopatra, etc. The verb is to *reincarnate* (ree'-IN'-kah-nayt), to bring (a soul) back in another bodily form.

6. *incarnate* (in-KAH'-nət) – in the *flesh*. If we use this adjective to call someone 'the devil *incarnate*', we mean that here is the devil in the *flesh*. Or we may say that someone is evil *incarnate*, that is, the personification of evil, evil invested with human or bodily form. The verb to *incarnate* (IN'-kah-nayt) is to embody, give bodily form to, or make real.

7. Dark secrets

Clandestine comes from Latin *clam*, secretly, and implies secrecy or concealment in the working out of a plan that is dangerous or illegal. *Clandestine* is a close synonym of *surreptitious* (sur'-əp-TISH'-əs), which means *stealthy, sneaky, furtive*, generally because of fear of detection.

The two words cannot always, however, be used interchangeably. We may speak of either *clandestine* or *surreptitious* meetings or arrangements; but usually only of *clandestine* plans and only of *surreptitious* movements or actions. Can you write the noun form of *surreptitious*? _____

Review of Etymology

Prefix, Root, Suffix	Meaning	English Word
1. *-ine*	like, similar to, characteristic of	_____
2. *leo*	lion	_____
3. *felis*	cat	_____
4. *porcus*	pig	_____
5. *canis*	dog	_____
6. *vulpus*	fox	_____
7. *ursus*	bear	_____

8. *lupus*	wolf	_____
9. *equus*	horse	_____
10. *piscis*	fish	_____
11. *nostos*	a return	_____
12. *algos*	pain	_____
13. *-ic*	adjective suffix	_____
14. *kakos*	bad, harsh, ugly	_____
15. *phone*	sound	_____
16. *xylon*	wood	_____
17. *carnis*	flesh	_____
18. *voro*	to devour	_____
19. *herba*	herb	_____
20. *omnis*	all	_____
21. *-ous*	adjective suffix	_____
22. *potens, potentis*	powerful	_____
23. *sciens*	knowing	_____
24. *ubique*	everywhere	_____
25. *-ity*	noun suffix	_____
26. *vale*	farewell	_____
27. *-al*	adjective suffix	_____
28. *re-*	again, back	_____
29. *-ate*	verb suffix	_____
30. *in-*	in	_____
31. *clam*	secretly	_____
32. *-ent*	adjective suffix	_____
33. *-ence*	noun suffix	_____

Using the Words

Can you pronounce the words? (I)

1. *leonine*	LEE'-ə-nīn'
2. *canine*	KAY'-nīn'
3. *feline*	FEE'-līn'
4. *porcine*	PAW'-sīn'
5. *vulpine*	VUL'-pīn'
6. *ursine*	əR'-sīn'
7. *lupine*	LŌŌ'-pīn'
8. *equine*	E'-kwīn'

9. *piscine*   PIS'-īn'
10. *nostalgic*   nos-TAL'-jik

Can you pronounce the words? (II)

1. *cacophonous*   kə-KOF'-ə-nəs
2. *phonetics*   fə-NET'-iks
3. *phonetic*   fə-NET'-ik
4. *phonetician*   fō-nə-TISH'-ən
5. *carnivore*   KAH'-ni-vaw
6. *herbivore*   HəR'-bi-vaw
7. *herbivorous*   hər-BIV'-ər-əs
8. *omnivorous*   om-NIV'-ər-əs
9. *voracious*   ·və-RAY'-shəs
10. *voracity*   və-RAS'-i-ti
11. *omnipotent*   om-NIP'-ə-tənt
12. *impotent*   IM -pə-tənt
13. *impotence*   IM'-pə-təns
14. *omnipotence*   om-NIP'-ə-təns

Can you pronounce the words? (III)

1. *omniscient*   om-NIS'-i-ənt
2. *omniscience*   om-NIS'-i-əns
3. *omnipresent*   om'-ni-PREZ'-ənt
4. *omnipresence*   om'-ni-PREZ'-əns
5. *ubiquitous*   yōō-BIK'-wi-təs
6. *ubiquity*   yōō-BIK'-wi-ti
7. *ubiquitousness*   yōō-BIK'-wi-təs-nəs
8. *omnibus*   OM'-ni-bəs

Can you pronounce the words? (IV)

1. *carnelian*   kah-NEEL yən
2. *carnal*   KAH'-nəl
3. *carnality*   kah-NAL.'-i-ti
4. *carnage*   KAH'-nij
5. *reincarnation*   ree'-in-kah-NAY'-shən
6. *reincarnate (v.)*   ree'-IN' kah-nayt
7. *incarnate (adj.)*   in-KAH ·nət

8. *incarnate (v.)*   IN'-kah-nayt
9. *surreptitious*   sur'-əp-TISH'-əs
10. *surreptitiousness*   sur'-əp-TISH'-əs-nəs

Can you work with the words? (I)

1. leonine		a.	doglike
2. canine		b.	greedy, devouring
3. feline		c.	foxlike
4. porcine		d.	all-powerful
5. vulpine		e.	stealthy, clandestine
6. ursine		f.	lionlike
7. voracious		g.	all-knowing
8. omnipotent		h.	bearlike
9. omniscient		i.	catlike
10. surreptitious		j.	piglike

Key: 1–f, 2–a, 3–i, 4–j, 5–c, 6–h, 7–b, 8–d, 9–g, 10–e

Can you work with the words? (II)

1. nostalgic		a.	harsh-sounding
2. cacophonous		b.	eating everthing
3. herbivorous		c.	lewd, lecherous, lubricious
4. omnivorous		d.	found everywhere
5. ubiquitous		e.	homesick
6. carnal		f.	grass-eating
7. incarnate		g.	in the flesh

Key: 1–e, 2–a, 3–f, 4–b, 5–d, 6–c, 7–g

Can you work with the words? (III)

1. phonetics		a.	universality
2. carnivore		b.	a gemstone
3. voracity		c.	infinite power
4. omnipotence		d.	furtiveness, stealth, sneakiness
5. omniscience		e.	lechery, lasciviousness, lubricity

6. omnipresence		f.	infinite wisdom
7. omnibus		g.	science of speech sounds
8. carnelian		h.	slaughter
9. carnality		i.	a collection of all things
10. carnage		j.	greediness
11. surreptitiousness		k.	meat-eater
12. reincarnation		l.	a return to life in a new body or form

Key: 1–g, 2–k, 3–j, 4–c, 5–f, 6–a, 7–i, 8–b, 9–e, 10–h, 11–d, 12–l

Can you work with the words? (IV)

1. lupine		a.	fishlike
2. equine		b.	powerless
3. piscine		c.	wolflike
4. phonetician		d.	bring back into a new body or form
5. impotent		e.	occurrence, or existence, everywhere
6. ubiquity		f.	horselike
7. reincarnate (v.)		g.	expert in speech sounds
8. incarnate (v.)		h.	embody; make real; put into bodily form

Key: 1–c, 2–f, 3–a, 4–g, 5–b, 6–e, 7–d, 8–h

Do you understand the words? (I)

1. A person of *leonine* appearance looks like a tiger.	TRUE	FALSE
2. *Canine* habits refers to the habits of dogs.	TRUE	FALSE
3. *Feline* grace means catlike grace.	TRUE	FALSE
4. *Porcine* appearance means wolflike appearance.	TRUE	FALSE
5. *Vulpine* craftiness means foxlike	TRUE	FALSE

6. *Ursine* means bearlike.	TRUE	FALSE
7. *Nostalgic* feelings refer to a longing for past experiences.	TRUE	FALSE
8. *Cacophonous* music is pleasant and sweet.	TRUE	FALSE
9. An elephant is a *carnivore*.	TRUE	FALSE
10. Deer are *herbivorous*.	TRUE	FALSE

Key: 1–F, 2–T, 3–T, 4–F, 5–T, 6–T, 7–T, 8–F, 9–F, 10–T

Do you understand the words? (II)

1. An *omnivorous* reader does very little reading.	TRUE	FALSE
2. A *voracious* eater is gluttonous.	TRUE	FALSE
3. True *omnipotence* is unattainable by human beings.	TRUE	FALSE
4. No one is *omniscient*.	TRUE	FALSE
5. Fear of economic ruin was practically *omnipresent* in the early 1930s.	TRUE	FALSE
6. As soon as warm weather arrives, the *ubiquitous* sound of the ice cream van can be heard.	TRUE	FALSE
7. An author's *omnibus* contains all his published writings.	TRUE	FALSE
8. *Carnelian* is a deep blue gemstone.	TRUE	FALSE
9. *Carnality* is much respected in a puritanical society.	TRUE	FALSE
10. There is considerable *carnage* in war.	TRUE	FALSE
11. A *surreptitious* glance is meant to be conspicous.	TRUE	FALSE
12. A person who is evil *incarnate* is a vicious character.	TRUE	FALSE

Key: 1–F, 2–T, 3–T, 4–T, 5–T, 6–T, 7–T, 8–F, 9–F,
         10–T, 11–F, 12–T

Can you recall the words?

I—adverbs

1–2. secretly (two forms)	1. C_____
	2. S_____
3. in a harsh and noisy manner	3. C_____
4. in a homesick manner	4. N_____
5. in a greedy, devouring manner	5. V_____

Key: 1–clandestinely, 2–surreptitiously, 3–cacophonously, 4–nostalgically, 5–voraciously

II—nouns

1. greediness	1. V_____
2. unlimited power	2. O_____
3. infinite knowledge	3. O_____
4. a gathering of all things	4. O_____
5. lechery; indulgence in fleshly pleasures	5. C_____
6. slaughter	6. C_____
7. stealthiness; secretiveness	7. S_____
8. harsh sound	8. C_____
9. science of speech sounds	9. P_____
10. a return to life in new form	10. R_____

Key: 1–voracity, 2–omnipotence, 3–omniscience, 4–omnibus, 5–carnality, 6–carnage, 7–surreptitiousness, 8–cacophony, 9–phonetics, 10–reincarnation

III—adjectives

1. lionlike	1. L_____
2. doglike	2. C_____

3. catlike   3. F_____
4. cowlike   4. B_____
5. foxlike   5. V_____
6. bearlike   6. U_____
7. homesick   7. N_____
8. grating in sound   8. C_____
9. meat-eating   9. C_____
10. grass-eating   10. H_____
11. all-eating; indiscriminate   11. O_____
12. devouring; greedy   12. V_____
13. in the flesh   13. I_____

Key: 1–leonine, 2–canine, 3–feline, 4–bovine, 5–vulpine,
       6–ursine, 7–nostalgic, 8–cacophonous, 9–carnivorous,
       10–herbivorous, 11–omnivorous, 12–voracious, 13–in-
       carnate

IV.   more adjectives

1. all-powerful   1. O_____
2. all-knowing   2. O_____
3. present or existing   3. O_____
   everywhere
4. found everywhere   4. U_____
5. lewd, lascivious, lecherous   5. C_____
6. secret   6. C_____

Key: 1–omnipotent, 2–omniscient, 3–omnipresent, 4–ubiq-
       uitous, 5–carnal, 6–clandestine

V.   final mop-up

1. wolflike   1. L_____
2. horselike   2. E_____
3. fishlike   3. P_____
4. referring to speech   4. P_____
   sounds
5. expert in speech sounds   5. P_____

6. powerless   6. I_____
7–8. existence everywhere   7. U_____
                                         or U_____
                                      8. O_____
9. to bring back into another   9. R_____
   body or form
10. to embody, make real, or   10. I_____
    put into bodily form

Key: 1–lupine, 2–equine, 3–piscine, 4–phonetic, 5–phone-
        tician, 6–impotent, 7–ubiquity *or* ubiquitousness,
        8–omnipresence, 9–reincarnate, 10–incarnate

Chapter Review

A.   Do you recognize the words?

1. Utter want:
   (a) affluence, (b) opulence, (c) penury
2. Experienced secondhand:
   (a) ephemeral, (b) vicarious, (c) evanescent
3. Inoffensive circumlocution:
   (a) badinage, (b) persiflage, (c) euphemism
4. Homesick:
   (a) nostalgic, (b) bromide, (c) clandestine
5. Meat-eating:
   (a) herbivorous, (b) voracious, (c) carnivorous
6. Stingy
   (a) indigent, (b) parsimonious, (c) opulent
7. Extreme financial need:
   (a) destitution, (b) affluence, (c) parsimony
8. Great and increasing wealth:
   (a) penuriousness, (b) affluence, (c) omnipresence
9. Remaining for a short time:
   (a) euphemistic, (b) evanescent, (c) eulogistic
10. Sweet-sounding:
    (a) euphonious, (b) cacophonous, (c) euphoric
11. Praise glowingly:

(a) evanesce, (b) eulogize, (c) reincarnate
12. Sense of physical well-being:
   (a) euthanasia, (b) euphoria, (c) persiflage
13. Hackneyed expression:
   (a) anodyne, (b) badinage, (c) cliché
14. catlike:
   (a) leonine, (b) feline, (c) canine
15. Bearlike:
   (a) vulpine, (b) ursine, (c) porcine
16. All-knowing:
   (a) omnipotent, (b) omniscient, (c) omnipresent
17. Found everywhere:
   (a) ubiquitous, (b) omnivorous, (c) omnibus
18. Destruction:
   (a) carnage, (b) carnality, (c) reincarnation
19. Stealthy:
   (a) voracious, (b) surreptitious, (c) incarnate

Key: 1–c, 2–b, 3–c, 4–a, 5–c, 6–b, 7–a, 8–b, 9–b, 10–a,
       11–b, 12–b, 13–c, 14–b, 15–b, 16–b, 17–a, 18–a,
       19–b

B.   Can you recognize roots?

Root	Meaning	Example
1. *penuria*	_____	penury
2. *fluo*	_____	affluent
3. *opulentus*	_____	wealthy
4. *ephemera*	_____	ephemeral
5. *vanesco*	_____	evanescent
6. *pheme*	_____	euphemism
7. *phone*	_____	phonetics
8. *logos*	_____	eulogy
9. *thanatos*	_____	euthanasia
10. *platys*	_____	platitude, platypus
11. *odyne*	_____	anodyne
12. *leo*	_____	leonine
13. *felis*	_____	feline

14. *porcus*	_____	porcine
15. *canis*	_____	canine
16. *vulpus*	_____	vulpine
17. *lupus*	_____	lupine
18. *equus*	_____	equine
19. *piscis*	_____	piscine
20. *nostos*	_____	nostalgia
21. *algos*	_____	nostalgic
22. *kakos*	_____	cacophonous
23. *xylon*	_____	xylophone
24. *carnis*	_____	carnivorous
25. *voro*	_____	omnivorous
26. *herba*	_____	herbivorous
27. *omnis*	_____	omnipotent
28. *potens, potentis*	_____	impotent
29. *sciens*	_____	omniscience
30. *ubique*	_____	ubiquitous
31. *vale!*	_____	carnival
32. *clam*	_____	clandestine

Key: 1—want, neediness, 2—to flow, 3—wealthy, 4—dayfly, 5—to vanish, 6—voice, 7—sound, 8—word, speech, 9—death, 10—flat, broad, 11—pain, 12—lion, 13—cat, 14—pig, 15—dog, 16—fox, 17—wolf, 18—horse, 19—fish, 20—a return, 21—pain, 22—bad, harsh, ugly, 23—wood, 24—flesh, 25—to devour, 26—herb, 27—all, 28—powerful, 29—knowing, 30—everywhere, 31—farewell, 32—secretly

Teaser Questions for the Amateur Etymologist

1. The American poet William Cullen Bryant wrote a poem in 1811 called *Thanatopsis*. You are familiar with both roots in the word. Can you work out the meaning?_____

2. If you wanted to coin a word for the study or science of death and dying, what would you come up with?

3. *Pheme*, as you know from *euphemism*, means *voice*. This root derives from a Greek verb *phanai*, to speak, which, as it travelled through Latin, Old French, and Middle English, finally took on the spelling *phet-*, *phec-*, or *phes-*. And you recall that the Greek prefix *pro-* means *beforehand* or *ahead* (as in *prognosis*, *prologue*, etc.). Can you now combine elements to form a word meaning:

       (a) to say beforehand; to foretell (an occurrence before it actually happens)? _____

       (b) the foretelling of such an occurrence?_____
_____

       (c) the person who foretells?_____

4. Can you combine a *Latin* prefix and root to form words of the same meaning?

       (a) to foretell:_____

       (b) the act of foretelling:_____

5. An eminent psychoanalyst, Richard Karpe of Connecticut, has coined the term *nostopathy* (nos-TOP'-ə-thi) for an emotional disorder he diagnosed among a number of his patients who were returning veterans of World War II and of the Korean and Vietnam wars. You know both roots in the word. Can you work out the meaning?_____
_____

6. Coin a word that means:

       (a) the killing of foxes:_____

       (b) the killing of wolves:_____

       (c) the killing of lions, tigers, and other cats:_____

       (d) the killing of bears:_____

7. Work out an adjective that means:

       (a) fish-eating:_____

       (b) insect-eating:_____

8. Have you ever wondered whether the Canary Islands were named after the Latin root *canis*, dog? They were. Large, wild dogs inhabited the area. Pretty songbirds also abounded there. What were these birds called?_____

9. A new verb was coined some years ago, based on the Latin root *potens*, *potentis*, meaning (of a drug) *to make more effective or powerful; to augment the effect of another drug*. Can you figure out what this verb would be?_____

(Answers in Chapter 18)

Getting Used to New Words

Reference has been made, in previous chapters, to the intimate relationship between reading and vocabulary building. Good books and the better magazines will not only acquaint you with a host of new ideas (and, therefore, new words, since every word is the verbalization of an idea), but also will help you gain a more complete and a richer understanding of the hundreds of words you are learning through your work in this book. If you have been doing a sufficient amoung of stimulating reading – and that means, at minimum, several magazines a week and at least three books of non-fiction a month – you have been meeting, constantly, over and over again, the new words you have been learning in these pages. Every such encounter is like seeing an old friend in a new place. You know how much better you understand your friends when you have a chance to see them react to new situations; similarly, you will gain a much deeper understanding of the friends you have been making among words as you see them in different contexts and in different places.

In the past, I have recommended reading non-fiction, but novels too are a rich source of additions to your vocabulary – provided you stay alert to the new words you will inevitably meet in reading novels.

The natural temptation, when you encounter a brand-new word in a novel, is to ignore it – the lines of the plot are perfectly clear even if many of the author's words are not.

I want to counsel strongly that you resist the temptation to ignore the unfamiliar words you may meet in your novel reading: resist it with every ounce of your energy, for only by such resistance can you keep building your vocabulary as you read.

What should you do? Don't rush to a dictionary, don't bother underlining the word don't keep long lists of words that you will eventually look up *en masse* – these activities are likely to become painful and you will not continue them for any great length of time.

Instead, do something quite simple – and very effective.

When you meet a new word, underline it with a *mental* pencil. That is, pause for a second and attempt to figure out its meaning from its use in the sentence or from its etymological root or prefix, if it contains one you have studied. Make a mental note of it, say it aloud once or twice – and then go on reading.

That's all there is to it. What you are doing, of course, is developing the same type of attitude towards the new word that you have developed towards the words you have studied in this book. And the result, of course, will be the same – you will begin to notice the word occurring again and again in other reading you do, and finally, having seen it in a number of varying contexts, you will begin to get enough of its connotation and flavour to come to a fairly accurate understanding of its meaning. In this way you will be developing alertness not only to the words you have studied in this book, but to all expressive and meaningful words. And your vocabulary will keep growing.

But of course that will happen only if you keep reading.

I do not wish to recommend any particular novels or novelists, since the type of fiction one enjoys is a very personal matter. You doubtless know the kind of story you like – mystery, science fiction, spy, adventure, historical, political, romantic, Western, biographical, one or all of the above. Or you may be entranced by novels of ideas, of sexual prowess, of fantasy, of life in different segments of society from your own. No matter. Find the kind of novel or novelist *you* enjoy by browsing in the public library or among the thousands of titles in bookshops that have a rich assortment of paperbacks as well as hardbacks.

And then read! And keep on the alert for new words! You will find them by the hundreds and thousands. Bear in mind: *people with rich vocabularies have been reading omnivorously, voraciously, since childhood* – including the ingredients listed in small print on bread wrappers and cereal boxes.

(End of Session 41)

How to spell a word

The spelling of English words is archaic, it's confusing, it's needlessly complicated, and, if you have a sense of humour, it's downright comical. In fact, any insulting epithet you might wish to level against our weird methods of putting letters together to form words would probably be justified – but it's our spelling, and we're stuck with it.

Many years ago, the Irish playwright George Bernard Shaw offered a dramatic proposal for reducing England's taxes. Just eliminate unnecessary letters from our unwieldy spelling, he said, and you'll save enough money in paper and printing to cut everyone's tax rate in half. Maybe it would work, but it's never been put to the test – and the way things look now, it never will be. Current practice more and more holds spelling exactly where it is, bad though it may be. It is a scientific law of language that if enough people make a 'mistake', the 'mistake' becomes acceptable usage. That law applies to pronunciation, to grammar, to word meanings, but not to spelling. Maybe it's because of our misbegotten faith in, and worship of, the printed word – maybe it's because written language tends to be relatively static, while spoken language constantly changes. Whatever the cause, spelling today successfully resists every logical effort at reform. 'English spelling', said the American sociologist and economist Thorstein Veblen, 'satisfies all the requirements of the canons of reputability under the law of conspicuous waste. It is archaic, cumbrous, and ineffective.' Perfectly true. Notwithstanding, it's here to stay.

Your most erudite friend doubtless misspells the name of the Hawaiian guitar. I asked half a dozen members of the English department of a large college to spell the word – without exception they responded with *ukelele*. Yet the only accepted form is *ukulele*.

Judging from my experience with my classes, half the population of the country must think the word is spelled *alright*. Seventy-five per cent of the members of my classes can't spell *embarrassing* or *coolly*. People will go on misspelling these four words, but the authorized spellings will remain impervious to change.

Well, you know the one about Mohammed and the mountain. If spelling won't change, as it probably won't, those of us who consider ourselves poor spellers will have to. We'll just have to get up and go to the mountain.

Is it hard to become a good speller? I have demonstrated over and over again in my classes that anyone of normal intelligence and average educational background can become a good speller in very little time.

What makes the task so easy?

First — investigations have proved that ninety-five per cent of the spelling errors that educated people make occur in just one hundred words. Not only do we all misspell the same words — but we misspell them in about the same way.

Second — correct spelling relies exclusively on memory, and the most effective way to train memory is by means of association or, to use the technical term, mnemonics.

If you fancy yourself an imperfect or even a terrible speller, the chances are very great that you've developed a complex solely because you misspell some or all of the hundred words with which this Intermission deals. When you have conquered this single list, and I shall immediately proceed to demonstrate how easy it is, by means of mnemonics, to do so, ninety-five per cent of your spelling difficulties will in all likelihood vanish.

Let us start with twenty-five words from the list. In the first column you will find the correct spelling of each, and in the second column the simple mnemonic that will forevermore fix that correct spelling in your memory.

Correct spelling	Mnemonic
1. all right	Two words, no matter what it means. Keep in mind that it's the opposite of *all wrong*.

2. coolly — Of course you can spell *cool* — simply add the adverbial ending -ly.

3. supersede — This is the only word in the language ending in *-sede* (the only one, mind you — there isn't a single other one so spelt).

4. succeed
5. proceed
6. exceed
{ The only three words in the entire language ending in *-ceed*. When you think of the three words in the order given here, the initial letters form the beginning of SPEED.

7. cede, precede, recede, etc. — All other words with a similar-sounding final syllable end in *-cede*.

8. procedure — One of the double *e*'s of *proceed* moves to the end in the noun form, *procedure*.

9. stationery — This is the word that means paper, and notice the *-er* in *paper*.

10. stationary — In this spelling, the words means standing, and notice the *-a* in *stand*.

11. recommend — *Commend,* which we all spell correctly, plus the prefix *re-*.

12. separate
13. comparative
{ Look for *a rat* in both words.

14. ecstasy — to *sy* (sigh) with ecstasy

15. analyse
16. paralyse
{ The only two non-technical words in the whole language ending in *-yse*.

17. repetition — First four letters indentical with those in the allied form *repeat*.

18. irritable
19. inimitable
{ Think of allied forms *irritate* and *imitate*.

20. absence — Think of the allied form *absent*, and you will not be tempted to misspell it *abscence*.

21. superintendent — A superintend*ent* manages a department *ent* — thus you avoid *superintendant*.

22. conscience — *Science* plus prefix *con-*.

23. anoint — Think of *an ointment*, hence no double *n*.

24. ridiculous   Think of the allied form *ridicule*, which we usually spell correctly, thus avoiding *rediculous*.

25. despair   Again, think of another form – *desperate* – and so avoid *dispair*.

Whether or not you have much faith in your spelling ability, you will need very little time to conquer the preceding twenty-five demons. Spend a few minutes, now, on each of those words in the list that you're doubtful of, and then test your success by means of the exercise below. Perhaps to your astonishment, you will find it easy to get a high score.

A test of your learning

Instructions: After studying the preceding list of words, fill in the missing letters correctly.

1. a_____right
2. coo_____y
3. super_____
4. suc_____
5. pro_____
6. ex_____
7. pre_____
8. proc_____dure
9. station_____ry (paper)
10. station_____ry (still)
11. sep_____rate
12. compar_____tive
13. re_____o_____end

14. ecsta_____y
15. anal_____e
16. paral_____e
17. rep_____tition
18. irrit_____ble
19. inimit_____ble
20. ab_____ence
21. superintend_____nt
22. con_____nce
23. a_____oint
24. r_____diculous
25. d_____spair

Mere repetitious drill is of no value in learning to spell a word correctly. You've probably heard the one about the youngster who was kept after school because he was in the habit of using the ungrammatical expression 'I have went'. Miss X was going to cure her pupil, even if it required drastic measures. So she ordered him to write 'I have gone' one thousand times. 'Just leave your work on my desk before you go home', she said 'and I'll find it when I come in tomorrow morning'. Well, there were twenty pages of neat script on her desk next morning, one thousand lines of 'I have gone's', and on the last sheet was a note from the child. 'Dear Teacher', it read, 'I have done the work and I have went home'. If this didn't actually happen, it logically could have, for in any exercise, if the mind is not actively engaged, no learning will result. If you drive a car, or sew, or do any familiar and repetitious manual work, you know how your hands can carry on an accustomed task while your mind is far away. And if you hope to learn to spell by filling pages with a word, stop wasting your time. All you'll get for your trouble is writer's cramp.

The only way to learn to spell those words that now plague you is to devise a mnemonic for each one.

If you are never quite sure whether it's *indispensible* or *indispensable*, you can spell it out one hundred, one thousand, or one million times – and the next time you have occasion to write it in a sentence, you'll still wonder whether to end it with *-ible* or *-able*. But if you say to yourself *just once* that *able* people are generally *indispensable*, that thought will come to you whenever you need to spell the word; in a few seconds you've conquered another spelling demon. By engineering your own mnemonic through a study of the structure of a troublesome word, you will become so quickly and completely involved with the correct spelling of that word that it will be impossible for you ever to be stumped again

Let us start at once. Below you will find another twenty-five words from the list of one hundred demons, each offered to you in both the correct form and in the popular misspelling. Go through the test quickly, ticking what you consider the proper choice in each case. In that way you will discover which of the twenty-five you would be likely to get caught on. Then devise a personal mnemonic for each word you missed, writing your ingenious result out in the margin of the page. And don't be alarmed if some of your mnemonics turn out rather silly – the sillier they are the more likely you are to recall them in an emergency. One of my pupils, who could not remember how many *l*'s to put into *tranquillity* (or is it *tranquility*?), shifted his mind into high gear and came up with this: 'In the old days life was more *tranquil* than today, and people wrote with *quills* instead of fountain pens. Hence – *tranquillity*.' Another pupil, a girl who always chewed her nails over *irresistible* before she could decide whether to end it with *-ible* or *-able*, suddenly realized that a certain brand of *lipstick* was called *irrestible*, the point being of course that the only vowel in *lipstick* is *i*

– hence, *-ible!* Silly, aren't they? But they work. Go ahead to the test now; and see how clever – or silly – you can be.

Spelling Test

1. a. supprise   b. surprise
2. a. inoculate   b. innoculate
3. a. definitely   b. definately
4. a. priviledge   b. privilege
5. a. incidently   b. incidentally
6. a. predictible   b. predictable
7. a. dissipate   b. disippate
8. a. descriminate   b. discriminate
9. a. description   b. discription
10. a. baloon   b. balloon
11. a. occurence   b. occurrence
12. a. truely   b. truly
13. a. argument   b. argument
14. a. assistant   b. asisstant
15. a. grammer   b. grammar
16. a. parallel   b. paralell
17. a. drunkeness   b. drunkenness
18. a. suddeness   b. suddenness
19. a. embarassment   b. embarrassment
20. a. weird   b. wierd
21. a. pronounciation   b. pronunciation
22. a. noticeable   b. noticable
23. a. developement   b. development
24. a. vicious   b. viscious
25. a. insistent   b. insistant

Key: 1–b, 2–a, 3–a, 4–b, 5–b, 6–b, 7–a, 8–b, 9–a, 10–b,
        11–b, 12–b, 13–b, 14–a, 15–b, 16–a, 17–b, 18–b,
        19–b, 20–a, 21–b, 22–a, 23–b, 24–a, 25–a

By now you're well on the way toward developing a definite superiority complex about your spelling – which isn't a bad thing, for I've learned, working with my students, that many people think they're awful spellers, and have completely lost faith in their ability, solely because they get befuddled over no more than two dozen or so common words that they use over and over again and always misspell. Every other word they spell perfectly, but they still think they're prize idiots in spelling until their self-confidence is restored. So if you're beginning to gain more assurance, you're on the right track. The conquest of the one hundred common words most frequently misspelt is not going to assure you that you will always come out top in a spelling competition, but it's certain to clean up your writing and bolster your ego.

So far you have worked with fifty of the one hundred spelling demons. Here, now, is the remainder of the list. Test yourself, or have someone who can keep a secret test you, and discover which ones are your Waterloo. Study each one you miss as if it were a problem in engineering. Observe how it's put together and devise whatever association pattern will fix the correct form in your mind.

Happy spelling!

Spelling Demons

These fifty words complete the list of one hundred words that most frequently stump the inexpert spellers:

1. embarrassing
2. indispensable
3. disappear
4. disappoint
5. corroborate
6. sacrilegious
7. tranquillity
8. exhilaration
9. newsstand
10. licence (n.)
11. license (v.)
12. irresistible
13. persistent
14. dilemma
15. perseverance
16. until (but till)
17. tyrannize
18. vacillate
19. oscillate
20. accommodate
21. dilettante
22. changeable
23. accessible
24. desirable
25. panicky
26. seize
27. leisure
28. receive
29. achieve
30. practise (v.)
31. practice (n.)
32. existence
33. pursue
34. pastime

35. possesses
36. professor
37. category
38. rhythmical
39. vacuum
40. benefited
41. committee
42. grievous
43. conscious
44. plebeian
45. tariff
46. sheriff
47. connoisseur
48. necessary
49. sergeant
50. misspelling

15

HOW TO TALK ABOUT
WHAT GOES ON

(Sessions 42—44)

Teaser preview

What verb, ending in -ate, means:

- *to exhaust?*
- *to scold severely?*
- *to deny oneself?*
- *to repeat the main points?*
- *to be a victim of mental or intellectual stagnation?*
- *to pretend?*
- *to hint?*
- *to make (something) easier to bear?*
- *to show sympathy?*
- *to waver indecisively?*

Session 42

WORDS are symbols of ideas – and we have been learning, discussing, and working with words as they revolve around certain basic concepts.

Starting with an idea (personality types, doctors, occupations, science, lying, actions, speech, insults, compliments, etc.), we have explored the meanings and uses of basic words; then, working from each word, we have wandered off towards any ideas and additional words that a basic word might suggest, or towards any *other* words built on the same Latin or Greek roots.

By this natural and logical method, you have been able to make lasting contact with fifty to a hundred or more words in each chapter. And you have discovered, I think, that while five *isolated* words may be difficult to learn in one day, fifty to a hundred or more *related* words are easy to learn in a few sessions.

In this session we learn words that tell what's going on, what's happening, what people do to each other or to themselves, or what others do to *them*.

Ideas

1.   Complete exhaustion

You have stayed up all night. And what were you doing? Playing poker, a very pleasant way of whiling away time? No. Engaging in some creative activity, like writing a short story, planning a political campaign, discussing fascinating questions with friends? No.

The examples I have offered are exciting or stimulating – as psychologists have discovered, it is not work or effort that causes fatigue, but boredom, frustration, or a similar feeling.

You have stayed up all night with a very sick husband, wife, child, or dear friend. And despite all your ministrations, the patient is sinking. You can see how this long vigil contains all the elements of frustration that contribute to mental, physical, and nervous fatigue.

And so you are exhausted – completely. Your exhaustion is mental, it is physiological, it is emotional.

What verb expresses the effect of the night's frustrations on you?

to enervate

2. Tongue-lashing

You suddenly see the flashing blue light as you glance in your rear-view mirror. It's the middle of the night, yet the police flasher is as clear as day – and then you hear the wail of the siren. So you pull over, knowing you were speeding along at 70 in a 50 mile-an-hour-limit area – after all, there was not another car in sight on the deserted stretch of road.

The police officer is pleasant, courteous, smiling; merely asks for your driver's licence and registration; even says 'Please'.

Feeling guilty and stupid, you become irritated. So what do you do?

You lash out at the officer with all the verbal vituperation welling up in you from your self-anger. You scold him harshly for not spending his time looking for violent criminals instead of harassing innocent motorists; you call into question his honesty, his ambition, his fairness, even his ancestry. To no avail, of course.

What verb describes how you reacted?

to castigate

3. Altruistic

Phyllis is selfless and self-sacrificing. Her husband's needs and desires come first – even when they conflict with her own. Clothes for her two daughters are her main concern – even if she has to wear a seven-year-old coat and outmoded dresses so that Paula and Evelyn can look smart and trim. At the dinner table, she heaps everyone's plate – while she herself often goes without. Phyllis will deny herself, will scrimp and save – all to the end that she may offer her husband and children the luxuries that her low self-esteem does not permit her to give herself.

What verb expresses what Phyllis does?

to self-abnegate

Repetition

You have delivered a long, complicated lecture to your class, and now, to make sure that they will remember the important points, you restate the key ideas, the main thoughts. You offer, in short, a kind of brief summary, step by step, omitting all extraneous details.

What verb best describes what you do?

to recapitulate

5.   No joie de vivre

Perhaps you wake up some gloomy Monday morning (why is it that Monday is always the worst day of the week?) and begin to think of the waste of the last five years. Intellectually, there has been no progress – you've read scarcely half a dozen books, haven't made one new, exciting friend, haven't had a startling or unusual thought. Economically, things are no better – same old debts to meet, same old hundred pounds in the bank, same old job, same old routine of the nine-to-five workdays, the cheese or ham salad sandwich for lunch, the same dreary ride home. What a life! No change, nothing but routine, sameness, monotony – and for what? (By now you'd better get up – this type of thinking never leads anywhere, as you've long since learnt.)

What verb describes how you think you live?

to vegetate

6.   Pretence

Your neighbour, Mrs. Brown, pops in without invitation to tell you of her latest troubles with (a) her boss, (b) her hairdresser, (c) her husband, (d) her children, and/or (e) her gynaecologist.

Since Florence Brown is dull to the point of ennui, and anyway you have a desk piled high with work you were planning to get stuck into, you find it difficult to concentrate on what she is saying. However, you do not wish to offend her by sending her packing, or even by appearing to be uninterested, so you pretend rapt attention, nodding wisely at what you hope are the right places.

What verb describes this feigning of interest?

to simulate

7.   Slight hint, no more

You are an author and are discussing with your editor the possible avenues of publicity and advertising for your new book. At one point in the conversation the editor makes several statements which might – or might not – be construed to mean that the company is going to promote the book heavily. For example, 'If we put some real money behind this, we might sell a few copies', or 'I wonder if it would be a good idea to get you on a few talk shows ...'. No unequivocal commitments, no clear-cut promises, only the slight and oblique mention of possibilities.

What verb expresses what the editor is doing?

to intimate

8.   Helpful

Aspirin doesn't cure any diseases. Yet this popular and inexpensive drug is universally used to lighten and relieve various unpleasant symptoms of disease: aches and pains, fever, inflammations, etc.

What verb expresses the action of aspirin?

to alleviate

9.   When the bell tolls

John Donne's lines (made famous by Ernest Hemingway):

No mane is an Iland, *intire of it selfe; every man is a peece of the* Continent, *a part of the* maine; *if a* Clod *bee washed away by the* Sea, Europe *is the lesse, as well as if a* Promontorie *were, as well as if a* Mannor *of thy* friends *or of thine owne* were; *any mans* death *diminishes me, because I am involved in* Mankinde; *And therefore never send to know for whom the* bell *tolls; It tolls for thee.*

are truer than you may think; any person who views another's pain with complete detachment or indifference is shutting off important feelings.

When people have suffered a bereavement (as through death), when they have been wounded by life or by friends, then is the time they most need to feel that they are not alone, that you share their misery with them even if you cannot directly alleviate their sorrow. Your sympathy and compassion are, of course, alleviation enough.

What verb signifies this vicarious sharing of sorrow with someone who directly suffers?

to commiserate

10.   When two men propose

Should you marry John or George? (You're strongly and equally attracted to both.) John is handsome, virile, tender; George is stable, reliable, dependable, always there when you need him. George loves you deeply; John is more exciting. You decide on John, naturally.

But wait – marrying John would mean giving up George, and with George you always know where you stand; he's like the Rock of Gibraltar (and sometimes almost as dull). So you change your mind – it's George, on more mature reflection.

But how happy can you be with a husband who is not exciting? Maybe John would be best after all . . . .

The pendulum swings back and forth – you cannot make up your mind and stick to it. (You fail to realize that your indecision proves that you don't want to marry either one, or perhaps don't want to give either one up, or possibly don't even want to get married.) First it's John, then it's George, then back to John, then George again. *Which is it, which is it?*

What verb describes your pendulum-like indecision?

to vacillate

Using the words

Can you pronounce the words?

1.	*enervate*	EN'-ə-vayt'
2.	*castigate*	KAS'-ti-gayt'
3.	*self-abnegate*	self-AB'-ni-gayt'
4.	*recapitulate*	ree'-kə-PIT'-yoŏ-layt
5.	*vegetate*	VEJ'-i-tayt'
6.	*simulate*	SIM'-yoŏ-layt'
7.	*intimate*	IN'-ti-mayt'
8.	*alleviate*	ə-LEE'-vi-ayt'
9.	*commiserate*	kə-MIZ'-ə-rayt
10.	*vacillate*	VAS'-i-layt'

Can you work with the words?

1.	enervate	a.	deny oneself
2.	castigate	b.	stagnate
3.	self-abnegate	c.	suggest; hint
4.	recapitulate	d.	sympathize
5.	vegetate	e.	waver
6.	simulate	f.	exhaust
7.	intimate	g.	lessen; lighten
8.	alleviate	h.	summarize
9.	commiserate	i.	pretend
10.	vacillate	j.	censure; scold; lash at verbally

Key: 1–f, 2–j, 3–a, 4–h, 5–b, 6–i, 7–c, 8–g, 9–d, 10–e

Do you understand the words? (I)

1. Should you feel *enervated* after a good night's sleep?	YES	NO
2. Do motorists who have been caught speeding sometimes start *castigating* the police officer?	YES	NO

3. Do people who are completely *self-abnegating* say 'No!' to their needs and desires?   YES   NO

4. When you *recapitulate*, do you cover new material?   YES   NO

5. Do people possessed of *joie de vivre* usually feel that they are *vegetating*?   YES   NO

6. When you *simulate* alertness, do you purposely act somnolent?   YES   NO

7. When you *intimate*, do you make a direct statement?   YES   NO

8. Does aspirin often have an *alleviating* effect on pain?   YES   NO

9. Do we naturally *commiserate* with people who have suffered a bereavement?   YES   NO

10. Do decisive people often *vacillate*?   YES   NO

Key: 1–no, 2–yes, 3–yes, 4–no, 5–no, 6–no, 7–no, 8–yes, 9–yes, 10–no

---

Do you understand the words? (II)

1. enervated – exhilarated   SAME   OPPOSITE
2. castigate – praise   SAME   OPPOSITE
3. self-abnegate – deny oneself   SAME   OPPOSITE
4. recapitulate – summarize   SAME   OPPOSITE
5. vegetate – stagnate   SAME   OPPOSITE
6. simulate – pretend   SAME   OPPOSITE
7. intimate – hint   SAME   OPPOSITE
8. alleviate – make worse   SAME   OPPOSITE
9. commiserate – sympathize   SAME   OPPOSITE
10. vacillate – decide   SAME   OPPOSITE

Key: 1–O, 2–O, 3–S, 4–S, 5–S, 6–S, 7–S, 8–O, 9–S, 10–O

Can you recall the words?

1.	pretend	1.	S_____
2.	scold	2.	C_____
3.	sacrifice one's desires	3.	S_____
4.	waver	4.	V_____
5.	exhaust	5.	E_____
6.	sympathize	6.	C_____
7.	summarize	7.	R_____
8.	lighten	8.	A_____
9.	hint	9.	I_____
10.	stagnate	10.	V_____

Key: 1–simulate, 2–castigate, 3–self-abnegate, 4–vacillate,
5–enervate, 6–commiserate, 7–-recapitulate, 8–alleviate, 9–intimate, 10–vegetate

(End of Session 42)

Session 43

Origins and related words

1. More than fatigue

When you are *enervated*, you feel as if your nerves have been ripped out — or so the etymology of the word indicates.

Enervate is derived from *e-* (*ex-*), out, and Latin *nervus*, nerve. *Enervation* (en'-ə-VAY'-shən) is not just fatigue, but complete de-vitalization — physical, emotional, mental — as if every ounce of the life force has been sapped out, as if the last particle of energy has been drained away.

Despite its similar appearance to the word *energy*, *enervation* is almost a direct antonym. *Energy* is derived from the Greek prefix *en-*, in, plus the root *ergon*, work; *erg* is the term used in physics for a unit of work or energy. *Synergism* (SIN'-ə-jiz-əm *or* SIN'-ər-jiz-əm) — the prefix *syn-*, together or with, plus *ergon* — is the process by which two or more substances or drugs, by working together, produce a greater effect in combination than the sum total of their individual effects.

Alcohol, for example, is a depressant. So are barbiturates and other soporifics. Alcohol and barbiturates work *synergistically* (sin'-ə-JIS'-tik'-li *or* sin'-ər-JIS'-tik'-li) — the effect of each is increased by the other if the two are taken together.

So if you're drinking, don't take a sleeping pill — or if you *must* take a pill for your insomnia, don't drink — the combination, if not lethal, will do more to you than you may want done!

Synergy (SIN'-ə-ji *or* SIN'-ər-ji), by the way, is an alternative form of *synergism*.

2.   Verbal punishment

Castigate is derived from a Latin verb meaning *to punish*; in pres-ent-day usage, the verb generally refers to verbal punishment, usually harsh and severe. It is somewhat synonymous with *scold, criticize, rebuke, censure, reprimand,* or *berate,* but much stronger than any of these – *rail at, rant at, lash out at,* or *tongue-lash* is a much closer synonym. When candidates for office *castigate* their opponents, they do not mince words.

Can you construct the noun form of *castigate?*_____

3.   Saying 'No!' to oneself

Abnegate is derived from Latin *ab-,* away (as in *absent*), plus *nego,* to deny – *self-abnegation* (self-ab'-ni-GAY'-shən), then, is self-denial. *Nego* itself is a contraction of Latin *neg-,* not, no, and *aio,* I say; to be *self-abnegating* is to say 'No!' to what you want, as if some inner censor were at work whispering, 'No, you can't have that, you can't do that, you don't deserve that, you're not good enough for that . . .'.

To *negate* (ni-GAYT') is to deny the truth or existence of, as in 'The atheist *negates* God'; or, by extension, to destroy by working against, as in, 'His indulgence in expensive hobbies *negates* all his wife's attempts to keep the family solvent.' Can you write the noun form of the verb *negate?*_____

Negative and *negativity* obviously spring from the same source as *negate.*

4.   Heads and headings

Latin *caput, capitis* means *head*. The *captain* is the *head* of any group; the *capital* is the *'head city'* of a state or nation; and to *decapitate* (di-KAP'-i-tayt') is to chop off someone's *head*, a popular activity during the French Revolution after the guillotine was invented. Write the noun form of *decapitate:*_____

Latin *capitulum* is a little head, or, by extension, the heading, or title, of a chapter. So when you *recapitulate*, you go through the chapter headings again (*re-*), etymologically speaking, or you sum-marize or review the main points.

Remembering how the noun and adjective forms are derived from *adulate* (Chapter 9), can you write the required forms of *recapitulate*?

NOUN: _____

ADJECTIVE: _____

When you *capitulate* (kə-PIT'-yŏŏ-layt'), etymologically you arrange in headings, or, as the meaning of the verb naturally evolved, you arrange conditions of surrender, as when an army *capitulates* to the enemy forces under prearranged conditions; or, by further natural extension, you stop resisting and give up, as in, 'He realized there was no longer any point in resisting her advances, so he reluctantly *capitulated*.' Can you write the noun form of *capitulate*? _____

5.   Mere vegetables

Vegetable is from Latin *vegeto*, to live and grow, which is what vegetables do – but that's *all* they do, so to *vegetate*, is, by implication, to do no more than stay alive, stuck in a rut, leading an inactive, unstimulating, emotionally and intellectually stagnant existence. *Vegetation* (vej'-i-TAY'-shən) is any dull, passive, stagnant existence; also any plant life, as the thick *vegetation* of a jungle.

Review of etymology

Prefix, Root, Suffix	Meaning	English Word
1. *e- (ex-)*	out	_____
2. *nervus*	nerve	_____
3. *en-*	in	_____
4. *ergon*	work	_____
5. *syn-*	with, together	_____
6. *–ic*	adjective suffix	_____
7. *–ion*	noun suffix	_____
8. *ab-*	away	_____
9. *nego*	to deny	_____
10. *caput, capitis*	head	_____
11. *de-*	negative prefix	_____
12. *capitulum*	little head, chapter heading	_____
13. *re-*	again	_____

14. *—ory*   adjective suffix   _____
15. *vegeto*   to live and grow   _____

Using the words

Can you pronounce the words?

1. *enervation*   en'-ə-VAY'-shən
2. *synergism*   SIN'-ə-jiz-əm *or* SIN'-ər-jiz-əm
3. *synergy*   SIN'-ə-ji *or* SIN'-ər-ji
4. *synergistic*   SIN'-ə-jis'-tik *or* sin'-ər-jis'-tik
5. *castigation*   kas'-ti-GAY'-shən
6. *self-abnegation*   self-ab'-ni-GAY'-shən
7. *negate*   ni-GAYT'
8. *negation*   ni-GAY'-shən
9. *decapitate*   di-KAP'-i-tayt'
10. *decapitation*   di-kap'-i-TAY'-shən
11. *recapitulation*   ree-kə-pit-yoo-LAY'-shən
12. *recapitulatory*   ree-kə-PIT'-yoo-lə-taw'-ri
13. *capitulate*   kə-PIT'-yoo-layt'
14. *capitulation*   kə-PIT'-yoo-LAY'-shən

Can you work with the words?

1. enervation   a. tongue-lashing
2. synergism, synergy   b. denial; destruction
3. castigation   c. a lopping off of one's head
4. self-abnegation   d. summary; review of main points
5. negation   e. self-denial
6. decapitation   f. utter exhaustion; mental, emotional, and physical drain
7. recapitulation   g. a working together for greater effect
8. capitulation   h. surrender

Key: 1–f, 2–g, 3–a, 4–e, 5–b, 6–c, 7–d, 8–h

Do you understand the words?

1. enervating –refreshing	SAME	OPPOSITE
2. synergistic – neutralizing	SAME	OPPOSITE
3. castigation – scolding	SAME	OPPOSITE
4. self-abnegation – egoism	SAME	OPPOSITE
5. negate – accept	SAME	OPPOSITE
6. decapitate – behead	SAME	OPPOSITE
7. recapitulatory – summarizing	SAME	OPPOSITE
8. capitulate – resist	SAME	OPPOSITE

Key: 1–O, 2–O, 3–S, 4–O, 5–O, 6–S, 7–S, 8–O

Can you recall the words?

1. to give in	1. C_____
2. working together for greater effect (*adj.*)	2. S_____
3. total fatigue	3. E_____
4. for the purpose of summarizing or review (*adj.*)	4. R_____
5. self-denial	5. S_____-A_____
6. deny; render ineffective; nullify	6. N_____
7. process by which two or more substances produce a greater effect than the sum of the individual effects	7. S_____ *or* S_____
8. to cut off the head of	8. D_____
9. strong censure	9. C_____
10. to surrender	10. C_____

Key: 1–capitulate, 2–synergistic, 3–enervation, 4–recapitulatory, 5–self-abnegation, 6–negate, 7–synergism *or* synergy, 8–decapitate, 9–castigation, 10–capitulate

(End of Session 43)

Session 44

1.   Not the real McCoy

Simulate is from Latin *simulo*, to copy; and *simulo* itself derives from the Latin adjective *similis*, like or similar.

Simulation (sim'-yoŏ-LAY'-shən), then, is copying the real thing, pretending to be the genuine article by taking on a similar appearance. The *simulation* of joy is quite a feat when you really feel depressed.

Genuine pearls grow inside oysters; *simulated* pearls are synthetic, but look like the ones from oysters. (Rub a pearl against your teeth to tell the difference – the natural pearl feels gritty.) So the frequent advertisement of an inexpensive necklace made of 'genuine *simulated* pearls' can fool you if you don't know the word – you're being offered a genuine fake.

Dissimulation (di-sim'-yoŏ-LAY'-shən) is something else! When you *dissimulate* (di-SIM'-yoŏ-layt') you hide your true feelings by making a pretence of opposite feelings.

Sycophants are great *dissimulators* – they may feel contempt but show admiration; they may feel negative, but express absolutely positive agreement.

A close synonym of *dissimulate* is *dissemble* (di-SEM'-bəl), which also is to hide true feelings by pretending the opposite; or, additionally, to conceal facts, or one's true intentions, by deception; or, still further additionally, to pretend ignorance of facts you'd rather not admit, when, indeed, you're fully aware of them.

The noun is *dissemblance* (di-SEM'-bləns).

In *dissimulate* and *dissemble*, the negative prefix *dis*-acts largely to make both words pejorative.

2.   Hints and helps

The verb *intimate* is from Latin *intimus*, innermost, the same root from which the adjective *intimate* (IN'-ti-mət) and its noun *intimacy* (IN'-ti-mə-si) are derived; but the relationship is only in etymology, not in meaning. An *intimation* (in'-ti-MAY'-shən) contains a significance buried deep in the innermost core, only a hint showing. As you grow older, you begin to have *intimations* that you are mortal; when someone aims a gun at you, or when a lorry comes roaring down at you as you drive absent-mindedly against a red light through an intersection, you are suddenly *very sure* that you are mortal.

Alleviate is a combination of Latin *levis*, light (not heavy), the prefix *ad-*, to, and the verb suffix. (*Ad-* changes to *al-*before a root starting with *l-*).

If something *alleviates* your pain, it makes your pain lighter for you; if I *alleviate* your sadness, I make it lighter to bear; and if you need some *alleviation* (ə-lee'-vi-AY'-shən) of your problems, you need them made lighter and less burdensome. To *alleviate* is to relieve only temporarily, not to cure or do away with. (*Relieve* is also from *levis*, plus *re-*, again – to make light or easy again.) The adjective form of *alleviate* is *alleviative* (ə-LEE'-vi-ay'-tiv) – aspirin is an *alleviative* drug.

Anything light will rise – so from the prefix *e-* (*ex-*), out, plus *levis*, we can construct the verb *elevate*, etymologically, to raise out, or, actually, raise up, as to *elevate* one's spirits, raise them up, make them lighter; or *elevate* someone to a higher position.

Have you ever seen a performance of magic in which a person or an object apparently rises in the air as if floating? That's *levitation* (lev'-i-TAY'-shən) – rising through no visible means. (I've watched it a dozen times and never *could* work it out!) The verb, so to rise, is *levitate* (LEV'-i-tayt').

And how about *levity* (LEV'-i-ti)? That's lightness too, but of a different sort – lightness in the sense of frivolity, flippancy, joking, or lack of seriousness, especially when solemnity, dignity, or formality is required or more appropriate, as in 'tones of *levity*', or as in, '*Levity* is out of place at a funeral or in a house of worship', or as in, 'Okay, enough *levity* – now let's get down to business!'

3.   Sharing someone's misery

Latin *miser*, wretched, the prefix *con-* (which, as you know, becomes *com-* before a root beginning with *m-*), together or with, and the verb suffix –*ate* are the building blocks from which *commiserate* is constructed. 'I *commiserate* with you', then, means, 'I am wretched together with you – I share your misery'. The noun form?

_____

Miser, miserly, miserable, misery all come from the same root.

4.   Swing and sway

Vacillate – note the single *c*, double *l* – derives from Latin *vacillo*, swing back and forth. The noun form?_____

People who swing back and forth in indecision, who are irresolute, who can, unfortunately, see both, or even three or four, sides of every question, and so have difficulty making up their mainds, are *vacillatory* (VAS'-i-lə-taw'-ri). They are also, usually, *ambivalent* (am-BIV'-ə-lənt) – they have conflicting and simultaneous emotions about the same person or thing; or they want to go but they also want to stay; or they love something, but they hate it too. The noun is *ambivalence* (am-BIV'-ə-ləns) – from *ambi* both. (Remember *ambivert* and *ambidextrous* from Chapter 3?)

Ambivalence has best been defined as watching your mother-in-law drive over a cliff in your new car.

To *vacillate* is to swing mentally or emotionally. To sway back and forth physically is *oscillate* – again note the double *l* – (OS'-i-layt'), from Latin *oscillum*, a swing. A pendulum *oscillates*, the arm of a metronome *oscillates*, and people who've had much too much to drink *oscillate* when they try to walk. The noun?_____

Review of etymology

Prefix, Root, Suffix	Meaning	English Word
1. *simulo*	to copy	_____
2. *similis*	like, similar	_____

3. *dis-*   pejorative prefix   _____
4. *ad- (al-)*   to, towards   _____
5. *levis*   light   _____
6. *—ate*   verb suffix   _____
7. *—ion*   noun suffix   _____
8. *e- (ex-)*   out   _____
9. *intimus*   innermost   _____
10. *miser*   wretched   _____
11. *vacillo*   to swing back and forth   _____
12. *ambi-*   both   _____
13. *oscillum*   a swing   _____

Using the words

Can you pronounce the words?

1. *simulation*   sim'-yoo-LAY'-shən
2. *dissimulate*   di-SIM'-yoo-layt'
3. *dissimulation*   di-sim'-yoo-LAY'-shən
4. *dissemble*   di-SEM'-bəl
5. *dissemblance*   di-SEM'-bləns
6. *intimation*   in'-ti-MAY'-shən
7. *alleviation*   ə-lee'-vi-AY'-shən
8. *alleviative*   ə-LEE'-vi-ay'-tiv
9. *levitate*   LEV'-i-tayt'
10. *levitation*   lev'-i-TAY'-shən
11. *levity*   LEV'-i-ti
12. *commiseration*   kə-miz'-ə-RAY'-shən
13. *vacillation*   vas'-i-LAY'-shən
14. *vacillatory*   VAS'-i-lə-taw'-ri
15. *ambivalent*   am-BIV'-ə-lənt
16. *ambivalence*   am-BIV'-ə-ləns
17. *oscillate*   OS'-i-layt'
18. *oscillation*   os'-i-LAY'-shən

Can you work with the words? (I)

1. simulation   a. hint

2. dissemble — b. flippancy or joking when seriousness is required

3. intimation — c. a sharing of grief
4. alleviation — d. physical swaying; swinging action, as of a pendulum

5. levitate — e. a swinging back and forth in indecision

6. levity — f. pretence
7. commiseration — g. conflicted and contrary feelings
8. vacillation — h. rise in the air (as by magic or illusion)

9. ambivalence — i. pretend
10. oscillation — j. a lightening; a making less severe

Key: 1–f, 2–i, 3–a, 4–j, 5–h, 6–b, 7–c, 8–e, 9–g, 10–d

Can you work with the words? (II)

1. dissimulate — a. pretence of ignorance
2. dissemblance — b. a rising and floating in air
3. alleviate — c. having simultaneous and contrary feelings

4. levitation — d. tending to swing back and forth in indecision

5. vacillatory — e. to swing back and forth like a pendulum

6. ambivalent — f. to hide real feelings by pretending opposite feelings

7. oscillate — g. tending to ease (pain, burdens, suffering, etc.)

Key: 1–f, 2–a, 3–g, 4–b, 5–d, 6–c, 7–e

Do you understand the words?

1. simulated – genuine   SAME   OPPOSITE
2. dissimulate – pretend   SAME   OPPOSITE

3. dissemble – be truthful   SAME   OPPOSITE
4. intimation – hint   SAME   OPPOSITE
5. alleviation – reduction   SAME   OPPOSITE
6. levitate – sink   SAME   OPPOSITE
7. levity – flippancy   SAME   OPPOSITE
8. vacillation – decisiveness   SAME   OPPOSITE
9. ambivalent – confused   SAME   OPPOSITE
10. oscillate – sway   SAME   OPPOSITE

Key: 1–O, 2–S, 3–O, 4–S, 5–S, 6–O, 7–S, 8–O, 9–S, 10–S

Can you recall the words?

1. to swing back and forth	1.	O_____
2. feeling both ways at the same time (*adj.*)	2.	A_____
3. to conceal real feelings	3.	D_____
	or	D_____
4. pretence	4.	S_____
5. to pretend ignorance though knowing the facts	5.	D_____
6. joking; frivolity; flippancy	6.	L_____
7. indecisive	7.	V_____
	or	V_____
8. to rise in the air, as by illusion	8.	L_____
9. tending to ease (pain, etc.) (*adj.*)	9.	A_____
	or	A_____
10. a sharing of another's grief (*n.*)	10.	C_____

Key: 1–oscillate, 2–ambivalent, 3–dissimulate *or* dissemble,
4–simulation, 5–dissemble, 6–levity, 7–vacillatory *or*
vacillating, 8–levitate, 9–alleviate *or* alleviating,
10–commiseration

Chapter review

A.   Do you recognize the words?

1. Complete exhaustion:
    (a) synergism, (b) enervation, (c) negation
2. Co-operation in producing effects:
    (a) synergy, (b) castigation, (c) capitulation
3. Lop off the head of:
    (a) castigate, (b) capitulate, (c) decapitate
4. deny; render ineffective:
    (a) castigate, (b) negate, (c) recapitulate
5. stagnate:
    (a) intimate, (b) simulate, (c) vegetate
6. concealment of true feelings:
    (a) simulation, (b) dissimulation, (c) dissemblance
7. sympathy:
    (a) levity, (b) ambivalence, (c) commiseration
8. indecisiveness:
    (a) vacillation, (b) oscillation, (c) dissimulation
9. aware of contrary feelings:
    (a) alleviate, (b) dissimulating, (c) ambivalent

Key: 1–b, 2–a, 3–c, 4–b, 5–c, 6–b *and* c, 7–c, 8–a, 9–c

B.   Can you recognize roots?

Roots	Meaning	Example
1. *nervus*	_____	enervate
2. *ergon*	_____	energy
3. *nego*	_____	self-abnegation
4. *caput, capitis*	_____	decapitate
5. *capitulum*	_____	recapitulate
6. *vegeto*	_____	vegetate
7. *simulo*	_____	dissimulate
8. *similis*	_____	similarity
9. *levis*	_____	levity
10. *intimus*	_____	intimation
11. *miser*	_____	commiserate

12. *vacillo*	_____	vacillate
13. *ambi-*	_____	ambivalent
14. *oscillum*	_____	oscillate

Key: 1−nerve, 2−work, 3−deny, 4−head, 5−little head, chapter heading, 6−live and grow, 7−to copy, 8−like, similar, 9−light, 10−innermost, 11−wretched, 12−swing back and forth, 13−both, 14−a swing

Teaser questions for the amateur etymologist

We have previously met the Greek prefix *syn-*, together or with, in *ynonym* ('names together') and *sympathy* ('feeling with'), and again n this chapter in *synergism* ('working together').

Syn- is a most useful prefix to know. Like Latin *con-*, (together or with) and *ad-* (to, towards), the final letter changes depending on the first letter of the root to which it is attached. *Syn-* becomes *sym-* before *b,m* and *p*.

Can you construct some words using *syn-*, or *sym-*?

1. Etymologically, Jews are 'led together' in a house of worship (*agogos*, leading). Can you construct the word for this temple or place of worship?_____

2. There is a process by which dissimilar organisms live together (*bios*, life) in close association, each in some way helping, and getting help from, the other (like the shark and the pilot fish). What word, ending in −*sis*, designates such a process?_____
What would the adjective form be?_____

3. Using Greek *phone*, sound, write the word that etymologically refers to a musical composition in which the sounds of all instruments are in harmony together._____
Using the suffix −*ic*, write the adjectival form of this word:

4. Combine *sym-* with *metron*, measurement, to construct a word designating similarity of shape on both sides (i.e., 'measurement together'): _____
Write the adjectival form of this word:_____

5. *Syn-* plus *dromos*, a running, are the building blocks of a medical word designating a group of symptoms that occur (i.e., run) together in certain diseases. Can you work out the word?

6. The same *dromos,* a running, combines with Greek *hippos,* horse, to form a word referring to a place in ancient Greece in which horse and chariot races were run. The word?_____

7. *Hippos,* horse, plus Greek *potamos,* river, combine to form a word designating one of the three pachyderms we discussed in an earlier chapter. The word?_____

(Answers in Chapter 18.)

Picking your friends' brains

You can build your vocabulary, I have said, by increasing your familiarity with new ideas and by becoming alert to the new words you meet in your reading of magazines and books.

There is still another productive method, one that will be particularly applicable in view of all the new words you are learning from your study of these pages.

That method is *picking your friends' brains.*

Intelligent people are interested in words because words are symbols of ideas, and the person with an alert mind is always interested in ideas.

You may be amazed, if you have never tried it, to find that you can stir up an animated discussion by asking, in a social group that you attend, 'What does_____ mean?' (Use any word that particularly fascinates you.) Someone in the group is likely to know, and almost everyone will be willing to make a guess. From that point on, others in the group will ask questions about their own favourite words (most people do have favourites), or about words that they themselves have in some manner recently learned. As the discussion continues along these lines, you will be introduced to new words yourself, and if your friends have fairly good vocabularies you may strike a rich vein and come away with a large number of words to add to your vocabulary.

This method of picking your friends' brains is particularly fruitful because you will be learning not from a page of print (as in this book or as in your other reading) but from real people – the same sources that children use to increase their vocabularies at such prodigious rates. No learning is quite as effective as the learning that comes from other people – no information in print can ever be as vivid as information that comes from another human being. And so the words you pick up from your friends will have an amazingly strong appeal, will make a lasting impression on your mind.

Needless to say, your own rich vocabulary, now that you have come this far in the book, will make it possible for you to contribute to your friends' vocabulary as much as, if not more than, you take away – but since giving to others is one of the greatest sources of a feeling of self-worth, you can hardly complain about this extra dividend.

(End of Session 44)

Take this spelling test

Even in the most painstakingly edited of magazines, a silly little misspelling of a perfectly common word will occasionally appear. How the error eluded the collective and watchful eyes of the editor, the associate editor, the assistant editor, the typesetter, and the proofreader, no one will ever know — for practically every reader of the magazine spots it at once and writes an indignant letter, beginning: 'Didn't you ever go to school . . . ?'

Even if you went to school, you're going to have plenty of trouble spotting the one misspelt word in each group below. And not one of these words will be a demon like *sphygmomanometer* (a device for measuring blood pressure) or *piccalilli* (a highly seasoned relish), which no one would ever dare spell without first checking with a dictionary. On the contrary, every word will be of the common or garden variety that you might use every day in your social or business correspondence.

Nevertheless, you're letting yourself in for ten minutes of real trouble, for you will be working with fifty particularly difficult spelling words. So put on your thinking cap before you begin.

Half a dozen secondary school teachers who took this test were able to make an average score of only five proper choices. Can you do better? Six or seven right is *very good*, eight or nine right is *excellent*, and 100 per cent success marks you as an absolute expert in English spelling.

Tick the only misspelt word in each group.

A: 1−surprise, 2−disappear, 3−innoculate, 4−description,
   5−recommend

B: 1−privilege, 2−separate, 3−incidentally, 4−dissipate,
   5−occurence

C: 1–analize, 2–argument, 3–assistant, 4–comparative,
5–truly
D: 1–grammar, 2–drunkeness, 4–parallel, 4–sacrilegious,
5–conscience
E: 1–precede, 2–exceed, 3–accede, 4–procede, 5–concede
F: 1–pronunciation, 2–noticable, 3–desirable, 4–holiday,
5–anoint
G: 1–wierd, 2–seize, 3–achieve, 4–receive, 5–leisure
H: 1–superintendent, 2–persistent, 3–resistant, 4–insistent,
5–perseverence
I: 1–accessible, 2–permissible, 3–inimitable, 4–irresistable,
5–irritable
J: 1–pursue, 2–pastime, 3–kidnapped, 4–rhythmical,
5–exhillarate

Key: A-3 (inoculate), B-5 (occurrence), C-1 (analyse), D-2
(drunkenness), E-4 (proceed), F-2 (noticeable), G-1
(weird), H-5 (perseverance), I-4 (irresistible), J-5 (exhilarate)

16

HOW TO TALK ABOUT A VARIETY OF PERSONAL CHARACTERISTICS

(Sessions 45—46)

Teaser preview

What word, ending in -ous, describes someone who is:

- *fawning, servilely attentive, transparently self-ingratiating?*
- *nagging, dissatisfied, complaining?*
- *snobbish, haughtily contemptuous, arrogant?*
- *noisily troublesome, unmanageable?*
- *habitually short of cash?*
- *attentive and courteous to women?*
- *harmless*
- *fond of drink?*
- *pale, gaunt, haggard?*
- *melancholy, sorrowful?*

Session 45

There are thousands of English words that end in the letters *—ous* — a Latin suffix meaning *full of*.

The central theme about which the words in this chapter revolve is the idea of 'fullness' — and as you will shortly see, you can be full of compliance and servility; full of complaints; full of snobbery; full of noise; full of no money; full of horsemanship; full of harmlessness; full of drink; full of deathly pallor; and full of sorrows.

For each of these ideas English has a word — and the person with a rich vocabulary knows the exact word to describe what someone is full of.

Ideas

1. Compliance

The Latin root *sequor* means *to follow* — and those who follow rather than lead are usually in a menial, subordinate, or inferior position. People who engage in certain fields of endeavour — waiters, clerks, and servants, for example — are forced, often contrary to their natural temperaments, to act in an excessively courteous, pleasant, obliging, even subservient and humble manner. They must follow the lead of their customers or employers, bending their own wills according to the desires of those they serve. They are, etymologically, *full of following after*, or —

obsequious

Related Words:

1. *obsequies* — In a funeral cortege, the mourners *follow after* the corpse. Hence, *obsequies* are the burial ceremonies, the funeral rites.
2. *subsequent* — A *subsequent* letter, paragraph, time, etc. is one that *follows* another.
3. *sequel* — A *sequel* may be a literary work, such as a novel, or a film that *follows* another, continuing the same subject, dealing with the same people or village, etc. or it may be an occurrence that grows out of or *follows* another, as in, 'Just wait until you hear the *sequel* to the story!'
4. *sequence* — In order, one item *following* another, as in, 'The *sequence* of events of the next few days left him breathless.'

Any other word containing the root *sequ-* is likely to have some relationship to the idea of *following*.

2.   Complaints

The Latin root *queror* means *to complain* — and anyone full of complaints, constantly nagging, harping, fretful, petulant, whining, never satisfied, may accordingly be called —

querulous

3.   Snobbery

The Latin root *cilium* means *eyelid; super* means *above;* and above the eyelid, as anyone can plainly see, is the eyebrow. Now there are certain obnoxious people who go around raising their eyebrows in contempt, disdain, and sneering arrogance at ordinary mortals like you and me. Such contemptuous, sneering, overbearingly conceited people are called —

supercilious

4.   Noise

The Latin root *strepo* means *to make a noise.* Anyone who is unruly, boisterous, resistant to authority, unmanageable — and in a noisy, troublesome manner — is

obstreperous

5.   Moneyless

The Latin root *pecus* means *cattle* — and at one time in human history a person's wealth was measured not by stocks and shares buy by stocks of domestic animals, which was a lot more logical, since you get milk and leather and meat from cattle — true wealth — and all you get from the stock market is a headache.

Someone who had lots of *pecus*, then, was rich — someone without *pecus* was indigent, destitute, 'broke'. And so today we call someone who is habitually without funds, who seems generally to be full of a complete lack of money —

impecunious

This word is not a synonym of *indigent, destitute,* or *poverty-stricken;* it does not necessarily imply living in reduced circumstances or want, but quite simply short of cash — habitually.

Related word:

1. *pecuniary* — pertaining to money, as in, a *pecuniary* consideration, *pecuniary* affairs, etc.

6.   Horses

The French word *cheval* means *horse;* and in medieval times only gentlemen and knights rode on horses — common people walked. Traditionally (but not, I understand, actually) knights were courteous to women, attentive to female desires, and self-sacrificing when their own interests came in conflict with those of the fair sex. Hence, we call a modern man who has a knightly attitude to women —

chivalrous

Related words:

(*Cheval*, horse, comes from Latin *caballus,* an inferior horse. *Caballus* is found in English words in the spelling *caval-*.)

1. *cavalcade* — A procession of persons on horseback, as in a parade.

2. *cavalier* — As a noun, a *cavalier* was once a mounted soldier. As an adjective, *cavalier* describes actions and attitudes that are haughty, unmindful of others' feelings, too offhand, such attrib-

utes often being associated with people in power (the military being one of the powers-that-be). Thus, 'He answered in a *cavalier* manner' would signify that he was arrogant in his answer, as if the questioner were being a little too familiar with him. Or, 'After the *cavalier* treatment I received, I never wished to return', signifying that I was pretty much made to feel unimportant and inferior. Or, 'After her *cavalier* refusal, I'll never invite her to another party', signifying that the refusal was, perhaps, curt, offhand, without any attempt at apology or courtesy.

3. *cavalry* – The mounted, or 'horsed' part of an army.

4. *chivalry* – Noun form of *chivalrous*. Can you write the alternate noun form ending in *–ness?* _____

5. *chivalric* – Less commonly used adjectival form, identical in meaning to *chivalrous*.

Another Latin root for *horse*, as you know, is *equus*, found in words we have already discussed:

1. *equestrian* – A horseman.

2. *equestrienne* – A horsewoman.

3. *equine* – Horselike.

7.   No harm done

The Latin root *noceo* means to *injure;* someone who need cause you no fear, so harmless is that person, so unable to interfere, so unlikely to get you into trouble, is called –

innocuous

Related words:

1. *innocent* – Not guilty of crime or injury.

2. *noxious* – Harmful, poisonous; unwholesome.

8.   alcoholic

The Latin root *bibo* means *to drink;* and one who is generally found propping up the bar, who likes to tipple beyond the point of sobriety – who, in short, has an overfondness for drinks with a pronounced alcoholic content, is called, usually humorously –

bibulous

Related words:

1. *imbibe* – To drink in, soak up, absorb. If we use this verb without specifying what is drunk, as in, 'He likes to *imbibe*,' the implication, of course, is always alcohol; but *imbibe* may also be used in patterns like '*imbibe* learning' or 'In early infancy she *imbibed* a respect for her parents.'

2. *bib* – Upper part of an apron, or an apronlike napkin tied around a child's neck. In either case, the *bib* prevents what is drunk (or eaten) from spilling over, or dribbling down, the wearer's clothing.

9.   Like death itself

The Latin root *cado* means *to fall* – one's final fall is of course always in death, and so someone who looks like a corpse (figuratively speaking), who is pale, gaunt, thin, haggard, with sunken eyes and wasted limbs, in other words the extreme opposite of the picture of glowing health, is called –

cadaverous

Related words:

1. *cadaver* – A corpse, literally, especially one used for surgical dissection.

2. *decadent* – Etymologically, '*falling down*' (*de-* is a prefix one meaning of which is *down*, as in *descend*, climb down; *decline*, turn down; etc.). If something is in a *decadent* state, it is deteriorating, becoming corrupt or demoralized. *Decadence* is a state of decay. Generally *decadent* and *decadence* are used figuratively – they refer not to actual physical decay (as of a dead body), but to moral or spiritual decay.

10.   Pain and misery

The Latin root *doleo* means to *suffer or grieve* – one who is mournful and sad, whose melancholy comes from physical pain or mental distress, who seems to be suffering or grieving, is called –

dolorous

Related words:

1. *dolour* – A poetic synonym of *grief*.

2. *doleful* – A word referring somewhat humorously to exaggerated dismalness, sadness, or dreariness.

3. *condole* – Etymologically, to suffer or grieve with (Latin *con-*, with, together). *Condole* is a somewhat less commonly used synonym of *commiserate*, a verb we discussed in Chapter 15. The noun *condolence* is much more frequently heard than the verb, as in, 'Let me offer you my *condolences*', usually said to someone mourning the death of a friend or relative. You have heard of *condolence* cards, and no doubt have sent your share of them. When you *condole* with somebody who has sustained a loss, usually by death, you are saying, in effect, 'I am suffering or grieving with you'.

Review of etymology

Prefix, Root, Suffix	Meaning	English Word
1. *sequor*	to follow	_____
2. *queror*	to complain	_____
3. *cilium*	eyelid	_____
4. *super*	above	_____
5. *strepo*	to make a noise	_____
6. *pecus*	cattle	_____
7. −*ary*	adjective suffix	_____
8. *im-* (*in-*)	negative prefix	_____
9. *cheval*	horse	_____
10. *caballus* (*caval-*)	inferior horse	_____
11. −*ous*	adjective suffix	_____
12. −*ic*	adjective suffix	_____
13. *equus*	horse	_____
14. −*ine*	like, similar to, characteristic of	_____
15. *bibo*	to drink	_____
16. *im-* (*in-*)	in	_____
17. *cado*	to fall	_____
18. *de-*	down	_____
19. −*ent*	adjective suffix	_____
20. −*ence*	noun suffix	_____
21. *con-*	with, together	_____

Word Power Made Easy

Using the words

A. The basic words

Can you pronounce the words?

1. *obsequious* — əb-SEEK'-wi-əs
2. *querulous* — KWER'-yŏŏ-ləs *or* KWER'-ŏŏ-ləs
3. *supercilious* — sōō-pə-SIL'-i-əs
4. *obstreperous* — əb-STREP'-ər-əs
5. *impecunious* — im'-pi-KYŌŌ'-ni-əs
6. *chivalrous* — SHIV'-əl-rəs
7. *innocuous* — i-NOK'-yŏŏ-əs
8. *bibulous* — BIB'-yŏŏ-ləs
9. *cadaverous* — kə-DAV'-ər-əs
10. *dolorous* — DOL'-ər-əs

Can you work with the words? (I)

1. obsequious	a.	snobbish
2. querulous	b.	harmless
3. supercilious	c.	gaunt
4. obstreperous	d.	short of funds
5. impecunious	e.	fawning; excessively, ingratiatingly, polite
6. chivalrous	f.	sorrowful
7. innocuous	g.	addicted to drink
8. bibulous	h.	courteous to women
9. cadaverous	i.	complaining
10. dolorous	j.	unmanageable

Key: 1–e, 2–i, 3–a, 4–j, 5–d, 6–h, 7–b, 8–g, 9–c, 10–f

Can you work with the words? (II)

Match each word in the first column with one from the second column that is *opposite* in meaning.

1. obsequious	a.	content; uncomplaining; satisifed
2. querulous	b.	affluent
3. supercilious	c.	healthy
4. obstreperous	d.	rude
5. impecunious	e.	sober
6. chivalrous	f.	dangerous
7. innocuous	g.	humble
8. bibulous	h.	misogynous
9. cadaverous	i.	happy; cheerful
10. dolorous	j.	quiet

Key: 1–d, 2–a, 3–g, 4–j, 5–b, 6–h, 7–f, 8–e, 9–c, 10–i

Do you understand the words?

1. Do *obsequious* people usually command our respect	YES	NO
2. Are *querulous* people satisfied?	YES	NO
3. Are *supercilivus* people usually popular?	YES	NO
4. Is a person of affluence *impecunious*?	YES	NO
5. Do some women like *chivalrous* men?	YES	NO
6. Are *innocuous* people dangerous?	YES	NO
7. Is a *bibulous* character a teetotaler?	YES	NO
8. Is a *cadaverous* – looking individual the picture of health?	YES	NO
9. Is a *dolorous* attitude characteristic of jovial people?	YES	NO
10. Is an *obstreperous* child difficult to manage?	YES	NO

Key: 1–no, 2–no, 3–no, 4–no, 5–yes, 6–no, 7–no, 8–no, 9–no, 10–yes

Can you recall the words?

1. sorrowful   1. D_____

2. servilely attentive; overly polite
    2. O_____

3. haggard; gaunt; pale
    3. C_____

4. complaining; whining
    4. Q_____

5. addicted to alcohol; likely to drink past the point of sobriety
    5. B_____

6. arrogant; haughty
    6. S_____

7. harmless
    7. I_____

8. noisily unmanageable
    8. O_____

9. attentive and courteous to women
    9. C_____

10. short of money; without funds
    10. I_____

Key: 1—dolorous, 2—obsequious, 3—cadaverous, 4—querulous, 5—bibulous, 6—supercilious, 7—innocuous, 8—obstreperous, 9—chivalrous, 10—impecunious

(End of Session 45)

Session 46

B. Related words

Can you pronounce the words? (I)

1. *obsequies*   OB'-si-kwiz
2. *subsequent*   SUB'-si-kwənt
3. *sequel*   SEE'-kwəl
4. *sequence*   SEE'-kwəns
5. *pecuniary*   pi-KYŌŌ-ni-ər'-i
6. *noxious*   NOK'-shəs
7. *imbibe*   im-BĪB'
8. *dolour*   DŌ-lə
9. *doleful*   DŌL'-fəl
10. *cavalcade*   KAV'-əl-kayd'
11. *cavalier* (*adj.*)   kav-ə-LI'-ə

Can you pronounce the words? (II)

1. *cavalry*   KAV'-əl-ri
2. *chivalry*   SHIV'-əl-ri
3. *chivalric*   SHIV'-əl-rik
4. *condole*   kən-DŌL'
5. *condolence*   kən-DŌ'-ləns
6. *equestrian*   i-KWES'-tri-ən
7. *equestrienne*   i-KWES'-tree-en
8. *equine*   E'-kwīn'
9. *cadaver*   kə-DAV'-ər *or* kə-DAY'-vər
10. *decadent*   DEK'-ə-dənt

11. *decadence*   DEK'-ə-dəns

Can you work with the words?

1. obsequies		a.	proper order
2. subsequent		b.	drink; absorb; take in
3. sequel		c.	harmful, poisonous
4. sequence		d.	pain, sorrow (*poetic*)
5. pecuniary		e.	coming late or afterwards
6. noxious		f.	procession of mounted riders
7. imbibe		g.	offhand, haughty
8. dolour		h.	a following event or literary work
9. doleful		i.	horsewoman
10. cavalcade		j.	pertaining to money
11. cavalier (*adj.*)		k.	mounted military division; soldiers on horseback
12. cavalry		l.	funeral rites
13. equestrian		m.	exaggeratedly sorrowful
14. equestrienne		n.	horselike
15. equine		o.	horseman
16. cadaver		p.	spiritual decline
17. decadent		q.	morally decaying
18. decadence		r.	corpse
19. chivalry		s.	expression of sympathy
20. condolence		t.	gallant courtesy to women

Key: 1–l, 2–e, 3–h, 4–a, 5–j, 6–c, 7–b, 8–d, 9–m, 10–f, 11–g, 12–k, 13–o, 14–i, 15–n, 16–r, 17–q, 18–p, 19–t, 20–s

Do you understand the words? (I)

1. Are speeches usually made during *obsequies*?	YES	NO
2. Is *Rocky II* a *sequel* to the film *Rocky*?	YES	NO
3. Are these numbers in *sequence*: 5, 6, 7, 8, 9, 10, 11?	YES	NO

4. Do banks often handle the *pecuniary*   YES   NO
details of an estate?

5. Is arsenic a *noxious* chemical?   YES   NO

6. Do children sometimes *imbibe*   YES   NO
wisdom from their parents?

7. If a song is sung in tones of *dolour*,   YES   NO
is it a happy song?

8. Is a *doleful* countenance a happy   YES   NO
one?

9. Does a *cavalcade* contain horses?   YES   NO

10. Does a *cavalier* attitude show a spirit   YES   NO
of humility?

Key: 1—yes, 2—no, 3—yes, 4—yes, 5—yes, 6—yes, 7—no, 8—no,
9—yes, 10—no

Do you understand the words? (II)

1. Is a *cavalry* officer usually a good   YES   NO
horseman?

2. Would an *equestrian* statue of   YES   NO
General Grant show him with or on
a horse?

3. Is an *equestrienne* a man?   YES   NO

4. Do humans possess many *equine*   YES   NO
characteristics?

5. Is a *cadaver* alive?   YES   NO

6. Is an iconoclast likely to consider   YES   NO
religion a *decadent* institution?

7. Is *decadence* a desirable quality?   YES   NO

8. Is *chivalry* dead?   YES   NO

9. Is it appropriate to *condole* with   YES   NO
someone who has suffered a loss
through death?

10. Are *condolences* appropriate at a   YES   NO
wedding ceremony?

Key: 1–yes, 2–yes, 3–no, 4–no, 5–no, 6–yes, 7–no, 8–yes,
         or no, depending on your point of view, 9–yes, 10–no
         (unless you're misogamous)

Do you understand the words? (III)

1. obsequies – rites	SAME	OPPOSITE
2. subsequent – preceding	SAME	OPPOSITE
3. pecuniary – financial	SAME	OPPOSITE
4. sequence – order	SAME	OPPOSITE
5. noxious – harmful	SAME	OPPOSITE
6. imbibe – drink	SAME	OPPOSITE
7. dolour – delight	SAME	OPPOSITE
8. doleful – merry	SAME	OPPOSITE
9. cavalier – courteous	SAME	OPPOSITE
10. cadaver – corpse	SAME	OPPOSITE
11. decadent – resurgent	SAME	OPPOSITE
12. chivalry – gallantry to women	SAME	OPPOSITE
13. condolences – congratulations	SAME	OPPOSITE

Key: 1–S, 2–O, 3–S, 4–S, 5–S, 6–S, 7–O, 8–O, 9–O, 10–S,
         11–O, 12–S, 13–O

Can you recall the words?

1. harmful	1. N_____
2. a literary work or an event that follows another	2. S_____
3. drink in	3. I_____
4. poetic word for sorrow	4. D_____
5. burial ceremonies	5. O_____
6. horseman	6. E_____
7. horsewoman	7. E_____
8. horselike	8. E_____
9. following (*adj.*)	9. S_____
10. relating to money (*adj.*)	10. P_____
11. exaggeratedly sad	11. D_____

12. proper order   12. S_____
13. parade of mounted riders   13. C_____
14. offhand; unmindful of   14. C_____
     another's feelings
15. mounted soldiers   15. C_____
16. a corpse   16. C_____
17. morally deteriorating   17. D_____
     (*adj.*)
18. spiritual decay   18. D_____
19. expression of sympathy   19. C_____
20. gallantry to women   20. C_____

Key: 1–noxious, 2–sequel, 3–imbibe, 4–dolour, 5–obsequies, 6–equestrian, 7–equestrienne, 8–equine, 9–subsequent, 10–pecuniary, 11–doleful, 12–seqeunce,
13–cavalcade, 14–cavalier, 15–cavalry, 16–cadaver,
17–decadent, 18–decadence, 19–condolence, 20–chivalry *or* chivalrousness

Chapter review

A.   Do you recognize the words?

1. Excessively polite and fawning:
   (a) querulous, (b) obsequious, (c) supercilious
2. Noisily troublesome:
   (a) querulous, (b) impecunious, (c) obstreperous
3. Courteous and attentive to women:
   (a) querulous, (b) chivalrous, (c) supercilious
4. Complaining, nagging:
   (a) querulous, (b) supercilious, (c) innocuous
5. Haughtily disdainful:
   (a) supercilious, (b) bibulous, (c) dolorous
6. Gaunt, corpselike:
   (a) noxious, (b) cadaverous, (c) doleful
7. Highhanded:
   (a) supercilious, (b) cavalier, (c) decadent
8. Moral decay:
   (a) decadence, (b) obsequies, (c) sequence

9. Expression of sympathy:
(a) bibulousness, (b) dolefulness, (c) condolence
10. Courtesy to women:
(a) dolour, (b) chivalry, (c) decadence

Key: 1–b, 2–c, 3–b, 4–a, 5–a, 6–b, 7–b, 8–a, 9–c, 10–b

Can you recognize roots?

Root	Meaning	Example
1. *sequor*	_____	subsequent
2. *queror*	_____	querulous
3. *cilium*	_____	supercilious
4. *super*	_____	supervision
5. *strepo*	_____	obstreperous
6. *pecus*	_____	pecuniary
7. *cheval*	_____	chivalry
8. *caballus (caval-)*	_____	cavalier
9. *equus*	_____	equine
10. *cado*	_____	decadence

Key: 1–to follow, 2–to complain, 3–eyelid, 4–above, 5–to make a noise, 6–cattle, 7–horse, 8–(inferior) horse, 9–horse, 10–to fall

Teaser questions for the amateur etymologist

1. In logic, a conclusion not based on the evidence is called a *non sequitur;* by extension, the term is applied to any statement that appears to have no connection or relevance to what was said before. Knowing the root *sequor*, how would you define this term etymologically?_____

2. *Sequor*, like many other Latin verbs, has another form somewhat differently spelled. (Remember *verto, versus* and *loquor, locutus?*) The other form of *sequor* is *secutus*. Can you define the following words in terms of the root?
          (a) second: _____

(b) consecutive: _____

(c) persecute: _____

(d) prosecute: _____

3. Latin *super*, above or over, is used as a prefix in hundreds of English words. Can you work out the word starting with *super*-that fits each etymological definition?

(a) above others (in quality, position, etc.) _____

(b) above the surface; not in depth (*adj.*) _____

(c) (flowing) above what is necessary; more than needed (*adj.*) _____

(d) above (or beyond) the natural (*adj.*) _____

(e) to oversee; be in charge of (*v.*) _____

4. *Cado*, to fall, is found in the following English words (sometimes the root is spelled *-cid*). Can you define each word in terms of its etymological parts?

(a) cadence: _____

(b) occidental: _____

(c) deciduous: _____

(d) incident: _____

(e) accident: _____

(f) coincidence: _____

5. The negative prefix *in-* plus *doleo*, to suffer, forms an adjective that *etymologically* means *not suffering (pain)*, but *actually* means *idle; lazy; disliking effort or work*. Can you work out the English word?_____

Can you write the noun form?_____

6. What does the feminine name Dolores mean etymologically?

_____

(End of Session 46)

Another check on your spelling

In each line you will find four words – one of them purposely, subtly, and perhaps unexpectedly misspelt. It's up to you to tick the single error. If you can come out on top at least fifteen times out of twenty, you're probably a better speller than you realize.

1. (a) alright, (b) coolly, (c) supersede, (d) disappear
2. (a) inoculate, (b) definately, (c) irresistible, (d) recommend
3. (a) incidentally, (b) dissipate, (c) seperate, (d) balloon
4. (a) argument, (b) ecstasy, (c) occurrance, (d) analyse
5. (a) sacrilegious, (b) weird, (c) pronunciation, (d) repitition
6. (a) drunkeness, (b) embarrassment, (c) weird, (d) irritable
7. (a) noticeable, (b) superintendant, (c) absence,
   (d) development
8. (a) vicious, (b) conscience, (c) panicy, (d) amount
9. (a) accessible, (b) pursue, (c) exhilarate, (d) insistant
10. (a) naïveté, (b) necessary, (c) catagory, (d) professor
11. (a) rhythmical, (b) sergeant, (c) vaccuum, (d) assassin
12. (a) benefitted, (b) allotted, (c) corroborate, (d) despair
13. (a) diphtheria, (b) grandeur, (c) rediculous, (d) license (v.)
14. (a) tranquillity, (b) symmetry, (c) occassionally, (d) privilege
15. (a) tarriff, (b) tyranny, (c) battalion, (d) archipelago
16. (a) bicycle, (b) geneology, (c) liquefy, (d) bettor
17. (a) defence, (b) batchelor, (c) stupefy, (d) parallel
18. (a) whisky, (b) likable, (c) bookkeeper, (d) accomodate
19. (a) comparitive, (b) mayonnaise, (c) indispensable,
    (d) dexterous
20. (a) dictionary, (b) cantaloupe, (c) existance, (d) ukulele

Key: 1–a (all right), 2–b (definitely), 3–c (separate), 4–c (occurrence), 5–d (repetition), 6–a (drunkenness), 7–b (superintendent), 8–c (panicky), 9–d (insistent), 10–c (category), 11–c (vacuum), 12–a (benefited), 13–c (ridiculous), 14–c (occasionally), 15–a (tariff), 16–b (genealogy), 17–b (bachelor), 18–d (accommodate), 19–a (comparative), 20–c (existence)

17

HOW TO CHECK YOUR PROGRESS

Comprehensive Test III

Session 47

I—Etymology

Root	Meaning	Example
1. *fluo*	_____	affluent
2. *pheme*	_____	euphemism
3. *platys*	_____	platitude
4. *felis*	_____	feline
5. *piscis*	_____	piscine
6. *nostos*	_____	nostalgia
7. *kakos*	_____	cacophony
8. *carnis*	_____	carnivorous
9. *voro*	_____	voracious
10. *omnis*	_____	omnivorous

12. *ubique*	_____	ubiquity
13. *lupus*	_____	lupine
14. *doleo*	_____	dolorous
15. *porcus*	_____	porcine
16. *thanatos*	_____	euthanasia
17. *canis*	_____	canine
18. *vulpus*	_____	vulpine
19. *algos*	_____	nostalgic
20. *odyne*	_____	anodyne
21. *logos*	_____	eulogy
22. *sciens, scientis*	_____	omniscient
23. *ursus*	_____	ursine
24. *phone*	_____	euphonious
25. *penuria*	_____	penury

II—More etymology

Root, Prefix	Meaning	Example
1. *nervus*	_____	enervate
2. *ergon*	_____	energy
3. *nego*	_____	negation
4. *caput, capitis*	_____	decapitate
5. *capitulum*	_____	recapitulate
6. *vegeto*	_____	vegetate
7. *simulo*	_____	simulate
8. *similis*	_____	similarity
9. *levis*	_____	alleviate
10. *intimus*	_____	intimate (*v.*)
11. *miser*	_____	commiserate
12. *vacillo*	_____	vacillate
13. *ambi-*	_____	ambivalent
14. *oscillum*	_____	oscillate
15. *sequor, secutus*	_____	obsequious
16. *queror*	_____	querulous
17. *cilium*	_____	supercilious
18. *super-*	_____	superior
19. *strepo*	_____	obstreperous
20. *pecus*	_____	impecunious
21. *equus*	_____	equine
22. *caballus (caval-)*	_____	cavalier

23. *loquor, locutus*   _____   circumlocution
24. *cado*   _____   decadence
25. *vanesco*   _____   evanescent

III—Same or opposite?

1. penury – affluence	SAME	OPPOSITE
2. vicarious – secondhand	SAME	OPPOSITE
3. ephemeral – evanescent	SAME	OPPOSITE
4. badinage – persiflage	SAME	OPPOSITE
5. cacophony – euphony	SAME	OPPOSITE
6. clandestine – surreptitious	SAME	OPPOSITE
7. parsimonious – extravagant	SAME	OPPOSITE
8. indigent – opulent	SAME	OPPOSITE
9. destitute – impecunious	SAME	OPPOSITE
10. euphemistic – indirect	SAME	OPPOSITE
11. cliché – bromide	SAME	OPPOSITE
12. platitudinous – original	SAME	OPPOSITE
13. voracious – gluttonous	SAME	OPPOSITE
14. omniscient – ignorant	SAME	OPPOSITE
15. omnipresent – ubiquitous	SAME	OPPOSITE
16. carnal – libidinous	SAME	OPPOSITE
17. carnage – slaughter	SAME	OPPOSITE
18. enervated – exhilarated	SAME	OPPOSITE
19. castigate – condone	SAME	OPPOSITE
20. simulate – pretend	SAME	OPPOSITE

IV—Matching

Words	Definitions
1. alleviating	a. excessively polite or servile
2. cavalier (*adj.*)	b. gaunt, corpselike
3. vacillating	c. noisy
4. obsequious	d. poisonous
5. querulous	e. highhanded
6. obstreperous	f. sad
7. innocuous	g. nagging; complaining
8. cadaverous	h. harmless
9. dolorous	i. soothing
10. noxious	j. constantly changing one's mind

V—More matching

1. condolence
2. decadent
3. levity
4. levitation
5. surreptitious
6. cacophony
7. reincarnation
8. omnivorous
9. impotence
10. bovine

a. a rising into the air
b. harsh sound
c. powerlessness
d. a return to life in a new form
e. devouring all; eating everything
f. expression of sympathy
g. cowlike; phlegmatic; stolid
h. morally deteriorating
i. joking
j. stealthy; secret

VI—Recall a word

1. lionlike
2. doglike
3. catlike
4. piglike
5. foxlike
6. bearlike
7. horselike
8. all-powerful
9. in the flesh
10. to stagnate
11. secret
12. meat-eating (*adj.*)
13. lasting a very short time
14. stingy; tight-fisted

15. feeling contradictory ways at the same time (*adj.*)
16. speech of praise
17. a feeling of well-being, both physical and emotional
18. statement intended to allay pain or anxiety
19. mercy death
20. science of speech sounds
21. all-powerful

1. L_____
2. C_____
3. F_____
4. P_____
5. V_____
6. U_____
7. E_____
8. O_____
9. I_____
10. V_____
11. C_____
12. C_____
13. E_____
14. P_____
    or P_____
15. _____

16. E_____
17. E_____

18. A_____

19. E_____
20. P_____
21. O_____

22. to give in; to stop   22. C_____
    resisting

23. a working together for   23. S_____
    greater effect   or S_____

24. to behead   24. D_____

25. relating to, pertaining to, 25. P_____
    or involving money (*adj.*)

26. harmless   26. I_____

27. tending to drink a lot   27. B_____
    (*adj.*)

28. to express sympathy; to   28. C_____
    share suffering, pain, or or C_____
    grief (with)

29. snobbish; contemptuous;   29. S_____
    haughty; arrogant

30. mounted soldiers   30. C_____

Key: A correct answer counts one point. Score your points for
        each part of the test, then add for a total.

I

1–to flow, 2–voice, 3–flat, broad, 4–cat, 5–fish, 6–a return,
7–harsh, bad, ugly, 8–flesh, 9–to devour, 10–all, 11–powerful,
12–everywhere, 13–wolf, 14–to suffer, grieve, 15–pig,
16–death, 17–dog, 18–fox, 19–pain, 20–pain, 21–word,
speech, 22–knowing, 23–bear, 24–sound, 25–want, neediness
        Your score:_____

II

1–nerve, 2–work, 3–to deny, 4–head, 5–little head, chapter
heading, 6–to live and grow, 7–to copy, 8–like, similar, 9–light,
10–innermost, 11–wretched, 12–to swing back and forth,
13–both, 14–a swing, 15–to follow, 16–to complain, 17–eyelid,
18–above, 19–to make a noise, 20–cattle, 21–horse, 22–(inferi-
or) horse, 23–to speak, 24–to fall, 25–to vanish
        Your score:_____

III

1–O, 2–S, 3–S, 4–S, 5–O, 6–S, 7–O, 8–O, 9–S, 10–S, 11–S,
12–O, 13–S, 14–O, 15–S, 16–S, 17–S, 18–O, 19–O, 20–S
        Your score:_____

IV

1–i, 2–e, 3–j, 4–a, 5–g, 6–c, 7–h, 8–b, 9–f, 10–d

       Your score:_____

V

1–f, 2–h, 3–i, 4–a, 5–j, 6–b, 7–d, 8–e, 9–c, 10–g

       Your score:_____

VI

1–leonine, 2–canine, 3–feline, 4–porcine, 5–vulpine, 6–ursine, 7–equine, 8–omnipotent, 9–incarnate, 10–vegetate, 11–clandestine, 12–carnivorous, 13–ephemeral, 14–penurious *or* parsimonious, 15–ambivalent, 16–eulogy, 17–euphoria, 18–anodyne, 19–euthanasia, 20–phonetics, 21–omnipotent, 22–capitulate, 23–synergism *or* synergy, 24–decapitate, 25–pecuniary, 26–innocuous, 27–bibulous, 28–condole *or* commiserate, 29–supercilious, 30–cavalry

       Your score:_____

       Your total score:_____

Significance of Your Total Score:

100–120: Masterly

80–99: Good

65–79: Average

50–64: Barely acceptable

35–49: Poor

0–34: Terrible!

Record your score in the appropriate space below as well as your scores from Chapters 8 and 13. You will then have a comparison chart of all three achievement tests.

      Scores

TEST I (Chapter 8):   _____   out of 120.

TEST II (Chapter 13):   _____   out of 120.

TEST III (Chapter 17):   _____   out of 120.

(End of Session 47)

18

HOW TO CHECK YOUR STANDING AS AN AMATEUR ETYMOLOGIST

(Answers to Teaser Questions in Chapters 3–7, 9–12, and 14–16)

Chapter 3:

1. *Anthropocentric* (an'-thrə-pə-SEN'-trik *or* an'-thrə-pō-SEN'-trik), an adjective built on *anthropos*, mankind; Greek *kentron*, centre, and the adjective suffix *–ic*, describes thinking, assumptions, reasoning, etc. that see mankind as the central fact, or ultimate aim, of the universe. The noun forms are either *anthropocentrism* (an'-thrə-pə-SEN'-triz-əm *or* an'-thrə-pō-SEN'-triz-əm) or *anthropocentricity* (an'-thrə-pō'-sən-TRIS'-ə-ti).

2. *Andromania* (an'-drō-MAY'-ni-ə), a combination of *andros*, man (male), plus *mania*, madness, signifies an obsession with males. Person: *andromaniac*, one who is mad about men; adjective: *andromaniacal* (an'-drō-mə-NI'-ə-kəl).

3. *Gynandrous* (jī-NAN''-drəs), combining *gyne*, woman, with *andros*, man (male), describes:

a. plants in which the male and female organs are united in the same column; *or*

b. people who physically have both male and female sexual organs, often one or both in rudimentary form; *or*

c. (*a more recent meaning*) people who exhibit, or are willing to own up to, the male *and* female *emotional* characteristics that everyone possesses.

The word may have the roots in reverse, becoming *androgynous* (an-DROJ'-ə-nəs), with all three meanings identical to those of *gynandrous*.

Hermaphroditic (hə-maf'-rə-DIT'–ik), a combination of *Hermes*, the Greek god who served as messenger or herald (in Roman mythology, this god was known as *Mercury*, and is conventionally pictured with wings on his heels), and *Aphrodite*, the Greek goddess of love and beauty (in Roman mythology, *Venus*), has either of the first two meanings of *gynandrous*.

The noun form of *gynandrous* is *gynandry* (jī-NAN'-dri); of *androgynous*, *androgyny* (an-DROJ'-ə-ni); of *hermaphroditic*, *hermaphroditism* (hər-MAF'-rə-dī'-tiz-əm).

The individual plant is an *androgyne* (AN'-drə-jīn); plant or person, a *hermaphrodite* (hər-MAF'-rə-dīt').

4. *Monomania* (mon-ō-MAY'-ni-ə), combining *monos*, one, and *mania*, madness, is an obsession with one thing, or obsessiveness in one area. Person: *monomaniac;* adjective: *monomaniacal* (mon'-ō-mə-NI'-ə-kəl).

5. A *misandrist* (mis-AN'-drist), combining *misein*, to hate, with *andros*, man (male), hates men. Noun: *misandry* (mis-AN'-dri). Adjective: *misandrous* (mis-AN'-drəs).

Check your learning

Root	Meaning	Example
1. *anthropos*	_____	anthropocentric
2. *kentron*	_____	anthropocentrism
3. *andros*	_____	andromania
4. *mania*	_____	andromaniac
5. *gyne*	_____	gynandrous
6. *Hermes*	_____	hermaphrodite
7. *Aphrodite*	_____	hermaphroditic
8. *monos*	_____	monomania
9. *misein*	_____	misandry

Key: 1—mankind, 2—centre, 3—man (male), 4—madness, 5—woman, 6—Hermes, the messenger of the gods, 7—Aphrodite, goddess of love and beauty, 8—one, 9—to hate

Chapter 4:

1. *Paedodontics* (pee'-də-DON'-tiks) is the speciality of child dentistry – *paidos*, child, plus *odontos*, tooth. Specialist: *paedodontist*. Adjective: *paedodontic*.

2. *Cardialgia* (kah'-di-AL'-ji-ə), heart pain – *kardia*, heart, plus *algos*, pain.

3. *Odontalgia* (ō'-don-TAL'-ji-ə), toothache.

4. *Nostalgia* (nos-TAL'-ji-ə *or* nos-TAL'-ji-ə). Adjective: *nostalgic*.

Check your learning

Prefix, Root	Meaning	Example
1. *padios (paed-)*	_____	paedodontics
2. *kardia*	_____	cardialgia
3. *algos*	_____	odontalgia
4. *odontos*	_____	paedodontist
5. *nostos*	_____	nostalgia

Key: 1–child, 2–heart, 3–pain, 4–tooth, 5–a return

Chapter 5:

1. Eighty to eighty-nine years old. From Latin *octoginta*, eighty. People of other ages are as follows:
(a) 50–59: *quinquagenarian* (kwin'-kwə-ji-NAIR'-i-ən)
(b) 60–69: *sexagenarian* (seks'-ə-ji-NAIR'-i-ən)
(c) 70–79: *septuagenarian* (sep'-tyoŏ-ə-ji-NAIR'-i-ən)
(d) 90–99: *nonagenarian* (nōn-ə-ji-NAIR'-i-ən)

2. *Cacophony* (kə-KOF'-ə-ni). Adjective: *cacophonous* (kə-KOF'-ə-nəs).

3. *Cacopygian* (kak'-ə-PIJ'-i-ən).

4. *Telescope* (*tele-* plus *skopein*, to view); *telephone; television*.

Check your learning

Prefix, Root	Meaning	Example
1. *octoginta*	_____	octogenarian
2. *quinquaginta*	_____	quinquagenarian
3. *sexaginta*	_____	sexagenarian

4. *septuaginta*	_____	septuagenarian
5. *nonaginta*	_____	nonagenarian
6. *centum*	_____	centenarian
7. *kakos*	_____	cacophony
8. *phone*	_____	cacophonous
9. *pyge*	_____	cacopygian
10. *tele-*	_____	television
11. *shopein*	_____	telescope

Key: 1–eighty, 2–fifty, 3–sixty, 4–seventy, 5–ninety, 6–one hundred, 7–ugly, harsh, bad, 8–sound, 9–buttock, 10–distance, from afar, 11–to view

Chapter 6:

1. *Sophisticated* (sə-FIS'-ti-kay'-tid). The verb is *sophisticate*, the noun *sophistication*. One who is worldly-wise is a *sophisticate* (sə-FIS'-ti-kət *or* sə-FIS'-ti-kayt).

Sophisticated has in recent years taken on the added meaning of *highly developed, nature, or complicated; appealing to a mature intellect;* or *aware and knowledgeable*. Examples: *sophisticated* machinery, electronic equipment; a *sophisticated* approach; a *sophisticated* audience, group, staff, faculty, etc.

2. One who is obsessed with books, especially with collecting books.

3. (a) speaking one language, (b) speaking two languages, (c) speaking three languages.

Multilingual (*multus*, many, plus *lingua*) – speaking many languages.

· A *linguist* is one who is fluent in many languages, or else an expert in *linguistics* (or both).

Multus, as indicated, means *many*, as in *multitude, multiply, multiple, multicoloured, multifarious, multilateral*, etc., etc.

4. (a) France, (b) Russia, (c) Spain, (d) Germany, (e) Japan, (f) China.

5. (a) *androphile*, (b) *gynaephile* (or *philogynist*), (c) *zoophile*, (d) *botanophile*.

But *paedophilia* (pee'-də-FIL'-i-ə) is another story. A *paedophile* or *paedophiliac* sexually molests young children.

Check your learning

Prefix, Root	Meaning	Example
1. *biblion*	_____	bibliomaniac
2. *mania*	_____	bibliomania
3. *lingua*	_____	linguist
4. *monos*	_____	monolingual
5. *bi-*	_____	bilingual
6. *tri-*	_____	trilingual
7. *multus*	_____	multilingual
8. *Franco-*	_____	Francophile
9. *Russo-*	_____	Russophile
10. *Hispano-*	_____	Hispanophile
11. *Germano-*	_____	Germanophile
12. *Nippono-*	_____	Nipponophile
13. *Sino-*	_____	Sinophile
14. *andros*	_____	androphile
15. *gyne*	_____	gynaephile
16. *philein*	_____	philogynist
17. *paidos (paed-)*	_____	paedophile
18. *zoion*	_____	zoophile
19. *botane*	_____	botanophile

Key: 1–book,   2–madness,   3–tongue,   4–one,   5–two,
6–three,   7–many,   8–France,   9–Russia,   10–Spain,
11–Germany,   12–Japan,   13–China,   14–man (male),
15–woman,   16–to love,   17–child,   18–animal,   19–plant

Chapter 7:

1. A *notable* is someone well-*known*.

2. To *notify* is, etymologically, to make *known* – *notus* + *-fy*, a derivation of *facio*, to make.

Notice, as a noun, is what makes something *known; to notice*, as a verb, is to observe (something or someone) so that it, he, or she becomes *known* to the observer.

–Fy, as a verb suffix, means *to make*. So *simplify* is to make simple, *clarify*, to make clear; *liquefy*, to make liquid; *putrefy*, to make (or become) rotten or putrid; *stupefy*, to make stupid, or dumb, with astonishment (note the *–e* preceding the suffix in *liquefy, putrefy,*

stupefy): fortify, to make strong; *rectify,* to make right or correct; etc., etc.

3. *Chronograph* (KRŌN'-ə-grɑhf') is an instrument that measures and records short intervals of time.

4. To *generate* is to give birth to, figuratively, or to create or produce, as a turbine *generates* power, a person's presence *generates* fear, etc. The noun is *generation,* which, in another context, also designates the people born and living about the same time (the older, previous, or next *generation,* the Depression *generation,* etc.), or a period, conventionally set at about thirty years, between such groups of people.

To *regenerate* is to give birth to again, or to be born again. Some creatures can *regenerate* new limbs or parts if these are lost or cut off – or the limbs or parts *regenerate.*

Re- means, of course, *again;* or, in some words, as *recede, regress,* etc., *back.*

5. *Omnipotent* (om-NIP'-ə-tənt) – all-powerful; *omnis* plus *potens, potentis,* powerful.

Omnipresent (om'-ni-PREZ'-ənt) – present all over, or everywhere.

Nouns: *omnipotence, omnipresence.*

6. *Anaphrodisiac* (ən-af'-rə-DIZ'-i-ak') – both a noun and an adjective. Saltpeter is supposedly an *anaphrodisiac;* so, some people say, is a cold shower, which is highly doubtful.

Check your learning

Prefix, Root	Meaning	Example
1. *notus*	_____	notify
2. *chronos*	_____	chronograph
3. *graphein*	_____	chronographic
4. *genesis*	_____	generate
5. *re-*	_____	regenerate
6. *omnis*	_____	omnipotent
7. *potens, potentis*	_____	omnipotence
8. *an-*	_____	anaphrodisiac

Key: 1–known, 2–time, 3–to write, 4–birth, 5–again, 6–all, 7–powerful, 8–not (negative)

Chapter 9:

1. *Magnanimity* (mag'-nə-NIM'-i-ti). Adjective: *magnanimous* (mag-NAN'-i-məs).

2. *Bilateral* (bī-LAT'-ər-əl), as in a *bilateral* decision, i.e., one made by the two sides or two people involved. On the other hand, a *unilateral* (yōō-ni-LAT'-ər-əl) decision is made by *one* person, without consultation with others.

3. *Transcribe*. Noun: *transcription*. A secretary *transcribes* shorthand notes into English words, or a musical *transcriber* arranges or adapts a musical composition for an instrument, group, etc. other than the one for which the work was originally written.

4. *Malaria* was once thought to have been caused by the 'bad air' of swamps; actually, it was (and is) transmitted to humans by infected anopheles mosquitoes breeding and living in swamps and other places where there is stagnant water.

5. *Confection*. The word is hardly used today with this meaning, except perhaps by members of an older generation who remember *confectioner's* shops.

Check your learning

Prefix, Root	Meaning	Example
1. *magnus*	_____	magnanimous
2. *animus*	_____	mangnanimity
3. *bi-*	_____	bilateral
4. *unus*	_____	unilateral
5. *latus, lateris*	_____	unilateral
6. *trans-*	_____	transcribe
7. *scribo, scriptus*	_____	transcription
8. *malus*	_____	malaria
9. *con-*	_____	confection
10. *facio (fec-)*	_____	confectionery

Key: 1—big, large, great, 2—mind, 3—two, 4—one, 5—side, 6—across, 7—to write, 8—bad, evil, 9—together, 10—to make

Chapter 10:

1. *Modus operandi*. Method (or mode) of working (or operating). Pronounced MŌ'-dəs op'-ə-RAN'-di, the word is not, of course, restricted to the special methods used by a criminal, but may refer to the method or style of operating characteristic of any other professional. *Modus vivendi* (MŌ'dəs vi-VEN'-di), etymologically 'method of living', is the style of life characteristic of a person or group.

2. *Circumscription*. To *circumscribe* also means, figuratively, to write (a line) *around* (*one's freedom of action*), so that one is restricted, limited, hemmed in, as in 'a life *circumscribed* by poverty, by parental injunctions, or by an overactive conscience, etc', or 'actions *circumscribed* by legal restraints'. The noun *circumscription* has the figurative meaning also.

3. *Somniloquent* (som-NIL'-ə-kwənt). Noun: *somniloquence* (som-NIL'-ə-kwəns) or *somniloquy* (som-NIL'-ə-kwi), the latter noun also designating the words spoken by the sleeper. One who habitually talks while asleep is a *somniloquist* (som-NIL'-ə-kwist).

4. An *aurist* is an ear specialist, more commonly called an *otologist* (ō-TOL'-ə-jist), from Greek *otos*, ear. Noun: *otology*. Adjective: *otological* (ō-tə-LOJ'-i-kəl).

It is difficult at this point to resist telling a well-known story about medical specialists. In fact it's impossible to resist, so here it is:

A dentist, doing his first extraction on a patient, was understandably nervous. When he got the molar out, his hand shook, he lost his grip on the instrument, and the tooth dropped down into the patient's throat.

'Sorry,' said the dentist. 'You're outside my speciality now. You should see a laryngologist! [lar'-ing-GOL'-ə-jist — a larynx or throat specialist]'

By the time the unfortunate victim got to the laryngologist, the tooth had worked its way much further down.

The laryngologist examined the man.

'Sorry,' said the doctor, 'You're outside my speciality now. You should see a gastrologist! [gas-TROL'-ə-jist — a stomach specialist]'

The gastrologist X-rayed the patient. 'Sorry,' said the doctor, 'the tooth has travelled into your lower intestines. You should see an enterologist [en'-tə-ROL'-ə-jist — an intestinal specialist]'

The enterologist took some X rays. 'Sorry, the tooth isn't there. It must have gone down farther. You should see a proctologist! [prok-TOL'-ə-jist -- a specialist in diseases of the rectum; from Greek *proktos*, anus]'

Our patient is now on the proctologist's examining table, in the proper elbow-knee position. The doctor has inserted a proctoscope and is looking through it.

'Good heavens, man! You've got a tooth up there! You should see a dentist!'

5. *Aural* (AW'-rəl) refers to the ears or to the sense or phenomenon of hearing. *Monoaural* reproduction, as of music over a radio or by a gramophone record, for example, has only one source of sound, and technically should be called *monophonic* (mon'-ō-FON'-ik) – *monos*, one, plus *phone*, sound. *Binaural* may means *having two ears* or *involving the use of both ears*, or, recently, *descriptive of sound from two sources*, giving a *stereophonic* (ster'-i-ō-FON'-ik) effect – *stereos*, deep, solid, plus *phone*.

6. A *noctambulist* (nok-TAM'-byoŏ-list) walks at night – *nox*, *noctis*, night, plus *ambulo*, to walk. Noun: *noctambulism* (nok-TAM'-byoŏ-liz-əm).

7. *Somnific* (som-NIF'-ik): *a somnific lecture, film, effect, etc.*

8. *Circumambulate* (sər'-kəm-AM'-byoŏ-layt'). To *circumnavigate* is to sail around – *circum*, around, plus *navis*, ship.

Check your learning

Prefix, Root	Meaning	Example
1. *modus*	_____	*modus operandi*
2. *operandi*	_____	*modus operandi*
3. *vivo*	_____	*modus vivendi*
4. *circum-*	_____	circumscribe
5. *scribo, scriptus*	_____	circumscription
6. *somnus*	_____	somniloquent
7. *liquor*	_____	somniloquence
8. *aurus*	_____	aurist
9. *otos*	_____	otology
10. *proktos*	_____	proctologist
11. *stereos*	_____	stereophonic
12. *phone*	_____	stereophonic
13. *monos*	_____	monaural

14. *bi-* _____ binaural
15. *nox, noctis* _____ noctambulist
16. *ambulo* _____ noctambulism
17. *facio (fic-)* _____ somnific

Key: 1—mode, method, 2—of working, 3—to live, 4—around,
        5—to write, 6—sleep, 7—to speak, to talk, 8—ear, 9—ear,
        10—anus, 11—deep, solid, 12—sound, 13—one, 14—two,
        15—night, 16—to walk, 17—to make

Chapter 11:

1. *Matronymic* (mat'-rə-NIM'-ik). Or, if you prefer to use the
   Greek root for mother (*meter, metr-*), *metronymic*. The Greek
   word *metra*, uterus, derives from *meter*, naturally enough, so
   metritis is inflammation of the uterus; *metralgia* is uterine pain;
   endometriosis (en'-dō-mee'-tri-Ō'-sis) is any abnormal
   condition of the uterine lining – *endo*, inside; *metra*, uterus;
   –osis, abnormal condition.
2. (a) An *incendiary* statement, remark, speech, etc. figuratively
       inflames an audience, sets them alight, gets them excited,
       galvanizes them into action, etc.
   (b) *Incense* (IN'-sens) is a substance that sends off a pleasant
       odour when burnt – often, but not necessarily, to mask
       unpleasant or telltale smells, as of marijuana smoke, etc.
   (c) To *incence* (in-SENS') is to anger greatly, i.e., to 'burn up'.
       'I'm all burnt up' is etymologically an accurate translation
       of 'I'm *incensed*'.
3. (a) *Ardent* (AH'-dənt) – burning with zeal, ambition, love,
       etc., as an *ardent* suitor, worker, etc.
   (b) *Ardor* (AH'-dər) – the noun form of *ardent* – burning
       passion, zeal, enthusiasm, etc. Alternate noun: *ardency*
       (AH'-dən-si).
4. *Megaphone.*
5. *Megalopolis* (meg'-ə-! OP'-ə-lis).
6. *Police. Politics.*

7. *Bibliokleptomaniac* (bib'-li-ō-klep'-tə-MAY'-ni-ak): one who has an obsession for stealing books. Not too many years ago, an author titled his book, *Steal This Book!*, perhaps hoping to appeal to *bibliokleptomaniacs;* if the appeal was unsuccessful enough, his royalty statements must have been miniscule indeed!

   Gynaekleptomaniac.
   Paedokleptomaniac.
   Androkleptomaniac.
   Demokleptomaniac.

   If you prefer to use shorter words, *compulsive kidnapper* or *obsessive abductor* will do as well for these words.

8. *Acromaniac.*
   Agoramaniac.
   Claustromaniac.

9. *Kleptophobe; pyrophobe; gynaephobe; androphobe; demophobe.*
   Triskaidekaphobia (tris'-kī-dek'-ə-FŌ'-bi-ə) is the morbid dread of the number 13, from Greek *triskai*, three, *deka*, ten, and *phobia.*

10. *Gnosiology* (nō'-si-OL'-ə-ji), the science or study of knowledge.

11. *Amadeus* is love (Latin *amor*) God (Latin *deus*). *Theophilus* is love (Greek *philos*) God (Greek *theos*). *Gottlieb* is love (German *Lieb*) God (German *Gott*). Perhaps this explains why he started composing at the age of four and wrote forty-one symphonies.

12. *Cellophane* – cellulose made to be transparent, i.e., to *show* what's wrapped in it.

13. *Hypoglycaemia* (hī-pō-glī-SEE'-mi-ə) – low blood sugar (Greek *hypos*, under: *glykys*, sweet: *haima*, blood).
    Haima, blood, is found in many English words, the root spelt either *haem* or *–aem*. Here are a few, with their etymological interpretations:

    (a) *Haemorrhage* – excessive blood flow.
    (b) *Anaemia* – 'no blood' – actually a pathological reduction of red blood corpuscles.
    (c) *Haematology* – science of blood (and its diseases).
    (d) *Haemophilia* – 'love of blood' – actually a hereditary condition, occurring in males, in which the blood clots too slowly.

(e) *Haemoglobin* – 'blood globules' – actually the red colouring matter of the red blood corpuscles.
Hyperglycaemia is the opposite of *hypoglycaemia*.

14. (a) *Pantheon* (PAN'-thi-ən') – a temple built in Rome in 27 B.C. for 'all the gods'.

(b) *Pandemonium* (pan'-di-MŌ'-ni-əm) – a word supposedly coined by poet John Milton in *Paradise Lost* to signify the dwelling place of all the demons; now any wild and noisy disorder.

(c) *Panorama* (pan'-ə-RAH'-mə) – a view (or a picture of such a view) all around – *pan*, all, plus *horama*, view. The adjective: *panoramic* (pan'-ə-RAM'-ik).

15. *Monarchy* – rule by one person.

Check your learning

Prefix, Root	Meaning	Example
1. *mater, matris*	_____	matronymic
2. *onyma*	_____	metronymic
3. *meter*	_____	metronymic
4. *metra*	_____	metritis
5. *endo-*	_____	endometriosis
6. *incendo, incensus*	_____	incendiary
7. *ardo*	_____	ardent
8. *megalo-*	_____	megalopolis
9. *polis*	_____	police
10. *demos*	_____	demokleptomaniac
11. *akros*	_____	acromaniac
12. *agora*	_____	agoramaniac
13. *claustrum*	_____	claustromaniac
14. *triskai*	_____	triskaidekaphobia
15. *deka*	_____	triskaidekaphobia
16. *gnosis*	_____	gnosiology
17. *amor*	_____	Amadeus
18. *deus*	_____	deity
19. *theos*	_____	Theophilus
20. *philos*	_____	haemophilia
21. *phanein*	_____	cellophane
22. *hypos*	_____	hypoglycaemia
23. *glykys*	_____	hypoglycaemia

24. *haima*	_____	haemorrhage
25. *an-*	_____	anaemia
26. *hyper-*	_____	hyperglycaemia
27. *pan*	_____	Pantheon
28. *horama*	_____	panorama
29. *archein*	_____	monarch
30. *monos*	_____	monarchy

Key: 1–mother, 2–name, 3–mother, 4–uterus, 5–inside,
6–to set on fire, 7–to burn, 8–big, large, great, 9–city,
10–people, 11–highest, 12–market place, 13–enclosed
place, 14–three, 15–ten, 16–knowledge, 17–love,
18–God, 19–God, 20–love, 21–to show, 22–under,
23–sweet, 24–blood, 25–not, negative, 26–over,
27–all, 28–view, 29–to rule, 30–one

Chapter 12:

1. *Survive.* **Noun:** *survival.*
2. *Vivarium* (vī-VAIR'-i-əm) – enclosed area in which plants and (small) animals live in conditions resembling their natural habitat. The suffix *–ium* usually signifies *place where* – *solarium*, a place for the sun to enter, or where one can sunbathe; *aquarium*, a place for water (Latin *aqua*, water), or fish tank; *podium*, a place for the feet (Greek *podos*, foot), or speaker's platform; *auditorium*, a place for hearing (or listening to) concerts, plays, etc. (Latin *audio*, to hear).
3. (a) *Unicorn* (Latin *cornu*, horn).
   (b) *Uniform.*
   (c) *Unify* (*–fy*, from *facio*, to make).
   (d) *Unity.*
   (e) *Unicycle* (Greek *kyklos*, circle, wheel).
4. *Anniversary* – a year has turned.
5. (a) *Universe* – everything turning as one.
   (b) *University* – highest institute of education – universal subjects taught, learned, etc., i.e. the curriculum covers the universe, is in no way restricted, etc.
6. (a) *Interstate.*
   (b) *International.*

(c) *Intermediate.*

(d) *Interrupt* (Latin *rumpo, ruptus,* to break).

(e) *Interpersonal.*

7. (a) *Intrastate.*

(b) *Intranational.*

(c) *Intrapersonal* or *intrapsychic.*

(d) *Intramuscular.*

Check your learning

Prefix, Root	Meaning	Example
1. *vivo*	_____	survive
2. *podos*	_____	podium
3. *cornu*	_____	unicorn
4. *kyklos*	_____	unicycle
5. *annus*	_____	anniversary
6. *verto, versus*	_____	universe
7. *unus*	_____	university
8. *inter-*	_____	interstate
9. *intra-*	_____	intrapsychic

Key: 1–to live, 2–foot, 3–horn, 4–circle, wheel, 5–year, 6–to turn, 7–one, 8–between, 9–within

Chapter 14:

1. 'View of Death'.

2. *Thanatology.*

3. (a) *Prophesy* (PROF'-i-sī').

   (b) *Prophecy* (PROF'-i-si).

   (c) *Prophet* (PROF'-it).

4. (a) *Predict.*

   (b) *Prediction.*

5. (a) *Vulpicide.*

   (b) *Lupicide.*

   (c) *Felicide.*

   (d) *Ursicide.*

6. (a) *Piscivorous* (pi-SIV"-ər-əs).

   (b) *Insectivorous* (in'-sek-TIV'-ər-əs).

7. *Canaries*, what else?
8. *Potentiate* (pə-TEN'-shi-ayt').

Check your learning

Prefix, Root	Meaning	Example
1. *thanatos*	_____	thanatology
2. *logos*	_____	thanatology
3. *opsis*	_____	thanatopsis
4. *pheme*	_____	prophecy
5. *pro-*	_____	prophet
6. *pre-*	_____	predict
7. *dico, dictus*	_____	predict
8. *vulpus*	_____	vulpicide
9. *lupus*	_____	lupicide
10. *felis*	_____	felicide
11. *ursus*	_____	ursicide
12. *piscis*	_____	piscivorous
13. *voro*	_____	insectivorous
14. *caedo (–cide)*	_____	insecticide
15. *canis*	_____	canary
16. *potens, potentis*	_____	potentiate

Key: 1–death, 2–science, study, 3–view, 4–voice, 5–beforehand, 6–before, 7–to say or tell, 8–fox, 9–wolf, 10–cat,
11–bear, 12–fish, 13–devour, 14–to kill (killing),
15–dog, 16–powerful

Chapter 15:

1. *Synagogue*.
2. *Symbiosis* (sim'-bī-Ō'-sis). Adjective: *symbiotic* (sim'-bī-OT'-ik).People (for example lovers, spouses, parent and child, etc.) also may live in a *symbiotic* relationship, each depending on the other for important services, emotional needs, etc.; each also providing these for the other.
3. *Symphony; symphonic*.
4. *Symmetry* (SIM'-i-tri); *symmetrical* (si-MET'-ri-kəl) or *symmetric* (si-MET'-rik).

5. *Syndrome* (SIN'-drōm).
6. *Hippodrome* (HIP'-ə-drōm'); the word today is often used as the name of a cinema or other place of entertainment.
7. *Hippopotamus.*

Check your learning

Prefix, Root	Meaning	Example
1. *syn-*	_____	synagogue
2. *agogos*	_____	synogogue
3. *bios*	_____	symbiosis
4. *phone*	_____	symphonic
5. *metron*	_____	symmetry
6. *dromos*	_____	syndrome
7. *hippos*	_____	hippodrome
8. *potamos*	_____	hippopotamus

Key: 1—with, together, 2—leader, leading, 3—life, 4—sound, 5—measurement, 6—a running, 7—horse, 8—river

Chapter 16:

1. *Non sequitur* (non SEK'-wi-tə) – 'it does not follow'.
2. (a) *Second* – following after the first.
   (b) *Consecutive* – following in proper order.
   (c) *Persecute* – to follow (i.e , pursue) through and through; hence to annoy, harass continually for no good reason.
   (d) *Prosecute* – to follow before; hence to pursue (something) diligently or vigorously in order to complete it successfully (*prosecute* a campaign); or to start, or engage in, legal proceedings against, especially in an official capacity.
3. (a) *Superior.*
   (b) *Superficial.*
   (c) *Superfluous* (soō-PƏR'-floŏ-əs *or* syoō-PƏR'-floŏ-əs). Noun: superfluity (soō'-pə FLOŌ'-i-ti).
   (d) *Supernatural.*
   (e) *Supervise.*

4. (a) *Cadence* (KAY'-dəns) – fall and rise of the voice in speaking; hence inflection, rhythm, beat, etc. of sound or music. Adjective: *cadent* (KAY'-dənt).

  (b) *Occidental* (ok'-si-DEN'-təl) – etymologically, falling. Hence relating to Western countries, since the sun falls in the west; also, a native of such a country. Noun: *Occident* (OK'-si-dənt). The sun rises in the east, so Latin *orior*, to rise, is the origin of the *Orient, oriental,* etc., and also of the verb *orient* (AW'-ri-ent'). To *orient* or *orientate* (AW'-ri-ənt'-ayt) is to adjust to a place or situation; etymologically, to turn, or face, east. Noun: *orientation.* 'I'm finally *oriented*' does not mean that I'm easternized or facing east, but that I have become familiar with, and comfortable in, a place, job, situation, etc. So to *disorient* (dis-AW'-ri-ənt') or *disorientate* (dis-AW'-ri-ənt'-ayt) is to remove (someone's) *orientation,* or to confuse or bewilder, especially in reference to locality, direction, etc. Noun: *disorientation.*

  (c) *Deciduous* (di-SID'-yŏŏ-əs) – falling down (Latin prefix *de-*). This adjective refers to trees whose leaves fall (down) every autumn.

  (d) *Incident* – that which falls upon, befalls, or happens.

  (e) *Accident* – that which falls to (*ac-* is a respelling of *ad-*, to, towards) someone or something (by chance).

  (f) *Coincidence* – *co-* is a respelling of *con-*, together. A *coincidence* occurs when two things befall, or happen, together, or at the same time, and by chance.

5. *Indolent* (IN'-də-lənt). Noun: *indolence* (IN'-də-ləns).

6. *Dolores* – from Spanish *María de los Dolores*, Mary of the Sorrows; hence, I suppose, someone who is generally sorrowful, though the few Doloreses I have known do not live up to their etymology.

Check your learning

Prefix, Root	Meaning	Example
1. *sequor, secutus*	_____	non sequitur, second
2. *per-*	_____	persecute
3. *pro-*	_____	prosecute

4. *super-*	_____	superior
5. *fluo*	_____	superfluous
6. *cado*	_____	cadence
7. *orio*	_____	Orient
8. *dis-*	_____	disorient
9. *ad-* (*ac-*)	_____	accident
10. *doleo*	_____	indolent
11. *in-*	_____	indolence

Key: 1—to follow, 2—through, 3—beforehand, 4—above, 5—to flow, 6—to fall, 7—to rise, 8—negative prefix, 9—to, towards, 10—to suffer, to grieve, 11—negative prefix

HOW TO KEEP BUILDING YOUR VOCABULARY

When you leave school, or college, someone will inevitably point out that this is not the end – not by a long shot. It is only the beginning.

Of course the speaker is right – no educative process is ever the end; it is always the beginning of more education, more learning, more living.

And that is the case here. What has happened to you as a result of your reaction to the material and suggestions in this book is only the beginning of your development. To stop increasing your vocabulary is to stop your intellectual growth. You will wish, I am sure, to continue growing intellectually as long as you remain alive. And with the momentum that your weeks of hard work have provided, continuing will not be at all difficult.

Let me offer, as a summary of all I have said throughout the book, a recapitulation of the steps you must take so that your vocabulary will keep growing and growing.

STEP ONE. *You must become actively receptive to new words.*

Words won't come chasing after you – you must train yourself to be on a constant lookout, in your reading and listening, for any words that other people know and you don't.

STEP TWO. *You must read more.*

As an adult, you will find most of the sources of your supply of new words in books and magazines. Is your reading today largely restricted to a quick perusal of the daily newspaper? Then you will have to change your habits. If your aim is to have a superior vocabulary, you will have to make the time to read at least one book and several magazines *every week*. Not just this week and next week – but every week for the rest of your life. I have never met a single person who possessed a rich vocabulary who was not also an omnivorous reader.

STEP THREE. *You must learn to add to your own vocabulary the new words you meet in your reading.*

When you see an unfamiliar word in a book or magazine, do not skip over it impatiently. Instead, pause for a moment and say it over to yourself – get used to its sound and appearance. Then puzzle out its possible meaning in the context of the sentence. Whether you come to the right conclusion or not, whether indeed you are able to come to any intelligent conclusion at all, is of no importance. What is important is that you are, by this process, becoming superconscious of the word. As a result, you will suddenly notice that this very word pops up unexpectedly again and again in all your reading – for now your mind has been alerted to notice it. And of course after you've seen it a few times, you will know fairly accurately not only what it means but the many ways in which it can be used.

STEP FOUR. *You must open your mind to new ideas.*

Every word you know is the translation of an idea.

Think for a few minutes of the areas of human knowledge that may possibly be unknown to you – psychology, semantics, science, art, music, or whatever. Then attack one of these areas methodically – by reading books in the field. In every field, from the simplest to the most abstruse, there are several books written for the average, untrained lay reader that will give you both a good grasp of the subject and at the same time add immeasurably to your vocabulary. College students have large vocabularies because they are required to expose themselves constantly to new areas of learning. You must do the same.

STEP FIVE. *You must set a goal.*

If you do *nothing* about your vocabulary, you will learn, at most, twenty-five to fifty new words in the next twelve months. *By conscious effort you can learn several thousand.* Set yourself a goal of finding several new words *every day.* This may sound ambitious – but you will discover as soon as you start actively looking for new words in your reading, and actively doing reading of a more challenging type, that new words are all around you – that is, if you're ready for them. And understand this: vocabulary building *snowballs.* The results of each new day's search will be greater and greater – once you provide the necessary initial push, once you gain momentum, once you *become addicted* to looking for, finding, and taking possession of new words.

And this is one addiction well worth cultivating!

Appendix

Some esoteric phobias

(You will recognize many of the Greek roots on which these words are constructed)

air: aerophobia
animals: zoophobia
beauty: callophobia
birth: genophobia
blood: haematophobia
breasts: mastophobia
burglars: scelerophobia
burial alive: taphephobia
cats: ailurophobia
change: neophobia
childbirth: maieusiophobia
children: paedophobia
colours: chromophobia
crowds: ochlophobia
darkness: nyctophobia
death: thanatophobia
depths: bathophobia
disease: pathophobia
doctors: iatrophobia
dogs: cynophobia
dying: thanatophobia
emptiness: kenophobia
everything: pantophobia
eyes: ophthalmophobia
fear: phobophobia
faeces: coprophobia
feet: podophobia
female genitals: eurotophobia
filth: mysophobia

fire: pyrophobia
fish: ichthyophobia
fog: homichlophobia
food: cibophobia
foreigners: xenophobia
freaks: teratophobia
frogs: batrachophobia
ghosts: phasmophobia
hands: chirophobia
hair: trichophobia
healers or healing: iatrophobia
heat: thermophobia
hell: stygiophobia
horses: hippophobia
insects: entomophobia
knives: aichmophobia
knowledge: gnosiophobia
large things: megalophobia
light: photophobia
lightning: astrophobia
males: androphobia
many things: polyphobia
marriage: gamophobia
medicine: pharmacophobia
mice: musophobia
mirrors: spectrophobia
mobs: ochlophobia
motherhood: metrophobia
motion: kinesophobia

nakedness: gymnophobia
needles: belonophobia
newness: neophobia
night: nyctophobia
oceans: thalassophobia
odours: osmophobia
old age: geraphobia
old men: gerontophobia
pain: algophobia; odynophobia triskaidekaphobia
people: demophobia
plants: botanophobia
pleasure: hedonophobia
poison: toxicophobia
poverty: peniophobia
prostitutes: pornophobia
punishment: poinophobia
rain: ombrophobia
red: erythrophobia
rivers: potamophobia
robbers: harpaxophobia
sameness: homophobia
sex: genophobia
sexual intercourse: coitophobia
sinning: peccatophobia
skin: dermatophobia
sleep: hypnophobia
small things: microphobia
smothering: pnigerophobia
snakes: ophidiophobia
snow: chionophobia
solitude: autophobia; monophobia
sounds: acousticophobia
speaking: lalophobia

speaking aloud: phonophobia
speech: logophobia
spiders: arachneophobia
stairs: climacophobia
stars: siderophobia
stealing: kleptophobia
stillness: eremiophobia
strangers: xenophobia
strength: sthenophobia
study: logophobia
sunlight: heliophobia
tapeworms: taeniophobia
taste: geumophobia
teeth: odontophobia
thieves: kleptophobia
thinking: phronemophobia
thirteen (the number): thirst: dipsophobia
thunder: brontophobia
time: chronophobia
togetherness: synophobia
travel: hodophobia
ugliness: cacophobia
voices: phemophobia
vomiting: emetophobia
walking: basiphobia
watching: scoptophobia
water: hydrophobia
weakness: asthenophobia
wealth: plutophobia
wind: anemophobia
women: gynaephobia
words: logophobia
work: ergophobia
writing: graphophobia

PRONUNCIATION KEY
of Word List

aa	as in	*cat*, pl*ai*d
ah	as in	*father*, *hearth*, *sergeant*
air	as in	*rare*, *air*, *prayer*, *there*, *wear*, *their*
ate	as in	*mate*, *straight*, *eight*
ay	as in	*gauge*, *way*, *steak*, *eh*, *obey*, *lane*, *rain*, *rein*
aw	as in	*tall*, *Utah*, *talk*, *fault*, *law*, *order*, *broad*, *fought*
b	as in	*book*, *hobby*
ch	as in	*chop*, *watch*, *righteous*, *question*, *nature*
d	as in	*day*, *ladder*, *pulled*
e	as in	*any*, *aesthetic*, *said*, *says*, *beg*, *leather*, *heifer*, *leopard*, *friend*, *bury*
ee	as in	*Caesar*, *evil*, *team*, *see*, *receive*, *people*, *key*, *machine*, *field*, *amoeba*
eye	as in	*aisle*, *aye*, *height*, *eye*, *ice*, *pie*, *buy*, *sky*, *lye*, *island*, *sigh*
f	as in	*fall*, *muffin*, *tough*, *physical*
g	as in	*gate*, *haggle*, *ghost*, *guard*, *catalogue*
h	as in	*happy*, *who*
i	as in	*England*, *been*, *ink*, *sieve*, *women*, *busy*, *build*, *hymn*
ih	as in	*attitude*
ize	as in	*lies*, *surprise*, *dyes*, *eyes*
j	as in	*graduate*, *judgment*, *ledge*, *soldier*, *cage*, *magic*, *exaggerate*, *jelly*
k	as in	*cook*, *account*, *saccharin*, *chronic*, *quick*, *liquor*, *acquaint*, *biscuit*
l	as in	*line*, *mellow*
m	as in	*calm*, *seam*, *limb*, *hammer*, *hymn*
n	as in	*know*, *now*, *runner*, *pneumonia*, *gnat*
ng	as in	*pink*, *hang*, *tongue*
ngg	as in	*linger*
o	as in	*beau*, *sew*, *note*, *road*, *toe*, *oh*, *brooch*, *soul*, *flow*
oo	as in	*maneuver*, *grew*, *move*, *wolf*, *canoe*, *ooze*, *look*, *troupe*, *should*, *rule*, *pull*, *flue*, *fruit*
p	as in	*pat*, *apple*
r	as in	*rat*, *carry*, *rhythm*
s	as in	*city*, *some*, *science*, *missile*

sh	as in	ocean, machine, special, sugar, conscience, nauseous, ship, mansion, tissue, mission, mention, fuchsia
t	as in	talked, bought, tip, thyme
th	as in	think
u	as in	come, does, flood, couple, up
uh	as in	ability, mountain, system, dungeon, comical, parliament. gallop, porpoise, obvious, circus
v	as in	of, Stephen, victory, flivver
w	as in	choir, quiet, work
y	as in	union, hallelujah, you, confuse
z	as in	has, discern, scissors, zoo, dazzle, xylophone
zh	as in	garage, measure, division

is substituted for a vowel before a consonant to indicate that the vowel is to be pronounced only briefly; for example **comical** (KAHM uh k'l), **session** (SESH'n), **reason** (REE z'n).

Syllables shown in CAPITAL LETTERS are given main stress: **living** (LIV ing), **president** (PREZ ih d'nt), **reside** (rih ZIDE).

WORD LIST
DICTIONARY OF
A # DIFFICULT WORDS

ABASH (uh BASH) *v* to make ashamed; to embarrass

Meredith felt *abashed* by her inability to remember her lines in the school chorus of "Old McDonald Had a Farm."

To do something without shame or embarrassment is to do it *unabashedly.* Ken handed in a term paper that he had *unabashedly* copied from the *National Enquirer.*

ABATE (uh BATE) *v* to subside; to reduce

George spilled a pot of hot coffee on his leg. It hurt quite a bit. Then, gradually, the agony *abated.*

Bad weather *abates* when good weather begins to return. A rain storm that does not let up continues *unabated.*

A tax *abatement* is a reduction in taxes. Businesses are sometimes given tax *abatements* in return for building factories in places where there is a particular need for jobs.

ABDICATE (AB duh KATE) *v* to step down from a position of power or responsibility

When King Edward VIII of England decided he would rather be married to Wallis Warfield Simpson, an American divorcée, than be king of England, he turned in his crown and *abdicated.*

Even people who aren't monarchs can *abdicate* duties and responsibilities. Mary *abdicated* her responsibility as a baby-sitter by locking the five-year-old in a closet and flying to the Bahamas.

ABERRATION (AB uh RAY shun) *n* something not typical; a deviation from the standard

Tom's bad behavior was an *aberration.* So was Harry's good behavior. That is, Tom was usually good and Harry was usually bad.

A snowstorm in June is an *aberration;* snow doesn't normally fall in June.

The chef at this restaurant is dreadful; the good meal we just had was an *aberration.*

An *aberration* is an *aberrant* (uh BER unt) occurrence. Tom's behavior was *aberrant.* The summer snowstorm was *aberrant.*

ABHOR (ab HAWR) *v* to hate very, very much; to detest

To *abhor* something is to view it with horror. Hating a person is almost friendly in comparison with *abhorring* him or her.

Emanuel *abhorred* having anvils dropped on his head.

To *abhor* raw chicken livers is to have an *abhorrence* of them or to find them *abhorrent.*

ABJECT (AB jekt) *adj* hopeless; extremely sad and servile; defeated; utterly bummed out

An *abject* person is one who is crushed and without hope. A slave would be *abject,* in all likelihood.

Perhaps 90 percent of the time, when you encounter this word it will be followed by the word *poverty*. *Abject poverty* is hopeless, desperate poverty. The phrase "abject poverty" is overused. Writers use it because they are too lazy to think of anything more novel.

ABNEGATE (AB nuh GATE) *v* to deny oneself things; to reject; to renounce

Samantha *abnegated* desserts for one month after getting on the scale.

Self-abnegation is giving up oneself, usually for some higher cause. Ascetics practice *self-abnegation* because they believe it will bring them closer to spiritual purity.

ABORTIVE (uh BAWR tiv) *adj* unsuccessful

Mary and Elisabeth made an *abortive* effort to bake a birthday cake; that is, their effort did not result in a birthday cake.

Fred's attempt to climb the mountain was *abortive;* he fell off when he was halfway up.

To *abort* something is to end it before it is completed. An *aborted* pregnancy, called an *abortion*, is one that is ended before the baby is born. An *abortion* in this sense doesn't have to be the result of a controversial medical procedure.

ABRIDGE (uh BRIJ) *v* to shorten; to condense

The thoughtful editor had *abridged* the massive book by removing the boring parts.

An *abridged* dictionary is one that has been shortened to keep it from crushing desks and people's laps.

An *abridgment* is a shortened or condensed work.

ABSOLUTE (AB suh LOOT) *adj* total; unlimited; perfect

An *absolute* ruler is one who is ruled by no one else. An *absolute* mess is a total mess. An absolute rule is one that has no exceptions and that you must follow, no two ways about it.

Absolute is also a noun. It means something that is total, unlimited, or perfect. Death, for living things, is an *absolute*. There just isn't any way around it.

ABSOLVE (ab ZOLV) *v* to forgive or free from blame; to free from sin; to free from an obligation

The priest *absolved* the sinner who had come to church to confess his sin.

Tom's admission of guilt *absolved* Dick, who had originally been accused of the crime.

It is also possible to *absolve* someone of a responsibility. Bill *absolved* Mary of her obligation to go to the prom with him. That is, he told her it was all right if she went with the captain of the football team instead.

The act of *absolving* is called *absolution* (AB suh LOO shun).

Q·U·I·C·K · Q·U·I·Z #1

Match each word in the first column with its definition in the second column. Check your answers in the back of the book.

1. abash		a. step down from power
2. abate		b. hopeless
3. abdicate		c. unsuccessful
4. aberration		d. forgive
5. abhor		e. total
6. abject		f. subside
7. abnegate		g. detest
8. abortive		h. shorten
9. abridge		i. deviation
10. absolute		j. embarrass
11. absolve		k. renounce

ABSTINENT (AB stuh nunt) *adj* abstaining; voluntarily not doing something, especially something pleasant that is bad for you or has a bad reputation

Beulah used to be a chain-smoker; now she's *abstinent* (it was just too hard to get those chains lit).

Cynthia, who was dieting, tried to be *abstinent,* but when she saw the chocolate cake she realized that she would probably have to eat the entire thing.

ABSTRACT (AB strakt) *adj* theoretical; impersonal

To like something in the *abstract* is to like the idea of it. He liked oysters in the *abstract,* but when he actually tried one he became nauseated.

ABSTRUSE (ab STROOS) *adj* hard to understand

The professor's article, on the meaning of meaning, was very *abstruse.* Michael couldn't even pronounce the words in it.

Nuclear physics is a subject that is too *abstruse* for most people.

ABYSMAL (uh BIZ mul) *adj* extremely hopeless or wretched; bottomless

An *abyss* is a bottomless pit, or something so deep that it seems bottomless. *Abysmal* despair is despair so deep that no hope seems possible.

The nation's debt crisis was *abysmal;* there seemed to be no possible solution to it.

Abysmal is often used somewhat sloppily to mean "very bad." You might hear a losing baseball team's performance referred to as *abysmal.* This isn't strictly correct, but many people do it.

ACCOLADE (AK uh LADE) *n* an award; an honor

This word is generally used in the plural. The first break-dancing troupe to perform in Carnegie Hall, the Teflon Toughs, received the *accolades* of the critics as well as of the fans.

ACCOST (uh KAWST) *v* to approach and speak to someone
Amanda karate chopped the stranger who *accosted* her in the street and was embarrassed to find he was an old blind man.

ACERBIC (uh SUR bik) *adj* bitter; sour; severe
Barry sat silently as our teacher read aloud her *acerbic* comments on his paper.
Acerb and *acerbic* are synonyms. *Acerbity* is bitterness.

ACQUIESCE (AK wee ES) *v* to comply passively; to accept; to assent; to agree
To *acquiesce* is to do something without objection—to do it *quietly*. As the similarity of their spellings indicates, the words *acquiesce* and *quiet* are closely related. They are both based on Latin words meaning "rest" or "be quiet."
The pirates asked Pete to walk the plank; he took one look at their swords and then *acquiesced*.
Acquiesce is sometimes used sloppily as a simple synonym for *agree* in situations where it isn't really appropriate. For example, it isn't really possible to *acquiesce* noisily, enthusiastically, or eagerly. Don't forget the *quiet* in the middle.
To *acquiesce* is to exhibit *acquiescence*.

ACRID (AK rid) *adj* harsh; like acid
The chile we had at the party had an *acrid* taste; it was harsh and unpleasant.
Long after the fire had been put out, we could feel the *acrid* sting of smoke in our nostrils.
Acrid is used most often with tastes and smells, but it can be used more broadly to describe anything that is offensive in a similar way. A comment that stung like acid could be called *acrid*. So could a harsh personality.

ACRIMONIOUS (AK ruh MOH nee us) *adj* full of spite; bitter; nasty
George and Elizabeth's discussion turned *acrimonious* when Elizabeth introduced the subject of George's perennial, incorrigible stupidity.
Relations between the competing candidates were so *acrimonious* that each refused to acknowledge the presence of the other.

ACUMEN (AK yuh mun) *n* keenness of judgment; mental sharpness
A woman who knows how to turn a dollar into a million dollars overnight might be said to have a lot of business *acumen*.
Ernie's near-total lack of *acumen* led him to invest all his money in a company that had already gone out of business.

Q·U·I·C·K · Q·U·I·Z #2

Match each word in the first column with its definition in the second column. Check your answers in the back of the book.

1. abstinent
2. abstract
3. abstruse
4. abysmal
5. accolade
6. accost
7. acerbic
8. acquiesce
9. acrid
10. acrimonious
11. acumen

a. hard to understand
b. voluntarily avoiding
c. wretched
d. bitter (2)
e. comply
f. harsh
g. mental sharpness
h. theoretical
i. award
j. approach someone

ACUTE (uh KYOOT) *adj* sharp; shrewd

If your eyesight is *acute*, you can see things that other people can't. You have visual *acuity*. An *acute* mind is a quick, intelligent one. You have mental *acuity*. An *acute* pain is a sharp pain.

Acute means sharp only in a figurative sense. A knife, which is sharp enough to *cut*, is never said to be *acute*.

Acute is a word doctors throw around quite a bit. An *acute* disease is one that reaches its greatest intensity very quickly and then goes away. What could a disease be if it isn't *acute*? See chronic.

ADAGE (AD ij) *n* an old saying; a familiar bit of wisdom

"For a happy life, eat figs" is not an *adage*. No one ever said it, until now. But "Honesty is the best policy" is. Very often an *adage* is also a cliché.

ADAMANT (AD uh munt, AD uh mant) *adj* stubborn; unyielding; completely inflexible

Candice was *adamant*: She would never go out with Paul again.

A very hard substance, like a diamond, is also *adamant*.

Adamantine and *adamant* are synonyms. *Adamancy* is being *adamant*.

ADDRESS (uh DRES) *v* to speak to; to direct one's attention to

To *address* a convention is to give a speech to the convention. To *address* a problem is to face it and set about solving it. Ernie *addressed* the problem of *addressing* the convention by sitting down and writing his speech.

ADHERENT (ad HEER unt) *n* follower; supporter; believer

The king's *adherents* threw a big birthday party for him, just to show how much they liked him.

To *adhere* to something is to stick to it. *Adherents* are people who *adhere* to, or stick to, something or someone.

A religion could be said to have *adherents*, assuming there are people who believe in it. Governments, causes, ideas, people, philosophies, and many other things can have *adherents*, too.

ADMONISH (ad MON ish) *v* to scold gently; to warn

The boys' mother *admonished* them not to eat the pie she had just baked. When they did so anyway, she *admonished* them for doing it. In the first sentence *admonish* means "warn"; in the second it means "scold gently." Consider yourself *admonished* not to misuse this word.

ADROIT (uh DROIT) *adj* skillful; dexterous; clever; shrewd; socially at ease

Adroit comes from *droit*, which is the French word for *right* (the opposite of *left*). *Dexterous*, which means pretty much the same thing as *adroit*, comes from *dexter*, which is the Latin word for *right* (the opposite of *left*). Right-handed people were once thought to be more *dexterous* and *adroit* than left-handed people. In fact, left-handed people were once thought to be downright evil, or *sinister*, which is the Latin word for *left* (the opposite of *right*). To say nowadays that right-handed people are better than left-handed people would be considered *gauche*, which means graceless, crude, socially awkward, or clumsy. *Gauche* is the French word for *left* (the opposite of *right*). A synonym for *gauche* is *maladroit*.

Got all that? Here it is again. It would be *gauche* to go to the ball wearing your right shoe on your left foot and your left shoe on your right foot. It would also be hard to dance *adroitly* with your shoes that way. If you were sufficiently *dexterous*, you might be able to switch and retie your shoes while you were dancing, but your dancing partner might think you were up to something *sinister* down there and ask you to keep both your right hand and your left hand to yourself.

ADULATION (AJ uh LAY shun) *n* wild or excessive admiration; flattery

The boss thrived on the *adulation* of his scheming secretary.

The rock star grew to *abhor* the *adulation* of his fans.

There is a note of insincerity in *adulation*, as there is in *flattery*.

Q·U·I·C·K · Q·U·I·Z #3

Match each word in the first column with its definition in the second column. Check your answers in the back of the book.

1. acute		a. shrewd
2. adage		b. follower
3 adamant		c. socially awkward
4. address		d. scold gently
5. adherent		e. speak to
6. admonish		f. skillful (2)
7. adroit		g. old saying
8. dexterous		h. wild admiration
9. gauche		i. unyielding
10. adulation		

ADULTERATE (uh DUL tuh RATE) *v* to contaminate; to make impure

We discovered that our orange juice had radioactive waste in it; we discovered, in other words, that our orange juice had been *adulterated*.

Vegetarians do not like their foods *adulterated* with animal fats.

Unadulterated means pure. *Unadulterated* joy is joy untainted by sadness.

ADVERSE (ad VURS) *adj* unfavorable; antagonistic

Airplanes often don't fly in *adverse* weather.

We had to play our soccer match under *adverse* conditions: it was snowing and only three members of our team had bothered to show up.

An airplane that took off in bad weather and reached its destination safely would be said to have overcome *adversity*. *Adversity* means misfortune or unfavorable circumstances. To do something "in the face of adversity" is to undertake a task despite obstacles. Some people are at their best in *adversity*, because they rise to the occasion.

A word often confused with *adverse* is *averse*. The two are related but they don't mean quite the same thing. A person who is *averse* to doing something is a person who doesn't want to do it. To be *averse* to something is to be opposed to doing it—to have an *aversion* to doing it.

AESTHETIC (es THET ik) *adj* having to do with artistic beauty; artistic

Our art professor had a highly developed *aesthetic* sense; he found things to admire in paintings that, to us, looked like garbage.

AFFABLE (AF uh bul) *adj* easy to talk to; friendly

Susan was an *affable* girl; she could strike up a pleasant conversation with almost anyone.

The Jeffersons' dog was big but *affable;* it liked to lick little children on the nose.

The noun is *affability*.

AFFECTATION (AF ek TAY shun) *n* unnatural or artificial behavior, usually intended to impress

Bucky's English accent is an *affectation*. He spent only a week in England, and that was several years ago.

Elizabeth had somehow acquired the absurd *affectation* of pretending that she didn't know how to turn on a television set.

A person with an *affectation* is said to be *affected*.

To *affect* a characteristic or habit is to adopt it consciously, usually in the hope of impressing other people. Edward *affected* to be more of an artist than he really was. Everyone hated him for it.

AFFINITY (uh FIN i tee) *n* sympathy; attraction; kinship; similarity

Ducks have an *affinity* for water; that is, they like to be in it.

Children have an *affinity* for trouble; that is, they often find themselves in it.

Magnets and iron have an *affinity* for each other; that is, each is attracted to the other.

Affinity also means similarity or resemblance. There is an *affinity* between snow and sleet.

AFFLUENT (AF loo unt) *adj* rich; prosperous

A person can be *affluent;* all it takes is money. A country can be *affluent*, too, if it's full of *affluent* people.

Affluence means the same thing as *wealth* or *prosperity*.

AGENDA (uh JEN duh) *n* program; the things to be done

What's on the *agenda* for the board meeting? A little gossip, then lunch.

A politician is often said to have an *agenda*. The politician's *agenda* consists of the things he or she wishes to accomplish.

An *agenda*, such as that for a meeting, is often written down, but it doesn't have to be. A person who has sneaky ambitions or plans is often said to have a secret or hidden *agenda*.

AGRARIAN (uh GRAR ee un) *adj* relating to land; relating to the management or farming of land

Agrarian usually has to do with farming. Think of agriculture. Politics in this country often pit the rural, *agrarian* interests against the urban interests.

```
                    Q·U·I·C·K · Q·U·I·Z  #4

    Match each word in the first column with its definition in the second
    column. Check your answers in the back of the book.

      1. adulterate              a. opposed to
      2. adverse                 b. friendly
      3. averse                  c. rich
      4. aesthetic               d. unnatural behavior
      5. affable                 e. artistic
      6. affectation             f. contaminate
      7. affinity                g. sympathy
      8. affluent                h. unfavorable
      9. agenda                  i. program
     10. agrarian                j. relating to land
```

AGGREGATE (AG ruh git, AG ruh GATE) *n* sum total; a collection of separate things mixed together

Chili is an *aggregate* of meat and beans.

Aggregate can also be a verb or an adjective. You would make chili by *aggregating* meat and beans. Chili is an *aggregate* food.

Similar and related words include *congregate*, *segregate*, and *integrate*. To *aggregate* is to bring together, to *congregate* is to get together, to *segregate* is to keep apart (or separate), to *integrate* is to unite.

A church's *congregation* is the group of people that gets together inside it on Sunday.

Racial *segregation* is the separation of different races. School systems in which blacks and whites attend different schools are called *segregated*.

The act of opening those schools to members of all races is called *integration*.

AGNOSTIC (ag NOS tik) *n* one who believes that the existence of a god can be neither proven nor disproven

An *atheist* is someone who does not believe in a god. An *agnostic*, on the other hand, isn't sure. He doesn't believe but he doesn't *not* believe, either.

ALACRITY (uh LAK ri tee) *n* cheerful eagerness or readiness to respond

David could hardly wait for his parents to leave; he carried their luggage out to the car with great *alacrity*.

ALLEGE (uh LEJ) *v* to assert without proof

If I say, "Bill *alleges* that I stole his hat," I am saying two things:

    1. Bill says I stole his hat
    2. I say I didn't do it

To *allege* something is to assert it without proving it. Such an assertion is called an *allegation*.

If the police accuse someone of having committed a crime, newspapers will usually refer to that person as an *alleged* criminal. The police have *alleged* that he or she committed the crime, but a jury hasn't made a decision yet.

ALLEVIATE (uh LEE vee ATE) *v* to relieve, usually temporarily or incompletely; to make bearable; to lessen

Aspirin *alleviates* headache pain. When your headache comes back, take some more aspirin.

Visiting the charming pet cemetery *alleviated* the woman's grief over the death of her canary.

ALLOCATE (AL uh KATE) *v* to distribute; to assign; to allot

The long car trip had been a big failure, and David, Doug, and Jan spent several hours attempting to *allocate* the blame. In the end, they decided it had all been Jan's fault.

The office manager had *allocated* just seven paper clips for our entire department.

ALLOY (AL oi) *n* a combination of two or more things, usually metals

Brass is an *alloy* of copper and zinc. That is, you make brass by combining copper and zinc.

Alloy (uh LOI) is often used as a verb. To *alloy* two things is to mix them together. There is usually an implication that the mixture is less than the sum of the parts. That is, there is often something undesirable or debased about an *alloy* (as opposed to pure substance).

Unalloyed means undiluted or pure. *Unalloyed* dislike is dislike undiminished by any positive feelings; *unalloyed* love is love undiminished by any negative feelings.

Q·U·I·C·K · Q·U·I·Z #5

Match each word in the first column with its definition in the second column. Check your answers in the back of the book.

1. aggregate	a.	get together
2. congregate	b.	unite
3. segregate	c.	someone unconvinced about the existence of a god
4. integrate		
5. agnostic	d.	relieve
6. alacrity	e.	keep apart
7. allege	f.	combination of metals
8. alleviate	g.	sum total
9. allocate	h.	distribute
10. alloy	i.	assert
	j.	cheerful eagerness

ALLUSION (uh LOO zhun) *n* an indirect reference (often to a literary work); a hint

To *allude* to something is to refer to it indirectly. When Ralph said, "I sometimes wonder whether to be or not to be," he was *alluding* to a famous line in *Hamlet*. If Ralph had said, "As Hamlet said, 'To be or not to be, that is the question'," his statement would have been a direct reference, not an *allusion*.

An *allusion* is an *allusion* only if the source isn't identified directly. Anything else is a reference or a quotation.

If Andrea says, "I enjoyed your birthday party," she isn't *alluding* to the birthday party; she's referring to it, or mentioning it. But if she says, "I like the way you blow out candles," she is *alluding* to the party.

ALOOF (uh LOOF) *adj* uninvolved; standing off; keeping one's distance

Al, on the roof, felt very *aloof*.

To stand *aloof* from a touch-football game is to stand on the sidelines and not take part.

Cats are often said to be *aloof* because they usually mind their own business and don't crave the affection of people.

ALTRUISM (AL troo IZ um) *n* selflessness; generosity; devotion to the interests of others

The private foundation depended on the *altruism* of the extremely rich old man. When he decided to start spending his money on his new eighteen-year-old girlfriend instead, the foundation went out of business.

To be *altruistic* is to help others without expectation of personal gain. Giving money to charity is an act of *altruism*. The *altruist* does it just to be nice, although he'll probably also remember to take a tax deduction.

An *altruistic* act is also an act of philanthropy, which means almost the same thing.

AMBIENCE (AM bee uns) *n* atmosphere; mood; feeling

By decorating their house with plastic beach balls and Popsicle sticks, the Cramers created a playful *ambience* that delighted young children.

A restaurant's *ambience* is the look, mood, and feel of the place. People sometimes say that a restaurant has "an atmosphere of ambience." To do so is redundant—*atmosphere* and *ambience* mean the same thing.

AMBIGUOUS (am BIG yoo us) *adj* unclear in meaning; confusing; capable of being interpreted in different ways

We listened to the weather report, but the forecast was *ambiguous;* we couldn't tell if the day was going to be rainy or sunny.

The poem we read in English class was *ambiguous;* no one had any idea what the poet was trying to say.

AMBIVALENT (am BIV uh lunt) *adj* undecided; neutral; wishy-washy

Susan felt *ambivalent* about George as a boyfriend. Her frequent desire to break up with him reflected this *ambivalence*.

Q·U·I·C·K · Q·U·I·Z #6

Match each word in the first column with its definition in the second column. Check your answers in the back of the book.

1. allusion   a. atmosphere
2. aloof   b. stand-offish
3. altruism   c. confusing
4. ambience   d. generosity
5. ambiguous   e. indirect reference
6. ambivalent   f. undecided

AMELIORATE (uh MEEL yuh RATE) *v* to make better or more tolerable

The condition of the prisoners was *ameliorated* when the warden gave them color television sets and keys to their cells.

My great-uncle's gift of several million dollars considerably *ameliorated* my financial condition.

AMENABLE (uh MEE nuh bul, uh MEN uh bul) *adj* obedient; willing to give in to the wishes of another; agreeable

I suggested that Bert pay for my lunch as well as for his own and, to my surprise, he was *amenable*.

The plumber was *amenable* to my paying my bill with jelly beans, which was lucky, because I had more jelly beans than money.

AMENITY (uh MEN i tee) *adj* pleasantness; attractive or comfortable feature

The *amenities* at the local club include a swimming pool, a golf course, and a fallout shelter.

If an older guest at your house asks you where the *amenities* are, he or she is probably asking for directions to the bathroom. Provide them.

Those little bars of soap and bottles of shampoo found in hotel rooms are known in the hotel business as *amenities*. They are meant to increase your comfort. People like them because people like almost anything that is free (although, of course, the cost of providing such *amenities* is simply added to the price of hotel rooms).

AMIABLE (AY mee uh bul) *adj* friendly; agreeable

Our *amiable* guide made us feel right at home in what would otherwise have been a cold and forbidding museum.

The drama critic was so *amiable* in person that even the subjects of negative reviews found it impossible not to like her.

Amicable is a similar and related word. Two not very *amiable* people might nonetheless make an *amicable* agreement. *Amicable* means politely friendly, or not hostile. Two countries might trade *amicably* with each other even while technically remaining enemies. Jeff and Clarissa had a surprisingly *amicable* divorce and remained good friends even after paying their lawyers' fees.

AMNESTY (AM ni stee) *n* an official pardon for a group of people who have violated a law or policy

Amnesty comes from the same root as *amnesia*, the condition that causes characters in movies to forget everything except how to speak English and drive their cars.

An *amnesty* is an official forgetting. When a state government declares a tax *amnesty*, it is saying that if people pay the taxes they owe, the government will officially "forget" that they broke the law by not paying them in the first place.

The word *amnesty* always refers to a pardon given to a group or class of people. A pardon granted to a single person is simply a pardon.

AMORAL (ay MAWR ul) *adj* lacking a sense of right and wrong; neither good nor bad, neither moral nor immoral; without moral feelings

Very young children are *amoral;* when they cry, they aren't being bad or good, they're merely doing what they have to do.

A *moral* person does right; an *immoral* person does wrong; an *amoral* person simply does.

AMOROUS (AM ur us) *adj* feeling loving, especially in a sexual sense; in love; relating to love

The *amorous* couple made quite a scene at the movie. The movie they were watching, *Love Story*, was pretty *amorous* itself. It was about an *amorous* couple, one of whom died.

AMORPHOUS (uh MAWR fus) *adj* shapeless; without a regular or stable shape; bloblike

Ed's teacher said that his term paper was *amorphous;* she said that it was as shapeless and disorganized as a cloud.

The sleepy little town was engulfed by an *amorphous* blob of glowing protoplasm—a higher intelligence from outer space.

To say that something has an "amorphous shape" is a contradiction. How can a shape be shapeless?

ANACHRONISM (uh NAK ruh NIZ um) *n* something out of place in time or history; an incongruity

In this day of impersonal hospitals, a family doctor who will visit you at home seems like an *anachronism.*

In these modern, liberated times, some women disdain the *anachronistic* practice of a man's holding open a door for a woman.

ANALOGY (uh NAL uh jee) *n* a comparison of one thing to another; similarity

To say having an allergy feels like being bitten by an alligator would be to make or draw an *analogy* between an allergy and an alligator. *Analogy* usually refers to similarities between things that are not otherwise very similar. If you don't think an allergy is at all like an alligator, you might say, "That *analogy* doesn't hold up." To say that there is no *analogy* between an allergy and an alligator is to say that they are not *analogous.*

Q·U·I·C·K · Q·U·I·Z #7

Match each word in the first column with its definition in the second column. Check your answers in the back of the book.

1. ameliorate		a.	pleasantness
2. amenable		b.	comparison
3. amenity		c.	obedient
4. amiable		d.	without moral feeling
5. amicable		e.	feeling loving
6. amnesty		f.	make better
7. amoral		g.	shapeless
8. amorous		h.	politely friendly
9. amorphous		i.	official pardon
10. anachronism		j.	friendly
11. analogy		k.	incongruity

ANARCHY (AN ur KEE) *n* absence of government or control; lawlessness; disorder

The country fell into a state of *anarchy* after the rebels kidnapped the president and locked the legislature inside the Capitol.

The word doesn't have to be used in its strict political meaning. You could say that there was *anarchy* in the kindergarten when the teacher stepped out of the door for a moment. You could say it, and you would probably be right.

The words *anarchy* and *monarchy* are closely related. *Anarchy* means no leader; *monarchy*, a government headed by a king or queen, means one leader.

ANECDOTE (AN ik DOTE) *n* a short account of a humorous or revealing incident

The old lady kept the motorcycle gang thoroughly amused with *anecdote* after *anecdote* about her cute little dog.

Fred told an *anecdote* about the time Sally got her big toe stuck in a bowling ball.

The vice-president set the crowd at ease with an *anecdote* about his childhood desire to become a vice-president.

To say that the evidence of life on other planets is merely *anecdotal* is to say that we haven't captured any aliens, but simply heard a lot of stories from people who claimed to have been kidnapped by flying saucers.

ANGUISH (ANG gwish) *n* agonizing physical or mental pain

Theresa had been a nurse in the emergency room for twenty years, but she had never gotten used to the *anguish* of accident victims.

ANIMOSITY (AN uh MOS i tee) *n* resentment; hostility; ill will

Loulou hates Eric so much that she would like to stuff him in a mail sack and throw him out of an airplane. Loulou is full of *animosity*.

A person whose look could kill is a person whose *animosity* is evident.

The rivals for the state championship felt great *animosity* toward each other. Whenever they ran into each other, they snarled.

ANOMALY (uh NOM uh lee) *n* an aberration; an irregularity; a deviation

A snowy winter day is not an *anomaly*, but a snowy July day is.

A house without a roof is an *anomaly*—a cold, wet *anomaly*. A roofless house could be said to be *anomalous*. Something that is *anomalous* is something that is not normal or regular.

ANTECEDENT (AN ti SEED unt) *n* someone or something that went before; something that provides a model for something that came after it

Your parents and grandparents could be said to be your *antecedents;* they came before you.

The horse-drawn wagon is an *antecedent* of the modern automobile.

Antecedent can also be used as an adjective. The oil lamp was *antecedent* to the light bulb.

In grammar, the *antecedent* of a pronoun is the person, place, or thing to which it refers. In the previous sentence, the *antecedent* of *it* is *antecedent*. In the sentence, "Bill and Harry were walking together, and then he hit him," it is impossible to determine what the *antecedents* of the pronouns (*he* and *him*) are.

Antecedent is related to a word that is similar in meaning: *precedent*.

ANTIPATHY (an TIP uh thee) *n* firm dislike; a dislike

I feel *antipathy* toward bananas wrapped in ham. I do not want them for dinner. I also feel a certain amount of *antipathy* toward the cook who keeps trying to force me to eat them. My feelings on these matters are quite *antipathetic*.

I could also say that ham-wrapped bananas and the cooks who serve them are among my *antipathies*. My *antipathies* are the things I don't like.

ANTITHESIS (an TITH i sis) *n* the direct opposite

Erin is the *antithesis* of Erika: Erin is bright and beautiful; Erika is dull and plain.

APARTHEID (uh PAHRT hate, uh PAHRT hite) *n* the abhorrent policy of racial segregation and oppression in the Republic of South Africa.

The word *apartheid* is related to the word *apart*. Under *apartheid* in South Africa, blacks are kept apart from whites and denied all rights.

The word *apartheid* is sometimes applied to less radical forms of racial injustice and to other kinds of separation. Critics have sometimes accused American public schools of practicing educational *apartheid*, by providing substandard schooling for nonwhites.

Q·U·I·C·K · Q·U·I·Z #8

Match each word in the first column with its definition in the second column. Check your answers in the back of the book.

1.	anarchy	a.	resentment
2.	monarchy	b.	racial oppression
3.	anecdote	c.	firm dislike
4.	anguish	d.	irregularity
5.	animosity	e.	what went before
6.	anomaly	f.	agonizing pain
7.	antecedent	g.	amusing account
8.	antipathy	h.	government by king or queen
9.	antithesis	i.	lawlessness
10.	apartheid	j.	direct opposite

APATHY (AP uh thee) *n* lack of interest; lack of feeling

The members of the student council accused the senior class of *apathy* because none of the seniors had bothered to sign up for the big annual Bake Sale.

Jill didn't care one bit about current events; she was entirely *apathetic*.

APHORISM (AF uh RIZ um) *n* a brief, often witty saying; a proverb

Benjamin Franklin was fond of *aphorisms*. He was frequently *aphoristic*.

APOCALYPSE (uh POK uh lips) *n* a prophetic revelation, especially one concerning the end of the world

In strict usage, *apocalypse* refers to specific Judeo-Christian writings from ancient times, but most people use it more generally in connection with predictions of things like nuclear war, the destruction of the ozone layer, and the spread of fast-food restaurants to every corner of the universe. To make such predictions, or to be deeply pessimistic, is to be *apocalyptic*.

APOCRYPHAL (uh POK ruh ful) *n* of dubious authenticity; fictitious; spurious

An *apocryphal* story is one whose truth is not proven or whose falsehood is strongly suspected. Like *apocalypse*, this word has a religious origin. The *Apocrypha* are a number of "extra" books of the Old Testament that Protestants and Jews don't include in their Bibles because they don't think they're authentic.

APOTHEOSIS (uh POTH ee OH sis) *n* elevation to divine status, the perfect example of something

Some people think that the Corvette is the *apotheosis* of American car making. They think it's the ideal.

Geoffrey is unbearable to be with. He thinks he's the *apotheosis* of masculinity.

APPEASE (uh PEEZ) *v* to soothe; to pacify by giving in to

Larry *appeased* his angry mother by promising to make his bed every morning without fail until the end of time.

The trembling farmer handed over all his grain, but still the emperor was not *appeased*.

We *appeased* the angry juvenile delinquents by permitting them to slash the tires of Jerry's father's car.

APPRECIATE (uh PREE shee ATE) *v* to increase in value

The Browns bought their house twenty years ago for a hundred dollars, but it has *appreciated* considerably since then; today it's worth almost a million dollars.

Harry bought Joe's collection of old chewing-tobacco tins as an investment. His hope was that the tins would *appreciate* over the next few years, enabling him to turn a profit by selling them to someone else.

The opposite of *appreciate* is *depreciate*. When a new car loses value over time, we say it has *depreciated*.

APPREHENSIVE (AP ri HEN siv) *adj* worried; anxious

The *apprehensive* child clung to his father's leg as the two of them walked into the main circus tent to watch the lion tamer.

Bill was *apprehensive* about the exam, because he had forgotten to go to class for several months. As it turned out, his *apprehensions* were justified. He couldn't answer a single question on the test.

A *misapprehension* is a misunderstanding. Bill had no *misapprehensions* about his lack of preparation; he knew perfectly well he would fail abysmally.

Q·U·I·C·K · Q·U·I·Z #9

Match each word in the first column with its definition in the second column. Check your answers in the back of the book.

1. apathy	a.	of dubious authenticity
2. aphorism	b.	misunderstanding
3. apocalypse	c.	increase in value
4. apocryphal	d.	lack of interest
5. apotheosis	e.	soothe
6. appease	f.	prophetic revelation
7. appreciate	g.	decrease in value
8. depreciate	h.	the perfect example
9. apprehensive	i.	witty saying
10. misapprehension	j.	worried

APPROBATION (AP ruh BAY shun) *n* approval; praise

The crowd expressed its *approbation* of what the team had done by gleefully covering the field with chicken carcasses.

The ambassador's actions met with the *approbation* of his commander in chief.

Approbation is a fancy word for *approval*, to which it is closely related. *Disapprobation* is disapproval.

APPROPRIATE (uh PROH pree ATE) *v* to take without permission; to set aside for a particular use

Nick *appropriated* my lunch; he grabbed it out of my hands and ate it. So I *appropriated* Ed's.

The deer and raccoons *appropriated* the vegetables in our garden last summer. This year we'll build a better fence.

Don't confuse the pronunciation of the verb *to appropriate* with the pronunciation of the adjective *appropriate* (uh PROH pree it). To *appropriate* has a different meaning as well. When Congress decides to buy some new submarines, it *appropriates* money for them. That is, it sets some money aside. The money thus set aside is called an *appropriation*.

When an elected official takes money that was supposed to be spent on submarines and spends it on a Rolls-Royce and a few mink coats, he is said to have *misappropriated* the money.

When the government decides to build a highway through your backyard, it *expropriates* your property for this purpose. That is, it uses its official authority to take possession of your property.

APTITUDE (AP ti TOOD) *n* capacity for learning; natural ability

Princeton Review students have a marked *aptitude* for taking the Scholastic Aptitude Test. They earn high scores.

I tried to repair my car, but as I sat on the floor of my garage surrounded by mysterious parts, I realized that I had no *aptitude* for automobile repair.

The opposite of *aptitude* is *ineptitude*.

ARBITER (AHR bi tur) *n* one who decides; a judge

A judge is an *arbiter*.

An *arbiter* of fashion is someone who determines what other people will wear by wearing it herself.

An *arbiter arbitrates*, or weighs opposing viewpoints and makes decisions. The words *arbiter* and *arbitrator* mean the same thing.

ARBITRARY (AHR bi TRER ee) *adj* random; capricious

The grades Mr. Simone gave his English students appeared to be *arbitrary;* they didn't seem to be related to anything the students had done in class.

The old judge was *arbitrary* in sentencing criminals; there was no sensible pattern to the sentences he handed down.

ARCANE (ahr KANE) *adj* mysterious; known only to a select few

The rites of the secret cult were *arcane;* no one outside the cult knew what they were.

The *arcane* formula for the cocktail was scrawled in blood on a faded scrap of paper.

We could make out only a little of the *arcane* inscription on the old trunk.

ARCHAIC (ahr KAY ik) *adj* extremely old; ancient; outdated

The tribe's traditions are *archaic*. They have been in force for thousands of years.

Archaic civilizations are ones that disappeared a long time ago.

An *archaic* meaning of a word is one that isn't used anymore.

Q·U·I·C·K · Q·U·I·Z #10

Match each word in the first column with its definition in the second column. Check your answers in the back of the book.

1. approbation	a. misuse public money
2. appropriate	b. extremely old
3. misappropriate	c. take without permission
4. expropriate	d. weigh opposing views
5. aptitude	e. mysterious
6. arbiter	f. approval
7. arbitrate	g. random
8. arbitrary	h. take property officially
9. arcane	i. judge
10. archaic	j. natural ability

ARCHETYPE (AHR ki TYPE) *n* an original model or pattern

An *archetype* is similar to a *prototype*. A *prototype* is a first, tentative model that is made but that will be improved in later versions. Henry Ford built a *prototype* of his Model T in his basement. His mother kicked him out so he had no choice but to start a motor car company.

An *archetype* is usually something that precedes something else. Plato is the *archetype* of all philosophers.

An *archetype* is *archetypal* or *archetypical*.

ARDENT (AHR dunt) *adj* passionate

Larry's *ardent* wooing finally got on Cynthia's nerves, and she told him to get lost.

Blanche happily stuffed badgers from morning to night. She was an *ardent* taxidermist.

To be *ardent* is to have *ardor*. The young lovers were oblivious to everything except their *ardor* for each other.

ARDUOUS (AHR joo us) *adj* hard; difficult

Climbing the mountain was *arduous*. We were so exhausted when we got to the top that we forgot to enjoy the view.

The *arduous* car trip was made even more difficult by the fact that all four tires went flat, one after another.

ARISTOCRATIC (uh RIS tuh KRAT ik) *adj* of noble birth; snobbish

Prince Charles is *aristocratic*. He is a member of the British *aristocracy*, a small class of privileged people.

Polo, which Prince Charles enjoys, is often said to be an *aristocratic* sport, because it is typically played by dukes, marquises, and other privileged people.

It is possible to be an *aristocrat* without being rich, although *aristocrats* tend to be quite wealthy. There is nothing you can do to become an *aristocrat*, short of being born into a family of them.

People who act as though they think they are better than everyone else are often said to be *aristocratic*. A person with an "aristocratic bearing" is a person who keeps his or her nose in the air and looks down on everyone else.

ARTFUL (AHRT ful) *adj* crafty; wily; sly

After dinner, the *artful* counselor told the campers that there was a madman loose in the woods, thus causing them to lie quietly in the tent. The *Artful Dodger* is a sly con man in Charles Dickens's *Oliver Twist*.

Artful does not mean artistic. If an artist is *artful*, it means not that she is talented but that she is in some way crafty or sneaky.

Someone who is *artless*, on the other hand, is simple and honest. Young children are charmingly *artless*.

ARTIFICE (AHRT uh fus) *n* a clever trick; cunning

The Trojan Horse was an *artifice* designed to get the soldiers inside the walls.

Mrs. Baker had to resort to *artifice* to get her children to take their baths: She told them that the bathtub was filled with sugar syrup and that they could drink it if they would take off their clothes and climb in.

Artifice and *artificial* are related words.

ASCENDANCY (uh SEN dun see) *n* supremacy; domination

Small computers have been in *ascendancy* for the last few years.

The *ascendancy* of the new regime had been a great boon for the economy of the tiny tropical kingdom.

When something is in *ascendancy*, it is *ascendant*.

ASCETIC (uh SET ik) *adj* hermitlike; practicing self-denial

The college professor's apartment, which contained no furniture except a single tattered mattress, was uncomfortably *ascetic*.

In his effort to save money, Roy led an *ascetic* existence: he never went out, he never ate anything but soup, and he never had any fun.

Ascetic can also be a noun. A person who leads an *ascetic* existence is an *ascetic*. An *ascetic* is someone who practices *asceticism*.

A similar-sounding word with a very different meaning is *aesthetic*. Don't be confused.

ASSIDUOUS (uh SIJ oo us) *adj* hardworking; busy; quite diligent

The workmen were *assiduous* in their effort to get nothing done; instead of working, they drank coffee all day long.

Wendell was the only *assiduous* student in the entire math class; all the other students had to copy their homework from him.

Q·U·I·C·K · Q·U·I·Z #11

Match each word in the first column with its definition in the second column. Check your answers in the back of the book.

1. archetype
2. ardent
3. arduous
4. aristocratic
5. artful
6. artifice
7. ascendancy
8. ascetic
9. assiduous

a. passionate
b. of noble birth
c. supremacy
d. hardworking
e. difficult
f. trickery
g. hermitlike
h. crafty
i. original model

ASSIMILATE (uh SIM uh LATE) *v* to take in; to absorb; to learn thoroughly

To *assimilate* an idea is to take it in as thoroughly as if you had eaten it. (Your body *assimilates* nutrients from the food you eat.) To *assimilate* knowledge is to absorb it, to let it soak in.

People can be *assimilated*, too. Margaret didn't have any friends when she first went to the new school, but she was gradually *assimilated*—she became part of the new community. When she was chosen for the cheerleading squad, her *assimilation* was complete.

ASSUAGE (uh SWAYJ) *v* to soothe; to pacify; to ease the pain of; to relieve

Beth was extremely angry, but I *assuaged* her by promising to leave the house and never return.

The thunderstorm made the baby cry, but I *assuaged* her fears by singing her a lullaby.

Assuage spelled sideways is *sausage*, a soothing food to some people.

ASTUTE (uh STOOT) *adj* shrewd; keen in judgment

Morris was an *astute* judge of character; he was very good at seeing what people are really like.

Amanda, who notices everything that is important and many things that other people don't see, is an *astute* observer.

ATTRITION (uh TRISH un) *n* gradual wearing away, weakening, or loss; a natural or expected decrease in numbers or size

Mr. Gregory did not have the heart to fire his workers even though his company was losing millions each year. He altruistically preferred to lose workers through *attrition* when they moved away, retired, or decided to change jobs.

AUDACITY (aw DAS i tee) *n* boldness; reckless daring; impertinence

Edgar's soaring leap off the top of the building was an act of great *audacity.*

Ivan had the *audacity* to tell that nice old lady to shut up.

A person with *audacity* is said to be *audacious.* Bert made the *audacious* decision to climb Mt. Everest in bowling shoes.

AUGMENT (awg MENT) *v* to make bigger; to add to; to increase

The army *augmented* its attack by sending in a few thousand more soldiers.

To *augment* a record collection is to add more records to it.

Adding another example to this definition would *augment* it.

The act of *augmenting* is called *augmentation.*

AUSPICIOUS (aw SPISH us) *adj* favorable; promising; pointing to a good result

A clear sky in the morning is an *auspicious* sign on the day of a picnic.

The first quarter of the football game was not *auspicious;* the home team was outscored by seventy points.

AUSTERE (aw STEER) *adj* unadorned; stern; forbidding; without excess

The Smiths' house was very *austere;* there was no furniture in it, and there was nothing hanging on the walls.

Quentin, with his *austere* personality, didn't make many friends. Most people were too intimidated by him to introduce themselves and say hello.

The noun *austerity* (aw STER i tee) is generally used to mean roughly the same thing as poverty. To live in *austerity* is to live without comforts. Conditions in Austria were very *austere* after the war.

AUTOCRATIC (AW tuh KRAT ik) *adj* ruling with absolute authority; extremely bossy

The ruthless dictator's *autocratic* reign ended when the rebels blew up his palace with a few thousand pounds of plastic explosive.

A two-year-old can be very *autocratic*—it wants what it wants when it wants it.

No one at our office liked the *autocratic* manager. She always insisted on having her own way, and she never let anyone make a decision without consulting her.

An *autocrat* is an absolute ruler. *Autocracy,* a system of government headed by an *autocrat,* is not democratic—the people don't get a say.

Q·U·I·C·K · Q·U·I·Z #12

Match each word in the first column with its definition in the second column. Check your answers in the back of the book.

1. assimilate		a. shrewd
2. assuage		b. boldness
3. astute		c. favorable
4. attrition		d. make bigger
5. audacity		e. soothe
6. augment		f. extremely bossy
7. auspicious		g. absorb
8. austere		h. unadorned
9. autocratic		i. gradual wearing away

AUTONOMOUS (aw TON uh mus) *adj* acting independently

The West Coast office of the law firm was quite *autonomous;* it never asked the East Coast office for permission before it did anything.

An *autonomous* nation is one that is independent—it governs itself. It is said to have *autonomy.*

To act *autonomously* is to act on your own authority. If something happens *autonomously,* it happens all by itself.

AVARICE (AV ur is) *n* greed; excessive love of riches

The rich man's *avarice* was annoying to everyone who wanted to lay hands on some of his money.

Avarice is the opposite of generosity or philanthropy.

To be *avaricious* is to love wealth above all else and not to share it with other people.

AVOW (uh VOW) *v* to claim; to declare boldly; to admit

At the age of twenty-five, Louis finally *avowed* that he couldn't stand his mother's apple pie.

To *avow* something is to declare or admit something that most people are reluctant to declare or admit. Mr. Smith *avowed* on television that he had never paid any income tax. Shortly afterward, he received a lengthy letter from the Internal Revenue Service.

An *avowed* criminal is one who admits he is a criminal. To *disavow* is to deny or repudiate someone else's claim. The mayor *disavowed* the allegation that he had embezzled campaign contributions.

AVUNCULAR (uh VUNG kyuh lur) *adj* like an uncle, especially a nice uncle

What's an uncle like? Kind, helpful, generous, understanding, and so on, in an uncle-y sort of way. This is a fun word to use, although it's usually hard to find occasions to use it.

AWRY (uh RYE) *adj* off course; twisted to one side

The hunter's bullet went *awry*. Instead of hitting the bear, it hit an-other hunter.

When we couldn't find a restaurant, our dinner plans went *awry*.

The old man's hat was *awry;* it had dipped in front of his left eye.

AXIOM (AK see um) *n* a self-evident rule or truth; a widely accepted saying

"Everything that is living dies" is an *axiom*.

An *axiom* in geometry is a rule that doesn't have to be proved, because its truth is accepted as obvious, self-evident, or unprovable.

That the rich get richer is an *axiom*. It is unquestionable; it is *axiomatic*.

Q·U·I·C·K · Q·U·I·Z #13

Match each word in the first column with its definition in the second column. Check your answers in the back of the book.

1. autonomous   a. greed
2. avarice   b. like an uncle
3. avow   c. self-evident truth
4. avuncular   d. acting independently
5. awry   e. claim
6. axiom   f. off course

B

BANAL (buh NAL, BANE ul) *adj* unoriginal; ordinary

The dinner conversation was so *banal* that Amanda fell asleep in her dessert dish.

A *banal* statement is a boring, trite, and uncreative statement. It is a *banality*.

What made Amanda fall asleep was the *banality* of the dinner conver-sation.

BANE (bane) *n* poison; torment; cause of harm

Bane means poison (wolfsbane is a kind of poisonous plant), but the word is usually used figuratively. To say that someone is the *bane* of your existence is to say that that person poisons your enjoyment of life.

Baneful means harmful.

BASTION (BAS chun) *n* stronghold; fortress; fortified place

Mrs. Garrett's classroom is a *bastion* of banality; that is, it's a place where originality seldom if ever makes its way inside.

The robbers terrorized the village for several weeks, then escaped to their *bastion* high in the treacherous mountains.

BEGET (bi GET) *v* to give birth to; to create; to lead to; to cause

Those who lie should be creative and have good memories, since one lie often *begets* another lie, which *begets* another.

BELABOR (bi LAY bur) *v* to go over repeatedly or to an absurd extent

For more than an hour, the boring speaker *belabored* his point about the challenge of foreign competition.

Mr. Irving spent the entire period *belaboring* the obvious; he made the same dumb observation over and over again.

BELEAGUER (bi LEE gur) *v* to surround; to besiege; to harass

No one could leave the *beleaguered* city; the attacking army had closed off all the exits.

Oscar felt *beleaguered* at work. He was months behind in his assignments, and he had little hope of catching up.

The *beleaguered* president seldom emerged from the Oval Office as he struggled to deal with the growing scandal.

BELIE (bi LYE) *v* to give a false impression of; to contradict

Melvin's smile *belied* the grief he was feeling; despite his happy expression he was terribly sad inside.

The messy appearance of the banquet table *belied* the huge effort that had gone into setting it up.

A word that is sometimes confused with *belie* is *betray*. To rework the first example above: Melvin was smiling, but a small tear in one eye *betrayed* the grief he was feeling.

The fact that the groom kept his fingers crossed during the wedding ceremony *betrayed* his true feelings about his bride; the loving look he gave his bride *belied* his true feelings.

BELITTLE (bi LIT ul) *v* to make to seem little; to put someone down

We worked hard to put out the fire, but the fire chief *belittled* our efforts by saying he wished he had brought some marshmallows.

The chairman's *belittling* comments made everyone feel small.

Q·U·I·C·K · Q·U·I·Z #14

Match each word in the first column with its definition in the second column. Check your answers in the back of the book.

1. banal
2. bane
3. bastion
4. beget
5. belabor
6. beleaguer
7. belie
8. belittle

a. make to seem little
b. unoriginal
c. go over repeatedly
d. stronghold
e. poison
f. give a false impression
g. surround
h. give birth to

BELLIGERENT (buh LIJ ur unt) *adj* combative; quarrelsome; waging war

A bully is *belligerent*. To be *belligerent* is to push other people around, to be noisy and argumentative, to threaten other people, and generally to make a nuisance of oneself.

Al was so *belligerent* that the convention had the feel of a boxing match.

Opposing armies in a war are referred to as *belligerents*. Sometimes one *belligerent* in a conflict is more *belligerent* than the other.

BEMUSED (bi MYOOZD) *adj* confused; bewildered

To muse is to think about or ponder things. To be *bemused*, then, is to have been thinking about things to the point of confusion.

The two stood *bemused* in the middle of the parking lot at Disneyland, trying to remember where they had parked their car.

Ralph was *bemused* when all the lights and appliances in his house began switching on and off for no apparent reason.

People often use the word *bemused* when they really mean "amused," but *bemusement* is no laughing matter. *Bemused* means confused.

BENEFACTOR (BEN uh FAK tur) *n* one who provides help, especially in the form of a gift or donation

To give benefits is to be a *benefactor*. To receive benefits is to be a *beneficiary*. People very, very often confuse these two words. It would be to their benefit to keep them straight.

If your next-door neighbor rewrites his life insurance policy so that you will receive all his millions when he dies, then you become the *beneficiary* of the policy. If your neighbor then dies, he is your *benefactor*.

A *malefactor* is a person who does bad things. Batman and Robin made life hell for malefactors in Gotham City.

BENEVOLENT (buh NEV uh lunt) *adj* generous; kind; doing good deeds

Giving money to the poor is a *benevolent* act. To be *benevolent* is to bestow benefits. The United Way, like any charity, is a *benevolent* organization.

BENIGN (bi NYNE) *adj* gentle; not harmful; kind; mild

Betty has a *benign* personality; she is not at all unpleasant to be with.

The threat of revolution turned out to be *benign;* nothing much came of it.

Charlie was worried that he had cancer, but the lump on his leg turned out to be *benign*.

The difference between a *benign* person and a *benevolent* (see separate entry) one is that the *benevolent* one is actively kind and generous while the *benign* one is more passive. *Benevolence* is usually active generosity or kindness, while *benignancy* tends to mean simply not causing harm.

The opposite of a *benign* tumor is a *malignant* one. This is a tumor that can kill you. A *malignant* personality is one you wish a surgeon would remove. *Malignant* means nasty, evil, and full of ill will. The word *malignant* also conveys a sense that the evil is spreading, as with a cancer. An adjective that means the same thing is *malign*.

As a verb, *malign* has a different meaning. To *malign* someone is to say unfa___d things about that person, to injure that person by telling evil lies ab___ him or her. Slander and *malign* are synonyms.

Q·U·I·C·K · Q·U·I·Z #15

Match each word in the first column with its definition in the second column. Check your answers in the back of the book.

1. belligerent	a. intending harm
2. bemused	b. donor
3. benefactor	c. not harmful
4. beneficiary	d. deadly
5. benevolent	e. confused
6. benign	f. generous
7. malignant	g. combative
8. malign	h. injure with lies
9. malevolent	i. one who receives benefits
10. malefactor	j. evildoer

BEQUEST (bi KWEST) *n* something left to someone in a will

If your next-door neighbor leaves you all his millions in a will, the money is a *bequest* from him to you. It is not polite to request a *bequest*. Just keep smiling and hope for the best.

To leave something to someone in a will is to *bequeath* it. A *bequest* is something that has been *bequeathed*.

BEREFT (bi REFT) *adj* deprived or left desolate, especially through death

Bereaved means the same thing as *bereft*.

The new widow was still *bereaved* when we saw her. Every time anyone mentioned her dead husband's name, she burst into tears.

The children were *bereaved* by the death of their pet. Then they got a new pet.

BESET (bi SET) *v* to harass; to surround

The *bereft* widow was *beset* by grief.

Problems *beset* the expedition almost from the beginning, and the mountain climbers soon returned to their base camp.

The little town was *beset* by robberies, but the police could do nothing.

BLASPHEMY (BLAS fuh mee) *n* irreverence; an insult to something held sacred; profanity

In the strictest sense, to commit *blasphemy* is to say nasty, insulting things about God. The word is used more broadly, though, to cover a wide range of nasty, insulting comments.

To *blaspheme* (blas FEEM, BLAS feem) is to use swear words or say deeply irreverent things. A person who says such things is *blasphemous*.

BLATANT (BLAT unt) *adj* unpleasantly or offensively noisy;

David was *blatantly* critical of our efforts; that is, he was ~~obnoxious~~ obnoxious in making his criticisms.

Blatant is often confused with *flagrant*, since both words mean glaring. A *blatant* act is usually also a *flagrant* one, but a *flagrant* act isn't necessarily *blatant*. You might want to refer to the listing for *flagrant*.

Q·U·I·C·K · Q·U·I·Z · #16

Match each word in the first column with its definition in the second column. Check your answers in the back of the book.

1.	bequest	a.	left desolate
2.	bequeath	b.	something left in a will
3.	bereft	c.	harass
4.	beset	d.	offensively noisy
5.	blasphemy	e.	leave in a will
6.	blatant	f.	irreverence

BLIGHT (blyte) *n* a disease in plants; anything that injures or destroys

An early frost proved a *blight* to the citrus crops last year, so we had no orange juice for breakfast.

BLITHE (blythe) *adj* carefree; cheerful

The *blithe* birds in the garden were making so much noise that Paul began to think about the shotgun in the attic.

The children were playing *blithely* in the hazardous-waste dump. While they played, they were *blithely* unaware that they were doing something dangerous.

To be *blithely* ignorant is to be happily unaware.

BOURGEOIS (boor ZHWAW) *adj* middle class, usually in a pejorative sense; boringly conventional

The original *bourgeoisie* (BOOR zhwaw ZEE) were simply people who lived in cities, an innovation at the time. They weren't farmers and they weren't nobles. They were members of a new class—the middle class. Now the word is used mostly in making fun of or sneering at people who seem to think about nothing but their possessions and other comforts and about conforming with other people who share those concerns.

A hip young city dweller might reject life in the suburbs as being too *bourgeois*. A person whose dream is to have a swimming pool in his backyard might be called *bourgeois* by someone who thinks there are more important things in life. Golf is often referred to as a *bourgeois* sport.

BOVINE (BOH vyne) *adj* cow related; cowlike

Cows are *bovine*, obviously. Eating grass is a *bovine* concern.

A fat or mooing person might be said to be *bovine*, too.

The woman's *bovine* figure made her very unpopular with the man sitting next to her on the airplane.

There are a number of similar words based on other animals:

canine: dogs
feline: cats
equine: horses
piscine: fish
porcine: pigs
ursine: bears

BREVITY (BREV i tee) *n* briefness

The audience was deeply grateful for the *brevity* of the after-dinner speaker's remarks.

The reader of this book may be grateful for the *brevity* of this example.

BROACH (broach) *v* to open up a subject for discussion, often a delicate subject

Henrietta was proud of her new dress, so no one knew how to *broach* the subject with her of how silly grandmothers look in leather.

BUCOLIC (byoo KOL ik) *adj* charmingly rural; rustic; countrylike

The changing of the autumn leaves, old stone walls, distant views, and horses grazing in green meadows are examples of *bucolic* splendor.

The *bucolic* scene didn't do much for the city child, who preferred screaming fire engines and honking horns to the sound of a babbling brook.

BUREAUCRACY (byoo ROK ruh see) *n* a system of government administration consisting of numerous bureaus or offices, especially one run according to inflexible and inefficient rules; any large administrative system characterized by inefficiency, lots of rules, and red tape

The Department of Motor Vehicles is a *bureaucracy.* Every clerk you speak with hands you a printed form and tells you to stand in line somewhere else. No one can answer all your questions. At lunchtime, when the lines are longest, half the clerks disappear. The forms you have to fill out all request unnecessary information. After you finally get everything all filled out and handed in, you don't hear another word from the Department for many months.

The people who work in a *bureaucracy* are called *bureaucrats.* These people and the inefficient procedures they follow might be called *bureaucratic.* Administrative systems outside the government can be *bureaucratic,* too. A high school principal who required teachers and students to fill out forms for everything might be called *bureaucratic.*

BURGEON (BUR jun) *v* to expand; to flourish

The *burgeoning* weeds in our yard soon overwhelmed the grass.

BURLESQUE (bur LESK) *n* a ludicrous, mocking, or exaggerated imitation

Vaudeville actors frequently performed *burlesque* works on the stage.

Burlesque, parody, lampoon, and caricature share similar meanings.

Q·U·I·C·K · Q·U·I·Z #17

*Match each word in the first column with its definition in the second
column. Check your answers in the back of the book.*

1. blight	a. flourish
2. blithe	b. bearlike
3. bourgeois	c. carefree
4. bovine	d. catlike
5. canine	e. cowlike
6. feline	f. charmingly rural
7. equine	g. middle class
8. piscine	h. horselike
9. porcine	i. briefness
10. ursine	j. piglike
11. brevity	k. inflexible administration
12. broach	l. fishlike
13. bucolic	m. doglike
14. bureaucracy	n. plant disease
15. burgeon	o. open a subject
16. burlesque	p. ludicrous imitation

C

CACOPHONY (kuh KOF uh nee) *n* harsh-sounding mixture of words,
voices, or sounds

A *cacophony* isn't just a lot of noise—it's a lot of noise that doesn't sound
good together. A steam whistle blowing isn't a *cacophony*. But a high
school orchestra that had never rehearsed together might very well produce a *cacophony*. The roar of engines, horns, and sirens arising from a
busy city street would be a *cacophony*. A lot of people all shouting at once
would produce a *cacophony*.

Euphony is the opposite of *cacophony*. *Euphony* is pleasing sound.

CADENCE (KADE uns) *n* rhythm; the rise and fall of sounds

We wished the tone of Irwin's words would have a more pleasing
cadence, but he spoke in a dull monotone.

CAJOLE (kuh JOHL) *v* to persuade someone to do something he or she
doesn't want to do

I didn't want to give the speech, but Joel *cajoled* me into doing it by
telling me what a good speaker I am. As it turned out, he simply hadn't
been able to find anyone else.

CALLOW (KAL oh) *adj* immature

To be *callow* is to be youthfully naïve, inexperienced, and unsophisticated.

A teenager might show *callow* disregard for the feelings of adults.

Driving fast cars and hanging out in the parking lot at the 7-Eleven are *callow* pursuits.

The patient was alarmed by the *callowness* of the medical staff. The doctors looked too young to have graduated from high school, much less from medical school.

CANDOR (KAN dur) *n* truthfulness; sincere honesty

My best friend exhibited *candor* when he told me that for many years now he has believed me to be a jerk.

Teddy appreciated Ross's *candor;* Teddy was glad to know that Ross thought Teddy's sideburns looked stupid.

To show *candor* is to be *candid.* What is *candid* about the camera on *Candid Camera?* The camera is *candid* because it is truthful in showing what people do when they can't turn off the coffee machine in the office where they're applying for a job. *Candid* does *not* mean "concealed" or "hidden," even though the camera on *Candid Camera* is concealed. To be *candid* is to speak frankly.

CAPITALISM (KAP i tuh LIZ um) *n* free enterprise; an economic system in which businesses are owned by private citizens (not by the government) and in which the resulting products and services are sold with relatively little government control.

The American economy is *capitalistic.* If you wanted to start a company to sell signed photographs of yourself, you could. You, and not the government, would decide how much you would charge for the pictures. Your success or failure would depend on how many people decided to buy your pictures.

CAPITULATE (kuh PICH uh LATE) *v* to surrender; to give up or give in

I urged him and urged him to take off his cap; when I threatened to knock his head off, he *capitulated.*

On the twentieth day of the strike, the workers *capitulated* and went back to work without a new contract.

To *recapitulate* is not to *capitulate* again. To *recapitulate* is to summarize.

So few students paid attention to Mr. Jones that he had to *recapitulate* his major points at the end of the class.

CAPRICIOUS (kuh PRISH us, kuh PREE shus) *adj* unpredictable; likely to change at any moment

Bill was very *capricious.* One minute he said his favorite car was a Chevy Caprice; the next minute he said it was a Camaro.

The weather is often said to be *capricious.* One minute it's snowing, the next minute it's 120 degrees in the shade.

A *caprice* is a whim.

Penny attempted a quadruple somersault off the ten-meter diving board as a *caprice.* It was a painful *caprice.*

CARICATURE (KAR uh kuh chur, KAR uh kuh choor) *n* a portrait or description that is purposely distorted or exaggerated, often to prove some point about its subject

Editorial cartoonists often draw *caricatures*. Big noses, enormous glasses, floppy ears, and other distortions are common in such drawings. A politician who has been convicted of bribery might be depicted in a prison uniform or with a ball and chain around his ankle. If the politician has big ears to begin with, the ears might be drawn vastly bigger.

A *caricature* uses exaggeration to bring out the hidden character of its subject.

The word can also be used as a verb. To *caricature* someone is to create such a distorted portrait.

CASTIGATE (KAS tuh GATE) *v* to criticize severely; to chastise

Jim's mother-in-law *castigated* him for forgetting to pick her up at the airport.

CATALYST (KAT uh list) *n* in chemistry, something that changes the rate of a chemical reaction without itself being changed; anyone or anything that makes something happen without being directly involved in it

When the mad scientist dropped a few grains of the *catalyst* into his test tube, the bubbling liquid began to boil furiously.

This word is often used outside the laboratory as well. The launching of Sputnik by the Russians provided the *catalyst* for the creation of the modern American space program.

The tragic hijacking provided the *catalyst* for Congress's new antiterrorist legislation.

Q·U·I·C·K · Q·U·I·Z #18

Match each word in the first column with its definition in the second column. Check your answers in the back of the book.

1. cacophony		a.	truthfulness
2. cadence		b.	harsh mixture of sounds
3. cajole		c.	surrender
4. callow		d.	distorted portrait
5. candor		e.	unpredictable
6. capitalism		f.	immature
7. capitulate		g.	free enterprise
8. recapitulate		h.	it makes things happen
9. capricious		i.	summarize
10. caricature		j.	persuade deceptively
11. castigate		k.	criticize severely
12. catalyst		l.	rhythm

CATEGORICAL (KAT uh GAWR i kul) *adj* unconditional; absolute

A *categorical* denial is one without exceptions—it covers every *category*. Crooked politicians often make *categorical* denials of various charges against them. Then they go to jail.

I *categorically* refuse to do anything whatsoever at any time, in any place, with anyone.

CATHARSIS (kuh THAR sis) *n* purification that brings emotional relief or renewal

To someone with psychological problems, talking to a psychiatrist can lead to a *catharsis*. A *catharsis* is a sometimes traumatic event after which one feels better.

A *catharsis* is *cathartic*. Some people find emotional movies *cathartic*—watching one often allows them to release buried emotions. *Cathartic* can also be a noun. Young Teddy swallowed the contents of a bottle of shoe polish, so his mother gave him a raw egg as a *cathartic* to make him vomit.

CATHOLIC (KATH uh lik) *adj* universal; embracing everything

Catholic with a small "c" means universal. Da Vinci was a *catholic* genius who excelled at everything he did. *Parochial* means narrow-minded, so *parochial* and *catholic* are almost opposites.

CAUSTIC (KAW stik) *adj* like acid; corrosive

Paint remover is a *caustic* substance; if you spill it on your skin, your skin will burn.

The *caustic* detergent ate right through Henry's laundry.

Caustic can be used figuratively as well. A *caustic* comment is one that is so nasty or insulting that it seems to sting or burn the person to whom it is directed. The teacher's *caustic* criticism of Sally's term paper left her in tears.

CELIBACY (SEL uh buh see) *n* abstinence from sex

People who practice *celibacy* don't practice sex.

To practice *celibacy* is to be *celibate*. You will look a very long time in Hollywood before you find a *celibate* celebrity.

Celibacy is one of the requirements for Catholic priesthood.

CENSURE (SEN shur) *v* to condemn severely for doing something bad

The Senate sometimes *censures* senators for breaking laws or engaging in behavior unbecoming to an elected official.

Censure can also be a noun. The clumsy physician feared the *censure* of his fellow doctors, so he stopped treating anything more complicated than the common cold.

A Senate that made a habit of *censuring* senators might be said to be *censorious*. To be *censorious* is to be highly critical—to do a lot of *censuring*.

CEREBRAL (SER uh brul, suh REE brul) *adj* brainy; intellectually refined

Your *cerebrum* is the biggest part of your brain. To be *cerebral* is to do and care about things that really smart people do and care about.

A *cerebral* discussion is one that is filled with big words and concerns abstruse matters that ordinary people can't understand.

Bill was too *cerebral* to be a baseball announcer; he kept talking about the existentialism of the outfield.

CHAGRIN (shuh. GRIN) *n* humiliation; embarrassed disappointment

Much to my *chagrin*, I began to giggle during the eulogy at the funeral.

Doug was filled with *chagrin* when he lost the race because he had put his shoes on the wrong feet.

The word *chagrin* is sometimes used incorrectly to mean "surprise." There is, however, a definite note of shame in *chagrin*.

To be *chagrined* is to feel humiliated or mortified.

CHARISMA (kuh RIZ muh) *n* a magical-seeming ability to attract followers or inspire loyalty

The glamorous presidential candidate had a lot of *charisma;* voters didn't seem to support him so much as be entranced by him.

The evangelist's undeniable *charisma* enabled him to bring in millions and millions of dollars in donations to his television show.

To have *charisma* is to be *charismatic*.

Q·U·I·C·K · Q·U·I·Z #19

Match each word in the first column with its definition in the second column. Check your answers in the back of the book.

1. categorical		a.	unconditional
2. catharsis		b.	relieving purification
3. catholic		c.	abstinence from sex
4. caustic		d.	brainy
5. celibacy		e.	humiliation
6. censure		f.	magical attractiveness
7. cerebral		g.	corrosive
8. chagrin		h.	condemn severely
9. charisma		i.	universal

CHARLATAN (SHAR luh tun) *n* fraud; quack; con man

Buck was selling what he claimed was a cure for cancer, but he was just a *charlatan* (the pills were jelly beans).

The flea market usually attracts a lot of *charlatans*, who sell phony products that don't do what they claim they will.

CHASM (KAZ um) *n* a deep, gaping hole; a gorge

Bill was so stupid that his girlfriend wondered whether there wasn't a *chasm* where his brain should be.

The bad guys were gaining, so the hero grabbed the heroine and swung across the *chasm* on a slender vine.

CHASTISE (chas TIZE) *v* to inflict punishment on; to discipline
Mother *chastised* us for firing our bottle rockets through the living-room window.
Chastising the dog for sleeping in the fireplace never seemed to do any good; the minute we turned our backs, he'd curl up in the ashes again.

CHICANERY (shi KAY nuh ree) *n* trickery; deceitfulness; artifice, especially legal or political
Political news would be dull were it not for the *chicanery* of our elected officials.

CHIMERA (kye MEER uh) *n* an illusion; a foolish fancy
Susan's dream of becoming a movie star was just a *chimera*.
Could you take a picture of a *chimera* with a camera? No, of course not. It wouldn't show up on the film.
Be careful not to mispronounce this word. Its apparent similarity to chimney is just a *chimera*.

CHOLERIC (KOL ur ik) *adj* hot-tempered; quick to anger
The *choleric* watchdog would sink his teeth into anyone who came within biting distance of his doghouse.
When the grumpy old man was in one of his *choleric* moods, the children refused to go near him.
The *choleric* administrator kept all the secretaries in a state of terror.

CHRONIC (KRON ik) *adj* constant; lasting a long time; inveterate
Someone who always comes in last could be called a *chronic* loser.
Chronic is usually associated with something negative or undesirable: *chronic* illness, *chronic* failure, *chronic* depression. You would be much less likely to encounter a reference to *chronic* success or *chronic* happiness, unless the writer or speaker was being ironic.
A *chronic* disease is one that lingers for a long time, doesn't go away, or keeps coming back. The opposite of a *chronic* disease is an *acute* disease. An *acute* disease is one that comes and goes very quickly. It may be severe, but it doesn't last forever.

CHRONICLE (KRON i kul) *n* a record of events in order of time; a history
Sally's diary provided her mother with a detailed *chronicle* of her daughter's extracurricular activities. *Chronicle* can also be used as a verb. The reporter *chronicled* all the events of the revolution. *Chronology* and *chronicle* are nearly synonyms: Both provide a *chronological* list of events. *Chronological* means in order of time.

Q·U·I·C·K · Q·U·I·Z #20

Match each word in the first column with its definition in the second column. Check your answers in the back of the book.

1. charlatan		a.	in order of occurrence
2. chasm		b.	constant
3. chastise		c.	hot-tempered
4. chicanery		d.	punish
5. chimera		e.	account of past times
6. chivalrous		f.	list in time order
7. choleric		g.	illusion
8. chronic		h.	fraud
9. chronological		i.	gallant
10. chronology		j.	gaping hole
11. chronicle		k.	trickery

CIRCUITOUS (sur KYOO i tus) *adj* roundabout; not following a direct path

The *circuitous* bus route between the two cities went here, there, and everywhere, and it took an extremely long time to get anywhere.

The salesman's route was *circuitous*—it wound aimlessly through many small towns.

A *circuitous* argument is one that rambles around for quite a while before making its point.

A *circuitous* argument is very similar to a *circular* argument, which is one that ends up where it begins or attempts to prove something without offering any new information. To say, "A majority is that which exists when there is a majority," is to give a *circular,* or tautological, definition of the word *majority.*

CIRCUMLOCUTION (SUR kum loh KYOO shun) *n* an indirect expression; use of wordy or evasive language

The lawyer's *circumlocution* left everyone in the courtroom wondering what had been said.

The indicted executive evaded the reporters' questions by resorting to *circumlocution.*

To use a lot of big, vague words and to speak in a disorganized way is to be *circumlocutory.*

CIRCUMSCRIBE (SUR kum SKRIBE) *v* to draw a line around; to set the limits; to define; to restrict

The Constitution clearly *circumscribes* the restrictions that can be placed on our personal freedoms.

A barbed-wire fence and armed guards *circumscribed* the movement of the prisoners.

CIRCUMSPECT (SUR kum SPEKT) *adj* cautious

As a public speaker, Nick was extremely *circumspect;* he always took great care not to say the wrong thing or give offense.

The *circumspect* general did everything he could not to put his soldiers at unnecessary risk.

The word *circumspect* comes from Greek roots meaning "around" and "look" (as do the words *circle* and *inspect*). To be *circumspect* is to look around carefully before doing something.

CIRCUMVENT (SUR kum VENT) *v* to frustrate as though by surrounding

Our hopes for an early end of the meeting were *circumvented* by the chairman's refusal to deal with the items on the agenda.

The angry school board *circumvented* the students' effort to install color television sets in every classroom.

CIVIL (SIV il) *adj* polite; civilized; courteous

Our dinner guests conducted themselves *civilly* when we told them we weren't going to serve them dinner after all. They didn't bang their cups on the table or throw their plates to the floor.

The word *civil* also has other meanings. *Civil* rights are rights established by law. *Civil* service is government service. Consult your dictionary for the numerous shades of meaning.

CLANDESTINE (klan DES tin) *adj* secret; sneaky; concealed and, usually, up to no good

The head of the CIA was upset when the agency's *clandestine* activities in Central America were discussed on *Donahue.*

Crimes are usually *clandestine*, because criminals usually don't want to get caught.

When a politician does something *clandestinely*, she doesn't want the voters to know about it.

The child ate the stolen cookies *clandestinely*, when no one was looking.

CLEMENCY (KLEM un see) *n* mercy; forgiveness; mildness

The judge displayed *clemency* in giving the student a suspended sentence for shooting Mr. Reed, his dreadful math teacher.

The governor committed an act of *clemency* when he released all the convicts from the state penitentiary.

Mild weather is called *clement* weather; bad weather is called *inclement*. You should wear a coat and carry an umbrella in *inclement* weather.

CLICHÉ (klee SHAY) *n* an overused saying or idea

The expression "You can't judge a book by its cover" is a *cliché*; it's been used so many times its freshness has been worn away.

Clichés are usually true. That's why they've been repeated often enough to become overused. But they are boring. A writer who uses a lot of *clichés*—referring to a foreign country as "a land of contrasts," describing spring as "a time of renewal," saying that a snowfall is a "blanket of white"—is not interesting to read, because there is nothing new about his observations.

CLIQUE (klik, kleek) *n* an exclusive group bound together by some shared quality or interest

The high school newspaper staff was a real *clique;* they all hung out together and wouldn't talk to anyone else. It's hard to have fun at that school if you aren't a member of the right *clique.*

The cheerleaders were *cliquish* as well.

Q·U·I·C·K · Q·U·I·Z #21

Match each word in the first column with its definition in the second column. Check your answers in the back of the book.

1. circuitous
2. circumlocution
3. circumscribe
4. circumspect
5. circumvent
6. civil
7. clandestine
8. clemency
9. inclement
10. cliché
11. clique

a. cautious
b. secret
c. mercy
d. polite
e. roundabout
f. frustrate
g. overused saying
h. indirect expression
i. exclusive group
j. bad, as in weather
k. draw a line around

COALESCE (KOH uh LES) *v* to come together as one; to fuse; to unite

When the dough *coalesced* into a big black blob, we began to wonder whether the cookies would be good to eat.

The people in our neighborhood *coalesced* into a powerful force for change in the community.

A *coalition* is a group of people that has come together for some purpose, often a political one. Coal miners and cola bottlers might *coalesce* into a *coalition* for the purpose of persuading coal mine owners to provide cola machines in coal mines.

The southern *coalition* in Congress is the group of representatives from southern states who often vote the same way.

COERCE (koh URS) *v* to force someone to do or not to do something

Darth Vader tried flattery, Darth Vader tried gifts, Darth Vader even tried to *coerce,* but Darth Vader was never able to make Han Solo reveal the hidden rebel base.

COGENT (KOH junt) *adj* powerfully convincing

Cogent reasons are extremely persuasive ones.

Kojak was *cogent* in explaining why he needed another lollipop, so we gave him one.

The lawyer's argument in his client's behalf was not *cogent*, so the jury convicted his client. The jury was persuaded by the *cogency* of the district attorney's argument.

COGNITIVE (KOG ni tiv) *adj* dealing with how we know the world around us through our senses; mental

Scientists study the *cognitive* apparatus of human beings to pattern how computers should gather information about the world.

Cognition is knowing.

COGNIZANT (KOG ni zunt) *adj* aware; conscious

To be *cognizant* of your responsibilities is to know what your responsibilities are.

Al was *cognizant* of the dangers of sword swallowing, but he tried it anyway and hurt himself quite badly.

COHERENT (koh HEER unt) *adj* holding together; making sense

A *coherent* wad of cotton balls is one that holds together.

A *coherent* explanation is an explanation that makes sense; the explanation holds together.

To hold together is to *cohere*.

COLLOQUIAL (kuh LOH kwee ul) *adj* conversational; informal in language

A writer with a *colloquial* style is a writer who uses ordinary words and whose writing seems as informal as common speech.

"The way I figure it" is a *colloquial* expression, or a *colloquialism:* people often say it but it isn't used in formal prose.

COLLUSION (kuh LOO zhun) *n* conspiracy; secret cooperation

The increase in oil prices was the result of *collusion* by the oil-producing nations.

There was *collusion* among the owners of the baseball teams; they agreed secretly not to sign any expensive free agents.

If the baseball owners were in *collusion,* then you could say that they had *colluded.* To *collude* is to conspire.

COMMENSURATE (kuh MEN sur it) *adj* equal; proportionate

Ernie's salary is *commensurate* with his abilities; like his abilities, his salary is small.

The number of touchdowns scored by the team and the number of its victories were *commensurate* (both zero).

COMPELLING (kum PEL ing) *adj* forceful; causing to yield

A *compelling* argument for buying a videocassette recorder is one that makes you go out and buy a videocassette recorder.

The recruiter's speech was so *compelling* that nearly everyone in the auditorium enlisted in the army when it was over.

To *compel* someone to do something is to force him or her to do it. Our consciences *compelled* us to turn the money we had found over to the authorities.

COMPENDIUM (kum PEN dee um) *n* a summary; an abridgment

A yearbook often contains a *compendium* of the offenses, foibles, and crimes of the members of the senior class.

Q·U·I·C·K · Q·U·I·Z #22

Match each word in the first column with its definition in the second column. Check your answers in the back of the book.

1. coalesce	a. perceptive
2. coalition	b. unite
3. coerce	c. conversational
4. cogent	d. force someone to do something
5. cognitive	e. proportionate
6. cognizant	f. making sense
7. coherent	g. group with a purpose
8. colloquial	h. powerfully convincing
9. collusion	i. summary
10. commensurate	j. forceful
11. compelling	k. conspiracy
12. compendium	l. dealing with how we know our environment

COMPLACENT (kum PLAY sunt) *adj* self-satisfied; overly pleased with oneself; contented to a fault

The *complacent* camper paid no attention to the bear prowling around his campsite, and the bear ate him up.

The football team won so many games that it became *complacent*, and the worst team in the league snuck up and beat it.

To fall into *complacency* is to become comfortably uncaring about the world around you.

The president of the student council was appalled by the *complacency* of his classmates; not one of the seniors seemed to care whether the theme of the prom was "You Light Up My Life" or "Color My World."

Don't confuse *complacent* with *complaisant* (kum PLAY zunt), which means eager to please.

COMPLEMENT (KOM pluh munt) *v* to complete or fill up; to be the perfect counterpart

This word is often confused with *compliment*, which means to praise. It's easy to tell them apart. *Complement* is spelled like *complete*. The flower arrangement *complemented* the table decorations.

Complement can also be a noun. Fish-flavored ice cream was a perfect *complement* to the seafood dinner.

COMPLICITY (kum PLIS i tee) *n* participation in wrongdoing; the act of being an accomplice

There was *complicity* between the bank robber and the dishonest teller. The teller neglected to turn on the alarm, and the robber rewarded him by sharing the loot.

Complicity among the students made it impossible to find out which of them had set fire to the Spanish teacher.

COMPREHENSIVE (KOM pri HEN siv) *adj* covering or including everything

The insurance policy was *comprehensive;* it covered all possible losses.

A *comprehensive* examination is one that covers everything in the course, or everything in a particular field of knowledge.

Mabel's knowledge of English was *comprehensive;* she even understood what *comprehensive* means.

COMPRISE (kum PRIZE) *v* to consist of

A football team *comprises* eleven players on offense and eleven players on defense.

A company *comprises* employees.

This word is very often misused. Be careful. Players do *not* "comprise" a football team, and employees do *not* "comprise" a company. Nor can a football team be said to be "comprised of" players, or a company to be "comprised of" employees. These are very common mistakes. Instead, you can say that players *constitute* or *compose* a team, and that employees *constitute* or *compose* a company. You can also say that a team *consists of* players or a company *consists of* employees.

CONCILIATORY (kun SIL ee uh tawr ee) *adj* making peace; attempting to resolve a dispute through goodwill

To be *conciliatory* is to kiss and make up. Come on—be *conciliatory!*

The formerly warring countries were *conciliatory* at the treaty conference.

After dinner at the all-you-can-eat pancake house, the divorced couple began to feel *conciliatory,* so they flew to Las Vegas and were remarried.

When peace has been made, we say that the warring parties have come to a *reconciliation.* To *reconcile* is to bring two things into agreement. The accountant managed to *reconcile* the company books with cash on hand only with great creativity.

CONCISE (kun SISE) *adj* brief and to the point; succinct

The scientist's explanation was *concise;* it was brief and it helped us understand the difficult concept.

To be *concise* is to say much with few words.

A *concise* speaker is one who speaks *concisely,* or who speaks with *concision.*

Q·U·I·C·K · Q·U·I·Z #23

Match each word in the first column with its definition in the second column. Check your answers in the back of the book.

1. complacent
2. complement
3. complicity
4. comprehensive
5. comprise
6. compose
7. constitute
8. conciliatory
9. concise

a. covering everything
b. complete
c. consist of
d. make up (2)
e. brief and to the point
f. making peace
g. participation in wrongdoing
h. self-satisfied

CONCORD (KON kawrd) *n* harmony; agreement

Nations that live in *concord* are nations that live together in peace.

The war between the neighboring tribes ended thirty years of *concord*.

The faculty meeting was marked by *concord;* no one yelled at anyone else.

Discord is the opposite of *concord*. A faculty meeting where everyone yelled at one another would be a faculty meeting marked by *discord*. It would be a *discordant* meeting.

CONCURRENT (kun KUR unt) *adj* happening at the same time; parallel

The criminal was sentenced to two *concurrent* fifteen-year sentences; the sentences will run at the same time, and he will be out of jail in fifteen years.

High prices, falling demand, and poor weather were three *concurrent* trends that made life especially difficult for popcorn farmers last month.

To *concur* means to agree. The assistant wanted to keep his job, so he always *concurred* with his boss.

CONDESCEND (KON di send) *v* to stoop to someone else's level, usually in an offensive way; to patronize

I was surprised that the president of the company had *condescended* to talk with me, a mere temporary employee.

Many grown-ups make the mistake of *condescending* to young children, who usually prefer to be treated as equals, or at least as rational beings.

CONDONE (kun DOHN) *v* to overlook; to permit to happen

To *condone* what someone does is to look the other way while it happens, or to permit it to happen by not doing anything about it.

The principal *condoned* the hoods' smoking in the bathroom; he simply ignored it.

CONDUCIVE (kun DOO siv) *adj* promoting

The chairs in the library are *conducive* to sleep. If you sit in them to study, you will fall asleep.

The foul weather was not *conducive* to our having a picnic.

The teacher's easygoing manner was *conducive* to chaos in the classroom.

CONFLUENCE (KON floo uns) *n* a flowing together, especially of rivers; the place where they begin to flow together

The *confluence* of the Missouri and Mississippi rivers is at St. Louis; that's the place where they join together.

There is a remarkable *confluence* in our thoughts: we think the same way about almost everything.

A *confluence* of many factors (no ice, bad food, terrible music) made it inevitable that the party would be a big flop.

CONGENIAL (kun JEEN yul) *adj* agreeably suitable; pleasant

The little cabin in the woods was *congenial* to the writer; he was able to get a lot of writing done there.

The new restaurant has a *congenial* atmosphere. We enjoy just sitting there playing with the ice in our water glasses.

When people get along together at a restaurant, and don't throw food at one another, they are being *congenial*.

Genial and *congenial* share similar meanings. *Genial* means pleasing, kind, sympathetic or helpful. You can be pleased by a *genial* manner or by a *genial* climate.

CONGENITAL (kun JEN i tul) *adj* a trait or condition acquired between conception and birth; innate

A *congenital* birth defect is one that is present at birth but was not caused by one's genes.

The word is also used more loosely to describe any (usually bad) trait or behavior that is so firmly fixed it seems to be a part of a person's nature.

A *congenital* liar is a natural liar, a person who can't help but lie.

Q·U·I·C·K · Q·U·I·Z #24

Match each word in the first column with its definition in the second column. Check your answers in the back of the book.

1. concord
2. discord
3. concurrent
4. condescend
5. condone
6. conducive
7. confluence
8. congenial
9. congenital

a. agreeably suitable
b. innate
c. harmony
d. flowing together
e. promoting
f. stoop or patronize
g. overlook
h. happening at the same time
i. disharmony

CONJECTURE (kun JEK chur) *v* to guess; to deduce or infer on slight evidence

If forced to *conjecture*, I would say the volcano will erupt in twenty-four hours.

Conjecture can also be a noun. The divorce lawyer for Mr. Davis argued that the putative cause of the lipstick on his collar was mere *conjecture*.

A *conjecture* is *conjectural*.

CONJURE (KON jur) *v* to summon or bring into being as if by magic

The chef *conjured* [or *conjured* up] a fabulous gourmet meal using nothing more than the meager ingredients in Lucy's kitchen.

The wizard *conjured* [or *conjured* up] an evil spirit by mumbling some magic words and throwing a little powdered eye of newt into the fire.

CONNOISSEUR (KON uh SUR) *n* an expert, particularly in matters of art or taste

The artist's work was very popular, but *connoisseurs* rejected it as amateurish.

Frank was a *connoisseur* of bad movies. He had seen them all and knew which ones were genuinely dreadful and which ones were merely poorly made.

The meal was exquisite enough to impress a *connoisseur*.

I like sculpture, but I'm no *connoisseur;* I couldn't tell you why one statue is better than another.

CONSECRATE (KON suh KRATE) *v* to make or declare sacred

The Veterans Day speaker said that the battlefield had been *consecrated* by the blood of the soldiers who had died there.

The priest *consecrated* the building by sprinkling holy water on it.

The college chaplain delivered a sermon at the *consecration* ceremony for the new chapel.

The opposite of *consecrate* is *desecrate*, which means to treat irreverently. The vandals desecrated the cemetery by knocking down all the tombstones. Their act of vandalism was a *desecration*.

Desecrate can also be applied to areas outside religion.

Doodling in a book *desecrates* the book, even if the book isn't a Bible.

The wife *desecrated* a photograph of her husband by drawing a mustache on it.

The graffiti on the front door of the school are a *desecration*.

CONSENSUS (kun SEN sus) *n* unanimity or general agreement

When there is a *consensus*, everybody feels the same way.

Contrary to how the word is often used, *consensus* implies more than just a rough agreement or a majority opinion. Election results don't reflect a *consensus* unless everyone or nearly everyone votes for the same candidate.

CONSONANT (KON suh nunt) *adj* harmonious; in agreement

Our desires were *consonant* with theirs; we all wanted the same thing.

The decision to construct a new gymnasium was *consonant* with the superintendent's belief in physical education.

The opposite of *consonant* is *dissonant*, which means inharmonious. *Dissonant* voices are voices that don't sound good together.

Q·U·I·C·K · Q·U·I·Z #25

Match each word in the first column with its definition in the second column. Check your answers in the back of the book.

1. conjecture	a. incompatible
2. conjure	b. harmonious
3. connoisseur	c. make sacred
4. consecrate	d. unanimity
5. desecrate	e. summon as if by magic
6. consensus	f. treat irreverently
7. consonant	g. artistic expert
8. dissonant	h. guess

CONSTRUE (kun STROO) *v* to interpret

The meaning of the poem, as I *construed* it, had to do with the love of a man for his dog.

Mickey *construed* his contract as giving him the right to do anything he wanted.

The law had always been *construed* as permitting the behavior for which Joe had been arrested.

To *misconstrue* is to misinterpret. Hank *misconstrued* Pamela's smile, but he certainly did not *misconstrue* the slap she gave him.

CONSUMMATE (kun SUM it) *adj* perfect; complete; supremely skillful

A *consummate* pianist is an extremely good one. Nothing is lacking from the way he or she plays.

Consummate (KON suh MATE) is also a verb. Notice the different pronunciation. To *consummate* something is to finish it or make it complete. Signing a contract would *consummate* an agreement.

CONTENTIOUS (kun TEN shus) *adj* argumentative; quarrelsome

A person looking for a fight is *contentious*.

Two people having a fight are *contentious*.

To be *contentious* in a discussion is to make a lot of noisy objections.

A *contender* is a fighter. To *contend* is to fight or argue for something. Someone who breaks the law may have to *contend* with the law.

CONTIGUOUS (kun TIG yoo us) *adj* side by side; adjoining

Two countries that share a border are *contiguous*. So are two events that happened one right after the other.

If two countries are *contiguous*, the territory they cover is continuous. That is, it spreads or continues across both countries without any interruption.

CONTINGENT (kun TIN junt) *adj* dependent; possible

Our agreement to buy their house is *contingent* upon the sellers' finding another house to move into. That is, they won't sell their house to us unless they can find another house to buy.

My happiness is *contingent* on yours; if you're unhappy, I'm unhappy.

A *contingency* is a possibility or something that may happen but is at least as likely not to happen. Several *contingencies* stand between us and the successful completion of our business; several things could happen to screw it up.

The Joneses were prepared for any *contingency*. Their front hall closet contained a first aid kit, a fire extinguisher, a life raft, a parachute, and a pack of sled dogs.

CONTRITE (kun TRITE) *adj* admitting guilt; especially feeling remorseful

To be *contrite* is to admit whatever terrible thing you did.

Sally was *contrite* about her mistake, so we forgave her.

A criminal who won't confess his crime is not *contrite*.

Saying that you're sorry is an act of *contrition*.

CONTRIVED (kun TRIVED) *adj* artificial; labored

Sam's acting was *contrived:* no one in the audience believed his character or enjoyed his performance.

The artist was widely admired for his originality, but his paintings seemed *contrived* to me.

No one laughed at Sue's *contrived* attempt at humor.

CONVENTIONAL (kun VEN shun nul) *adj* common; customary; unexceptional

The architect's *conventional* designs didn't win him awards for originality.

Tipping the waiter in a restaurant is a *conventional* courtesy.

Conventional wisdom is what everyone thinks. The bland politician maintained his popularity by never straying far from the *conventional* wisdom about any topic.

CONVIVIAL (kun VIV ee ul) *adj* fond of partying; festive

A *convivial* gathering is one in which the people present enjoy eating, drinking, and being together.

To be *convivial* is to be an eager but generally well-behaved party animal.

A *convivial* person is the opposite of an antisocial person.

COPIOUS (KOH pee us) *adj* abundant; plentiful

The champagne at the wedding reception was *copious* but not very good.

Harry had a *copious* supply of nails in his workshop. Everywhere you stepped, it seemed, there was a pile of nails.

We ate *copiously* at the banquet and went home feeling quite sick.

Q·U·I·C·K · Q·U·I·Z #26

Match each word in the first column with its definition in the second column. Check your answers in the back of the book.

1. construe		a. admitting guilt
2. consummate		b. interpret
3. contentious		c. perfect
4. contiguous		d. labored
5. contingent		e. dependent
6. contrite		f. abundant
7. contrived		g. adjoining
8. conventional		h. argumentative
9. convivial		i. festive
10. copious		j. common

COROLLARY (KAWR uh LER ee) *n* something that follows; a natural consequence

In mathematics, a *corollary* is a law that can be deduced without further proof from a law that has already been proved.

Bloodshed and death are *corollaries* of any declaration of war.

Higher prices were a *corollary* of the two companies' agreement not to compete.

CORROBORATE (kuh ROB uh RATE) *v* to confirm; to back up with evidence

I knew my statement was correct when my colleague *corroborated* it.

Henny Penny's contention that the sky was falling could not be *corroborated*. That is, no one was able to find any fallen sky.

The police could find no evidence of theft and thus could not *corroborate* Bill's claim that he had been robbed.

COSMOPOLITAN (KOZ muh POL i tun) *adj* at home in many places or situations; internationally sophisticated

Huey's interests were *cosmopolitan*—he liked Greek wine, German beer, Dutch cheese, Japanese cars, and french fries.

A truly *cosmopolitan* traveler never feels like a foreigner anywhere on earth.

New York is a *cosmopolitan* city; you can hear nearly every language in the world spoken there.

COUNTENANCE (KOUN tuh nuns) *n* face; facial expression, especially an encouraging one

His father's confident *countenance* gave Lou the courage to persevere.

Ed's harsh words belied his *countenance*, which was kind and encouraging.

Countenance can also be a verb. To *countenance* something is to condone it or tolerate it.

Dad *countenanced* our backyard rock fights even though he didn't really approve of them.

COUP (koo) *n* a brilliant victory or accomplishment; the violent overthrow of a government by a small internal group

Winning a gold medal at the Olympics was a real *coup* for the skinny, sick, fifty-year-old man.

The student council's great *coup* was persuading the Rolling Stones to play at our prom.

In the attempted *coup* in the Philippines, some army officers tried to take over the government. The full name for this type of coup is coup d'état (koo day TAH).

COVENANT (KUV i nint) *n* a solemn agreement; a contract; a pledge

The warring tribes made a *covenant* in which they agreed not to fight each other anymore.

We signed a *covenant* in which we promised never to drive Harry's father's car into the Murphys' living room ever again.

COVERT (KUV urt, KOH vurt) *adj* secret; hidden

To be *covert* is to be *covered*.

Covert activities are secret activities.

A *covert* military operation is one the public knows nothing about.

Most of the activities of spies are *covert*.

The opposite of *covert* is *overt*. *Overt* (OH vurt) means open or unconcealed.

COVET (KUV it) *v* to wish for enviously

To *covet* thy neighbor's wife is to want thy neighbor's wife for thyself.

Billy *coveted* Bobby's bicycle and very nearly decided to steal it.

To be *covetous* is to be envious.

Q·U·I·C·K · Q·U·I·Z #27

Match each word in the first column with its definition in the second column. Check your answers in the back of the book.

1. corollary	a. worldly and sophisticated
2. corroborate	b. face
3. cosmopolitan	c. wish for enviously
4. countenance	d. confirm
5. coup	e. solemn agreement
6. covenant	f. brilliant victory
7. covert	g. natural consequence
8. covet	h. secret

CREDULOUS (KREJ uh lus) *adj* eager to believe; gullible

The *credulous* postal patron believed that he had won a million dollars from Publishers Clearing House.

Paula was so *credulous* that she simply nodded happily when Ralph told her he could teach her how to fly.

Credulous should not be confused with *credible*. To be *credible* is to be believable.

Almost anything, however *incredible*, is *credible* to a *credulous* person.

Larry's implausible story of heroism was not *credible*. Still, *credulous* old Louis believed it.

A story that cannot be believed is *incredible*. If you don't believe that story someone just told you, you are *incredulous*.

If something is *credible*, it may gain *credence* (KREED uns), which means belief or intellectual acceptance. The chemist's sound techniques inspired *credence* in the scientific world.

No one could prove Frank's theory, but his standing at the university helped it gain *credence*.

Another similar word is *creditable*, which means worthy of *credit* or praise. Frances made a *creditable* effort to play on the boys' football team, even though she was ultimately forced to sit on the bench.

Our record in raising money was very *creditable;* we raised several thousand dollars every year.

CRITERION (kyre TEER ee un) *n* standard; basis for judgment

When Garfield judges a meal, he has only one *criterion:* Is it edible?

In choosing among the linemen, the most important *criterion* was quickness.

The plural of *criterion* is *criteria*. You can't have one *criteria;* you can only have one *criterion*. If you have two or more, you have *criteria*. There is no such thing as *criterions* and no such thing as a *criteria*.

CRYPTIC (KRIP tik) *adj* mysterious; mystifying

Elaine's remarks were *cryptic;* everyone was baffled by what she said.

A *cryptic* statement is one in which something important remains hidden. The ghost made *cryptic* comments about the *crypt* from which he had just emerged; that is, no one could figure out what the ghost meant.

CULINARY (KYOO luh NER ee) *adj* relating to cooking or the kitchen

A cooking school is sometimes called a *culinary* institute. Stan pursued his *culinary* interests by attending the *culinary* institute. His first meal, which was burned beyond recognition, was a *culinary* disaster.

CULMINATE (KUL muh NATE) *v* to climax; to reach full effect

Susan's years of practice *culminated* in a great victory at the international blow ball championship.

The masked ball was the *culmination* of our fund-raising efforts.

Q·U·I·C·K · Q·U·I·Z #28

Match each word in the first column with its definition in the second column. Check your answers in the back of the book.

1. credulous	a.	related to cooking
2. credible	b.	believable
3. incredible	c.	believability
4. incredulous	d.	worthy of praise
5. credence	e.	eager to believe
6. creditable	f.	unbelieving
7. criterion	g.	unbelievable
8. cryptic	h.	climax
9. culinary	i.	standard
10. culminate	j.	mysterious

CULPABLE (KUL puh bul) *adj* deserving blame; guilty

A person who is *culpable* (a *culprit*) is one who can be blamed for doing something.

The accountant's failure to spot the errors made him *culpable* in the tax-fraud case.

We all felt *culpable* when the homeless old man died in the doorway of our apartment building.

To decide that a person is not *culpable* after all is to *exculpate* that person. Lou's confession didn't *exculpate* Bob, because one of the things that Lou confessed was that Bob had helped him do it.

CURSORY (KUR suh ree) *adj* hasty; superficial

To give a book a *cursory* reading is to skim it quickly without comprehending much.

To make a *cursory* attempt at learning French is to memorize a couple of easy words and then say the heck with it.

The *cursor* on Dave's computer made a *cursory* sweep across the data as he scrolled down the page.

CURTAIL (kur TALE) *v* to shorten; to cut short

The vet *curtailed* his effort to cut the cat's tail with the lawn mower. That is, he stopped trying.

To *curtail* a tale is to cut it short.

CYNIC (SIN ik) *n* one who deeply distrusts human nature; one who believes humans are motivated only by selfishness

When the rich man gave a million dollars to the museum, *cynics* said he was merely trying to buy himself a reputation as a cultured person.

To be *cynical* is to be extremely suspicious of the motivation of other people.

Cynicism is general grumpiness and pessimism about human nature.

Q·U·I·C·K · Q·U·I·Z #29

Match each word in the first column with its definition in the second column. Check your answers in the back of the book.

1. culpable   a. free from guilt
2. exculpate   b. shorten
3. cursory   c. one who distrusts humanity
4. curtail   d. hasty
5. cynic   e. guilty

D

DAUNT (dawnt) *v* to make fearful; to intimidate

The steepness of the mountain *daunted* the team of amateur climbers, who hadn't realized what they were in for.

The size of the players on the visiting team was *daunting;* the players on the home team began to perspire nervously.

To be *dauntless* or *undaunted* is to be fearless or unintimidated. The rescue crew was *undaunted* by the flames and ran into the burning house to look for survivors. They were *dauntless* in their effort to save the people inside.

DEARTH (durth) *n* lack; scarcity

There is no *dearth* of comedy at a convention of clowns.

When there is a *dearth* of food, many people may starve.

There was a *dearth* of gaiety at the boring Christmas party.

DEBACLE (day BAH kul, day BAK ul, di BAH kul) *n* violent breakdown; sudden overthrow

A football game can turn into a *debacle* if one team is suddenly being clobbered.

A political debate would become a *debacle* if the candidates began screaming and throwing dinner rolls at each other.

The government fell as a result of a *debacle* instigated by a scheming general.

DEBAUCHERY (di BAW chuh ree) *n* wild living; excessive intemperance

Debauchery can be expensive; fortunately for William, his wallet matched his appetite for extravagant pleasures. He died a poor, albeit happy, man.

To *debauch* is to seduce or corrupt. Someone who is *debauched* has been seduced or corrupted.

DEBILITATE (di BIL i TATE) *v* to weaken; to cripple

Hank *debilitated* Stu by hitting him on the head with a skillet.

The football player's career was ended by a *debilitating* injury to his knee.

To become *debilitated* is to suffer a *debility*, which is the opposite of an ability. A surgeon who becomes *debilitated* is one who has lost the ability to operate on the *debilities* of other people.

DECADENT (DEK uh dunt) *adj* decaying or decayed, especially in terms of morals

A person who engages in *decadent* behavior is a person whose morals have decayed or fallen into ruin.

Carousing in local bars instead of going to class is *decadent*.

Decadent behavior is often an affectation of bored young people.

DECIMATE (DES uh MATE) *v* to kill or destroy a large part of

To *decimate* an army is to come close to wiping it out.

When locusts attack a crop, they sometimes *decimate* it, leaving very little that's fit for human consumption.

You might say in jest that your family had *decimated* its turkey dinner on Thanksgiving, leaving nothing but a few crumbs and a pile of bones.

DECOROUS (DEK ur us, di KORE us) *adj* proper; in good taste; orderly

Decorous behavior is good, polite, orderly behavior.

To be *decorous* is to be sober and tasteful.

The New Year's Eve crowd was relatively *decorous* until midnight, when they went wild.

To behave *decorously* is to behave with *decorum*.

DEDUCE (di DOOS) *v* to conclude from the evidence; to infer

To *deduce* something is to conclude it without being told it directly.

From the footprints on the ground, the detective *deduced* that the criminal had feet.

Nancy *deduced* from the gun in Sluggo's hand that all was not well with their relationship.

Daffy *deduced* from the shape of its bill that the duck was really a chicken.

That the duck was really a chicken was Daffy's *deduction*.

DEFAME (di FAME) *v* to libel or slander; to ruin the good name of

To *defame* someone is to make accusations that harm the person's reputation.

The local businessman accused the newspaper of *defaming* him by publishing an article that said his company was poorly managed.

To *defame* is to take away fame, to take away a good name.

To suffer such a loss of reputation is to suffer *defamation*. The businessman who believed he had been *defamed* by the newspaper sued the paper's publisher for *defamation*.

Q·U·I·C·K · Q·U·I·Z #30

Match each word in the first column with its definition in the second column. Check your answers in the back of the book.

1. daunt	a. conclude from evidence
2. dearth	b. lack
3. debacle	c. kill a large part of
4. debauchery	d. libel or slander
5. debilitate	e. make fearful
6. decadent	f. decaying or decayed
7. decimate	g. proper
8. decorous	h. weaken
9. deduce	i. violent breakdown
10. defame	j. wild living

DEFERENCE (DEF ur uns) *n* submission to another's will; respect; courtesy

To show *deference* to another is to place that person's wishes ahead of your own.

The young man showed *deference* to his grandfather: he let the old man have first dibs on the birthday cake.

Herbie stopped yodeling at the dinner table in *deference* to the wishes of his mother.

To show *deference* to another is to *defer* to that person. Joe was supposed to go first, but he *deferred* to Steve, who had been waiting longer.

To show *deference* is also to be *deferential*. Joe was being *deferential* when he allowed Steve to go first.

DEFINITIVE (di FIN uh tiv) *adj* conclusive; providing the last word

Walter wrote the *definitive* biography of Keats; nothing more could have been added by another book.

The army completely wiped out the invaders; its victory was *definitive*.

No one could find anything to object to in Cindy's *definitive* explanation of how the meteorite had gotten into the bathtub.

DEGENERATE (di JEN uh RATE) *v* to break down; to deteriorate

The discussion quickly *degenerated* into an argument.

Over the years, the nice old neighborhood had *degenerated* into a terrible slum.

The fans' behavior *degenerated* as the game went on.

A person whose behavior has *degenerated* can be referred to as a *degenerate* (di JEN ur it). The mood of the party was spoiled when a drunken *degenerate* wandered in from off the street.

Degenerate (di JEN ur it) can also be an adjective, meaning *degenerated*. The slum neighborhood was degenerate. The fans' *degenerate* behavior prompted the police to make several arrests.

DELETERIOUS (DEL i TEER ee us) *adj* harmful

Smoking cigarettes is *deleterious* to your health. So is brushing your teeth with oven cleaner or washing your hair with gasoline.

Is watching *Family Feud deleterious*? Of course not.

DELINEATE (di LIN ee ATE) *v* to describe accurately; to draw in outline

After Jack had *delineated* his plan, we had no doubt about what he intended to do.

Sharon's peculiar feelings about her pet gorilla were *delineated* in the newspaper article about her.

The portrait artist *delineated* Sarah's features, then filled in the shading.

DELUDE (di LOOD) *v* to deceive

The con man *deluded* us into thinking that he would make us rich. Instead, he tricked us into giving him several hundred dollars.

The *deluded* mental patient believed that he was a chicken sandwich.

Betty is so persuasive that she was able to *delude* Henrietta into thinking she was a countess.

To be *deluded* is to suffer from a *delusion*. That he was a great poet was the *delusion* of the English teacher, who could scarcely write two complete sentences in a row.

Bert, the well-known jerk, suffered from the *delusion* that he was a very great man.

DELUGE (DEL yooj) *n* a flood; an inundation

A *deluge* is a flood, but the word is often used figuratively. The $1 million reward for the lost poodle brought in a *deluge* of hot leads. The distraught owner was *deluged* by phone calls all week.

DEMAGOGUE (DEM uh GAWG) *n* a leader of the people, but more a rabble rouser

A *demagogue* is a leader, but not in a good sense of the word. He manipulates the public to support his aims, but he is little different from a dictator. A *demagogue* is often a despot.

DENIZEN (DEN i zun) *n* inhabitant

To be a *denizen* of a country is to live there. A citizen of a country is usually also a *denizen*.

To be a *denizen* of a restaurant is to go there often—so often that people begin to wonder whether you live there.

Fish are sometimes referred to as "*denizens* of the deep." Don't refer to them this way yourself; the expression is a cliché.

DEPRAVITY (di PRAV i tee) *n* extreme wickedness or corruption

Mrs. Prudinkle wondered whether the *depravity* of her class of eight-year-olds was the result of their watching Saturday morning television.

To exhibit *depravity* is to be *depraved*.

DEPRECATE (DEP ruh KATE) *v* to express disapproval of

To *deprecate* a colleague's work is to risk making yourself unwelcome in your colleague's office.

"This stinks!" is a *deprecating* remark.

The critic's *deprecating* comments about my new novel put me in a bad mood for an entire month.

To be *self-deprecating* is to make little of one's own efforts, often in the hope that someone else will say, "No, you're swell!"

A very similar word is *depreciate* (di PREE shee ATE). To *depreciate* a colleague's work would be to represent it as being of little value.

For another meaning of *depreciate*, see *appreciate*.

DERIDE (di RIDE) *v* to ridicule; to laugh at contemptuously

Barry *derided* Barbara's driving ability after their hair-raising trip down the twisting mountain road.

Sportswriters *derided* Columbia's football team, which hadn't won a game in many years.

The boss *derided* his secretary mercilessly, so she poisoned him. She was someone who could not accept *derision* (di RIZH un).

Q·U·I·C·K · Q·U·I·Z #31

Match each word in the first column with its definition in the second column. Check your answers in the back of the book.

1. deference	a. deteriorate
2. definitive	b. ridicule
3. degenerate	c. describe accurately
4. deleterious	d. respect
5. delineate	e. conclusive
6. delude	f. express disapproval of
7. deluge	g. harmful
8. demagogue	h. inhabitant
9. denizen	i. deceive
10. depravity	j. flood
11. deprecate	k. extreme wickedness
12. deride	l. rabble-rousing leader

DEROGATORY (di ROG uh TOHR ee) *adj* disapproving; degrading

Derogatory remarks are negative remarks expressing disapproval. They are nastier than merely critical remarks.

Oliver could never seem to think of anything nice to say about anyone; virtually all his comments were *derogatory*.

DESICCATE (DES uh KATE) *v* to dry out

The hot wind *desiccated* the few grapes remaining on the vine; after a day or two, they looked like raisins.

After a week without water, the *desiccated* plant fell over and died.

Plums become prunes through a process of *desiccation*.

DESPONDENT (di SPON dunt) *adj* extremely depressed; full of despair

The cook became *despondent* when the wedding cake exploded fifteen minutes before the reception.

After the death of his wife, the man was *despondent* for many months.

The team fell into *despondency* after losing the state championship by a single point.

DESPOT (DES put) *n* an absolute ruler; an autocrat

The manager of the office was a *despot;* workers who disagreed with him were fired.

The island kingdom was ruled by a ruthless *despot* who executed suspected rebels at noon each day in the village square.

To act like a *despot* is to be *despotic.* There was cheering in the street when the country's *despotic* government was overthrown.

DESTITUTE (DES ti TOOT) *adj* extremely poor; utterly lacking

Destitute people are people without money or possessions, or with very little money and very few possessions.

To be left *destitute* is to be left without money or property.

The word can also be used figuratively. A teacher might accuse her students of being *destitute* of brains, or intellectually *destitute.*

DESULTORY (DES ul TOHR ee) *adj* without a plan or purpose; disconnected; random

Phil made a few *desultory* attempts to start a garden, but nothing came of them.

In his *desultory* address, Jake skipped from one topic to another and never came to the point.

The discussion at our meeting was *desultory;* no one's comments seemed to bear any relation to anyone else's.

DIALECTICAL (DYE uh LEK ti kul) *adj* relating to discussions; relating to the rules and methods of reasoning; approaching truth in the middle of opposing extremes

The game of Twenty Questions is *dialectical,* in that the participants attempt to narrow down a chosen object by asking a series of even more specific questions.

The noun is *dialectics.*

DICTUM (DIK tum) *n* an authoritative saying; an adage; a maxim; a proverb

No pain no gain is a hackneyed *dictum* of sadistic coaches everywhere.

DIDACTIC (dye DAK tik) *adj* intended to teach; morally instructive; pedantic

Luther's seemingly amusing talk had a *didactic* purpose; he was trying to show his listeners the difference between right and wrong.

The priest's conversation was always *didactic.* He never said anything that wasn't intended to teach a lesson.

The new novel is painfully *didactic;* the author's aim is always to instruct and never to entertain.

DIFFIDENT (DIF i dunt) *adj* timid; lacking in self-confidence

The *diffident* student never made a single comment in class. *Diffident* and *confident* are opposites.

Mary's stammer made her *diffident* in conversation and shy in groups of strangers.

Amos's *diffidence* led many participants to believe he hadn't been present at the meeting, even though he had.

DIGRESS (di GRESS) *v* to stray from the main subject

Speaking metaphorically, to *digress* is to leave the main highway in order to travel aimlessly on back roads. When a speaker *digresses*, he departs from the main topic and tells a story only distantly related to it.

Such a story is called a *digression*. Sometimes a writer's or speaker's *digressions* are more interesting than his or her main points.

After a lengthy *digression*, the lecturer returned to his speech and brought it to a conclusion.

DILETTANTE (DIL i TAHNT) *n* someone with superficial knowledge of the arts; an amateur; a dabbler

To be a *dilettante* is to dabble in something rather than doing it in a serious way.

Reginald said he was an artist, but he was merely a *dilettante;* he didn't know a pencil from a paintbrush.

Helen dismissed the members of the ladies' sculpture club as nothing more than a bunch of *dilettantes.*

Q·U·I·C·K · Q·U·I·Z #32

Match each word in the first column with its definition in the second column. Check your answers in the back of the book.

1. derogatory	a. without purpose
2. desiccate	b. extremely depressed
3. despondent	c. amateur
4. despot	d. stray from main subject
5. destitute	e. extremely poor
6. desultory	f. timid
7. dialectical	g. dry out
8. dictum	h. disapproving
9. didactic	i. absolute ruler
10. diffident	j. intended to teach
11. digress	k. relating to discussions
12. dilettante	l. authoritative saying

DISCERN (di SURN) *v* to have insight; to see things clearly, to discriminate; to differentiate

To discern something is to perceive it clearly. A writer whose work demonstrates *discernment* is a writer who is a keen observer.

The ill-mannered people at Louise's party proved that she had little *discernment* when it came to choosing friends.

DISCREET (di SKREET) *adj* prudent; judiciously reserved

To make *discreet* inquiries is to ask around without letting the whole world know you're doing it.

The psychiatrist was very *discreet;* no matter how much we pestered him, he wouldn't gossip about the problems of his famous patients. He had *discretion* (di SKRESH un).

To be *indiscreet* is to be imprudent and especially to say or do things you shouldn't. It was *indiscreet* of Laura to tell Sally how much she hated Betty's new hairdo, because Sally always tells Betty everything.

When Laura told that to Sally, she committed an *indiscretion.*

DISCRETE (di SKREET) *adj* unconnected; separate; distinct

Do not confuse *discrete* with *discreet.* The twins were identical but their personalities were *discrete.*

The drop in the stock market was not the result of any single force but of many *discrete* trends.

When things are all jumbled up together, they are said to be *indiscrete,* which means not separated or sorted.

DISCRIMINATE (di SKRIM uh NATE) *v* to notice or point out the difference between two or more things; to discern; to differentiate

A person with a refined aesthetic sense is able to *discriminate* subtle differences where a less observant person would see nothing. Such a person is *discriminating.* This kind of *discrimination* is a good thing. To *discriminate* unfairly, though, is to dwell on differences that shouldn't make a difference. It is unfair—and illegal—to *discriminate* between black people and white people in selling a house. Such a practice is not *discriminating* (which is good) but *discriminatory* (which is wrong).

DISDAIN (dis DANE) *n* arrogant scorn; contempt

Bertram viewed the hot dog with *disdain,* believing that to eat such a disgusting food was beneath him.

The millionaire looked upon the poor workmen with evident *disdain.*

Disdain can also be a verb. The millionaire in the previous example could be said to have *disdained* those workmen.

To be filled with *disdain* is to be *disdainful.*

DISINTERESTED (dis IN tri stid) *adj* not taking sides; unbiased

Disinterested should *not* be used to mean *uninterested.* If you don't care about knowing something, you are uninterested, not disinterested.

A referee should be *disinterested.* He or she should not be rooting for one of the competing teams.

A *disinterested* observer is one who has no personal stake in or attachment to what is being observed.

Agatha claimed that the accident had been Lester's fault, but several *disinterested* witnesses said that Agatha had actually bashed into his car after jumping the median and driving in the wrong lane for several miles.

DISPARAGE (di SPAIR ij) *v* to belittle; to say uncomplimentary things about, usually in a somewhat indirect way

The mayor *disparaged* our efforts to beautify the town square by saying that the flower bed we had planted looked somewhat worse than the weeds it had replaced.

My guidance counselor *disparaged* my high school record by telling me that not everybody belongs in college.

Q·U·I·C·K · Q·U·I·Z #33

Match each word in the first column with its definition in the second column. Check your answers in the back of the book.

1. discern
2. discreet
3. discrete
4. indiscrete
5. discriminate
6. disdain
7. disinterested
8. disparage

a. insight
b. belittle
c. not separated
d. not taking sides
e. arrogant scorn
f. prudent
g. unconnected
h. differentiate

DISPARATE (DIS pur it) *adj* different; incompatible; unequal

Our interests were *disparate*: Cathy liked to play with dolls and I liked to throw her dolls out the window.

The *disparate* interest groups were united only by their intense dislike of the candidate.

The novel was difficult to read, because the plot consisted of dozens of *disparate* threads that never came together.

The noun form of *disparate* is *disparity* (di SPAR i tee). *Disparity* means inequality. The opposite of *disparity* is *parity*.

DISSEMINATE (di SEM uh NATE) *v* to spread the seeds of something; to scatter; to make widely known

News is *disseminated* through many media: radio, television, newspapers, magazines, and gossips.

DISSIPATE (DIS uh PATE) *v* to thin out, drift away, or dissolve; to cause to thin out, drift away, or dissolve; to waste or squander

The smoke *dissipated* as soon as we opened the windows.

Rex's anger *dissipated* as the day wore on and he gradually forgot what had upset him.

The police *dissipated* the riotous crowd by spraying the demonstrators with fire hoses and firing bullets over their heads.

Alex won the weekly lottery but *dissipated* the entire winnings in one abandoned, fun-filled weekend. We can also say that a person is *dissipated*, by which we mean that he indulges in wild living. Alex is *dissipated*.

DISSOLUTION (DIS uh LOO shun) *n* the breaking up or *dissolving* of something into parts; disintegration

Nothing could prevent the *dissolution* of the Pee Wee Herman Fan Club after he retired to seek a political career.

A person who is *dissolute* has lived life in the fast lane too long. *Dissolute* and *dissipated* are synonyms in this sense.

DISTEND (di STEND) *v* to swell; to extend a great deal

The tire *distended* alarmingly as the forgetful gas station attendant kept pumping more and more air into it.

A *distended* belly is one symptom of malnutrition.

A swelling is a *distension*.

DISTINGUISH (di STING gwish) *v* to tell apart; to cause to stand out

The rodent expert's eyesight was so *acute* that he was able to *distinguish* between a shrew and a vole at more than a thousand paces.

I studied and studied but I was never able to *distinguish* between *discrete* and *discreet*.

His face had no *distinguishing* characteristics; there was nothing about his features that stuck in your memory.

Lou's uneventful career as dogcatcher was not *distinguished* by adventure or excitement.

DOCILE (DOS ul) *adj* easily taught; obedient; easy to handle

The *docile* students quietly memorized all the lies their teacher told them.

The baby raccoons appeared *docile* at first, but they were almost impossible to control.

Louise's *docility* fooled the professor into believing that she was incapable of thinking for herself.

DOCTRINAIRE (DOK truh NAIR) *adj* inflexibly committed to a doctrine or theory without regard to its practicality; dogmatic

A *doctrinaire* supporter of manned space flights to Pluto would be someone who supported such space flights even though it might be shown that such lengthy journeys could never be undertaken.

A *doctrinaire* opponent of fluoridation of water would be someone whose opposition could not be shaken by proof that fluoride is good for teeth and not bad for anything else.

A person with *doctrinaire* views can be called a *doctrinaire*.

DOGMATIC (dawg MAT ik) *adj* arrogantly assertive of unproven ideas; stubbornly claiming that something (often a system of beliefs) is beyond dispute

A *dogma* is a belief. A *dogmatic* person, however, is stubbornly convinced of his beliefs.

Marty is *dogmatic* on the subject of the creation of the world; he sneers at anyone whose views are not identical to his.

The philosophy professor became increasingly *dogmatic* as he grew older and became more firmly convinced of his strange theories.

The opinions or ideas *dogmatically* asserted by a *dogmatic* person are known collectively as *dogma*.

DOMESTIC (duh MES tik) *adj* having to do with the household or family; not foreign

A home that enjoys *domestic* tranquility is a happy home.

A maid is sometimes referred to as a *domestic* engineer or simply as a domestic.

To be *domestic* is to enjoy being at home or to be skillful at doing things around the house.

Domestic wine is wine from this country, as opposed to wine imported from, say, France.

The *domestic* steel industry is the steel industry in this country.

A country that enjoys *domestic* tranquility is a happy country.

Q·U·I·C·K · Q·U·I·Z #34

Match each word in the first column with its definition in the second column. Check your answers in the back of the book.

1. disparate		a.	inharmonious
2. disseminate		b.	committed to a theory
3. dissipate		c.	thin out
4. dissolution		d.	of the household
5. dissonant		e.	firmly held system of ideas
6. distend		f.	easily taught
7. distinguish		g.	arrogantly assertive
8. docile		h.	swell
9. doctrinaire		i.	tell apart
10. dogmatic		j.	incompatible
11. dogma		k.	spread seeds
12. domestic		l.	disintegration

DORMANT (DAWR munt) *adj* inactive; as though asleep; asleep

Dormant, like *dormitory,* comes from a root meaning "sleep."

The volcano erupted violently and then fell *dormant* for several hundred years.

Many plants remain *dormant* through the winter; that is, they stop growing until spring.

Frank's interest in playing the piano was *dormant* and, quite posssibly, dead.

The snow fell silently over the *dormant* village, which became snarled in traffic jams the following morning.

DUBIOUS (DOO bee us) *adj* full of doubt; uncertain

I was fairly certain that I would be able to fly if I could merely flap my arms hard enough, but Mary was *dubious;* she said I'd better flap my legs as well.

We were *dubious* about the team's chance of success and, as it turned out, our *dubiety* was justified: the team lost.

Dubious and *doubtful* don't mean exactly the same thing. A *dubious* person is a person who has *doubts.* A *doubtful* outcome is an outcome that isn't certain to occur.

Sam's chances of getting the job were *doubtful,* because the employer was *dubious* of his claim that he had been president of the United States while in high school.

Something beyond *doubt* is *indubitable*. A dogmatic person believes his opinions are *indubitable*.

DUPLICITY (doo PLIS i tee) *n* the act of being two-faced; double-dealing; deception

Dave, in his *duplicity*, told us he wasn't going to rob the bank and then went right out and robbed it.

Liars engage in *duplicity* all the time; they say one thing and do another.

The *duplicitous* salesman sold the stuffed camel to someone else even though he had promised to sell it to us.

Q·U·I·C·K · Q·U·I·Z #35

Match each word in the first column with its definition in the second column. Check your answers in the back of the book.

1. dormant   a. uncertainty

2. dubiety   b. double-dealing

3. duplicity   c. inactive

E

EBULLIENT (i BUL yunt) *adj* boiling; bubbling with excitement; exuberant

A boiling liquid can be called *ebullient*. More often, though, this word describes excited or enthusiastic people.

The roaring crowd in a full stadium before the World Series might be said to be *ebullient*.

A person overflowing with enthusiasm might be said to be *ebullient*.

Mabel was *ebullient* when her fairy godmother said she could use one of her three wishes to wish for three more wishes.

Someone or something that is *ebullient* is characterized by *ebullience*.

ECCENTRIC (ik SEN trik) *adj* not conventional; a little kooky; irregular

The *eccentric* inventor spent all his waking hours fiddling with what he said was a time machine but was actually just an old telephone booth.

Fred's political views are *eccentric:* he believes that we should have kings instead of presidents and that the government should raise money by holding bake sales.

The rocket followed an *eccentric* course; first it veered in one direction, then it veered in another, then it crashed.

An *eccentric* person is a person who has *eccentricities*.

ECLECTIC (i KLEK tik) *adj* choosing the best from many sources; drawn from many sources

Zeke's taste in art was *eclectic*. He liked the Old Masters, the Impressionists, and Walt Disney.

The *eclectic* menu included dishes from many different countries.

George's *eclectic* reading made him well rounded.

EDIFY (ED uh FYE) *v* to enlighten; to instruct, especially in moral or religious matters

We found the pastor's sermon on the importance of not eating beans to be most *edifying*.

The teacher's goal was to *edify* her students, not to force a handful of facts down their throats.

We would have felt lost at the art show had not the excellent and informative programs been provided for our *edification*.

EFFACE (i FASE) *v* to erase; to rub away the features of

The inscription on the tombstone had been *effaced* by centuries of weather.

The vandals *effaced* the delicate carving by rubbing it with sandpaper.

We tried to *efface* the dirty words that had been written on the front of our house, but nothing would remove them.

To be *self-effacing* is to be modest. Jennings is *self-effacing*: He won an Olympic gold medal and all he said was "Aw, shucks. I'm just a regular fella."

EFFUSION (i FYOO zhun) *n* a pouring forth

When the child was rescued from the well, there was an intense *effusion* of emotion from the crowd that had gathered around the hole.

The madman's writings consisted of a steady *effusion* of nonsense.

To be *effusive* is to be highly emotional. Sally's *effusive* thanks for our silly little present made us feel somewhat embarrassed, so we decided to move to a different city.

EGALITARIAN (i GAL i TAIR ee un) *adj* believing in the social and economic equality of all people

People often lose interest in *egalitarian* measures when such measures interfere with their own interests.

Egalitarian can also be used as a noun to characterize a person. An *egalitarian* advocates *egalitarianism*.

EGOCENTRIC (EE goh SEN trik) *adj* selfish; believing that one is the center of everything

Lou was so *egocentric* that he could never give anyone else credit for doing anything.

Egocentric Bill never read the newspaper unless there was something in it about him.

It never occurred to the *egocentric* musician that his audiences might like to hear someone else's songs every once in a while.

An *egoist* is an *egocentric* person. He believes the entire universe exists for his benefit.

An *egotist* is another type of *egocentric*. An *egotist* is an egoist who tells everyone how wonderful he is.

EGREGIOUS (i GREE jus) *adj* extremely bad; flagrant

Save this word for things that are worse than bad.

The mother's *egregious* neglect was responsible for her child's accidental cross-country ride on the freight train.

Stephen's manners were *egregious;* he ate his mashed potatoes with his fingers and slurped the peas right off his plate.

Q·U·I·C·K · Q·U·I·Z #36

Match each word in the first column with its definition in the second column. Check your answers in the back of the book.

1. ebullient	a. pouring forth
2. eccentric	b. self-obsessed person
3. eclectic	c. extremely bad
4. edify	d. not conventional
5. efface	e. drawn from many sources
6. effusion	f. bubbling with excitement
7. egalitarian	g. erase
8. egocentric	h. selfish
9. egotist	i. enlighten
10. egregious	j. believing in social equality

ELICIT (i LIS it) *v* to bring out; to call forth

The interviewer skillfully *elicited* our true feelings by asking us questions that got to the heart of the matter.

The defendant tried to *elicit* the sympathy of the jury by appearing at the trial in a wheelchair, but the jury convicted him anyway.

Don't confuse this word with *illicit.*

ELLIPTICAL (i LIP ti kul) *adj* oval; missing a word or words; obscure

This word has several meanings. Consult a dictionary if you are uncertain.

The orbit of the earth is not perfectly round; it is *elliptical.*

An egg may have an *elliptical* shape.

An *elliptical* statement is one that is hard or impossible to understand, either because something is missing from it or because the speaker or writer is trying to be hard to understand. The announcement from the State Department was purposely *elliptical*—the government didn't really want reporters to know what was going on.

ELUSIVE (i LOO siv) *adj* hard to pin down; evasive

To be *elusive* is to *elude,* which means to avoid, evade, or escape.

The answer to the problem was *elusive;* every time the mathematician thought he was close, he discovered another error. (Or, one could say that the answer to the problem *eluded* the mathematician.)

The *elusive* criminal was next to impossible for the police to catch. (The criminal *eluded* the police.)

The team played hard, but victory was *elusive* and they suffered another defeat. (Victory *eluded* the hard-playing team.)

EMIGRATE (EM uh GRATE) *v* to move to a new country; to move to a new place to live; to expatriate

At the heart of this word is the word *migrate*, which means to move from one place or country to another. *Emigrate* adds to migrate the sense of moving *out of* some place in particular. Pierre *emigrated* from France because he had grown tired of speaking French. Pierre became an *émigré*.

The Soviet dissidents were persecuted by the secret police, so they sought permisssion to *emigrate*.

On the other end of every *emigration* is an *immigration*, or *"in-migration."* When Pierre *emigrated* from France, he *immigrated* to the United States.

To *emigrate* is to leave one country for another; to *immigrate* is to arrive in one country from another.

EMINENT (EM uh nunt) *adj* well known and respected; standing out from all others in quality or accomplishment; outstanding

The visiting poet was so *eminent* that our English teacher fell to the ground before him and licked his shoes. Our English teacher thought the poet was *preeminent* in his field.

The entire audience fell silent when the *eminent* musician walked onto the stage and picked up his banjo and bongo drums.

Don't confuse this word with *imminent*.

EMPIRICAL (em PIR i kul) *adj* relying on experience or observation; not merely theoretical

The apple-dropping experiment gave the scientists *empirical* evidence that gravity exists.

Huey's idea about the moon being made of pizza dough was not *empirical*.

We proved the pie's deliciousness *empirically*, by eating it.

Q·U·I·C·K · Q·U·I·Z #37

Match each word in the first column with its definition in the second column. Check your answers in the back of the book.

1. elicit   a. well known
2. elliptical   b. bring out
3. elusive   c. hard to pin down
4. emigrate   d. relying on experience
5. immigration   e. move from a country
6. eminent   f. move into a country
7. empirical   g. obscure

EMULATE (EM yuh LATE) *v* to strive to equal or excel, usually through imitation

To *emulate* someone is to try to be just as good as, or better than, him or her.

The American company *emulated* its successful Japanese competitor but never quite managed to do as well.

Little Joey imitated his athletic older brother in the hope of one day *emulating* his success.

I got ahead by *emulating* those who had gone before me.

ENCROACH (en KROCH) *v* to make gradual or stealthy inroads into; to trespass

As the city grew, it *encroached* on the countryside surrounding it.

With an *encroaching* sense of dread, I slowly pushed open the blood-spattered door.

My neighbor *encroached* on my yard by building his new stockade fence a few feet on my side of the property line.

ENDEMIC (en DEM ik) *adj* native; restricted to a particular region or era; indigenous

You won't find that kind of tree in California; it's *endemic* in our part of the country.

That peculiar strain of influenza was *endemic* in a small community in South Carolina; there were no cases anywhere else.

The writer Tom Wolfe coined the term "Me Decade" to describe the egocentricity *endemic* in the 1970s.

ENERVATE (EN ur VATE) *v* to reduce the strength or energy of, especially to do so gradually

Mark felt *enervated* by his long ordeal and couldn't make himself get out of bed.

Clinging to a flagpole for a month without food or water *enervated* me, and one day I fell asleep and fell off.

Life itself seemed to *enervate* the old man. He grew weaker and paler with every breath he drew.

ENFRANCHISE (en FRAN chize) *v* to grant the privileges of citizenship, especially the right to vote

In the United States, citizens become *enfranchised* on their eighteenth birthdays. American women were not *enfranchised* until the adoption of the Nineteenth Amendment in 1920, which gave them the right to vote.

To *disfranchise* (not *disenfranchise*) someone is to take away the privileges of citizenship or take away the right to vote. One of the goals of the reform candidate was to *disfranchise* the bodies at the cemetery, which had had a habit of voting for the crooked mayor.

ENGENDER (en JEN dur) *v* to bring into existence; to create; to cause

My winning lottery ticket *engendered* a great deal of envy among my co-workers; they all wished that they had won.

Smiles *engender* smiles.

The bitter lieutenant *engendered* discontent among his troops.

ENIGMA (uh NIG muh) *n* a mystery

Hal is an *enigma;* he never does any homework but he always gets good grades.

The wizard spoke in riddles and *enigmas,* and no one could understand what he was saying.

An *enigma* is *enigmatic* (EN ig MAT ik). Hal's good grades were *enigmatic.* So was the wizard's speech.

ENORMITY (i NAWR mi tee) *n* extreme evil; a hideous offense; immensity

Hitler's soldiers stormed through the village, committing one *enormity* after another.

Enormity does *not* mean hugeness or great size, although it is often misused in this way. Use *immensity* instead.

EPHEMERAL (i FEM ur al) *adj* lasting a very short time

Ephemeral comes from the Greek and means "lasting a single day." The word is usually used more loosely to mean lasting a short time.

Youth and flowers are all *ephemeral.* They're gone before you know it.

Some friendships are *ephemeral.*

The tread on those used tires will probably turn out to be *ephemeral.*

Q·U·I·C·K · Q·U·I·Z #38

Match each word in the first column with its definition in the second column. Check your answers in the back of the book.

1. emulate
2. encroach
3. endemic
4. enervate
5. enfranchise
6. disfranchise
7. engender
8. enigma
9. enormity
10. ephemeral

a. cause to exist
b. mystery
c. remove voting rights
d. reduce the strength of
e. native
f. grant voting rights
g. strive to equal
h. lasting a very short time
i. extreme evil
j. trespass

EPIGRAM (EP uh GRAM) *n* a brief and usually witty or satirical saying

People often find it difficult to remember the difference between an *epigram* and an:

epigraph: an apt quotation placed at the beginning of a book or essay
epitaph: a commemorative inscription on a grave
epithet: a term used to characterize the nature of something, or a *disparaging* term used to describe a person.

There. Now you know.

An *epigram* is *epigrammatic.*

EPITOME (i PIT uh mee) *n* a brief summary that captures the meaning of the whole; the perfect example of something; a paradigm

The first paragraph of the new novel is an *epitome* of the entire book; you could read it and understand what the author was trying to get across. It *epitomized* the entire work.

Luke's freshman year was an *epitome* of the college experience. He made friends, missed classes, fell in love, and flunked out.

Eating corn dogs and drinking root beer is the *epitome* of the good life, as far as Wilson is concerned.

EQUANIMITY (EE kwuh NIM i tee) *n* composure; calm

The entire apartment building was crumbling, but Rachel faced the disaster with *equanimity*. She ducked out of the way of a falling beam and made herself a chocolate sundae.

The mother of twelve boys viewed the mudball fight with *equanimity*; at least they weren't shooting bullets at one another.

EQUITABLE (EK wi tuh bul) *adj* fair

King Solomon's decision was certainly *equitable*; each mother would receive half the child.

The pirates distributed the loot *equitably* among themselves, so that each pirate received the same share as every other pirate.

The divorce settlement was quite *equitable*. Sheila got the right half of the house and Tom got the left half.

Equity is fairness; *inequity* is unfairness. *Iniquity* and *inequity* both mean unfair, but *iniquity* implies wickedness as well. By the way, *equity* has a meaning in business. See our business listing at the end of the book.

EQUIVOCAL (i KWIV uh kul) *adj* ambiguous; intentionally confusing; capable of being interpreted in more than one way

Ambiguous means unclear. To be *equivocal* is to be intentionally ambiguous. Joe's response was *equivocal*; we couldn't tell whether he meant yes or no, which is precisely what Joe wanted.

The doctor's *equivocal* diagnosis made us think that he had no idea what Mrs. Johnson had.

To be *equivocal* is to *equivocate*. To *equivocate* is to mislead by saying confusing or ambiguous things. When we asked Harry whether that was his car that was parked in the middle of the hardware store, he *equivocated* and asked, "In which aisle?"

ERUDITE (ER yoo DITE) *adj* scholarly; deeply learned

The professor said things so *erudite* that none of us had the slightest idea of what he was saying.

The *erudite* biologist was viewed by many of his colleagues as a likely winner of the Nobel Prize.

To be *erudite* is to possess *erudition*, or extensive knowledge. Mr. Jones's vast library was an indication of his *erudition*.

Q·U·I·C·K · Q·U·I·Z #39

Match each word in the first column with its definition in the second column. Check your answers in the back of the book.

1. epigram	a. brief summary
2. epigraph	b. fair
3. epitaph	c. composure
4. epithet	d. intentionally confusing
5. epitome	e. apt quotation
6. equanimity	f. say confusing things
7. equitable	g. inscription on a grave
8. equivocal	h. scholarly
9. equivocate	i. brief, witty saying
10. erudite	j. disparaging term

ESOTERIC (ES uh TER ik) *adj* hard to understand; understood by only a select few; peculiar

Chicken wrestling and underwater yodeling were just two of Bob's *esoteric* hobbies.

The author's books were so *esoteric* that no one except his mother ever bought any of them.

ESPOUSE (e SPOUZ) *v* to support; to advocate

The Mormons used to espouse bigamy, or marriage to more than one woman.

Bert *espoused* so many causes that he sometimes had trouble remembering which side he was on.

The candidate for governor *espoused* a program in which all taxes would be abolished and all the state's revenues would be supplied by income from Bingo and horse racing.

ETHEREAL (i THIR ee ul) *adj* heavenly; as light and insubstantial as a gas or ether

The *ethereal* music we heard turned out to be not angels plucking on their harps but the wind blowing past our satellite-television antenna.

The *ethereal* mist on the hillside was delicate and beautiful.

EUPHEMISM (YOO fuh miz um) *n* a pleasant or inoffensive expression used in place of an unpleasant or offensive one

Aunt Gladys, who couldn't bring herself to say the word *death*, said that Uncle George had taken the big bus uptown. "Taking the big bus uptown" was her *euphemism* for dying.

The sex-education instructor wasn't very effective. She was so embarrassed by the subject that she could only bring herself to speak *euphemistically* about it.

EVANESCENT (EV uh NES unt) *adj* fleeting; vanishing; happening for only the briefest period

Meteors are *evanescent:* They last so briefly that it is hard to tell whether one has actually appeared.

EXACERBATE (ek ZAS ur bate) *v* to make worse

Dipping Austin in lye *exacerbated* his skin condition.

The widow's grief was *exacerbated* by the minister's momentary inability to remember her dead husband's name.

The fender-bender was *exacerbated* when a line of twenty-five cars plowed into the back of Margaret's car.

EXACTING (ig ZAK ting) *adj* extremely demanding; difficult; requiring great skill or care

The *exacting* math teacher subtracted points for even the most unimportant errors.

Weaving cloth out of guinea-pig hair is an *exacting* occupation, because guinea pigs are small and their hair is short.

The surgeon's *exacting* task was to reconnect the patient's severed eyelashes.

EXALT (ig ZAWLT) *v* to raise high; to glorify

The manager decided to *exalt* the lowly batboy by asking him to pitch in the opening game of the World Series.

The adjective *exalted* is used frequently. Being Queen of England is an exalted occupation.

Larry felt *exalted* when he woke up to discover that his great-uncle had left him a hundred million dollars.

Cleaning out a septic tank is not an *exalted* task.

Be careful not to confuse this word with *exult*.

EXASPERATE (ig ZAS puh RATE) *v* to annoy thoroughly; to make very angry; to try the patience of

The child's insistence on hopping backward on one foot *exasperated* his mother, who was in a hurry.

The algebra class's refusal to answer any questions was extremely *exasperating* to the substitute teacher.

EXEMPLIFY (ig ZEM pluh FYE) *v* to illustrate by example; to serve as a good example

Fred participated in every class discussion and typed all of his papers. His teacher thought Fred *exemplified* the model student; Fred's classmates thought Fred was sycophantic.

An *exemplar* is an ideal model or a paradigm. *Exemplary* means outstanding, or worthy of imitation.

EXHAUSTIVE (ig ZAWS tiv) *adj* thorough; rigorous; complete; painstaking

Before you use a parachute, you should examine it *exhaustively* for defects. Once you jump, your decision is irrevocable.

EXHORT (ig ZAWRT) *v* to urge strongly; to give a serious warning to

The coach used his bullhorn to *exhort* us to try harder.

The fearful forest ranger *exhorted* us not to go into the cave, but we did so anyway and became lost in the center of the earth.

Q·U·I·C·K · Q·U·I·Z #40

Match each word in the first column with its definition in the second column. Check your answers in the back of the book.

1. esoteric		a.	peculiar
2. espouse		b.	make worse
3. ethereal		c.	extremely demanding
4. euphemism		d.	raise high
5. evanescent		e.	inoffensive expression
6. exacerbate		f.	urge strongly
7. exacting		g.	annoy thoroughly
8. exalt		h.	heavenly
9. exasperate		i.	advocate
10. exemplify		j.	fleeting
11. exhaustive		k.	illustrate by example
12. exhort		l.	thorough

EXIGENCY (EK si jen see). *n* an emergency; an urgency

An academic *exigency:* You haven't opened a book all term and the final is tomorrow morning.

Exigent means urgent.

EXISTENTIAL (EG zi STEN shul) *adj* having to do with existence; having to do with the body of thought called *existentialism*, which basically holds that human beings are responsible for their own actions but is otherwise too complicated to summarize in a single sentence

This word is overused but under-understood by virtually all of the people who use it. Unless you have a very good reason for throwing it around, you should probably avoid it.

EXONERATE (ig ZON uh RATE) *v* to free completely from blame; to exculpate

The suspect was *exonerated* when the district attorney's fingerprints were found on the murder weapon.

The defendant, who had always claimed he wasn't guilty, expected to be *exonerated* by the testimony of his best friend.

Our dog was *exonerated* when we discovered that it was in fact the cat who had eaten all the chocolate-chip cookies.

EXPATRIATE (eks PAY tree ATE) *v* to throw (someone) out of his or her native land; to move away from one's native land; to emigrate

The rebels were *expatriated* by the nervous general, who feared that they would cause trouble if they were allowed to remain in the country.

Hugo was fed up with his native country and so *expatriated* to America. In doing so, Hugo became an *expatriate*.

EXPEDIENT (ik SPEE dee unt) *adj* providing an immediate advantage; serving one's immediate self-interest; practical

Since the basement had nearly filled with water, the plumber felt it would be *expedient* to clear out the drain.

The candidate's position in favor of higher pay for teachers was an *expedient* one adopted for the national teachers' convention and abandoned shortly afterward.

Expedient can also be used as a noun. The car repairman did not have his tool kit handy, so he used chewing gum as an expedient to patch a hole.

EXPEDITE (EK spi DITE) *v* to speed up or ease the progress of

The post office *expedited* mail delivery by hiring more letter carriers.

The lawyer *expedited* the progress of our case through the courts by bribing a few judges.

Our wait for a table was *expedited* by a waiter who mistook Angela for a movie star.

EXPLICIT (ik SPLIS it) *adj* clearly and directly expressed

The sexually *explicit* movie received an X rating.

The machine's instructions were *explicit*—they told us exactly what to do.

No one *explicitly* asked us to set the barn on fire, but we got the impression that that was what we were supposed to do.

Implicit means indirectly expressed or implied. Gerry's dissatisfaction with our work was implicit in his expression, although he never criticized us directly.

EXTOL (ik STOHL) *v* to praise highly; to laud

The millionaire *extolled* the citizen who returned his gold watch, and then rewarded him with a heartfelt handshake.

EXTRANEOUS (ik STRAY nee us) *adj* unnecessary; irrelevant; extra

To be *extra*neous is to be *extra*, but always with the sense of being unnecessary. Extra ice cream would never be *extraneous*, unless everyone had already eaten so much that no one wanted any more.

The book's feeble plot was buried in a lot of *extraneous* material about a talking dog.

The soup contained several *extraneous* ingredients, including hair, sand, and a single dead fly.

EXTRAPOLATE (ik STRAP uh LATE) *v* to project or deduce from something known; to infer

George's estimates were *extrapolated* from last year's data; he simply took all the old numbers and doubled them.

Jacob came up with a probable recipe by *extrapolating* from the taste of the cookies he had eaten at the store.

By *extrapolating* from a handful of pottery fragments, the archaeologists formed a possible picture of the ancient civilization.

To *extrapolate*, a scientist uses the facts he has to project to facts outside; to *interpolate*, he tries to fill the gaps within his data.

EXTRICATE (EK struh KATE) *v* to free from a difficulty

It took two and a half days to *extricate* the little girl from the abandoned well into which she had fallen.

Sam had to pretend to be sick to *extricate* himself from the blind date with the mud wrestler.

Mary had no trouble driving her car *into* the ditch, but she needed a tow truck to *extricate* it.

EXTROVERT (EK stroh vurt) *n* an open, outgoing person; a person whose attention is focused on others rather than on himself or herself

The little girl was quite an *extrovert;* she walked boldly into the roomful of strange adults and struck up a friendly conversation.

Hal was an *extrovert* in the sense that he was always more interested in other people's business than in his own.

An *introvert* is a person whose attention is directed inward and who is concerned with little outside himself or herself. Bud was an *introvert;* he spent virtually all his time in his room, writing in his diary and talking to himself. An *introvert* is usually introspective.

EXULT (ig ZULT) *v* to rejoice; to celebrate

Exult and *exalt* have distinct though similar meanings. The spelling team *exulted* in its victory over the pronunciation club at the badminton finals. They were *exalted* by the spectators as true champions.

Q·U·I·C·K · Q·U·I·Z #41

Match each word in the first column with its definition in the second column. Check your answers in the back of the book.

1. exigency	a.	free from blame
2. existential	b.	clearly expressed
3. exonerate	c.	indirectly expressed
4. expatriate	d.	having to do with existence
5. expedient	e.	outgoing person
6. expedite	f.	speed up
7. explicit	g.	infer
8. implicit	h.	free from difficulty
9. extol	i.	immediately advantageous
10. extraneous	j.	unnecessary
11. extrapolate	k.	inward-directed person
12. extricate	l.	throw out of native land
13. extrovert	m.	emergency
14. introvert	n.	rejoice
15. exult	o.	praise highly

F

FABRICATION (FAB ruh KAY shun) *n* a lie; something made up

My story about being the Prince of Wales was a *fabrication*. I'm really the King of Denmark.

The suspected murderer's alibi turned out to be an elaborate *fabrication;* in other words, he was lying when he said that he hadn't killed the victim.

To create a fabrication is to *fabricate.*

FACETIOUS (fuh SEE shus) *adj* humorous; not serious; clumsily humorous

David was sent to the principal's office for making a *facetious* remark about the intelligence of the French teacher.

Our proposal about shipping our town's garbage to the moon was *facetious,* but the first selectman took it seriously.

FACILE (FAS il) *adj* fluent; skillful in a superficial way; easy

To say that a writer's style is *facile* is to say both that it is skillful and that it would be better if the writer exerted himself or herself more. The word *facile* almost always contains this sense of superficiality.

Joe's poems were *facile* rather than truly accomplished; if you read them closely, you soon realized they were filled with clichés.

The bank president was a *facile* speaker. He could speak engagingly on almost any topic with very little preparation. He spoke with great *facility.*

FACTION (FAK shun) *n* a group, usually a small part of a larger group, united around some cause; disagreement within an organization.

At the Republican National Convention, the Ford *faction* spent much of its time shouting at the Reagan *faction.*

The faculty was relatively happy, but there was a *faction* that called for higher pay.

When the controversial topic of the fund drive came up, the committee descended into bitterness and *faction*. It was a *factious* topic.

FARCICAL (FARS i kul) *adj* absurd; ludicrous

Farcical means like a *farce,* which is a mockery or a ridiculous satire.

The serious play quickly turned *farcical* when the leading man's belt broke and his pants fell to his ankles.

The formerly secret documents detailed the CIA's *farcical* attempt to discredit Fidel Castro by sprinkling his shoes with a powder that was supposed to make his beard fall out.

FASTIDIOUS (fa STID ee us) *adj* meticulous; demanding; finicky

Mrs. Brown was a *fastidious* housekeeper; she cleaned up our crumbs almost before they hit the floor.

Jeb was so *fastidious* in his work habits that he needed neither a wastebasket nor an eraser.

The *fastidious* secretary was nearly driven mad by her boss, who used the floor as a file cabinet and his desk as a pantry.

FATALIST (FATE uh list) *n* someone who believes that future events are already determined and that humans are powerless to change them

Fatalist is closely related to the word *fate*. A *fatalist* is someone who believes that fate determines everything.

The old man was a *fatalist* about his illness, believing there was no sense in worrying about something over which he had no control.

Bill was such a *fatalist* that he never wore a seat belt; he said that if he was meant to die in a car accident, there was nothing he could do to prevent it.

To be a *fatalist* is to be *fatalistic*.

FATUOUS (FACH oo us) *adj* foolish; silly; idiotic

Pauline is so pretty that her suitors are often driven to *fatuous* acts of devotion. They are infatuated with her.

FAUNA (FAW nuh) *n* animals

We saw little evidence of *fauna* on our walk through the woods. We did, however, see plenty of *flora*, or plants.

"Flora and *fauna"* means plants and animals. The terms are used particularly in describing what lives in a particular region or environment.

Arctic *fauna* are very different from tropical fauna.

In Jim's yard, the *flora* consists mostly of weeds.

It's easy to remember which of these words means what. Just remember *fawns* and *flowers*.

FECUND (FEE kund, FEK und) *adj* fertile; productive

The *fecund* mother rabbit gave birth to hundreds and hundreds of little rabbits.

The philosopher's imagination was so *fecund* that ideas hopped out of him like so many baby rabbits.

Our compost heap became increasingly *fecund* as it decomposed.

The state of being *fecund* is *fecundity* (fi KUN di tee).

Q·U·I·C·K · Q·U·I·Z #42

Match each word in the first column with its definition in the second column. Check your answers in the back of the book.

1.	fabrication	a.	plants
2.	facetious	b.	fertile
3.	facile	c.	absurd
4.	faction	d.	one who believes in fate
5.	farcical	e.	humorous
6.	fastidious	f.	animals
7.	fatalist	g.	superficially skillful
8.	fatuous	h.	group with a cause
9.	fauna	i.	lie
10.	flora	j.	meticulous
11.	fecund	k.	foolish

FELICITY (fi LIS i TEE) *n* happiness; skillfulness, especially at expressing things; adeptness

Love was not all *felicity* for Glen and Pam; they argued all the time. In
fact their relationship was characterized by *infelicity*.

Shakespeare wrote with great *felicity*. His works are filled with *felicitous*
expressions.

FERVOR (FUR vur) *n* great warmth or earnestness; ardor; zeal

Avid baseball fans frequently display their *fervor* for the game by
throwing food at bad players.

FETTER (FET ur) *v* to restrain; to hamper

In his pursuit of the Nobel Prize for physics, Professor Jenkins was
fettered by his near-total ignorance of the subject.

To be *unfettered* is to be unrestrained or free of hindrances. When his
parents went to Europe for a few months, Jimmy invited all his friends
for some unfettered partying in the empty house.

A *fetter* is literally a chain (attached to the foot) that is used to restrain
a criminal or, for that matter, an innocent person. A figurative *fetter* can
be anything that hampers or restrains someone. The housewife's young
children were the *fetters* that prevented her from pursuing her love affair
with the washing-machine repairman.

FIDELITY (fi DEL i TEE) *n* faithfulness; loyalty

The motto of the United States Marine Corps is *semper fidelis*, which is
Latin for "always loyal."

A high-*fidelity* record player is one that is very faithful in reproducing
the original sound of whatever was recorded.

The crusader's life was marked by *fidelity* to the cause of justice.

The soldiers couldn't shoot straight, but their *fidelity* to the cause of
freedom was never in question.

Infidelity means faithlessness or disloyalty. *Marital infidelity* is another
way of saying *adultery*. Early phonograph records were marked by *infidelity*
to the original.

FIGURATIVE (FIG yur uh tiv) *adj* based on figures of speech; expressing
something in terms usually used for something else; metaphorical

To say that the autumn hillside was a blaze of color is to use the word
blaze in a *figurative* sense. The hillside wasn't really on fire, but the colors
of the leaves made it appear (somewhat) as though it were.

When the mayor said that the housing market had sprouted wings, he
was speaking *figuratively*. The housing market hadn't really sprouted
wings; it had merely grown so rapidly that it had almost seemed to fly.

A *figurative* meaning of a word is one that is not *literal*. A *literal* statement is one in which every word means exactly what it says. If the housing
market had *literally* sprouted wings, genuine wings would somehow have
popped out of it.

People very, very often confuse these words, using one when they
really mean the other. Andy could *literally* eat money if he chewed up and
swallowed a dollar bill. Andy's car eats money only *figuratively*, in the sense
that it is very expensive to operate.

FINESSE (fi NES) *n* skillful maneuvering; subtlety; craftiness

The doctor sewed up the wound with *finesse*, making stitches so small one could scarcely see them.

The boxer moved with such *finesse* that his opponent never knew what hit him.

FLAGRANT (FLAY grunt) *adj* glaringly bad; notorious; scandalous

A *flagrant* theft is stealing a car, for example, from the lot behind the police station. A *flagrant* spelling error is one that jumps right off the page. See the listing for *blatant*.

FLAUNT (flawnt) *v* to show off; to display ostentatiously

The brand-new millionaire annoyed all his friends by driving around his old neighborhood to *flaunt* his new Rolls-Royce.

Colleen *flaunted* her engagement ring, shoving it in the face of almost anyone who came near her.

This word is very often confused with *flout*.

FLOUT (flout) *v* to disregard something out of disrespect

A driver *flouts* the traffic laws by driving through red lights and knocking down pedestrians.

To *flaunt* success is to make certain everyone knows that you are successful. To *flout* success is to be contemptuous of success or to act as though it means nothing at all.

FOIBLE (FOI bul) *n* a minor character flaw

Barbara's *foibles* included a tendency to prefer dogs to people.

The delegates to the state convention ignored the candidates' positions on the major issues and concentrated on their *foibles*.

FOMENT (foh MENT) *v* to stir up; to instigate

The bad news from abroad *fomented* pessimism among professional investors.

The radicals set off several bombs in an effort to *foment* rebellion among the peasants.

Q·U·I·C·K · Q·U·I·Z #43

Match each word in the first column with its definition in the second column. Check your answers in the back of the book.

1. felicity	a. loyalty
2. fervor	b. stir up
3. fetter	c. restrain
4. fidelity	d. meaning what it says
5. figurative	e. minor character flaw
6. literal	f. show off
7. finesse	g. based on figures of speech
8. flagrant	h. to disregard contemptuously
9. flaunt	i. skillful maneuvering
10. flout	j. happiness
11. foible	k. glaringly bad
12. foment	l. zeal

FORBEAR (fawr BAIR) *v* to refrain from; to abstain

Stephen told me I could become a millionaire if I joined him in his business, but his company makes me nervous so I decided to *forbear*.

George *forbore* to punch me in the nose, even though I had told him that I thought he was a sniveling idiot.

A *forebear* (FORE bair)—sometimes also spelled *forbear*—is an ancestor. William's forebears came to America on the *Mayflower*.

FORGO (fohr GOH) *v* to do without; to forbear

We had some of the chocolate cake, and some of the chocolate mousse, and some of the chocolate cream pie, but we were worried about our weight so we decided to *forgo* the chocolate-covered potato chips. That is, we *forwent* them.

FORSAKE (fawr SAKE) *v* to abandon; to renounce; to relinquish

We urged Buddy to *forsake* his life with the alien beings and return to his job at the drugstore.

All the guru's followers had *forsaken* him, so he became a real estate developer and turned his temple into an apartment building.

FORTUITOUS (fawr TOO i tus) *adj* accidental; occurring by chance

The program's outcome was not the result of any plan but was entirely *fortuitous*.

The object was so perfectly formed that its creation could not have been *fortuitous*.

Fortuitous is often misused to mean lucky or serendipitous. Don't make that same mistake. It means merely accidental.

FOUNDER (FOUN dur) *v* to fail; to collapse; to sink

The candidate's campaign for the presidency *foundered* when it was revealed that he had once been married to an orangutan.

Zeke struggled through the first part of the course but *foundered* when the final examination was given.

The ship *foundered* shortly after its hull fell off.

Be careful not to confuse this word with *flounder*, which means to move clumsily or in confusion. Our field hockey team *floundered* helplessly around the field while the opposing team scored point after point.

The witness began to *flounder* as the attorney fired question after question.

If you want to remember the difference between the two words, think that when a person *flounders*, he is flopping around like a *flounder*.

FRATERNAL (fruh TUR nul) *adj* like brothers

The *fraternal* feeling among the meeting's participants disappeared when one of them stood up at dinner and began firing a machine gun.

A *fraternity* is an organization of men who have bound themselves together in a relationship analogous to that of real brothers.

FRENETIC (fruh NET ik) *adj* frantic; frenzied

There was a lot of *frenetic* activity in the office, but nothing ever seemed to get accomplished.

The bird's *frenetic* attempt to free itself from the thorn bush finally exhausted it. Then the cat strolled over and ate it.

FRUGAL (FROO gul) *adj* economical; penny-pinching

Laura was so *frugal* that she even tried to bargain with the checkout girl at the supermarket.

We were as *frugal* as we could be, but we still ended up several thousand dollars in debt.

Hannah's *frugality* annoyed her husband, who loved nothing better than spending money.

FURTIVE (FUR tiv) *adj* secretive; sly

Cal wiggled his ears while the countess was talking to him in a *furtive* attempt to catch our attention.

The burglars were *furtive*, but not *furtive* enough; the alert policeman grabbed them as they carried the color TV through the Washingtons' back door.

Q·U·I·C·K · Q·U·I·Z #44

Match each word in the first column with its definition in the second column. Check your answers in the back of the book.

1.	forbear	a.	economical
2.	forebear	b.	ancestor
3.	forgo	c.	move in confusion
4.	forsake	d.	do without
5.	fortuitous	e.	refrain from
6.	founder	f.	sink
7.	flounder	g.	secretive
8.	frenetic	h.	accidental
9.	frugal	i.	abandon
10.	furtive	j.	frantic

FUTILE (FYOOT il) *adj* useless; hopeless
   A D+ average and no extracurricular interests to speak of meant that applying to Harvard was *futile*, but Lucinda hoped against hope.
   Something *futile* is a *futility*. Lucinda doesn't know what *futility* it is.

G

GARRULOUS (GAR uh lus) *adj* talkative; chatty
   Gillette is gregarious and *garrulous;* he loves to hang out with the gang and gab.
   The noun is *garrulity*.

GENRE (ZHAHN ruh) *n* a type or category, especially of art or writing
   The novel is one *genre*. Poetry is another. Alan displayed a great talent for a particular *genre:* the bawdy limerick.

GENTEEL (jen TEEL) *adj* refined; polite; aristocratic; affecting refinement
   The ladies at the ball were too *genteel* to accept our invitation to the wrestling match.
   Jake had been born in a slum but now, in his mansion, his life was *genteel*.
   A person who is *genteel* has *gentility*.

GESTICULATE (je STIK yuh LATE) *v* to make gestures, especially when speaking or in place of speaking
   Harry *gesticulated* wildly on the other side of the theater in an attempt to get our attention.

The after-dinner speaker *gesticulated* in such a strange way that the audience paid more attention to his hands than to his words.

A person who *gesticulates* makes *gesticulations*.

GLUT (glut) *n* surplus; an overabundance

The international oil shortage turned into an international oil *glut* with surprising speed.

We had a *glut* of contributions but a *dearth*, or scarcity, of volunteers; it seemed that people would rather give their money than their time.

GRANDILOQUENT (gran DIL uh kwunt) *adj* pompous; using a lot of big, fancy words in an attempt to sound impressive

The president's speech was *grandiloquent* rather than eloquent; there were some six-dollar words and some impressive phrases, but he really had nothing to say.

The new minister's *grandiloquence* got him in trouble with deacons, who wanted him to be more restrained in his sermons.

GRANDIOSE (GRAN dee ohs) *adj* absurdly exaggerated

The scientist's *grandiose* plan was to build a huge shopping center on the surface of the moon.

Their house was genuinely impressive, although there were a few *grandiose* touches: a fireplace the size of a garage, a kitchen with four ovens, and a computerized media center in every room.

To be *grandiose* is to be characterized by *grandiosity*.

GRATUITOUS (gruh TOO i tus) *adj* given freely (said of something bad); unjustified; unprovoked; uncalled for

The scathing review of the movie contained several *gratuitous* remarks about the sex life of the director.

Their attack against us was *gratuitous;* we had never done anything to offend them. *Gratuitous* is often misunderstood because it is confused with *gratuity*.

A *gratuity* is a tip, like the one you leave in a restaurant. A *gratuity* is a nice thing. *Gratuitous*, however, is not nice. Don't confuse these words.

GRAVITY (GRAV i tee) *n* seriousness

Not the force that makes apples fall down instead of up, but a different sort of weightiness.

The anchorman's nervous giggling was entirely inappropriate, given the *gravity* of the situation.

No one realized the *gravity* of Myron's drug addiction until it was much too late to help him.

At the heart of the word *gravity* is the word *grave*, which means serious.

GREGARIOUS (gri GAIR ee us) *adj* sociable; enjoying the company of others

Dirk was too *gregarious* to enjoy the fifty years he spent in solitary confinement.

Anna wasn't very *gregarious;* she went to the party, but she spent most of her time hiding in the closet.

In biology, *gregarious* is used to describe animals that live in groups. Bees, which live together in large colonies, are said to be *gregarious* insects.

GUILE (gile) *n* cunning, duplicity; artfulness

José used *guile*, not intelligence, to win the spelling bee; he cheated.

Stuart was shocked by the *guile* of the automobile mechanic, who had poked a hole in his radiator and then told him that it had sprung a leak.

To be *guileless* is to be innocent or naïve. *Guileless* and artless are synonyms.

The word *beguile* also means to deceive, but in a charming and not always bad way. Clarence found Mary's beauty so *beguiling* that he did anything she asked of him.

Q·U·I·C·K · Q·U·I·Z #45

Match each word in the first column with its definition in the second column. Check your answers in the back of the book.

1. futile		a. chatty
2. garrulous		b. surplus
3. genre		c. cunning
4. genteel		d. unjustified
5. gesticulate		e. seriousness
6. glut		f. make gestures
7. grandiloquent		g. hopeless
8. grandiose		h. refined
9. gratuitous		i. sociable
10. gravity		j. pompous
11. gregarious		k. absurdly exaggerated
12. guile		l. type of art

H

HACKNEYED (HAK need) *adj* overused; trite; stale

"As cold as ice" is a *hackneyed* expression.

Michael's book was full of clichés and *hackneyed* phrases.

The creationism issue had been discussed so much as to become *hackneyed*.

HAPLESS (HAP lis) *adj* unlucky

Joe's *hapless* search for fun led him from one disappointment to another.

Alex led a *hapless* existence that made all his friends' lives seem fortunate by comparison.

HARBINGER (HAR bin jur) *n* a forerunner; a signal of
Be careful with the pronunciation of this word. Many people pronounce it incorrectly.
Warm weather is the *harbinger* of spring.
A cloud of bad breath and body odor, which preceded him by several yards everywhere he went, was Harold's *harbinger*.

HEDONISM (HEED uh niz um) *n* the pursuit of pleasure as a way of life
A *hedonist* practices *hedonism* twenty-four hours a day.

HEGEMONY (hi JEM uh nee) *n* leadership, especially of one nation over another
America's nuclear *hegemony* has been challenged and perhaps usurped by the Soviets.
Japan and Germany vie for *hegemony* in the foreign-car market.

HERESY (HER i see) *n* any belief that is strongly opposed to established beliefs
Galileo was tried for the *heresy* of suggesting that the sun did not revolve around the earth. He was almost convicted of being a *heretic*, but he recanted his *heretical* view.

HERMETIC (hur MET ik) *adj* impervious to external influence; airtight
The president led a *hermetic* existence in the White House, as his advisers attempted to seal him off from the outside world.
The old men felt vulnerable and unwanted outside the *hermetic* security of their club.
The poisonous substance was sealed *hermetically* inside a glass cylinder.

HEYDAY (HAY DAY) *n* golden age; prime
In his *heyday*, Vernon was a world-class athlete; today he's just Vernon.
The *heyday* of the British Navy ended a long, long time ago.

HIATUS (hye AY tus) *n* a break or interruption, often from work
Spencer looked forward to spring break as a welcome *hiatus* from the rigors of campus parties.

HIERARCHY (HYE uh RAHR kee) *n* an organization based on rank or degree; pecking order
George was very low in the State Department *hierarchy*. In fact, his phone number wasn't even listed in the State Department directory.
There appeared to be no *hierarchy* in the newly discovered tribe; there was no leader and, for that matter, no followers.

HISTRIONIC (HIS tree ON ik) *adj* overly dramatic; theatrical
Adele's *histrionic* request for a raise embarrassed everyone in the office. She gesticulated wildly, jumped up and down, pulled out handfuls of hair, threw herself to the ground, and groaned in agony.
The chairman's *histrionic* presentation convinced no one.
Histrionic behavior is referred to as *histrionics*. The young actor's *histrionics* made everyone in the audience squirm.

HOMILY (HOM ul lee) *n* a sermon

The football coach often began practice with a lengthy *homily* on the virtues of clean living.

HOMOGENEOUS (HOH muh JEE nee us) *adj* uniform; made entirely of one thing

Homogenized milk is milk in which the cream, which usually floats on top, has been permanently mixed with the rest of the milk. (Skim milk is milk from which the layer of cream has been skimmed off.) When milk is *homogenized*, it becomes a homogeneous substance—that is, it's the same throughout, or uniform.

The kindergarten class was extremely *homogeneous:* all the children had blond hair, blue eyes, red shoes, and the same last name.

To be *heterogeneous* is to be mixed or varied. On Halloween the children amassed a *heterogeneous* collection of candy, chewing gum, popcorn, cookies, and razor blades.

HUSBANDRY (HUZ bun dree) *n* thrifty management of resources; livestock farming

Husbandry is the practice of conserving money or resources. To husband is to economize. Everyone *husbanded* oil and electricity during the energy crisis of the seventies.

HYPERBOLE (hye PUR buh lee) *n* an exaggeration used as a figure of speech; exaggeration

When Joe said, "I'm so hungry I could eat a horse," he was using a *hyperbole* to convey the extent of his hunger.

The candidate was guilty of *hyperbole;* all the facts in his speech were exaggerated.

HYPOTHETICAL (hye puh THET i kul) *adj* uncertain; unproven

Ernie's skill as a baseball player was entirely *hypothetical,* since he had never played the game.

There were several *hypothetical* explanations for the strange phenomenon, but no one could say for certain what had caused it.

Q·U·I·C·K · Q·U·I·Z #46

Match each word in the first column with its definition in the second column. Check your answers in the back of the book.

1. hackneyed
2. hapless
3. harbinger
4. hedonism
5. hegemony
6. heresy
7. hermetic
8. heyday
9. hiatus
10. hierarchy
11. hindrance
12. histrionic
13. homily
14. homogeneous
15. heterogeneous
16. husbandry
17. hyperbole
18. hypothetical

a. leadership
b. uniform
c. airtight
d. forerunner
e. pecking order
f. overused, trite
g. exaggeration
h. golden age
i. varied
j. obstruction
k. unlucky
l. uncertain
m. overly dramatic
n. break
o. sermon
p. thrifty management of resources
q. lifelong pursuit of pleasure
r. strongly contrary belief

I

ICONOCLAST (iye KON uh KLAST) *n* one who attacks popular beliefs or institutions

Iconoclast comes from Greek words meaning "image breaker." The original *iconoclasts* were opponents of the use of *icons*, or sacred images, in certain Christian churches. Today the word is used to refer to someone who attacks popular figures and ideas—a person to whom "nothing is sacred."

The popular columnist was an inveterate *iconoclast*, avidly attacking public figures no matter what their party affiliation.

To study and go to class is to be an *iconoclast* on that campus, which has a reputation for being the biggest party school in the country if not the world.

Herbert's *iconoclastic* views were not popular with the older members of the board.

IDEOLOGY (IYE dee OL uh JEE) *n* a system of social or political ideas

Conservatism and liberalism are competing *ideologies*.

The candidate never managed to communicate his *ideology* to the voters, so few people were able to grasp what he stood for.

The senator's tax proposal had more to do with *ideology* than with common sense; his plan, though consistent with his principles, was clearly impractical.

A dogmatic person attached to an *ideology* is an *ideologue*. An *ideologue* is doctrinaire.

IDIOSYNCRASY (ID ee oh SINK ruh see) *n* a peculiarity; an eccentricity

Eating green beans drenched in ketchup for breakfast was one of Jordana's *idiosyncrasies*.

The doctor's interest was aroused by an *idiosyncrasy* in Bill's skull: there seemed to be a coin slot in the back of his head.

A person who has an *idiosyncrasy* is said to be *idiosyncratic*. Tara's driving was somewhat *idiosyncratic;* she sometimes seemed to prefer the sidewalk to the street.

IDYLLIC (iye DIL ik) *adj* charming in a rustic way; naturally peaceful

They built their house in an *idyllic* spot. There was a babbling brook in back and an unbroken view of wooded hills in front.

Our vacation in the country was *idyllic;* we went for long walks down winding dirt roads and didn't see a newspaper all week.

An *idyllic* vacation or other experience could also be called an *idyll*.

IGNOMINY (IG nuh MIN ee) *n* deep disgrace

After the big scandal, the formerly high-flying investment banker fell into a life of shame and *ignominy*.

The *ignominy* of losing the spelling bee was too much for Arnold, who decided to give up spelling altogether.

Something that is deeply disgraceful is *ignominious*. The massacre of the farm family was an *ignominious* act.

ILLICIT (i LIS it) *adj* illegal; not permitted

Criminals engage in *illicit* activities.

Don't confuse this word with *elicit*. The police interviewed hundreds of witnesses, trying to *elicit* clues that might help them stop an *illicit* business.

IMMINENT (IM uh nunt) *adj* just about to happen

The pink glow in the east made it clear that sunrise was *imminent*.

George had a feeling that disaster was *imminent*, but he couldn't figure out why; then the jumbo jet crashed into his garage.

Don't confuse this word with *eminent*.

IMMUTABLE (i MYOO tuh bul) *adj* unchangeable

Jerry's mother had only one *immutable* rule: no dancing on the dinner table.

The statue of the former principal looked down on the students with an *immutable* scowl.

Something that *is* changeable is said to be *mutable*. The *mutable* shoreline shifted continually as the tides moved sand first in one direction and then in another.

Helena's moods were *mutable;* one minute she was kind and gentle, the next minute she was screaming with anger.

Both *immutable* and *mutable* are based on a Latin root meaning "change." So are *mutation* and *mutant.*

IMPARTIAL (im PAHR shul) *adj* fair; not favoring one side or the other; unbiased

Jurors are supposed to be *impartial* rather than *partial;* they aren't supposed to make up their minds until they've heard all the evidence.

Beverly tried to be an *impartial* judge at the beauty contest, but in the end she couldn't help selecting her own daughter to be the new Pork Queen.

IMPECCABLE (im PEK uh bul) *adj* flawless; entirely without sin

The children's behavior was *impeccable;* they didn't set fire to the cat, and they didn't pour naval dye into the swimming pool.

Hal's clothes were always *impeccable;* even the wrinkles were perfectly creased.

By the way, *peccable* means liable to sin. And while we're at it, *peccadillo* is a minor sin.

IMPERIAL (im PEER ee ul) *adj* like an emperor or an empire

Imperial, emperor, and *empire* are all derived from the same root.

England's *imperial* days are over, now that the British Empire has crumbled away.

The palace was decorated with *imperial* splendor.

George's *imperial* manner was inappropriate, since he was nothing more exalted than the local dogcatcher.

A similar word is *imperious,* which means bossy and, usually, arrogant. The director's *imperious* style rubbed everyone the wrong way; he always seemed to be giving orders, and he never listened to what anyone said.

Q·U·I·C·K · Q·U·I·Z #47

Match each word in the first column with its definition in the second column. Check your answers in the back of the book.

1. iconoclast		a. peculiarity
2. ideology		b. naturally peaceful
3. idiosyncrasy		c. like an emperor
4. idyllic		d. flawless
5. ignominy		e. attacker of popular beliefs
6. illicit		f. just about to happen
7. imminent		g. fair
8. immutable		h. system of social ideas
9. impartial		i. bossy
10. impeccable		j. deep disgrace
11. imperial		k. unchangeable
12. imperious		l. illegal

IMPERVIOUS (im PUR vee us) *adj* not allowing anything to pass through; impenetrable

A raincoat, if it is any good, is *impervious* to water. It is made of an *impervious* material.

David was *impervious* to criticism—he did what he wanted to do no matter what anyone said.

IMPETUOUS (im PECH oo us) *adj* impulsive; extremely impatient

Impetuous Dick always seemed to be running off to buy a new car, even if he had just bought one the day before.

Samantha was so *impetuous* that she never took more than a few seconds to make up her mind.

IMPLEMENT (IM pluh munt) *v* to carry out

Leo developed a plan for shortening the grass in his yard, but he was unable to *implement* it, because he didn't have a lawn mower.

The government was better at creating new laws than at *implementing* them.

IMPOTENT (IM puh tunt) *adj* powerless; helpless; unable to perform sexual intercourse

Impotent means not potent—not powerful.

Joe and Betty made a few *impotent* efforts to turn aside the steamroller, but it squished their vegetable garden anyway.

We felt *impotent* in the face of their overpowering opposition to our plan.

Omnipotent means all powerful. After winning a dozen games in a row, the football team began to feel *omnipotent*.

IMPUGN (im PYOON) *v* to attack, especially to attack the truth or integrity of something

The critic *impugned* the originality of Jacob's novel, claiming that long stretches of it had been lifted from the work of someone else.

Fred said I was *impugning* his honesty when I called him a dirty liar, but I told him he had no honesty to *impugn*. This just seemed to make him angrier, for some reason.

INANE (i NANE) *adj* silly; senseless

Their plan to make an indoor swimming pool by flooding their basement was *inane*.

Mel made a few *inane* comments about the importance of chewing only on the left side of one's mouth, and then he passed out beneath the table.

Something that is *inane* is an *inanity*.

INAUGURATE (in AW gyuh RATE) *v* to begin officially; to induct formally into office

The mayor *inaugurated* the new no-smoking policy and then celebrated by lighting up a big cigar.

The team's loss *inaugurated* an era of defeat that lasted for several years.

To *inaugurate* a president is to make him take the oath of office and then give him the keys to the White House.

Q·U·I·C·K · Q·U·I·Z #48

Match each word in the first column with its definition in the second column. Check your answers in the back of the book.

1. impervious   a. begin officially
2. impetuous   b. carry out
3. implement   c. powerless
4. impotent   d. impenetrable
5. impugn   e. silly
6. inane   f. attack the truth of
7. inaugurate   g. impulsive

INCANDESCENT (in kun DES unt) *adj* brilliant; giving off heat or light

An *incandescent* light bulb is one containing a wire or filament that gives off light when it is heated. An *incandescent* person is one who gives off light or energy in a figurative sense.

Jan's ideas were so *incandescent* that simply being near her made you feel as though you understood the subject for the first time.

INCANTATION (IN kan TAY shun) *n* a chant; the repetition of statements or phrases in a way reminiscent of a chant

Much to our delight, the wizard's *incantation* eventually caused the small stone to turn into a sleek black BMW.

The students quickly became deaf to the principal's *incantations* about the importance of school spirit.

INCENSE (in SENS) *v* to make very angry

Jeremy was *incensed* when I told him that even though he was stupid and loathsome, he would always be my best friend.

My comment about his lovely painting of a tree *incensed* the artist, who said it was actually a portrait of his mother.

INCESSANT (in SES unt) *adj* unceasing

I will go deaf and lose my mind if you children don't stop your *incessant* bickering.

The noise from the city street was *incessant;* there always seemed to be a fire engine or a police car screaming by.

INCIPIENT (in SIP ee unt) *adj* beginning; emerging

Sitting in class, Henrietta detected an *incipient* tingle of boredom that told her she would soon be asleep.

Support for the plan was *incipient,* and the planners hoped it would soon grow and spread.

INCISIVE (in SYE siv) *adj* cutting right to the heart of the matter

When a surgeon cuts into you, he or she makes an *incision.* To be *incisive* is to be as sharp as a scalpel in a figurative sense.

After hours of debate, Louis offered a few *incisive* comments that made it immediately clear to everyone how dumb the original idea had been.

Lloyd's essays were always *incisive;* he never wasted any words, and his reasoning was always sharp and persuasive.

INCONGRUOUS (in KON groo us) *adj* not harmonious; not consistent; not appropriate; not fitting in

The ultra-modern kitchen seemed *incongruous* in the restored eighteenth-century farmhouse. It was an incongruity.

Bill's membership in the motorcycle gang was *incongruous* with his mild personality and his career as a management consultant.

INCORRIGIBLE (in KAWR i juh bul) *adj* incapable of being reformed

The convict was an *incorrigible* criminal; as soon as he got out of prison, he said, he was going to rob another donut store.

Bill is *incorrigible*—he eats three bags of potato chips every day even though he knows that eating two would be better for him.

Ever-cheerful Annie is an *incorrigible* optimist. .

Think of *incorrigible* as incorrectable. The word *corrigible* is rarely seen or used these days.

INCREMENT (IN kruh munt) *n* an increase; one in a series of increases

Bernard received a small *increment* in his salary each year, even though he did less and less work with every day that passed.

This year's fund-raising total represented an *increment* of 1 percent over last year's. This year's total represented an *incremental* change from last year's.

Orville built up his savings account *incrementally,* one dollar at a time.

INDIFFERENT (in DIF ur unt) *adj* not caring one way or the other; apathetic; mediocre

Red was *indifferent* about politics; he didn't care who was elected to office so long as no one passed a law against Monday Night Football.

Henry's *indifference* was extremely annoying to Melissa, who loved to argue but found it difficult to do so with people who had no opinions.

We planted a big garden but the results were *indifferent;* only about half of the flowers came up.

The painter did an *indifferent* job, but it was good enough for Susan, who was *indifferent* about painting.

Q·U·I·C·K · Q·U·I·Z #49

Match each word in the first column with its definition in the second column. Check your answers in the back of the book.

1.	incandescent	a.	increase
2.	incantation	b.	make very angry
3.	incense	c.	beginning
4.	incessant	d.	chant
5.	incipient	e.	not harmonious
6.	incisive	f.	incapable of being reformed
7.	incongruous	g.	not caring; mediocre
8.	incorrigible	h.	cutting right to the heart
9.	increment	i.	unceasing
10.	indifferent	j.	brilliant

INDIGENOUS (in DIJ uh nus) *adj* native; originating in that area

Fast-food restaurants are *indigenous* to America, where they were invented.

The grocer said the corn had been locally grown, but we didn't believe him because it didn't appear to be *indigenous*.

The botanist said that the small cactus was *indigenous* but that the large one had been introduced to the region by Spanish explorers.

INDIGENT (IN di junt) *adj* poor

The *indigent* family had little to eat, nothing to spend, and virtually nothing to wear.

Rusty had once been a lawyer but now was *indigent;* he spent most of his time sleeping on a bench in the park.

Don't confuse this word with *indigenous*.

INDIGNANT (in DIG nunt) *adj* angry, especially as a result of something unjust or unworthy; insulted

Bruno became *indignant* when the policeman accused him of stealing the nuclear weapon.

Isabel was *indignant* when we told her all the nasty things that Blake had said about her over the public address system at the big party.

INDOLENT (IN duh lunt) *adj* lazy

The *indolent* teenagers slept late, moped around, and never looked for summer jobs.

Inheriting a lot of money enabled Rodney to do what he loved most: pursue a life of *indolence*.

INDULGENT (in DUL junt) *adj* lenient; yielding to desire

The nice mom was *indulgent* of her children, letting them have all the candy, cookies, and ice cream that they wanted, even for breakfast.

Our *indulgent* teacher never punished us for not turning in our homework. She was nice. She didn't want us to turn into ascetic grinds.

INEFFABLE (in EF uh bul) *adj* incapable of being expressed or described

The simple beauty of nature is often so *ineffable* that it brings tears to our eyes.

The word *effable*—expressible—is rarely used.

INEPT (in EPT) *adj* clumsy; incompetent; gauche

Joshua is an *inept* dancer; he is as likely to stomp on his partner's foot as he is to step on it.

Julia's *inept* attempt at humor drew only groans from the audience.

To be *inept* is to be characterized by *ineptitude*, which is the opposite of aptitude. The woodworking class's ineptitude was both broad and deep; there was little that they were able to do, and nothing that they were able to do well.

The opposite of *inept* is *adept*. *Adept* and *adroit* are synonyms.

INERT (in URT) *adj* inactive; sluggish; not reacting chemically

The baseball team seemed strangely *inert;* it was as though they had lost the will not only to win but even to play.

Having colds made the children *inert* and reluctant to get out of bed.

Helium is an *inert* gas: it doesn't burn, it doesn't explode, and it doesn't kill you if you inhale it.

To be *inert* is to be characterized by *inertia*. As it is most commonly used, *inertia* means lack of get up and go, or an inability or unwillingness to move.

In physics, *inertia* refers to an object's tendency to continue doing what it's doing (either moving or staying still) unless it's acted on by something else.

INEXORABLE (in EK sur uh bul) *adj* relentless; inevitable; unavoidable

The *inexorable* waves pounded the shore, as they have always pounded it and as they always will pound it.

Eliot drove his father's car slowly but *inexorably* through the grocery store, wrecking aisle after aisle despite the manager's anguished pleading.

Inexorable death finds everyone sooner or later.

INFAMOUS (IN fuh mus) *adj* shamefully wicked; having an extremely bad reputation; disgraceful

Be careful with the pronunciation of this word.

To be *infamous* is to be *famous* for being evil or bad. An *infamous* cheater is one whose cheating is well known.

Deep within the prison was the *infamous* torture chamber, where hooded guards tickled their prisoners with feathers until they confessed.

Infamy is the state of being *infamous*. The former Nazi lived the rest of his life in *infamy* after the court convicted him of war crimes and atrocities.

President Roosevelt said that the date of the Japanese attack on Pearl Harbor would "live in *infamy*."

INFATUATED (in FACH oo AY tid) *adj* foolish; foolishly passionate or attracted; made foolish; foolishly in love

To be *infatuated* is to be *fatuous* or foolish. I was so *infatuated* with Polly that I drooled and gurgled whenever she was near.

The *infatuated* candidate thought so highly of himself that he had the ceiling of his bedroom covered with his campaign posters.

My ride in Boris's racing car *infatuated* me; I knew immediately that I would have to have a racing car too.

Q·U·I·C·K · Q·U·I·Z #50

Match each word in the first column with its definition in the second column. Check your answers in the back of the book.

1. indigenous   a. native
2. indigent   b. inactive
3. indignant   c. lazy
4. indolent   d. foolish
5. indulgent   e. shamefully wicked
6. ineffable   f. poor
7. inept   g. relentless
8. inert   h. angry
9. inexorable   i. clumsy
10. infamous   j. lenient
11. infatuated   k. inexpressible

INFER (in FUR) *v* to conclude; to deduce

Ruth said she loved the brownies, but I *inferred* from the size of the piece left on her plate that she had actually despised them.

She hadn't heard the score, but the silence in the locker room led her to *infer* that we had lost.

Infer is often confused with *imply*. To *imply* something is to hint at it, suggest it, or state it indirectly. To *infer* something is to figure out what it is without being told directly.

INFINITESIMAL (IN fin i TES uh mul) *adj* very, very, very small; infinitely small

Infinitesimal does not mean "huge," as some people incorrectly believe.

Dumb old Willy's brain, if he had one at all, was undoubtedly *infinitesimal.*

An *infinitesimal* bug of some kind crawled into Heather's ear and bit her in a place she couldn't scratch.

Our chances of winning were *infinitesimal,* but we played our hearts out anyway.

INGENUOUS (in JEN yoo us) *adj* frank; without deception; simple; artless; charmingly naïve

A young child is *ingenuous.* He doesn't know much about the ways of the world, and certainly not enough to deceive anyone.

An *ingenue* is a somewhat naïve young woman, especially a young actress.

Disingenuous means crafty or artful. The movie producer was being *disingenuous* when he said, "I don't care if I make a cent on this movie. I just want every man, woman and child in the country to see it."

INHERENT (in HEER unt, in HER unt) *adj* part of the essential nature of something; intrinsic

Wetness is an *inherent* quality of water. (You could also say that wetness is *inherent* in water.)

There is an *inherent* strength in steel that is lacking from cardboard. (Strength is *inherent* in steel.)

The man's *inherent* fatness, jolliness, and beardedness made it easy for him to play the part of Santa Claus.

INJUNCTION (in JUNGK shun) *n* a command or order, especially a court order

Wendy's neighbors got a court *injunction* prohibiting her from playing her radio loud.

Herbert, lighting up, disobeyed his doctor's *injunction* to stop smoking.

INNATE (i NATE) *adj* existing since birth; inborn; inherent

Joseph's kindness was *innate;* it was part of his natural character.

Bill has an apparently *innate* ability to throw a football. You just can't teach someone to throw a ball as well as he can.

There's nothing *innate* about good manners; all children have to be taught to say please and thank you.

INNOCUOUS (i NOK yoo us) *adj* harmless; banal

Innocuous is closely related, in both origin and meaning, to *innocent.*

The supposedly obscene record sounded pretty *innocuous* to us; there weren't even any four-letter words in it.

The speaker's voice was loud but his words were *innocuous;* there was nothing to get excited about.

Meredith took offense at Bruce's *innocuous* comment about the saltiness of her soup.

INORDINATE (in AWR duh nit) *adj* excessive; unreasonable

The young math teacher paid an *inordinate* amount of attention to the pretty blond senior.

The limousine was *inordinately* large, even for a limousine; there was room for more than a dozen passengers.

Romeo's love for Juliet was perhaps a bit *inordinate,* given the outcome of their relationship.

INSATIABLE (in SAY shuh bul) *adj* hard or impossible to satisfy; greedy; avaricious

Peter had an *insatiable* appetite for chocolate macadamia ice cream; he could never get enough. Not even a gallon of chocolate macadamia was enough to *sate* or *satiate* his craving. Peter's addiction never reached *satiety.*

Q·U·I·C·K · Q·U·I·Z #51

Match each word in the first column with its definition in the second column. Check your answers in the back of the book.

1. infer		a.	hard or impossible to satisfy
2. imply		b.	intensify
3. infinitesimal		c.	part of the nature of
4. inflame		d.	hint at
5. ingenuous		e.	artless
6. inherent		f.	inborn
7. injunction		g.	conclude
8. innate		h.	excessive
9. innocuous		i.	harmless
10. inordinate		j.	infinitely small
11. insatiable		k.	court order

INSIDIOUS (in SID ee us) *adj* treacherous; sneaky

The spy's *insidious* plan was to steal all the kryptonite in Metropolis.

Winter was *insidious;* it crept in under the doors and through cracks in the windows.

Cancer, which can spread rapidly from a small cluster of cells, is an *insidious* disease.

INSINUATE (in SIN yoo ATE) *v* to hint; to creep in

When I told her that I hadn't done any laundry in a month, Valerie *insinuated* that I was a slob.

He didn't ask us outright if we would leave; he merely *insinuated,* through his tone and his gestures, that it was time for us to go.

Jessica *insinuated* her way into the conversation by moving her chair closer and closer to where we were sitting.

Before we realized what was happening, the stray cat had *insinuated* itself into our household.

To *insinuate* is to make an *insinuation.*

INSIPID (in SIP id) *adj* dull; bland; banal

Barney's jokes were so *insipid* that no one in the room managed to force out so much as a chuckle.

We were bored to death at the party; it was full of *insipid* people making *insipid* conversation.

The thin soup was so *insipid* that all the spices in the world could not have made it interesting.

INSOLENT (IN suh lunt) *adj* arrogant; insulting

The ill-mannered four-year-old was so *insolent* that even adults were tempted to kick him in the rear end.

The *insolent* sales clerk said she was sorry but the store did not accept cash.

INSTIGATE (IN stuh GATE) *v* to provoke; to stir up

The strike was *instigated* by the ambitious union president, who wanted to get his name into the newspapers.

The CIA tried unsuccessfully to *instigate* rebellion in the tiny country by distributing pamphlets that, as it turned out, were printed in the wrong language.

INSULAR (IN suh lur) *adj* like an island; isolated

The Latin word for island is *insula*. From it we get the words *peninsula* ("almost an island"), *insulate* (*insulation* makes a house an island of heat), and *insular*, among others.

Lying flat on his back in bed for twenty-seven years, the 1,200-pound man led an *insular* existence.

The *insular* little community had very little contact with the world around it.

Something that is *insular* has *insularity*. The *insularity* of the little community was so complete that it was impossible to buy a big-city newspaper there.

INSURGENT (in SUR junt) *n* a rebel; someone who revolts against a government

The heavily armed *insurgents* rushed into the presidential palace, but they paused to taste the fresh blueberry pie on the dinner table and the president's bodyguards captured them.

This word can also be an adjective. A rebellion is an *insurgent* activity.

Insurgency is another word for rebellion.

INTEGRAL (IN tuh grul) *adj* essential

A solid offense was an *integral* part of our football team; so was a strong defense.

Dave was *integral* to the organization; it could never have gotten along without him.

INTRACTABLE (in TRAK tuh bul) *adj* uncontrollable; stubborn; disobedient

The *intractable* child was a torment to his nursery school teacher.

Bill was *intractable* in his opposition to ·pay increases for the library employees; he swore he would never vote to give them a raise.

The disease was *intractable*. None of the dozens of medicines the doctor tried had the slightest effect on it.

The opposite of *intractable* is *tractable*.

INTRANSIGENT (in TRAN si junt) *adj* uncompromising; stubborn

Roy was an *intransigent* hard-liner, and he didn't care how many people he offended with his views.

The jury was unanimous except for one *intransigent* member, who didn't believe that anyone should ever be forced to go to jail.

Q·U·I·C·K · Q·U·I·Z #52

Match each word in the first column with its definition in the second column. Check your answers in the back of the book.

1. insidious		a. hint
2. insinuate		b. uncontrollable
3. insipid		c. treacherous
4. insolent		d. essential
5. instigate		e. provoke
6. insular		f. like an island
7. insurgent		g. rebel
8. integral		h. dull
9. intractable		i. uncompromising
10. intransigent		j. arrogant

INTRINSIC (in TRIN sik) *adj* part of the essential nature of something; inherent

Larry's *intrinsic* boldness was always getting him into trouble.

There was an *intrinsic* problem with Owen's alibi: it was a lie.

The opposite of *intrinsic* is *extrinsic*.

INTROSPECTIVE (IN truh SPEC tiv) *adj* tending to think about oneself; examining one's feelings

The *introspective* six-year-old never had much to say to other people but always seemed to be turning over something in her mind.

Randy's *introspective* examination of his motives led him to conclude that he must have been at fault in the breakup of his marriage.

See *extrovert*.

INUNDATE (IN un DATE) *v* to flood; to cover completely with water; to overwhelm

The tiny island kingdom was *inundated* by the tidal wave. Fortunately, no one died from the deluge.

The fifteen-year-old girl was *inundated* with telegrams and gifts after she gave birth to octuplets.

INVECTIVE (in VEK tiv) *n* insulting or abusive speech

The critic's searing review was filled with bitterness and *invective*.

Herman wasn't much of an orator, but he was brilliant at *invective*.

INVETERATE (in VET ur it) *adj* habitual; firm in habit; deeply rooted

Eric was such an *inveterate* liar on the golf course that when he finally made a hole-in-one, he marked it on his score card as a zero.

Larry's practice of spitting into the fireplace became *inveterate* despite his wife's protestations.

IRASCIBLE (i RAS uh bul) *adj* easily angered or provoked; irritable

A grouch is *irascible*. The students generally abused substitute teachers, but they knew that even substitute teachers become *irascible* on Monday mornings.

IRONIC (iye RON ik) *adj* meaning the opposite of what you seem to say; using words to mean something other than what they seem to mean

Don't use the alternate form, *ironical*.

Eddie was being *ironic* when he said he loved Peter like a brother; in truth, he hated him.

Blake's discussion of Reagan's brilliance was, of course, *ironic;* he really thinks that Reagan is idiotic. Blake is a writer known for his *irony*.

Credulous George never realized that the speaker was being *ironic* as he discussed what he called his plan to put a nuclear-missile silo in every backyard in America.

IRREVOCABLE (i REV uh kuh bul) *adj* irreversible

To *revoke* (ri VOKE) is to take back. Something *irrevocable* cannot be taken back. My decision not to wear a Tarzan costume and ride on a float in the Macy's Thanksgiving Day Parade is *irrevocable;* there is absolutely nothing you could do or say to make me change my mind.

Shortly after his car began to plunge toward the sea, Tom decided not to drive off the cliff after all, but by that point his decision to do so was *irrevocable*.

ITINERANT (iye TIN ur unt) *adj* moving from place to place

The life of a traveling salesman is an *itinerant* one.

The *itinerant* junk dealer passes through our neighborhood every month or so, pulling his wagon of odds and ends.

The international banker's *itinerant* lifestyle began to seem less glamorous to him after his first child was born.

A closely related word is *itinerary*, which is the planned route or schedule of a trip. The traveling salesman taped his *itinerary* to the refrigerator before every trip so that his wife would know how to reach him on the telephone.

Q·U·I·C·K · Q·U·I·Z #53

Match each word in the first column with its definition in the second column. Check your answers in the back of the book.

1. intrinsic
2. introspective
3. inundate
4. invective
5. inveterate
6. irascible
7. ironic
8. irrevocable
9. itinerant
10. itinerary

a. irreversible
b. insulting speech
c. planned trip route
d. flood
e. inherent
f. examining one's feelings
g. meaning other than what's said
h. moving from place to place
i. irritable
j. habitual

J

JUDICIOUS (joo DISH us) *adj* exercising sound judgment

The judge was far from *judicious;* he told the jury that he thought the defendant looked guilty and said that anyone who would wear a red bow tie into a courtroom deserved to be sent to jail.

The fire fighters made *judicious* use of flame-retardant foam as the burning airplane skidded along the runway.

The mother of twin boys *judiciously* used an electron microscope and a laser to divide the ice cream into equal parts.

The word *judicial* is obviously closely related, but there is a critically important difference in meaning between it and *judicious*. A judge is *judicial* simply by virtue of being a judge; *judicial* means having to do with judges, judgment, or justice. But a judge is *judicious* only if he or she exercises sound judgment.

JUXTAPOSE (JUK stuh POSE) *v* to place side by side

Comedy and tragedy were *juxtaposed* in the play, which was alternately funny and sad.

Juxtaposing the genuine painting and the counterfeit made it much easier to tell which was which.

The final examination requires students to *juxtapose* two unrelated works of fiction.

K

KINETIC (ki NET ik) *adj* having to do with motion; lively; active

Kinetic energy is energy associated with motion. A speeding bullet has a lot of *kinetic* energy.

Kinetic art is art with things in it that move. A mobile is an example of *kinetic* art.

A *kinetic* personality is a lively, active, moving personality.

L

LABYRINTH (LAB uh rinth) *n* a maze; something like a maze

Each of the fifty floors in the office building was a *labyrinth* of dark corridors and narrow passageways.

The bill took many months to pass through the *labyrinth* of congressional approval.

A *labyrinth* is *labyrinthine*, or mazelike. Before beginning construction on the new house, the contractor had to weave his way through the *labyrinthine* bureaucracy in order to obtain a building permit.

LACONIC (luh KON ik) *adj* using few words, especially to the point of seeming rude

The manager's *laconic* dismissal letter left the fired employees feeling angry and hurt.

When she went backstage, June discovered why the popular rock musician was so *laconic* in public: his voice was high and squeaky.

LAMENT (luh MENT) *v* to mourn

From the balcony of the bullet-pocked hotel, the foreign correspondents could hear hundreds of women and children *lamenting* the fallen soldiers.

As the snowstorm gained in intensity, Stan *lamented* his decision that morning to dress in shorts and a T-shirt.

Lamentable means regrettable.

LAMPOON (lam POON) *v* to satirize; to mock; to parody

The irreverent students mercilessly *lampooned* their Latin teacher's lisp in a skit at the school talent show.

The Harvard Lampoon, the nation's oldest humor magazine, has *lampooned* just about everything there is to *lampoon* in its 112-year history.

LANGUISH (LANG gwish) *v* to become weak, listless, or depressed

The formerly eager and vigorous accountant *languished* in his tedious job at the international conglomerate.

The longer Jill remained unemployed, the more she *languished* and the less likely it became that she would find another job.

To *languish* is to be *languid*. The child seemed so *languid* that his father thought he was sick and called the doctor. It turned out that the little boy had simply had an overdose of television.

LARGESS (lahr JES) *n* generous giving of gifts (or the gifts themselves); generosity; philanthropy

Sam was marginally literate at best. Only the *largess* of his uncle got Sam into Princeton.

Largess can also be spelled *largesse*.

LATENT (LAYT unt) *adj* present but not visible or apparent; potential

A photographic image is *latent* in a piece of exposed film; it's there, but you can't see it until the film is developed.

LAUD (lawd) *v* to praise; to applaud; to extol; to celebrate

The bank manager *lauded* the hero who trapped the escaping robber. The local newspaper published a *laudatory* editorial on this intrepid individual. *Laudatory* means praising.

Giving several million dollars to charity is a *laudable* act of philanthropy. *Laudable* means praiseworthy.

LEGACY (LEG uh see) *n* something handed down from the past; a bequest

The *legacy* of the corrupt administration was chaos, bankruptcy, and despair.

A shoebox full of baseball cards was the dead man's only *legacy*.

To be a *legacy* at a college sorority is to be the daughter of a former sorority member.

LETHARGY (LETH ur jee) *n* sluggishness; laziness; drowsiness; indifference

The couch potato had fallen into a state of such total *lethargy* that he never moved except to change channels or get another bag of Doritos from the kitchen.

The *lethargy* of the library staff caused what should have been a quick errand to expand into a full day's work.

To be filled with *lethargy* is to be *lethargic*. The *lethargic* teenagers took all summer to paint the Hendersons' garage.

LEVITY (LEV i tee) *n* lightness; frivolity; unseriousness

To *levitate* something is to make it so light that it floats up into the air. *Levity* comes from the same root and has to do with a different kind of lightness.

The speaker's *levity* was not appreciated by the convention of funeral directors, who felt that a convention of funeral directors was no place to tell jokes.

The judge's attempt to inject some *levity* into the dreary court proceedings (by setting off a few firecrackers in the jury box) was entirely successful.

Q·U·I·C·K · Q·U·I·Z #54

Match each word in the first column with its definition in the second column. Check your answers in the back of the book.

1. judicious		a.	sluggishness
2. juxtapose		b.	lightness
3. kinetic		c.	using few words
4. labyrinth		d.	maze
5. laconic		e.	place side by side
6. lament		f.	present but not visible
7. lampoon		g.	bequest
8. languish		h.	active
9. latent		i.	become weak
10. laud		j.	satirize
11. legacy		k.	mourn
12. lethargy		l.	praise
13. levity		m.	exercising sound judgment

LIBEL (LYE bul) *n* a written or published falsehood that injures the reputation of, or defames, someone

The executive said that the newspaper had committed *libel* when it called him a stinking, no-good, corrupt, incompetent, overpaid, lying, worthless moron. He claimed that the newspaper had *libeled* him, and that its description of him had been *libelous*. At the trial, the jury disagreed, saying that the newspaper's description of the executive had been substantially accurate.

Don't confuse this word with *liable*, which means something else entirely.

Slander is just like *libel* except that it is spoken instead of written. To slander someone is to say something untrue that injures that person's reputation.

LITIGATE (LIT uh GATE) *v* to try in court; to engage in legal proceedings

His lawyer thought a lawsuit would be fruitless, but the client wanted to *litigate*. He was feeling *litigious*; that is, he was feeling in a mood to go to court.

When the company was unable to recover its money outside of court, its only option was to *litigate*.

To *litigate* is to engage in *litigation*; a court hearing is an example of *litigation*.

LOQUACIOUS (loh KWAY shus) *adj* talking a lot or too much

The child was surprisingly *loquacious* for one so small.

Mary is so *loquacious* that Belinda can sometimes put down the telephone receiver and run a load of laundry while Mary is talking.

A *loquacious* person is one who is characterized by *loquaciousness* or *loquacity*.

The English teacher's *loquacity* in class left little time for any of the students to speak, which was fine with most of the students.

LUCID (LOO sid) *adj* clear; easy to understand

The professor's explanation of the theory of relativity was so astonishingly *lucid* that even I could understand it.

Hubert's remarks were few but *lucid:* he explained the complicated issue with just a handful of well-chosen words.

The extremely old man was *lucid* right up until the moment he died; his body had given out but his mind was still going strong.

To *elucidate* something is to make it clear, to explain it. The poem was an enigma until a second grader in Encino, California, *elucidated* it for his admiring elders.

LUGUBRIOUS (loo GOO bree us) *adj* exaggeratedly mournful

To be mournful is to be sad and sorrowful. To be *lugubrious* is to make a big show of being sad and sorrowful.

Harry's *lugubrious* eulogy at the funeral of his dog eventually made everyone start giggling.

The valedictorian suddenly turned *lugubrious* and began sobbing and tearing his hair at the thought of graduating from high school.

LUMINOUS (LOO muh nus) *adj* giving off light; glowing; bright

The moon was a *luminous* disk in the cloudy nighttime sky.

The snow on the ground appeared eerily *luminous* at night—it seemed to glow.

The dial on my watch is *luminous;* it casts a green glow in the dark.

Q·U·I·C·K · Q·U·I·Z #55

Match each word in the first column with its definition in the second column. Check your answers in the back of the book.

1. libel   a. giving off light

2. slander   b. try in court

3. litigate   c. exaggeratedly mournful

4. loquacious   d. easy to understand

5. lucid   e. written injurious falsehood

6. lugubrious   f. spoken injurious falsehood

7. luminous   g. talking a lot

M

MACHINATION (MAK uh NAY shun) *n* scheming activity for an evil purpose

This word is almost always used in the plural—*machinations*—in which form it means the same thing.

The ruthless *machinations* of the mobsters left a trail of blood and bodies.

The *machinations* of the conspirators were aimed at nothing less than the overthrow of the government.

This word is often used imprecisely to mean something like "machine-like activity." It should not be used in this way.

MAGNANIMOUS (mag NAN uh mus) *adj* forgiving; unresentful; noble in spirit; generous

The boxer was *magnanimous* in defeat, telling the sports reporters that his opponent had simply been too talented for him to beat.

Mrs. Jones *magnanimously* offered the little boy a cookie when he came over to confess that he had broken her window while attempting to shoot her cat with his pellet gun.

To be *magnanimous* is to have *magnanimity*. The *magnanimity* of the conquering general was much appreciated by the defeated soldiers.

MAGNATE (MAG nate) *n* a rich, powerful, or very successful business-person

John D. Rockefeller was a *magnate* who was never too busy to give a shoeshine boy a dime for his troubles.

MALAISE (ma LAYZ) *n* feeling uneasy or queasy

Malaise descended on the calculus class when the teacher announced a quiz.

MALFEASANCE (mal FEE zuns) *n* an illegal act, especially by a public official

President Ford officially pardoned former President Nixon before the latter could be convicted of any *malfeasance*.

MALINGER (mul LING ger) *v* to pretend to be sick to avoid doing work

Indolent Leon always *malingered* when it was his turn to clean up the house. Arthur is artful and he always manages to *malinger* before a big exam.

MALLEABLE (MAL ee uh bul) *adj* easy to shape or bend

Modeling clay is very *malleable*.

So is Stuart. We can make him do whatever we want him to do.

MANDATE (MAN date) *n* a command or authorization to do something; the will of the voters as expressed by the results of an election

Our *mandate* from the executive committee was to find the answer to the problem as quickly as possible.

The newly elected president felt that the landslide vote had given him a *mandate* to do whatever he wanted to do.

Mandate can also be a verb. To *mandate* something is to command or require it.

A closely related word is *mandatory*, which means required or obligatory.

MANIFEST (MAN uh FEST) *adj* visible; evident

Daryl's anger at us was *manifest:* you could see it in his expression and hear it in his voice.

There is *manifest* danger in riding a pogo stick along the edge of a cliff.

Manifest can also be a verb, in which case it means to show, to make visible, or to make evident. Rusty has been sick for a very long time, but it was only recently that he began to *manifest* symptoms.

Rebecca *manifested* alarm when we told her that the end of her ponytail was on fire, but she didn't do anything to put it out.

A visible sign of something is called a *manifestation* of it. A lack of comfort and luxury is the most obvious *manifestation* of poverty.

MANIFESTO (MAN uh FES toh) *n* a public declaration of beliefs or principles, usually political ones

The *Communist Manifesto* was a document that spelled out Karl Marx's vision of a Communist world.

Jim's article about the election was less a piece of reporting than a *manifesto* of his political views.

MARSHAL (MAHR shul) *v* to arrange in order; to gather together for the purpose of doing something

The statistician *marshaled* his facts before making his presentation.

The general *marshaled* his troops in anticipation of making an attack on the enemy fortress.

We *marshaled* half a dozen local groups in opposition to the city council's plan to bulldoze our neighborhood.

MARTIAL (MAHR shul) *adj* warlike; having to do with combat

Martial is often confused with *marital*, which means having to do with marriage. Marriages are sometimes *martial*, but don't confuse these words.

Karate and judo are often referred to as *martial* arts.

The parade of soldiers was *martial* in tone; the soldiers carried rifles and were followed by a formation of tanks.

The school principal declared *martial* law when food riots erupted in the cafeteria.

MARTYR (MAHR tur) *n* someone who gives up his or her life in pursuit of a cause, especially a religious one; one who suffers for a cause; one who makes a show of suffering in order to arouse sympathy

Many of the saints were also *martyrs;* they were executed, often gruesomely, for refusing to renounce their religious beliefs.

Jacob is a *martyr* to his job; he would stay at his desk twenty-four hours a day if his wife and the janitor would let him.

Eloise played the *martyr* during hay fever season, trudging wearily from room to room with a jumbo box of Kleenex in each hand.

MATRICULATE (muh TRIK yuh LATE) *v* to enroll, especially at a college

Benny told everyone he was going to Harvard, but when he actually *matriculated* it was at the local junior college.

Q·U·I·C·K · Q·U·I·Z #56

Match each word in the first column with its definition in the second column. Check your answers in the back of the book.

1.	machination	a.	forgiving
2.	macroeconomic	b.	easy to shape
3.	magnanimous	c.	queasiness
4.	magnate	d.	command to do something
5.	malaise	e.	scheming evil activity
6.	malfeasance	f.	public declaration
7.	malinger	g.	pretend to be sick
8.	malleable	h.	visible
9.	mandate	i.	one who dies for a cause
10.	manifest	j.	arrange in order
11.	manifesto	k.	illegal act
12.	marshal	l.	enroll
13.	martial	m.	warlike
14.	martyr	n.	rich businessman
15.	matriculate	o.	dealing with the economy at large

MAUDLIN (MAWD lin) *adj* silly and sentimental

The high school reunion grew more and more *maudlin* as the participants had more and more to drink.

The old lady had a *maudlin* concern for the worms in her yard; she would bang a gong before walking in the grass in order to give them a chance to get out of her way.

MAVERICK (MAV ur ik) *n* a nonconformist; a rebel

The word *maverick* originated in the Old West. It is derived from the name of Samuel A. Maverick, a Texas banker who once accepted a herd of cattle in payment of a debt. Maverick was a banker, not a rancher. He failed to confine or brand his calves, which habitually wandered into his neighbors' pastures. Local ranchers got in the habit of referring to any unbranded calf as a *maverick*. The word is now used for anyone who has refused to be "branded"---who has refused to conform.

The political scientist was an intellectual *maverick;* most of his theories had no followers except himself.

Maverick can also be an adjective. The *maverick* police officer got in trouble with the department for using illegal means to track down criminals.

MAXIM (MAK sim) *n* a fundamental principle; an old saying

We always tried to live our lives according to the *maxim* that it is better to give than to receive.

No one in the entire world is entirely certain of the differences in meaning among the words *maxim, adage, proverb,* and *aphorism.*

MEDIATE (MEE dee ATE) *v* to help settle differences

The United Nations representative tried to *mediate* between the warring countries, but the soldiers just kept shooting at each other.

Joe carried messages back and forth between the divorcing husband and wife in the hope of *mediating* their differences.

To *mediate* is to engage in *mediation.* When two opposing groups, such as a trade union and the management of a company, try to settle their differences through *mediation*, they call in a *mediator* to listen to their cases and make an equitable decision.

MELLIFLUOUS (muh LIF loo us) *adj* sweetly flowing

Mellifluous comes from Greek words meaning, roughly, "honey flowing." We use the word almost exclusively to describe voices, music, or sounds that flow sweetly, like honey.

Melanie's clarinet playing was *mellifluous;* the notes flowed smoothly and beautifully.

The choir's *mellifluous* singing made us feel as though we were being covered with a sticky yellow liquid.

MENDACIOUS (men DAY shus) *adj* lying; dishonest

Children are naturally *mendacious.* If you ask them what they are doing, they will automatically answer, "Nothing."

The jury saw through the *mendacious* witness and convicted the defendant.

To be *mendacious* is to engage in *mendacity,* or lying. I have no flaws, except occasional *mendacity.* Don't confuse this word with *mendicant.*

MENDICANT (MEN duh kunt) *n* a beggar

The presence of thousands of *mendicants* in every urban area is a sad commentary on our national priorities.

MENTOR (MEN tur) *n* a teacher, tutor, counselor, or coach; especially in business, an experienced person who shows an inexperienced person the ropes

Mentor is too big a word to apply to just an ordinary teacher. A student might have many teachers but only one *mentor*—the person who taught him what was really important.

Chris's *mentor* in the pole vault was a former track star who used to hang out by the gym and give the students pointers.

Young men and women in business often talk about the importance of having a *mentor*—usually an older person at the same company who takes an interest in them and helps them get ahead by showing them the ropes.

Mentor is often used as a verb, but you shouldn't do it.

MERCENARY (MUR suh NER ee) *n* a hired soldier; someone who will do anything for money

If an army can't find enough volunteers or draftees, it will sometimes hire *mercenaries*. The magazine *Soldier of Fortune* is aimed at *mercenaries* and would-be *mercenaries;* it even runs classified advertisements by soldiers looking for someone to fight.

You don't have to be a soldier to be a *mercenary*. Someone who does something strictly for the money is often called a *mercenary*. Our business contains a few dedicated workers and many, many *mercenaries*, who want to make a quick buck and then get out.

Mercenary can also be used as an adjective. Larry's motives in writing the screenplay for the trashy movie were strictly *mercenary*—he needed the money.

MERCURIAL (mur KYOOR ee ul) *adj* emotionally unpredictable; rapidly changing in mood

A person with a *mercurial* personality is one who changes rapidly and unpredictably between one mood and another.

Mercurial Helen was crying one minute, laughing the next.

METAMORPHOSIS (MET uh MAWR fuh sis) *n* a magical change in form; a striking or sudden change

When the magician passed his wand over Eileen's head, she underwent a bizarre *metamorphosis:* she turned into a hamster.

Damon's *metamorphosis* from college student to Hollywood superstar was so sudden that it seemed a bit unreal.

To undergo a *metamorphosis* is to *metamorphose*. No matter how hard he tried, the accountant was unable to *metamorphose* the losses into gains.

Q·U·I·C·K · Q·U·I·Z #57

Match each word in the first column with its definition in the second column. Check your answers in the back of the book.

1.	maudlin	a.	teacher
2.	maverick	b.	fundamental principle
3.	maxim	c.	lying
4.	mediate	d.	help settle differences
5.	mellifluous	e.	sweetly flowing
6.	mendacious	f.	nonconformist
7.	mendicant	g.	emotionally unpredictable
8.	mentor	h.	magical change in form
9.	mercenary	i.	silly and sentimental
10.	mercurial	j.	hired soldier
11.	metamorphosis	k.	beggar

MICROCOSM (MYE kruh KOZ um) *n* the world in miniature

The *cosmos* is the heavens, *cosmopolitan* means worldly, and a *microcosm* is a miniature version of the world. All three words are related.

MILIEU (mil YOO) *n* environment; surroundings

A caring and involved community is the proper *milieu* for raising a family.

The farmer on vacation in the big city felt out of his *milieu*.

MINUSCULE (MIN uh SKYOOL) *adj* very tiny

Be careful with the spelling of this word. People tend to spell it "miniscule." Think of *minus*.

Bob's *minuscule* brain was just enough to get him out of junior high school and into a job at the gas station.

Hank's salary was *minuscule*, but the benefits were pretty good: he got to sit next to the refrigerator and eat all day long.

Minute is a synonym for *minuscule*. The small details of something are the *minutiae*.

MISANTHROPIC (MIS un THROP ik) *adj* hating mankind

A misogynist hates women. A *misanthropic* person doesn't make distinctions; he or she hates everyone. The opposite of a *misanthrope* is a philanthropist. Curiously, there is no word for someone who hates men only.

MITIGATE (MIT uh GATE) *v* to moderate the effect of something

The sense of imminent disaster was *mitigated* by the guide's calm behavior and easy smile.

The effects of the disease were *mitigated* by the experimental drug treatment.

Nothing Trip said could *mitigate* the enormity of what he had done.

MOLLIFY (MOL uh FYE) *v* to soften; to soothe; to pacify

Lucy *mollified* the angry police officer by kissing him on the tip of his nose.

My father was not *mollified* by my promise never to crash his car into a brick wall ever again.

The baby-sitter was unable to *mollify* the cranky child, so she put him in the clothes dryer and spun him around for a little while.

MONOLITHIC (MON uh LITH ik) *adj* massive, solid, uniform, and unyielding

A *monolith* is a huge stone shaft or column. Many other things can be said to be *monolithic*.

A huge corporation is often said to be *monolithic*, especially if it is enormous and powerful and all its parts are dedicated to the same purpose.

If the opposition to a plan were said to be *monolithic*, it would probably consist of a very large group of people who all felt the same way.

MORIBUND (MAWR uh BUND) *adj* dying

The steel industry in this country was *moribund* a few years ago, but now it seems to be reviving somewhat.

The senator's political ideas were *moribund;* no one thinks that way anymore.

A dying creature could be said to be *moribund*, too, although this word is usually used in connection with things that die only figuratively.

MOROSE (muh ROHS) *adj* gloomy; sullen

Louise was always so *morose* about everything that she was never any fun to be with.

New Yorkers always seemed *morose* to the writer who lived in the country; they seemed beaten down by the vast, unfriendly city in which they lived.

MORTIFY (MAWR tuh FYE) *adj* to humiliate

I was *mortified* when my father asked my girlfriend whether she thought I was a dumb, pathetic wimp.

We had a *mortifying* experience at the opera; when Stanley sneezed, the entire orchestra stopped playing and stared at him for several minutes.

MUNDANE (mun DANE) *adj* ordinary; pretty boring; not heavenly and eternal

My day was filled with *mundane* chores: I mowed the lawn, did the laundry, fed the dog, and fed the dog to the gorilla.

Dee's job was so *mundane* she sometimes had trouble remembering whether she was at work or asleep.

The monk's thoughts were far removed from *mundane* concerns; he was contemplating all the fun he was going to have in heaven.

MUNIFICENT (myoo NIF i sunt) *adj* very generous; lavish

The *munificent* millionaire gave lots of money to any charity that came to him with a request.

Mrs. Bigelow was a *munificent* hostess; there was so much wonderful food and wine at her dinner parties that the guests had to rest between courses. She was known for her *munificence.*

MYOPIA (mye OH pee uh) *adj* nearsightedness; lack of foresight

Myopia is the fancy medical name for the inability to see clearly at a distance. It's also a word used in connection with people who lack other kinds of visual acuity.

The president suffered from economic *myopia;* he was unable to see the consequences of his fiscal policies.

The workers' dissatisfaction was inflamed by management's *myopia* on the subject of wages.

To suffer *myopia* is to be *myopic.* Some people who wear glasses are *myopic.* So are the people who can't see the consequences of their actions.

MYRIAD (MIR ee ud) *n* a huge number

A country sky on a clear night is filled with a *myriad* of stars.

There are *myriad* reasons why I don't like school.

This word can also be used as an adjective. *Myriad* stars is a lot of stars. The teenager was weighted down by the *myriad* anxieties of adolescence.

Q·U·I·C·K · Q·U·I·Z #58

Match each word in the first column with its definition in the second column. Check your answers in the back of the book.

1. microcosm	a. a huge number
2. milieu	b. moderate the effect of
3. minuscule	c. massive and unyielding
4. misanthropic	d. humiliate
5. mitigate	e. ordinary
6. mollify	f. soften
7. monolithic	g. nearsightedness
8. moribund	h. very tiny
9. morose	i. gloomy
10. mortify	j. environment
11. mundane	k. very generous
12. munificent	l. dying
13. myopia	m. world in miniature
14. myriad	n. hating mankind

N

NARCISSISM (NAHR si SIZ um) *n* excessive love of one's body or oneself

In Greek mythology, Narcissus was a boy who fell in love with his own reflection and, after lying around for a long time staring at it, turned into a flower. To engage in *narcissism* is to be like Narcissus.

Throwing a kiss to your reflection in the mirror is an act of *narcissism.* So is filling your living room with all your bowling trophies or telling everyone how smart and good-looking you are.

Someone who suffers from *narcissism* is said to be *narcissistic.* The selfish students were bound up in *narcissistic* concerns and gave no thought to other people.

NEBULOUS (NEB yuh lus) *adj* vague; hazy; indistinct

Oscar's views are so *nebulous* that no one can figure out what he thinks about anything.

The community's boundaries are somewhat *nebulous;* where they are depends on whom you ask.

Molly's expensive new hairdo was a sort of *nebulous* mass of wisps, waves, and hair spray.

NEFARIOUS (ni FAIR ee us) *adj* evil; flagrantly wicked

The radicals' *nefarious* plot was to destroy New York by filling the reservoir with strawberry Jello.

The convicted murderer had committed a myriad of *nefarious* acts.

NEOLOGISM (nee OL uh JIS um) *n* a new word or phrase; a new usage of a word

Pedants don't like *neologisms*. They like the words we already have. But at one time every word was a *neologism*. Someone somewhere had to be the first to use it.

NEPOTISM (NEP uh TIZ um) *n* showing favoritism to friends or family in business or politics

Clarence had no business acumen, so he was counting on *nepotism* when he married the boss's daughter.

NIHILISM (NYE uh LIZ um) *n* the belief that there are no values or morals in the universe

A *nihilist* does not believe in any objective standards of right or wrong. *Nihilism* and *annihilate* are related words.

NOMINAL (NOM uh nul) *adj* in name only; insignificant; A-OK (during rocket launches)

Bert was the *nominal* chairman of the committee, but Sue was really the one who ran things.

The cost was *nominal* in comparison with the enormous value of what you received.

"All systems are *nominal*," said the NASA engineer as the space shuttle successfully headed into orbit.

NOSTALGIA (no STAL juh) *n* sentimental longing for the past; home-sickness

A wave of *nostalgia* overcame me when the old Temptations song came on the radio; hearing it took me right back to 1967.

Some people who don't remember what the decade was really like feel a misplaced *nostalgia* for the 1950s.

To be filled with *nostalgia* is to be *nostalgic*. As we talked about the fun we'd had together in junior high school, we all began to feel a little *nostalgic*.

NOTORIOUS (noh TOHR ee us) *adj* famous for something bad

A well-known actor is famous; a well-known criminal is *notorious*.

No one wanted to play poker with Jeremy, because he was a *notorious* cheater.

Luther's practical jokes were *notorious;* people always kept their distance when he came into the room.

To be *notorious* is to have *notoriety*. Jesse's *notoriety* as a bank robber made it difficult for him to find a job in banking.

NOVEL (NOV ul) *adj* new; original

Ray had a *novel* approach to homework: he didn't do it. Ray failed geometry as a result of this *novelty*.

There was nothing *novel* about the author's latest novel; the characters were old and the plot was borrowed.

NOXIOUS (NOK shus) *adj* harmful; offensive
Smoking is a *noxious* habit in every sense.
Poison ivy is a *noxious* weed.
Carbon monoxide is a *noxious* gas.
The mothers' committee believed that rock 'n' roll music exerted a *noxious* influence on their children.

NUANCE (NOO ahns) *n* a subtle difference or distinction
The artist's best work explored the *nuance* between darkness and deep shadow.
Harry was incapable of *nuance;* everything for him was either black or white.
In that Chinese dialect, the difference between one word and its opposite is sometimes nothing more than a *nuance* of inflection.

Q·U·I·C·K · Q·U·I·Z #59

Match each word in the first column with its definition in the second column. Check your answers in the back of the book.

1. narcissism		a.	excessive love of self
2. nebulous		b.	in name only
3. nefarious		c.	harmful
4. neologism		d.	original
5. nepotism		e.	evil
6. nihilism		f.	subtle difference
7. nominal		g.	famous for something bad
8. nostalgia		h.	vague
9. notorious		i.	longing for the past
10. novel		j.	favoritism
11. noxious		k.	belief in the absence of all values and morals
12. nuance		l.	new word

O

OBDURATE (OB doo rit) *adj* stubborn and insensitive
Obdurate contains one of the same roots as *durable* and *endurance;* each word conveys a different sense of "hardness."
The committee's *obdurate* refusal to listen to our plan was heartbreaking to us, since we had spent ten years coming up with it.
The child begged and begged to have a bubble-gum machine installed in his bedroom, but his parents were *obdurate* in their insistence that he have a soft-drink machine instead.

OBFUSCATE (ob FUS kate) *v* to darken; to confuse; to make confusing

The spokesman's attempt to explain what the president had meant merely *obfuscated* the issue further. People had hoped the spokesman would elucidate the issue.

Too much gin had *obfuscated* the old man's senses.

The professor's inept lecture gradually *obfuscated* a subject that had been crystal clear to us before.

To *obfuscate* something is to engage in *obfuscation*. Lester called himself a used-car salesman, but his real job was *obfuscation:* he sold cars by confusing his customers.

OBLIQUE (uh BLEEK) *adj* indirect; at an angle

In geometry, lines are said to be *oblique* if they are neither parallel nor perpendicular to each other. The word has a related meaning outside of mathematics. An *oblique* statement is one that does not directly address the topic at hand, that approaches it as if from an angle.

An allusion could be said to be an *oblique* reference.

An *oblique* argument is one that does not directly confront its true subject.

To insult someone *obliquely* is to do so indirectly.

Harry sprinkled his student council speech with *oblique* references to the principal's new toupee; the principal is so dense that he never figured out what was going on, but the rest of us were rolling on the floor.

OBLIVION (uh BLIV ee un) *n* total forgetfulness; the state of being forgotten

A few of the young actors would find fame, but most were headed for *oblivion*.

After tossing and turning with anxiety for most of the night, Richie finally found the *oblivion* of sleep.

To be *oblivious* is to be forgetful or unaware. Old age had made the retired professor *oblivious* of all his old theories.

The workmen stomped in and out of the room, but the happy child, playing on the floor, was *oblivious* of all distraction.

OBSCURE (ub SKYOOR) *adj* unknown; hard to understand; dark

The comedy nightclub was filled with *obscure* comedians who stole each other's jokes and seldom got any laughs.

The artist was so *obscure* that even his parents had trouble remembering his name.

The noted scholar's dissertation was terribly *obscure;* it had to be translated from English into English before anyone could make head or tail of it.

Some contemporary poets apparently believe that the only way to be great is to be *obscure*.

The features of the forest grew *obscure* as night fell.

The state of being *obscure* in any of its senses is called *obscurity*.

OBSEQUIOUS (ub SEE kwee us) *adj* fawning; subservient; sucking up to

Ann's assistant was so *obsequious* that she could never tell what he really thought about anything.

My *obsequious* friend seemed to live only to make me happy and never wanted to do anything if I said I didn't want to do it.

OBTUSE (ub TOOS) *adj* insensitive; blockheaded

Mabel was so *obtuse* that she didn't realize for several days that Carl had asked her to marry him.

The *obtuse* student couldn't seem to grasp the difference between addition and subtraction.

OFFICIOUS (uh FISH us) *adj* annoyingly eager to help or advise

The *officious* officer could never resist sticking his nose into other people's business.

The *officious* salesperson refused to leave us alone, so we finally left without buying anything.

ONEROUS (OHN ur us) *adj* burdensome; oppressive

We were given the *onerous* task of cleaning up the fairgrounds after the carnival.

The job had long hours but the work wasn't *onerous;* Bill spent most of his time sitting with his feet on the desk.

OPAQUE (oh PAKE) *adj* impossible to see through; impossible to understand

The windows in the movie star's house were made not of glass but of some *opaque* material that was intended to keep his fans from spying on him.

We tried to figure out what Horace was thinking, but his expression was *opaque:* it revealed nothing.

Marvin's mind, assuming he had one, was *opaque*.

The statement was *opaque;* no one could make anything of it.

The noun form of *opaque* is *opacity* (oh PAS i tee).

OPULENT (OP yuh lunt) *adj* luxurious

Everything in the *opulent* palace was made of gold—except the toilet-paper holder, which was made of platinum.

The investment banker had grown so accustomed to an *opulent* lifestyle that he had trouble adjusting to the federal penitentiary.

Opulence is often ostentatious.

ORTHODOX (AWR thuh DOKS) *adj* conventional; adhering to established principles or doctrines, especially in religion; by the book

The doctor's treatment for Lou's cold was entirely *orthodox:* plenty of liquids and aspirin, and lots of rest.

Austin's views were *orthodox;* there was nothing shocking about any of them.

The body of what is *orthodox* is called *orthodoxy*. The teacher's lectures were characterized by strict adherence to *orthodoxy*.

To be unconventional is to be *unorthodox*. "Green cheese" is an *unorthodox* explanation for the composition of the moon.

OSTENSIBLE (ah STEN suh bul) *adj* apparent (but misleading); professed

Blake's *ostensible* mission was to repair a broken telephone, but his real goal was to plant a bomb that would blow up the building.

Trevor's *ostensible* kindness to squirrels belied his deep hatred of them.

OSTENTATIOUS (AHS ten TAY shus) *adj* excessively conspicuous; showing off

The designer's use of expensive materials was *ostentatious;* every piece of furniture was covered with silk or velvet, and every piece of hardware was made of silver or gold.

The donor was *ostentatious* in making his gift to the hospital. He held a big press conference to announce it and then walked through the wards to give patients an opportunity to thank him personally.

The young lawyer had *ostentatiously* hung his Harvard diploma on the door to his office.

To be *ostentatious* is to engage in *ostentation.* Jerry wore solid-gold shoes to the party; I was shocked by his *ostentation.*

P

PACIFY (PAS uh FYE) *v* to calm someone down; to placate

A parent gives a baby a *pacifier* to *pacify* him or her. A *pacifist* is someone who does not believe in war.

Q·U·I·C·K · Q·U·I·Z #60

Match each word in the first column with its definition in the second column. Check your answers in the back of the book.

1. obdurate	a forgetfulness
2. obfuscate	b. hard to understand
3. oblique	c. stubborn
4. oblivion	d. insensitive
5. obscure	e. burdensome
6. obsequious	f. luxurious
7. obtuse	g. indirect
8. officious	h. misleadingly apparent
9. onerous	i. showing off
10. opaque	j. impossible to see through
11. opulent	k. calm someone down
12. orthodox	l. confuse
13. ostensible	m. fawning
14. ostentatious	n. conventional
15. pacify	o. annoyingly helpful

PAINSTAKING (PANE STAY king) *adj* extremely careful; taking pains

Painstaking = pains-taking = taking pains.

The jeweler was *painstaking* in his effort not to ruin the $50 million diamond.

We made a *painstaking* effort to move the piano without harming it; first we wrapped it in Kleenex, then we covered it with balloons, then we put it on roller skates and pushed it down the ramp.

PALLIATE (PAL ee ATE) *v* to relieve or alleviate something without getting rid of the problem; to assuage; to mitigate

You take aspirin in the hope that it will *palliate* your headache. Aspirin is a *palliative*.

PALPABLE (PAL puh bul) *adj* capable of being touched; obvious; tangible

The tumor was *palpable;* the doctor could feel it with his finger.

Harry's disappointment at being rejected by every college in America was *palpable;* it was so obvious that you could almost reach out and touch it.

There was *palpable* danger in flying the kite in a thunderstorm.

The opposite of *palpable* is *impalpable*.

PALTRY (PAWL tree) *adj* insignificant; worthless

The lawyer's efforts in our behalf were *paltry;* they didn't add up to anything.

The *paltry* fee he paid us was scarcely large enough to cover our expenses.

PANACEA (PAN uh SEE uh) *n* something that cures everything

The administration seemed to believe that a tax cut would be a *panacea* for the country's economic ills.

Granny believed that her "rheumatiz medicine" was a *panacea*. No matter what you were sick with, that was what she prescribed.

PARADIGM (PAR uh dime) *n* a model or example

Mr. King is the best teacher in the whole world; his classroom should be the *paradigm* for all classrooms.

In selecting her wardrobe, messy Gertrude apparently used a scarecrow as her *paradigm*.

A paradigm is *paradigmatic* (PAR uh dig MAT ik). Virtually all the cars the company produced were based on a single, *paradigmatic* design.

PARADOX (PAR uh DOKS) *n* a true statement or phenomenon that nonetheless seems to contradict itself; an untrue statement or phenomenon that nonetheless seems logical

Mr. Cooper is a political *paradox;* he's a staunch Republican who votes only for Democrats.

One of Xeno's *paradoxes* seems to prove the impossibility of an arrow's ever reaching its target: if the arrow first moves half the distance to the target, then half the remaining distance, then half the remaining distance, and so on, it can never arrive.

A *paradox* is *paradoxical*. Hubert's dislike of ice cream was *paradoxical*, considering that he worked as an ice cream taster.

PAROCHIAL (puh ROH kee ul) *adj* narrow or confined in point of view; provincial

The townspeople's concerns were entirely *parochial;* they worried only about what happened in their town and not about the larger world around it.

The journalist's *parochial* point of view prevented him from becoming a nationally known figure.

A lot of people think the *parochial* school is the religious school. Actually, the parochial school is the school of the parish or neighborhood. In other contexts, though, *parochial* has negative connotations.

PARODY (PAR uh dee) *n* a satirical imitation

On the cover of *The Harvard Lampoon's parody* of *People* magazine was a photograph of Brooke Shields holding a great big fish.

At the talent show the girls sang a terrible *parody* of a Beatles song called "I Want to Hold Your Foot."

Some *parodies* are unintentional and not very funny. The unhappy student accused Mr. Benson of being not a teacher but a *parody* of one.

Parody can also be a verb. To *parody* something is to make a *parody* of it. A *parody* is *parodic*.

PARSIMONIOUS (PAHR suh MOH nee us) *adj* stingy

The old widow was so *parsimonious* that she hung used teabags out to dry on her clothesline so that she would be able to use them again.

We tried to be *parsimonious*, but without success. After just a couple of days at the resort we realized that we had spent all the money we had set aside for our entire month-long vacation.

To be *parsimonious* is to practice *parsimony*.

PARTISAN (PAHR ti zun) *n* one who supports a particular person, cause, or idea

Henry's plan to give himself the award had no *partisan* except himself.

I am the *partisan* of any candidate who promises not to make promises.

The mountain village was attacked by *partisans* of the rebel chieftain.

Partisan can also be used as an adjective meaning biased, as in *partisan* politics. An issue that everyone agrees on regardless of the party he or she belongs to is a *nonpartisan* issue. *Bipartisan* means supported by two (bi) parties. Both the Republican and Democratic senators voted to give themselves a raise. The motion had *bipartisan* support.

Q·U·I·C·K · Q·U·I·Z #61

Match each word in the first column with its definition in the second column. Check your answers in the back of the book.

1. painstaking		a. obvious
2. palliate		b. model
3. palpable		c. supporter of a cause
4. paltry		d. narrow in point of view
5. panacea		e. contradictory truth
6. paradigm		f. stingy
7. paradox		g. cure for everything
8. parochial		h. insignificant
9. parody		i. extremely careful
10. parsimonious		j. satirical imitation
11. partisan		k. alleviate

PATENT (PATE unt) *adj* obvious

To say that the earth is flat is a *patent* absurdity, since the world is obviously spherical.

It was *patently* foolish of Lee to think that he could sail across the Pacific Ocean in a washtub.

PATERNAL (puh TUR nul) *adj* fatherly; fatherlike

Fred is *paternal* toward his niece. Maternal means motherly or momlike.

PATHOLOGY (puh THOL uh jee) *n* the science of diseases

Pathology is the science or study of diseases, but not necessarily in the medical sense. *Pathological* means relating to *pathology*, but it also means arising from a disease. So if we say Brad is an inveterate, incorrigible, *pathological* liar, we are saying that Brad's lying is a sickness.

PATRIARCH (PAY tree AHRK) *n* the male head of a family or tribe

A *patriarch* is generally a strong male head of a family or tribe.

PATRICIAN (puh TRISH un) *n* a person of noble birth; an aristocrat

Mr. Anderson was a *patrician*, and he was never truly happy unless his place at the dinner table was set with at least half a dozen forks.

Patrician can also be an adjective. Polo is a *patrician* sport.

The noisy crowd on the luxury ocean liner was *patrician* in dress but not in behavior; they were wearing tuxedos but throwing deck chairs into the ocean.

PATRONIZE (PAY truh NIZE) *v* to treat as an inferior; to condescend to

Our guide at the art gallery was extremely *patronizing*, treating us as though we wouldn't be able to distinguish a painting from a piece of sidewalk without her help.

We felt *patronized* by the waiter at the fancy French restaurant; he ignored all our efforts to attract his attention and then pretended not to understand our accents.

(*Patronize* also means to frequent or be a regular customer of. To *patronize* a restaurant is to eat there often, not to treat it as an inferior.)

PAUCITY (PAW si tee) *n* scarcity

There was a *paucity* of fresh vegetables at the supermarket so we had to buy frozen.

The plan was defeated by a *paucity* of support.

There is no *paucity* of water in the ocean.

PECCADILLO (PEK uh DIL oh) *n* a minor offense

The smiling defendant acted as though first-degree murder were a mere *peccadillo* rather than a hideous crime.

The reporters sometimes seemed more interested in the candidates' sexual *peccadillos* than in their inane programs and proposals.

PEDANTIC (puh DAN tik) *adj* boringly scholarly or academic

The discussion quickly turned *pedantic* as each participant tried to sound more learned than all the others.

Percival's feelings about love were mostly *pedantic;* he'd read about love in books but had never really encountered it in his life.

The professor's interpretation of the poem was *pedantic* and empty of genuine feeling.

A *pedantic* person is called a *pedant*.

PEDESTRIAN (puh DES tree un) *adj* unimaginative; banal

This is one of the favorite words of the people who write the SAT. A *pedestrian* is someone walking, but to be *pedestrian* is to be something else altogether.

Mary Anne said the young artist's work was brilliant, but I found it to be *pedestrian;* I've seen better paintings in kindergarten classrooms.

The menu was *pedestrian;* I had encountered each of the dishes dozens of times before.

PEJORATIVE (pi JAWR uh tiv) *adj* negative; disparaging

"Hi, stupid" is a *pejorative* greeting.

"Loudmouth" is a nickname with a *pejorative* connotation.

Abe's description of the college as "a pretty good school" was unintentionally *pejorative*.

PENCHANT (PEN chunt) *n* a strong taste or liking for something; a predilection

Dogs have a *penchant* for chasing cats and mailmen.

PENITENT (PEN i tunt) *adj* sorry; repentant; contrite

Julie was *penitent* when Hank explained how much pain she had caused him.

The two boys tried to sound *penitent* at the police station, but they weren't really sorry that they had herded the sheep into Mr. Ingersoll's house. They were *impenitent*.

PENSIVE (PEN siv) *adj* thoughtful and sad

Norton became suddenly *pensive* when Jack mentioned his dead father.

The gloomy weather made everyone feel *pensive*, so we cheered them up by shooting off a few firecrackers in the living room.

Q·U·I·C·K · Q·U·I·Z #62

Match each word in the first column with its definition in the second column. Check your answers in the back of the book.

1. patent		a.	male head of a family
2. paternal		b.	minor offense
3. pathology		c.	unimaginative
4. patriarch		d.	thoughtful and sad
5. patrician		e.	boringly scholarly
6. patronize		f.	science of diseases
7. paucity		g.	treat as an inferior
8. peccadillo		h.	negative
9. pedantic		i.	obvious
10. pedestrian		j.	aristocrat
11. pejorative		k.	scarcity
12. penchant		l.	fatherly
13. penitent		m.	sorry
14. pensive		n.	strong liking

PEREMPTORY (puh REMP tuh ree) *adj* final; categorical; dictatorial

Someone who is *peremptory* says or does something without giving anyone a chance to dispute it. Frank's father *peremptorily* banished him to his room.

PERENNIAL (puh REN ee ul) *adj* continual; happening again and again or year after year

Mr. Phillips is a *perennial* favorite of students at the high school, because he always gives everyone an A.

Milton was a *perennial* candidate for governor; every four years he printed up another batch of his "Bingo and horse-racing" bumper stickers.

Perennial flowers—called *perennials*—are flowers that bloom year after year without being replanted.

Biennial and *centennial* are related words. *Biennial* means happening once every two years (biannual means happening twice a year). *Centennial* means happening once every century.

PERFIDY (PUR fi dee) *n* treachery

It was the criminals' natural *perfidy* that finally did them in, as each one became an informant on the other.

I was appalled at Al's *perfidy*. He had sworn to me that he was my best friend, but then he asked my girlfriend to the prom.

To engage in *perfidy* is to be *perfidious*.

PERFUNCTORY (pur FUNGK tuh ree) *adj* unenthusiastic; careless

Larry made a couple of *perfunctory* attempts at answering the questions on the test, but then he put down his pencil and his head and slept until the end of the period.

Sandra's lawn mowing was *perfunctory* at best: she skipped all the difficult parts and didn't rake up any of the clippings.

PERIPATETIC (PER uh peh TET ik) *adj* wandering; traveling continually; itinerant

Groupies are a *peripatetic* bunch, traveling from concert to concert to follow their favorite rock stars.

PERIPHERY (puh RIF uh ree) *n* the outside edge of something

José never got involved in any of our activities; he was always at the *periphery*.

The professional finger painter enjoyed his position at the *periphery* of the art world.

To be at the *periphery* is to be *peripheral* (puh RIF uh rul). A *peripheral* interest is a secondary or side interest.

Your *peripheral* vision is your ability to see to the right and left while looking straight ahead.

PERJURY (PUR jur ee) *n* lying under oath

The defendant was acquitted of bribery but convicted of *perjury*, because he had lied on the witness stand during his trial.

To commit *perjury* is to *perjure* oneself. The former cabinet official *perjured* himself when he said that he had not committed *perjury* during his trial for bribery.

PERMEATE (PUR mee ATE) *v* to spread or seep through; to penetrate

A stinky smell quickly *permeated* the room after Jock lit a cigarette.

Corruption had *permeated* the company; every single one of its executives belonged in jail.

Something that can be *permeated* is said to be *permeable*. A *permeable* raincoat is one that lets water seep through.

PERNICIOUS (pur NISH us) *adj* deadly; extremely evil

The drug dealers conducted their *pernicious* business on every street corner in the city.

Lung cancer is a *pernicious* disease.

PERQUISITE (PUR kwi zit) *n* a privilege that goes along with a job; a "perk"

Free access to a photocopier is a *perquisite* of most office jobs.

The big corporate lawyer's *perquisites* included a chauffeured limousine, a luxurious apartment in the city, and all the chocolate ice cream he could eat.

A *perquisite* should not be confused with a *prerequisite*, which is a necessity. Health and happiness are two *prerequisites* of a good life.

A college degree is a *prerequisite* for many high-paying jobs.

PERTINENT (PUR tuh nunt) *adj* relevant; dealing with the matter at hand

The suspect said that he was just borrowing the jewelry for a costume ball. The cop said he did not think that was *pertinent*.

By the way, *impertinent* means disrespectful.

PERTURB (pur TURB) *v* to disturb greatly

Rudolph's mother was *perturbed* by his aberrant behavior at the dinner table. Rudolph's father was not bothered. Nothing bothered Rudolph Sr. He was *imperturbable*.

PERUSE (puh ROOZ) *v* to read carefully

This word is misused more often than it is used correctly. To *peruse* something is *not* to skim it or read it quickly. To *peruse* something is to study it or read it with great care.

The lawyer *perused* the contract for many hours, looking for a loophole that would enable his client to back out of the deal.

To *peruse* something is to engage in *perusal*. My *perusal* of the ancient texts brought me no closer to my goal of discovering the meaning of life.

Q·U·I·C·K · Q·U·I·Z #63

Match each word in the first column with its definition in the second column. Check your answers in the back of the book.

1. peremptory		a. outside edge of something
2. perennial		b. unenthusiastic
3. perfidy		c. penetrate
4. perfunctory		d. lying under oath
5. peripatetic		e. job-related privilege
6. periphery		f. continual
7. perjury		g. disturb greatly
8. permeate		h. necessity
9. pernicious		i. read carefully
10. perquisite		j. treachery
11. prerequisite		k. final
12. pertinent		l. wandering
13. perturb		m. relevant
14. peruse		n. deadly

PERVADE (pur VADE) *v* to spread throughout

A terrible smell *pervaded* the apartment building after the sewer main exploded.

On examination day, the classroom was *pervaded* by a sense of imminent doom.

Something that *pervades* is *pervasive*. There was a *pervasive* feeling of despair on Wall Street on the day the Dow Jones industrial average fell more than 500 points.

There was a *pervasive* odor of fuel oil in the house, and we soon discovered why: the basement was filled with the stuff.

PETULANT (PECH uh lunt) *adj* rude; cranky; ill-tempered

Gloria became *petulant* when we suggested that she leave her pet cheetah at home when she came to spend the weekend; she said that we had insulted her cheetah and that an insult to her cheetah was an insult to her.

The *petulant* waiter slammed down our water glasses and spilled a tureen of soup onto Roger's toupee.

To be *petulant* is to engage in *petulance*, or rudeness.

PHILANTHROPY (fi LAN thruh pee) *n* love of mankind, especially by doing good deeds

A charity is a *philanthropic* institution. An altruist is someone who cares about other people. A *philanthropist* is actively doing things to help, usually by giving time or money.

PHILISTINE (FIL i steen) *n* a smugly ignorant person with no appreciation of intellectual or artistic matters

The novelist dismissed his critics as *philistines*, saying they wouldn't recognize a good book if it crawled up and bit them on the nose; the critics, in reply, dismissed the novelist as a *philistine* who wouldn't recognize a good book if it crawled up and rolled itself into his typewriter.

Philistine can also be an adjective. To be *philistine* is to act like a *philistine*.

PIOUS (PYE us) *adj* reverent or devout; outwardly (and sometimes falsely) reverent or devout; hypocritical

This is a sometimes confusing word with meanings that are very nearly opposite each other.

A *pious* Presbyterian is one who goes to church every Sunday and says his prayers every night before bed. *Pious* in this sense means something like religiously dutiful.

Pious can also be used to describe feelings or behavior that aren't religious at all but are quite hypocritical. The adulterous minister's sermon on marital fidelity was filled with *pious* disregard for his own sins.

The state of being *pious* is *piety*. The opposite of *pious* is *impious* (IM pee us). Note the pronunciation.

PIVOTAL (PIV uh tul) *adj* crucial

Pivotal is the adjective form of the verb to *pivot*. To *pivot* is to turn on a single point or shaft. A basketball player *pivots* when he turns while leaving one foot planted in the same place on the floor.

A *pivotal* comment is a comment that turns on a discussion. It is a very important comment.

A *pivotal* member of a committee is a crucial or extremely important member of a committee.

Harry's contribution was *pivotal;* without it, we would have failed.

PLACATE (PLAY kate) *v* to pacify; to appease; to soothe

The tribe *placated* the angry volcano by tossing a few teenagers into the raging crater.

The beleaguered general tried to *placate* his fierce attacker by sending him a pleasant flower arrangement. His duplicitous enemy decided to attack anyway. He was *implacable*.

PLAINTIVE (PLAIN tiv) *adj* expressing sadness or sorrow

The lead singer's *plaintive* love song expressed his sorrow at being abandoned by his girlfriend for the lead guitarist.

The chilly autumn weather made the little bird's song seem *plaintive*.

You could also say that there was *plaintiveness* in that bird's song.

Don't confuse *plaintive* with *plaintiff*. A *plaintiff* is a person who takes someone to court—who makes a legal com*plaint*.

PLATITUDE (PLAT i TOOD) *n* a dull or trite remark; a cliché

The principal thinks he is a great orator, but his loud, boring speech was full of *platitudes*.

Instead of giving us any real insight into the situation, the lecturer threw *platitudes* at us for the entire period. It was a *platitudinous* speech.

PLEBIAN (pluh BEE un) *adj* common; vulgar; low class; bourgeois

Plebian is the opposite of *aristocratic*. Sarah refused to eat frozen dinners, saying they were too *plebian* for her discriminating palate.

PLETHORA (PLETH ur uh) *n* an excess

Be careful not to mispronounce this word.

We ate a *plethora* of candy on Halloween and a *plethora* of turkey on Thanksgiving.

Letting the air force use our backyard as a bombing range created a *plethora* of problems.

POIGNANT (POIN yunt) *adj* painfully emotional; extremely moving; sharp or astute

The words *poignant* and *pointed* are very closely related, and they share much of the same range of meaning.

A *poignant* scene is one that is so emotional or moving that it is almost painful to watch.

All the reporters stopped taking notes as they watched the old woman's *poignant* reunion with her daughter, whom she hadn't seen in eighty-five years.

Poignant can also mean *pointed* in the sense of sharp or astute. A *poignant* comment might be one that shows great insight.

To be *poignant* is to have *poignancy*.

Q·U·I·C·K · Q·U·I·Z #64

Match each word in the first column with its definition in the second column. Check your answers in the back of the book.

1.	pervade	a.	painfully emotional
2.	petulant	b.	spread throughout
3.	philanthropy	c.	pacify
4.	philistine	d.	smugly ignorant person
5.	pious	e.	excess
6.	pivotal	f.	expressing sadness
7.	placate	g.	reverent
8.	plaintive	h.	trite remark
9.	platitude	i.	rude
10.	plebeian	j.	crucial
11.	plethora	k.	love for mankind
12.	poignant	l.	low class

POLARIZE (POH luh RIZE) *v* to break up into opposing factions or groupings

The issue of what kind of sand to put in the sandbox *polarized* the nursery school class; some students would accept nothing but wet, while some wanted only dry.

The increasingly acrimonious debate between the two candidates *polarized* the political party.

POLEMIC (puh LEM ik) *n* a powerful argument made in refutation of something

The book was a convincing *polemic* that revealed the fraud at the heart of the large corporation.

Instead of the traditional Groundhog's Day address, the state senator delivered a *polemic* against the sales tax.

A *polemic* is *polemical*.

PONDEROUS (PON dur us) *adj* so large as to be clumsy; massive; dull

The wedding cake was a *ponderous* blob of icing and jelly beans.

The fat man was unable to type, because his *ponderous* belly prevented him from pushing his chair up to his desk.

The chairman, as usual, gave a *ponderous* speech that left half his listeners snoring in their plates.

PORTENT (POR tent) *n* an omen; a sign of something coming in the future

The distant rumbling we heard this morning was a *portent* of the thunderstorm that hit our area this afternoon.

Stock-market investors looked for *portents* in their complicated charts and graphs; they hoped that the market's past behavior would give them a clue as to what would happen in the future.

Portentous is the adjective form of *portent*, meaning ominous or filled with *portent*. But it is very often used to mean pompous, or self-consciously serious or ominous-sounding. It can also mean amazing or prodigious.

A *portentous* speech is not one that you would enjoy listening to.

A *portentous* announcement might be one that tried to create an inappropriate sense of alarm in those listening to it.

Portentous can also mean amazing or astonishing. A *portentous* sunset might be a remarkably glorious one rather than an ominous or menacing one.

POSTULATE (POS chuh LATE) *n* something accepted as true without proof; an axiom

A *postulate* is taken to be true because it is convenient to do so. We might be able to prove a *postulate* if we had the time, but not now. A theorem is something that is proven using *postulates*.

Postulate can be used as a verb, too. Sherlock Holmes rarely *postulated* things, waiting for evidence before he made up his mind.

PRAGMATIC (prag MAT ik) *adj* practical; down to earth; based on experience rather than theory

A *pragmatic* person is one who deals with other things as they are rather than as they might be or should be.

Erecting a gigantic dome of gold over our house would have been the ideal solution to the leak in our roof, but the small size of our bank account forced us to be *pragmatic*; we patched the hole with a dab of tar instead.

PRECEDENT (PRES i dunt) *n* an earlier example or model of something

Precedent is a noun form of the verb *to precede*, or go before. To set a *precedent* is to do something that sets an example for what may follow.

Last year's million-dollar prom set a *precedent* that the current student council hopes will not be followed in the future. That is, the student council hopes that future proms won't cost a million dollars.

To be *unprecedented* is to have no *precedent*, to be something entirely new. George's consumption of 10,677 hot dogs was *unprecedented*; no one had ever eaten so many hot dogs before.

PRECEPT (PREE sept) *n* a rule to live by; a principle establishing a certain kind of action or behavior; a maxim

"Love thy neighbor" is a *precept* we have sometimes found difficult to follow; our neighbor is a noisy oaf who painted his house electric blue and who throws his empty beer cans in our yard.

PRECIPITATE (pri SIP i TATE) *v* to cause to happen abruptly

A panic among investors *precipitated* last Monday's crisis in the stock market.

The police were afraid that distributing machine guns to the angry protestors might *precipitate* a riot.

Precipitate (pri SIP i tit) can also be an adjective, meaning unwisely hasty or rash. A *precipitate* decision is one made without enough thought beforehand.

The guidance counselor, we thought, was *precipitate* when he had the tenth grader committed to a mental hospital for saying that homework was boring.

PRECIPITOUS (pri SIP i tus) *adj* steep

Precipitous means like a precipice, or cliff. It and *precipitate* are very closely related, as you probably guessed. But they don't mean the same thing, even though *precipitous* is often used loosely to mean the same thing as *precipitate*.

A mountain can be *precipitous*, meaning either that it is steep or that it comprises lots of steep cliffs.

Precipitous can also be used to signify things that are only figuratively steep. For example, you could say that someone had stumbled down a *precipitous* slope into drug addiction.

Q·U·I·C·K · Q·U·I·Z #65

Match each word in the first column with its definition in the second column. Check your answers in the back of the book.

1.	polarize	a.	massive and clumsy
2.	polemic	b.	rule to live by
3.	ponderous	c.	practical
4.	portent	d.	powerful refutation
5.	portentous	e.	steep
6.	postulate	f.	cause to happen abruptly
7.	pragmatic	g.	cause opposing positions
8.	precedent	h.	ominous
9.	precept	i.	earlier example
10.	precipitate	j.	omen
11.	precipitous	k.	axiom

PRECLUDE (pri KLOOD) *v* to prevent something from ever happening

Ann feared that her abysmal academic career might *preclude* her becoming a brain surgeon.

PRECURSOR (pri KUR sur) *n* forerunner; something that goes before and anticipates or paves the way for whatever it is that follows

The arrival of a million-dollar check in the mail might very well be the *precursor* of a brand-new car.

A sore throat is often the *precursor* of a cold.

Hard work on the practice field might be the *precursor* of success on the playing field.

PREDILECTION (PRED uh LEK shun) *n* a natural preference for something

The impatient judge had a *predilection* for well-prepared lawyers who said what they meant and didn't waste his time.

Joe's *predilection* for saturated fats has added roughly a foot to his waistline in the last twenty years.

PREEMINENT (pree EM uh nunt) *adj* better than anyone else; outstanding; supreme

The nation's *preeminent* harpsichordist would be the best harpsichordist in the nation.

The Nobel Prize-winning physicist was *preeminent* in his field but he was still a lousy teacher.

PREEMPT (pree EMPT) *v* to seize something by prior right

When television show A *preempts* television show B, television show A is shown at the time usually reserved for television show B. The word *preempt* implies that television show A is more important than television show B and thus has a greater right to the time slot.

A *preemptive* action is one that is undertaken in order to prevent some other action from being undertaken. When the air force launched a *preemptive* strike against the missile base, the air force was attacking the missiles in order to prevent the missiles from attacking the air force.

PREMISE (PREM is) *n* an assumption; the basis for a conclusion

In deciding to eat all the ice cream in the freezer, my *premise* was that if I didn't do it, you would.

Based on the *premise* that two wrongs don't make a right, I hit him three times.

PREPOSSESS (PREE puh ZES) *v* to preoccupy; to influence beforehand or prejudice; to make a good impression on beforehand

This word has several common meanings. Be careful.

When a person is *prepossessed* by an idea, he or she can't get it out of his or her mind. My dream of producing energy from old chewing-gum wrappers *prepossessed* me, and I lost my job, my home, my wife, and my children.

Experience has *prepossessed* Larry's mother not to believe him when he said that someone else had broken the window; Larry had broken it every other time, so she assumed that he had broken it this time.

The new girl in the class was extremely *prepossessing*. The minute she walked into the room, all the boys rushed over to introduce themselves. *Unprepossessing* means unimpressive, but the word is only mildly negative. The quaint farmhouse had an *unprepossessing* exterior, but a beautiful interior. Who would have imagined?

PREROGATIVE (pri ROG uh tiv) *n* a right or privilege connected exclusively with a position, a person, a class, a nation, or some other group or classification

Giving traffic tickets to people he didn't like was one of the *prerogatives* of Junior's job as a policeman.

Sentencing people to death is a *prerogative* of kings and queens.

Big mansions and fancy cars are among the *prerogatives* of wealth.

PREVAIL (pri VALE) *v* to triumph; to overcome rivals; (with *on, upon,* or *with*) to persuade

When justice *prevails*, it means that good defeats evil.

The prosecutor *prevailed* in the murder trial; the defendant was found guilty.

My mother *prevailed* on me to make my bed. She told me she would belt me if I didn't, so I did.

The adjective *prevailing* means most frequent or predominant. The *prevailing* opinion on a topic is the one that most people hold. If the *prevailing* winds are out of the north, then the wind is out of the north most of the time. A *prevailing* theory is the one most widely held at the time. It is *prevalent*.

PRISTINE (PRIS teen) *adj* original; unspoiled; pure

An antique in *pristine* condition is one that hasn't been tampered with over the years. It's still in its original condition.

A *pristine* mountain stream is a stream that hasn't been polluted.

PRODIGAL (PROD uh gul) *adj* wastefully extravagant

The chef was *prodigal* with his employer's money, spending thousands of dollars on ingredients for what was supposed to be a simple meal.

The young artist was *prodigal* with his talents, wasting time and energy on greeting cards that might have been devoted to serious paintings.

The *prodigal* gambler soon found that he couldn't afford even a two-dollar bet.

To be *prodigal* is to be characterized by *prodigality*.

Q·U·I·C·K · Q·U·I·Z #66

Match each word in the first column with its definition in the second column. Check your answers in the back of the book.

1. preclude	a.	outstanding
2. precursor	b.	triumph
3. predilection	c.	seize by prior right
4. preeminent	d.	wastefully extravagant
5. preempt	e.	unspoiled
6. premise	f.	natural preference
7. prepossess	g.	preoccupy
8. prerogative	h.	right or privilege
9. prevail	i.	assumption
10. pristine	j.	forerunner
11. prodigal	k.	prevent

PRODIGIOUS (pruh DIJ us) *adj* extraordinary; enormous

To fill the Grand Canyon with Ping-Pong balls would be a *prodigious* undertaking; it would be both extraordinary and enormous.

The little boy caught a *prodigious* fish—it was ten times his size and might more easily have caught him had their situations been reversed.

See also *prodigy*.

PRODIGY (PROD i jee) *n* an extremely talented child; an extraordinary accomplishment or occurrence

The three-year-old *prodigy* could play all of Beethoven and most of Brahms on his harmonica.

Larry was a mathematical *prodigy;* he had calculated *pi* to 100 decimal places almost before he could walk.

Josephine's tower of dominoes and Popsicle sticks was a *prodigy* of engineering.

PROFANE (pruh FANE) *adj* not having to do with religion; irreverent; blasphemous

Profane is the opposite of sacred. Worshipping the almighty dollar is *profane. Profane* can also mean disrespectful of religion. Sticking out your tongue in church would be a *profane* gesture.

Profane can also be a verb. You *profaned* the church by sticking out your tongue in it. Nick *profaned* his priceless Egyptian statue by using it as a doorstop.

The noun form of *profane* is *profanity.* Throwing a gallon of red paint at the front door of the church was an act of *profanity.*

PROFESS (pruh FESS) *v* to declare; to declare falsely or pretend

Jason *professed* to teach himself calculus; he declared that he was going to do it.

No one in our town was fooled by the candidate's *professed* love for llama farmers; everyone knew he was just trying to win votes with all those pro-llama positions.

PROFICIENT (pruh FISH unt) *adj* thoroughly competent; skillful; very good (at something)

Jerry was a *proficient* cabinetmaker. He could make a cabinet that would make you sit back and say, "Now, there's a cabinet."

I fiddled around at the piano for many years but never became *proficient* at playing.

Lucy was merely competent but Molly was *proficient* at plucking canaries.

Proficiency is the state of being *proficient.*

PROFLIGATE (PROF luh git) *adj* extravagantly wasteful and, usually, wildly immoral

The fraternity members were a *profligate* bunch; they held all-night orgies on weeknights and nearly burned down their fraternity house with their parties every weekend.

The young heir was *profligate* with his fortune, spending millions on champagne and racehorses.

PROFOUND (pruh FOUND) *adj* deep (in several senses)

Profound understanding is deep understanding.

To say something *profound* is to say something deeply intelligent or discerning.

Profound dislike is deep dislike. The noun of *profound* is *profundity* (pruh FUN di tee).

Profound horror is deep horror.

PROFUSE (pruh FYOOS) *adj* flowing; extravagant

When we gave Marian our house, our car, and all our clothes, her gratitude was *profuse*.

My teacher said I had done a good job, but his praise was far from *profuse*. I got the feeling he hadn't really liked my epic poems about two dinosaurs who fall in love just before they go extinct.

The grieving widow's tears were *profuse*. She had tears in *profusion*.

PROLETARIAT (PROH li TAIR ee ut) *n* the industrial working class

The *proletariat* is the laboring class—blue-collar workers or people who roll up their shirt sleeves to do an honest day's work.

PROLIFERATE (proh LIF uh RATE) *v* to spread or grow rapidly

Honey bees *proliferated* when we filled our yard with flowering plants.

Coughs and colds *proliferate* when groups of children are cooped up together during the winter.

The police didn't know what to make of the *proliferation* of counterfeit money in the north end of town.

PROLIFIC (proh LIF ik) *adj* abundantly productive; fruitful or fertile

A *prolific* writer is a writer who writes a lot of books. A prolific artist is an artist who paints a lot of pictures.

The old man had been extraordinarily *prolific;* he had thirty children and more than one hundred grandchildren.

Q·U·I·C·K · Q·U·I·Z #67

Match each word in the first column with its definition in the second column. Check your answers in the back of the book.

1. prodigious	a. declare
2. prodigy	b. irreverent
3. profane	c. abundantly productive
4. profess	d. flowing
5. proficient	e. extremely talented child
6. profligate	f. extraordinary
7. profound	g. spread rapidly
8. profuse	h. deep
9. proletariat	i. thoroughly competent
10. proliferate	j. extravagantly wasteful
11. prolific	k. industrial working class

PROMULGATE (PROM ul GATE) *v* to proclaim; to publicly or formally declare something

The principal *promulgated* a new dress code over the loudspeaker system: red, green, yellow, and blue were the only permissible artificial hair colors.

PROPENSITY (pruh PEN si tee) *n* a natural inclination or tendency; a predilection

Jessie has a *propensity* for saying stupid things: every time she opens her mouth, something stupid comes out.

Bill's *propensity* to sit around all day doing nothing came into conflict with his mother's *propensity* to kick him out of the house.

PROPITIOUS (pruh PISH us) *adj* marked by favorable signs or conditions

Rush hour is not a *propitious* time to drive into the city.

The early negotiations between the union and the company had been so *propitious* that no one was surprised when a new contract was announced well before the strike deadline.

PROPONENT (pruh POH nunt) *n* an advocate; a supporter of a position

Proponent and *opponent* are antonyms.

PROPRIETARY (pruh PRYE i TER ee) *adj* characteristic of an owner of property; constituting property

To take a *proprietary* interest in something is to act as though you own it. George felt very *proprietary* about the chocolate-cookie recipe; he had invented it himself.

The company's design for musical toilet paper is *proprietary;* the company owns it, and outsiders can't look at it for nothing.

PROPRIETY (pruh PRYE i tee) *n* properness; good manners

The old lady viewed the little girl's failure to curtsy as a flagrant breach of *propriety*. She did not approve of or countenance such *improprieties*.

Propriety prevented the young man from trashing the town in celebration of his unexpected acceptance by the college of his choice.

PROSAIC (proh ZAY ik) *adj* dull; unimaginative; like prose (as opposed to poetry)

His description of the battle was so *prosaic* that it was hard for his listeners to believe that any of the soldiers had even been wounded, much less blown to smithereens.

The little boy's ambitions were all *prosaic*: he said he wanted to be an accountant, an auditor, or a claims adjustor.

PROSCRIBE (proh SCRIBE) *v* to outlaw; to prohibit

Spitting on the sidewalk and shooting at road signs were both *proscribed* activities under the new administration.

The young doctor *proscribed* smoking in the waiting room of his office.

The act of *proscribing* is *proscription;* an individual act of *proscribing* is also a *proscription*.

PROSELYTIZE (PROS uh li TIZE) *v* to convert (someone) from one religion or doctrine to another; to recruit converts to a religion or doctrine.

The former Methodist had been *proselytized* by a Lutheran deacon.

The airport terminal was filled with *proselytizers* from a dozen different sects, cults, and religions. They were attempting to *proselytize* the passengers walking through the terminal.

PROTAGONIST (proh TAG uh nist) *n* the leading character in a novel, play, or other work; a leader or champion

Martin Luther King, Jr., was a *protagonist* in the long and continuing struggle for racial equality.

The *protagonist* of the movie was an eleven-year-old boy who saved his hometown from destruction by eating all the donuts that the mad scientist had been using to fuel his nuclear reactor. The mad scientist was the boy's chief *antagonist*. An *antagonist* is an opponent or adversary.

PROTRACT (proh TRACT) *v* to prolong

The trial was so *protracted* that one of the jurors died of old age and another gave birth.

The commencement speaker promised not to *protract* his remarks, but then he spoke for two solid hours. It was a *protracted* speech.

PROVIDENT (PROV i dunt) *adj* preparing for the future; providing for the future; frugal

We were *provident* with our limited food supplies, knowing that the winter ahead would be long and cold.

The *provident* father had long ago set aside money for the college educations of each of his children.

To be *improvident* is to fail to provide for the future. It was *improvident* of the grasshopper not to store any food for the winter, unlike his acquaintance the *provident* ant.

Q·U·I·C·K · Q·U·I·Z #68

Match each word in the first column with its definition in the second column. Check your answers in the back of the book.

1. promulgate	a.	natural inclination
2. propensity	b.	good manners
3. propitious	c.	advocate
4. proponent	d.	prohibit
5. proprietary	e.	prolong
6. propriety	f.	leading character
7. prosaic	g.	constituting property
8. proscribe	h.	frugal
9. proselytize	i.	dull
10. protagonist	j.	marked by favorable signs
11. protract	k.	convert
12. provident	l.	proclaim

PROVINCIAL (pruh VIN shul) *adj* limited in outlook to one's own small corner of the world; narrow

The farmers were very *provincial;* they had no opinions about anything but the price of corn and no interest in anything except growing more of it.

New Yorkers have reputations for being very sophisticated and cosmopolitan, but most of them are actually very *provincial;* they act as though nothing of interest had ever happened on the other side of the Hudson River.

PROVISIONAL (pruh VIZH uh nul) *adj* conditional; temporary; tentative

Louis had been accepted as a *provisional* member of the club. He wouldn't become a permanent member until the other members had had a chance to see what he was really like.

The old man's offer to donate $10,000 to the charity was *provisional;* he said that he would give the money only if the charity could manage to raise a matching sum.

PROXIMITY (prok SIM i tee) *n* nearness

I can't stand being in the *proximity* of a nuclear explosion. The radiation leaves my hair a mess.

In a big city, one is almost always in the *proximity* of a restaurant.

PRUDENT (PROOD unt) *adj* careful; having foresight

Joe is a *prudent* money manager. He doesn't invest heavily in racehorses, and he puts only a small part of his savings in the office football pool. Joe is the epitome of *prudence*.

The opposite of *prudent* is *imprudent*. It was *imprudent* of us to pour gasoline all over the floor of our living room and then light a fire in the fireplace.

PURPORTED (pur PORT id) *adj* rumored; claimed

The heiress is *purported* to have been kidnaped by adventurers and buried in a concrete vault beneath the busiest intersection in Times Square. No one believes this story except the psychic who was consulted by the police.

To *purport* something is to claim or allege it.

PUTATIVE (PYOO tuh tiv) *adj* commonly accepted; supposed; reputed

The *putative* reason for placing the monument downtown is that nobody had wanted it uptown. When you use the word *putative*, you emphasize that the reason is only supposed, not proven.

Q·U·I·C·K · Q·U·I·Z #69

Match each word in the first column with its definition in the second column. Check your answers in the back of the book.

1. provincial
2. provisional
3. proximity
4. prudent
5. purported
6. putative

a. commonly accepted
b. nearness
c. narrow in outlook
d. rumored
e. careful
f. conditional

Q

QUALIFY (KWOL uh FYE) *v* to modify or restrict

You already know the primary meaning of *qualify.* Here's another meaning.

Susan *qualified* her praise of Judith by saying that her kind words applied only to Judith's skillful cooking and not to her abhorrent personality. Judith was upset by Susan's *qualification.*

The library trustees rated their fund-raiser a *qualified* success; many more people than expected had come, but virtually no money had been raised.

An *unqualified* success is a complete, unrestricted success.

QUALITATIVE (KWOL i TAY tiv) *adj* having to do with the *quality* or *qualities* of something (as opposed to the *quantity*)

If a school achieves a *qualitative* improvement in attendance, it means the school is being attended by better students. If the school achieves a *quantitative* improvement, it means the school is being attended by more students.

The difference between the two restaurants was *quantitative* rather than *qualitative.* Both served the same dreadful food, but the second restaurant served more of it.

QUERULOUS (KWER uh lus) *adj* complaining; grumbling; whining

Although a query is a question, *querulous* does not mean questioning.

The exasperated mother finally managed to hush her *querulous* child.

The *querulous* voices of the students, who believed that their quiz had been graded too harshly, could be heard all the way at the other end of the school building.

QUIXOTIC (kwik SOT ik) *adj* romantic or idealistic to a foolish or impractical degree

The word *quixotic* is derived from the name of Don Quixote, the protagonist of Miguel de Cervantes's classic seventeenth-century novel. Don Quixote had read so many romances about the golden age of chivalry that he set out to become a knight himself and have chivalrous adventures. Instead, his romantic idealism almost invariably got him into trouble. To be *quixotic* is to be as foolish or impractical as Don Quixote in pursuing an ideal.

For many years Mr. Morris had led a *quixotic* effort to repeal the federal income tax.

The political organization had once been a powerful force in Washington, but its membership had dwindled and its causes had become increasingly *quixotic.*

Q·U·I·C·K · Q·U·I·Z #70

Match each word in the first column with its definition in the second column. Check your answers in the back of the book.

1. qualify
2. qualitative
3. quantitative
4. querulous
5. quixotic

a. having to do with quantity
b. foolishly romantic
c. complaining
d. modify or restrict
e. having to do with quality

RAMIFICATION (RAM uh fuh KAY shun) *n* a consequence; a branching out

A tree could be said to *ramify*, or branch out, as it grows. A *ramification* is a consequence that grows out of something in the same way that a tree branch grows out of a tree trunk.

The professor found a solution to the problem, but there are many *ramifications;* some experts are afraid that he has created more problems than he has solved.

RANCOR (RANG kur) *n* bitter, long-lasting ill will or resentment

The mutual *rancor* felt by the two nations eventually led to war.

Jeremy's success produced such feelings of *rancor* in Jessica, his rival, that she was never able to tolerate being in the same room with him again.

To feel *rancor* is to be *rancorous*. The *rancorous* public exchanges between the two competing boxers are strictly for show; outside the ring, they are the best of friends.

RAPACIOUS (ruh PAY shus) *adj* greedy; plundering; avaricious

Wall Street investment bankers are often accused of being *rapacious*, but they claim they are performing a valuable economic function.

The noun form is *rapacity*.

REBUKE (ri BYOOK) *v* to criticize sharply

The judge *rebuked* the convicted murderer for chopping up so many people and burying them in the woods.

We trembled as Mr. Solomon *rebuked* us for flipping over his car and taking off the tires.

A piece of sharp criticism is called a *rebuke*. When the students pushed their French teacher out the window, the principal delivered a *rebuke* that made their ears twirl.

REBUT (ri BUT) *v* to contradict; to argue in opposition to; to prove to be false

They all thought I was crazy, but none of them could *rebut* my argument.

The defense attorney attempted to *rebut* the prosecutor's claim that the defendant's fingerprints, hair, clothing, signature, wallet, wristwatch, credit cards, and car had been found at the scene of the crime.

An act or instance of *rebutting* is called a *rebuttal*. *Rebut* and *refute* are synonyms.

RECALCITRANT (ri KAL si trunt) *adj* stubbornly defiant of authority or control; disobedient

The *recalcitrant* cancer continued to spread through the patient's body despite every therapy and treatment the doctors could think to try.

The country was in a turmoil, but the *recalcitrant* dictator refused even to listen to the pleas of the international representatives.

RECANT (ri KANT) *v* to publicly take back and deny (something previously said or believed); to openly confess error

The chagrined scientist *recanted* his theory that mice originated on the moon; it turned out that he had simply mixed up the results of two separate experiments.

The secret police tortured the intellectual for a week, by tickling his feet with a feather duster, until he finally *recanted*.

An act of *recanting* is called a *recantation*.

RECIPROCAL (ri SIP ruh kul) *adj* mutual; shared; interchangeable

The Rochester Club had a *reciprocal* arrangement with the Duluth Club. Members of either club had full privileges of membership at the other.

Their hatred was *reciprocal;* they hated each other.

To *reciprocate* is to return in kind, to interchange, or to repay.

Our new neighbors had had us over for dinner several times, but we were unable to *reciprocate* immediately because our dining room was being remodeled.

Peter hit Paul over the head with a stick. Paul *reciprocated* by punching Peter in the nose.

A *reciprocity* is a *reciprocal* relation between two parties, often whereby both parties gain.

RECLUSIVE (ri KLOOS iv) *adj* hermitlike; withdrawn from society

The crazy millionaire led a *reclusive* existence, shutting himself up in his labyrinthine mansion and never setting foot in the outside world.

Our new neighbors were so *reclusive* that we didn't even meet them until a full year after they had moved in.

A *reclusive* person is a *recluse*. After his wife's death, the grieving old man turned into a *recluse* and seldom ventured out of his house.

RECONDITE (REK un DITE) *adj* hard to understand; over one's head

The philosopher's thesis was so *recondite* that I couldn t get past the first two sentences.

Every now and then the professor would lift his head from his desk and deliver some *recondite* pronouncement that left us scratching our heads and trying to figure out what he meant.

The scholarly journal was so *recondite* as to be utterly incomprehensible.

Q·U·I·C·K · Q·U·I·Z #71

Match each word in the first column with its definition in the second column. Check your answers in the back of the book.

1. ramification		a.	hard to understand
2. rancor		b.	criticize sharply
3. rapacious		c.	consequence
4. rebuke		d.	mutual
5. rebut		e.	hermitlike
6. recalcitrant		f.	bitter resentment
7. recant		g.	stubbornly defiant
8. reciprocal		h.	publicly deny
9. reclusive		i.	contradict
10. recondite		j.	greedy

RECRIMINATION (ri KRIM uh NAY shun) *n* a bitter counteraccusation, or the act of making a bitter counteraccusation

The word is often used in the plural. Mary was full of *recrimination*. When I accused her of stealing my pen, she angrily accused me of being careless, evil, and stupid.

The courtroom echoed with the *recriminations* of the convicted defendant as he was taken off to the penitentiary.

To make a *recrimination* is to *recriminate*. The adjective is *recriminatory*.

REDOLENT (RED uh lunt) *adj* fragrant

The air in autumn is *redolent* of wood smoke and fallen leaves.

The flower arrangements on the tables were both beautiful and *redolent*.

Something that is *redolent* has *redolence*.

Redolent also means suggestive. The new play was *redolent* of one I had seen many years ago.

REDUNDANT (ri DUN dunt) *adj* unnecessarily repetitive; excessive; excessively wordy

Bill had already bought paper plates, so our purchase of paper plates was *redundant*.

Harry's article was *redundant*—he kept saying the same thing over and over again.

An act of being *redundant* is a *redundancy*. The title "Department of Redundancy Department" is *redundant*.

REFUTE (ri FYOOT) *v* to prove to be false; to disprove

His expensive suit and imported shoes clearly *refuted* his claim that he was poor.

I *refuted* Larry's mathematical proof by showing him that it depended on two and two adding up to five.

An act of *refuting* is called a *refutation*. The audience enjoyed the panelist's humorous *refutation* of the main speaker's theory about the possibility of building an antigravity airplane.

Something that is indubitable, something that cannot be disproven, is *irrefutable*. Carrie's experiments with jelly beans and pencil erasers offered *irrefutable* proof that jelly beans taste better than pencil erasers.

REITERATE (ree IT uh RATE) *v* to say again; to repeat
The candidate had *reiterated* his position so many times on the campaign trail that he sometimes even muttered it in his sleep.

To *reiterate*, let me say once again that I am very happy to have been invited to the birthday celebration of your adorable Pekingese.

An act of *reiterating* is called a *reiteration*. Bobby's *reiteration* of his demands was entirely unnecessary, since we already knew what they were.

RELEGATE (REL uh GATE) *v* to banish; to send away
The most junior of the junior executives was *relegated* to a tiny, windowless office that had once been a broom closet.

The new father's large collection of jazz records was *relegated* to the cellar to make room for the new baby's larger collection of stuffed animals. The father objected to the *relegation* of his record collection to the cellar, but his objection did no good.

RELENTLESS (ri LENT lis) *adj* continuous; unstoppable
To *relent* is to stop or give up. *Relentless*, or *unrelenting*, means not stopping. The insatiable rabbit was *relentless*; it ate and ate until nothing was left in the botanical garden. The torrential rains were *relentless*, eventually creating a deluge.

RELINQUISH (ri LING kwish) *v* to release or let go of; to surrender; to stop doing
The hungry dog refused to *relinquish* the enormous beef bone that he had stolen from the butcher's shop.

The retiring president *relinquished* control of the company only with the greatest reluctance.

Sandra was forty-five years old before she finally *relinquished* her view of herself as a glamorous teenaged beauty.

REMONSTRATE (ri MON strate) *v* to argue against; to protest; to raise objections
My boss *remonstrated* with me for telling all the secretaries they could take the rest of the week off.

The manager *remonstrated*, but the umpire continued to insist that the base runner had been out at third. When the manager continued to *remonstrate*, the umpire threw him out of the game.

An act of *remonstrating* is a *remonstration*.

RENAISSANCE (REN i SAHNS) *n* a rebirth or revival
The capital R *Renaissance* was a great blossoming of art, literature, science, and culture in general that transformed Europe between the

fourteenth and seventeenth centuries. The word is also used in connection with lesser rebirths.

The declining neighborhood underwent a *renaissance* when a group of investors bought several crumbling tenements and turned them into attractive apartment buildings.

The small college's football team had endured many losing seasons but underwent a dramatic *renaissance* when the new coach recruited half a dozen 400-pound freshmen.

Renaissance can also be spelled *renascence*.

RENOUNCE (ri NOWNCE) *v* to formally give up or resign; to disown; to have nothing to do with anymore

Despite the pleadings and protestations of her parents, Deborah refused to *renounce* her love for the leader of the motorcycle gang.

The presidential candidate *renounced* his manager after it was revealed that the zealous manager had tried to murder the candidate's opponent in the primary.

To *renounce* is to make a *renunciation* (ri NUN see AY shun).

Q·U·I·C·K · Q·U·I·Z #72

Match each word in the first column with its definition in the second column. Check your answers in the back of the book.

1.	recrimination	a.	surrender
2.	redolent	b.	disown
3.	redundant	c.	rebirth
4.	refute	d.	argue against
5.	reiterate	e.	fragrant
6.	relegate	f.	banish
7.	relinquish	g.	say again
8.	remonstrate	h.	bitter counteraccusation
9.	renaissance	i.	unnecessarily repetitive
10.	renounce	j.	prove to be false

REPARATION (REP uh RAY shun) *n* paying back; making amends; compensation

To make a *reparation* is to *repair* some damage that has occurred.

This word is often used in the plural. The defeated country demanded *reparation* for the destruction it had suffered at the hands of the victorious army.

After the accident we sought *reparation* in court, but our lawyer was not competent and we didn't win a cent.

Something that cannot be *repaired* is *irreparable* (i REP ur uh bul).

REPERCUSSION (REE pur KUSH un) *n* a consequence; an indirect effect

One *repercussion* of the new tax law was that accountants found themselves with a lot of new business.

The declaration of war had many *repercussions*, including a big increase in production at the bomb factory.

REPLENISH (ri PLEN ish) *v* to fill again; to resupply; to restore

The manager of the hardware store needed to *replenish* his stock; quite a few of the shelves were empty.

The commanding general *replenished* his army with a trainload of food and other supplies.

After the big Thanksgiving meal, everyone felt *replenished*.

An act of *replenishing* is a *replenishment*. The *replenishment* of our firewood supply was our first thought after the big snowstorm.

REPLETE (ri PLEET) *adj* completely filled; abounding

The once polluted stream was now *replete* with fish of every description.

The bride wore a magnificent sombrero *replete* with fuzzy dice and campaign buttons.

Tim ate all nine courses at the wedding banquet. He was filled to the point of *repletion*.

REPREHENSIBLE (REP ri HEN suh bul) *adj* worthy of blame or censure

He put the cat in the laundry chute, tied the dog to the chimney, and committed several other *reprehensible* acts.

Malcolm's manners were *reprehensible:* He ate his soup by drinking it from his empty wineglass and flipped his peas into his mouth with the back of his salad fork.

REPRISAL (ri PRYE zul) *n* a military action undertaken in revenge for another; an act of taking "an eye for an eye"

The raid on the Iranian oil-drilling platform was a *reprisal* for the Iranians' earlier attack on the American tanker.

Fearing *reprisals* from the terrorists, the CIA beefed up its security after capturing the terrorist leader.

REPROACH (ri PROACH) *v* to scold, usually in disappointment; to blame; to disgrace

My doctor *reproached* me for gaining twenty pounds after he had advised me to lose fifteen.

The police officer *reproached* me for leaving my car parked overnight in a no-standing zone.

Reproach can also be a noun. To look at someone with *reproach* is to look at that person critically or accusingly. To be filled with *self-reproach* can mean to be ashamed.

Impeccable behavior is beyond fault, it is *irreproachable*. Even though Jerome did split Aunt Mabel's skull with an ax, his motive was *irreproachable:* He had merely been trying to kill a fly perched on her hairnet.

REPROVE (ri PROOV) *v* to criticize mildly

Aunt May *reproved* us for eating too much, but we could tell she was actually thrilled that we had enjoyed the meal.

My wife *reproved* me for leaving my dirty dish in the sink.

An act of *reproving* is called a *reproof*. The judge's decision was less a sentence than a gentle *reproof;* He put Jerry on probation and told him never to get in trouble again.

REPUDIATE (ri PYOO dee ATE) *v* to reject; to renounce; to disown; to have nothing to do with

Hoping to receive a lighter sentence, the convicted gangster *repudiated* his former connection with the mob.

REQUISITE (REK wi zit) *adj* required; necessary

Howard bought a hunting rifle and the *requisite* ammunition.

The *requisite* number of members not being in attendance, the chairman adjourned the meeting just after it had begun.

Requisite can also be a noun, meaning a requirement or a necessity. A hammer and a saw are among the *requisites* of the carpenter's trade.

A *prerequisite* is something required before you can get started. A high school diploma is usually a *prerequisite* to entering college.

RESOLUTE (REZ uh LOOT) *adj* determined; firm; unwavering

Uncle Ted was *resolute* in his decision not to have a good time at our Christmas party; he stood alone in the corner and muttered to himself all night long.

The other team was strong, but our players were *resolute*. They kept pushing and shoving until, in the final moments, they won the roller-derby tournament.

Someone who sticks to his New Year's resolution is *resolute*.

To be *irresolute* is to be wavering or indecisive. Our *irresolute* leader led us first one way and then the other way in the process of getting us thoroughly and completely lost.

Q·U·I·C·K · Q·U·I·Z   #73

Match each word in the first column with its definition in the second column. Check your answers in the back of the book.

1. reparation	a. act of revenge
2. repercussion	b. determined
3. replenish	c. worthy of blame
4. replete	d. consequence
5. reprehensible	e. scold
6. reprisal	f. completely filled
7. reproach	g. paying back
8. reprove	h. necessary
9. repudiate	i. criticize mildly
10. requisite	j. fill again
11. resolute	k. reject

RESPITE (RES pit) *n* a period of rest or relief

We worked without *respite* from five in the morning until five in the afternoon.

The new mother fell asleep when her baby stopped crying, but the *respite* was brief; the baby started up again almost immediately.

RETICENT (RET i sunt) *adj* quiet; restrained; reluctant to speak, especially about oneself

Luther's natural *reticence* made him an ideal speaker: His speeches never lasted more than a few minutes.

Jeffrey was *reticent* on the subject of his accomplishments; he didn't like to talk about himself.

To be *reticent* is to be characterized by *reticence*.

REVERE (ri VEER) *v* to respect highly; to honor

Einstein was a preeminent scientist who was *revered* by everyone, even his rivals. Einstein enjoyed nearly universal *reverence*. To be *irreverent* is to be mildly disrespectful. Peter made jokes about his younger sister's painting. Peter's sister was perturbed at his *irreverence* and began to cry.

RHETORIC (RET ur ik) *n* the art of formal speaking or writing; inflated discourse

A talented public speaker might be said to be skilled in *rhetoric*.

The word is often used in a pejorative sense to describe speaking or writing that is skillfully executed but insincere or devoid of meaning. A political candidate's speech that was long on drama and promises but short on genuine substance might be dismissed as "mere *rhetoric*."

To use *rhetoric* is to be *rhetorical*. A *rhetorical* question is one the speaker intends to answer himself or herself—that is, a question asked only for *rhetorical* effect.

RIGOROUS (RIG ur us) *adj* strict; harsh; severe

To be *rigorous* is to act with *rigor*.

Our exercise program was *rigorous* but effective; after just a few months, our eighteen hours of daily exercise had begun to pay off.

The professor was popular largely because he wasn't very *rigorous;* there were no tests in his course and only one paper, which was optional.

ROBUST (roh BUST) *adj* strong and healthy; vigorous

The hundred-year-old man was still *robust.* Every morning he ran several miles down to the ocean and jumped in.

The tree we planted last year isn't looking very *robust.* Most of the leaves have fallen off, and the bark has begun to peel.

ROGUE (rohg) *n* a criminally dishonest person; a scoundrel

A *rogue* is someone who can't be trusted. It is often used, however, to characterize a playfully mischievous person.

RUDIMENTARY (ROO duh MEN tuh ree) *adj* basic; crude; unformed or undeveloped

The primitive tribe's tools were very *rudimentary.* In fact, they looked more like rocks than like tools.

The boy who had lived with wolves for fifteen years lacked even the most *rudimentary* social skills.

The strange creature had small bumps on its torso that appeared to be *rudimentary* limbs.

RUMINATE (ROO muh NATE) *v* to contemplate; to ponder; to mull over

Ruminate comes from a Latin word meaning "to chew cud." Cows, sheep, and other cud-chewing animals are called *ruminants.* To *ruminate* is to quietly chew on or ponder your own thoughts.

The teacher's comment about the causes of weather set me to *ruminating* about what a nice day it was and to wishing that I were outside.

The very old man spent his last days *ruminating* about death and eating box after box of vanilla wafers.

An act of *ruminating* is called a *rumination.* Serge was a very private man; he kept his *ruminations* to himself.

RUSTIC (RUS tik) *adj* rural; lacking urban comforts or sophistication; primitive

Life in the log cabin was too *rustic* for Leah; she missed hot showers, cold beer, and electricity.

Rustic can be used as a noun. A *rustic* is an unsophisticated person from the country. We enjoyed the *rustic* scenery as we traveled through the countryside.

Q·U·I·C·K · Q·U·I·Z #74

Match each word in the first column with its definition in the second column. Check your answers in the back of the book.

1. respite		a.	basic
2. reticent		b.	contemplate
3. retract		c.	vigorous
4. reverberate		d.	withdraw
5. revere		e.	formal writing or speaking
6. rhetoric		f.	restrained
7. rigorous		g.	rural
8. robust		h.	period of rest
9. rogue		i.	echo
10. rudimentary		j.	strict
11. ruminate		k.	honor
12. rustic		l.	scoundrel

S

SACCHARINE (SAK uh rin) *adj* sweet; excessively or disgustingly sweet

Saccharin is a calorie-free sweetener; *saccharine* means sweet. Except for the spelling, this is one of the easiest to remember words there is. Don't screw up.

Saccharine can be applied to things that are literally sweet, such as sugar, Saccharin, fruit, and so on. It can also be applied to things that are sweet in a figurative sense, such as children, personalities, and sentiments —especially things that are *too* sweet, or sweet in a sickening way.

We wanted to find a nice card for Uncle Moe, but the cards in the display at the drugstore all had such *saccharine* messages that we would have been too embarrassed to send any of them.

The love story was so *saccharine* that I ended up loathing the heroine and wishing the hero would belch or pick his nose just to break the gooey monotony.

SACRILEGE (SAK ruh lij) *n* a violation of something sacred; blasphemy

The minister committed the *sacrilege* of delivering his sermon while wearing his golf shoes; he didn't want to be late for his tee-off time, which was just a few minutes after the scheduled end of the service.

The members of the fundamentalist sect believed that dancing, going to movies, and watching television were *sacrileges*.

To commit a *sacrilege* is to be *sacrilegious*. Be careful with the spelling of these words.

SACROSANCT (SAK roh SANGKT) *adj* sacred; held to be inviolable

A church is *sacrosanct.* So, for Christians, is belief in the divinity of Jesus Christ.

Sacrosanct is also used loosely, and often ironically, outside of religion. Mr. Peters's lunchtime trip to his neighborhood bar was *sacrosanct;* he would no sooner skip it than he would skip his mother's funeral.

SAGACIOUS (suh GAY shus) *adj* discerning; shrewd; keen in judgment; wise

Edgar's decision to move the chickens into the barn turned out to be *sagacious;* about an hour later, the hailstorm hit.

The announcer's *sagacious* commentary made the baseball game seem vastly more interesting than we had expected it to be.

To be *sagacious* is to have *sagacity.* A similar word is *sage,* which means wise; possessing wisdom derived from experience or learning.

When we were contemplating starting our own popcorn business, we received some *sage* advice from a man who had lost all his money selling candied apples.

The professor's critique, which consisted of just a few *sage* comments, sent me back to my room feeling pretty stupid.

Sage can also be a noun. A wise person, especially a wise old person, is often called a *sage.*

SALIENT (SAYL yunt) *adj* sticking out; conspicuous; leaping

A *salient* characteristic is one that leaps right out at you.

Ursula had a number of *salient* features including, primarily, her nose, which stuck out so far that she was constantly in danger of slamming it in doors and windows.

SALUTARY (SAL yuh TER ee) *adj* healthful; remedial; curative

Lowered blood pressure is among the *salutary* effects of exercise.

The long sea voyage was *salutary;* when Elizabeth landed she looked ten years younger than she had when she set sail.

SANCTIMONIOUS (SANGK tuh MOH nee us) *adj* pretending to be devout; affecting religious feeling

The *sanctimonious* old bore pretended to be deeply offended when Lucius whispered a mild swearword after dropping the anvil on his bare foot.

Simon is an egoist who speaks about almost nothing but caring for one's fellowman. His altruism is *sanctimonious.*

SANGUINE (SANG gwin) *adj* cheerful; optimistic; hopeful

Peter was *sanguine* about his chances of winning the Nobel Peace Prize, even though, as an eighth grader, he hadn't really done anything to deserve it.

The ebullient checkers champion remained *sanguine* in defeat; he was so sure of himself that he viewed even catastrophe as merely a temporary setback.

Don't confuse *sanguine* (a nice word) with *sanguinary* (not a nice word). *Sanguinary* means bloodthirsty.

SARDONIC (sahr DON ik) *adj* mocking; scornful

Robert's weak attempts at humor were met by nothing but a few scattered pockets of *sardonic* laughter.

Even George's friends found him excessively *sardonic;* he couldn't discuss anything without mocking it, and there was almost nothing about which he could bring himself to say two nice words in a row.

Q·U·I·C·K · Q·U·I·Z #75

Match each word in the first column with its definition in the second column. Check your answers in the back of the book.

1. saccharine   a. blasphemy
2. sacrilege   b. wise
3. sacrosanct   c. sweet
4. sagacious   d. pretending to be devout
5. sage   e. healthful
6. salient   f. mocking
7. salutary   g. cheerful
8. sanctimonious   h. sacred
9. sanguine   i. sticking out
10. sardonic   j. discerning

SCINTILLATE (SIN tuh LATE) *v* to sparkle, either literally or figuratively

Stars and diamonds *scintillate*. So do witty comments, charming personalities, and anything else that can be said to sparkle.

Warner was a quiet drudge at home, but at a party he could be absolutely *scintillating*, tossing off witty remarks and charming everyone in the room.

Benny's grades last term weren't *scintillating*, to put it mildly; he had four Ds and an F.

The act of *scintillating* is called *scintillation*.

SCRUPULOUS (SKROO pyuh lus) *adj* strict; careful; hesitant for ethical reasons

Doug was *scrupulous* in keeping his accounts; he knew where every penny came from and where every penny went.

We tried to be *scrupulous* about not dripping paint, but by the time the day was over there was nearly as much paint on the floor as there was on the walls.

Philip was too *scrupulous* to make a good armed robber; every time he started to point his gun at someone, he was overcome by ethical doubts.

A *scruple* is a qualm or moral doubt. To have no *scruples*—to be *unscrupulous*—is to have no conscience.

SCRUTINIZE (SKROOT uh NIZE) *v* to examine very carefully

I *scrutinized* the card catalog at the library but couldn't find a single book on the topic I had chosen for my term paper.

The rocket scientists *scrutinized* thousands of pages of computer printouts, looking for a clue to why the rocket had exploded.

My mother *scrutinized* my clothes and my appearance before I left for the evening, but even after several minutes of careful analysis she was unable to find anything to complain about.

To *scrutinize* something is to subject it to *scrutiny*. The clever forgery fooled the museum curator but did not withstand the *scrutiny* of the experts; after studying for several weeks, the experts pronounced the painting to be a fake.

Something that cannot be examined is *inscrutable*. *Inscrutable* means mysterious, impossible to understand. We had no idea what Bill was thinking since his smile was *inscrutable*. Poker players try to be *inscrutable* to their opponents.

SECULAR (SEK yuh lur) *adj* having nothing to do with religion or spiritual concerns

The halfway house had several nuns on its staff, but it was an entirely *secular* operation; it was run by the city, not the church.

The priest's *secular* interests include German food and playing the trombone.

SEDITION (si DISH un) *n* treason; the incitement of public disorder or rebellion

Revolutions usually begin as a small band of *seditious* individuals plot to change the established order.

SENSORY (SEN suh ree) *adj* having to do with the senses or sensation

Babies enjoy bright colors, moving objects, pleasant sounds, and other forms of *sensory* stimulation.

Your ears, eyes, and tongue are all *sensory* organs. It is through them that your senses operate.

Extrasensory perception is the supposed ability of some people to perceive things without using the standard *senses* of sight, hearing, smell, touch, or taste.

Two similar-sounding and often confusing words are *sensual* and *sensuous*. To be *sensual* is to be devoted to gratifying one's senses through physical pleasure, especially sexual pleasure; to be *sensuous* is to delight the senses. A *sensual* person is one who eagerly indulges his or her physical desires. A *sensuous* person is one who stimulates the senses of others (sometimes, though by no means invariably, inspiring in them thoughts of *sensual* gratification).

SENTIENT (SEN shunt) *adj* able to perceive by the senses; conscious

Human beings are *sentient*. Rocks are not.

SEQUESTER (si KWES tur) *v* to set or keep apart

Since much of the rest of the city had become a battle zone, the visiting entertainers were *sequestered* in the international hotel.

The struggling writer *sequestered* himself in his study for several months, trying to produce the Great American Novel.

Juries are sometimes *sequestered* during trials to prevent them from talking to people or reading newspapers.

Q·U·I·C·K · Q·U·I·Z #76

Match each word in the first column with its definition in the second column. Check your answers in the back of the book.

1. scintillate
2. scrupulous
3. scrutinize
4. secular
5. sedition
6. sensory
7. sensual
8. sensuous
9. sentient
10. sequester

a. sparkle
b. having nothing to do with religion
c. treason
d. having to do with the senses
e. set apart
f. strict
g. delighting the senses
h. examine very carefully
i. devoted to pleasure
j. conscious

SERENDIPITY (SER un DEP i tee) *n* accidental good fortune; discovering good things without looking for them

It was *serendipity* rather than genius that led the archaeologist to his breathtaking discovery of the ancient civilization. While walking his dog in the desert, he tripped over the top of a buried tomb.

Something that occurs through *serendipity* is *serendipitous*. Our arrival at the airport *serendipitously* coincided with that of the Queen, and she offered us a ride to our hotel in her carriage.

SERVILE (SUR vil) *adj* submissive and subservient; like a servant

Cat lovers sometimes say that dogs are too *servile;* they follow their owners everywhere and slobber all over them at every opportunity.

The horrible boss demanded *servility* from his employees; when he said, "Jump!" he expected them to ask, "How high?"

A very similar word is *slavish* (SLAY vish), which means even more subservient than *servile. Slavish* devotion to a cause is devotion in spite of everything. An artist's *slavish* imitator would be an imitator who imitated everything about the artist.

SINGULAR (SING gyuh lur) *adj* unique; superior; exceptional; strange

Dale had the *singular* ability to stand on one big toe for several hours at a stretch.

The man on the train had a *singular* deformity: both of his ears were on the same side of his head.

A *singularity* is a unique occurrence. *Singularity* is also the quality of being unique.

SLANDER (SLAN dur) *v* to speak badly about someone publicly; to defame; to spread malicious rumor

Jonathan *slandered* Mr. Perriwinkle by telling everyone in school that the principal wore a toupee; Mr. Perriwinkle resented this *slander*. Since he was the principal, he expelled the *slanderous* student.

SLOTH (slawth) *n* laziness; sluggishness

You may have seen a picture of an animal called a *sloth*. It hangs upside down from tree limbs and is never in a hurry to do anything. To fall into *sloth* is to act like a *sloth*.

Ivan's weekends were devoted to *sloth*. He never arose before noon, and he seldom left the house before Monday morning.

To be lazy and sluggish is to be *slothful*. Ophelia's *slothful* husband virtually lived on the couch in the living room, and the television remote-control device was in danger of becoming grafted to his hand.

SOBRIETY (suh BRYE i tee) *n* the state of being *sober;* seriousness

A *sober* person is a person who isn't drunk. A *sober* person can also be a person who is serious, solemn, or not ostentatious. *Sobriety* means both "undrunkness" and seriousness or solemnity.

Sobriety was such an unfamiliar condition that the reforming alcoholic didn't recognize it at first.

Sobriety of dress is one characteristic of the hardworking Amish.

SOLICITOUS (suh LIS i tus) *adj* eager and attentive, often to the point of hovering; anxiously caring or attentive

Every time we turned around, we seemed to step on the foot of the *solicitous* salesman, who appeared to feel that if he left us alone for more than a few seconds we would decide to leave the store.

When the sick movie star sneezed, half a dozen *solicitous* nurses came rushing into his hospital room.

SOLVENT (SOL vent) *adj* not broke or bankrupt; able to pay one's bills

Jerry didn't hope to become a millionaire; all he wanted to do was remain *solvent*.

The struggling company was battered but still *solvent* after it paid its billion-dollar fine for selling exploding Christmas ornaments.

To be broke is to be *insolvent*. An *insolvent* company is one that can't cover its debts.

The state of being *solvent* is called *solvency;* the state of being *insolvent* is called *insolvency*.

SOPORIFIC (SOP uh RIF ik) *adj* sleep inducing; extremely boring; very sleepy

The doctor calmed his hysterical patient by injecting him with some sort of *soporific* medication.

Sam's *soporific* address was acknowledged not by applause but by a chorus of snores.

The *soporific* creature from the bottom of the sea lay in a gigantic blob on the beach for several days, and then roused itself enough to consume the panic-stricken city.

Q·U·I·C·K · Q·U·I·Z #77

Match each word in the first column with its definition in the second column. Check your answers in the back of the book.

1. serendipity		a.	accidental good fortune
2. servile		b.	sleep-inducing
3. singular		c.	eager and attentive
4. slavish		d.	not bankrupt
5. sloth		e.	submissive
6. sobriety		f.	broke
7. solicitous		g.	laziness
8. solvent		h.	state of being sober
9. insolvent		i.	extremely subservient
10. soporific		j.	unique

SORDID (SAWR did) *adj* vile; filthy; squalid

The college roommates led a *sordid* existence whose principal ingredients were dirty laundry, rotting garbage, and body odor.

The conspirators plotted their *sordid* schemes at a series of secret meetings in an abandoned warehouse.

The drug dealers had turned a once-pretty neighborhood into a *sordid* outpost of despair and crime.

SPAWN (spawn) *v* to bring forth; to produce a large number

A best-selling book or blockbuster movie will *spawn* dozens of imitators.

SPECIOUS (SPEE shus) *adj* deceptively plausible or attractive

The charlatan's *specious* theories about curing baldness with used teabags charmed the television studio audience but did not convince the experts, who believed that fresh teabags were more effective.

The river's beauty turned out to be *specious;* what had looked like churning rapids from a distance was, on closer inspection, some sort of foamy industrial waste.

· To be *specious* is to be characterized by *speciousness.*

SPORADIC (spoh RAD ik) *adj* stopping and starting; scattered; occurring in bursts every once in a while

The bathers were made jittery by *sporadic* gunfire that peppered the beach.

Kyle's attention to his schoolwork was *sporadic* at best; he tended to lose his concentration after a few minutes of effort.

SPURIOUS (SPYOOR ee us) *adj* false; fake

An apocryphal story is one whose truth is uncertain. A *spurious* story, however, is out and out false, no doubt about it. The political candidate attributed his loss to numerous *spurious* rumors that hounded him throughout his campaign.

SQUALOR (SKWOL ur) *n* filth; wretched, degraded, or repulsive living conditions

If people live in *squalor* for too long, the ruling elite can count on an insurgency.

SQUANDER (SKWON dur) *v* to waste

Jerry failed to husband his inheritance; instead, he *squandered* it on stuffed toys.

STAGNATION (stag NAY shun) *n* motionlessness; inactivity

The company grew quickly for several years, then fell into *stagnation*.

Many years of carelessly dumping pollutants led to the gradual *stagnation* of the river.

To fall into *stagnation* is to *stagnate*. To be in a state of *stagnation* is to be *stagnant*.

STATIC (STAT ik) *adj* stationary; not changing or moving

Sales of the new book soared for a few weeks, then became *static*.

The movie was supposed to be a thriller, but we found it to be tediously *static;* nothing seemed to happen from one scene to the next.

STAUNCH (STAWNCH) *adj* firmly committed; firmly in favor of; steadfast

A *staunch* Republican is someone who always votes for Republican candidates. A *staunch* supporter of tax reform would be someone who firmly believes in tax reform. To be *staunch* in your support of something is to be unshakable.

STEADFAST (STED fast) *adj* loyal; faithful

Steadfast love is love that never wavers. To be *steadfast* in a relationship is to be faithfully committed. To be *steadfast* is to be like a rock: unchanging, unwavering, unmoving.

STIGMATIZE (STIG muh TIZE) *v* to brand with disgrace; to set a mark of disgrace upon

Steve's jeans were Lee's instead of Levi's, and this mistake *stigmatized* him for the rest of his high school career.

STIPULATE (STIP yuh LATE) *v* to require something as part of an agreement

You are well advised to *stipulate* the maximum amount you will pay in any car-repair contract.

Guarantees often *stipulate* certain conditions that must be met if the guarantee is to be valid.

STOIC (STOH ik) *adj* indifferent (at least outwardly) to pleasure or pain, to joy or grief, to fortune or misfortune

Nina was *stoic* about the death of her canary; she went about her business as though nothing sad had happened.

We tried to be *stoic* about our defeat, but as soon as we got into the locker room, we all began to cry and bang our foreheads on the floor.

STRATUM (STRAT um, STRAY tum) *n* a layer; a level

The middle class is one *stratum* of society.

The plural of *stratum* is *strata*. A hierarchy is composed of *strata*.

To *stratify* is to make into layers.

STRICTURE (STRIK chur) *n* a restriction; a limitation; a negative criticism

Despite the *strictures* of apartment living, we enjoyed the eight years we spent in New York City.

The unfavorable lease placed many *strictures* on how the building could be used.

The poorly prepared violinist went home trembling after his concert to await the inevitable *strictures* of the reviewers.

Q·U·I·C·K · Q·U·I·Z #78

Match each word in the first column with its definition in the second column. Check your answers in the back of the book.

1. sordid		a. disgrace
2. spawn		b. stopping and starting
3. specious		c. restriction
4. sporadic		d. inactivity
5. spurious		e. require
6. squander		f. indifferent to pain, pleasure
7. stagnation		g. bring forth
8. static		h. vile
9. staunch		i. firmly committed (2)
10. steadfast		j. layer
11. stigmatize		k. stationary
12. stipulate		l. deceptively plausible
13. stoic		m. false
14. stratum		n. waste
15. stricture		

STRIFE (strife) *n* bitter conflict; discord; a struggle or clash

Marital *strife* often leads to divorce.

STRINGENT (STRIN junt) *adj* strict; restrictive

The restaurant's *stringent* dress code required diners to wear paper hats, army boots, and battery-operated twirling bow ties.

The IRS accountant was quite *stringent* in his interpretation of the tax code; he disallowed virtually all of Leslie's deductions.

STYMIE (STYE mee) *v* to thwart; to get in the way of; to hinder

Stymie is a golfing term. A golfer is *stymied* when another player's ball lies on the direct path between his or her own ball and the cup.

Off the golf course, one might be *stymied* by one's boss: In my effort to make a name for myself in the company, I was *stymied* by my boss, who always managed to take credit for all the good things I did and to blame me for his mistakes.

SUBJUGATE (SUB juh GATE) *v* to subdue and dominate; to enslave

I bought the fancy riding lawn mower because I thought it would make my life easier, but it quickly *subjugated* me; all summer long, it seems, I did nothing but change its oil, sharpen its blades, and drive it back and forth between my house and the repair shop.

The tyrant *subjugated* all the peasants living in the kingdom; once free, they were now forced to do his bidding.

SUBLIME (suh BLIME) *adj* awesome; extremely exalted; lofty; majestic

After winning $70 million in the lottery and quitting our jobs as sewer workers, our happiness was *sublime*.

Theodore was a *sublime* thinker; after pondering even a difficult problem for just a few minutes, he would invariably arrive at a concise and elegant solution.

The soup at the restaurant was *sublime*. I've never tasted anything so good in my life.

The noun form of *sublime* is *sublimity* (suh BLIM i tee). Don't confuse *sublime* with *subliminal*, which means subconscious, or *sublimate*, which means to suppress one's subconscious mind.

SUBORDINATE (suh BAWR duh nit) *adj* lower in importance, position, or rank; secondary

My desire to sit on the couch and watch television all night long was *subordinate* to my desire to stand in the kitchen eating junk food all night long, so I did the latter instead of the former.

A vice president is *subordinate* to a president.

Subordinate (suh BAWR duh NATE) can also be a verb. To *subordinate* something in relation to something else is to make it secondary or less important.

To be *insubordinate* (in suh BAWR duh nit) is not to acknowledge the authority of a superior. An army private who says "Bug off!" when ordered to do something by a general is guilty of being *insubordinate* or of committing an act of *insubordination*.

SUBSTANTIVE (SUB stan tiv) *adj* having *substance*; real; essential; solid; *substantial*

The differences between the two theories were not *substantive;* in fact, the two theories said the same thing with different words.

The gossip columnist's wild accusations were not based on anything *substantive;* her source was a convicted criminal, and she had made up all the quotations.

SUBTLE (SUT ul) *adj* not obvious; able to make fine distinctions; ingenious; crafty

The alien beings had created a very shrewd replica of Mr. Jenson, but his wife did notice a few *subtle* differences, including the fact that the new Mr. Jenson had no pulse or internal organs.

Joe's *subtle* mind enables him to see past problems that confuse the rest of us.

The burglar was very *subtle;* he had come up with a plan that would enable him to steal all the money in the world without arousing the suspicions of the authorities.

Something *subtle* is a *subtlety.*

SUBVERSIVE (sub VUR siv) *adj* corrupting; overthrowing; undermining; insurgent

The political group planted bombs in the White House, destroyed the Pentagon's computer files, hijacked Air Force One, and engaged in various other *subversive* activities.

Madeline's efforts to teach her first-grade students to read were thwarted by that most *subversive* of inventions, the television set.

SUCCINCT (suk SINGKT) *adj* brief and to the point; concise

Harry's *succinct* explanation of why the moon doesn't fall out of the sky and crash into the earth quickly satisfied even the dullest of the anxious investment bankers.

We were given so little room in which to write on the examination that we had no choice but to keep our essays *succinct.*

Q·U·I·C·K · Q·U·I·Z · #79

Match each word in the first column with its definition in the second column. Check your answers in the back of the book.

1. strife	a.	not obvious
2. stringent	b.	awesome
3. stymie	c.	brief and to the point
4. subjugate	d.	thwart
5. sublime	e.	subdue
6. subordinate	f.	corrupting
7. insubordinate	g.	not respectful of authority
8. substantive	h.	strict
9. subtle	i.	lower in importance
10. subversive	j.	having substance
11. succinct	k.	bitter conflict

SUCCUMB (suh KUM) *v* to yield or submit; to die

I had said I wasn't going to eat anything at the party, but when Ann held the tray of imported chocolates under my nose, I quickly *succumbed* and ate all of them.

The Martians in *The War of the Worlds* survived every military weapon known to man but *succumbed* to the common cold.

When Willard reached the age of 110, his family began to think that he would live forever, but he *succumbed* not long afterwards.

SUPERCILIOUS (SOO pur SIL ee us) *adj* haughty; patronizing

The *supercilious* Rolls-Royce salesman treated us like peasants until we opened our suitcase full of one-hundred-dollar bills.

The newly famous author was so *supercilious* that he pretended not to recognize members of his own family, whom he now believed to be beneath him.

SUPERFICIAL (SOO pur FISH ul) *adj* on the surface only; shallow; not thorough

Tom had indeed been shot, but the wound was *superficial;* the bullet had merely creased the tip of his nose.

The mechanic, who was in a hurry, gave my car what appeared to be a very *superficial* tune-up. In fact, if he checked the oil, he did it without opening the hood.

A person who is *superficial* can be accused of *superficiality.* The *superficiality* of the editor's comments made us think that he hadn't really read the manuscript.

SUPERFLUOUS (soo PUR floo us) *adj* extra; unnecessary; redundant

Andrew's attempt to repair the light bulb was *superfluous*, since the light bulb had already been repaired.

Roughly 999 of the 1,000-page book's pages were *superfluous*.

SURFEIT (SUR fit) *n* excess; an excessive amount; excess or overindulgence in eating or drinking

Thanksgiving meals are usually a *surfeit* for everyone involved.

SURREPTITIOUS (SUR up TISH us) *adj* sneaky; secret

The dinner guest *surreptitiously* slipped a few silver spoons into his jacket as he was leaving the dining room.

The baby-sitter mixed herself a *surreptitious* cocktail as soon as Mr. and Mrs. Robinson had driven away.

SURROGATE (SUR uh GATE, SUR uh GIT) *adj* substitute

A *surrogate* mother is a woman who bears a child for someone else.

This word is often a noun. A *surrogate* is a substitute. The nice father offered to go to prison as a surrogate for his son, who had been convicted of extortion.

SYCOPHANT (SIK uh funt) *n* one who sucks up to others

The French class seemed to be full of *sycophants;* the students were always bringing apples to the teacher and telling her how nice she looked.

A *sycophant* is *sycophantic.* The exasperated boss finally fired his *sycophantic* secretary because he couldn't stand being around someone who never had anything nasty to say.

SYNTHESIS (SIN thi sis) *n* the combining of parts to form a whole

It seemed as though the meeting might end in acrimony and confusion until Raymond offered his brilliant *synthesis* of the two diverging points of view.

A hot fudge sundae is the perfect *synthesis* of hot fudge and vanilla ice cream.

Q·U·I·C·K · Q·U·I·Z #80

Match each word in the first column with its definition in the second column. Check your answers in the back of the book.

1.	succumb	a.	haughty
2.	supercilious	b.	yield
3.	superficial	c.	flatterer
4.	superfluous	d.	substitute
5.	surfeit	e.	unnecessary
6.	surreptitious	f.	on the surface only
7.	surrogate	g.	sneaky
8.	sycophant	h.	excess

T

TACIT (TAS it) *adj* implied; not spoken

Mrs. Rodgers never formally asked us to murder her husband, but we truly believed that we were acting with her *tacit* consent.

There was *tacit* agreement among the men that women had no business at their weekly poker game.

TACITURN (TAS i TURN) *adj* untalkative by nature

The chairman was so *taciturn* that we often discovered that we had absolutely no idea what he was thinking.

The *taciturn* physicist was sometimes thought to be brilliant simply because no one had ever heard him say anything stupid. Everyone miscontrued his *taciturnity;* he was actually quite stupid. *Taciturn* is related to *tacit*.

TANGENTIAL (tan JEN schul) *adj* only superficially related to the matter at hand; not especially relevant; peripheral

The mayor's speech bore only a *tangential* relationship to the topic that had been announced.

Stuart's connection with our organization is *tangential;* he once made a phone call from the lobby of our building, but he never worked here.

When a writer or speaker "goes off on a *tangent*," he or she is making a digression or straying from the original topic.

TANGIBLE (TAN juh bul) *adj* touchable; palpable

A mountain of cigarette butts was the only *tangible* evidence that Luther had been in our house.

There was no *tangible* reason I could point to, but I did have a sneaking suspicion that Ernest was an ax murderer.

TANTAMOUNT (TAN tuh MOUNT) *adj* equivalent to

Waving a banner for the visiting team at that football game would be *tantamount* to committing suicide; the home-team fans would tear you apart in a minute.

Yvonne's method of soliciting donations from her employees was *tantamount* to extortion; she clearly implied that she would fire them if they didn't pitch in.

TAUTOLOGICAL (TAWT uh LOG i kul) *adj* redundant; circular

"When everyone has a camera, cameras will be universal" is a *tautological* statement, because "everyone having a camera" and "cameras being universal" mean the same thing.

The testing company's definition of intelligence—"that which is measured by intelligence tests"—is *tautological*.

A *tautology* is a needless repetition of words, or saying the same thing using different words. For example: The trouble with bachelors is that they aren't married.

TEMERITY (tuh MER i tee) *n* boldness; recklessness; audacity

Our waiter at the restaurant had the *temerity* to tell me he thought my table manners were atrocious.

The mountain climber had more *temerity* than skill or sense. He tried to climb a mountain that was much too difficult and ended up in a heap at the bottom.

TEMPERATE (TEM pur it) *adj* mild; moderate; restrained

Our climate is *temperate* during the spring and fall, but very nearly unbearable during the summer and winter.

The teacher's *temperate* personality lent a feeling of calm and control to the kindergarten class.

The opposite of *temperate* is *intemperate*, which means not moderate. Bucky's intemperate use of oregano ruined the chili.

To *temper* something is to make it milder. Wilma laughed and shrieked so loudly at every joke that even the comedian wished she would *temper* her appreciation.

TENABLE (TEN uh bul) *adj* defensible, as in one's position in an argument; capable of being argued successfully; valid

Members of the Flat Earth Society continue to argue that the earth is flat, although even children dismiss their arguments as not *tenable*.

TENACIOUS (tuh NAY shus) *adj* persistent; stubborn; not letting go

The foreign student's *tenacious* effort to learn English won him the admiration of all the teachers at our school.

Louise's grasp of geometry was not *tenacious*. She could handle the simpler problems most of the time, but she fell apart on quizzes and tests.

The ivy growing on the side of our house was so *tenacious* that we had to tear the house down to get rid of it.

To be *tenacious* is to have *tenacity* (tuh NAS uh tee).

Q·U·I·C·K · Q·U·I·Z #81

Match each word in the first column with its definition in the second column. Check your answers in the back of the book.

1.	tacit	a.	persistent
2.	taciturn	b.	naturally untalkative
3.	tangential	c.	boldness
4.	tangible	d.	equivalent to
5.	tantamount	e.	not deeply relevant
6.	tautological	f.	redundant
7.	temerity	g.	mild
8.	temperate	h.	defensible
9.	tenable	i.	implied
10.	tenacious	j.	touchable

TENET (TEN it) *n* a shared principle or belief

One of the most important *tenets* of our form of government is that people can be trusted to govern themselves.

The *tenets* of his religion prevented him from dancing and going to movies.

TENTATIVE (TEN tuh tiv) *adj* experimental; temporary; uncertain

George made a *tentative* effort to paint his house by himself; he slapped some paint on the front door and his clothes, tipped over the bucket, and called a professional.

Our plans for the party are *tentative* at this point, but we are considering hiring a troupe of accordionists to play polkas while our guests are eating dessert.

Hugo believed himself to be a great wit, but his big joke was rewarded by nothing more than a very *tentative* chuckle from his audience.

TENUOUS (TEN yoo us) *adj* flimsy; extremely thin

The organization's financial situation has always been *tenuous;* the balance of the checking account is usually close to zero.

The hostess's *tenuous* gown, which had been made from a sheet of clear plastic, certainly made her popular with her male guests.

To *attenuate* is to make thin. *Extenuating* circumstances are those that lessen the magnitude of something, especially a crime. Percy admitted that he stole the Cracker Jacks but claimed that there were *extenuating* circumstances: He had no money to buy food for his pet armadillo.

TERSE (turs) *adj* using no unnecessary words; succinct

The new recording secretary's minutes were so *terse* that they were occasionally cryptic.

Terseness is not one of Rex's virtues; he would talk until the crack of doom if someone didn't stop him.

THEOLOGY (thee OL uh jee) *n* the study of god or religion
Ralph was a paradox: He was an atheist yet he passionately studied *theology*.

TIRADE (TYE rade) *n* prolonged, bitter speech
Percival launched into a *tirade* against imitation cheese on the school lunch menu.

TORPOR (TAWR pur) *n* sluggishness; inactivity; apathy
After consuming the guinea pig, the boa constrictor fell into a state of contented *torpor* that lasted several days.
The math teacher tried to reduce the *torpor* of his students by setting off a few firecrackers on his desk, but the students scarcely blinked.
To be in a state of *torpor* is to be *torpid*.

TOUCHSTONE (TUCH STONE) *n* a standard; a test of authenticity or quality
In its original usage, a *touchstone* was a dark stone against which gold and other precious metals were rubbed in order to test their purity. Now the word is used more loosely to describe a broad range of standards and tests.
The size of a student's vocabulary is a useful *touchstone* for judging the quality of his or her education.
A candidate's pronouncements about the economy provided a *touchstone* by which his or her fitness for office could be judged.

TOUT (tout) *v* to praise highly; to brag publicly about
Advertisements *touted* the chocolate-flavored toothpaste as getting rid of your sweet tooth while saving your teeth.

TRANSCEND (tran SEND) *v* to go beyond or above; to surpass
The man who claimed to have invented a perpetual motion machine believed that he had *transcended* the laws of physics.
The basketball player was so skillful that he seemed to have *transcended* the sport altogether; he was so much better than his teammates that he seemed to be playing an entirely different game.
To be *transcendent* is to be surpassing or preeminent. Something *transcendent* is *transcendental*.

TRANSGRESS (trans GRES) *v* to violate (a law); to sin
The other side had *transgressed* so many provisions of the treaty that we had no choice but to go to war.
We tried as hard as we could not to transgress their elaborate rules, but they had so many prohibitions that we couldn't keep track of all of them.
An act of *transgressing* is a *transgression*. The bully's innumerable *transgressions* included breaking all the windows in the new gymnasium and pushing several first graders off the jungle gym.

TRANSIENT (TRAN shunt) *adj* not staying for a long time; temporary
The transient breeze provided some relief from the summer heat, but we were soon perspiring again.

The child's smile was *transient;* it disappeared as soon as the candy bar was gone.

A hotel's inhabitants are *transient;* they come and go and the population changes every night.

Transient can also be a noun. A *transient* person is sometimes called a *transient.* Hoboes, mendicants, and other homeless people are often called *transients.*

A very similar word is *transitory,* which means not lasting very long. A *transient* breeze might provide *transitory* relief from the heat. The breeze didn't stay very long; the relief didn't last very long.

TREPIDATION (TREP i DAY shun) *n* fear; apprehension; nervous trembling

The nursery school students were filled with *trepidation* when they saw the other children in their class dressed in their Halloween costumes.

The *trepidation* of the swimming team was readily apparent: their knees were knocking as they lined up along the edge of the pool.

To be fearless is to be *intrepid.* The *intrepid* captain sailed his ship around the world with only a handkerchief for a sail.

TURPITUDE (TUR pi TOOD) *n* shameful wickedness; depravity

Larry was sacked by his boss because of a flagrant act of *turpitude:* He slept with the boss's wife.

Q·U·I·C·K · Q·U·I·Z #82

Match each word in the first column with its definition in the second column. Check your answers in the back of the book.

1. tenet		a.	without unnecessary words
2. tentative		b.	go beyond
3. tenuous		c.	brag publicly about
4. terse		d.	fearless
5. torpor		e.	experimental
6. theology		f.	not lasting long (2)
7. tirade		g.	bitter speech
8. touchstone		h.	shared principle
9. tout		i.	wickedness
10. transcend		j.	sluggishness
11. transgress		k.	flimsy
12. transient		l.	fear
13. transitory		m.	study of religion
14. trepidation		n.	standard
15. intrepid		o.	violate
16. turpitude			

U

UBIQUITOUS (yoo BIK wi tus) *adj* being everywhere at the same time

The new beer commercial was *ubiquitous*—it seemed to be on every television channel at once.

Personal computers, once a rarity, have become *ubiquitous*.

To be *ubiquitous* is to be characterized by *ubiquity*. The *ubiquity* of fast-food restaurants is one of the more depressing features of American culture.

UNCONSCIONABLE (un KON shuh nuh bul) *adj* not controlled by conscience; unscrupulous

Leaving a small child unattended all day long is an *unconscionable* act.

Murdering every citizen of that town was *unconscionable*. Bert should be ashamed of himself for doing it.

Don't confuse this word with *unconscious*.

UNCTUOUS (UNGK choo us) *adj* oily, both literally and figuratively; insincere

Salad oil is literally *unctuous*. A used-car salesman might be figuratively *unctuous*—that is, oily in the sense of being slick, sleazy, and insincere.

UNIFORM (YOO ni FAWRM) *adj* consistent; unchanging; the same for everyone

Traffic laws are similar from one state to the next, but they aren't *uniform*; each state has its own variations.

The school did not have a *uniform* grading policy; each teacher was free to mark students according to any system that he or she thought appropriate.

Something that is *uniform* has *uniformity*.

Uniforms are suits of clothing that are *uniform* in appearance from one person to the next.

UNREMITTING (UN ri MIT ing) *adj* unceasing; unabated; relentless

Superman waged an *unremitting* battle against evildoers everywhere.

UNWITTING (un WIT ing) *adj* unintentional; ignorant; not aware

When Leo agreed to hold open the door of the bank, he became an *unwitting* accomplice to the bank robbery.

My theft was *unwitting;* I hadn't meant to steal the car, but had unintentionally driven it away from the automobile dealership and parked it in my garage.

On the camping trip, Josephine *unwittingly* stepped into a bear trap and remained stuck in it for several days.

URBANE (ur BANE) *adj* poised; sophisticated; refined

The British count was witty and *urbane;* all the hosts and hostesses wanted to have him at their parties.

The new magazine was far too *urbane* to appeal to a wide audience outside of the big city.

Urbanity is a quality more often acquired in an *urban* setting than in a rural one.

USURP (yoo SURP) *v* to seize wrongfully

The children believed that their mother's new boyfriend had *usurped* their real father's rightful place in their family.

The founder's scheming young nephew *usurped* a position of power in the company.

UTILITARIAN (yoo TIL i TAIR ee un) *adj* stressing usefulness or *utility* above all other qualities; pragmatic

Jason's interior-decorating philosophy was strictly *utilitarian;* if an object wasn't genuinely useful, he didn't want it in his home.

Utilitarian can also be a noun. Jason, just mentioned, could be called a *utilitarian.*

UTOPIA (yoo TOH pee uh) *n* an ideal society

A country where nobody had to work and Monday Night Football was on television every night would be Quentin's idea of *utopia.*

The little town wasn't just a nice place to live, as far as Ed was concerned; it was *utopia.*

A *utopian* is someone with unrealistic or impractical plans or expectations for society. Such plans or expectations are *utopian* plans or expectations.

Q·U·I·C·K · Q·U·I·Z #83

Match each word in the first column with its definition in the second column. Check your answers in the back of the book.

1. ubiquitous   a. oily
2. unconscionable   b. poised and sophisticated
3. unctuous   c. everywhere at once
4. uniform   d. pragmatic
5. unremitting   e. seize wrongfully
6. unwitting   f. unscrupulous
7. urbane   g. an ideal society
8. usurp   h. unintentional
9. utilitarian   i. consistent
10. utopia   j. unceasing

V

VACILLATE (VAS uh LATE) *v* to be indecisive; to waver

We invited James to spend Thanksgiving with us, but he *vacillated* for so long about whether he would be able to come that we finally became annoyed and disinvited him.

Tyler *vacillated* about buying a new car. He couldn't decide whether to get one or not.

The act of *vacillating* is called *vacillation*.

VAPID (VAP id) *adj* without liveliness; dull; spiritless

An apathetic person just doesn't care about anything, and everything he does is *vapid*.

The novelist's prose was so *vapid* that Mary couldn't get beyond the first page.

VEHEMENT (VEE uh munt) *adj* intense; forceful; violent

Shaking his fist and stomping his foot, Gerry was *vehement* in his denial.

VENAL (VEEN ul) *adj* capable of being bribed; willing to do anything for money; corrupt

The *venal* judge reversed his favorable ruling when the defendant refused to make good on his promised bribe.

The young man's interest in helping the sick old woman was strictly *venal;* he figured that if he was kind to her, she would leave him a lot of money in her will.

A *venal* person is a person characterized by *venality*.

Don't confuse this word with *venial*, which means trivial or pardonable. A peccadillo is a *venial*, harmless sin.

VENERATE (VEN uh RATE) *v* to revere; to treat as something holy, especially because of great age

Lester *venerated* his grandfather; he worshipped the very ground the old man limped on.

The members of the curious religion *venerated* Elvis Presley and hoped that the Pope would declare him a saint.

A person who is worthy of being *venerated* is said to be *venerable*.

VERACITY (vuh RAS i tee) *n* truthfulness

The *veracity* of young George Washington is legendary, but it may be apocryphal.

VERBOSE (vur BOHS) *adj* using too many words; not succinct; circumlocutory

Someone who is *verbose* uses too many words when fewer words would suffice. Lee handed in a 178-word final assignment; no one ever accused him of *verbosity*.

VERISIMILITUDE (VER i si MIL i TOOD) *n* similarity to reality; the appearance of truth; looking like the real thing

They used pinecones and old truck tires to make statues of Hollywood celebrities that were remarkable for their *verisimilitude*.

The *verisimilitude* of counterfeit eleven-dollar bills did not fool the eagle-eyed treasury officer, who recognized them immediately for what they were.

VERNACULAR (vur NAK yuh lur) *n* everyday speech; slang; idiom

Our teacher said that we should save our *vernacular* for the street; in the classroom we should use proper grammar.

VESTIGE (VES tij) *n* a remaining bit of something; a last trace

The unhappy young man found *vestiges* of his fiancée in the rubble, but the explosion had effectively ended their romance.

An old uniform and a tattered scrapbook were the only *vestiges* of the old man's career as a professional athlete.

Your appendix is a *vestige*: It used to have a function, but now this organ does nothing.

The adjective form of *vestige* is *vestigial*. The appendix is referred to as a *vestigial* organ. It is still in our bodies, although it no longer has a function. It is a mere *vestige* of some function our digestive systems no longer perform.

VEX (veks) *v* to annoy, to pester; to confuse

Margaret *vexed* me by poking me with a long, sharp stick.

Stuck at the bottom of a deep well, I found my situation extremely *vexing*.

The act of *vexing*, or the state of being *vexed*, is *vexation*. Both the person who *vexes* and the person who is *vexed* can be said to exhibit *vexation*.

VIABLE (VYE uh bul) *adj* capable of living; workable

When a doctor says that a patient is no longer *viable*, it's time to begin planning a funeral.

A fetus is said to be *viable* when it has developed to the point where it is capable of surviving outside the womb.

Harry's plan for storing marshmallows in the dome of the Capitol just wasn't *viable*.

Something that is *viable* has *viability*.

VICARIOUS (vye KAIR ee us) *adj* experienced, performed, or suffered through someone else; living through the experiences of another as though they were one's own experiences

To take *vicarious* pleasure in someone else's success is to enjoy that person's success as though it were your own.

We all felt a *vicarious* thrill when the mayor's daughter won fourth prize in the regional kick-boxing competition.

VICISSITUDE (vi SIS i TOOD) *n* upheaval; natural change; change in fortune

The *vicissitudes* of the stock market were too much for Penny; she decided to look for a job that would stay the same from one day to the next.

The *vicissitudes* of the local political machine were such that one could never quite be certain whom one was supposed to bribe.

VILIFY (VIL uh FYE) *v* to say vile things about; to defame

The teacher was reprimanded for *vilifying* the slow student in front of the rest of the class.

Our taxi driver paused briefly on the way to the airport in order to *vilify* the driver of the car that had nearly forced him off the road.

The political debate was less a debate than a *vilification* contest. At first the candidates took turns saying nasty things about each other; then they stopped taking turns.

Q·U·I·C·K · Q·U·I·Z #84

Match each word in the first column with its definition in the second column. Check your answers in the back of the book.

1. vacillate	a. annoy
2. vapid	b. be indecisive
3. vehement	c. defame
4. venal	d. capable of living
5. venerate	e. experienced through another
6. veracity	f. dull
7. verbose	g. upheaval
8. verisimilitude	h. revere
9. vernacular	i. last trace
10. vestige	j. similarity to reality
11. vex	k. truthfulness
12. viable	l. corrupt
13. vicarious	m. wordy
14. vicissitudes	n. slang
15. vilify	o. intense

VINDICATE (VIN duh KATE) *v* to clear from all blame or suspicion; to justify

Tony, having been accused of stealing money from the cash register, was *vindicated* when the store manager counted the money again and found that none was missing after all.

Inez's claim of innocence appeared to be *vindicated* when several dozen inmates at the state mental hospital confessed to the crime of which she had been accused.

A person who has been *vindicated* is a person who has found *vindication*.

VINDICTIVE (vin DIK tiv) *adj* seeking revenge

Jeremy apologized for denting the fender of my car, but I was feeling *vindictive* so I filed a $30 million lawsuit against him.

Samantha's *vindictive* ex-husband drove all the way across the country just to punch her in the nose.

To feel *vindictive* is to be filled with *vindictiveness*.

VIRTUOSO (VUR choo OH soh) *n* a masterful musician; a masterful practitioner in some other field

The concert audience fell silent when the *virtuoso* stepped forward to play the sonata on his electric banjo.

As an artist, he was a *virtuoso;* as a husband, he was a chump.

Virtuoso can also be an adjective. A *virtuoso* performance is a performance worthy of a *virtuoso.*

VIRULENT (VIR uh lunt) *adj* extremely poisonous; malignant; full of hate

The *virulent* disease quickly swept through the community, leaving many people dead and many more people extremely ill.

The snake was a member of a particularly *virulent* breed; its bite could kill an elephant.

Jonathan is a *virulent* antifeminist; he says that all women should sit down and shut up and do what he tells them to.

To be *virulent* is to be characterized by *virulence. Virulent* is related to *virus,* not to *virile,* which means manly.

VISIONARY (VIZH uh NER ee) *n* a dreamer; someone with impractical goals or ideas about the future

My uncle was a *visionary,* not a businessman; he spent too much time tinkering with his antigravity generator and not enough time working in his plumbing business.

The candidate was a *visionary;* he had a lot of big ideas but no realistic plan for putting them into practice.

Visionary can also be an adjective. A *visionary* proposal is an idealistic and usually impractical proposal.

VITIATE (VISH ee ATE) *v* to make impure; to pollute

For years a zealous group of individuals has campaigned against the use of fluoride in water, claiming that it has *vitiated* our bodies as well as our morals.

Vitiate can be used figuratively.

VITRIOLIC (VI tree OL ik) *adj* caustic; full of bitterness

Vitriol is another name for sulfuric acid. To be *vitriolic* is to say or do something so nasty that your words or actions burn like acid.

The review of the new book was so *vitriolic* that we all wondered whether the reviewer had some personal grudge against the author.

VOCATION (voh KAY shun) *n* an occupation, a job

Your *vocation* is what you do for a living.

If Stan could figure out how to make a *vocation* out of watching television and eating potato chips, he would be one of the most successful people in the world.

Vocational training is job training.

Since your *vocation* is your job, your *avocation* is your hobby. The accountant's *vocation* bored her, but her *avocation* of mountain climbing did not.

VOCIFEROUS (voh SIF ur us) *adj* loud, noisy

Randy often becomes *vociferous* during arguments. He doesn't know what he believes but he states it loudly nevertheless.

VOLATILE (VOL uh tile) *adj* quick to evaporate; highly unstable; explosive

A *volatile* liquid is one that evaporates readily. Gasoline is a *volatile* liquid. It evaporates very readily, and then the vapor poses a great danger of explosion.

A *volatile* crowd is one that seems to be in imminent danger of getting out of control, or exploding.

The situation in the Middle East was highly *volatile;* the smallest incident could have set off a war.

To be *volatile* is to be characterized by *volatility.*

VOLITION (voh LISH un) *n* will; conscious choice

Insects, lacking *volition*, simply aren't as interesting as humans are.

The question the jury had to decide was whether the killing had been an accident or an act of *volition.*

Q·U·I·C·K · Q·U·I·Z · #85

Match each word in the first column with its definition in the second column. Check your answers in the back of the book.

1. vindicate	a. extremely poisonous
2. vindictive	b. masterful musician
3. virtuoso	c. dreamer
4. virulent	d. caustic
5. visionary	e. clear from suspicion
6. vitiate	f. will
7. vitriolic	g. quick to evaporate
8. vocation	h. seeking revenge
9. vociferous	i. occupation
10. volatile	j. make impure
11. volition	k. noisy

W

WANTON (WON tun) *adj* malicious; unjustifiable; unprovoked; egregious

Terrorists commit *wanton* acts on a helpless populace to make their point.

Wanton also means intemperate. A hedonist lives a *wanton* life in the relentless, unremitting pursuit of pleasure; an ascetic does not.

WILLFUL (WIL ful) *adj* deliberate; obstinate; insistent on having one's way

The mother insisted that the killing committed by her son had not been *willful*, but the jury apparently believed that he had known what he was doing.

When her mother told her she couldn't have a cookie, the *willful* little girl simply snatched the cookie jar and ran out of the room with it. She had stolen the cookies *willfully*.

WISTFUL (WIST ful) *adj* yearning; sadly longing

I felt *wistful* when I saw Herb's fancy new car. I wished that I had enough money to buy one for myself.

The boys who had been cut from the football team watched *wistfully* as the team put together an undefeated season and won the state championship.

Q·U·I·C·K · Q·U·I·Z #86

Match each word in the first column with its definition in the second column. Check your answers in the back of the book.

1. wanton   a. yearning
2. willful   b. deliberate
3. wistful   c. malicious

Z

ZEALOUS (ZEL us) *adj* enthusiastically devoted to something; fervent

The *zealous* young policeman made so many arrests that the city jail soon became overcrowded.

The dictator's followers were so *zealous* that if he had asked them all to jump off a cliff, most of them would have done so.

To be *zealous* is to be full of *zeal*, or fervent enthusiasm. An overly *zealous* person is a *zealot*.

THE ANSWERS

Quick Quiz #1
1. j
2. f
3. a
4. i
5. g
6. b
7. k
8. c
9. h
10. e
11. d

Quick Quiz #2
1. b
2. h
3. a
4. c
5. i
6. j
7. d
8. e
9. f
10. d
11. g

Quick Quiz #3
1. a
2. g
3. i
4. e
5. b
6. d
7. f

8. f
9. c
10. h

Quick Quiz #4
1. f
2. h
3. a
4. e
5. b
6. d
7. g
8. c
9. i
10. j

Quick Quiz #5
1. g
2. a
3. e
4. b
5. c
6. j
7. i
8. d
9. h
10. f

Quick Quiz #6
1. e
2. b
3. d
4. a

5. c
6. f

Quick Quiz #7
1. f
2. c
3. a
4. j
5. h
6. i
7. d
8. e
9. g
10. k
11. b

Quick Quiz #8
1. i
2. h
3. g
4. f
5. a
6. d
7. e
8. c
9. j
10. b

Quick Quiz #9
1. d
2. i
3. f
4. a
5. h

6. e
7. c
8. g
9. j
10. b

Quick Quiz #10
1. f
2. c
3. a
4. h
5. j
6. i
7. d
8. g
9. e
10. b

Quick Quiz #11
1. i
2. a
3. e
4. b
5. h
6. f
7. c
8. g
9. d

Quick Quiz #12
1. g
2. e
3. a
4. i

5. b
6. d
7. c
8. h
9. f

Quick Quiz #13
1. d
2. a
3. e
4. b
5. f
6. c

Quick Quiz #14
1. b
2. e
3. d
4. h
5. c
6. g
7. f
8. a

Quick Quiz #15
1. g
2. e
3. b
4. i
5. f
6. c
7. d
8. h
9. a
10. j

Quick Quiz #16
1. b
2. e
3. a
4. c
5. f
6. d

Quick Quiz #17
1. n
2. c
3. g
4. e
5. m
6. d
7. h
8. l
9. j
10. b
11. i
12. o
13. f
14. k
15. a
16. p

Quick Quiz #18
1. b
2. l
3. j
4. f
5. a
6. g
7. c
8. i
9. e
10. d
11. k
12. h

Quick Quiz #19
1. a
2. b
3. i
4. g
5. c
6. h
7. d
8. e
9. f

Quick Quiz #20
1. h
2. j

3. d
4. k
5. g
6. i
7. c
8. b
9. a
10. f
11. e

Quick Quiz #21
1. e
2. h
3. k
4. a
5. f
6. d
7. b
8. c
9. j
10. g
11. i

Quick Quiz #22
1. b
2. g
3. d
4. h
5. l
6. a
7. f
8. c
9. k
10. e
11. j
12. i

Quick Quiz #23
1. h
2. b
3. g
4. a
5. c
6. d
7. d
8. f
9. e

Quick Quiz #24
1. c
2. i
3. h
4. f
5. g
6. e
7. d
8. a
9. b

Quick Quiz #25
1. h
2. e
3. g
4. c
5. f
6. d
7. b
8. a

Quick Quiz #26
1. b
2. c
3. h
4. g
5. e
6. a
7. d
8. j
9. i
10. f

Quick Quiz #27
1. g
2. d
3. a
4. b
5. f
6. e
7. h
8. c

Quick Quiz #28
1. e
2. b

3. g
4. f
5. c
6. d
7. i
8. j
9. a
10. h

Quick Quiz #29
1. e
2. a
3. d
4. b
5. c

Quick Quiz #30
1. e
2. b
3. i
4. j
5. h
6. f
7. c
8. g
9. a
10. d

Quick Quiz #31
1. d
2. e
3. a
4. g
5. c
6. i
7. j
8. l
9. h
10. k
11. f
12. b

Quick Quiz #32
1. h
2. g
3. b

4. i
5. e
6. a
7. k
8. l
9. j
10. f
11. d
12. c

Quick Quiz #33
1. a
2. f
3. g
4. c
5. h
6. e
7. d
8. b

Quick Quiz #34
1. j
2. k
3. c
4. l
5. a
6. h
7. i
8. f
9. b
10. g
11. e
12. d

Quick Quiz #35
1. c
2. a
3. b

Quick Quiz #36
1. f
2. d
3. e
4. i
5. g
6. a

7. j
8. h
9. b
10. c

Quick Quiz #37
1. b
2. g
3. c
4. e
5. f
6. a
7. d

Quick Quiz #38
1. g
2. j
3. e
4. d
5. f
6. c
7. a
8. b
9. i
10. h

Quick Quiz #39
1. i
2. e
3. g
4. j
5. a
6. c
7. b
8. d
9. f
10. h

Quick Quiz #40
1. a
2. i
3. h
4. e
5. j
6. b
7. c

8. d
9. g
10. k
11. l
12. f

Quick Quiz #41
1. m
2. d
3. a
4. l
5. i
6. f
7. b
8. c
9. o
10. j
11. g
12. h
13. e
14. k
15. n

Quick Quiz #42
1. i
2. e
3. g
4. h
5. c
6. j
7. d
8. k
9. f
10. a
11. b

Quick Quiz #43
1. j
2. l
3. c
4. a
5. g
6. d
7. i
8. k
9. f
10. h

11. e
12. b

Quick Quiz #44
1. e
2. b
3. d
4. i
5. h
6. f
7. c
8. j
9. a
10. g

Quick Quiz #45
1. g
2. a
3. l
4. h
5. f
6. b
7. j
8. k
9. d
10. e
11. i
12. c

Quick Quiz #46
1. f
2. k
3. d
4. q
5. a
6. r
7. c
8. h
9. n
10. e
11. j
12. m
13. o
14. b
15. i
16. p

17. g
18. l

Quick Quiz #47
1. e
2. h
3. a
4. b
5. j
6. l
7. f
8. k
9. g
10. d
11. c
12. i

Quick Quiz #48
1. d
2. g
3. b
4. c
5. f
6. e
7. a

Quick Quiz #49
1. j
2. d
3. b
4. i
5. c
6. h
7. e
8. f
9. a
10. g

Quick Quiz #50
1. a
2. f
3. h
4. c
5. j
6. k
7. i

8. b
9. g
10. e
11. d

Quick Quiz #51
1. g
2. d
3. j
4. b
5. e
6. c
7. k
8. f
9. i
10. h
11. a

Quick Quiz #52
1. c
2. a
3. h
4. j
5. e
6. f
7. g
8. d
9. b
10. i

Quick Quiz #53
1. e
2. f
3. d
4. b
5. j
6. i
7. g
8. a
9. h
10. c

Quick Quiz #54
1. m
2. e
3. h

4. d
5. c
6. k
7. j
8. i
9. f
10. l
11. g
12. a
13. b

Quick Quiz #55
1. e
2. f
3. b
4. g
5. d
6. c
7. a

Quick Quiz #56
1. e
2. o
3. a
4. n
5. c
6. k
7. g
8. b
9. d
10. h
11. f
12. j
13. m
14. i
15. l

Quick Quiz #57
1. i
2. f
3. b
4. d
5. e
6. c
7. k
8. a
9. j

10. g
11. h

Quick Quiz #58
1. m
2. j
3. h
4. n
5. b
6. f
7. c
8. l
9. i
10. d
11. e
12. k
13. g
14. a

Quick Quiz #59
1. a
2. h
3. e
4. l
5. j
6. k
7. b
8. i
9. g
10. d
11. c
12. f

Quick Quiz #60
1. c
2. l
3. g
4. a
5. b
6. m
7. d
8. o
9. e
10. j
11. f
12. n
13. h

14. i
15. k

Quick Quiz #61
1. i
2. k
3. a
4. h
5. g
6. b
7. e
8. d
9. j
10. f
11. c

Quick Quiz #62
1. i
2. l
3. f
4. a
5. j
6. g
7. k
8. b
9. e
10. c
11. h
12. n
13. m
14. d

Quick Quiz #63
1. k
2. f
3. j
4. b
5. l
6. a
7. d
8. c
9. n
10. e
11. h
12. m
13. g
14. i

Quick Quiz #64
1. b
2. i
3. k
4. d
5. g
6. j
7. c
8. f
9. h
10. l
11. e
12. a

Quick Quiz #65
1. g
2. d
3. a
4. j
5. h
6. k
7. c
8. i
9. b
10. f
11. e

Quick Quiz #66
1. k
2. j
3. f
4. a
5. c
6. i
7. g
8. h
9. b
10. e
11. d

Quick Quiz #67
1. f
2. e
3. b
4. a
5. i

6. j
7. h
8. d
9. k
10. g
11. c

Quick Quiz #68
1. l
2. a
3. j
4. c
5. g
6. b
7. i
8. d
9. k
10. f
11. e
12. h

Quick Quiz #69
1. c
2. f
3. b
4. e
5. d
6. a

Quick Quiz #70
1. d
2. e
3. a
4. c
5. b

Quick Quiz #71
1. c
2. f
3. j
4. b
5. i
6. g
7. h
8. d

9. e
10. a

Quick Quiz #72
1. h
2. e
3. i
4. j
5. g
6. f
7. a
8. d
9. c
10. b

Quick Quiz #73
1. g
2. d
3. j
4. f
5. c
6. a
7. e
8. i
9. k
10. h
11. b

Quick Quiz #74
1. h
2. f
3. d
4. i
5. k
6. e
7. j
8. c
9. l
10. a
11. b
12. g

Quick Quiz #75
1. c
2. a

3. h
4. j
5. b
6. i
7. e
8. d
9. g
10. f

Quick Quiz #76
1. a
2. f
3. h
4. b
5. c
6. d
7. i
8. g
9. j
10. e

Quick Quiz #77
1. a
2. e
3. j
4. i
5. g
6. h
7. c
8. d
9. f
10. b

Quick Quiz #78
1. h
2. g
3. l
4. b
5. m
6. n
7. d
8. k
9. i
10. i
11. a
12. e
13. f

14. j
15. c

Quick Quiz #79
1. k
2. h
3. d
4. e
5. b
6. i
7. g
8. j
9. a
10. f
11. c

Quick Quiz #80
1. b
2. a
3. f
4. e
5. h
6. g
7. d
8. c

Quick Quiz #81
1. i
2. b
3. e
4. j
5. d
6. f
7. c
8. g
9. h
10. a

Quick Quiz #82
1. h
2. e
3. k
4. a
5. j
6. m
7. g

8. n
9. c
10. b
11. o
12. f
13. f
14. l
15. d
16. i

Quick Quiz #83
1. c
2. f
3. a
4. i
5. j
6. h
7. b
8. e
9. d
10. g

Quick Quiz #84
1. b
2. f
3. o
4. l
5. h
6. k
7. m
8. j
9. n
10. i
11. a
12. d
13. e
14. g
15. c

Quick Quiz #85
1. e
2. h
3. b
4. a
5. c

6. j
7. d
8. i
9. k
10. g
11. f

Quick Quiz
#86
1. c
2. b
3. a

Published in India
by

GOYL SaaB

W.R. GOYAL Publishers & Distributors

86, U.B. (University Block) Jawahar Nagar, Delhi - 110007,
Tel.: 23852986, 23858342, 23858983, Fax : 23850961,
E-mail : goyal@vsnl.com Website : www.goylsaab.com

Distributed by

GENERAL BOOK DEPOT

1691, Nai Sarak, Post Box 1220, Delhi - 110006
Tel. : 011-23263695, 23250635, Fax : 23940861
E-mail : kaushalgoyal@yahoo.com

(GBD) BOOKS

16, Ansari Road, New Delhi - 110002
Tel. : 011-23260022, 011-31086851
Website : www.gbdbooks.com

Showrooms

OCM BOOKS

P-7,CIT Road, Entally, Kolkatta - 700014
Tel. : 22465542, 22445008, Fax : 22448950

THE GERMAN BOOK SHOP

Der Buchladen at Max Mueller Bhavan
3,Kasturba Gandhi Marg, New Delhi - 110001
Tel. : 011-23358534, 23329506

SANSKAR BOOKS

SF-211, Sahajanand Palace,
Sanjay Sachin Road, Ahmedabad - 380051
Tel. : 26779866

Merriam-Webster's Dictionaries

America's Best-Selling Dictionaries

	Rs.
Merriam-Webster's Collegiate Dictionary-11th edition - hard cover, 1665 pages, 2,25000 definitions.	495/-
With CD-ROM & Online -Free one-year subscription to www.Merriam-WebsterCollegiate.com	550/-
Merriam-Webster's Collegiate Thesaurus - hard cover, 894 pages, over 340,000 synonyms, antonyms	495/-
Merriam-Webster's Concise Dictionary - 720 pages, 65,000 definitions	295/-
Merriam-Webster's Pocket Dictionary - 896 pages, 70,000 definitions	150/-
Merriam-Webster's Mini Pocket Dictionary - 416 pages 40,000 definitions	75/-
Merriam-Webster's Pocket Thesaurus - 672 pages, over 1,57,000 synonyms, antonyms	150/-
Merriam-Webster's Pocket Vocabulary Builder - 576 pages, over 3000 vocabulary words	150/-
Merriam-Webster's Pocket Dictionary of Quotation - 512 pages, over 4000 quotations	150/-
Merriam-Webster's Crossward Puzzle Dictionary - 784 pages, over 30,0000 ans. word.	150/-
Merriam-Webster's Medical Dictionary - 800 pages, over 35,000 entires.	195/-

GOYL SABB — ENGLISH LANGUAGE & QUOTATION DICTIONARIES

	Rs.
Bloomsbury Dictionary of Word Origins	180/-
Bloomsbury Dictionary of Contemporary Slang	195/-
Bloomsbury Dictionary of Phrase & Allusion	95/-
Bloomsbury Dictionary of Differences	95/-
Bloomsbury Dictionary of New Words since 1960	90/-
Bloomsbury Dictionary of Popular Phrases	75/-
Bloomsbury Good Word Guide	125/-
Bloomsbury Crossword Lists	75/-
Bloomsbury Dictionary of Quotations	295/-
Bloomsbury Thematic Dictionary of Quotations	250/-
Bloomsbury Chronological Dictionary of Quotations "Who Said What When"	250/-
Hutchinson Pocket Dictionary of Quotations	60/-
A.T.Morgan HandBook of Quotations	100/-

GOYL SABB — Mini Dictionaries

Compact design and suitable for home and school use

	Rs.		Rs.
Dictionary of Biology	60/-	Dictionary of Confuiable Words	70/-
Dictionary of Chemistry	60/-	Dictionary of Spelling	60/-
Dictionary of Physics	60/-	Dictionary of the Environment	60/-
Dictionary of Science	70/-	Pocket Hutchinson Encyclopedia	90/-
Dictionary of Geography	60/-	Pocket Guide to Countries of the World	70/-
Dictionary of Mathematics	60/-	Pocket English Usage	60/-
Dictionary of Computers	60/-	Pocket Quiz Book	60/-
Dictionary of Medical Terms	60/-	Dictionary of Quotations	60/-

Subject Dictionaries

			Rs.
W.P. Scott	☐	Dictionary of Sociology	175/-
E.B. Tylor	☐	Dictionary of Anthropology	250/-
Woodworth et al	☐	Dictionary of Psychology	195/-
M. Hoffman	☐	Dictionary of Geology	160/-
Hutchinson	☐	Dictionary of Difficult Words	175/-
Hutchinson	☐	Dictionary of Science	350/-

General Interest
Self Improvement, Personal Growth and Health Care

			Rs.
Dale Carnegie	•	Little Known Facts About Well Known People	125/-
Murphy's Law Book	•	& Other Reasons Why Things go Wrong (1, 2, 3)	75/-
Paramhansa Yogananda	•	Autobiography of a yogi	95/-
Swami Kriyananda	•	The Path Autobiography of a Western Yogi	150/-
Swami Kriyananda (J. Donald Walter)	•	Conversation with Yogananda	295/-
Paramhansa Yogananda	•	God Is For Everyone	195/-
Thomson	•	Better Speeches Made Easy	95/-
Charles Darwin	•	The Origin of Species	100/-
Miller	•	Dictionary of Dreams	150/-
Susan Stern	•	These Strange German Ways	85/-
Bloomsbury (U.K.)	•	Good Health Guide	200/-
Bloomsbury (U.K.)	•	Dictionary of Sex	90/-
Kathleen Roquemore	•	Numerology Made Easy It's All in your Numbers	95/-
Suhani Activity & Colouring Books (8 Different Books of 44 page each)			15/-

Teach Yourself in 10 Minute™ Series

*From Macmilan Spectrum/Alpha Books, (U.S.A.) the Creators of the Complete
Idiot's guides comes this all-new series for people who want to learn fast and accomplish the feat without
outside assistance. With only a smidgen of time
spent on these quick and easy guides, anyone can gain working
knowledge of a subject in ten (one minute) lessons.*

Over 2 Million 10 Minute Guides Sold !

	Rs.
10 Minute Guide to Leadership	95/-
10 Minute Guide to Motivating People	95/-
10 Minute Guide to Business Communication	95/-
10 Minute Guide to Job Interviews	95/-
10 Minute Guide to Negotiating	95/-
10 Minute Guide to Teams & Team Works	95/-
10 Minute Guide to Building Your Vocabulary	95/-
10 Minute Guide to Planning	95/-
10 Minute Guide to Accounting for Non-Accountants	95/-
10 Minute Guide to Annual Reports and Prospectuses	95/-

The Core Knowledge Series™
Complete General Knowledge Books for Children of 1ˢᵗ to 6ᵗʰ Standard

		Rs.
E.D. Hirsch	☐ What Your 1st Grader Needs to Know	150/-
E.D. Hirsch	☐ What Your 2nd Grader Needs to Know	150/-
E.D. Hirsch	☐ What Your 3rd Grader Needs to Know	150/-
E.D. Hirsch	☐ What Your 4th Grader Needs to Know	150/-
E.D. Hirsch	☐ What Your 5th Grader Needs to Know	150/-
E.D. Hirsch	☐ What Your 6th Grader Needs to Know	150/-

K. Sree Bhargava

French Language Books
Textbook used by Alliance Franchise & Universities

		Rs.
Panorama 1	Textbook	250/-
	Excercise book	150/-
Panorama 1	Study Guide & Workbook	195/-
Le Nouveau Sans Frontieres 1	Textbook	190/-
	Workbook	100/-
	4 Audio Cassettes	200/-
Le Nouvel Espaces-1	Textbook	425/-
Campus 1	Textbook	395/-
Forum 1	Textbook	425/-

TEXTBOOKS FOR SCHOOLS (C.B.S.E.)

		Rs.
G. Mauger : Cours de langue et de civilisation francaises	Text Book-1	85/-
	2 Audio Cassettes	100/-
G. Mauger : Cours de langue et de civilisation francaises	Text Book-2	120/-
French C.B.S.E. Board Papers for X Class with solutions		90/-
Entre Jeunes C.B.S.E. IX Class Guide		90/-

Textbooks for Professional Studies

		Rs.
Bon Voyage 1	Textbook	200/-
	Audio Cassette	50/-
	Teacher's Guide	150/-
A Votre Service 1	Textbook	150/-
	Audio Cassette	50/-
	Teacher's Guide	100/-
A Votre Service 2	Textbook	180/-
	Audio Cassette	70/-
	Teacher's Guide	100/-

Reference Books

	Rs.
Webster's French Grammar and Exercises	125/-
Webster's French Vocabulary and Verbs	140/-
Larousse Dictionnaire General (Over 400, 000 Translations)	795/-
Larousse Compact/Concise Dictionary (Over 120,000 Translations)	350/-
Larousse Pocket Dictionary (Over 20,00 Translations)	225/-
Larousse Mini Dictionary (Over 46,000 Translations)	100/-
Le Robert & Collins Cadet (Over 65,000 Translations)	495/-
Le Petit Robert (French-French)	3330/-
Le Robert Micro French (French-French)	885/-
Le Robert Micro Poche (French-French)	595/-
Le Robert Mini (French-French)	370/-
My First Trillingual Dictionary (French-English-Hindi)	150/-
Le Robert & Nathan : La Conjugaison (with English Translation)	170/-
Larousse French Grammar	95/-
Larousse Pocket Encyclopedia of Wine	175/-

Foreign Language Self-Study Packs Foreign

			Rs.
Langenscheidt/Humboldt	☐	German in 30 days *(Book + Cassette)*	250/-
Hachette	☐	French Made Easy *(Book + 2 Cassette)*	350/-
Martinez	☐	Spanish Made Easy	195/-
Y. Masuda	☐	Japanese Made Easy (2 Books + 2 Cassettes)	395/-
Langenscheidt	☐	Jiffy Travel Pack Spanish (Book + Cassette)	250/-
Langenscheidt	☐	Jiffy Travel Pack Italian (Book + Cassette)	250/-
Langenscheidt	☐	Jiffy Travel Pack German (Book + Cassette)	250/-
Langenscheidt	☐	Jiffy Travel Pack French (Book + Cassette)	250/-
Langenscheidt	☐	Universal Phrasebook German: (Over 1000 Essential Phrases	95/-
Langenscheidt	☐	Universal Phrasebook French : (Over 1000 Essential rases)	95/-
Langenscheidt	☐	Universal Phrasebook Spanish :(Over 1000 Essential Phrases)	95/-
Langenscheidt	☐	Universal Phrasebook Italian :(Over 1000 Essential phrases)	95/-

Foreign Language Dictionaries

			Rs.
Larousse General French	☐	*French-English/English-French*	795/-
Larousse Compact French	☐	*French-English/English-French*	350/-
Larousse Pocket Dictionary	☐	*French-English/English-French*	225/-
Larousse Mini Dictionary	☐	*French-English/English-French*	100/-
Langenscheidt Pocket French	☐	*French-English/English-French*	200/-
Langenscheidt Universal French	☐	*French-English/English-French*	90/-
Langenscheidt Compact German	☐	*German-English/English-German*	350/-
Langenscheidt Pocket German	☐	*German-English/English-German*	200/-
Langenscheidt Universal German	☐	*German-English/English-German*	100/-
Langenscheidt Pocket Spanish	☐	*Spanish-English/English-Spanish*	200/-
Langenscheidt Pocket Russian	☐	*Russian-English/English-Russian*	180/-
Langenscheidt Universal Italian	☐	*Italian-English/English-Italian*	100/-
Langenscheidt Pocket Italian	☐	*Italian English/English-Italian*	250/-
Langenscheidt Pocket Japanese	☐	*Japanese-English/English-Japanese*	250/-
Langenscheidt Pocket Chinese	☐	*Chinese-English/English-Chinese*	250/-

Textbooks

			Rs.
Burns et al	☐	World Civilization Vol. A (Ancient)	250/-
Burns et al	☐	World Civilization Vol. B (Medieval)	250/-
Burns et al	☐	World Civilization Vol. C (Modern)	295/-
S.P.Gupta & D.K.Gupta	☐	Medical Emergencies in General Practice (6th Edn.)	250/-
I. D. Aggarwal	☐	Current Drug Therapy for General Practitioner (2nd Edn.)	275/-
Hughs	☐	News Writing, 4th Edition	195/-
Defleur	☐	Understanding Mass Communications, 3rd Edn.	195/-

UPTEC & GBD BOOKS

Information Technology for School Series (Based on CBSE & ISC Syllabus)

	Rs.
Introductory Informatic Practices-I for Class IX	150/-
Introductory Informatic Practices-II for Class X	135/-
Computer Science-I for Class XI	150/-
Computer Science-II for Class XII	150/-